Lecture Notes in Computer Science 785

Edited by G. Goos and J. Hartmanis

Hartmut Ehrig Fernando Orejas (Eds.)

Recent Trends in Data Type Specification

9th Workshop on Specification of Abstract Data Types
Joint with the 4th COMPASS Workshop
Caldes de Malavella, Spain, October 26-30, 1992
Selected Papers

Springer-Verlag
Berlin Heidelberg New York
London Paris Tokyo
Hong Kong Barcelona
Budapest

Series Editors

Gerhard Goos
Universität Karlsruhe
Postfach 69 80
Vincenz-Priessnitz-Straße 1
D-76131 Karlsruhe, Germany

Juris Hartmanis
Cornell University
Department of Computer Science
4130 Upson Hall
Ithaca, NY 14853, USA

Volume Editors

Hartmut Ehrig
Institut für Software und Theoretische Informatik, Technische Universität Berlin
Franklinstraße 28/29, D-10587 Berlin, Germany

Fernando Orejas
Departament de Llenguatges i Sistemes Informatics
Universitat Politecnica de Catalunya
Pau Gargallo, 5, E-08028 Barcelona, Spain

CR Subject Classification (1991): D.2.1-2, D.2.4, D.2.10-m, D.3.1, F.3.1-2

ISBN 3-540-57867-6 Springer-Verlag Berlin Heidelberg New York
ISBN 0-387-57867-6 Springer-Verlag New York Berlin Heidelberg

CIP data applied for

Printed in Germany

Typesetting: Camera-ready by author
SPIN: 10132053 45/3140-543210 - Printed on acid-free paper

Preface

Research in the area of algebraic specification of abstract data types started about twenty years ago. Since then, there has been continuous activity with strong influence both on the applications and the theoretical foundations of methodologies for software design. The Ninth Workshop on Specification of Abstract Data Types was held jointly with the Fourth COMPASS Workshop in Caldes de Malavella (about 100 km from Barcelona), October 26-30, 1992, and was organized by Fernando Orejas. The main topics covered were:

- object oriented specifications
- rewriting methods
- specification languages and associated tools
- type systems
- algebraic specification of concurrency

The program consisted of 46 presentations describing ongoing work and 5 invited lectures from Michel Bidoit, Joseph Goguen, Jean Pierre Jouannaud, Axel Poigné and Eric Wagner surveying different topics in the area. Altogether, it was considered that the scientific level of the Workshop was very high. Afterwards, a selection committee (Michel Bidoit, Hartmut Ehrig, Bernd Krieg-Bruckner, Fernando Orejas, Horst Reichel and Andrzej Tarlecki) selected the talks that were considered to represent the most interesting ideas and to reflect the main trends in current research. This volume contains the final version of the selected papers, describing the current status of their work, together with the written version of four invited surveys. All of them underwent a careful refereeing process. In this sense we are grateful to the following people who acted as referees:

E. Astesiano, H. Ganzinger, P. Lescanne, M. Bidoit, C. Choppy, C. Delgado-Kloos, H.-D. Ehrich, H. Ehrig, J. Farrés, S. Gilmore, M. Gogolla, M. Grosse-Rhode, V. Holten, R. Jiménez, J.-P. Jouannaud, H.-J. Kreowski, B. Krieg-Bruckner, U. Lechner, S. Matthews, R. Nieuwenhuis, F. Orejas, J. Padberg, F. Parisi, H. Peterreins, H. Reichel, M. Rodríguez-Artalejo, R. Socher-Ambrosius, A. Tarlecki and B. Wolff

We are also grateful to Silvia Clerici, Laura Espitia, Rosa Jiménez, Nikos Mylonakis, Robert Nieuwenhuis, Pilar Nivela, Jose Miguel Rivero and Albert Rubio for helping in the Workshop organization and to Springer-Verlag for agreeing to publish this volume. The Workshop received financial support by the ESPRIT Basic Research Working Group COMPASS, the Universitat Politècnica de Catalunya, the Comissió Interdepartamental de Recerca i Innovació Tecnològica (CIRIT) and the Comisión Interministerial de Ciencia y Tecnología (CICYT).

Berlin — Hartmut Ehrig

Barcelona — Fernando Orejas

Table of Contents

Invited Papers

Contributed Papers

Towards an Algebraic Semantics for the Object Paradigm*

Joseph A. Goguen and Răzvan Diaconescu
Programming Research Group, Oxford University

Abstract: This paper surveys our current state of knowledge (and ignorance) on the use of hidden sorted algebra as a foundation for the object paradigm. Our main goal is to support equational reasoning about properties of concurrent systems of objects, because of its simple and efficient mechanisation. We show how equational specifications can describe objects, inheritance and modules; our treatment of the latter topic emphasises the importance of reuse, and the rôle of the so-called Satisfaction Condition. We then consider how to prove things about objects, how to unify the object and logic paradigms by using logical variables that range over objects, and how to connect objects into concurrent systems. We provide a universal characterisation of parallel connection, and more generally, of parallel connection with synchronisation, and show how the former construction gives a class manager that provides unique identifiers for its objects. The paper concludes with some topics for further research.

1 Introduction

This paper presents some initial steps towards an algebraic foundation for what we will call the *object paradigm.* This paradigm consists of specification, programming and refinement, in the context of objects, classes, inheritance and concurrency. These issues are increasingly important for applications to information systems, operating systems, protocols, programming languages, and more generally, to distributed systems of any kind, as well as to aspects of areas like conceptual modelling, natural language processing, knowledge representation and software engineering.

There are several reasons for preferring an algebraic approach. Perhaps the most compelling is the extensive algorithmic and theoretical support available for equational reasoning. This includes algorithms for term rewriting, unification, narrowing and completion, and theorems for the completeness of equational reasoning with respect to algebras, and the soundness of constructor induction. Many important problems are decidable or semi-decidable for equational logic that are not for more complex logics. Also, efficient implementations of many useful algorithms are available in a variety of tools. It follows that we should use equational logic wherever possible. Of course, it is *not* always possible; but this paper will show that many aspects of the object paradigm can be treated with equational reasoning.

This paper continues the programme initially sketched in [11], formally begun in [15], and further elaborated in [19]. This programme aims to generalise and integrate the classical initial algebraic semantics for Abstract Data Types (ADTs) with relevant aspects of process algebra, such as concurrency, hiding, non-determinism, complex data structures, complex objects, and sharing for objects and methods (i.e., synchronisation), while avoiding the *ad hoc* combination of process algebra and ADTs that is found for example in LOTOS.

*The research reported in this paper has been partially supported by the Science and Engineering Research Council, Fujitsu Laboratories Limited, the Information Technology Promotion Agency, Japan, as part of the R & D of Basic Technology for Future Industries "New Models for Software Architecture" project sponsored by NEDO (New Energy and Industrial Technology Development Organization), and the CEC under ESPRIT-2 BRA Working Groups 6071, IS-CORE (Information Systems Correctness and REusability) and 6112, COMPASS (COMPrehensive Algebraic Approach to System Specification and development).

It seems important to consider complex systems that are built from several objects. For this purpose, we should have *modules* for the object paradigm, including *parameterised* modules, and not just inheritance; and for verification, we will of course need to have *semantics* for objects, modules, and their interconnections. An important property of modules in this context is that whatever we prove about a module remains true of that module wherever it is used; we will call this property *encapsulation*; it is vital for the reuse of modules, and differs from the weaker sense of encapsulation that refers to merely hiding the representation of data items. We will see that the so-called Satisfaction Condition plays an important rôle here. Our approach is "constraint based" rather than oriented towards input-output, in that we use equations to describe relationships that necessarily hold among attributes, methods, and processes.

Section 5 discusses how to prove things about objects, while Section 6 unifies the object and logic paradigms with logical variables that range over objects, and Section 7 considers the parallel connection of objects to form systems. The main results here are universal characterisations for parallel connection, and more generally, for parallel connection with synchronisation. We use the former construction to define a class manager for objects, each having a unique identifier. Because the result of a parallel connection (with or without synchronisation) is given by an equational specification, we can again apply equational reasoning to systems.

It is worth noting that the goal of our general programme for semantics, of which this paper is a part, is not to model the warts and tumours of existing languages (such as C++ or Smalltalk), but rather to construct simple but powerful new theories that will guide the design of new languages, and support efficient calculational reasoning about properties of their programs. Thus, our notions of inheritance and module are not merely based upon those of existing languages. Nevertheless, our notions can be used to give semantics for existing languages, although the details will necessarily involve a degree of awkwardness matching that of the language involved. We feel that the cleanliness of semantic-based design is particularly appropriate for languages (like FOOPS [23, 35] and OOZE [2, 1]) that are intended to be used for specification and prototyping[1].

2 Prerequisites and Preliminaries

We assume familiarity with basics of the object paradigm (e.g., the notions of object, class, attribute, method and inheritance), with overloaded many sorted algebra, and with the notation of OBJ (for which see [25]). In order to fix notation, and also to set the stage for later developments, we briefly review some basics of overloaded many sorted algebra; further details may be found in [16] and [30]. We emphasise overloading because of its importance for the object paradigm. Many readers may wish to skip directly to Section 3.

2.1 Overloaded Many Sorted Algebra

Given a **sort set** S, an S-**indexed** (or **sorted**) **set** A is a family $\{A_s \mid s \in S\}$ of sets indexed by the elements of S. In this context, $a \in A$ means that $a \in A_s$ for some $s \in S$. Similarly, $A \subseteq B$ means that $A_s \subseteq B_s$ for each $s \in S$, and an S-**indexed** (or **sorted**) **function** $f\colon A \to B$ is a family $\{f_s\colon A_s \to B_s \mid s \in S\}$. Also, we let S^* denote the set of all finite sequences of elements from S, with $[]$ the empty sequence. Given an S-indexed set A and $w = s_1 \ldots s_n \in S^*$, we let $A^w = A_{s_1} \times \cdots \times A_{s_n}$; in particular, we let $A^{[]} = \{\star\}$, some one point set.

A (n S-**sorted**) **signature** (S, Σ) is an $S^* \times S$-indexed set $\Sigma = \{\Sigma_{w,s} \mid w \in S^*,\ s \in S\}$; we often write just Σ instead of (S, Σ). Note that this definition permits *overloading*, in that the sets $\Sigma_{w,s}$ need *not* be disjoint. Call $\sigma \in \Sigma_{[],s}$ a **constant symbol** of sort s. A **signature morphism** Φ from a signature (S, Σ) to a signature (S', Σ') is a pair (f, g) consisting of a map

[1] These remarks are in response to a criticism of the paper raised by one of its referees.

$f\colon S \to S'$ of sorts and an $S^* \times S$-indexed family of maps $g_{w,s}\colon \Sigma_{w,s} \to \Sigma'_{f^*(w),f(s)}$ on operation symbols, where $f^*\colon S^* \to S'^*$ is the extension of f to strings[2]. We may write $\Phi(s)$ for $f(s)$, $\Phi(w)$ for $f^*(w)$, and $\Phi(\sigma)$ for $g_{w,s}(\sigma)$ when $\sigma \in \Sigma_{w,s}$.

A **Σ-algebra** A consists of an S-indexed set A and a function $\sigma_A\colon A^w \to A_s$ for each $\sigma \in \Sigma_{w,s}$; the set A_s is called the **carrier** of A of sort s. If $\sigma \in \Sigma_{[],s}$ then σ_A determines a point in A_s which may also be denoted σ_A. A **Σ-homomorphism** from one Σ-algebra A to another B is an S-indexed function $h\colon A \to B$ such that

$$h_s(\sigma_A(a_1, ..., a_n)) = \sigma_B(h_{s_1}(a_1), ..., h_{s_n}(a_n))$$

for each $\sigma \in \Sigma_{w,s}$ and $(a_1, ..., a_n) \in A^w$. (When $n = 0$, this condition just says that $f(\sigma_A) = \sigma_B$.) A Σ-homomorphism $h\colon A \to B$ is a **Σ-isomorphism** iff each function $h_s\colon A_s \to B_s$ is bijective (i.e., one-to-one and onto, in an older terminology).

Given a many sorted signature Σ, an S-indexed set X will be called a set of **variable symbols** if the sets X_s are disjoint from each other and from all of the sets $\Sigma_{w,s}$. Given a set X of variable symbols, we let $\Sigma(X)$ denote the signature formed by adding the elements of X to Σ as new constants, and we let $T_\Sigma(X)$ denote $T_{\Sigma(X)}$ viewed as a Σ-algebra. It is called the **Σ-term algebra** or **free Σ-algebra** generated by X, and has the property that if $\theta\colon X \to A$ is an **assignment**, i.e., a (S-sorted) function to a Σ-algebra A, then there is a unique extension of θ to a Σ-homomorphism $\theta^*\colon T_\Sigma(X) \to A$. (Strictly speaking, the usual term algebra is not free unless the constant symbols in Σ are mutually disjoint; however, even if they are not disjoint, a closely related term algebra, with each constant annotated by its sort, is free.) Also, we let T_Σ denote the **initial** term Σ-algebra $T_\Sigma(\emptyset)$, noting that this means there is a unique Σ-homomorphism $T_\Sigma \to A$ for any Σ-algebra A. Call $t \in T_\Sigma$ a **ground Σ-term**.

A special case of free extension is **substitution**, where the target algebra A is a term algebra, often $T_\Sigma(X)$ itself; in this case, we may use the notation $t(x_1 \leftarrow t_1, ..., x_n \leftarrow t_n)$ for $\theta^*(t)$ when $\theta(x_i) = t_i$ and the elements of X are $x_1, ..., x_n$. The following result is often useful:

Lemma 1 Given an assignment $\theta\colon X \to A$ and a Σ-homomorphism $f\colon A \to B$, then

$$(\theta; f)^* = \theta^*; f\colon T_\Sigma(X) \to B.$$

Proof: By freeness, there is exactly one Σ-homomorphism from $T_\Sigma(X)$ to B extending $\theta; f$. □

A **conditional Σ-equation** consists of a variable set X, terms $t, t' \in T_\Sigma(X)_s$ for some sort s, and terms $t_j, t'_j \in T_\Sigma(X)_{s_j}$ for $j = 1, ..., m$. Such an equation is generally written in the form

$$(\forall X)\, t = t' \textbf{ if } t_1 = t'_1, ..., t_m = t'_m\ .$$

The special case where $m = 0$ is called an **(unconditional) equation**, written $(\forall X)\, t = t'$. A **ground equation** has $X = \emptyset$. A Σ-algebra A **satisfies** a conditional equation, written

$$A \models_\Sigma (\forall X)\, t = t' \textbf{ if } t_1 = t'_1, ..., t_m = t'_m\ ,$$

iff for all assignments $\theta\colon X \to A$, we have $\theta^*(t) = \theta^*(t')$ whenever $\theta^*(t_j) = \theta^*(t'_j)$ for $j = 1, ..., m$. Given a set E of (possibly conditional) Σ-equations, we call any Σ-algebra that satisfies E a (Σ, E)-algebra.

---

[2]This extension is defined by $f^*([]) = []$ and $f^*(ws) = f^*(w)f(s)$, for w in S^* and s in S.

2.2 Congruence and Quotient

A Σ-**congruence** on a Σ-algebra A is an S-sorted family of relations, $\equiv_s$ on A_s, each of which is an equivalence relation, and which also satisfy the **congruence property**, that given any $\sigma \in \Sigma_{s_1...s_n,s}$ and any $a_i, a_i' \in A_{s_i}$ for $i = 1, ..., n$, then $\sigma_A(a_1, ..., a_n) \equiv_s \sigma_A(a_1', ..., a_n')$ whenever $a_i \equiv_{s_i} a_i'$ for $i = 1, ..., n$. The **quotient** of A by $\equiv$, denoted $A/\equiv$, has carriers $(A/\equiv)_s = A_s/\equiv_s$, which inherit a Σ-algebra structure by defining $\sigma_{A/\equiv}([a_1], \ldots, [a_n]) = [\sigma_A(a_1, \ldots, a_n)]$, where $\sigma \in \Sigma_{s_1...s_n,s}$ and $a_i \in A_{s_i}$, where $[a]$ denotes the $\equiv$-equivalence class of a.

2.3 Equational Deduction

We now consider the *logic* of many sorted algebra, that is, rules for deducing new equations from old ones.

Definition 2 Given a set E of (possibly conditional) Σ-equations, we define the (unconditional) Σ-equations that are **derivable** from E recursively, by the following **rules of deduction**:

(0) Base: Each unconditional equation in E is derivable.

(1) Reflexivity: Each equation $(\forall X)\, t = t$ is derivable.

(2) Symmetry: If $(\forall X)\, t = t'$ is derivable, then so is $(\forall X)\, t' = t$.

(3) Transitivity: If $(\forall X)\, t = t'$ and $(\forall X)\, t' = t''$ are derivable, then so is $(\forall X)\, t = t''$.

(4) Congruence: If $(\forall X)\, t_i = t_i'$ is derivable, where $t_i, t_i' \in T_\Sigma(X)_{s_i}$ for $i = 1, ..., n$, then for any $\sigma \in \Sigma_{s_1...s_n,s}$, the equation $(\forall X)\, \sigma(t_1, \ldots, t_n) = \sigma(t_1', \ldots, t_n')$ is also derivable.

(5) Modus Ponens: Given $(\forall X)\, t = t'$ **if** $t_1 = t_1', \ldots, t_m = t_m'$ in E and given a substitution $\theta\colon X \to T_\Sigma(Y)$ such that $(\forall Y)\, \theta^*(t_j) = \theta^*(t_j')$ is derivable for $j = 1, ..., m$, then $(\forall Y)\, \theta^*(t) = \theta^*(t')$ is also derivable.

Given a set E of Σ-equations, let $E^{\bigcirc}$ denote the S-sorted set of pairs (t, t') of *ground* Σ-terms such that $(\forall\emptyset)\, t = t'$ is derivable from E. Then $E^{\bigcirc}$ is a Σ-congruence by rules (1)–(4). □

The following completeness result was first proved by Goguen and Meseguer [20], although the unconditional one sorted form is very well known, going back to Birkhoff [4] in 1935:

Theorem 3 Given a set E of (possibly conditional) Σ-equations, an unconditional Σ-equation is satisfied by every (Σ, E)-algebra iff it is derivable from E using the rules (0)–(5). □

Goguen and Meseguer [20] use the above to prove the following basic result:

Theorem 4 The Σ-algebra $T_{\Sigma,E} = T_\Sigma/E^{\bigcirc}$ is an initial (Σ, E)-algebra, in the sense that for any (Σ, E)-algebra A there is a unique Σ-homomorphism $h\colon T_{\Sigma,E} \to A$. □

Of course, there are many other initial Σ, E-algebras, but they are all Σ-isomorphic to this one. Also, there are many other complete sets of rules of deduction, some of which are more convenient in practice; but the above rules are especially convenient for proving Theorem 4.

2.4 The Satisfaction Condition

Given signatures $\Sigma \subseteq \Sigma'$ and a Σ'-algebra M', let us write $M'\lceil_\Sigma$ for M' viewed as a Σ-algebra by dropping any operations in Σ' that are not in Σ, and also dropping any carriers of sorts in Σ' that are not in Σ; call this the **reduct** of M' to Σ. Moreover, given a Σ'-homomorphism $h\colon M_1' \to M_2'$, we can form $h\lceil_\Sigma\colon M_1'\lceil_\Sigma \to M_2'\lceil_\Sigma$ by defining $(h\lceil_\Sigma)_s = h_s$ for $s \in S$ (the sort set of Σ); it is not difficult to show that this is a Σ-homomphism.

More generally, given a signature morphism $\Phi\colon \Sigma \to \Sigma'$ and a Σ'-algebra M', we can define the **reduct** of M' to Σ, denoted $\Phi(M')$ or $M'\lceil_\Phi$, to have carriers $M'_{\Phi(s)}$ for $s \in S$, and to have operations $\sigma_{\Phi(M')}$ for $\sigma \in \Sigma_{w,s}$ defined by $\sigma_{\Phi(M')}(m) = \Phi(\sigma)_{M'}(m)$ for $m \in M^w$. Also, given a Σ'-homomorphism $h\colon M_1' \to M_2'$, we can define $h\lceil_\Phi\colon M_1'\lceil_\Phi \to M_2'\lceil_\Phi$ by $(h\lceil_\Phi)_s = h_{\Phi(s)}$ for $s \in S$.

Similarly, given a Σ-equation e of the form $(\forall X)\ t = t'$, we define $\Phi(e)$ to be the Σ'-equation $(\forall X')\ \overline{\Phi}(t) = \overline{\Phi}(t')$, where X' is the S'-indexed set, also denoted $\Phi(X)$, with $X'_{s'} = \bigcup_{\Phi(s)=s'} X_s$ for $s' \in S'$, and where $\overline{\Phi}\colon T_{\Sigma(X)} \to T_{\Sigma'(X')}$ is the S-indexed function defined by viewing $T_{\Sigma'(X')}$ as a $\Sigma(X)$-algebra using the reduct construction given above, and then the initiality of $T_{\Sigma(X)}$.

An important property of these translations on algebras and equations under signature morphisms is called the **Satisfaction Condition**, which expresses the invariance of satisfaction under change of notation:

Theorem 5 Given an overloaded many sorted signature morphism $\Phi\colon \Sigma \to \Sigma'$, a Σ'-algebra M', and a Σ-equation e, then

$$\Phi(M') \models_\Sigma e \text{ iff } M' \models_{\Sigma'} \Phi(e).$$

□

This theorem was first proved in the original version of [18]. We will later relate the Satisfaction Condition to the encapsulation of modules, and in Section 4.1, we will see that it is an important part of the formalisation of logical system called an *institution* by Burstall and Goguen [6, 17, 18].

2.5 Other Topics

Section 3.1 assumes familiarity with basic order sorted algebra, as given for example in [22]. For simplicity of exposition, this paper will first treat the many sorted case, and then treat the order sorted case more briefly afterwards. Some examples assume familiarity with some basics of term rewriting, including confluence, termination and narrowing; these are explained, for example, in [7] and [16].

We sometimes use basic notions from category theory, including category, functor, and initial object. For an introduction to category theory, see [3] or [27]. We use the "bbold" font to denote categories, e.g., C. Given morphisms $f\colon A \to B$ and $g\colon B \to C$, we let $f;g$ denote their composition, a morphism $A \to C$; also, we let 1_A denote the identity morphism at an object A. Sections 4.1 and 7 use colimits, and Section 7 also uses universal constructions. A general discussion of category theory for Computing Science is given in [14].

3 Hidden Sorted Algebra

This section gives a brief summary of basic concepts from (overloaded many sorted) hidden sorted algebra, with some motivation, following the lines of [15]. The basic intuition is that an object has a *state*, which is *hidden*, i.e., only *observed* through the effect of methods on attributes. This approach is a variant of algebra that:

0. fixes an algebra D of data values; in typical applications, D might include natural numbers, booleans, character strings, etc.;

1. models states with *hidden sorts*;

2. models data with *visible sorts*;

3. models attributes with visible valued functions that are *monadic* in states, in the sense of having exactly one hidden sorted argument; and

4. models methods with hidden valued functions that are monadic in states.

The following is our first step in making this precise:

Definition 6 **A hidden sorted signature** consists of

1. a set S of **sorts**,

2. a subset $V \subseteq S$ of **visible** sorts, where $H = S - V$ is called the set of **hidden** sorts,

3. an S-sorted signature Σ,

4. a V-sorted subsignature $\Psi \subseteq \Sigma$ called the **data signature**, and

5. a Ψ-algebra D, called the **data algebra**,

such that

(S1) for each $d \in D_v$ with $v \in V$ there is some $\psi \in \Psi_{[],v}$ such that ψ is interpreted as d in D; for simplicity, we can assume that $D_v \subseteq \Psi_{[],v}$ for each $v \in V$,

(S2) each $\sigma \in \Sigma_{w,s}$ with $w \in V^*$ and $s \in V$ lies in $\Psi_{w,s}$, and

(S3) each $\sigma \in \Sigma_{w,s}$ has at most one element of w in H.

To indicate this entire situation, we may write (S, Σ, V, Ψ, D) or (Σ, D), or even just Σ if context permits. If $w \in S^*$ contains a hidden sort, then $\sigma \in \Sigma_{w,s}$ is called a **method** if $s \in H$ and an **attribute** if $s \in V$.

A **hidden sorted specification** is a tuple $(S, \Sigma, V, \Psi, D, E)$, where (S, Σ, V, Ψ, D) is a hidden sorted signature and E is a set of Σ-equations; we may abbreviate this (Σ, D, E) or even just (Σ, E) if the context permits. We will also call it a **module**. □

Condition (S1) says that all data items are named by constants in Ψ, while (S2) is a data encapsulation condition, that Σ cannot add any new operations on data items. Condition (S3) says that methods and attributes act on (the states of) single objects.

The following example may help to clarify this definition. The code in this and subsequent examples uses the syntax of OBJ3 [25], but the intended semantics is not initial algebra semantics, but rather a loose hidden sorted semantics that we will soon explain.

Example 7 We specify a flag object, where the intuitive idea is that a flag is either up or down, and there are methods to put it into either state, and also to reverse its state; when initially created, the flag is down.

```
obj FLAG is
   pr DATA .
   sort Flag .
   op newf : -> Flag .
   ops (up_) (dn_) (rev_) : Flag -> Flag .
   op up?_ : Flag -> Bool .
   var F : Flag .
   eq up? up F = true .
   eq up? dn F = false .
   eq up? rev F = not up? F .
   eq up? newf = false .
endo
```

Here FLAG is the name of the module and Flag is the name of the class of flag objects, representing the states of such objects. Then newf is a constant which represents the initial state of a flag object, while up, dn and rev are methods which change the state of flag objects, and up? is an attribute that tells whether or not the flag is up. The underbar characters indicate where an argument goes, so that all three methods and the attribute have prefix syntax.

The imported module DATA defines the data types that will be used, which should include at least the Booleans. Then Ψ is the signature of DATA, and D is some standard model for the given data types. Later, we will see that a model of this FLAG specification is an algebra such that its restriction to Ψ is D, providing functions for the given methods and attributes, and behaving as if it satisfied the given equations; i.e., it is an implementation that provides the given data, the one attribute, the three methods, and the desired behaviour.

In ordinary programming notation, one would write things like

```
up.F; dn.F; rev.F; up?.F
```

where F is some particular flag object, but in the more algebraic notation that we are using here, the above instead takes the form

```
up? rev dn F
```

□

To make our notion of model precise, we must first define behavioural satisfaction. Intuitively, this means that the two terms of an equation "look the same" under every "experiment," consisting of some methods, followed by an observation of some attribute. More formally, such an "experiment" is given by a *context*, which is a term of visible sort having one free variable of hidden sort. This motivates the following:

Definition 8 Given a hidden sorted signature (S, Σ, V, Ψ, D) and an S-sorted set X of variable symbols, then a **Σ-context** is a visible sorted Σ-term having a single occurrence of a new variable symbol z. Call such a context **appropriate** for a term t iff the sort of t matches the sort of z.

A Σ-algebra A **behaviourally satisfies** a Σ-equation $(\forall X)\, t = t'$ iff A satisfies each equation $(\forall X)\, c(t) = c(t')$ where c is an appropriate Σ-context; in this case, we may write $A \models_\Sigma (\forall X)\, t = t'$, and we may drop the subscript Σ if it is not needed.

Similarly, A **behaviourally satisfies** a conditional equation e of the form

$$(\forall X)\, t = t' \textbf{ if } t_1 = t'_1, \ldots, t_m = t'_m$$

iff for every interpretation $\theta : X \to A$, we have

$$\theta^*(c(t)) = \theta^*(c(t'))$$

for all appropriate contexts c whenever, for $j = 1, ..., m$,

$$\theta^*(c_j(t_j)) = \theta^*(c_j(t'_j))$$

for all appropriate contexts c_j. As with unconditional equations, we write $A \models_\Sigma e$. □

The algebraic approach to the object paradigm is prefigured in work of Goguen and Meseguer on (what they then called) abstract machines [20, 30]; the hidden sorted algebra approach differs from this mainly in its use of behavioural satisfaction for equations, an idea introduced by Reichel [32] in the context of partial algebras. Reichel [33] later introduced the related idea of behavioural equivalence for states, which we also use here later on.

Example 9 The following are some contexts for `FLAG`:

```
c(z) = up? z
c(z) = up? up rev z
c(z) = up? dn dn z
```

□

We can now make the idea of model precise:

Definition 10 Given a hidden sorted specification $(S, \Sigma, V, \Psi, D, E)$, then a **model** of that specification is a Σ-algebra A such that

1. $A\restriction_\Psi = D$, and
2. each equation in E is behaviourally satisfied.

A model of $(S, \Sigma, V, \Psi, D, E)$ is also called a $(S, \Sigma, V, \Psi, D, E)$-**algebra**, or a (Σ, D, E)-algebra for short. A Σ-algebra that satisfies just the first condition is called a (S, Σ, V, Ψ, D)-algebra, or for short, a (Σ, D)-algebra, or a **hidden sorted algebra.** □

The following gives some (abstract) implementations of flag objects to illustrate the above:

Example 11 Let's first define a simple Boolean cell C as a hidden sorted algebra. Here, $C_{\texttt{Flag}} = C_{\texttt{Bool}} = \{true, false\}$, up $F = true$, dn $F = false$, up? $F = F$, **rev** $F = not\ F$, and **newf** $= false$.

A more complex implementation H keeps complete histories of interactions, so that the action of a method is merely to concatenate its name to the front of a list of method names. Then $H_{\texttt{Flag}} = \{up, dn, rev\}^*$, the lists from $\{up, dn, rev\}$, while $H_{\texttt{Bool}} = \{true, false\}$, up $F = up^\frown F$, dn $F = dn^\frown F$, **rev** $F = rev^\frown F$, while up? $up^\frown F = true$, up? $dn^\frown F = false$, and up? $rev^\frown F =$ *not* up? F, where $^\frown$ is the concatenation operation.

Note that C and H are not isomorphic. □

For visible sorted equations, there is no difference between ordinary satisfaction and behavioural satisfaction. But these concepts can be different for hidden sorted equations. For example, the equation

```
eq rev rev F = F .
```

is strictly satisfied by the Boolean cell model C, but it is *not* satisfied by the history model H (however, it is *behaviourally* satisfied by both models).

3.1 The Order Sorted Case

We first consider a simple example, and then give the general definitions.

Example 12 It is very traditional to consider the stack object, which is interesting because one of its equations, namely

```
eq pop push(N,S) = S .
```

is not actually satisfied by some important models, including the traditional pointer-array pair implementation. Here is the code:

```
obj STACK is
  pr DATA .
  sorts NeStack Stack .
  subsort NeStack < Stack .
  op push : Nat Stack -> NeStack .
  op empty : -> Stack .
  op pop_ : NeStack -> Stack .
  op top_ : NeStack -> Nat .
  var S : Stack . var N : Nat .
  eq pop push(N,S) = S .
  eq top push(N,S) = N .
endo
```

Notice that this specification involves a subsort `NeStack` of the basic sort `Stack` of stack states; this subsort is for those stack states that are non-empty. Thus, this specification uses order sorted equational logic to classify the possible states of objects. A model is an order sorted algebra with the appropriate data subalgebra, having the `push` and `pop` methods and the `top` attribute (plus the constant `empty`), and behaving as if it satisfies the two equations.

The following contexts are appropriate for terms of the class `Stack`:

```
c(z) = top z
c(z) = top pop z
c(z) = top pop pop z
```

These contexts respectively select the top, second and third elements on a stack, if they exist. (Strictly speaking, the above are not really contexts for `STACK`, but rather for the enrichment of `STACK` by retracts, as described for example in [22], and implemented in OBJ3.) □

We are now ready to define hidden order sorted signatures and algebras; these extend our previous definitions for the many sorted case by adding an ordering relation $\leq$ on sorts.

Definition 13 Given an order sorted signature $(V, \leq, \Psi)$ with set V of visible sorts and an order sorted Ψ-algebra D, then $(S, \leq, \Sigma, V, \Psi, D)$ is a **hidden order sorted signature** if $(V, \leq, \Psi) \subseteq (S, \leq, \Sigma)$ as order sorted signatures, and (S, Σ, V, Ψ, D) is a hidden many sorted signature, such that no visible sort is related (by $\leq$) to any hidden sort.

A **hidden order sorted specification** or **module** is a tuple $(S, \leq, \Sigma, V, \Psi, D, E)$ where $(S, \leq, \Sigma, V, \Psi, D)$ is a hidden order sorted signature and E is a set of Σ-equations. We may abbreviate this to just (Σ, D, E), as in the many sorted case.

A **hidden order sorted** $(S, \leq, \Sigma, V, \Psi, D)$**-algebra** is an order sorted $(S, \leq, \Sigma)$-algebra M that is also a hidden many sorted (Σ, D)-algebra. A **homomorphism** of hidden order sorted algebras $h: M \to M'$ is a homomorphism of order sorted algebras that is also a homomorphism of hidden sorted algebras. □

The condition that visible and hidden sorts are unrelated under $\leq$ has the intuitive meaning that nothing visible can be a subsort of something hidden, and *vice versa*.

3.2 Inheritance and Modularity

There are many opinions about what inheritance is or should be. We believe that much confusion has resulted from not distinguishing carefully between subclasses and imported modules, or more fundamentally, between classes and modules (see [26] for a more detailed discussion of this). We believe that each of these is needed, and that they are different. Similarly, there are many different notions of encapsulation, which can also become confused by failure to distinguish between modules and classes. In our opinion, the fundamental notion of inheritance is at the module level rather than at the class level. Also, we believe that modules should support the declaration of more than one class (examples showing the need for this are given in [26]).

The basic intuition about modules is that they should support the reuse or replacement of code [31]. This requires that the *properties* of an imported module should be preserved by its importing module: we want old classes to behave the same way in their new context as they did in their original context. In fact, this requirement is often not satisfied by code that is written in the usual object oriented languages.

The following example will help us get started on our quest to formalise these issues.

Example 14 The module CFLAG below introduces a new subclass CFlag of Flag having a new attribute count that counts up's and down's (but ignores rev's):

```
obj CFLAG is
   pr DATA .
   sort Flag .
   op newf : -> Flag .
   ops (up_) (dn_) (rev_) : Flag -> Flag .
   op up?_ : Flag -> Bool .
   var F : Flag .
   eq up? up F = true .
   eq up? dn F = false .
   eq up? rev F = not up? F .
   eq up? newf = false .

   sort CFlag .
   subsort CFlag < Flag .
   op newc : -> CFlag .
   ops (up_) (dn_) (rev_) : CFlag -> CFlag .
   op count_ : CFlag -> Nat .
   var C : CFlag .
   eq count newc  = 0 .
   eq up? newc = false .
   eq count up  C = count C + 1 .
   eq count dn  C = count C + 1 .
   eq count rev C = count C .
endo
```

The first part of this module is exactly the same as FLAG; in particular, the second line says that it has the same data algebra (which should include at least the Booleans and natural numbers). The rest of the module defines the new subclass CFlag with its new constant newc, new attribute count, and with new (overloaded) versions of all the methods in FLAG. Notice that the subsort relationship here between Flag and CFlag is used to introduce a new class of object, without disturbing the old class Flag. It is also interesting to notice that the Boolean cell algebra C

cannot be extended with a count attribute that will make it a model of CFLAG. but the history algebra H can be so extended.

By using OBJ's module import notation, we can simplify the above code:

```
obj CFLAG is
   pr DATA .
   pr FLAG .
   sort CFlag .
   subsort CFlag < Flag .
   op newc : -> CFlag .
   ops (up_) (dn_) (rev_) : CFlag -> CFlag .
   op count_ : CFlag -> Nat .
   var C : CFlag .
   eq count newc  = 0 .
   eq up? newc = false .
   eq count up  C = count C + 1 .
   eq count dn  C = count C + 1 .
   eq count rev C = count C .
endo
```

The line[3] pr FLAG above indicates that the code for FLAG is imported in such a way that every model of CFLAG also gives a model of FLAG (as already noted, the converse of this does not hold). □

The claim that properties of FLAG-models should also hold for the FLAG-part of a CFLAG-model expresses the encapsulation of the module FLAG within the module CLFAG. To formalise this, notice that there is an *inclusion* from the signature of FLAG into the signature of CFLAG, and that this inclusion satisfies some rather special conditions, which are given in the following:

Definition 15 Given hidden order sorted signatures Σ and Σ', then a **hidden order sorted signature morphism** $\Phi : \Sigma \to \Sigma'$ is an order sorted signature morphism $\Phi = (f, g) : \Sigma \to \Sigma'$ such that:

(M1) $f(v) = v$ for each $v \in V$;

(M2) $g(\psi) = \psi$ for each $\psi \in \Psi$;

(M3) $f(H) \subseteq H'$ (where $H' = S' - V$ and S' is the sort set of Σ');

(M4) if $\sigma' \in \Sigma'_{w',s'}$ and some sort in w' lies in $f(H)$, then $\sigma' = g(\sigma)$ for some $\sigma \in \Sigma$; and

(M5) for any hidden sorts h, h', if $f(h) < f(h')$ then $h < h'$.

For the many sorted case, the condition (M5) is omitted. □

The first three conditions say that hidden sorted signature morphisms preserve visibility and invisibility for both sorts and operations, while the fourth and fifth conditions express the *encapsulation* of classes and subclasses, in the sense that no new methods or attributes can be defined on any imported class, and that any sublcass relation between images of hidden sorts comes from a relation between their sources. A morphism of modules, i.e., of hidden sorted specifications, must satisfy an additional condition:

[3]This declaration differs from the previous declaration "pr DATA" in that DATA has an initial semantics, whereas FLAG has a loose behavioural semantics.

Definition 16 Given hidden sorted specifications (Σ, D, E) and (Σ', D, E'), then a hidden sorted signature morphism $\Phi: (\Sigma, D) \to (\Sigma', D)$ is a **morphism** $\Phi: (\Sigma, D, E) \to (\Sigma', D, E')$ iff

(M6) $M' \models_{\Sigma'} E'$ implies $\Phi(M') \models_{\Sigma} E$,

for all Σ'-algebras M', where the **reduct** $\Phi(M')$ of M' to Σ is M' viewed as a Σ-algebra, just as in many sorted algebra. □

The following diagram may help to visualise this situation:

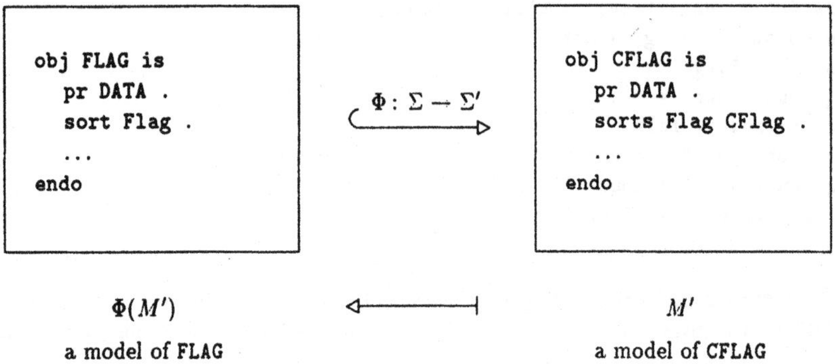

4 The Hidden Equational Institution

This section shows that the Satisfaction Condition (previously stated as Theorem 5 for overloaded many sorted algebra) also holds for hidden sorted algebra. This condition has methodological significance, because it implies that whatever we prove about the objects defined by some module P remains true in the context of some module P' that imports P. This property is crucial to the reuse of modules: if we define stacks and then use them in some new program, but they no longer behave the same way, then we will have to start from scratch in trying to understand the new code; we want to import not just code, but also *properties* of code.

Theorem 17 Given a hidden many sorted signature morphism $\Phi: \Sigma \to \Sigma'$, a Σ'-algebra M', and a Σ-equation $e = (\forall X)\ t_0 = t_1$, then

$$\Phi(M') \models_{\Sigma} e \text{ iff } M' \models_{\Sigma'} \Phi(e).$$

Proof: We have to show that for all appropriate contexts c and c',

$$\Phi(M') \models_{\Sigma} (\forall X)\ c(t_0) = c(t_1)$$

iff

$$M' \models_{\Sigma'} (\forall X')\ c'(\Phi(t_0)) = c'(\Phi(t_1)).$$

The "if" direction follows from Theorem 5, the Satisfaction Condition for ordinary many sorted equational logic, plus the fact that $\Phi(c(t_i)) = \Phi(c)(\Phi(t_i))$.

For the converse, conditions (S3) and (M4) of the definitions of hidden sorted signature and morphism imply that every context c' for $\Phi(e)$ is of the form $c''(\Phi(c))$ where $c'' \in T_{\Psi \cup \{z'\}}$ and c is a context for e. Therefore it suffices to show that

$$M' \models_{\Sigma'} (\forall X')\ \Phi(c)(\Phi(t_0)) = \Phi(c)(\Phi(t_1)).$$

But this follows from Theorem 5 plus the assumption, again using the fact that $\Phi(c(t_i)) = \Phi(c)(\Phi(t_i))$. □

We find it rather exciting that the conditions (S0–S3) and (M1–M4), which express encapsulation in the object paradigm, can be (and in fact, were) determined by the need to make the above proof of the Satisfaction Condition work. This derivation of the methodological principle of encapsulation from the metamathematical principle of the invariance of truth under change of notation seems to confirm the naturalness of both principles.

Note that the result and proof given above treat the many sorted case, following [15]. Although the result generalises to the order sorted case, the proof does not, and the interested reader should instead consult the proof of Burstall and Diaconescu in [5]. The result also generalises to conditional equations.

The next result makes precise our intuition that properties true of an imported module in isolation remain true of that module in its new context. To state this result, we must first explain what it means for an equation to be true of a module: it is just that the equation is satisfied by all correct implementations of the module. This semantic entailment relation is obtained from our basic behavioural satisfaction relation as follows:

Definition 18 Let $P = (\Sigma, D, E)$ be a specification and let M be a (Σ, D)-algebra. Then we let $M \models\!\!\equiv_\Sigma P$ mean that $M \models\!\!\equiv_\Sigma e$ for each $e \in E$. If e is a Σ-equation, then we let $P \models\!\!\equiv_\Sigma e$ mean that for any (Σ, D)-algebra M, if $M \models\!\!\equiv_\Sigma P$ then $M \models\!\!\equiv_\Sigma e$. □

Corollary 19 Let $P = (\Sigma, D, E)$ and $P' = (\Sigma', D, E')$ be hidden sorted specifications with $P \subseteq P'$ (i.e., with $\Sigma \subseteq \Sigma'$ and $E \subseteq E'$); let $\Phi : \Sigma \to \Sigma'$ denote the inclusion, and let e be a Σ-equation. Then

$$P \models\!\!\equiv_\Sigma e \text{ implies } P' \models\!\!\equiv_{\Sigma'} e.$$

Proof: First note that $\Phi(e) = e$ for any Σ-equation e, and thus that $\Phi(E) = E$. Now let M' be a Σ'-algebra satisfying E'. Because $E \subseteq E'$, we have $M' \models\!\!\equiv_{\Sigma'} E$, so that $\Phi(M') \models\!\!\equiv_\Sigma E$, by the Satisfaction Condition. Therefore $\Phi(M') \models\!\!\equiv_\Sigma e$ by hypothesis, and hence $M' \models\!\!\equiv_{\Sigma'} e$, again by the Satisfaction Condition. □

4.1 Institutions

We now have all the ingredients from hidden sorted algebra needed to form what is called an *institution*, which is a formalisation of the notion of "logic." These ingredients are as follows:

- signatures and their morphisms,
- Σ-sentences, for each signature Σ, and
- Σ-models, for each Σ,

such that

- signatures form a category, denoted ***Sign***,
- sentences are functorial on signatures,
- models are functorial on signatures, and
- the Satisfaction Condition holds,

$$\Phi(M') \models_\Sigma e \text{ iff } M' \models_{\Sigma'} \Phi(e).$$

where M' is a Σ'-model, e is a Σ-sentence, and $\Phi : \Sigma \to \Sigma'$ is a signature morphism.

A formalisation of logic that is adequate for Computing Science should encompass both syntax and semantics. On the one hand, *syntax is fundamental*, because we must say things in a finite amount of space: we manipulate finite texts, which (partially) describe real world entities, such as VLSI chips, bank balances, and computations, and we perform computations on such texts, such as proofs, translations, and type checks.

On the other hand, *semantics is fundamental*, because we are really interested in the *models*, rather than their descriptions; that is, we are really interested in chips, computations, etc.; we manipulate the syntactic representations only because we hope they correspond to the reality[4].

There is a reconciliation of these two views of what is fundamental that has been traditional since Tarski's classic semantic definition of truth for first order logic [37], based on the notion of *satisfaction*, seen as a binary relation between models and sentences (or more generally, sets of models and sets of sentences). Some such notion is needed for the basic notions of soundness and completeness of logical systems, because these notions depend in an essential way on the relationship between provability (which is syntactic) and satisfaction (which is semantic, i.e., concerns "truth" in Tarski's sense). In turn, these notions are fundamental to classical treatments of the adequacy of rules of deduction for logical systems: soundness and completeness with respect to an intuitively plausible class of models gives us confidence in some set of rules of deduction[5].

The theory of institutions allows us to discuss the pivotal relationship between specifications and models without committing to either side at the expense of the other. Institutions are much more abstract than Tarski's classical approach to truth, and also add another basic ingredient: signatures, and the possibility of translating sentences and models from one signature to another. The Satisfaction Condition, that truth is invariant under change of notation, is surely a very basic intuition for all classical logics.

Signatures are important for Computing Science because we consider not just "pure" logics, but rather "applied" logics, that use special "non-logical" symbols to capture the particularities of application areas, e.g., VLSI chip design for a fast Fourier transform. Category theory suggests treating not just the objects, which in this case are signatures, but also the relevant structure preserving morphisms, i.e., signature morphisms; it is these that enable us to consider how sentence, model, and satisfaction vary under change of notation.

Definition 20 An **institution** consists of

1. a category $\mathbf{Sign}$, whose objects are called **signatures**,
2. a functor $Sen: \mathbf{Sign} \to \mathbf{Set}$, giving for each signature a set whose elements are called **sentences** over that signature,

[4]Actually, this is a somewhat naive view, because we never really "have" the models, but only descriptions of models. Moreover, these descriptions generally use powerful idealistic constructions, such as power sets and dependent types, whose ultimate consistency cannot be resolved.

[5]There are also non-classical approaches to mathematics, e.g., the type theories of Martin-Löf, which do not appeal to notions of satisfaction, soundness and completeness, but rather regard their rules of inference as intuitively self-evident. There is room to doubt such claims, because of the contradictions that have been found in some such systems. However, it may be possible to construct appropriate set theories for such systems, and then construct appropriate models within such set theories.

3. a functor Mod: $\mathbf{Sign}^{op} \to \mathbf{Cat}$ giving for each signature Σ a category whose objects are called **Σ-models**, and whose arrows are called **Σ-(model) morphisms**, and

4. a relation $\models_\Sigma \subseteq |Mod(\Sigma)| \times Sen(\Sigma)$ for each $\Sigma \in |\mathbf{Sign}|$, called **Σ-satisfaction**,

such that for each morphism $\Phi: \Sigma \to \Sigma'$ in $\mathbf{Sign}$, the **Satisfaction Condition**

$$M' \models_{\Sigma'} Sen(\Phi)(e) \text{ iff } Mod(\Phi)(M') \models_\Sigma e$$

holds for each $M' \in |Mod(\Sigma')|$ and $e \in Sen(\Sigma)$. We may write $\Phi(e)$ for $Sen(\Phi)(e)$, and $\Phi(M')$ for $Mod(\Phi)(M')$. □

A perhaps surprising amount of Computing Science can be done over any institution; [18, 9] and [34] give many results. For example, a version of Corollary 19 holds for any institution. For this paper, it is especially significant that the notions of module, generic (parameterised) module, sum (combination) of modules, importation (inheritance) of modules, etc. can all be defined (using colimits of specifications) over any institution whose signatures admit colimits (details are given in [6, 18, 10]). This includes all the institutions that interest us, such as hidden sorted equational logic over over a fixed Ψ and D. The following result (from [18]) supports this approach, and is also used in Section 7.

Theorem 21 If the category $\mathbf{Sign}$ of signatures of an institution $\mathcal{I}$ has all (finite) colimits, then so does the category $\mathbf{Spec}(\mathcal{I})$ of all specifications over $\mathcal{I}$. □

Some researchers have argued that hidden sorted algebra is not really an institution, because without conditions like (M1–M4) the Satisfaction Condition does not hold. However, the most general possible morphisms are *not* necessarily the right ones. For example, although functions work well for sets, they are not the right morphisms for groups, because arbitrary functions do not preserve the group structure. Similarly for Banach spaces, morphisms should preserve all the relevant structure – not just the algebraic structure of vector spaces, but also the norm, in an appropriate sense. Thus, because the purpose of hidden sorts in hidden sorted algebra is to encapsulate states, we should expect to preserve the structure relating to encapsulation, and not just the operations in signatures.

5 Techniques for Verification

This section considers how to prove things about objects. The approach is to try to reduce reasoning about behavioural satisfaction to reasoning about ordinary satisfaction using ordinary equational deduction. The results in this section and the next are joint work with Tom Kemp, and follow [19].

Theorem 22 Ordinary equational reasoning (substituting equals for equals) is sound for behaviourally satisfied equations. □

But it is not complete. For example, we can prove

```
eq up? up dn F = true .
```

just by substitution, but we cannot prove

```
eq rev rev F = F .
```

in this way. The following result is originally due to Burstall and Diaconescu [5]; a more concrete proof is given in [19]:

Theorem 23 Given a hidden sorted Σ-algebra A, there is an ordinary Σ-algebra $\beta_\Sigma(A)$ such that

$$A \models\!\!\equiv e \text{ iff } \beta_\Sigma(A) \models e,$$

for any equation (or conditional equation) e. □

This result allows us to reason about $\beta_\Sigma(A)$ instead of A. Moreover, it extends to all first order sentences. Here is how $\beta_\Sigma(A)$ is constructed:

Given $a, a' \in A_s$ define $a \equiv_s a'$, and say a and a' are **behaviourally equivalent**, iff $c_A(a) = c_A(a')$ in A, for any s-sorted context c. Then $\equiv$ is a Σ-congruence relation on A, and so we can form the quotient $A/\equiv$, another Σ-algebra, denoted $\beta_\Sigma(A)$.

Unfortunately, it can be hard to see exactly what $\beta_\Sigma(A)$ looks like, and thus hard to use this result for practical reasoning. There is another construction that often yields a term algebra that is more convenient for reasoning. Let E be a set of Σ-equations, and let $\mathrm{Eq}(D)$ be the set of Ψ-equations satisfied by D. Now let Q be the Σ-congruence relation on T_Σ defined by

$$tQt' \text{ iff } (\forall\emptyset)\ t = t' \text{ is deducible from } E \cup \mathrm{Eq}(D).$$

Finally, let $T = T_\Sigma/Q$. This is almost what we want; it can be given the structure of a hidden sorted algebra under certain modest conditions.

Definition 24 A set E of Σ-equations is D-**protecting** iff

- for all $d, d' \in D$, if dQd' then $d = d'$, and
- for any $t \in T_{\Sigma,v}$ with $v \in V$, there is some $d \in D_v$ such that tQd.

□

Theorem 25 Let (Σ, D) be a hidden sorted signature and E a D-protecting set of Σ-equations, then:

(0) There is a hidden sorted Σ-algebra $G^D_{\Sigma,D,E}$ (denoted just G for short) that behaviourally satisfies E, and that is Σ-isomorphic to T_Σ/Q as an ordinary Σ-algebra.

(1) If G satisfies some (possibly conditional) Σ-equation then every reachable (Σ, D, E)-algebra behaviourally satisfies it.

(2) If G behaviourally satisfies some (possibly conditional) ground Σ-equation then every (Σ, D, E)-algebra behaviourally satisfies it.

(3) If all equations in E are unconditional, then (1) and (2) above can be made "iff" rather than "if ... then" assertions.

□

In general, proving behavioural satisfaction for G requires induction over all possible contexts.

Example 26 Suppose we want to establish that the equation

```
eq rev rev F = F .
```

is (behaviourally) satisfied by all models of FLAG.

The equations in FLAG are a canonical term rewriting system, so we can use the canonical (i.e., reduced) terms as (an algebra Σ-isomorphic to) G. Any appropriate context must be of the form up?($c(z)$). Then we use induction on the form of c to prove that

$$\texttt{up?}(c(\texttt{rev rev } F)) = \texttt{up?}(c(F))$$

for all appropriate terms $c(z)$.

(0) The base case is $c(z) = z$, in which each side reduces to up? F.

(1) For the induction step, there are three cases,

(a) $c(z) = \texttt{up } c'(z)$,
(b) $c(z) = \texttt{dn } c'(z)$, and
(c) $c(z) = \texttt{rev } c'(z)$,

where in each case the equation to be proved is assumed for c'.

All four cases can be proved by reduction, because the two sides have the same canonical form. The transcript of an OBJ3 proof score for this is given in Appendix A. □

6 Existential Queries

Our motivation is to unify the object and logic paradigms, by allowing *queries* over (systems of) objects involving so-called "logical variables" that can range over objects. This will support a novel programming style, in which framing a query can activate methods that change the world so that a solution object actually comes to exist. In applications, this can be realised over an object oriented data base. Let us consider two examples:

- *A travel agency.* Consider a query about a holiday package, having constraints on cost, flight times, seat assignments, hotels, expected weather, and so on; then a solution to this query would be an actual holiday package, providing tickets, reservations, visas, etc. that satisfy the constraints (of course, subject to user approval before commitment).

- *A software factory.* Consider a query about an operating system, with constraints on number of disc drives, amount of core memory, external connections, etc.; then a solution would be a loadable image of an actual properly configured operating system, assembled from generic components in the software library.

One can easily imagine other applications where answering an active query over a domain specific objectbase actually creates new objects that satisfy the given constraints; for example, there are many such applications in the area of Computer Aided Design. This new paradigm differs from traditional logic programming in that permanent storage is permanently altered; for example, seats may be reserved in an airline database. or an executable core image of an operating system may be created. The particular way that this approach is based on logic means that it supports the powerful generic module facilities of parameterised programming, in the sense of [10, 12].

In order to know that this new paradigm for computing works as desired, we need a *hidden Herbrand theorem*, which reduces reasoning over arbitary implementations (e.g., of object oriented databases) to reasoning over a single term algebra (a "Herbrand universe"). The result below is joint work with Tom Kemp, and follows [19].

Definition 27 An **(existential) Σ-query** is a sentence of the form

$$(\exists X)\, t_1 = t'_1, \ldots, t_m = t'_m$$

and it is **behaviourally satisfied** by a Σ-algebra A iff there is some substitution $\theta: X \to A$ such that, for $j = 1, ..., m$,

$$\theta^*(c_j(t_j)) = \theta^*(c_j(t'_j))$$

for all appropriate contexts c_j. □

The following is the basic result:

Theorem 28 If (Σ, D) is a hidden sorted signature and E is a D-protecting set of Σ-equations, then whenever G behaviourally satisfies a Σ-query q, so does every (Σ, D, E)-algebra. □

When G is (isomorphic to) a canonical term algebra, we can use narrowing to solve queries, for example, over arbitrary implementations of object oriented databases (narrowing is described in [7], among other places, and the use of narrowing to solve queries is illustrated in [19].)

We note that the definitions and results in this and the previous section extend to Horn clause logic with equality, by applying a construction that reduces that logic to hidden sorted equational logic. This is described in [19], extending some earlier work of Diaconescu [8].

7 Concurrent Systems of Objects

To motivate the general constructions that are given below, we first consider a parallel connection of two simple objects:

Example 29 We begin by defining an integer cell X with the following OBJ3 code:

```
obj X is
  pr DATA .
  sort X .
  op init : -> X .
  op putx : Nat X -> X .
  op getx_ : X ->  Nat .

  var X : X .  vars M N : Nat .
  eq getx init      = 0 .
  eq getx putx(N,X) = N .
endo
```

It is interesting to notice that the equation

```
eq putx(M,putx(N,X)) = putx(M,X) .
```

is a behavioural consequence of the above specification. Also, it is interesting that the integer-valued expressions in one hidden variable X (of sort `X`), i.e., the *contexts*, are the polynomials in the variable X. We may also call these *attribute expressions*; they form a polynomial ring $\mathbf{Z}[X]$. Next, let us define the cell Y in exactly the same way that we did X, but with `X` and `x` everywhere replaced by `Y` and `y`, respectively.

The parallel connection of X and Y should be described by a specification $X \parallel Y$ that has a single hidden sort, with all the operations of X and Y having the same semantics as before, in such a way that the operations in X and Y do not interfere with each other. Thus it seems intuitively clear that $X \parallel Y$ should be just the union of the specifications X and Y, with their sorts identified, and with some new equations to express the independence of X and Y:

```
obj XY is
  pr DATA .
  sort S .
  op init : -> S .
  ops putx puty : Nat S -> S .
  ops (getx_) (gety_) : S -> Nat .

  var S : S .  vars M N : Nat .
  eq getx init = 0 .
  eq gety init = 0 .
  eq getx putx(N,S) = N .
  eq gety puty(N,S) = N .
  eq getx puty(N,S) = getx S .
  eq gety putx(N,S) = gety S .
endo
```

The last equations equations, plus

```
eq putx(M,puty(N,S)) = puty(N,putx(M,S)).
```

(which is a behavioural consequence of the specification XY) express the independence of X and Y within their parallel connection. Notice that the attribute expressions for XY form a ring $\mathbf{Z}[X, Y]$ of polynomials in two variables, X, Y. Notice that the init methods from X and Y have been identified to a single method in XY. □

It is fairly straightforward to generalise the above construction of XY to the parallel connection of any set of specifications; Section 7.1 below gives the precise details, and also provides a suitable universal characterisation of the construction. But first, let us consider a somewhat more sophisticated example:

Example 30 Consider a simple manager for a class of objects, each of which is a cell that can hold one natural number. There is a method for updating the value in a cell, and an attribute that gives the value stored in a cell. We will use OBJ3's built-in module QID (for identifiers as strings with an initial quote symbol) to supply unique identifiers for objects.

```
obj NAT? is
  pr NAT + QID .
  sort Nat? .
  subsort Nat < Nat? .
  op bad : -> Nat? .
endo

obj MGR is
  pr NAT? .
  sort St .
  op init : -> St .
  op put : Id Nat St -> St .
  op get : Id St -> Nat? .

  vars I J : Id .  var N : Nat .  var S : St .
  eq get(I,init)       = bad .
  eq get(I,put(I,N,S))  = N .
  cq get(I,put(J,N,S))  = get(I,S) if I =/= J .
endo
```

The attribute expressions for MGR form a ring Z[Id] of polynomials in variables corresponding to the unique identifiers for the cells, where each cell has the following form:

```
obj CELL is
  pr NAT? .
  sort St .
  op init : -> St .
  op put  : Nat St -> St .
  op get_ : St ->  Nat? .

  var N : Nat .  var S : St .
  eq get init     = bad .
  eq get put(N,S) = N .
endo
```

This kind of cell is more sophisticated than the simple cells X and Y considered in Example 29 above, because of the error handling capability; in particular, there is an "inactive" state before a value is assigned. The next subsection defines a way to connect a number of copies of CELL in parallel to form a system that (in some appropriate sense) is the same as the system specified by MGR. The following equation, which together with the last equation of MGR expresses independence, is a behavioural consequence of MGR:

```
cq put(I,N,put(J,M,S)) = put(J,M,put(I,N,S)) if I =/= J .
```

Note that it would not be very difficult to enrich this specification with "meta level" methods, for example, to increment all currently active cells. □

It seems reasonable to expect that this approach will generalise to the dynamic creation and destruction of objects in more complex systems; the approach can also be considered a (weak form of) reflection, because it provides a "metaobject" for managing each class.

7.1 Universal Property for Parallel Connection

This subsection provides a universal characterisation for the parallel connection of hidden sorted specifications having just one hidden sort, which is denoted h. A basic semantic property of the parallel connection is that its components do not interact. Definition 31 below expresses this property precisely; in it, the notation $(\forall \underline{X})$ stands for $(\forall x_1)(\forall x_2)...(\forall x_n)$ where each x_i is a visible sorted variable and $n > 0$.

Definition 31 Given hidden sorted specifications P_1 and P_2 (with just one hidden sort), then hidden sorted specification morphisms of the form $P_1 \xrightarrow{\varphi_1} P \xleftarrow{\varphi_2} P_2$ are **independent** iff $\varphi_1(h) = \varphi_2(h)$, and for all $i, j \in \{1,2\}$ with $i \neq j$, we have

$$P \models (\forall \underline{X})(\forall \underline{Y})(\forall S)\ \varphi_i(a_i)(\underline{X}, \varphi_j(m_j)(\underline{Y}, S)) = \varphi_i(a_i)(\underline{X}, S),$$

$$P \models (\forall \underline{X})(\forall \underline{Y})(\forall S)\ \varphi_i(m_i)(\underline{X}, \varphi_j(m_j)(\underline{Y}, S)) = \varphi_j(m_j)(\underline{Y}, \varphi_i(m_i)(\underline{X}, S)),$$

where S is an h-sorted variable, where m_k is a method symbol of P_k, and where a_i is an attribute symbol of P_i. In this case, we will write $\varphi_1 \perp \varphi_2$. □

Example 32 If X and Y are the integer cells in Example 29, but without the **init** methods, and if XY is specification XY, again without the **init** method, let ι_X and ι_Y be the insertion morphisms defined by ι_X(X) = ι_Y(Y) = S, ι_X(get) = getx, ι_X(put) = putx, ι_Y(get) = gety, and ι_Y(put) = puty. Then ι_X and ι_Y are independent. An equation of the first kind required by Definition 31 is

```
eq getx puty(N,S) = getx S .
```

while an equation of the second kind is

```
eq putx(M,puty(N,S)) = puty(N,putx(M,S)).
```

which is a behavioural consequence of the specification XY. □

The intuitive idea behind the following universal characterisation of the parallel connection of systems P_i is simply that it is initial among all specifications that have independent insertions of the P_i.

Definition 33 Given a collection $\mathcal{P} = \{P_i \mid i \in I\}$ of hidden sorted specifications (each having just one hidden sort), let $\mathbf{Ind}(\mathcal{P})$ be the full subcategory of co-cones φ over $\mathcal{P}$ such that $\varphi_i \perp \varphi_j$ for all $i, j \in I$ with $i \neq j$; i.e., $\mathbf{Ind}(\mathcal{P})$ is the category whose objects are families $\varphi_i \colon P_i \to P$ for $i \in I$ of specification morphisms such that $\varphi_i \perp \varphi_j$ for all $i, j \in I$ with $i \neq j$, and whose morphisms $\rho\colon \varphi \to \varphi'$ are the specification morphisms $\rho\colon P \to P'$ such that $\varphi_i; \rho = \varphi'_i$ for all $i \in I$.

Let us call an initial object in $\mathbf{Ind}(\mathcal{P})$ an **independent sum** or **parallel connection** of the P_i for $i \in I$, and let us denote it by $\|_{i\in I} P_i$ or by $\|\mathcal{P}$. □

Note that although the components P_i are required to have just one hidden sort, the candidates P for the independent sum are not required to satisfy this property. However, the proof of Theorem 35 below shows that in fact the independent sum of components having just one hidden sort also has just one hidden sort. But first, we should state the following, the proof of which is similar to proofs in [18]:

Theorem 34 The category of hidden sorted signatures has colimits. □

Now the main result of this subsection:

Theorem 35 Any collection $\mathcal{P} = \{P_i \mid i \in I\}$ of hidden sorted specifications having just one hidden sort has an independent sum.

Proof: For any specification P, let $\Sigma(P)$ denote its signature. Now define $(\Sigma(P_i) \xrightarrow{\iota_i} \Sigma)_{i\in I}$ to be the colimit of the cone $(\Upsilon \hookrightarrow \Sigma(P_i))_{i\in I}$ in the category of hidden sorted signatures, where Υ is the hidden sorted signature with hidden part consisting of just the sort h, and with no method or attribute symbols. Then we define the specification $\|\mathcal{P}$ to have Σ as its signature and to have

$$\bigcup_{i\in I} \iota_i(P_i) \cup \bigcup_{i\neq j\in I} (A_{ij} \cup M_{ij})$$

as its sentences, where

$$A_{ij} = \{(\forall \underline{X})(\forall \underline{Y})(\forall S)\ \iota_i(a_i)(\underline{X}, \iota_j(m_j)(\underline{Y}, S)) = \iota_i(a_i)(\underline{X}, S) \mid a_i \in A_i \text{ and } m_j \in M_j\}$$

and

$$M_{ij} = \{(\forall \underline{X})(\forall \underline{Y})(\forall S)\ \iota_i(m_i)(\underline{X}, \iota_j(m_j)(\underline{Y}, S)) = \iota_j(m_j)(\underline{Y}, \iota_i(m_i)(\underline{X}, S)) \mid m_k \in M_k\},$$

where A_k is the set of attributes of P_k and M_k is the set of methods of P_k for each $k \in I$. Now it is not difficult to see that $\iota_i \perp \iota_j$ for all $i \neq j \in I$.

Next, consider a co-cone $(P_i \xrightarrow{\varphi_i} P)_{i\in I}$ such that $\varphi_i \perp \varphi_j$ for all $i \neq j \in I$. Then we have to show that there is a unique specification morphism $\rho\colon \|\mathcal{P} \to P$ such that $\iota_i; \rho = \varphi_i$ for all $i \in I$.

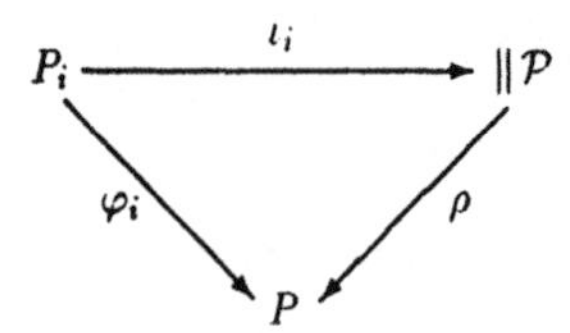

Because $\varphi_i(h) = \varphi_j(h)$ for all $i, j \in I$, we conclude that $(\Sigma(P_i) \xrightarrow{\varphi_i} \Sigma(P))_{i \in I}$ is a co-cone over $(\Upsilon \hookrightarrow \Sigma(P_i))_{i \in I}$. Therefore there is a unique hidden sorted signature morphism $\rho\colon \Sigma \to \Sigma(P)$ such that $\iota_i; \rho = \varphi_i$ for all $i \in I$.

Now it only remains to show that ρ is a specification morphism $\|\mathcal{P} \to P$. Let q be a sentence in $\|\mathcal{P}$. If $q \in \iota_i(P_i)$ for some $i \in I$, then $\rho(q) \in (\iota_i; \rho)P_i = \varphi_i(P_i)$. Therefore $P \models \rho(q)$. Also, if $q \in A_{ij}$ for some $i, j \in I$, then q is of the form

$$(\forall \underline{X})(\forall \underline{Y})(\forall S)\ (\iota_i(a))(\underline{X}, (\iota_j(m))(\underline{Y}, S)) = (\iota_i(a))(\underline{X}, S)$$

for some attribute symbol a of $\Sigma(P_i)$ and some method symbol m of $\Sigma(P_j)$. Therefore $\rho(q)$ is of the form

$$(\forall \underline{X})(\forall \underline{Y})(\forall S)\ (\varphi_i(a))(\underline{X}, (\varphi_j(m))(\underline{Y}, S)) = (\varphi_i(a))(\underline{X}, S).$$

Since $\varphi_i \perp \varphi_j$, we have $P \models \rho(q)$.

The case where $q \in M_{ij}$ for some $i, j \in I$ follows in a similar way. □

For example, if ι_X and ι_Y are the insertion morphisms defined in Example 32, then the diagram $X \xrightarrow{\iota_X} XY \xleftarrow{\iota_Y} Y$ satisfies the universal property for being an independent sum. Similarly, the specification MGR of Example 30 is (in some appropriate sense) the independent sum of a (potentially infinite) collection of CELL objects, indexed over their unique identifiers.

We expect that the construction and result of this section will generalise to the case where there may be more than one hidden sort in the component specifications.

7.2 Universal Property for Parallel Connection with Synchronisation

This subsection extends the previous subsection to situations where some methods and/or attributes are shared among the component specifications; this corresponds to what is called *synchronisation* in concurrency theory; it provides a very convenient way for communication among objects that would otherwise be independent. We first define the kind of situation in which synchronised parallel connection occurs.

Definition 36 Given a collection $\mathcal{P} = \{P_i \mid i \in I\}$ of hidden sorted specifications, then a **synchronisation** τ of $\mathcal{P}$ is a cone $(Q \xrightarrow{\tau_i} P_i)_{i \in I}$. The hidden sorted specification Q is called the **shared part** of the synchronisation.

Now let $P_1 \xleftarrow{\tau_1} Q \xrightarrow{\tau_2} P_2$ be a synchronisation τ of P_1 and P_2. Then hidden sorted specification morphisms of the form $P_1 \xrightarrow{\varphi_1} P \xleftarrow{\varphi_2} P_2$ are **independent over** τ iff $\tau_1; \varphi_1 = \tau_2; \varphi_2$, and for all $i, j \in \{1, 2\}$ with $i \neq j$, we have

$$P \models (\forall \underline{X})(\forall \underline{Y})(\forall S)\ \varphi_i(a_i)(\underline{X}, \varphi_j(m_j)(\underline{Y}, S)) = \varphi_i(a_i)(\underline{X}, S),$$

$$P \models (\forall \underline{X})(\forall \underline{Y})(\forall S)\ \varphi_i(m_i)(\underline{X}, \varphi_j(m_j)(\underline{Y}, S)) = \varphi_j(m_j)(\underline{Y}, \varphi_i(m_i)(\underline{X}, S)),$$

where S is an h-sorted variable, where m_k is a method symbol of P_k, where a_i is an attribute symbol of P_i, and where none of these symbols lie in the image of τ. In this case, we will write $\varphi_1 \perp^\tau \varphi_2$. □

The result below generalises Theorem 35 to synchronised parallel connections of hidden sorted specifications. Its proof follows the same lines as that of Theorem 35, and is therefore omitted.

Theorem 37 Given a collection $\mathcal{P} = \{P_i \mid i \in I\}$ of hidden sorted specifications (each having just one hidden sort) and a synchronisation τ of $\mathcal{P}$, let $\mathsf{Ind}^\tau(\mathcal{P})$ be the full subcategory of co-cones φ over $\mathcal{P}$ such that $\varphi_i \perp^\tau \varphi_j$ for all $i, j \in I$ with $i \neq j$.

Then $\mathsf{Ind}^\tau(\mathcal{P})$ has an initial object, called the **independent sum over** τ, or the **synchronised parallel connection over** τ, denoted $\|^\tau_{i\in I}\, P_i$ or $\|^\tau \mathcal{P}$. □

For example, the specification **XY** of Example 29 is the parallel connection of the specifications **X** and **Y** in that example, with synchronisation over the **init** method.

8 Further Research

It seems reasonable to expect that further aspects of concurrency could be treated in our hidden sorted framework in a natural way. However, we should also expect to find some difficult problems; in particular, it seems likely that combining object-valued logical variables with concurrency will raise some challenging theoretical problems concerning what may be an interesting new style for concurrent programming.

Non-determinism is another area that could be challenging. Notice that our way of describing objects with equational specifications is already non-deterministic, in the sense that there is no fixed starting state, and no fixed input-output relations; instead, we just describe the set of possible states, and how methods affect them. Then interconnecting objects with synchronisation may impose constraints that cut down on the possible states of the component objects. Combining this "internal non-determinism" with our constraint oriented approach to interconnection gives a situation similar to so-called "external non-determinism."

Another interesting problem is to characterise the interleaving parallel connection, which we might denote $X \otimes Y$, as opposed to the true concurrent connection that we have denoted $X \parallel Y$ and for which we have given a universal characterision above.

It is interesting to note that forming the so-called Lawvere algebraic theory (in the sense of [28] and [29]) of a hidden sorted specification gives rise to a structure generalising some traditional structures of process algebra, in that there is an action of the monoid of all method expressions (in the sense of FOOPS [21]) on the collection of all attribute expressions (again in the sense of FOOPS). This construction is similar to one used in [5], except that there only ground method and attribute expressions were used. Complex method and attribute expressions bring us closer to concurrent systems programming than the usual process algebra approaches, which only consider ground methods and attributes, ignoring the structure of data, and ignoring the relationships between methods and attributes that allow forming complex method expressions. On the other hand, traditional process algebra seems well suited to exploring concurrency as such, and it has been applied to some important issues that are not directly addressed in this paper, such as non-determinism and non-termination.

Finally, we expect soon to do some simple proofs of concurrent object systems using the 2OBJ metalogical framework theorem prover [24, 36] to support hidden sorted equational reasoning. This should provide a good test of how viable the approach suggested in this paper can be in practice.

Acknowledgements

We wish to thank Dr. Grant Malcolm for several important suggestions, and Ms. Frances Page for cheerfully typing many drafts, and for preparing the figure.

References

[1] Antonio Alencar. *OOZE: An Object Oriented Specification Language*. PhD thesis, Programming Research Group, Oxford University Computing Lab, to appear 1994.

[2] Antonio Alencar and Joseph Goguen. Specification in OOZE with examples. In *Object Oriented Specification Case Studies*, pages 158–183. Prentice Hall, 1993. Programming Research Group, Oxford University Computing Lab, Report PRG–TR–7–92, 1992.

[3] Michael Barr and Charles Wells. *Category Theory for Computing Science*. Prentice-Hall, 1990.

[4] Garrett Birkhoff. On the structure of abstract algebras. *Proceedings of the Cambridge Philosophical Society*, 31:433–454, 1935.

[5] Rod Burstall and Răzvan Diaconescu. Hiding and behaviour: an institutional approach. Technical Report ECS-LFCS-8892-253, Laboratory for Foundations of Computer Science, University of Edinburgh, 1992. To appear in *A Classical Mind: Essays in Honour of C.A.R. Hoare*, Prentice Hall, 1993.

[6] Rod Burstall and Joseph Goguen. The semantics of Clear, a specification language. In Dines Bjorner, editor, *Proceedings, 1979 Copenhagen Winter School on Abstract Software Specification*, pages 292–332. Springer, 1980. Lecture Notes in Computer Science, Volume 86; based on unpublished notes handed out at the Symposium on Algebra and Applications, Stefan Banach Center, Warsaw, Poland, 1978.

[7] Nachum Dershowitz and Jean-Pierre Jouannaud. Rewriting systems. In Jan van Leeuwen, editor, *Handbook of Theoretical Computer Science, Volume B*, pages 244–320. Elsevier Science, 1990.

[8] Răzvan Diaconescu. The logic of Horn clauses is equational. Technical Report PRG-TR-3-93, Programming Research Group, University of Oxford, 1993. Written in 1990.

[9] Răzvan Diaconescu, Joseph Goguen, and Petros Stefaneas. Logical support for modularisation. In Gerard Huet and Gordon Plotkin, editors, *Logical Environments*, pages 83–130. Cambridge, 1993. Proceedings of a Workshop held in Edinburgh, Scotland, May 1991.

[10] Joseph Goguen. Principles of parameterized programming. In Ted Biggerstaff and Alan Perlis, editors, *Software Reusability, Volume I: Concepts and Models*, pages 159–225. Addison Wesley, 1989.

[11] Joseph Goguen. An algebraic approach to refinement. In Dines Bjorner, C.A.R. Hoare, and Hans Langmaack, editors, *Proceedings, VDM'90: VDM and Z – Formal Methods in Software Development*, pages 12–28. Springer, 1990. Lecture Notes in Computer Science, Volume 428.

[12] Joseph Goguen. Hyperprogramming: A formal approach to software environments. In *Proceedings, Symposium on Formal Approaches to Software Environment Technology*. Joint System Development Corporation, Tokyo, Japan, January 1990.

[13] Joseph Goguen. Proving and rewriting. In Hélène Kirchner and Wolfgang Wechler, editors, *Proceedings, Second International Conference on Algebraic and Logic Programming*, pages 1–24. Springer, 1990. Lecture Notes in Computer Science, Volume 463.

[14] Joseph Goguen. A categorical manifesto. *Mathematical Structures in Computer Science*, 1(1):49–67, March 1991. Also, Programming Research Group Technical Monograph PRG–72, Oxford University, March 1989.

[15] Joseph Goguen. Types as theories. In George Michael Reed, Andrew William Roscoe, and Ralph F. Wachter, editors, *Topology and Category Theory in Computer Science*, pages 357–390. Oxford, 1991. Proceedings of a Conference held at Oxford, June 1989.

[16] Joseph Goguen. *Theorem Proving and Algebra*. MIT, 1994.

[17] Joseph Goguen and Rod Burstall. Introducing institutions. In Edward Clarke and Dexter Kozen, editors, *Proceedings, Logics of Programming Workshop*, pages 221–256. Springer, 1984. Lecture Notes in Computer Science, Volume 164.

[18] Joseph Goguen and Rod Burstall. Institutions: Abstract model theory for specification and programming. *Journal of the Association for Computing Machinery*, 39(1):95–146, January 1992. Draft appears as Report ECS-LFCS-90-106, Computer Science Department, University of Edinburgh, January 1990; an early ancestor is "Introducing Institutions," in *Proceedings, Logics of Programming Workshop*, Edward Clarke and Dexter Kozen, Eds., Springer Lecture Notes in Computer Science, Volume 164, pages 221–256, 1984.

[19] Joseph Goguen and Tom Kemp. A hidden Herbrand theorem, 1993. Submitted to special issue of *Theoretical Computer Science*, edited by A. William Roscoe and Michael W. Mislove.

[20] Joseph Goguen and José Meseguer. Universal realization, persistent interconnection and implementation of abstract modules. In M. Nielsen and E.M. Schmidt, editors, *Proceedings, 9th International Conference on Automata, Languages and Programming*, pages 265–281. Springer, 1982. Lecture Notes in Computer Science, Volume 140.

[21] Joseph Goguen and José Meseguer. Unifying functional, object-oriented and relational programming, with logical semantics. In Bruce Shriver and Peter Wegner, editors, *Research Directions in Object-Oriented Programming*, pages 417–477. MIT, 1987. Preliminary version in *SIGPLAN Notices*, Volume 21, Number 10, pages 153–162, October 1986.

[22] Joseph Goguen and José Meseguer. Order-sorted algebra I: Equational deduction for multiple inheritance, overloading, exceptions and partial operations. *Theoretical Computer Science*, 105(2):217–273, 1992. Also, Programming Research Group Technical Monograph PRG–80, Oxford University, December 1989, and Technical Report SRI-CSL-89-10, SRI International, Computer Science Lab, July 1989; originally given as lecture at *Seminar on Types*, Carnegie-Mellon University, June 1983; many draft versions exist, from as early as 1985.

[23] Joseph Goguen and Adolfo Socorro. Module composition and system design for the object paradigm. *Journal of Object Oriented Programming*, to appear 1994. Technical Report, Oxford University Computer Lab, 1993.

[24] Joseph Goguen, Andrew Stevens, Keith Hobley, and Hendrik Hilberdink. 2OBJ, a metalogical framework based on equational logic. *Philosophical Transactions of the Royal Society, Series A*, 339:69–86, 1992. Also in *Mechanized Reasoning and Hardware Design*, edited by C.A.R. Hoare and M.J.C. Gordon, Prentice-Hall, 1992, pages 69–86.

[25] Joseph Goguen, Timothy Winkler, José Meseguer, Kokichi Futatsugi, and Jean-Pierre Jouannaud. Introducing OBJ. In Joseph Goguen, editor, *Applications of Algebraic Specification using OBJ*. Cambridge, to appear 1993. Also to appear as Technical Report from SRI International.

[26] Joseph Goguen and David Wolfram. On types and FOOPS. In Robert Meersman, William Kent, and Samit Khosla, editors, *Object Oriented Databases: Analysis, Design and Construction*, pages 1–22. North Holland, 1991. Proceedings, IFIP TC2 Conference, Windermere, UK, 2–6 July 1990.

[27] Robert Goldblatt. *Topoi, the Categorial Analysis of Logic.* North-Holland, 1979.

[28] F. William Lawvere. Functorial semantics of algebraic theories. *Proceedings, National Academy of Sciences, U.S.A.*, 50:869–872, 1963. Summary of Ph.D. Thesis, Columbia University.

[29] Ernest Manes. *Algebraic Theories.* Springer, 1976. Graduate Texts in Mathematics, Volume 26.

[30] José Meseguer and Joseph Goguen. Initiality, induction and computability. In Maurice Nivat and John Reynolds, editors, *Algebraic Methods in Semantics*, pages 459–541. Cambridge, 1985.

[31] David Parnas. Information distribution aspects of design methodology. *Information Processing '72*, 71:339–344, 1972. Proceedings of 1972 IFIP Congress.

[32] Horst Reichel. Behavioural equivalence – a unifying concept for initial and final specifications. In *Proceedings, Third Hungarian Computer Science Conference.* Akademiai Kiado, 1981. Budapest.

[33] Horst Reichel. Behavioural validity of conditional equations in abstract data types. In *Contributions to General Algebra 3.* Teubner, 1985. Proceedings of the Vienna Conference, June 21-24, 1984.

[34] Donald Sannella and Andrzej Tarlecki. Specifications in an arbitrary institution. *Information and Control*, 76:165–210, 1988. Earlier version in *Proceedings, International Symposium on the Semantics of Data Types*, Lecture Notes in Computer Science, Volume 173, Springer, 1985.

[35] Adolfo Socorro. *Design, Implementation, and Evaluation of a Declarative Object Oriented Language.* PhD thesis, Programming Research Group, Oxford University, 1993.

[36] Andrew Stevens and Joseph Goguen. Mechanised theorem proving with 2OBJ: A tutorial introduction. Technical report, Programming Research Group, University of Oxford, 1993.

[37] Alfred Tarski. The semantic conception of truth. *Philos. Phenomenological Research*, 4:13–47, 1944.

A Transcript of an OBJ3 Proof Score

The following is the actual output produced by OBJ3 when given a proof score for showing that the equation

```
eq rev rev F = F .
```

is behaviourally satisfied by **FLAG**, according to the method discussed in Example 26 above. (Unfortunately, it does require some familiarity with OBJ3 and its use for theorem proving; the necessary details can be found in [13], [16], and [25]. The module **PROPC** that is used here provides a decision procedure for the Booleans.)

```
ruby: obj
                    \|||||||||||||||||/
                   --- Welcome to OBJ3 ---
                    /|||||||||||||||||\
       OBJ3 version 2.02 built: 1992 Jul 11 Sat 18:44:17
           Copyright 1988,1989,1991 SRI International
                   1993 Apr 23 Fri 10:24:39
OBJ> in tasop-pf
==========================================
***> file: ~goguen/oo/papers/tasop-pf.obj
==========================================
in /users/goguen/obj/prop/propc
Reading in file : "/users/goguen/obj/prop/propc"
==========================================
***> this file is /users/goguen/prop/propc.obj
==========================================
***> decision procedure for the propositional calculus
==========================================
obj PROPC
Done reading in file: "/users/goguen/obj/prop/propc"
==========================================
obj DATA
==========================================
obj FLAG
==========================================
***> to show: for all c, F: up? c rev rev F = up? c F
==========================================
openr
==========================================
***> common notation
==========================================
vars F z : Flag .
==========================================
op f : -> Flag .
==========================================
ops ( LHS _ ) ( RHS _ ) : Flag -> Bool .
==========================================
ops ( c _ ) ( c' _ ) : Flag -> Flag .
==========================================
```

```
eq LHS F = up? c rev rev F .
============================================
eq RHS F = up? c F .
============================================
close
============================================
open
============================================
***> base case:
============================================
var z : Flag .
============================================
eq c z = z .
============================================
reduce in FLAG : LHS f == RHS f
rewrites: 10
result Bool: true
============================================
close
============================================
***> induction steps:
============================================
openr
============================================
***> induction hypothesis:
============================================
var F : Flag .
============================================
eq up? c' rev rev F = up? c' F .
============================================
close
============================================
***> first up:
============================================
open
============================================
var z : Flag .
============================================
eq c z = up c' z .
============================================
reduce in FLAG : LHS f == RHS f
rewrites: 7
result Bool: true
============================================
close
============================================
***> second dn:
============================================
open
============================================
```

```
var z : Flag .
==========================================
eq c z = dn c' z .
==========================================
reduce in FLAG : LHS f == RHS f
rewrites: 7
result Bool: true
==========================================
close
==========================================
***> third rev:
==========================================
open
==========================================
var z : Flag .
==========================================
eq c z = rev c' z .
==========================================
reduce in FLAG : LHS f == RHS f
rewrites: 10
result Bool: true
==========================================
close
OBJ> q
Bye.
```

This only took about 4.6 seconds to run, and much of that was consumed by I/O. By including this detailed example, the authors hope to reinforce their basic contention that the hidden sorted algebra semantics for the object paradigm supports a simple calculational style of reasoning that is both more convenient and more efficient than currently known alternatives. Furthermore, it seems clear that it should be straightforward to totally automate this kind of proof using the 2OBJ theorem prover [36, 24].

Rewriting Techniques for Software Engineering *

Jean-Pierre Jouannaud[1]

Laboratoire de Recherche en Informatique, Bat. 490, Université de Paris Sud, 91405 Orsay, France, jouannau@lri.lri.fr

Abstract. This paper surveys the use of rewriting for prototyping languages based on equations as are algebraic specifications. The option is to stress the variety of questions expressed as logical queries that can be solved by using rewriting techniques, without hiding the limitations of the method. Using rewriting itself as a specification language is investigated next. Recent trends in rewriting are briefly sketched.

1 Introduction

The use of equations in computer science has culminated with the success of algebraic specifications, a method of specifying software by encapsulating datas defined abstractly by means of constructors, operations, and equations defining the action of the operations on the constructor expressions. The goal of this survey is to describe how rewriting techniques allow to prove properties of such specifications and prototype them into programs.

Equations can be used for reasoning, by using Leibnitz's law of replacing equals by equals, a highly non-deterministic way of using equations. In contrast, rewriting uses the equations in one way, hence eliminating one source of non-determinism. This one way use is achieved by rewriting according to a well-founded ordering on terms, hence it is called a reduction. The other sources of non-determinism, choice of an equation, and of a subterm where to rewrite can be eliminated as well if every expression has a unique irreducible form. In this case, rewriting defines a functional computation. These questions are investigated in section 2, including in the context of modular specifications.

The theory of rewriting centers therefore around the notion of normal form, an expression that cannot be reduced any further. How to obtain normal forms is described in section 3. Section 4 then describes all kinds of logical queries that can be solved by rewriting, provided normal forms exist. These queries can be used to formulate various questions in the theory of algebraic specifications, such as logical consequence or sufficient completeness.

Rewriting can also be used as a specification language itself when the specification problem centers around the computation of a normal form by means of equivalence transformations. This is of course the case for a number of problems, and we will show in section 5 several such uses of rewriting. Recent developments of rewriting are discussed in section 6.

---

* This work was parly supported by the "Greco de programmation du CNRS", and the ESPRIT working group COMPASS.

2 Rewriting

We will assume the standard notions of universal algebra, such as signature, terms, substitutions, etc. If necessary, the reader may refer to [19]. Key notations are the following: $s|_p$ denotes the subterm of s at position p, $s[t]_p$ the term obtained by replacing the subterm $s|_p$ by t, $s\sigma$ the instance of the term s by the substitution σ.

2.1 Equations and Rules

Traditionaly, rewrite rules are seen as object that differ from equations, even if what really differs is their use.

Definition 1. *Equation* and *rewrite rule* are pairs of terms written respectively $l \simeq r$ and $l \to r$. Let E be a set of equations, and R be a set of rules.

A term s rewrites to a term t at position p using an equation $l \simeq r \in E$, if there exist a substitution σ such that $s|_p = l\sigma$, and $t = s[r\sigma]_p$, or $s|_p = r\sigma$, and $t = s[l\sigma]_p$. We write $s \xleftrightarrow[l \simeq r]{p} t$ in the first case, and $s \xleftrightarrow[r \simeq l]{p} t$ in the second. We may drop the subscripts or superscripts, use E as a subscript if the actual equation is not important, as well as describe a position by a predicate if necessary.

A term s rewrites to a term t at position p using a rule $l \to r$ if there exist a substitution σ such that $s|_p = l\sigma$, and $t = s[r\sigma]_p$. We write $s \xrightarrow[l \to r]{p} t$. We may also write $s \xleftrightarrow[R]{} t$ for $s \xrightarrow[R]{}$ or $t \xrightarrow[R]{} s$, hence using rules as equations.

The *derivation relation* $\xrightarrow[R]{*}$ is the reflexive transitive closure of the above rewrite relation, while $\xleftrightarrow[E]{*}$ or $\xleftrightarrow[R]{*}$ are the congruence relations generated by respectively E and R.

At the heart of rewriting is the *encompassment* relation: s encompasses l, written $s \trianglerighteq l$, if a subterm of s is an instance of l, that is $s|_p = l\sigma$ for some position p and substitution σ.

2.2 Termination

A rewrite relation is said to be *terminating* (or *strongly normalizing* in the λ-calculus jargon) if there are no infinite sequences of rewrites.

Definition 2. A *rewrite ordering* is a well-founded ordering on terms which is closed both under context application ($s > t \Rightarrow f(\ldots, s, \ldots) > f(\ldots, t, \ldots)$) and under substitutions ($s > t \Rightarrow s\sigma > t\sigma$).

It can easily be seen that rewriting terminates iff there exists a rewrite ordering able to orient the rules in the right direction. We therefore simply need to provide with powerful enough rewrite orderings that will enable us to solve the practical cases we may face with. A popular method for designing rewrite orderings is by interpreting terms in some well-founded set, the set of terms being a particular case, see e.g. [17].

We will insist here in *divide and conquer* methods for building orderings, based on the use of functionals that preserve well-founded orderings. There are three major ones.

The *lexicographic extension* transforms n well-founded orderings $>_1, \ldots, >_n$ on n sets $S_1, \ldots, S_n$ into a well-founded ordering $(>_1, \ldots, >_n)_{lex}$ on the product $S_1 \times \ldots \times S_n$, by letting:

$$(a_1, \ldots, a_n)(>_1, \ldots, >_n)_{lex}(b_1, \ldots, b_n) \text{ if}$$

$$a_1 >_1 b_1 \text{ or } a_1 = b_1 \text{ and } (a_2, \ldots, a_n)(>_2, \ldots, >_n)_{lex}(b_2, \ldots, b_n)$$

We use to write $>_{lex}$ when all orderings $>_1, \ldots, >_n$ are the same ordering $>$. This definition extends to quasi-orderings, by using the equivalences associated to the quasi-orderings instead of the syntactic equality.

The *multiset extension* transforms any well-founded ordering $>$ on a set S into a well-founded ordering $\geq_{mul}$ on multisets on S. It is defined as the reflexive transitive closure of the relation between two multisets, say M_1 and M_2 such that M_2 is obtained from M_1 by replacing any element x by a finite number (possibly zero) of elements strictly smaller than x in the ordering on S.

The *term extension*, also called *recursive path ordering* transforms any well-founded ordering $\succ$ (called a *precedence*) on an alphabet $\mathcal{F}$ of function symbols into a rewrite-ordering $\succ_{rpo}$ on terms in $\mathcal{T}(\mathcal{F})$. To define it, we must first assign a status, lexicographic or multiset to all function symbols in $\mathcal{F}$, therefore split into two subsets Lex and Mul. The induced ordering is as follows:

$$s = f(s_1, \ldots, s_m) \succeq_{rpo} g(t_1, \ldots, t_n) = t$$

if either of the following (1 or 2 or 3) hold:

(1) $s_i \succeq_{rpo} t$ for some s_i, $i \in [1..m]$
(2) $f = g$ and
case a: $f \in Lex$, and $s \succ_{rpo} t_1, \ldots, s \succ_{rpo} t_n$ and $(s_1, \ldots, s_n)(\succeq_{rpo})_{lex}(t_1, \ldots, t_n)$
case b: $f \in Mul$, and $(s_1, \ldots, s_n)(\succeq_{rpo})_{mul}(t_1, \ldots, t_n)$
(3) $f \succ g$ and $s \succ_{rpo} t_i$ for all $i \in [1..n]$;

where $s \succ t$ if $s \succeq t$, but $s \not\preceq t$. When the precedence on function symbols is total, then the recursive path ordering is total. The ordering is strict if there are no multiset symbols, and its equivalence is generated by Malcev's permutative axioms for the multiset symbols otherwise.

See [18] for a more general version of this ordering mixing syntactic and semantic considerations.

There are two ways to extend the recursive path ordering to a rewrite ordering on terms with variables. By defining $s \succ_{rpo} t$ iff $s\sigma \succ_{rpo} t\sigma$ for all substitutions σ such that $s\sigma$ and $t\sigma$ are ground, we obtain the finest possible such extension [12; 40]. A less powerful but of lesser complexity one is obtained by considering the variables as new constants which do not compare with other function symbols nor between themselves in the precedence.

Example 1 [16]. The following is a "rewrite program" to sort a list of numbers by inserting elements one by one into position, with lists represented in "cons" notation and numbers in successor notation. The equations are written as rules by using the term extension generated by the precedence $sort > insert > max > min > s > cons$. insert is given a right-to-left (and not left-to-right as in the definition) lexicographic status. Other statuses are arbitrary.

$$\begin{array}{rcl} max(0,x) & \rightarrow & x \\ max(x,0) & \rightarrow & x \\ max(s(x),s(y)) & \rightarrow & s(max(x,y)) \\ min(0,x) & \rightarrow & 0 \\ min(x,0) & \rightarrow & 0 \\ min(s(x),s(y)) & \rightarrow & s(min(x,y)) \\ sort(nil) & \rightarrow & nil \\ sort(cons(x,y)) & \rightarrow & insert(x,sort(y)) \\ insert(x,nil) & \rightarrow & cons(x,nil) \\ insert(x,cons(y,z)) & \rightarrow & cons(max(x,y),insert(min(x,y),z)) \end{array}$$

2.3 Confluence

We say that s and t are: *convertible*, if $s \overset{*}{\leftrightarrow} t$; *divergent* if $u \overset{*}{\rightarrow} s$ and $u \overset{*}{\rightarrow} t$, for some u; *joinable*, if $s \overset{*}{\rightarrow} v$ and $t \overset{*}{\rightarrow} v$, for some v. In the latter case, we also say that $s \overset{*}{\leftrightarrow} t$ has a *rewrite proof*.

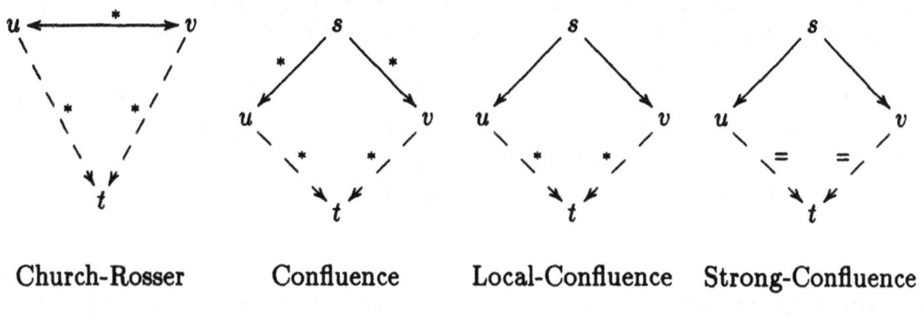

Fig. 1. Confluence Properties.

The following two properties are equivalent:

Definition 3. A rewrite system is *Church-Rosser* if convertible terms are joinable, and *confluent* if divergent terms are joinable.

Often, we are only interested in confluence for ground (variable-free) terms. If s and t are joinable for all ground u, we say the system is *ground confluent*.

When a rewrite system is confluent, a term may have at most one normal form.

Definition 4. A rewrite system is *functional* if any ground term has a unique normal form.

Functional systems are of course ground confluent. Conversely, if a rewrite system is ground confluent, and if any ground term has a normal form, then it is functional. Functional systems play a major role, since they allow to define a unique term for each equivalence class of ground terms with respect to the equations, which can be obtained by rewriting from any term of the class (provided normalization is decidable). These normal form terms are used to define the *normal form algebra*, which is equivalent to the initial algebra defined by the equations [27]. As a consequence, rewriting is the main paradigm used for prototyping algebraic specifications.

In the following, we investigate two cases of confluent systems. In both cases, we focus on confluence which can be more easily decided under additional assumptions.

Orthogonal Systems

Definition 5. A rewrite system is *orthogonal* if no left-hand side unifies with a renamed non-variable subterm of any other left-hand side or with a renamed proper subterm of itself, and no variable appears more than once on any left-hand side.

The importance of orthogonal systems lies in the following result:

Theorem 6 [31]. *Every orthogonal system is confluent.*

Example 2 [16]. The state of a machine with three integer-valued registers can be represented as a triple $\langle x,\ y,\ z\rangle$. The semantics of its instruction set can be defined by the interpreter shown in Figure 2. Note that the next to the last rule, for example, can clearly be applied *ad infinitum*.

When given an orthogonal system, the question is what strategy of rule application, if any, will lead to a normal form whenever there is one. This difficult question is investigated in detail in [34] and related works, where it is shown that indeed there are sound strategies, and even optimal ones for *sequential systems* [34; 43].

Terminating Systems In this section, we restrict our attention to terminating relations. Terminating confluent systems are of course functional. Besides, confluence can indeed be restricted to a weaker form under the termination assumption:

Definition 7. A proof pattern of the form $s \longleftarrow_R u \longrightarrow_R t$ is called a *peak*. A rewrite system is *locally confluent* if all peaks have a rewrite proof.

Theorem 8 [56]. *A terminating rewrite system is Church-Rosser if and only if it is locally confluent.*

For terminating confluent systems, any rewriting strategy will lead to the unique normal form. Besides, local confluence can itself be restricted to finitely many distinguished peaks, as shown now:

$$
\begin{array}{rcl}
eval(\mathbf{set0}\ n, \langle x,\ y,\ z\rangle) & \rightarrow & \langle n,\ y,\ z\rangle \\
eval(\mathbf{set1}\ n, \langle x,\ y,\ z\rangle) & \rightarrow & \langle x,\ n,\ z\rangle \\
eval(\mathbf{set2}\ n, \langle x,\ y,\ z\rangle) & \rightarrow & \langle x,\ y,\ n\rangle \\
eval(\mathbf{inc0}, \langle x,\ y,\ z\rangle) & \rightarrow & \langle s(x),\ y,\ z\rangle \\
eval(\mathbf{inc1}, \langle x,\ y,\ z\rangle) & \rightarrow & \langle x,\ s(y),\ z\rangle \\
eval(\mathbf{inc2}, \langle x,\ y,\ z\rangle) & \rightarrow & \langle x,\ y,\ s(z)\rangle \\
eval(\mathbf{dec0}, \langle s(x),\ y,\ z\rangle) & \rightarrow & \langle x,\ y,\ z\rangle \\
eval(\mathbf{dec1}, \langle x,\ s(y),\ z\rangle) & \rightarrow & \langle x,\ y,\ z\rangle \\
eval(\mathbf{dec2}, \langle x,\ y,\ s(z)\rangle) & \rightarrow & \langle x,\ y,\ z\rangle \\
eval(\mathbf{ifpos0}\ p, \langle 0,\ y,\ z\rangle) & \rightarrow & \langle 0,\ y,\ z\rangle \\
eval(\mathbf{ifpos0}\ p, \langle s(x),\ y,\ z\rangle) & \rightarrow & eval(p, \langle s(x),\ y,\ z\rangle) \\
eval(\mathbf{ifpos1}\ p, \langle x,\ 0,\ z\rangle) & \rightarrow & \langle x,\ 0,\ z\rangle \\
eval(\mathbf{ifpos1}\ p, \langle x,\ s(y),\ z\rangle) & \rightarrow & eval(p, \langle x,\ s(y),\ z\rangle) \\
eval(\mathbf{ifpos2}\ p, \langle x,\ 0,\ z\rangle) & \rightarrow & \langle x,\ 0,\ z\rangle \\
eval(\mathbf{ifpos2}\ p, \langle x,\ s(y),\ z\rangle) & \rightarrow & eval(p, \langle x,\ s(y),\ z\rangle) \\
\mathbf{whilepos0}\ p & \rightarrow & \mathbf{ifpos0}\ (p;\ \mathbf{whilepos0}\ p) \\
\mathbf{whilepos1}\ p & \rightarrow & \mathbf{ifpos1}\ (p;\ \mathbf{whilepos1}\ p) \\
\mathbf{whilepos2}\ p & \rightarrow & \mathbf{ifpos2}\ (p;\ \mathbf{whilepos2}\ p) \\
eval((p;\ q), u) & \rightarrow & eval(q, eval(p, u))
\end{array}
$$

Fig. 2. Three-register machine interpreter.

Definition 9. Let $l \rightarrow r$ and $g \rightarrow d$ be two rewrite rules (with variables renamed apart) and σ a most general unifier of g and a nonvariable subterm $l|_p$ of l.

Then the peak $r\sigma \xleftarrow[l\rightarrow r]{\Lambda} l\sigma \xrightarrow[g\rightarrow d]{p} l\sigma[d\sigma]_p$ is said *critical*, and the equation $r\sigma \simeq l\sigma[d\sigma]_p$ is called a *critical pair*.

Note that a finite rewrite system R has a finite set $cp(R)$ of critical pairs, and that there are "trivial" critical pairs in the above definition, when overlapping a rule with itself at the root.

Theorem 10 [44]. *A rewrite system is locally confluent if and only if all its critical pairs are joinable.*

Therefore, a terminating system is confluent if and only if all its critical pairs are joinable, a decidable property.

Insertion Sort has one trivially joinable critical pair, $0 = 0$, formed from either the first two rules, or the fourth and fifth.

2.4 Canonical systems

Rewrite systems which are both terminating and confluent are called *convergent*. We now consider an additional property in order to characterize a rewrite system under a given order.

Definition 11. A term s *encompasses* a term t if a subterm of s is an instance of t. We write $s \rhd t$ if s encompasses t, but not vice-versa.

Definition 12. A system R is *reduced* if, for each rule $l \rightarrow r$ in R, the right-hand side r is irreducible (unrewritable) and if $l \rhd l'$, for the left-hand side l, then l' is irreducible (proper subterms of l are in normal form, as is any term more general than l).

Definition 13. A rewrite system that is confluent, terminating, and reduced is called *canonical.*

Canonical systems have an interesting uniqueness property, an observation first made by Lankford:

Theorem 14 [51]. *Suppose R and S are two canonical (not necessarily finite) rewrite systems having the same equational theory. Suppose further that the combined system $R \cup S$ is terminating. Then R and S must be the same (up to renaming of variables).*

This result has important consequences to be developped in section 3.

2.5 Modularity

In most applications rewrite systems tend to become quite large, but are usually obtained by a stepwise construction. A property is called *modular* when it follows for the whole system from the same property for its components.

Traditional results apply to disjoint systems, that is systems that do not share any function symbol. These results actually extend to systems sharing constructors, where constructors are those symbols that do not appear as left-hand sides of rules.

Theorem 15. *Confluence [66] and functionality [52] are modular properties of disjoint systems.*

This is actually also true of systems sharing constructors [54]. But surprisingly, this is false for termination, as shown by the following example [23]:

Example 3.

$$R_1 = \{f(0,1,x) \rightarrow f(x,x,x), f(x,y,z) \rightarrow 2, 0 \rightarrow 2, 1 \rightarrow 2\}$$
$$R_2 = \{g(x,y,y) \rightarrow x, g(y,y,x) \rightarrow x\}$$

A infinite derivation is then the following:

$$f(g(0,0,1),g(0,0,1),g(0,0,1)) \xrightarrow{*} f(g(0,2,2),g(2,2,1),g(0,0,1)) \rightarrow$$
$$f(0,1,g(0,0,1)) \rightarrow f(g(0,0,1),g(0,0,1),g(0,0,1)) \rightarrow \ldots$$

The previous example is made of convergent systems, improving over Toyama's original example [65]. It can be adapted to yield canonical systems. On the other hand, it suffices to *share* variables in the right hand side in order to restore termination. In the above example, the term $f(g(0,0,1),g(0,0,1),g(0,0,1)) \rightarrow \ldots$ would have a unique subterm $g(0,0,1)$ and the above derivation could not apply once again.

Theorem 16 [46]. *Termination is a modular property of shared rewriting for disjoint systems.*

This property again extends to systems sharing constructors. For a more general case, see [53].

2.6 Generalizations

The results of the previous sections generalize to many situations for which the above techniques fail, because either termination is not satisfied, or more expressivity is needed.

There are two techniques to address the case where termination is not satisfied: rewriting modulo, and ordered rewriting.

Ordered rewriting uses directly the equations for rewriting, provided their instances are directed by means of an appropriate ordering.

Definition 17. A term s rewrites to a term t at position p with respect to a rewrite ordering $\succeq$ using an equation $l \simeq r \in E$, if there exists a substitution σ such that $s|_p = l\sigma, t = s[r\sigma]_p$, and $l\sigma \succ r\sigma$, or $s|_p = r\sigma, t = s[l\sigma]_p$, and $r\sigma \succ l\sigma$. We write $s \xrightarrow[l\simeq r]{p} t$ in the first case, and $s \xrightarrow[r\simeq l]{p} t$ in the second.

In the latter view of rewriting, an equation $l \simeq r$ is indeed a *rewrite rule* $l \rightarrow r$ if there are pairs s, t such that $s \xrightarrow[l\simeq r]{p} t$, but no pairs u, v such that $u \xrightarrow[r\simeq l]{p} v$.

Although commutativity can be used for ordered rewriting as defined above, for example $a+b \xrightarrow[x+y\simeq y+x]{} b+a$ if $a+b > b+a$ in the given ordering, it is in practice useful to separate the equations into two sets denoted by R and S. Equations in R will be used for rewriting. Equations in S will be used to find R-redexes by equational reasoning. This general principle known under the name of *rewriting modulo* has been proved very efficient in a number of cases by appropriately choosing R and S.

Definition 18 [60]. Let R be a set of rules and S be a set of equations. A term s rewrites to a term t at position p using a rule $l = r$ by using *extended rewriting* with S if there exist a substitution σ such that $s|_p \xleftrightarrow[S]{*} l\sigma$ and $t = s[r\sigma]_p$.

There are other definitions of rewriting modulo. In the above, a redex at position p is obtained by restricting the search to terms that differ from s by applying S-equalities under the position p only. This allows to obtain the substitution σ by S-pattern matching instead of equational search. The case where the whole term is searched is called *class-rewriting*, but its efficiency is dubious. The search can be restricted even more than in the above definition, for example to the positions of non-linear variables of the left hand side of the equation [21]. Although much more efficient (only standard pattern matching is used in conjunction with S-equality tests), the latter variant has not yet demonstrated its usefulness.

Termination for whatever variant of rewriting modulo S needs an *S-rewrite ordering*, that is a quasi ordering whose strict part is a rewrite ordering and whose equivalence contains the congruence generated by S. This is an area where research is still actively going on. On the other hand, most problems relating to confluence are basically solved [37; 2]. Orthogonal systems have received little attention, though. For ordered rewriting, joinability of an appropriate notion of critical pairs is a sufficient condition for confluence [30]. An interesting conjecture is the decidability of ground confluence for ordered rewriting when the ordering used is a total recursive path ordering with all statuses lexicographic.

The above definitions can be extended to more sophisticated notions of equations, such as conditional equations, order-sorted equations, and constrained equations. We refer to [19] for the definitions.

3 Completion of a set of rules

When a terminating set of rules is not confluent, critical pairs may be oriented and added as new rules, a process called Knuth-Bendix completion [44]. In completion, the axioms used are therefore in a constant state of flux; these changes are expressed as inference rules, which add a dynamic character to establishing the existence of rewrite proofs. This view of completion, then, has two main components: an inference system, used in the completion process to generate new rewrite rules, and a rewrite relation on proofs, that shows how any proof can be normalized to a rewrite proof, as long as the appropriate rules have been generated.

An *inference rule* (for our purposes) is a binary relation between pairs $(E; R)$, where E is a set of equations and R is a set of rewrite rules. Let $\succ$ be a reduction ordering, and $\gg$ the well-founded ordering on rules defined as follows: $s \rightarrow t \gg l \rightarrow r$ if (i) $s \blacktriangleright l$ under the encompassment ordering, or else (ii) $s \doteq l$ (s and l are literally similar) and $t \succ r$. We define the following set KB of six inference rules:

Delete:	$(E \cup \{s \simeq s\}; R) \vdash (E; R)$
Compose:	$(E; R \cup \{s \rightarrow t\}) \vdash (E; R \cup \{s \rightarrow u\})$ if $t \rightarrow_R u$
Simplify:	$(E \cup \{s \simeq t\}; R) \vdash (E \cup \{s \simeq u\}; R)$ if $t \rightarrow_R u$
Orient:	$(E \cup \{s \simeq t\}; R) \vdash (E; R \cup \{s \rightarrow t\})$ if $s \succ t$
Collapse:	$(E; R \cup \{s \rightarrow t\}) \vdash (E \cup \{u \simeq t\}; R)$ if $s \xrightarrow[l \rightarrow r]{p} u$ with $s \rightarrow t \gg l \rightarrow r$
Deduce:	$(E; R) \vdash (E \cup \{s \simeq t\}; R)$ if $s = t \in \mathrm{cp}(R)$

We write $(E; R) \vdash_{KB} (E'; R')$ if the latter may be obtained from the former by one application of a rule in KB. **Delete** removes a trivial equation $s \simeq s$. **Compose** rewrites the right-hand side t of a rule $s \rightarrow t$, if possible. **Simplify** rewrites either side of an equation $s \simeq t$. **Orient** turns an equation $s \simeq t$ that is orientable ($s \succ t$ or $t \succ s$) into a rewriting rule. **Collapse** rewrites the left-hand side of a rule $s \rightarrow t$ and turns the result into an equation $u \simeq t$, but only when the rule $l \rightarrow r$ being applied to s is smaller than the rule being removed under the rule ordering. **Deduce** adds equational consequences to E, but only those that follow from critical peaks $s \leftarrow_R u \rightarrow_R t$.

In practice, the completion rules are usually applied in some order, yielding a *completion sequence* $(E_0; \emptyset) \vdash_{KB} (E_1; R_1) \vdash_{KB} \cdots \vdash_{KB} (E_n; R_n) \cdots$ which may be infinite (completion *diverges*) or finite in case there are no possible non-redundant inferences after some finite step n. In the latter case, completion *succeeds* if $E_n = \emptyset$, and *fails* otherwise.

Let us now give a taste of the proof rewrite relation $\Rightarrow_{KB}$. The rûles come in two parts. The first set expresses commutation properties of rewrites. For example,

$$s \xleftarrow[l \rightarrow r]{p} u \xrightarrow[g \rightarrow d]{q} t \Rightarrow_{KB} s \xrightarrow[g \rightarrow d]{p} v \xleftarrow[l \rightarrow r]{q} t$$

for some $v = u[r\sigma]_p[d\theta]_q$ if p and q are incomparable in the prefix ordering.

The second encodes the effect of the inference rules on proofs, obtained by deleting some axioms, while adding new ones:

$$v \xrightarrow[s\to t]{q} w \Rightarrow_{KB} v \xrightarrow[l\to r]{q\cdot p} v[u]_p \xleftrightarrow[u\simeq t]{q} w$$

is the rule associated to **Collapse**. Such a rule replaces a small left-hand side by a seemingly bigger right-hand side using the generated equation. However, it can indeed be proved smaller in some well-chosen well-founded ordering [4]. See, e.g., [2] for a complete description of the rules and the ordering used to prove their termination.

The role of the rewrite rules on proofs is to show that every proof is eventually normalized, this is why termination of these rules is crucial, and that normal form proofs are indeed rewrite proofs. For this latter property to hold, an hypothesis is needed, called *fairness*. Let us call *persisting* a rule which is never reduced on the left nor on the right once it has been generated:

$$E_\infty = \bigcup_{i\geq 0} \bigcap_{j\geq i} E_j$$

$$R_\infty = \bigcup_{i\geq 0} \bigcap_{j\geq i} R_j$$

Then, a completion sequence is *fair* if the critical peaks formed with the persisting rules are all reducible with respect to the rewrite rules on proofs. This is in particular so, if the corresponding critical pairs have been computed, but this may not be always necessary.

If success occurs after a finite number n of steps, then the resulting system is a decision procedure for E_0. In case of divergence, a semi-decision procedure can be obtained if the completion sequence is *fair*:

Theorem 19 [32]. *Given two terms s and t such that $s \longleftrightarrow^*_{E_0} t$, and a fair completion sequence $(E_0; \emptyset) \vdash_{KB} (E_1; R_1) \vdash_{KB} \cdots \vdash_{KB} (E_n; R_n) \cdots$ such that E_∞ is empty, there exists an integer i such that s and t have the same normal form with respect to R_j for all $j \geq i$.*

The strategy described below, by a regular expression of the inference rules names, is fair:

$$((\textbf{Collapse}^*; \textbf{Compose}^*; \textbf{Simplify}^*; \textbf{Delete}^*; \textbf{Orient}^*)^*; \textbf{Deduce})^*$$

Completion has been extended to handle various situations, in particular to cope with associative-commutative axioms [60] which cannot be handled as rules. More generally, completion frameworks for rewriting modulo are described in [37; 4; 48], for ordered rewriting in [30; 57], and for constraint rewriting in [14]. Ordered completion, the variant based on ordered rewriting, has the important property that it always succeeds if it terminates. In addition, if the ordering used has the subterm property and a *canonical* set of rules exists for the considered theory, then ordered completion is garanteed to find it [2].

Efficiency of completion is strongly related to the possibility of eliminating redundant critical pair computations, especially in the context of completion modulo. See [3; 68] for various critical pair criteria and [5; 58; 48] for completion strategies which eliminate redundancy.

4 Rewriting: a tool for solving queries in algebraic specifications

A convergent set R of rewrite rules for some equational theory E allows one to solve various kinds of queries. A query will be a logical formula built over the equality predicate, to be interpreted in some term algebra ($\mathcal{T}(\mathcal{F})$ or $\mathcal{T}(\mathcal{F},\mathcal{X})$) by the congruence generated by the set E (equivalently R) of axioms. Accordingly, the query will be solved in the quotient under consideration (we may simply say in $\mathcal{T}(\mathcal{F})$ or $\mathcal{T}(\mathcal{F},\mathcal{X})$ in the following, leaving the quotient implicit). We will distinguish queries after their logical complexity. Since conjunctions and disjunctions do not cause particular problems, we will simplify our notations by forgetting about these two connectives, hence consider quantified atomic formulae.

4.1 Normalization queries

We apologize to the reader if the formulation of normalization in terms of a logical query appears somewhat artificial. We think it may actually help the understanding.

Query: $x = s$, where s is ground, and x is a free variable.

This query is solved in $\mathcal{T}(\mathcal{F})$ by returning the normal form of s for the value of the free variable x. The same technique applies to a non-ground term s, provided x is not a variable of s. In this case, the precise form of the query should be

Query: $\exists \mathcal{V}ar(s)\ \ x = s$, where $x \notin \mathcal{V}ar(s)$.

To solve this query in $\mathcal{T}(\mathcal{F},\mathcal{X})$, variables are in $\mathcal{V}ar(s)$ are considered as new constants, and the same process as above applies.

4.2 Word problems and universal queries

Query: $s = t$, where s and t are ground.

This query is solved by computing the normal forms of s and t and comparing them. Such a query is usually called a word problem. Since the convergence property of the set R of rules yields a decision procedure for equality, we can also answer to negative such queries:

Query: $s \neq t$, where s and t are ground.

Word problems generalize easily to universal queries:

Query: $\forall \mathcal{V}ar(s,t)\ \ s = t$

and its negation:

Query: $\exists \mathcal{V}ar(s,t)\ \ s \neq t$

This is of course done as above by considering the variables as new constants. This can be justified by looking at the latter query, where existential variables can be first skolemized into constants, and we are back to a ground query. This remark applies to the former query, by using a double negation. Note that the equality predicate is implicitely interpreted here in $\mathcal{T}(\mathcal{F},\mathcal{X})$, an algebra with infinitely many free constants. Adding new constants in an arbitrary algebra may not be sound: there are indeed pathological algebras with a decidable word problem for which universal queries are undecidable.

4.3 Existential queries

These queries may have free variables as well as existentially quantified ones:

Query: $\exists X \;\; s = t$, where $X \subseteq Var(s,t)$

The goal here is to find (ground) values for the free variables that make the formula true in the quotient of the Herbrand universe by the congruence generated by a convergent set of rules R. Variables in X are auxiliary variables (*parameters*) whole value is useless. The values of the free variables are supposed to be enumerated by the resolution process. This will be achieved by means of a set of non-deterministic transformation rules.

Due to the existence of a rewrite proof for an arbitrary valid equation, instead of solving a goal $\exists X \;\; s = t$, one solves a pair of "directed" goals,

$$\exists X, z \;\; s \rightarrow z \wedge t \rightarrow z$$

for some new variable z. The coming rules transform such a query into a substitution encoded as a formula of the form $x_1 \rightarrow u_1 \wedge \ldots \wedge x_n \rightarrow u_n$, where the x_i are distinct free variables of the query, and do not belong to any u_j.

Decompose:	$f(s_1,\ldots,s_m) \rightarrow f(t_1,\ldots,t_m) \Rightarrow \bigwedge_{i=1}^{i=n} s_i \rightarrow t_i$
Delete:	$s \rightarrow s \Rightarrow T$
Eliminate:	$x \rightarrow s \wedge P \Rightarrow x \rightarrow s \wedge P\{x \mapsto s\}$ if $x \in \mathcal{X}$, and $x \notin Var(s)$
Mutate:	$f(s_1,\ldots,s_n) \rightarrow t \Rightarrow s_1 \rightarrow l_1 \wedge \ldots \wedge s_n \rightarrow l_n \wedge r \rightarrow t$ if $f(l_1,\ldots,l_n) \rightarrow r$ is a copy of a rule in R with its variables renamed apart $Var(P,t,s_1,\ldots,s_n)$
Imitate:	$f(s_1,\ldots,s_n) \rightarrow y \Rightarrow \exists y_1,\ldots,y_n \;\; y \rightarrow f(y_1,\ldots,y_n) \wedge \bigwedge_{i=1}^{i=n} s_i \rightarrow y_i$ if $y \in \mathcal{X}$, $y_i \notin Var(y,s_1,\ldots,s_n)$
Parameters:	$\exists X, y \;\; y \rightarrow u \wedge P \Rightarrow \exists X \;\; P$ if $y \notin Var(P,u)$ $\exists X, y \;\; u \rightarrow y \wedge P \Rightarrow \exists X \;\; P$ if $y \notin Var(P,u)$ $\exists X, y \;\; P \Rightarrow \exists X \;\; P$ if $y \notin Var(P)$

For example, if R is $\{f(x,x) \rightarrow c(x), a \rightarrow b\}$, then the query $f(y,a) = c(y)$ can be solved by the following sequence of rewrites:

$$\exists z \;\; f(y,a) \rightarrow z \wedge c(y) \rightarrow z \Rightarrow_{Mutate}$$

$$\exists z, x \;\; y \rightarrow x \wedge a \rightarrow x \wedge c(x) \rightarrow z \wedge c(y) \rightarrow z \Rightarrow_{Eliminate}$$

$$\exists z, x \;\; y \rightarrow x \wedge a \rightarrow x \wedge c(x) \rightarrow z \Rightarrow_{Imitate}$$

$$\exists z, x \;\; y \rightarrow x \wedge x \rightarrow a \wedge c(x) \rightarrow z \Rightarrow_{Eliminate}$$

$$\exists z, x \;\; y \rightarrow a \wedge x \rightarrow a \wedge c(a) \rightarrow z \Rightarrow_{Parameters}$$

$$\exists z \;\; y \rightarrow a \wedge c(a) \rightarrow z \Rightarrow_{Parameters}$$

$$y \rightarrow a$$

The solution $\{y \mapsto b\}$ can be obtained with an application of *Mutate* replacing the application of *Imitate*:

$$\exists z, x \;\; y \rightarrow x \wedge a \rightarrow x \wedge c(x) \rightarrow z \Rightarrow_{Mutate}$$

$$\exists z, x \;\; y \rightarrow x \wedge x \rightarrow b \wedge c(x) \rightarrow z \Rightarrow_{Eliminate}$$

$$\exists z, x \;\; y \rightarrow b \wedge x \rightarrow b \wedge c(b) \rightarrow z \Rightarrow_{Parameters}$$

$$\exists z \;\; y \rightarrow b \wedge c(b) \rightarrow z \Rightarrow_{Parameters}$$

$$y \rightarrow b$$

Theorem 20 [19]. *Let R be a convergent rewrite system and Q the existential query* $\exists X, z \;\; s \rightarrow z \wedge t \rightarrow z$. *Then, for every solution* γ *of Q, there exists a sequence of rewrites from Q whose result is a substitution more general than* γ.

By exhibiting more primitive transformation rules, this set of rules subsumes *narrowing*, as used for this purpose in [24]:

Definition 21. A term s *narrows* to a term t, via substitution $\sigma = mgu(s|_p, l)$, at position p using the rule $l \rightarrow r$, symbolized $s \overset{p}{\underset{l \rightarrow r, \sigma}{\rightsquigarrow}} t$, if $t = s\sigma[r\sigma]_p$.

By encoding each narrowing step by appropriate sequences of the rules, the above theorem can now be reformulated as follows: For every solution γ of the above existential query Q, there exists a narrowing derivation from $s = t$:

$$s_0 = t_0 \underset{\sigma_0}{\rightsquigarrow} s_1 = t_1 \underset{\sigma_1}{\rightsquigarrow} \dots \underset{\sigma_{n-1}}{\rightsquigarrow} s_n = t_n$$

such that $s = s_0$, $t = t_0$, $\theta = mgu(s_n, t_n)$ and $\sigma = \sigma_1 \dots \sigma_{n-1}\theta$ is more general than γ.

Variations on narrowing include: *normal narrowing* [24] (in which terms are normalized via $\rightarrow^!_R$ before narrowing), *basic narrowing* [35] (in which the substitution part of prior narrowings is not subsequently narrowed), and their combination [59]. Basic narrowing can be elegantly formulated by the following two inference rules operating on pairs of equations $s = t$ (assuming $=$ commutative) and substitutions θ, with $s = t, \emptyset$ as the initial pair:

Narrowing:	$s = t \; ; \; \theta \;\; \Rightarrow \;\; \exists Var(l, r) s[r]_p = t \; ; \; \theta\sigma$
	if σ is the most general unifier of s_p and l
Success:	$s = t \; ; \; \theta \;\; \Rightarrow \;\; T \; ; \; \theta\sigma$
	if σ is the most general unifier of s and t

4.4 Negative queries

The above technique extends to negative queries, by making use of ground reducibility tests:

Query: $\exists X \;\; s \neq t$, where $X \subseteq Var(s,t)$

Definition 22. An equation $s \simeq t$ is *ground reducible* iff for all substitutions γ such that $s\gamma$ and $t\gamma$ are both ground, either $s\gamma = t\gamma$ or one of $s\gamma, t\gamma$ is reducible. In case $s\eta$ and $t\eta$ are different and irreducible, $s = t$ is not ground reducible *because of* η.

Narrowing:	$s \neq t \; ; \; \theta \;\; \Rightarrow \;\; s' \neq t' \; ; \; \theta\sigma$
	if σ is the most general unifier of s_p and l
Success:	$s \neq t \; ; \; \theta \;\; \Rightarrow \;\; T \; ; \; \theta\eta$
	if $s = t$ is not ground reducible because of η

Ground reducibility is indeed decidable [62; 41; 10; 9], and substitutions because of which an equation is not ground reducible are enumerable [25]. The test is however NP-hard. Actually, all algorithms published so far are doubly exponential with respect to the hight of terms.

4.5 Inductive queries

These queries have all their variables universally quantified over ground terms. Inductive queries do not differ from universal queries at the syntactic level, but the equality predicate is interpreted in the quotient of the ground term algebra. Answering to an inductive query normally requires an induction scheme (over the term algebra). This induction scheme can actually be hidden in a completion process.

Query: $\forall X \in \mathcal{T}(\mathcal{F}) \;\; s = t$, where $X \subseteq Var(s,t)$

For convergent systems R_0, any equation between distinct ground-normal forms is considered to be inconsistent with R_0. The observation that an equation $s = t$ is valid in the initial algebra associated with R_0 iff no inconsistency follows from $R_0 \cup \{s \simeq t\}$ is the basis of the method of inductive theorem proving pioneered by Musser [55]: if there exists a ground-convergent system with the same ground normal forms as R_0, and which presents the same equational theory as $R_0 \cup \{s \simeq t\}$, then inconsistency is precluded.

Solving these queries will therefore be done by adding the equation $s = t$ to the algebra, and completing the set $R_0, \{s \simeq t\}$. To ensure that normal forms are not changed during completion, it will be enough to check the left hand sides of the added rules for ground-reducibility [15; 38].

Definition 23. A term s is *ground reducible* by R at a set of *covering positions* S iff all its ground instances by irreducible substitutions are reducible by R at a position in S.

For example, $s(s(x))$ is ground reducible by $s(s(0)) \rightarrow 0$ at the set $\{\Lambda, 1\}$ of positions.

Since we are only interested in ground-normal forms, ground-convergence will actually be enough. As a consequence, not all critical pairs are actually needed.

Only those obtained by overlapping with R_0 at a set of covering positions of the generated rules are necessary. In the rules below, R denotes the set of added rules only:

Delete:	$(E \cup \{s \simeq s\}; R) \vdash (E; R)$
Compose:	$(E; R \cup \{s \rightarrow t\}) \vdash (E; R \cup \{s \rightarrow u\})$ if $t \rightarrow_{R \cup R_0} u$
Simplify:	$(E \cup \{s \simeq t\}; R) \vdash (E \cup \{s \simeq u\}; R)$ if $t \rightarrow_{R \cup R_0} u$
Orient:	$(E \cup \{s \simeq t\}; R) \vdash (E; R \cup \{s \rightarrow t\})$ if $s \succ t$ and s is ground-reducible by R_0
Disprove:	$(E \cup \{s \simeq t\}; R) \vdash$ False if $s \succ t$ and s is not ground-reducible by R_0
Collapse:	$(E; R \cup \{s \rightarrow t\}) \vdash (E \cup \{u \simeq t\}; R)$ if $s \longrightarrow^{p}_{l \rightarrow r} u$ with $s \rightarrow t \gg l \rightarrow r$
Deduce:	$(E; R) \vdash (E \cup \{s \simeq t\}; R)$ if $s \simeq t$ is a critical pair of R_0 at a covering position in R

Theorem 24 [26]. *An equation $s \simeq t$ is not an inductive consequence of a ground-convergent set R_0 of rules iff inductive completion returns false, provided it does not fail.*

This result can be made into a refutationally complete procedure by adopting the variant of completion based on ordered rewriting [1].

4.6 Normal form queries

Ground reducibility refers to the language of terms in normal form which are instances of a given term. Describing this language is a key to a decision procedure for ground reducibility. Ground reducibility can be expressed by means of a logical formula, whose set of solutions can be recognized by a bottom-up tree automaton of some form. To put this classical technique at work requires a class of tree automata closed under the formulae constructors such as the Boolean connectives, see e.g. [64] for a survey on this question.

Let $R = \{l_i \rightarrow r_i\}_{i \in [1..n]}$.

Note first that the set of ground terms in R-normal form wich are instances of a given term s is given as the set of solutions of the following first-order formula:

$$\exists \mathcal{V}ar(s) \;\; x = s \wedge \bigwedge_{i=1}^{i=n} x \not\trianglerighteq l_i$$

Assuming that a (bottom up) tree automaton can be constructed for these formulae, and that the class of these automata has the appropriate closure properties (including with respect to Boolean connectives, projection, ...), it will be possible to construct an automaton recognizing the language of solutions of the above formula. Since s is inductively reducible iff this language is empty, it will also be necessary to decide the emptyness problem for an automaton in that class. This approach is taken in [9]. These automata include (some bounded number of) "equality tests" along a path. The emptiness problem for automata with equality tests is NP-hard, but the actual algorithm based on pumping properties of these automata is doubly exponential as already mentioned. A simply exponential algorithm based on more sophisticated pumping techniques has been announced very recently by Comon and Jacquemart.

Note that the above formula uses a finite set of unary predicates $\trianglerighteq l_i$ rather than one binary predicate $\trianglerighteq$, whose first-order language is indeed undecidable as a consequence of the undecidability of the Σ_3 fragment of the theory of subterm [67].

Ground reducibility being an expensive test, it is worth avoiding it. Fortunately, this test is not necessary for (most) specifications whose set of function symbols can be split into constructors and defined symbols in the sens of Huet [33]: defined symbols generate inductive reducibility tests that are automatically satisfied as soon as the test applies to a term containing such a defined symbol.

Plaisted was the first to prove the decidability of inductive reducibility [61], and Comon to consider the problem in terms of formal language theory (using grammars and reachability techniques instead of automata and pumping techniques).

4.7 Limitations of rewriting techniques

Although rewriting appears as a very general and powerful technique for solving such problems in a uniform manner, it may not always apply: there are computable (with a decidable word problem) algebras, for which the word problem cannot be decided by means of (plain) rewriting in any presentation of the algebra [63].

However, Squier's example can be solved in a conservative extension of the algebra, by choosing a different set of generators as recently shown by Lafont at the "Ecole de Printemps d'Informatique Théorique".

4.8 Application to algebraic specifications

Sufficient completeness The problem of *sufficient completeness* relates to *ground reducibility*, hence may be decidable once a convergent system is known for the equations of the specification:

Definition 25. Let $\mathcal{F} = \mathcal{C} \cup \mathcal{D}$ be a finite set of function symbols split into constructors ($\mathcal{C}$) and defined symbols ($\mathcal{D}$), and E be a set of axioms. Then E is a *complete definition* of the symbols in $\mathcal{D}$ iff

$$\forall s \in \mathcal{T}(\mathcal{D} \cup \mathcal{C}) \;\; \exists t \in \mathcal{T}(\mathcal{C}) \text{ such that } t \xleftrightarrow[E]{*} s$$

The set E of axioms is also called sufficiently complete after Guttag. Note that the constructors may not be free in this general definition (different constructor terms may be E-equal).

Theorem 26 [38]. *Assume a specification as above such that there is a convergent set of rules R for E with the property that the normal form of a constructor term is a constructor term. Then the specification is sufficiently complete iff all terms of the form $f(x_1, \ldots, x_n)$ for $f \in \mathcal{D}$ are ground reducible.*

As a consequence, sufficient completeness becomes decidable when the left hand sides of rules are headed by defined symbols. This result generalizes to more complex situations where there are non-orientable axioms [38].

Relative consistency The notion of relative consistency relates to hierarchical specifications. A base specification with set of symbols F_0 and set of equations E_0 being given, a new set of symbols F_1 is added and a new set of equations E_1 is given to constrain the symbols in F_1. We will not require that these symbols are completely defined in the above sense. But we now want that the addition of these new symbols and equations does not change the base ground term algebra.

Definition 27. Let F_0, E_0, F_1, E_1 be a hierarchical specification. F_1, E_1 is *consistent* with respect to the base F_0, E_0 iff

$$\forall s,t \in \mathcal{T}(F_0) \;\; s \xleftrightarrow[E_0 \cup E_1]{*} t \text{ iff } s \xleftrightarrow[E_0]{*} t$$

So, non-equal ground terms in the base specification cannot be made equal in the extended specification. As one can guess, this principle relates to inductive queries. A precise procedure based on inductive reducibility with respect to a ground convergent set of rules for E_0 is given in [38].

Derivation of specifications with free constructors A quotient algebra may sometimes be freely generated by appropriately choosing the generators. For example, the algebra of integers is usually specified by giving 0, *succ*, *pred* as constructors, and $succ(pred(x)) = x, pred(succ(x)) = x$ as equations. It can however alternatively be specified in the form of a free order-sorted algebra as follows (using obj syntax [28]):

```
obj         INTEGERS
sorts       ZERO, POS, NEG
subsorts    ZERO < POS, ZERO < NEG
op          0 : -> ZERO
op          succ : ZERO -> POS
op          succ : POS -> POS
op          pred : ZERO -> NEG
op          pred : NEG -> NEG
endobj
```

Since inductive queries can be answered more efficiently in an specification with free constructors (inductive reducibility tests are trivial), it is helpful to compute the latter specification from the former whenever possible. This computation can be seen as a compilation of all possible inductive reducibility tests. In our example, a (ground) term of the former specification is in POS iff its normal form is either 0, or contains *succ* symbols only. Computing the *succ* of a POS term now yields a POS term. To do this automatically can be achieved by deriving an automaton recognizing the set of ground terms in normal form [11]. Using Comon's remark, this automaton is indeed an order sorted specification. So, this will be possible provided the language of terms in normal form is recognizable by a finite bottom up tree automaton, a property recently shown decidable by Kucherov and Tajine [45]. Note that the property is indeed true of sets of left linear rules.

5 Rewriting as a specification language

Up to now, rewriting has been seen as a tool for prototyping interpretors of algebraic specifications, or answering various queries about the specification. But rewriting can also be seen as a specification language on its own. In this context, rewriting is seen as a means to specify a subset of a given set of terms as the set of irreducible terms with respect to the specification (the reader must now think of a rewrite system as a specification). The left-hand sides of the rewrite rules are therefore those patterns that must be eliminated, in the sense that they do not belong to the subset of terms to be specified. Each right-hand side is of course related to the corresponding left-hand side by some equivalence depending on the particular problem under investigation.

There are many examples of use of rewrite specifications. The most familiar one is unification: a unification problem is a conjunction of equations and a unifier can be seen as a particular unification problem of the form $x_1 = u_1 \wedge \ldots \wedge x_n = u_n$ such that $x_i \neq x_j$ for $i \neq j$ and $x_i \notin Var(u_j)$ for all i, j. The empty conjunction is identified to T. F denotes a problem without solution. Such problems are also called *solved forms*. The computation of the most general unifier of a given unification problem can be specified by a particular set of rewrite rules, by eliminating appropriate patterns, that is unification problems that are not in solved form. $f(u_1, \ldots, u_m) = g(v_1, \ldots, v_n)$ is such a pattern, since the left hand side is not a variable. The right hand side for this pattern must be chosen so as to keep the set of solutions unchanged. This requires splitting the pattern into two, depending on the operators f and g. If they are different, this unification problem has no solution, so the right hand side is F. If they are equal, then $m = n$, and the corresponding subterms must be equal, so the appropriate right hand side is $u_1 = v_1 \wedge \ldots \wedge u_n = v_n$. Note that these rules encode actually a set of rules, for all possible operators f and g. With these two rules, normal forms are now conjunctions of equalities of the form $x = u$ or $u = x$, where x is a variable. Some more rules are now needed to eliminate other undesirable patterns. The full set of rules (where $=$ is supposed commutative) is borrowed from [36]:

Delete :	$s = s \wedge P \Longrightarrow$	P
Decompose :	$f(s_1, \ldots, s_n) = f(t_1, \ldots, t_n) \Longrightarrow$	$s_1 = t_1 \wedge \ldots \wedge s_n = t_n$
Conflict :	$f(s_1, \ldots, s_m) = g(t_1, \ldots, t_n) \wedge P \Longrightarrow$	F
		if $f \neq g$
Coalesce :	$x = y \wedge P \Longrightarrow$	$x = y \wedge P\{x \mapsto y\}$
		if $x \in Var(P)$, $y \in Var(P)$ *and* $x \neq y$
Check :	$x = s \Longrightarrow$	F
		if $x \in Var(s)$ *and* $s \notin \mathcal{X}$
Eliminate :	$x = s \wedge P \Longrightarrow$	$x = s \wedge P\{x \mapsto s\}$
		if $x \notin Var(s), s \notin \mathcal{X}$, *and* $x \in Var(P)$

In general, rewrite specifications are very useful to specify incremental algorithms for solving symbolic constraints, see [13] for a survey. But they are also very useful to specify proof transformations. Proofs are algebraic objects, and proof transformations can therefore be seen encoded as term rewritings. For example, natural deduction proofs can be encoded as lambda terms, and equational proofs as first-order terms. In the latter case, these terms are actually concatenations of elementary proof steps, each proof step being the application of an equation or rule. A proof step is indeed a ternary operator whose arguments are an equation or rule, the position where the equation or rule is applied, and the associated substitution. The direction of use of a rule is reflected by choosing different operators ($\rightarrow$ or $\leftarrow$). One may have a single operator for an equation ($\longleftrightarrow$) if an equation is handled as a pair of ordered pairs. This is indeed what we did with completion. Now, the quest for completion rules can be performed in a way similar to the quest for unification rules. In the usual view developed so far, completion rules are inference rules reflected at the proof level by proof rewrite rules. An alternative view is that completion rules are inference rules reflecting a given set of proof rewrite rules. These proof rewrite rules are easy to come up with, just as before for the case of unification. Normal form proofs are simply rewrite proofs, and they can be specified by giving an appropriate set of transformation rules. The inference rules can now be obtained as follows. If the right hand side uses the same axioms (rules or equations) as the left hand side, there is no corresponding inference rule. If the right hand side uses new axioms, then these new axioms must be added to the existing set, so an inference rule is needed. In general, the axioms used in the left-hand side cannot be eliminated, unless they become useless. This is the case if the transformation rule can be applied at once to all proofs steps that use these axioms. The corresponding inference rule is then a simplification rule. This point of view is developed in [21].

6 Conclusion

Rewriting has become a very powerful tool both for prototyping algebraic specifications, and for specifying various kind of algorithms for symbolic computations. Powerful environments exist that may help the user in building rewrite-oriented algebraic specifications. But the research is still very active in various directions. Let us mention a few of them.

Modularity problems are now investigated for combinations of first-order rewrite rules, higher-order rewrite rules, and various kinds of typed lambda-calculi. This direction is quite relevant for the software engineer since it opens the way to prototyping higher-order specifications. For example, recursors on lists can be specified by higher-order rules:

```
obj     LIST
import  NAT
sorts   List
op      nil : -> List
op      cons : Nat, List -> List
op      map  : Nat->Nat, List -> List
var     x:Nat, l:List, F:Nat->Nat
eq      map(F,nil) == nil
eq      map(F,cons(x,l)) == cons(F(x),map(F,l))
endobj
```

Now, F can be instantiated as a particular function on natural numbers, or by a lambda-expression denoting some function on natural numbers, provided its type (for example in Curry's type system) is `Nat->Nat`.

These combinations are all modular with respect to confluence and termination under quite reasonable properties for practice [8; 39; 6; 7].

The other directions are not directly linked to algebraic specifications, but are nevertheless worth mentioning. One is a quest for an abstract framework for rewriting that would capture the essence of the key theorems which are common to orthogonal systems and lambda calculi, such as the Church-Rosser property and the standard reduction theorem [29].

Up to now, we have considered finite computations only. Considering infinite computations is an interesting subject connected to various considerations, among which models for concurrency. In this context, even very basic concepts need new definitions. In particular, normal forms need not be attained in finite time [20; 42].

The kind of rewriting we have considered operates on terms. But rewriting is a very general idea of replacing equals by (smaller) equals, and can be used in a very general context. Rewriting on traces (as they are called in concurrency) yields very interesting new questions [22], as well as rewriting Penrose diagrams originating from Physics [47]. These are two very recent lines of research.

In the last section, we have considered the possibility of using rewriting as a specification language. But rewriting is a computation mechanism, not a logic. Since specifications should be based on a logic in the traditional sense, it should be useful to study what kind of logic is related to rewriting in a general sense. Work in this area has been started by Meseguer [49; 50].

References

1. Leo Bachmair. Proof by consistency in equational theories. In *Proc. 3rd IEEE Symp. Logic in Computer Science, Edinburgh*, July 1988.
2. Leo Bachmair. *Canonical Equational Proofs*. Birkhäuser, Boston, 1991.
3. Leo Bachmair and Nachum Dershowitz. Critical pair criteria for completion. *Journal of Symbolic Computation*, 6(1):1–18, 1988.
4. Leo Bachmair, Nachum Dershowitz, and Jieh Hsiang. Orderings for equational proofs. In *Proc. 1st IEEE Symp. Logic in Computer Science, Cambridge, Mass.*, pages 346–357, June 1986.
5. Leo Bachmair, Harald Ganzinger, Christopher Lynch, and Wayne Snyder. Basic paramodulation and superposition. In Deepak Kapur, editor, *Proc. 11th Int. Conf. on Automated Deduction, Saratoga Springs, NY, LNCS 607*. Springer-Verlag, June 1992.
6. Franco Barbanera and Maribel Fernández. Combining first and higher order rewrite systems with type assignment systems. In *Proceedings of the International Conference on Typed Lambda Calculi and Applications, Utrecht, Holland*, 1993.
7. Franco Barbanera and Maribel Fernández. Modularity of termination and confluence in combinations of rewrite systems with λ_ω. In *Proceedings of the 20th International Colloquium on Automata, Languages, and Programming*, 1993.
8. Val Breazu-Tannen and Jean Gallier. Polymorphic rewriting conserves algebraic confluence. *Information and Computation*. to appear.

9. A-C. Caron, J.-L. Coquidé, and M. Dauchet. Encompassment properties and automata with constraints. In *Proc. RTA 93*, 1993.
10. Hubert Comon. Unification et disunification: Théorie et applications. Thèse de Doctorat, Institut National Polytechnique de Grenoble, France, 1988.
11. Hubert Comon. Inductive proofs by specifications transformation. In *Proc. 3rd Rewriting Techniques and Applications, Chapel Hill, LNCS 355*, pages 76–91. Springer-Verlag, April 1989.
12. Hubert Comon. Solving symbolic ordering constraints. *International Journal of Foundations of Computer Science*, 1(4):387–411, 1990.
13. Hubert Comon. Disunification: a survey. In Jean-Louis Lassez and Gordon Plotkin, editors, *Computational Logic: Essays in Honor of Alan Robinson*. MIT Press, 1991.
14. Hubert Comon. Completion of rewrite systems with membership constraints. In W. Kuich, editor, *Proc. 19th Int. Coll. on Automata, Languages and Programming, LNCS 623*, Vienna, 1992. Springer-Verlag. An extended version is available as LRI Research Report number 699, Sept. 1991.
15. Nachum Dershowitz. Applications of the Knuth-Bendix completion procedure. In *Proceedings of the Seminaire d'Informatique Theorique*, pages 95–111, Paris, France, December 1982.
16. Nachum Dershowitz. A taste of rewrite systems. In *Proc. Functional Programming, Concurrency, Simulation and Automated Reasonning*, 1993.
17. Nachum Dershowitz. Trees, ordinals and termination. In *Proc. CAAP 93, LNCS 668*, 1993.
18. Nachum Dershowitz and Charles Hoot. Topics in termination. In *Proc. 5th Rewriting Techniques and Applications, Montréal, LNCS 690*, 1993.
19. Nachum Dershowitz and Jean-Pierre Jouannaud. Rewrite systems. In J. van Leeuwen, editor, *Handbook of Theoretical Computer Science*, volume B, pages 243–309. North-Holland, 1990.
20. Nachum Dershowitz, Stéphane Kaplan, and David A. Plaisted. Infinite normal forms. In *Proc. 16th Int. Coll. on Automata, Languages and Programming, LNCS 372*, pages 249–262, Stresa, Italy, July 1989. European Association of Theoretical Computer Science.
21. Hervé Devie. Une approche algébrique de la réécriture de preuves équationnelles et son application à la dérivation de procédures de complétion. Thèse de Doctorat, Université de Paris-Sud, France, Octobre 1991.
22. Volker Diekert. On the Knuth-Bendix completion for concurrent processes. Universität München.
23. K. Drosten. On termination in combined term rewriting systems:theoretical background and application to prototyping parametric algebraic specifications. TU Braunshweig.
24. M. Fay. First-order unification in an equational theory. In *Proc. 4th Workshop on Automated Deduction, Austin, Texas*, pages 161–167, 1979.
25. Maribel Fernández. Narrowing based procedures for equational disunification. *Applicable Algebra in Engineering Communication and Computing*, 3:1–26, 1992.
26. Laurent Fribourg. A strong restriction of the inductive completion procedure. *Journal of Symbolic Computation*, 8:253–276, 1989.
27. J. A. Goguen. How to prove inductive hypothesis without induction. In *Proc. 5th Conf. on Automated Deduction, Les Arcs, France, LNCS 87*, July 1980.
28. J. A. Goguen, T. Winkler, José Meseguer, K. Futatsugi, and Jean-Pierre Jouannaud. *Applications of Algebraic Specifications Using OBJ*, chapter Introducing OBJ*. Cambridge University Press, 1991. D. Coleman, R. Gallimore and J. Goguen eds.

29. G. Gonthier, J.-J. Lévy, and P.-A. Mellies. An abstract standardisation theorem. In *Proc. 7th IEEE Symp. on Logic in Computer Science*, Santa Cruz, CA, 1992.
30. Jieh Hsiang and Michaël Rusinowitch. On word problems in equational theories. In *Proc. in 14th ICALP Karlsruhe*, July 1987.
31. Gérard Huet. Confluent reductions: abstract properties and applications to term rewriting systems. *Journal of the ACM*, 27(4):797–821, October 1980.
32. Gérard Huet. A complete proof of correctness of the Knuth-Bendix completion algorithm. *Journal of Computer and System Sciences*, 23:11–21, 1981.
33. Gérard Huet and J.-M. Hullot. Proofs by induction in equational theories with constructors. *Journal of Computer and System Sciences*, 25(2), 1982.
34. Gérard Huet and Jean-Jacques Lévy. Computations in orthogonal term rewriting systems. In Gordon Plotkin and Jean-Louis Lassez, editors, *Computational Logic: essays in Honour of Alan Robinson*. MIT Press, 1990.
35. J.-M. Hullot. Canonical forms and unification. In *Proc. 5th Conf. on Automated Deduction, Les Arcs, France, LNCS 87*. Springer-Verlag, July 1980.
36. Jean-Pierre Jouannaud and Claude Kirchner. Solving equations in abstract algebras: A rule-based survey of unification. In Jean-Louis Lassez and Gordon Plotkin, editors, *Computational Logic: Essays in Honor of Alan Robinson*. MIT-Press, 1991.
37. Jean-Pierre Jouannaud and Hélène Kirchner. Completion of a set of rules modulo a set of equations. *SIAM Journal on Computing*, 15(4):1155–1194, 1986.
38. Jean-Pierre Jouannaud and Emmanuel Kounalis. Automatic proofs by induction in theories without constructors. *Information and Computation*, 82(1), July 1989.
39. Jean-Pierre Jouannaud and Mitsuhiro Okada. Executable higher-order algebraic specification languages. In *Proc. 6th IEEE Symp. Logic in Computer Science, Amsterdam*, pages 350–361, 1991.
40. Jean-Pierre Jouannaud and Mitsuhiro Okada. Satisfiability of systems of ordinal notations with the subterm property is decidable. In *Proc. 18th Int. Coll. on Automata, Languages and Programming, Madrid, LNCS 510*, 1991.
41. Deepak Kapur, Paliath Narendran, and Hantao Zhang. On sufficient completeness and related properties of term rewriting systems. *Acta Informatica*, 24(4):395–415, 1987.
42. J. R. Kennaway, J. W. Klop, M. R. Sleep, and F. J. de Vries. Transfinite reductions in orthogonal term rewriting systems. In *Proc. 4th Rewriting Techniques and Applications, Como, LNCS 488*, 1991.
43. Jan Willem Klop and Aart Middeldorp. Sequentiality in orthogonal term rewriting systems. Technical report, CWI, Amsterdam, 1989.
44. Donald E. Knuth and Peter B. Bendix. Simple word problems in universal algebras. In J. Leech, editor, *Computational Problems in Abstract Algebra*, pages 263–297. Pergamon Press, 1970.
45. G. Kucherov and M. Tajine. Decidability of regularity and related properties of ground normal form languages. Research Report 92-R-062, CRIN, Nancy, France, 1992. To appear in Information and Computation.
46. Mahahito Kurihara and Azuma Ohuchi. Non-copying term rewriting and modularity of termination. Hokkaido University.
47. Yves Lafont. Penrose diagrams and 2-dimensional rewriting, October 1991. extended abstract.
48. Claude Marché. Réécriture modulo une théorie présentée par un système convergent et décidabilité des problèmes du mot dans certains classes de théories équationnelles. Thèse de Doctorat, Université de Paris-Sud, France, 1993.
49. José Meseguer. General logics. Technical Report SRI-CSL-89-05, SRI International, March 1989. Proc. Logic Colloquium'87.

50. José Meseguer. Conditional rewriting logic as a unified model of concurrency. Technical Report SRI-CSL-91-05, SRI International, February 1991. TCS 96 (1992) 73-155.
51. Y. Métivier. About the rewriting systems produced by the knuth-bendix completion algorithm. *Information Processing Letters*, 16(1):31–34, 1983.
52. A. Middeldorp. Modular aspects of properties of term rewriting systems related to normal forms. In *Proc. 3rd Rewriting Techniques and Applications, Chapel Hill, LNCS 355*, pages 263–277. Springer-Verlag, 1989.
53. A. Middeldorp and Y. Toyama. Completeness of combinations of constructor systems. In *Proc. 4th Rewriting Techniques and Applications, Como, LNCS 488*, 1991.
54. Aart Middeldorp. *Modular Properties of Term Rewriting Systems*. PhD thesis, Free University of Amsterdam, Netherland, 1990.
55. D. Musser. Proving inductive properties of abstract data types. In *Proc. 7th ACM Symp. Principles of Programming Languages, Las Vegas*, 1980.
56. M. H. A. Newman. On theories with a combinatorial definition of 'equivalence'. *Ann. Math.*, 43(2):223–243, 1942.
57. Robert Nieuwenhuis and Albert Rubio. Completion of first-order clauses by basic superposition with ordering constraints. Tech. report, Dept. L.S.I., Univ. Polit. Catalunya, 1991. To appear in Proc. 11th Conf. on Automated Deduction, Saratoga Springs, 1992.
58. Robert Nieuwenhuis and Albert Rubio. Basic superposition is complete. In B. Krieg-Bruckner, editor, *Proc. European Symp. on Programming, LNCS 582*, pages 371–389, Rennes, 1992. Springer-Verlag.
59. W. Nutt, P. Réty, and Gert Smolka. Basic narrowing revisited. *Journal of Symbolic Computation*, 7(3/4):295–318, 1989.
60. Gerald E. Peterson and Mark E. Stickel. Complete sets of reductions for some equational theories. *Journal of the ACM*, 28(2):233–264, April 1981.
61. David Plaisted. Semantic confluence tests and completion methods. *Information and Control*, 65:182–215, 1985.
62. David A. Plaisted. Semantic confluence tests and completion methods. *Information and Control*, 65(2-3):182–215, May/June 1985.
63. C. C. Squier. Word problems and a homological finiteness condition for monoids. *Journal of Pure and Applied Algebra*, 49:201–217, 1987.
64. W. Thomas. Automata on infinite objects. In J. van Leeuwen, editor, *Handbook of Theoretical Computer Science*, pages 134–191. Elsevier, 1990.
65. Y. Toyama. Counterexamples to termination for the direct sum of term rewriting systems. *Information Processing Letters*, 25:141–143, April 1987.
66. Y. Toyama. On the Church-Rosser property for the direct sum of term rewriting systems. *Journal of the ACM*, 34(1):128–143, April 1987.
67. Ralf Treinen. A new method for undecidability proofs of first order theories. Tech. Report A-09/90, Universität des Saarladandes, Saarbrücken, May 1990.
68. H. Zhang. Automated proof of ring commutativity problems by algebraic methods. *Journal of Symbolic Computation*, 9:423–427, 1990.

Identity and Existence, and Types in Algebra

- A Survey of Sorts - [1]

Axel Poigné

German National Research Centre of Computer Science (GMD)
Schloß Birlinghoven,
D-53757 Sankt Augustin, Germany

Abstract We survey partiality as found in algebra covering the various approaches which have surfaced and are being used in computer science, particularly in the data type community.

0. Introduction

Algebra is about equational reasoning. Though indisputably a tautology, the variance and extent of "algebra" is underestimated if equational reasoning is equated with many-sorted algebra.

Shortcomings of many-sorted algebra have been noticed right from the beginning [1, 12]. Abstractly, the problem is thus : beside inherent infrastructure, logic provides a language format for a user to specify particular theories. The language format usually includes some principle for generation of *names*. There may be many names for the same entity, or there might be a name but no entity named. Mathematically speaking, a *theory of identity* caters for the first, and a *theory of existence* for the second, the latter being obviously related to *partiality*. Partiality may occur for at least two reasons, the obvious one being that a term is inherently meaningless under certain assumptions, such as division by *0*. On the other hand, meaning may not be fixed yet, for instance in the design phase. As Fourman and Scott [9] put it : 'When we talk about something, we cannot always presuppose its existence. Well-formed terms in a language may fail to denote'.

Let us consider the notorious example of stacks

spec STACK **is**	
NAT **with**	
sorts	<u>stack</u>
ops	*empty* : → <u>stack</u>
	push : <u>stack</u> <u>nat</u> → <u>stack</u>
	pop : <u>stack</u> → <u>stack</u>
	top : <u>stack</u> → <u>nat</u>
vars	*s* : <u>stack</u>, *d* : <u>nat</u>
axs	*pop(push(s,d)) = s*
	top(push(s,d)) = d

[1] Partially supported by the ESPRIT WG COMPASS and by the Verbundprojekt KORSO, funded by the German Ministery of Research and Technology, grant No. ITS 900 1A7

pop(*empty*) may denote an error, may be considered as undefined, or may be avoided entirely. For the latter, subsorting has been introduced (cf. [14])

```
spec STACK is
NAT with
sorts   nestack < stack
ops     empty : → stack
        push : stack nat → nestack
        pop : nestack → stack
        top : stack → nat
vars    s : stack, d : nat
axs     pop(push(s,d)) = s
        top(push(s,d)) = d
```

but at an expense: meaningful terms such as *pop*(*pop*(*push*(*push*(*empty*, *1*), 2)))) are no longer well-formed. In a way, some degree of partiality seems unavoidable because notation and denotation, respectively syntax and semantics, are incongruent.

This paper aims for a more comprehensive view of partiality, surveying some developments to be found in literature. The first section gives a rather special account of partial algebras, while the second shows how to avoid partiality by introducing sophisticated typing facilities. The third section comments on subsorting, and the fourth deals with expressiveness and pragmatics.

1. Partial Algebras

1.1 A View of Partiality

We reiterate that given a naming facility names may either denote the same entity or fail to denote at all. Interaction of the theory of equality and that of existence gives rise to a variety of axiomatizations, even with different, though equivalent semantics.

Let a supply A of names to be given. Let the notation Ea state that the name $a \in A$ denotes some entity, and let us use $a = b$ if the names a and b denote the same entity. We note a few consequences:

$$\begin{array}{lll} E\,a & \text{if} & a = b \\ a = b & \text{if} & a = b \\ a = c & \text{if} & a = b \text{ and } b = c. \end{array}$$

Reflexivity does not hold in general since then all names denote. Those entities which are named exactly correspond to *elements* (or *singletons*) of A, i.e. sets $[a] = \{a' \mid a = a'\}$. Hence we can forget about the mysterious entities, and distinguish between names and elements only. We may also equate reflexivity and existence since $a = a$ whenever Ea. Such a structure $(A, =)$, a set with a *partial equivalence relation* (a symmetric and transitive binary relation) is called a *per*.

Let us use A to refer to a per $(A, =)$, but to avoid confusion, $|A|$ will explicitly denote the underlying set of names if necessary, i.e. $A = (|A|, =)$. The set of elements will be denoted by EA.

Pers support two sorts of functions: those on names we will henceforth call *operations* and those on singletons we continue to refer to as *functions*[2]. Let A and B be pers.

- An operation is a mapping $\sigma : |A| \to |B|$ which preserve *equivalence*, i.e.

$$\sigma(a) \equiv \sigma(a') \text{ if } a \equiv a'$$

  where $a \equiv a' \Leftrightarrow (E\,a \vee E\,a' \Rightarrow a = a')$, implying that names which fail to denote are handled uniformly.
- Functions are strict and total functional relations $h : |A| \times |B|$, i.e.
  - h is *strict if* Ea and Eb whenever $(a, b) \in h$,
  - h is *total* if, for all $a \in A$ such that Ea, there exists $b \in B$ such that $(a, b) \in h$, and
  - h is *functional* if $(a, b), (a, b') \in h$ implies $b = b'$.

Once again, operations are naming procedures which generate new names from given ones, while functions relate elements in the usual way.

The reader will have noticed that we are just talking about sets (of elements) and of (total) functions, with operations being partial functions[3]. So why all the fuss?

Even though equivalent as categories, pers and sets support different (though equivalent) logics of partiality. As an example, consider the operators

$$0,\ suc, pred$$

and the following two "models" :

- as a set model : $\mathbb{N}_\bullet$ with the "predecessor" being a partial mapping, and
- as a per model : $\mathbb{Z}$ with partial equivalence $z = z$ if $z \geq 0$ (the operations being successor and predecessor).

The equations $pred(suc(x)) = x$ holds for all values of $\mathbb{N}_\bullet$ (equality being interpreted as identity), while it does not for $\mathbb{Z}$ with equality being interpreted as partial equivalence (since $pred(suc(-1)) = -1$ would imply $E\,\text{-}1$). The set model, however, is *not* closed under substitution. The equality $pred(suc(pred(x))) = pred(x)$ (obtained by substitution) fails to hold in $\mathbb{N}_\bullet$. We have a discrepancy between syntax and semantics in the case of set models; semantically, variables refer to the elements of $\mathbb{N}_\bullet$ while, syntactically, terms are substituted which may fail to denote. In our terminology, syntax refers to names, and semantics to elements only. This discrepancy disappears in case of per models where names are available on the level of syntax and semantics (the syntactic $pred(0)$ has a corresponding name -1 in the semantic domain).

The difference is reflected by the proof systems corresponding to the set models and the per models. The proof systems depend on the choice of interpretation for "equality". The

---

[2] A "function" $f : (A, =) \to (B, =)$ corresponds to a mapping $f : EA \to EB$ such that $f(a) = f(b)$ if $a = b$.

[3] Every per is isomorphic to its set of elements (with identity relation), an isomorphism being a bijective function on pers.

set-related logic is based on *strong* equivalence $\equiv$ and an additional existence predicate E. Then the ***substitution rule***, for instance, is defined by

$$\frac{\varphi\ [\Gamma] \quad Et\ [\Gamma]}{\varphi(x/t)\ [\Gamma]}$$

In contrast, the per-related logic only uses the "weak" equality = with a *substitution rule* being defined by the standard

$$\frac{\varphi\ [\Gamma]}{\varphi(x/t)\ [\Gamma(x/t)]}$$

There is a price to pay in that the *equivalence rule*

$$\frac{\varphi(x/t)\ [\Gamma] \quad t=t'\ [\Gamma, Et] \quad t=t'\ [\Gamma, Et']}{\varphi(x/t')\ [\Gamma]}$$

replaces the standard *identity rule*

$$\frac{\varphi(x/t)\ [\Gamma] \quad t=t'\ [\Gamma]}{\varphi(x/t')\ [\Gamma]}$$

The latter is sound, however, if all operators are *strict in each component*, i.e.

$$E\sigma(a_1,\ldots,a_n) \vdash \bigwedge_{i=1}^{n} E\, a_i$$

(which holds for partial algebras)[4].

Though being a matter of taste, I favour the per approach for a variety of reasons:

- Firstly, if restricted to partial operations, the standard rules of equational reasoning apply except that we have to abandon reflexivity. Explicitly the proof system is thus :

$$\frac{t=t'\ [\Gamma]}{t'=t\ [\Gamma]} \qquad \frac{t=t'\ [\Gamma] \quad t'=t''\ [\Gamma]}{t=t''\ [\Gamma]}$$

$$\frac{\varphi\ [\Gamma]}{\varphi(x/t)\ [\Gamma(x/t)]} \qquad \frac{\varphi(x/t)\ [\Gamma] \quad t=t'\ [\Gamma]}{\varphi(x/t')\ [\Gamma]}$$

$$\frac{E\sigma(t_1,\ldots,t_n)\ [\Gamma]}{Et_i\ [\Gamma]} \quad \text{for } i = 1,\ldots,n$$

where we refer to the last rule as the strictness rule.

As a consequence, whatever is implemented of equational deduction and rewriting may be kept at no expense (at least, I am not aware of any system which makes essential usage of reflexivity).

- Secondly, operations applied to arguments which fail to denote, such as pop(empty), have a natural interpretation as *errors* as advocated in [25] (see also below).

[4] A very thorough discussion of the options are to be found in [30], the semantics being discussed in [9]. Note that the setup may handle non-strict operations in a perfectly reasonable way, providing a natural semantics for an "algebraic" semantics of the kind discussed in [3].

We also note an apparent disadvantage:

- Equational axioms of the form

$$pop(push(s, d)) = s$$

(where s is of sort stack, and d is of sort nat) imply existence of all subterms. Especially, it follows that Es and Ed, i.e. all stacks and all data, are defined. For partiality, we need careful guarding of axioms, e.g.

$$pop(push(s, d)) = s \ \ [E\,s, E\,d]$$[5]

but we will learn about better notation below. The trade-off in relation to the set-related logic is minimal if there is one at all; in this logic the axiom

$$pop(push(x, d)) \equiv s$$

leaves open the existence of subterms. Conditional declarations of the form

$$E\,push(s, d)\ [E\,s, E\,d]$$

$$E\,pop(push(s, d))\ [E\,s, E\,d]$$

are necessary to ensure that the respective names denote at all.

1.2 Partial Algebras

On reflection, we have not spelled out what we mean by a partial algebra in our setting. First, we do need a construction to support "arity". There are two product constructions available in the setting. Let $(A, =)$ and $(B, =)$ be pers.

- The *cartesian product*
  Let the per $A \times B$ have the carrier $|A| \times |B|$ and the partial equality $(a, b) = (a', b')$ iff $a = a'$ and $b = b'$. It is easy to check that $E(A \times B) = EA \times EB$.

- The *partial product*
  Let the per $A \times_p B$ have the carrier $|A| \times |B|$ and the partial equality $(a, b) = (a', b')$ iff $a \equiv a'$ and $b \equiv b'$. Here we have $E(A \times_p B) = EA \times EB + EA + EB$, the product in the category of partial functions (+ denotes the disjoint union of sets).

Which one is appropriate? By common consent, we should use the cartesian product. The informal argument in favour of this choice is that, for instance, defining an operation *push* : stack $\times_p$ nat $\to$ stack would allow to push some data on top of an undefined stack yielding a well-defined stack, quite in contrast to one's ideas about stacks. More abstractly, operations are supposed to be ***strict in each argument***; i.e. we say that an n-ary operation $\sigma : |A| \times ... \times |A| \to |A|$ is ***strict*** if $E\sigma(a_1,...,a_n)$ implies Ea_i for all i = 1,...,n (and ***total*** if the converse holds) which is equivalent to: $\sigma : A \times ... \times A \to A$ is an operation. This is exactly

[5] Note the consequences $E\,push(s, d)\ [E\,s, E\,d]$ and $E\,pop(push(s, d))\ [E\,s, E\,d]$.

what the cartesian product supports (which is a *tensor product* in the category of partial functions)

Definition Given a (standard) many-sorted signature SIG, a ***partial*** SIG-***model*** $\mathcal{A}$ consists of a per $s^{\mathcal{A}}$ for every sort s, and a strict operation $\sigma^{\mathcal{A}} : s_1^{\mathcal{A}} \times ... \times s_n^{\mathcal{A}} \rightarrow s^{\mathcal{A}}$ for every operator $\sigma : s_1...s_n \rightarrow s$ (a strict relation $\rho^{\mathcal{A}} \subseteq s_1^{\mathcal{A}} \times ... \times s_n^{\mathcal{A}}$ for each relation symbol $\rho : s_1...s_n$ where a relation is ***strict*** if $\rho(a_1,...,a_n)$ implies Ea_i for all $i = 1,...,n$).

Definition *A specification* SPEC *consists of a signature plus a set of conditional clauses of the form* φ **if** Φ[6], *where satisfaction is defined as follows* :

$$[\![x]\!]_{\mathcal{A}}\xi := \xi(x)$$
$$[\![\sigma(t_1,...,t_n)]\!]_{\mathcal{A}}\xi := \sigma^{\mathcal{A}}([\![t_1]\!]_{\mathcal{A}}\xi,..., [\![t_n]\!]_{\mathcal{A}}\xi)$$
$$[\![\varphi[\Phi]]\!]_{\mathcal{A}}\xi := [\![\Phi]\!]_{\mathcal{A}}\xi \Rightarrow [\![\varphi]\!]_{\mathcal{A}}\xi$$
$$[\![\varphi \text{ if } \Phi]\!]_{\mathcal{A}}\xi := [\![\varphi[\Phi]]\!]_{\mathcal{A}}\xi$$

where $$[\![\Phi]\!]_{\mathcal{A}}\xi = \bigwedge_{\varphi \in \Phi} [\![\varphi]\!]_{\mathcal{A}}\xi$$
$$[\![\rho(t_1,...,t_n)]\!]_{\mathcal{A}}\xi := \rho[\![t_1]\!]_{\mathcal{A}}\xi,..., [\![t_n]\!]_{\mathcal{A}}\xi)$$
$$[\![t = t']\!]_{\mathcal{A}}\xi := [\![t]\!]_{\mathcal{A}}\xi = [\![t']\!]_{\mathcal{A}}\xi$$

$\mathcal{A} \models \varphi$ **if** Φ *if, for all substitutions* ξ, $[\![\varphi$ **if** $\Phi]\!]_{\mathcal{A}}\xi$ *holds.*
(*A* substitution $\xi : X \rightarrow A$ *maps the variable* x *of sort* s *to an element* $\xi(x) \in A_s$.)

Considering homomorphisms, a homomorphism should map elements to elements, i.e. it should be a function. Then the homomorphism diagram

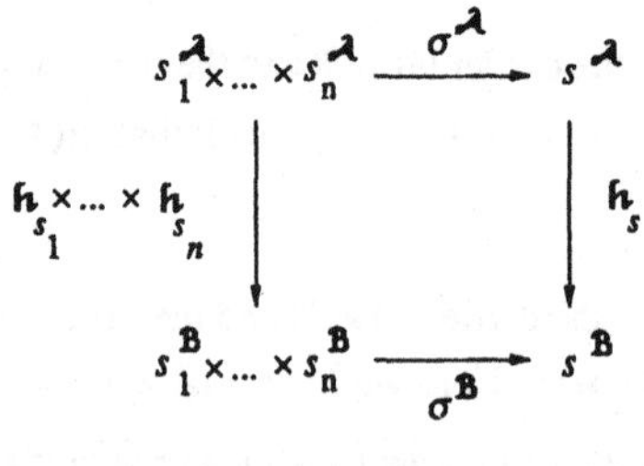

involves operations as well as functions which leaves a variety of choices.

Definition *A* (***weak***) ***homomorphism*** *is a family of functions such that*

$$\mathfrak{h}_s(\sigma^{\mathcal{A}}(a_1,...,a_n)) = \sigma^{\mathcal{B}}(\mathfrak{h}_{s_1}(a_1),...,\mathfrak{h}_{s_n}(a_n))$$

whenever $E\sigma^{\mathcal{A}}(a_1,...,a_n)$. *A homomorphism is* ***strong*** *if*

$$\mathfrak{h}_s(\sigma^{\mathcal{A}}(a_1,...,a_n)) = \sigma^{\mathcal{B}}(\mathfrak{h}_{s_1}(a_1),...,\mathfrak{h}_{s_n}(a_n))$$

whenever $E\sigma^{\mathcal{B}}(\mathfrak{h}_{s_1}(a_1),...,\mathfrak{h}_{s_n}(a_n))$.

---

[6] If Φ is empty, we use the notation φ instead of φ if $\emptyset$.

The homomorphisms have unexpected properties. Let us look at an example borrowed from [29]:

$$E\,k$$

$$E\,f(x) \textbf{ if } f(x) = k.$$

We claim existence of models which are related by a bijective homomorphism, but which are not isomorphic. Consider one algebra $\mathcal{B}$ with a carrier $(\{0\}, 0 = 0)$ and with the operators being totally defined, i.e. $k^{\mathcal{B}} = 0$ and $f^{\mathcal{B}}(0) = 0$, and another algebra $\mathcal{A}$ with the same carrier, and with $k^{\mathcal{A}} = 0$ and $f^{\mathcal{A}}(0)$ being undefined. The axioms hold in both cases, in the latter $f^{\mathcal{A}}(0)$ may be undefined since the premise does not hold, again due to undefinedness. The unique mapping from $\mathcal{A}$ to $\mathcal{B}$ is a bijective homomorphism but not an isomorphism. In contrast, strong bijective homomorphisms are isomorphisms since strongness implies that $\mathfrak{h}$ is an isomorphism on $E\,s_i^{\mathcal{A}}$, for all i.

Similarly, other standard properties of categories of algebras turn out not to behave as usually, or rather, each property has various instantiations depending on the notion of homomorphism. This is to be expected having, for each operator σ, a "virtual definedness predicate" $Def(\sigma)$ which is not explicitly considered when stating properties of homomorphisms, as e.g. bijectivity, injectivity, quotients etc. The taxonomy of the resulting phenomena is explained at length in [4], and, to some extent, in [16] (which is probably more accessible).

Reichel [29] has asked for suitable constraints which would at least guarantee that injective (bijective) homomorphisms become monomorphisms (isomorphisms). His guiding example is that of categories

```
spec CATEGORY is
sorts   ob , mor
decls   idA : mor       if A : ob
        dom(f) : ob     if f : mor
        cod(f) : ob     if f : mor
        f ; g  : mor    if f : mor, g : mor, cod(f) = dom(g)
axs     dom(f ; g) = dom(f)     if f, g : mor
        cod(f ; g) = cod(g)     if f, g : mor
        dom(idA) = A            if A : ob
        cod(idA)  = A           if A : ob
        f ; (g ; h) = (f ; g) ; h
                        if f,g,h : mor, cod(f) = dom(g), cod(g) = dom(h)
        idA ; f = f     if A : ob, f : mor, dom(f) = A
        f ; idB = f     if B : ob, f : mor, cod(f) = B
```

Here declarations provide sort information as well as stating existence, e.g.

$$f\,;g\ :\underline{mor} \textbf{ if } f:\underline{mor},\ g:\underline{mor},\ cod(f) = dom(g)$$

states that $f\,;g$ is of sort $\underline{mor}$ and that $E f\,;g$. This specification is well behaved since existence of an entity does not reflexively depend on its own existence as in

$$E\,f(x) \textbf{ if } f(x) = k.$$

Reichel introduces hierarchy conditions which, roughly, state the following: if we say that an operator σ *depends* on those which occur in the condition clause Γ of its declaration

$\sigma(_1,...,x_n) : s$ **if** Γ, and if we iterate the definition, an operator satisfies the *hierarchy condition* if it never depends on itself.

Theorem [29] *Let* SIG *be signature with (existence) declaration of the form*

$$\sigma(x_1,...,x_n) : s \textbf{ if } t_1 = t_1',..., t_n = t_n',$$

and let a SIG-algebra be a partial algebra which satisfies $E\sigma(x_1,...,x_n)$ **if** $t_1 = t_1',..., t_n = t_n'$, *for each declaration. Then injective (bijective) homomorphisms are monomorphisms (isomorphisms) iff* SIG *satisfies the hierarchy condition.*

Whether all this is irritating or not, may be a matter of taste. Otherwise there is nothing wrong with partial algebras; we have term construction as well as all sorts of subobject and quotient constructions which provide a rich infrastructure for all purposes. Just in order to give an example we consider *free generation.* We should note that the naming of a variable x is not sufficient for it to be a generator since only elements generate. More generally, we consider free algebras which are generated by a set Ψ of formulas.

Definition *Let* Ψ *be a set of formulas. A substitution* $\xi : X \to A$ *is called a solution of* Ψ *in an algebra* $\mathcal{A}$ *if* $\bigwedge_{\psi \in \Psi} [\![\psi]\!]_{\mathcal{A}} \xi$ *is true. A partial* SPEC-*model* $\mathcal{A}$ *is* ***freely generated*** *by* Ψ if there exists a solution ξ *of* Ψ *in* $\mathcal{A}$ *such that for every* SPEC-*model* $\mathbf{B}$ *and every solution* ζ *of* Ψ *in* $\mathbf{B}$ *there exists a unique homomorphism* $\mathfrak{h} : \mathcal{A} \to \mathbf{B}$ *such that* $\mathfrak{h}(\xi(x)) = \zeta(x)$.

Proposition *Let* $T_{SPEC+\Psi}$ *be the partial algebra with* $|T_{SPEC+\Psi}| = T_{SIG}(X)$ *where a formula* φ *holds if* $\vdash^{SPEC+\Psi}\varphi[]$ (by abuse of language).*Then* $T_{SPEC+\Psi}$ *is freely generated by* Ψ.[7]

Corollary $\mathrm{T}_{SPEC} := T_{SPEC}$ *is an initial* SPEC-*model.*

In fact, we use freely generated models to prove completeness, quite in the standard way (the proof can be found in [25], or [29] for the equational setup).

Proposition *Deduction is sound and complete.* I.e. $\Phi \vdash^{SPEC} \psi$ iff $\Phi \models^{SPEC} \psi$.

We will comment on the expressiveness of identity and existence restricted to an algebraic setting below (section 4).

---

7 $\vdash^{SPEC}\varphi[\Phi]$ states that $\varphi[\Phi]$ can be deduced from the axioms in SPEC. SPEC+Ψ extends the axioms of SPEC by those in Ψ.

2. Extending the Type System[8]

2.1 Some Examples

We now discuss strategies to avoid partiality. Accommodation of partiality within the world of total functions is a familiar idea: every partial function $f : A \to B$ can be presented by its domain of definition $Def(f)$ and a total function $f : Def(f) \to B$. We may name the domain of definition explicitly by introducing new sorts of the form $\{a \in A \mid \varphi\}$ where φ is some predicate. As a claim, we tag type systems as *(essentially) algebraic* where all types are of the form $\{a \in A \mid \varphi\}$ with φ being equational. This allows to write specifications the expressive power of which is well beyond that of the standard many-sorted idiom. Let us again look at the example of categories[9]

spec CATEGORY **is**
types *ob* , *mor*
decls $id_A : mor$ **if** $A : ob$
$dom(f) : ob$ **if** $f : mor$
$cod(f) : ob$ **if** $f : mor$
$f ; g : mor$ **if** $f : mor, g : mor, cod(f) = dom(g)$
axs $dom(f ; g) = dom(f)$ **if** $f, g : mor$
$cod(f ; g) = cod(g)$ **if** $f, g : mor$
$dom(id_A) = A = cod(id_A)$ **if** $A : ob$
$f ; (g ; h) = (f ; g) ; h$
if $f,g,h : mor, cod(f) = dom(g), cod(g) = dom(h)$
$id_A ; f = f$ **if** $A : ob, f : mor, dom(f) = A$
$f ; id_B = f$ **if** $B : ob, f : mor, cod(f) = B$

The semantics of such a specification appears to be straightforward. As usual, every type τ is interpreted by a set τ^A. *Conditional declarations* of the form $f(x_1,...,x_n) : \tau$ **if** $x_1 : \tau_1, ..., x_n : \tau_n, t_1 = t_1', ..., t_n = t_n'$ should be interpreted by functions $f^A : \{ (a_1,...,a_n) \in \tau_1^A \times ... \times \tau_n^A \mid t_1 = t_1', ..., t_n = t_n' \} \to \tau^A$. We encounter familiar problems. Consider the declaration $f(x) : \tau$ **if** $x : \tau, f(x) = f(x)$. For an interpretation of f, we first have to determine its domain of definition which, reflexively, depends on the interpretation of f.

There are a variety of proposals to avoid such reflexive dependencies, for instance Reichel's hierarchy constraints mentioned above. Whatever the syntax looks like, there is a common drawback in practical terms; checking definedness relies on the full computational power of equational reasoning, hence is no longer decidable.

There are other familiar examples such as bounded stacks which seem to follow the same scheme though not exactly being equational:

8 There is a fine distinction between *sorts* and *types*, the former refering to the syntactical level and the latter to the semantical level. I will comment on this distinction further below.

9 The change of format is deliberate since we want to distinguish between sorts and types below.

```
spec BOUNDEDSTACK is
NAT with
types   stack
decls   bound : nat
        length(s) : nat    if s : stack
        empty : stack
        push(s, d) : stack       if s : stack, d : nat, length(s) < bound
        pop(s) : stack           if s : stack, 0 < length(s)
        top(s) : nat             if s : stack, 0 < length(s)
axs     length(empty) = 0
        length(push(s,d)) = suc(length(s))
                                 if s : stack, d : nat, length(s) < bound
        pop(push(s,d)) = s       if s : stack, d : nat, length(s) < bound
        top(push(s,d)) = d       if s : stack, d : nat, length(s) < bound
```

In fact, we could have used equations instead, though some coding is required: let $\rho : \tau_1 ... \tau_n$ be some (sorted) relation symbol. We introduce a new type R and an operation $m_R : \tau_1 \times ... \times \tau_n$ **if** $x : R$ where

axs $x = y$ **if** $x{:}R,\ y{:}R,\ m_R(x) = m_R(y)$

and where the product type is determined by the following "generic" script:

```
types   τ1×...×τn
decls   <_,...,_> : τ1×...×τn if x1 : τ1,..., xn : τn
axs     xi = xi' if x1:τ1,..., xn:τn, < x1, ..., xn> = < x1', ..., xn'>.
```

Then we may replace every atomic proposition of the form $\rho(t_1,...,t_n)$ by the equality $<t_1,..., t_n> = m_R(x)$ without changing the semantic content, the additional variable x being of type R.

There is yet another way to write equational specifications, namely using dependent types.

```
spec STRATSTACK is
NAT with
types   stack if d : nat
decls   empty : stack(0)
        push(s, d) : stack(suc(n))  if n : nat, s : stack(n), d : nat
        pop(s) : stack(n)            if n : nat, s : stack(suc(n))
        top(s) : nat                 if n : nat, s : stack(n)
axs     pop(push(s,d)) = s           if n : nat, s : stack(n), d : nat
        top(push(s,d)) = d           if n : nat, s : stack(n), d : nat
```

The translation into our original style of specification is straightforward. For the dependant type *stack* **if** *d* : *nat* we introduce a new type *stack* and an operator *length*(*s*) : *nat*. **if** *s* : *stack*. Terms of the form *stack*(*t*) are translated to equalities *length*(*t*) = *s* where *s* is a variable of type *stack*. Systematic translation yields the specification

```
spec STRATSTACK is
NAT with
types   stack
decls   empty : stack
        push(s, d) : stack    if n : nat, s : stack, length(s) = n, d : nat
        pop(s) : stack        if n : nat, s : stack, length(s) = suc(n)
        top(s) : nat          if n : nat, s : stack, length(s) = suc(n)
```

axs	$pop(push(s,d)) = s$	**if** $n : nat, s : stack, length(s) = n, d : nat$
	$pop(push(s,d)) = d$	**if** $n : nat, s : stack, length(s) = n, d : nat$
	$length(empty) = 0$	
	$length(push(s,d) = n$	**if** $n : nat, s : stack, length(s) = n, d : nat$
	$length(pop(s)) = n$	**if** $n : nat, s : stack, length(s) = suc(n)$

Note that the operator declarations need to be split into an operator declaration and an equation circumscribing the type dependency. All these formats are semantically equivalent in that the respective categories of models are equivalent but have quite different syntactic and pragmatic aspects. This remark will be discussed more extensively below (section 4).

2.2 A System for Typing

Operators and terms cannot be introduced independently of each other since the domain of operators has to be defined a priori. To this effect, we use a predicate "well-formed". I recommend to compute a few examples in order to appreciate the definition.

Definition *A* ***prespecification*** SPEC = (Σ, D, Ax) *consists of a signature* Σ, *comprising type constructors* δ, *operators* σ, *and relation symbols* ρ, *a set D of* ***declarations*** *of the form*

types	$\delta(x_1,...,x_n)$ **if** Γ
operators	$\sigma(x_1,...,x_n) : \tau$ **if** Γ
relators	$\rho(x_1,...,x_n) : \tau$ **if** Γ

and a set Ax of axioms of the form φ **if** Γ *(where the atomic proposition* φ *are in the usual format).*

Definition *A context* $\Gamma = \gamma_1,...,\gamma_n$, *resp. a declaration or axiom,* γ **if** Γ *is* ***well-formed*** *(with regard to* SPEC*) if the predicates* $wf(\Gamma)$ *resp.* $wf(\gamma$ **if** $\Gamma)$ *hold which are defined inductively via a proof system (type and operator declarations are handled uniformly for technical convenience, we use* γ *to range over types* τ, *typed terms* $t : \tau$, *and atomic propositions* φ*) :*

- $wf([])$	
- $wf(\Gamma, x : \tau)$	if $\vdash \tau [\Gamma]$
- $wf(\Gamma, t = t' : \tau)$	if $\vdash t : \tau [\Gamma]$ and $\vdash t' : \tau [\Gamma]$
- $wf(\Gamma, \rho(t_1,...,t_n))$	if $\vdash t_i : \tau_i [\Gamma]$ for all $i = 1,...,n$
- $wf(\delta(x_1,...,x_n)$ **if** $\Gamma)$	if $wf(\Gamma)$
- $wf(\sigma(x_1,...,x_n) : \tau$ **if** $\Gamma)$	if $\vdash \tau [\Gamma]$
- $wf(\rho(x_1,...,x_n)$ **if** $\Gamma)$	if $\vdash \tau_i [\Gamma]$ for all $i = 1,...,n$
- $wf(t = t' : \tau$ **if** $\Gamma])$	if $\vdash t : \tau [\Gamma]$ and $\vdash t' : \tau [\Gamma]$
- $wf(\varphi [\Gamma])$	if $\vdash t : \tau [\Gamma]$ and $\vdash t' : \tau [\Gamma]$

where

(refl) $$\frac{t : \tau\,[\Gamma]}{t = t : \tau\,[\Gamma]}$$ (sym) $$\frac{t = t' : \tau\,[\Gamma]}{t' = t : \tau\,[\Gamma]}$$

(trans) $$\frac{t = t' : \tau\,[\Gamma] \quad t' = t'' : \tau\,[\Gamma]}{t = t'' : \tau\,[\Gamma]}$$

(id) $$\frac{(x/t)^{*}\gamma\,[\Gamma] \quad t = t' : \tau\,[\Gamma]}{(x/t')^{*}\gamma\,[\Gamma]}$$

(mon) $\gamma\,[\Gamma, \gamma, \Gamma']$ if $wf(\Gamma, \gamma, \Gamma')$

(axintro) $$\frac{\Theta^{*}\Gamma\,[\Gamma']}{\Theta^{*}\gamma\,[\Gamma']}$$ *where* γ **if** Γ *is a declaration or an axiom of* SPEC.

$\Theta^{*}\Gamma\,[\Gamma']$ *is an abbreviation for:* $\Theta^{*}\gamma_i\,[\Gamma']$ for all $i = 1,\ldots,n$. $\Theta^{*}\gamma$ *denotes the result of substituting all variables x in* γ *by terms* $\Theta(x)$. $\vdash \gamma[\Gamma]$ *states that we can deduce* $\gamma[\Gamma]$. *Note that the deduction system depends on* SPEC.

Definition *A* ***specification*** SPEC *is a prespecification such that all declarations and axioms are well-formed.*

Let us consider some examples. In order to check well-formedness of the axiom

$$pop(push(s, d)) = s \ \textbf{if}\ s : stack,\ d : nat,\ length(s) < bound$$

we have to prove that the terms have the same type, namely *stack*. We only pursue the more difficult argument. Assume that $0 < suc(n)\,[n : nat]$ is an axiom of NAT, we use

$$\cfrac{\cfrac{\cfrac{\cfrac{s : stack\,[s : stack, d : nat, length(s) < bound]}{length(s) : nat\,[s : stack, d : nat, length(s) < bound]}}{0 < suc(length(s))[s : stack, d : nat, length(s) < bound]}}{length(push(s, d)) = suc(length(s))\,[s : stack, d : nat, length(s) < bound]}}{0 < length(push(s, d))\,[s : stack, d : nat, length(s) < bound]}$$

provided that the axiom

$$length(push(s,d)) = suc(length(s)) \ \textbf{if}\ s : stack,\ d : nat,\ length(s) < bound$$

is well-formed (the proof of which is left to the reader). The conclusion is the essential condition needed to apply the introduction rule to deduce (in shorthand notation)

$$\frac{s : stack,\ 0 < length(push(s, d))\,[s : stack, d : nat, length(s) < bound]}{pop(s) : stack\,[s : stack, d : nat, length(s) < bound]}$$

The proof demonstrates the inductive nature of well-formedness: all the ingredients of the environment have to be established as well-formed in order to determine well-formedness of the conclusions. This becomes even more apparent if dependent types are considered. For instance, trying to establish that $pop(push(s, d)) : stack(n)$ **if** $n : nat,\ s : stack(n),\ d : nat$

is well-formed, we need the following proof tree which for didactic reasons is displayed in its full glory :

$$\frac{n : nat\ ,\ s : stack(n)\ ,\ d : nat\ [n : nat,\ s : stack(n),\ d : nat]}{push(s,d) : stack(suc(n))\ [n : nat,\ s : stack(n),\ d : nat]}$$

is used in

$$\frac{n : nat\ ,\ push(s,d) : stack(suc(n))\ [n : nat,\ s : stack(n),\ d : nat]}{pop(push(s,d)) : stack(n\ )\ [n : nat,\ s : stack(n),\ d : nat]}\ .$$

However, this presumes well-definedness of the declarations : for the push operation we have to establish that

$$\frac{\dfrac{n : nat\ [n : nat,\ s : stack(n),\ d : nat]}{suc(n) : nat\ [n : nat,\ s : stack(n),\ d : nat]}}{stack(suc(n))\ [n : nat,\ s : stack(n),\ d : nat]}$$

clearly depending on well-formedness of $suc(n) : nat$ **if** $n : nat$ and $stack(n)$ **if** $n : nat$. But $\vdash nat$ since the empty environment is well-formed.

As pointed out above, there is a need for efficient proof technology, probably based on rewriting. The use of equations in determining the type as in the example of the bounded stack is, of course, the crux. But in many cases type checking may still be efficient which seems to be the main argument in favour of a restriction to total functions.

2.3 A General Abstract Nonsense Point of View

Category theory has identified *(finite) limits*, in other words equationally defined subtypes of (finite) products, as the infrastructure needed to accommodate this variety of "algebra" semantically. For convenience (and for the sake of the not so initiated), we restrict ourselves to the domain of sets, though talking categorical language.

Definition *Let $f : A \to B$ and $g : A \to B$ be functions. Then the* ***equality type*** *$Eq(f,g)$ is defined to be the subset $Eq(f,g) := \{a \in A \mid f(a) = g(a)\}$. The prominent property is that every mapping $h : X \to A$ such that, for all $x \in X$, $f(h(x)) = g(h(x))$ uniquely restricts to a mapping $<h> : X \to Eq(f,g)$* with *$<h>(x) = h(x)$. A particular equality type $Pb(f,g)$ generated by functions $f : A \to C$ and $g : B \to C$ is defined by $Pb(f,g) := \{(a,b) \in A{\times}B \mid f(p_1(a,b)) = g(p_2(a,b))\} = \{(a,b) \in A{\times}B \mid f(a) = g(b)\}$ with p_1 and p_2 being the projections.*

We sketch the general idea for the interpretation of our logic. A dependent type like $stack(n)\ [n : nat]$ determines a family of sets $(B_a \mid a \in A)$, the set A being an interpretation of nat, and B_a being the interpretation of $stack(n)$ for "actual" parameter $a \in A$. Such a family of sets will be represented as a function $first : \{(a,b) \mid b \in B_a\} \to A$ with $first(a, b) = a$.[10] *Dependent elements* are of the form $(b_a \mid a \in A)$, i.e. for every index a there is an element $b_a \in B_a$. This will be equivalently represented by a function $b : A \to \{(a,b) \mid b \in$

[10] In fact, the argument may be prejudiced by set theory; the obvious isomorphism may not work as easily in more general structures [5].

$B_a\}$, $a \mapsto (a,b_a)$. Similarly, a dependent type $\delta_3(x, y)$ $[x : \delta_1, y : \delta_2(x)]$ is interpreted as a family of sets $\{C_{a,b} \mid a \in A, b \in B_a\}$, which can be represented by a pair of functions g : $\{(a,b,c) \mid a \in A, b \in B_a, c \in C_{a,b}\} \to \{(a,b) \mid b \in B_a\}$ and f: $\{(a,b) \mid b \in B_a\} \to A$, and so on.

More abstractly, a dependent type τ $[\Gamma]$ will be interpreted by a function $[\![\tau\,[\Gamma]]\!] : A_{\tau[\Gamma]} \to A_\Gamma$, in particular *constant* types $\tau\,[]$ (such as *nat* $[]$) as functions $[\![\tau\,[]]\!]: A_\tau \to 1$ where 1 is some one-element set (or terminal object, categorically speaking). The latter only states that the interpretation of a constant type is supposed to be a set. Dependent elements $t{:}\tau\,[\Gamma]$ determine functions $[\![t : \tau\,[\Gamma]]\!] : A_\Gamma \to A_{\tau[\Gamma]}$ such that the diagram

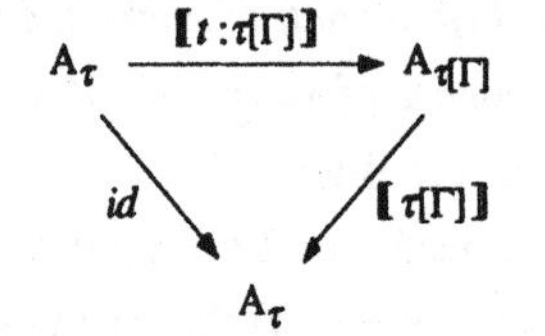

commutes (meaning that $[\![\tau\,[\Gamma]]\!] \circ [\![t{:}\tau\,[\Gamma]]\!](x) = x$).

Next we have to provide a means to define substitution. In the most elementary case, a variable x of type τ_1 may be replaced in $\tau_2(x)$ by a constant term c of type τ_1 to yield the type $\tau_2(c)$. Semantically, c denotes some element $[\![c]\!]$ of A_{τ_1}, and the type $\tau_2(c)$ the set $B_{[\![c]\!]}$ where $B = A_{\tau_2[x:\tau_1]}$. More generally, if we substitute a term $t(y)$ of type τ_1, with the free variable y being of type τ, to obtain the dependent type $\tau_2(t(y))$ $[y : \tau]$, the corresponding family is $\{B_{[\![t:\tau_1[y:\tau]]\!](c)} \mid c \in A_\tau\}$ where $[\![t : \tau_1[y{:}\tau]]\!]\,(c) \in A_{\tau_1}$ for every $c \in A_\tau$.

In terms of functions, given $[\![\tau_2(x)[x{:}\tau_1]]\!] : A_{\tau_2[x:\tau_1]} \to A_{\tau_1}$ and $[\![t : \tau_1[y{:}\tau]]\!] : A_\tau \to A_{\tau_1}$, we can define the function $[\![\tau_2(t(y))[y{:}\tau]]\!] : \{(c,b) \in A_\tau{\times}A_{\tau_2[x:\tau_1]} \mid [\![t : \tau_1[y{:}\tau]]\!](c) = [\![\tau_2(x)[x{:}\tau_1]]\!](b)\} \to A_\tau$, $(c,b) \mapsto c$ to provide the proper meaning. This may look pretty complicated but allows to express substitution in terms of equationally defined subtypes of products, as claimed above.

Remark Categorically, we pull back $[\![\tau_2[x{:}\tau_1]]\!]$ along $[\![t : \tau_1[y{:}\tau]]\!] : A_\tau \to A_{\tau_1}$ in that the left vertical arrow in the pullback diagram

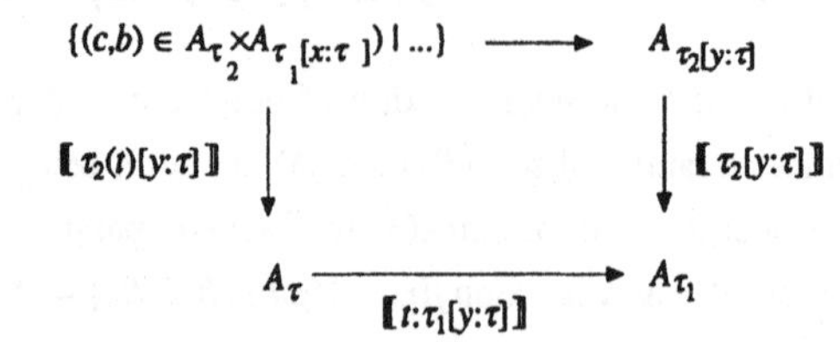

corresponds to $\{B_{[\![t]\!](c)} \mid c \in A_\tau\}$.

Notation If we have such a pullback square (*), and if $f \circ h = g \circ k$ in

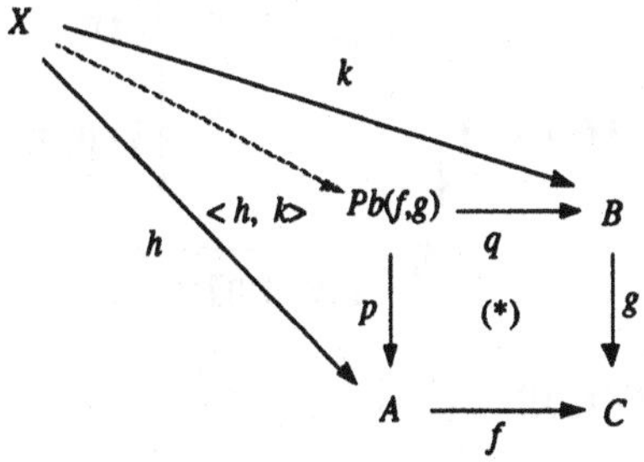

then we use the notation $<h, k>$ for the uniquely induced function such that $p \circ <h, k> = h$ and $q \circ <h, k> = k$

The general pattern of the formal interpretation is thus :

- the semantics of a type $\tau[\Gamma]$ is a function $[\![\tau[\Gamma]]\!] : A_{\tau[\Gamma]} \to A_\Gamma$,
- the semantics of a typed term $t : \tau[\Gamma]$ is a function $[\![t : \tau[\Gamma]]\!] : A_\Gamma \to A_{\tau[\Gamma]}$ such that $[\![\tau[\Gamma]]\!] \circ [\![t : \tau[\Gamma]]\!] = id_{A_\Gamma}$,
- the semantics of a *relation type* $\delta_\varphi[\Gamma]$ is an injective function $[\![\delta_\varphi[\Gamma]]\!] : A_{\delta_\varphi[\Gamma]} \to A_\Gamma$ where $\varphi[\Gamma]$ is a dependent proposition,
- the semantics of an *equality type* $Eq_\tau(t, t')[\Gamma]$ is defined by $eq([\![t : \tau[\Gamma]]\!], [\![t' : \tau[\Gamma]]\!]) : Eq([\![t : \tau[\Gamma]]\!], [\![t' : \tau[\Gamma]]\!]) \to A_\Gamma$.

The dependent type constructors δ_φ and Eq_τ are introduced for technicalities. Moreover

- the semantics of a type declaration $\tau(x_1,\ldots,x_n)$ **if** Γ is a function $[\![\tau(x_1,\ldots,x_n) \text{ if } \Gamma]\!] : A_{\tau(x_1,\ldots,x_n) \text{ if } \Gamma} \to A_\Gamma$, for some set $A_{\tau(x_1,\ldots,x_n) \text{ if } \Gamma}$,
- the semantics of a operator declaration $[\![\sigma(x_1,\ldots,x_n) : \tau \text{ if } \Gamma]\!]$ is a function $[\![\sigma(x_1,\ldots,x_n) : \tau \text{ if } \Gamma]\!] : A_\Gamma \to A_{\tau[\Gamma]}$ s.t. $[\![\tau[\Gamma]]\!] \circ [\![\sigma(x_1,\ldots,x_n) : \tau \text{ if } \Gamma]\!] = id_{A_\Gamma}$
- the semantics of a relator declaration $[\![\rho(x_1,\ldots,x_n) \text{ if } \Gamma]\!]$ is an injective function $[\![\rho(x_1,\ldots,x_n) \text{ if } \Gamma]\!] : A_{\rho(x_1,\ldots,x_n) \text{ if } \Gamma} \to A_\Gamma$

The semantics of *contexts* is inductively defined by

$$[\![()]\!] = id_1 : 1 \to 1$$
$$[\![\Gamma, x : \tau]\!] = [\![\tau[\Gamma]]\!] : A_{\tau[\Gamma]} \to A_\Gamma$$
$$[\![[\Gamma, t{=}t' : \tau]]\!] = [\![Eq_\tau(t,t')[\Gamma]]\!] : A_{Eq_\tau(t,t')[\Gamma]} \to A_\Gamma$$
$$[\![[\Gamma, \varphi]]\!] = [\![\delta_\varphi[\Gamma]]\!] : A_{\delta_\varphi[\Gamma]} \to A_\Gamma$$

where φ is of the form $\rho(t_1,\ldots,t_n)$. By definition $A_\Gamma := dom([\![\Gamma]\!])$.

The only proof rule to generate types is **axintro**. The *semantics of types* thus is defined by $[\![\delta(\Theta(x_1),\ldots,\Theta(x_n))[\Gamma']]\!] : A_{\tau[\Gamma']} \to A_{\Gamma'}$ which is uniquely induced by the pullback in

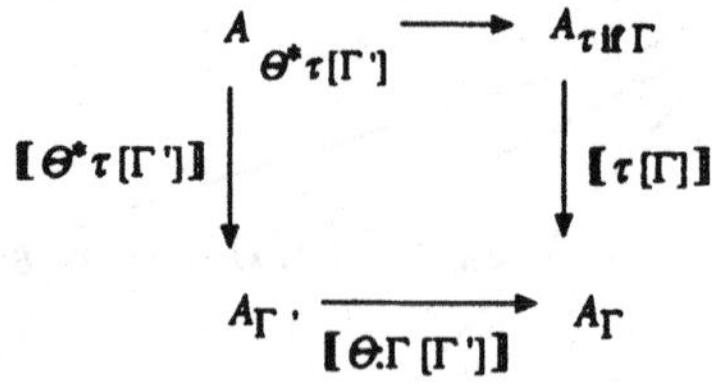

(where $\tau = \delta(\Theta(x_1),...,\Theta(x_n)))$.

The *semantics of terms* is defined by induction on the proof rules which generate terms, i.e. the rules **mon** and **axintro**

- $[\![x{:}\tau[\Gamma,\gamma]]\!] = id_{A_{\gamma[\Gamma]}} : A_{\gamma[\Gamma]} \to A_{\gamma[\Gamma]}$ if $\gamma = x{:}\tau$
$= <[\![x{:}\tau[\Gamma]]\!] \circ [\![\gamma[\Gamma]]\!], id_{A_{\gamma[\Gamma]}}> : A_{\gamma[\Gamma]} \to A_{\tau[\Gamma,\gamma]}$ otherwise

The latter case is visualized by the diagram, the dashed arrow being the one used

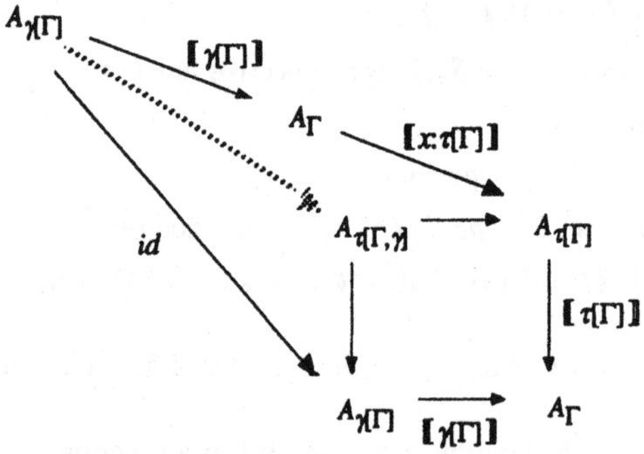

- $[\![\sigma(\Theta(x_1),...,\Theta(x_n)){:}\Theta^*\tau[\Gamma']]\!]$
$= <[\![\Theta^*t{:}\Theta^*\tau[\Gamma']]\!], [\![t{:}\tau \text{ if } \Gamma]\!] \circ [\![\Theta.\Gamma[\Gamma']]\!] : A_{\Gamma'} \to A_{\Theta^*\tau[\Gamma']}$
is uniquely induced by the pullback in

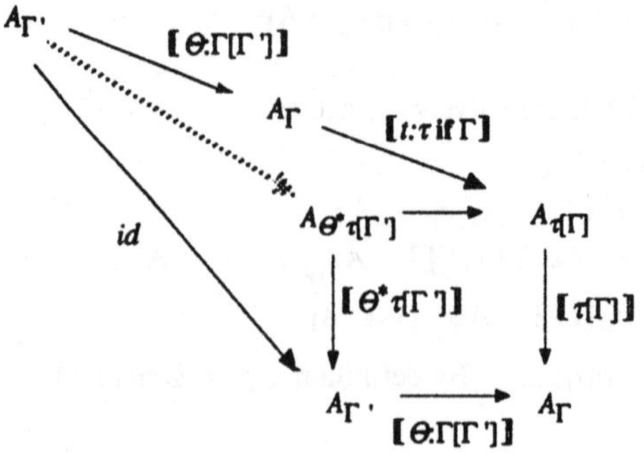

where t abbreviates $\sigma(x_1,...,x_n)$.

We use the syntactical construct

$$\Theta : \Gamma\,[\Gamma']$$

which informally states that the substitution Θ "satisfies" the context Γ in the context Γ'. The semantics will be a morphism $[\![\Theta{:}\Gamma\,[\Gamma']]\!] : A_{\Gamma'} \to A_{\Gamma}$ which is inductively defined by:

(i) $[\![\Theta : ()\,[\Gamma']\,]\!] : A_{\Gamma'} \to 1$

(ii) for a context of the form $\Gamma, x{:}\tau$, we use a pullback diagram,

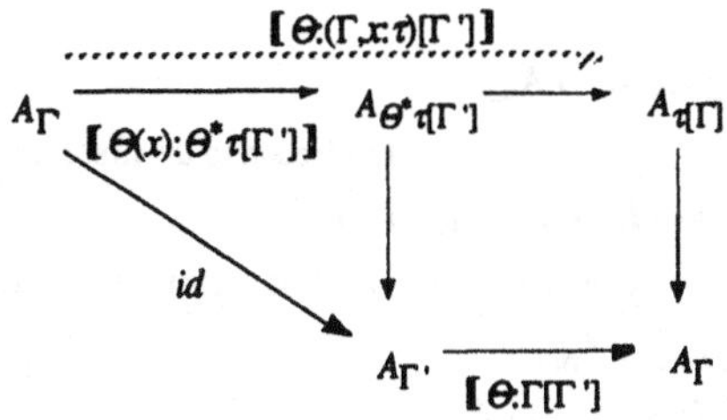

(iii) for a context of the form $\Gamma, t = t'{:}\tau$, we assume that $[\![\Theta{:}\Gamma\,[\Gamma']]\!]$ "satisfies" the proposition $t = t'{:}\tau\,[\Gamma]$. By this we mean that

$$[\![t:\tau\,[\Gamma']]\!] \circ [\![\Theta{:}\Gamma\,[\Gamma']]\!] = [\![t':\tau\,[\Gamma']]\!] \circ [\![\Theta{:}\Gamma\,[\Gamma']]\!].$$

This induces a unique function $[\![\Theta{:}(\Gamma, t = t'{:}\tau)[\Gamma']]\!] : A_{\Gamma'} \to A_{Eq_\tau(t,t')[\Gamma]}$ such that

$$[\![\Theta{:}(\Gamma, t = t'{:}\tau)[\Gamma']]\!] \circ [\![Eq_\tau(t,t')[\Gamma]]\!] = [\![\Theta{:}\Gamma[\Gamma']]\!]$$

by the properties of the equality type (equalizer),

(iv) for a context of the form Γ, φ with $\varphi = \rho(t_1,...,t_n)$, we assume that $[\![\Theta{:}\Gamma[\Gamma']]\!]$ "satisfies" the proposition $\rho(t_1,...,t_n)[\Gamma]$. By this we mean that there exists an function $[\![\Theta{:}(\Gamma,\varphi)[\Gamma']]\!] : A_{\Gamma'} \to A_{\delta_\varphi[\Gamma]}$ such that $[\![\delta_\varphi[\Gamma]]\!] \circ [\![\Theta{:}(\Gamma,\varphi)[\Gamma']]\!] = [\![\Theta{:}\Gamma[\Gamma']]\!]$.

We now define *satisfaction* formally:

- $t = t' : \tau\,[\Gamma]$ holds in a model if $[\![t\ :\ \tau\,[\Gamma]]\!] = [\![t'\ :\ \tau\,[\Gamma]]\!] : A_\Gamma \to A_{\tau[\Gamma]}$
- an atomic proposition $\rho(\Theta(x_1),...,\Theta(x_n))[\Gamma']$ holds if the function $[\![\Theta{:}\Gamma[\Gamma']]\!] : A_{\Gamma'} \to A_\Gamma$ induces a function $[\![\Theta{:}(\Gamma,\varphi)[\Gamma']]\!] : A_{\Gamma} \to A_{\varphi\,\mathbf{if}\,\Gamma}$ such that $[\![\varphi\,\mathbf{if}\,\Gamma]\!] \circ [\![\Theta{:}(\Gamma,\varphi)[\Gamma']]\!] = [\![\Theta{:}\Gamma\,[\Gamma']]\!]$, diagrammatically

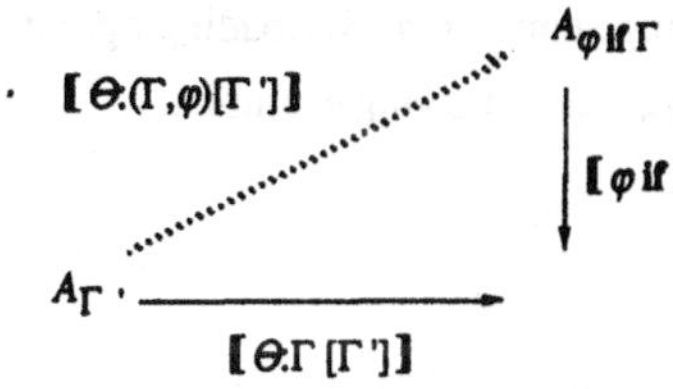

The definitions are consistent because substitution corresponds to composition, i.e. one can prove

- $[\![\Theta{:}\Gamma\,[\Gamma']]\!] \circ [\![\Theta'{:}\Gamma'[\Gamma'']]\!] = [\![\Theta \circ \Theta'{:}\Gamma\,[\Gamma'']]\!]$
- $[\![t{:}\tau\,[\Gamma]]\!] \circ [\![\Theta{:}\Gamma\,[\Gamma']]\!] = [\![\Theta^* t{:}\Theta^*\tau\,[\Gamma']]\!]$

This completes the definition of the semantics. One should try to compute the semantics of an example such as $pop(push(s, d)) : stack(n)\ [n : nat, s : stack(n), d : nat]$ the first steps of which are:

$[\![\ nat\ ]\!] : A_{nat} \to 1$

$[\![\ nat\ [n : nat]\ ]\!] = p : A_{nat} \times A_{nat} \to A_{nat}$

(projection to the first component)

$[\![\ suc(n) : nat\ \textbf{if} n : nat\ ]\!] = \langle id, suc\rangle : A_{nat} \to A_{nat} \times A_{nat}$

(where $suc : A_{nat} \to A_{nat}$ is determined by the specific mode)

$[\![\ stack(n)\ \textbf{if}\ n : nat\ ]\!] : A_{stack} \to A_{nat}$

$[\![\ n : nat\ [n : nat\ ]\!] = \langle id, id\rangle : A_{nat} \to A_{nat} \times A_{nat}$

$[\![\ nat\ [n : nat\ , s : stack(n)]\ ]\!] = p : A_{nat} \times A_{stack} \to A_{nat}$

$[\![\ n : nat\ [n : nat\ , s : stack(n)]\ ]\!] = \langle [\![stack(n)[n{:}nat]]\!], id_{A_{stack}}\rangle : A_{stack} \to A_{nat} \times A_{stack}$

I like to remark that the definition works provided the existence, categorically speaking, of finite limits. However, the typed language has more structure because of the inherent syntactical knowledge of the type declarations. Cartmell [5] has pointed out that "contextual categories" are the right framework.

3. An In-Between : Subsorting or, rather, Subtyping

Subsorting [12] is another particular scheme for avoiding partiality. Sorts are partially ordered, the proviso being that $s^{\mathcal{A}} \subseteq s'^{\mathcal{A}}$ if $s \leq s'$. We have already seen in the introduction how partial operations can be defined using subsorts when we discussed the stack. Whether subsorting is more general than standard "many-sorted" algebra with conditional equations may be a matter of opinion. Conditional equations provided, subsorting can be expressed in terms of injective operations $m : s \to s'$ whenever $s \leq s'$ without losing expressiveness on the semantic side [14].

The real attraction of subtyping stems from overloading operators which is not necessarily related to subsorting. Consider the following example:

spec NUMBERS **is**

sorts	<u>nat</u>, <u>int</u>
ops	0 : <u>nat</u>
	0 : <u>int</u>
	suc : <u>nat</u> $\to$ <u>nat</u>
	suc : <u>int</u> $\to$ <u>int</u>
	pred : <u>int</u> $\to$ <u>int</u>
vars	*z* : <u>int</u>

axs $pred(suc(z)) = z$
$suc(pred(z)) = z$

Since terms of the form $suc^n(0)$ may denote natural numbers as well as integers there is no harm in overloading the operators. If overloading is accidental in that by chance the same name is used, for instance by adding a "predecessor" $pred : nat \to nat$ on the natural numbers with the proviso that $pred(0) = 0$, we have a problem; the term $pred(0)$ has two different meanings depending on the context. Conventional term construction

(i) $x \in T_{SIG}(X)_s$

(ii) $\sigma(t_1,...,t_n) \in T_{SIG}(X)_{s'}$ if $\sigma : s_1...s_n \to s$ and $t_i \in T_{SIG}(X)_{s_i}$

(where X_s, $s \in S$, is a sorted set of generators) assumes that no overloading takes place, otherwise operators and generators are suitably annotated by type information, e.g. $pred_{nat}$, $pred_{int}$, 0_{nat}, 0_{int}.

Disambiguation by type (sort) information is an inherent assumption of all typed (sorted) languages, or, equivalently, that all terms have a unique type (sort). Even if carriers $s^{\mathcal{A}}$ and $s'^{\mathcal{A}}$ of types s and s' may have a non-empty intersection, the convention is that the carriers should be considered as disjoint by type information. Overloading may cause a term to have several types which is harmless in general since a type checking algorithm can easily be adapted to cope with lists of types.

Coexistence of deliberate and accidental overloading poses the question of how to decide what sort of overloading applies. Here subsorting plays its role. While, in the example above, all operators may be considered as independent, the subsorting in

spec NUMBERS **is**
sorts $\underline{nat} \leq \underline{int}$
ops $0 : \underline{nat}$
$suc : \underline{nat} \to \underline{nat}$
$suc : \underline{int} \to \underline{int}$
$pred : \underline{int} \to \underline{int}$
vars $z : \underline{int}$
axs $pred(suc(z)) = z$
$suc(pred(z)) = z$

suggests that the overloading of operators is deliberate. Unfortunately, a term construction which only refers to operator names (and not to additional typing information) yields the same results. This has been a matter of some discussion (most recent proponents of which are [15], [27]). There are basically two choices: either to restrict signatures so that overloaded operators are related by subtyping [14] as in the second version of our example, or to argue that overloading of operators is always deliberate [11, 22]. Each of the approaches has its relative merits. The latter guarantees that term construction always coincides with free generation, but accidental overloading may cause damage, and standard many-sorted algebra is not subsumed (which may be fixed at little cost [27]). The former needs checks to establish that certain constraints are met, specifically when specifications are constructed out of given ones by amalgamation.

While these subtleties may be interesting or not, the combination of subsorting and overloading is attractive for technical reasons. Firstly, terms are stripped of sometimes annoying type annotation, but, more importantly, type checking and (equational) deduction can be separated in a sense made precise below.

I did not yet mention the modification of term construction related to subsorting and overloading

$$\sigma(t_1,\ldots,t_n) \in T_{SIG}(X)_{s'} \text{ if } \sigma : s_1 \ldots s_n \to s,\ s \leq s' \text{ and } t_i \in T_{SIG}(X)_{s_i}$$

which guarantees terms of the form *pred(0)* cannot be formed with regard to

spec NAT **is**
sorts $\underline{nat+} \leq \underline{nat}$
ops $0 : \underline{nat}$
$suc : \underline{nat} \to \underline{nat+}$
$pred : \underline{nat+} \to \underline{nat}$
vars $n : \underline{nat}$
axs $pred(suc(n)) = n$
$suc(pred(n)) = n$

Similarly, *pred(pred(suc(suc(0))))* is syntactically wrong though meaningful if equational rewriting is applied

$$pred(pred(suc(suc(0)))) = pred(suc(0)) = 0.$$

Of course, this is not proper equational reasoning because terms are not well-formed. An apparently minor change of language, replacing sorts by types, helps. The following argument, in the typed variety of logic,

$$\cfrac{\cfrac{0 : nat[]}{suc() : nat+[]}\,(\text{axintro}) \qquad \cfrac{0 : nat[]}{pred(suc(suc(0))) \;=\; suc(0) : nat[]}\,(\text{axintro})}{\cfrac{pred(suc(suc(0))) : nat+[]}{pred(pred(suc(suc(0)))) : nat[]}\,(\text{axintro})}\,(\text{id})$$

establishes well-formedness of *pred(pred(suc(suc(0))))*. Here type checking and equational reasoning are intertwined but can still be separated provided that all type declarations of the form $\sigma(x_1,\ldots,x_n) : \tau$ **if** $x_1 : \tau_1,\ldots,x_n : \tau_n$ with the τ's being atomic types (constants).

Proposition [25] *If* $\vdash t : \tau\,[\Gamma]$ *then* $\vdash_{type} t' : \tau\,[\Gamma_{type}]$ *and* $\vdash t = t'\,[\Gamma]$ *for some term t'.*

where the subscript $_{type}$ refers to the restriction of deduction to typing (i.e. the type checking), e.g. $\Gamma_{type} := \{\, t : \tau \mid t : \tau \text{ occurs in } \Gamma\}$. We speak of this restriction as *type checking*. So, in other words, whenever a term can be typed we can apply equational reasoning to generate an equal term which can be type checked. Practically, if type checking of a term fails it is rewritten on the subterms which are already type checked. As typing is monotone under rewriting, the result will be a term, type checking of which may give better results. Given that rewriting is confluent one has got an efficient procedure for typing a term. One should note that confluence only depends on standard techniques provided that the equations are well-formed. I should add that the result also holds for subtyping which is introduced via declarations of the form

$$x : \tau \text{ if } \Gamma$$

e.g. $x : int$ **if** $x : nat$.

Separation of type checking fails immediately for more general operator declarations. For instance, well-typing of the axioms $pop(push(s,d)) = s$ **if** $(s : stack, d : nat, length(s) < b)$ requires a proof of $0 < length(push(s,d))$ for which the equality $length(push(s,d)) = suc(length(s))$ is needed. We do not claim that type checking is not feasible, but it would be substantially more sophisticated (and probably less efficient).

The result suggests distinguishing between types and sorts as in:

spec NAT **is**	
sorts	$\underline{nat}$
ops	$0 : \underline{nat}$
	$suc : \underline{nat} \rightarrow \underline{nat}$
	$pred : \underline{nat} \rightarrow \underline{nat}$
vars	$n : \underline{nat}$
types	$nat, nat+ : \underline{nat}$
decls	$n : nat$ **if** $n : nat+$
	$0 : nat$
	$suc(n) : nat+$ **if** $n : nat$
	$pred(n) : nat$ **if** $n : nat+$
axs	$pred(suc(n)) = n$ **if** $n : nat$
	$suc(pred(n)) = n$ **if** $n : nat+$

where terms such as $pred(0)$, $pred(pred(suc(suc(0))))$ are syntactically admissable, i.e. sorted, but of which one needs to establish by type checking whether they are meaningful or not. The next section elaborates on this theme.

4. About Expressiveness and Pragmatics

We have looked at partiality from different angles which raises the question whether the various idioms discussed are equally expressive. We suspect (and I claimed above) that many-sorted total algebra is less expressive. Such results typically depend on semantic closure properties, e.g. Birkhoff's variety theorem. We do not have the space to cover this theme; hence focus on more superficial arguments and observations.

At a first glance one might suspect that partial algebra can be well embedded into the total framework provided we allow for conditional equations, or subsorts; for every partial operator $\sigma : s_1 ... s_n \rightarrow s$, we define a new sort E_σ which is a subsort of the product sort $s_1 \times ... \times s_n$[11], and then restrict the operator to $\sigma : E_\sigma \rightarrow s$. This is the standard procedure to define partial functions as a total function on its domain of definition. So, do we have a category of models which is equivalent to that of the respective partial algebras? Yes, but! We cannot interpret terms if we stick to the idiom of total functions. To simplify the issue we consider unary operations. If we interpret the term $\sigma_2(\sigma_1(x))$ in total algebra we implicitly

[11] which has been defined above.

use composition of total functions, namely $\sigma_2(\sigma_1(x)) = \sigma_2 \circ \sigma_1(x)$. This does not work for our representation of partial functions, domain and range do not fit. This is trivial, but I want to stress that algebra is not only about models but some implicit infrastructure like closure under composition of operators.

If we try to characterise total algebra in this respect we should realise that closure under composition of total functions is a prerequisite, as well as closure under cartesian product, which allows to give a semantics of n-ary functions. In fact, it is well known that the logical infrastructure of many-sorted total algebra is that of (categories with) finite products (or infinite products if infinitary operators are considered).[12]

In order to define the composition of partial functions, we need certain equality types. The domain of $g \circ f$, for partial functions f, g, is defined by $E_{g \circ f} = \{x \in E_f \mid f(x) \in E_g\}$ which as an equality type is defined by $E_{g \circ f} = \{ (x, y) \in E_f \times E_g \mid f(x) = m(y)\}$ where $m : E_g \to Y$ is the subset inclusion. The logic of partial algebra thus appears to be a sublogic of that of (categories with) finite limits, i.e. finite products and equality types.[13]

On the other hand, restricting existence equations to those which are hierarchy constrained [29] yields a language which is equivalent to the typed logic we have introduced above. I do not know about a full proof though the proof idea is indicated in [23]). So, are the typed idiom and the idiom of partiality equivalent? I am afraid not. The nature of homomorphisms is different. An isomomorphism in the typed language would for instance imply that existence of a bijection on the "existence types" E_σ, while in partial algebra bijectivity only holds for the sorts. Morphisms (and isomorphisms) in the typed world correspond to strong (iso-) morphisms in the partial world. Again, this may be of interest or not, but one should keep it in mind.

Let us turn to some more pragmatic issues. I have promised in a footnote to comment on *sorts* as compared to *types*. If I recollect correctly, logicians have used "sorts" as synonym for syntactical categories[14] and "types" to refer to what might be called "semantic categories". In our context, sorts can be considered to categorise names, and types to categorise semantic entities, that is: types denote sets while sorts denote pers. For instance, in

```
spec NAT is
sorts nat
ops     0 : nat
        suc : nat → nat
        pred : nat → nat
vars    n : nat
types   nat, nat+ : nat
decls   0 : nat
        suc (n ) : nat+        if n : nat
        pred(n) : nat          if n : nat+
```

[12] By the way, the relation between categorical language and, for instance, the language of algebra (but others as well) is spelled out in some detail in [28].

[13] The relationship of partial algebra and finite limit theories is worked out carefully in [9]. An early, but sketchy discussion of the subject can be found in [23].

[14] in the logician's sense of categorisation of syntactical entities.

axs $pred(suc(n)) = n$ if $n : nat$
$suc(pred(n)) = n$ if $n : nat+$

the name $pred(0)$ is of sort $\underline{nat}$ while it fails to be an element in that we cannot prove it to have a type. On the other hand, names which do have a type, such as 0 or $suc(0)$, should refer to elements.

The latter is formally achieved by adding the axiom

$$\frac{x{:}\tau\,[\Gamma]}{Ex[\Gamma]}$$

which provides us with a more sophisticated mechanism to deal with definedness (as remarked above, similar results may achieved by hierarchy conditions within the framework of partial algebras [29]). Of course, in case of total "many-sorted" algebra "sorts" coincide with "types", justifying the practice of this paper.

I do not claim the argument to be conclusive, but at least it appears reasonable. Sorts tell us about the admissable syntax, types about admissable meanings. We leave it to the reader to amalgamate the proof systems of partial algebra and the typing system of section 2, or refer the reader to [26] (for the one-sorted case), where the typing discipline has been extended to cover *parametric types*, such as list in

spec LIST **is**
NAT **with**
ops $type : \rightarrow \underline{kinds}$
$list : \underline{types} \rightarrow \underline{types}$
$list{+}: \underline{types} \rightarrow \underline{types}$
$nil : \rightarrow \underline{list}$
$app : \underline{list}\ \underline{data} \rightarrow \underline{list}$
$head : \underline{list} \rightarrow \underline{data}$
$tail: \underline{list} \rightarrow \underline{list}$
decls $type\,!$
$nat :: type$
$list(\tau) : type$ if $\tau :: type$
$list{+}(\tau) : type$ if $\tau :: type$
$nil : list(\tau)$ if $\tau :: type$
$app(d,l) : list{+}(\tau)$ if $\tau :: type,\ l : list(\tau),\ d : \tau$
$head(l) : list(\tau)$ if $\tau :: type,\ l : list{+}(\tau)$
$tail(l) : \tau$ if $\tau :: type,\ l : list{+}(\tau)$
axs $head(app(d,l)) = d$ if $\tau :: type,\ l : list(\tau),\ d : \tau$
$tail(app(d,l)) = l$ if $\tau :: type,\ l : list(\tau),\ d : \tau$

The notation distinguishes between data ("$d : \tau$"), types ("$\tau :: \kappa$") and orders ("$\kappa\,!$") reflecting to the typical three-tiered hierarchy of type systems, e.g. elements, sets and universes in set theory.

There is another of these pragmatic distinctions. Types may be encoded as unary relations without changing the category of models (up to equivalence).

spec NAT **is**
sorts $\underline{nat}$
ops $0 : \underline{nat}$
$suc : \underline{nat} \rightarrow \underline{nat}$
$pred : \underline{nat} \rightarrow \underline{nat}$
rels $isnat,\ isnat{+} : \underline{nat}$

vars	n : <u>*nat*</u>	
axs	*isnat(0)*	
	isnat+(suc (n))	**if** *isnat(n)*
	isnat+(pred(n))	**if** *isnat+(n)*
	pred(suc(n)) = *n*	**if** *isnat(n)*
	suc(pred(n)) = *n*	**if** *isnat+(n)*

The difference is in usage. Atomic proposition can be used in axioms rather freely while the usage of types is more restricted. For instance,

isnat(n) **if** *isnat+(n)*

is an admissable axiom, while the declaration

n : *nat* **if** x : *nat+*

substantially changes the nature of declarations as we have seen in our discussion of subsorting.

What this means is that we have different *data types*. Even though the same entities may be addressed, the operations on these data are different. Sorts cater for elementary term construction, types also imply existence (and more sophisticated well-formedness conditions) while the inherent logical infrastructure applies to (unary) relations.[15] In presence of the dependent types, the distinction of the latter is not so clear-cut since type checking and deductive capabilities are inherently the same (which is the advantage or disadvantage of constructive type theory à la Martin-Löf).

Finally, we notice that the distinction between sorts and types allows to disambiguate accidental and deliberate overloading since sorting takes care of the accidental overloading, and overloading on the level of types is supposed to be deliberate, so giving a precise meaning to a specification such as the one considered at the end of section 3.[16]

5. A Concluding Remark

The language of limits is a yardstick, and a borderline, when implementing algebra in that it provides a Herbrand universe for free, meaning that term construction and type checking is algorithmic (but unfortunately not decidable in general which is the price to pay for equality types). Languages such as OBJ [10] approach this borderline though, I believe they are still a good way off, concerning the type checking facilities, for instance.

6. (Sketchy) Historical Notes

There is little need to mention the genesis of dependent types due to Per Martin-Löf [20, 21]. The reduction to its algebraic ingredients was achieved by John Cartmell in [5].

[15] The latter distinction is reminiscent of the classical variety of type theory, i.e. Russel's, which distinguishes between "types" and "sets", sets being obtained from types by means of comprehension $\{x : \tau | \varphi\}$ (types are generated by $\tau \times \tau'$ and $P(\tau)$). In particular every type generates a set via $\{x : \tau | tt\}$.

[16] A simplified version is discussed in [26] where the relevant mathematics is developed in elementary form.

Theories with limits as basic infrastructure have been named *essentially algebraic* by Peter Freyd [8] though probably being folklore for some time. The first logical language I am aware of has been defined by Coste [6]. A good overview over the relations to type theory are given in [17]. Recently, essentially algebraic theories are considered in a couple of publications on category theory and type theory (references can be found in [17]).

Horst Reichel was the first to introduce the respective class of algebras to the data type community though in the somewhat muted dialect of hep-varieties [29] which more reflect the optics of partial algebra. By now, the theme is well established, but may not be in the data type community. Hence little originality is claimed for my own efforts [25, 26] (including this paper). All the details of the categorical interpretation of partial algebras have recently been carefully worked out in [7]. Partiality has also been advocated by Broy, an early paper being [3].

The particular view of partiality is in this paper is due to Scott [30] (which I regard as a paper necessary and most pleasant to read). The corresponding semantics has been developed in [9].

The theme of subsorting was first stated in [12] and then developed in a several papers ([11, 14, 22, 25, 31, 32, 33] to name only a few). More recently, various new approaches to typing and partiality have been discussed [18, 34]).

Acknowledgement I thank the anonymous referee and Matthew Morley for careful reading.

References

1. J.A.Goguen, J.W.Thatcher, E.G.Wagner, J.B.Wright, A Uniform Approach to Inductive Posets and Inductive Closure, Proc. MFCS'77, LNCS 53, 1977, and TCS 7, 1978
2. K.Benecke, H.Reichel, Equational Partiality, Algebra Universalis 16, 1983
3. M.Broy, Partial Interpretation of Higher Order Algebraic Types, Int. Summer School, Marktoberdorf, 1986
4. P.Burmeister, A Model Theoretic Oriented Approach to Partial Algebras, Akademie Verlag, Berlin 1986
5. J.Cartmell, Generalised Algebraic Theories and Contextual Categories, PhD thesis, Oxford, Short version: Annals Pure Appl. Logic 32, 1986
6. M.Coste, Une Approche Logique des Théories Definissable par Limites Projectives Finies, Manuscript 1976
7. I.Claßen, M.Groß-Rhode, U.Wolter, Categorical Concepts for Parameterized Partial Specifications, Bericht-Nr. 92-42, TU Berlin, 1992
8. P.Freyd, Aspects of Topoi, Bull. Austral. Math. Soc. 7, 1972
9. M.Fourman, D.S.Scott, Sheaves and Logic, In: Applications of Sheaves, Proc. Durham, LNiMath 753, 1979
10. K.Futatsugi, J.A.Goguen, J.P.Jouannaud, J.Meseguer, Principles of OBJ2, CLSI Rep. No. 85-22, Stanford University, 1985
11. M.Gogolla, Algebraic Specifications with Subsorts and Declarations, FB Nr. 169, Abt.Informatik, Universität Dortmund, 1983, also: Proceedings CAAP'84, Cambridge University Press, 1984

12. J.A.Goguen, Abstract Errors for Abstract Data Types, IFIP Working Conf. on Formal description of Programming Concepts, MIT, 1977
13. J.A.Goguen, Order Sorted Algebras, UCLA Comp. Sci. Dept., Semantics and Theory of Comp. Rep. 14, 1978
14. J.A.Goguen, J.Meseguer, Order-Sorted Algebra I: Equationaal Deduction for Multiple Inheritance, Overloading, Exceptions, and Partial Operations, Techn.Rep. SRI-CSL-89-10, SRI International, Computer Science Lab, 1989
15. J.A.Goguen,R.,Diaconescu, A Survey of Order-Sorted Algebra, manuscript, 1992
16. G.Grätzer, Universal Algebra, Princeton 1978
17. J.M.E.Hyland, A.M.Pitts, The Theory of Constructions : Categorical Semantics and Topos-theoretic Models, *Contemporary Math. 92, 1989*
18. V.Manca, A.Salibra, G.Scollo, DELTA: A Deduction System Integrating Equational Logic and Type Assignment, Draft 1988
19. P.Mosses, Unified Algebras and Modules, In POPL'89, ACM, 1989
20. P.Martin-Löf, An Intuitionistic Theory of Types, Proc. Bristol Logic Coll. '73, North Holland 1973
21. P.Martin-Löf, Constructive Mathematics and Computer Programming, in : L.J.Cohen et al (eds), *Sixth International Congress for Logic Methodology and Philosophy of Science*, North Holland, 1982
22. A.Poigné, Another Look at Parameterization Using Algebraic Specifications with Subsorts, Proc. MFCS, LNCS 176, 1984, long version : Parameterization for Order-Sorted Algebra, JCCS, Vol.40, 1990
23. A.Poigné, Error Handling for Parameterized Data Types, Proc.3rd Workshop on Abstract Data Types, Bremen 1984, GI-Fachbericht 116, 1985
24. A.Poigné, Algebra Categorically (Tutorial), Workshop on Category and Computer Programming, Guildford 1985, LNCS240, 1986
25. A.Poigné, Partial Algebras, Subsorting and Dependent Types, Proc. ADT-Workshop, LNCS 332, 1988, full version : Arbeitsberichte der GMD, Nr. 446, 1990
26. A.Poigné, Typed Horn Logic, MFCS'90, LNCS 452, 1990, full version : Arbeitsberichte der GMD, Nr. 447, 1990
27. A.Poigné, Once more on Order-sorted Algebra, MFCS'91, LNCS 520, 1991, full version : Arbeitsberichte der GMD, Nr. 512 1991
28. A.Poigné, Basic Category Theory, in: Handbook of Logic in Computer Science, S.Abramsky, D.Gabbai, T.Maibaum (eds.), Oxford University Press, 1992
29. H.Reichel, Initial Computability, Algebraic Specifications, and Partial algebras, Oxford University press, 1987
30. D.S.Scott, Identity and Existence in Intutionistic Logic, In: Applications of Sheaves, Proc. Durham, LNiMath 753, 1979
31. G.Smolka, Order-Sorted Horn Logic Semantics and Deduction, SEKI-Rep. SR-86-17, Universität Kaiserslautern 1986
32. G.Smolka, W.Nutt, J.A.Goguen, J.Meseguer, Order-Sorted Equational Computation, To appear in: H.Ait-Kaci, M.Nivat (eds.) Resolution of Equations in Algebraic Structures, Academic Press 1988
33. G.Smolka, Logic Programming with Polymorphically Order-Sorted Types, In: J.Grabowski, P.Lescanne, W.Wechler, *Algebraic and Logic Programming*, Akademie Verlag, Berlin 1988
34. G.Smolka, Type Logic, Abstract 6th Workshop on Abstract Data Types, Berlin 1988

Overloading and Inheritance

Eric G. Wagner

Mathematical Sciences Department
IBM Research Division
T. J. Watson Research Center
Yorktown Heights, NY 10598, USA
Wagner@watson.ibm.com

Abstract. This paper reports on some recent investigations aimed at separating and clarifying a number of concepts that frequently appear in object-based and object-oriented languages. Concepts considered include are overloading, encapsulation, the message paradigm, and a limited form of inheritance. We also introduce formulations of the concepts of overload-systems and coercion-systems, and we present a treatment of $(+, \times)$-recursive classes and the definition of primitive recursive functions over such classes.

1 Introduction

There are a number of well-known object-oriented programming languages such as Smalltalk [6], Eiffel [8], C++ [10, 11], and Turbo Pascal® 6.0 [7], and a quantity of lesser known ones such as Amber [1]. All these languages make use of various terms, the most ubiquitous being "inheritance" with, perhaps, "encapsulation" being a close second. Unfortunately these terms are bandied about rather carelessly, and there is clearly no great agreement as to their precise meaning. One reason for this is that the developers and practitioners of object-oriented programming tend to think of these concepts in terms of HOW they are implemented rather than in terms of WHAT it is that is being implemented. This isn't necessarily bad, but it tends to obscure the underlying concept under a mass of details and accidental elaborations. In some cases it leads to confusing disparate ideas. In my opinion, the treating of "virtual methods" as "inheritance" in C++ is an example.

Of course there have been many attempts by the theoretical community to provide clarification of object-oriented concepts – indeed there are far to many to cite. However, for a spectrum of approaches and references, see [9, 2, 3, 4, 5]. What is different here, if anything, is that I am applying mathematics in the context of language development rather than in the context of pure theory. I think that this has a positive influence on both the questions asked and the answers given.

The emphasis in this paper, as the name implies, is on the concepts of overloading and inheritance. My interest in these topics arose in connection with my developing of the language LD^3 [14, 16, 18, 20, 19]. While LD^3 as presented in those papers, is object-based it lacks inheritance, and the work reported here is part of my investigation into how LD^3 might, could, and should be extended to include one, or more, inheritance concepts. However, this paper can be read without any knowledge of LD^3.

The underlying framework behind LD^3 and the work reported here – the abstract framework for dealing with data types, memory, pointer-like constructs, assignments, declarations, etc. – comes out of my earlier work [12, 13, 15, 17]. Here again I have tried to write this paper in a manner that does not require prior knowledge of that work.

Section 2 provides some preliminary material, in particular some notation, a review of strings and strings-of-strings, and a relatively informal sketch of some of the above mentioned framework.

Section 3 introduces the concept of an overload system, and presents a number of simple examples.

Section 4 is more background material, namely an introduction to the notion of primitive recursive functions over data types defined via products and coproducts (+ and $\times$).

Section 5 gives a mathematical treatment of "the Message Paradigm" as an approach to overload resolution. It also indicates how encapsulation can be achieved within this context. The languages looked at are purely functional, i.e., we are not yet talking about objects as entities with their own memory.

Section 6 investigates some notions of inheritance based on coercions. Actually, what is presented is a way of using systems of coercions to facilitate overloading – it is up to the reader to decide if he or she wants to call this "inheritance". In the framework employed here, which is essentially functional, coercions do not really provide an adequate treatment of inheritance (see [9] for a discussion of this), however, in more imperative context, such as employed in LD^3, coercions do suffice, as I will show in a subsequent paper.

2 Preliminaries

2.1 Some Notational Conventions

We write $f : A \rightarrow B$ for a total function and $f : A \rightharpoonup B$ for a partial function.

Let N denote the set of natural numbers, $N = \{0, 1, \cdots\}$. For $n \in N$ let $[n]$ denote the set $[n] = \{1, \cdots, n\}$, so $[0] = \emptyset$.

We shall write 1 for "the" singleton set – and write $\star$ for its unique element.

2.2 Strings and Strings-of-Strings

For any set K, a *string of length n over K* is a mapping $s : [n] \rightarrow K$. Let K^* denote the *set of all strings over K*. Let Str_K denote the *category of strings over K* with, as objects, all strings over K, and, as morphisms, $\alpha : u \rightarrow v$, where $u : [n] \rightarrow K$ and $v : [p] \rightarrow K$, all triples $\alpha = \langle u, \overline{\alpha} : [n] \rightarrow [p], v\rangle$ where $\overline{\alpha}$ is a mapping from $[n]$ to $[p]$ such that $v \bullet \overline{\alpha} = u$.

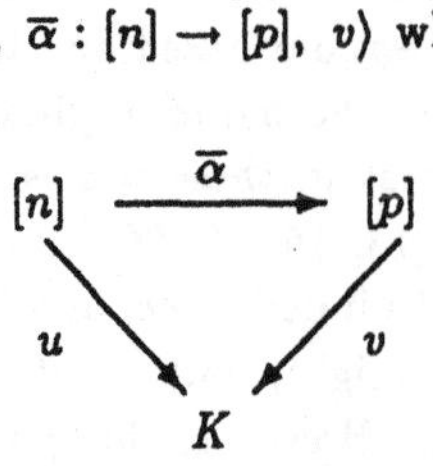

Given a set K, $k \in K$ and a string $u \in K^*$, we write $k \cdot u$, for the string resulting from appending k to the front of u.

For any string $u \in K^*$ we write $|u|$ for the length of u. Thus, for any $u \in K^*$, $u : [|u|] \to K$.

Let $(K^*)^*$ denote the *set of strings-of-strings* over K, i.e., all mappings $u : [n] \to K^*$ for all $n \in \mathrm{N}$. We will frequently write $(u_1)(u_2)\cdots(u_n)$ for the string $u : [n] \to K^*$ where $u(i) = u_i \in K^*$, for $i \in [n]$. We often write $(\ )$ for the mapping $[1] \to K^*$ taking 1 to the unique string $\lambda : [0] \to K$ (the empty string on K).

Define $\mathbf{SStr}_K$, *the category of strings-of-strings over* K, to have, as objects, all $u \in (K^*)^*$, and, as morphisms $\alpha : u \to v$ for $u : [n] \to K^*$ and $v : [p] \to K^*$, all triples $\langle u, \langle \alpha_0, \alpha_1, \cdots, \alpha_n \rangle, v \rangle$ where α_0 is a mapping $\alpha_0 : [n] \to [p]$, and for $i = 1, \cdots, n$, $\alpha_i : v_{\alpha_0(i)} \to u_i$ in $\mathbf{Str}_K$.

Proposition 1. *The category* $\mathbf{SStr}_K$ *has products and coproducts. Given strings-of-strings* $u = (u_1)(u_2)\cdots(u_n)$ *and* $w = (w_1)(w_2)\cdots(w_p)$, *their product object is*

$$(u_1w_1)(u_1w_2)\cdots(u_1w_p)(u_2w_1)\cdots(u_nw_p)$$

and their coproduct object is

$$(u_1)\cdots(u_n)(w_1)\cdots(w_p)$$

the initial object is $\mathbf{0} : [0] \to K^*$ *and the terminal object is* $\mathbf{1} = (\ ) : [1] \to K^*$, *as above.*

Proposition 2. *The category* $\mathbf{SStr}_K$ *is the free distributive category generated by* K. *So, in particular, viewing* K *as a discrete category, any functor* $F : K \to \mathbf{Set}$ *extends uniquely to a functor* $\widehat{F} : \mathbf{SStr}_K \to \mathbf{Set}$ *preserving products and coproducts. Furthermore, the construction "$\widehat{\ }$" is functorial in that if* $F, G : K \to \mathbf{Set}$ *and* η *is a natural transformation,* $\eta : F \to G$, *then* η *extends to a natural transformation* $\widehat{\eta} : \widehat{F} \to \widehat{G}$.

2.3 An Abstract Framework for Computing

Some underlying ideas are:

- The informal concept of encapsulation is that the data type or class is accessed and modified through a fixed interface that makes it impossible (or at least "illegal") for a user to exploit the representation of the elements of the class or the implementation of the methods. In a mathematical framework this means restricting the operations that can be applied to, or yield, elements of the class – that is, if we forget about memory, a class something like an algebra (a collection of named sets and named operations between those sets).
- Note that the "design unit" is not the individual class, but rather a collection of inter-related classes – a *class-system*.
- Using encapsulation we can implement any data type or class by means of sums of products of elements of other classes. The form of the representations can be presented recursively. For example:

$$\begin{aligned} \mathtt{BOOL} &\cong 1+1, \\ \mathtt{NAT} &\cong 1+\mathtt{NAT} \\ \mathtt{STKNAT} &\cong 1+(\mathtt{NAT}\times\mathtt{STKNAT}) \\ \mathtt{LINE} &\cong \mathtt{STKNAT}\times\mathtt{NAT}\times\mathtt{STKNAT} \end{aligned}$$

Now we could define a class SETNAT, which is supposed to be "finite sets of natural numbers", wherein the sets are represented by LINEs. By appropriately restricting the set of methods (functions) that can be applied to, or yield, such SETs (i.e., by encapsulating the class) we get an "external behavior" that is just what we would expect SETs to be based on our mathematical intuition. This is, of course, the same idea as that underlies the traditional equational specification techniques.

- The injections and projections associated with the $(+, \times)$-representation of data types frequently correspond to significant operations on the data types (the more encapsulation the less likely is this to be the case). Examples:
  For $\mathtt{BOOL} = 1+1$ the evident injections are $true, false : 1 \rightarrow \mathtt{BOOL}$.
  For $\mathtt{NAT} = 1 + \mathtt{NAT}$ the evident injections are $zero : 1 \rightarrow \mathtt{NAT}$ and $succ : \mathtt{NAT} \rightarrow \mathtt{NAT}$.
  For $\mathtt{STKNAT} = 1 + (\mathtt{NAT} \times \mathtt{STKNAT})$ the injections are $empty : 1 \rightarrow \mathtt{STKNAT}$, $push : \mathtt{NAT}\times\mathtt{STKNAT} \rightarrow \mathtt{STKNAT}$, and the projections are $top : \mathtt{NAT}\times\mathtt{STKNAT} \rightarrow \mathtt{NAT}$ and $pop : \mathtt{NAT} \times \mathtt{STKNAT} \rightarrow \mathtt{STKNAT}$.
  This is still an algebraic approach in that the resulting structure is an algebra (but not an equationally specified algebra).
- If the representation of objects is done by using sums of products then the methods can be implemented (defined) by means of recursion equations. One way to achieve encapsulation, is to impose the restriction that only the methods belonging to k (encapsulated by k) are allowed to make use of the injections, projections and mediating morphisms associated with the sum of products comprising the representation of the objects of class k. Examples:
  - $not = [false, true] : \mathtt{BOOL} \rightarrow \mathtt{BOOL}$
  - $add = [q_{1,NAT}, succ \bullet add] : \mathtt{NAT}\times\mathtt{NAT} \rightarrow \mathtt{NAT}$ where we are making use of the fact that $\mathtt{NAT}\times\mathtt{NAT} \cong (1\times\mathtt{NAT})+(\mathtt{NAT}\times\mathtt{NAT})$, and taking $q_{q,NAT} : 1\times\mathtt{NAT} \rightarrow \mathtt{NAT}$ to be the evident projection.

  Note, in particular, how the necessary conditionals are provided by the coproduct mediators. This yields a strictly functional language.
- The same basic framework can be employed to model imperative languages where there is a concept of memory involved in addition to the concept of data type. I treat such languages in an algebraic framework. However the imperative operations such as assignment and declaration are operations that transform one algebra into another rather than, as above, operations defined within an algebra. The approach is to introduce, for each class, k, a new carrier, O_k, consisting of the "current memory *locations*" for that class, a new carrier, V_k consisting of the "current possible values" that can be held by locations of that class, and an operator $\eta_k : O_k \rightarrow V_k$ that "takes each location to its *current value*".
  - A *variable* A of class k is a constant of sort O_k.

- The value of a variable A of class k is $\eta_k(\mathtt{A})$.
- Declaring a variable A of class k corresponds to changing the algebra by:
  * Adding a new element, $\star$ to O_k (i.e., producing a new location).
  * Adding a new constant operator, A, to the signature for class k, and letting its value be $\star$.
  * "Initializing A" by a suitable modification of η_k (i.e., defining $\eta_k(\star)$.
- An assignment statement to a variable A of class k is modeled by a suitable modification of η_k. It thus changes the algebra.

As described, this is just a mathematical model for imperative languages.

– More sophisticated languages result from allowing the "location carriers" to be used in the definitions of classes as summands and/or factors. To put it slightly more formally, the idea is to allow V_k, the set of current possible values, to contain locations, that is, elements of $\bigcup\langle O_j \mid j \in K\rangle$. This is where object based, and object-oriented, languages and languages "with pointers", can be modeled. See the language LD[3] for an example of a language where this possibility is exploited and combined with the above use of $(+, \times)$-represented data types.

3 Overload Systems

The idea of an overload system is that it is a way to overload the names of methods in such a way that we can always resolve the overloading by looking at the arguments "at run time".

Definition 3. An *overload system* is given by the following data:

K a set (of *class names*).
Σ a set (of *method names*).
$M \subseteq \Sigma \times K^\star$ called *the set of actual methods.*

Think of K as a set if names for classes of elements (or, later on in the development, as names for classes of objects). Think of Σ as a set of names for methods (functions, procedures). Finally, think of M as the actual set of methods. If $\langle\sigma, u\rangle \in M$ then it is a method with *name* σ and *arguments of type* u that is, with $|u|$ arguments where, for $i = 1\ldots, |u|$, the ith argument is of type (class) $u(i)$.

Definition 4. A *classified overload system* is given by the following data:

K a set (of *class names*).
Σ a set (of *method names*).
$\omega : \Sigma \times K^* \rightharpoonup K$, a partial function called the *ownership function.*

The set of actual methods for the overload system is defined to be the set $M = \bigcup\langle\omega^{-1}(k) \mid k \in K\rangle$. That is, $\langle\sigma, u\rangle \in M$ iff $\omega(\sigma, u)$ is defined. If $\omega(\sigma, u) = k$ we say that $\langle\sigma, u\rangle$ is *owned by*, or *belongs to*, k.

Note that for any $k \in K$, $\omega^{-1}(k)$ is the set of all methods belonging to k. The intuition is that if $\langle\sigma, u\rangle$ belongs to k then the code for the method $\langle\sigma, u\rangle$ resides in the class k. Going one step further, we might expect the methods belong to k to be, in some sense, encapsulated within the class k.

Example 1. Assume that for every $\sigma \in \Sigma$ there is exactly one $u \in K^*$ such that $\omega(\sigma, u)$ is defined. This is the traditional, non-overloaded case.

Example 2. We impose the following additional condition:

For all $\sigma \in \Sigma$, and $u \in K^*$, if $\omega(\sigma, u) = k$ then $u = k{\cdot}u'$, for some $u' \in K^*$.

This is a first approximation to the overload resolution scheme used in Smalltalk, where the first argument of a method indicates to which class it belongs. This condition has the immediate consequence

For all $\sigma \in \Sigma$, $\omega(\sigma, \lambda)$ is undefined.

This makes it impossible to have any constants (operations without arguments). This produces the somewhat awkward situation, found in many object oriented languages, that while everything is supposed to be done using "messages" some special "non-messages" are needed in order to create and initialize objects.

Example 3. A more appropriate choice for the condition would appear to be

For all $\sigma \in \Sigma$ and $u \in K^*$, if $u \neq \lambda$ then $\omega(\sigma, u) = k$ implies $u = k \cdot v$ for some $v \in V^*$.

Then it is perfectly possible to have $\omega(\sigma, \lambda) = k$ for some $k \in K$ – thus instead of having "no constants" we have "typed constants".

Example 4. We can restrict ourselves to a system where for each $\sigma \in \Sigma$ and each class $k \in K$, there is exactly one method in k with name σ. This is the same as saying that we have a total mapping $\delta : \Sigma \times K \rightarrow K^*$ such that $\omega(\sigma, u) = k$ iff $u = \delta(\sigma, k)$.

Example 5. We require that there exists a mapping $\nu : \Sigma \rightarrow \mathrm{N}$ such that, for each $\sigma \in \Sigma$ and $u \in K^*$, $\omega(\sigma, u) = k$ if, and only if, $u \in \{k\} \cdot K^{\nu(\sigma)}$. This is a more refined version of the Smalltalk overload resolution scheme than the one given above in Example 3.6.

Example 6. We require that there exists a mapping $\nu : \Sigma \rightarrow \mathrm{N}$ such that, $\omega(\sigma, u)$ is defined if, and only if $u \in K^{\nu(\sigma)}$, and, for $\nu(\sigma) > 0$, $\omega(\sigma, u) = k$ if, and only if, $u \in \{k\} \cdot K^{\nu(\sigma)-1}$. This is a more refined version of the Smalltalk overload resolution scheme than the one given above in Example 3.7.

Example 7. The most familiar use of a classified overload system is probably a typing system, that is, a situation where $\omega(\sigma, u) = k$ iff applying σ to arguments of type u (i.e., where the ith argument if of type $u(i)$ for $i = 1, \ldots, |u|$) gives a result of type k.

4 Primitive Recursion on (+, ×)-Recursive Types

4.1 (+, ×)-recursive types

Definition 5. A *specification of* (+, ×)*-recursive classes* consists of

K a set of *class names.*
$\iota : K \to (K^*)^*$ called the *form function.*

Given a K-ary set (a K-indexed family of sets) $A = \langle A_k \mid k \in K\rangle$, and given $k \in K$ with $\iota(k) = (u_1)(u_2)\cdots(u_n)$ with $u_i = k_{i,1}\cdots k_{i,p_i}$ for $i = 1, \ldots, n$, define

$$A^{\iota(k)} = A^{(u_1)} + A^{(u_2)} + \cdots + A^{(u_n)}$$

where, for $i = 1, \ldots, n$,

$$A^{(u_i)} = A_{k_{i,1}} \times \cdots \times A_{k_{i,p_i}}.$$

Proposition 6. *Given a class specification* $\langle K, \iota\rangle$ *there exists a* K*-ary set* $A = \langle A_k \mid k \in K\rangle$ *with the property that* $A_k \cong A^{\iota(k)}$ *for each* $k \in K$ *and that* A *is the smallest* K*-ary set with this property (i.e., if* B *is a* K*-ary set such that* $B_k \cong B^{\iota(k)}$ *for all* $k \in K$ *then* A *is isomorphic to a* K*-ary subset of* B*).*

We call A *a* least solution *for* $\langle K, \iota\rangle$*.*

The coproduct injections from the summands of $A^{\iota(k)}$ *to* A_k *are called the* the implicit injections. *The projections from the summands of* $A^{\iota(k)}$ *to its factors are called* the implicit projections.

Proposition 7. *Let* K *be a set and let* $\iota_1, \iota_2 : K \to (K^*)^*$ *be form functions and for* $i = 1, 2$ *let* A_i *be the least solution for* $\langle K, \iota_i\rangle$*. If* $\iota_1(k) \cong \iota_2(k)$ *in* $\mathbf{SStr}_K$ *for all* $k \in K$ *then* $A_1 \cong A_2$*.*

Definition 8. Let $\langle K, \iota\rangle$ be a specification with least solution A.

A function $f : A^v \to A_k$ ($v \in K^*$), will be said to be *primitive recursive* in $\langle K, \iota\rangle$ and A if:

1. it is an implicit injection or projection.
2. It is a projection $p_i^v : A^v \to A_{v(i)}$.
3. It is a composite of functions that are primitive recursive in $\langle K, \iota\rangle$ and A.
4. There is an isomorphism $I : \iota(k) \cong (u_1)\cdots(u_n)(k\cdot v_1)\cdots(k\cdot v_p)$ in $\mathbf{SStr}_K$, where u_i is k-free for $i = 1, \ldots, n$, and for some $m \in K$ and $w \in K^*$ we have functions

   $$g_i : A^{u_i} \times A^w \to A_m, \; i = 1, \ldots, n$$

   and

   $$h_j : A_k \times A^{v_j} \times A_w \times A_m \to A_m, \; j = 1, \ldots, p$$

   that are primitive recursive in $\langle K, \iota\rangle$ and A. In which case we get an additional function

$$f : A_k \times A^w \to A_m$$
$$f = [g_1, \ldots, g_n, \overline{h_1}, \ldots, \overline{h_p}] \bullet I$$

where, for $j = 1, \ldots, p$.

$$\overline{h_j} = h \bullet (1 \times f) \bullet \langle p_1, p_2, p_3, p_1, p_3 \rangle.$$

Proposition 9. *The concept of a primitive recursive function in $\langle K, \iota \rangle$ is well-defined.*

Example 8. Let $K = \{\mathtt{NAT}, \mathtt{STR}\}$ with

$\iota(\mathtt{NAT}) = (\ )(\mathtt{NAT})$
$\iota(\mathtt{STR}) = (\ )(\mathtt{STR} \cdot \mathtt{NAT})$

Then we claim that "the" least solution is A with $A_{NAT} = \mathrm{N}$, the set of natural numbers, and $A_{STR} = \mathrm{N}^*$, the set of strings on N. The corresponding implicit injections and projections are:

$0 : 1 \to \mathrm{N}$, the constant zero.
$succ : \mathrm{N} \to \mathrm{N}$, the successor function.
$\lambda : 1 \to \mathrm{N}^*$, the empty string.
$append : \mathrm{N}^* \times \mathrm{N} \to \mathrm{N}^*$.
$head : \mathrm{N}^* \times \mathrm{N} \to \mathrm{N}$.
$tail : \mathrm{N}^* \times \mathrm{N} \to \mathrm{N}^*$.

Examples of functions that are primitive recursive in $\langle K, \iota \rangle$ and A include:

1. $pred : \mathrm{N} \to \mathrm{N}$, $pred = [0, 1_N]$.
2. $add : \mathrm{N} \times \mathrm{N} \to \mathrm{N}$, $add = [p_2, succ \bullet add]$.
3. $concat : \mathrm{N}^* \times \mathrm{N}^* \to \mathrm{N}^*$, $concat = [p_2, append \bullet (concat \times 1) \bullet \langle p_1, p_3, p_1 \rangle]$.

5 The Message Paradigm

We show how to construct functional languages fitting an overload scheme of the sort given in Example 3.10. Recall that in that example, what we have is an overload system $\langle K, \Sigma, \omega : \Sigma \times K^* \to K \rangle$ where there exists a mapping $\nu : \Sigma \to \mathrm{N}$ such that, $\omega(\sigma, u)$ is defined if, and only if $u \in K^{\nu(\sigma)}$, and, for $\nu(\sigma) > 0$, $\omega(\sigma, u) = k$ if, and only if, $u \in \{k\} \cdot K^{\nu(\sigma)-1}$.

- We start from a specification $\langle K, \iota \rangle$ of $(+, \times)$-recursive classes. This gives us a K-indexed family of sets $A = \langle A_k \mid k \in K \rangle$, together with the associated collection of implicit injections and projections. Think of A_k as the set of "elements of class k", and of the implicit injections and projections for A_k as "the given or ground operations of class k".

- Let $\coprod A =_{def} \coprod\langle A_k \mid k \in K\rangle$ with an injection $i_k : A_k \to \coprod A$ for each $k \in K$. It is convenient to think of $\coprod A$ concretely as the set $\{\langle a, k\rangle \mid k \in K,\ a \in A_k\}$. We make use of this, in particular, in the example shown in Figure 1.
- For each $\sigma \in \Sigma$ its meaning is a function

$$\xi(\sigma) : (\coprod A)^{\nu(\sigma)} \to \coprod A.$$

  * If $\nu(\sigma) = 0$ then we require that "$\xi(\sigma) \in A_{\omega(\sigma,\lambda)}$" in the sense that $\xi(\sigma)$ is a mapping $\xi(\sigma) : 1 \to \coprod A$ that factors through i_k.
  * Observe that if $\nu(\sigma) > 0$ then, by the distributivity of $\times$ over $+$, we have
  $$(\coprod A)^{\nu(\sigma)} \cong \coprod\langle(A_k \times (\coprod A)^{\nu(\sigma)-1}) \mid k \in K\rangle.$$
  with an injection $\bar{i}_k = (i_k \times 1_{(\coprod A)^{\nu(\sigma)-1}}) : A_k \times (\coprod A)^{\nu(\sigma)-1} \to \coprod A$ for each $k \in K$. Thus $\xi(\sigma)$ can be expressed as the mediating morphism corresponding to the K-ary set of mappings $\langle \xi(\sigma)_k =_{def} \xi(\sigma) \bullet \bar{i}_k \mid k \in K\rangle$. That is, if $K = \{k_1, \ldots, k_n\}$ then
  $$\xi(\sigma) = [\![\xi(\sigma)_{k_1}, \ldots, \xi(\sigma)_{k_n}]\!].$$
  where $[\![\cdots]\!]$ is the indicated coproduct mediator.
  * A first approximation of the intuitive meaning of the phrase "$\langle\sigma, u\rangle$ belongs to $\omega(\sigma, u)$" is captured in this context by the fact that for $\nu(\sigma) > 0$ and $u = k \cdot v$ we have $\omega(\sigma, u) = k$ and, loosely speaking, the method $\langle\sigma, u\rangle$ is the restriction of $\xi(\sigma)_k$ to A^u. This is the formal counterpart of the "Message Paradigm".
  * In the example given below we utilize the generalized notion of primitive recursion described in section 4 to define the functions $\xi(\sigma)_k$. We extend the approach by allowing the use of the injections $i_k : A_k \to \coprod A$, and the following truly polymorphic functions for arbitrary sets X and Y:
    $tr : X \to 1$ is the unique function to the singleton set 1.
    $p_i : X_1 \times \cdots \times X_n \to X_i$, for $i = 1, \ldots, n$, is the indicated projection.
    $id : X \to X$ is the identity function on X.
  * We can, and will, introduce encapsulation by limiting the use of the implicit injections and implicit projections that are associated with A_k, and associated mediating morphisms, to the definitions of methods belonging to k. This provides a strong form of encapsulation and gives further intuitive meaning to the phrase, "$\langle\sigma, u\rangle$ belongs to $\omega(\sigma, u)$".

Example 9. For this example we take

$K = \{\mathtt{NAT}, \mathtt{BOOL}, \mathtt{STR}\}$.
$\Sigma = \{0, true, false, empty, succ, pred, add, mult\}$.
$\nu(0) = \nu(true) = \nu(false) = \nu(empty) = 0$.
$\nu(succ) = \nu(pred) = 1$.
$\nu(add) = \nu(mult) = 2$.

The semantics goes as follows:

The necessary sets for the classes NAT, BOOL, and STR are defined using the approach sketched in Section 4. That is we take A_{NAT}, A_{BOOL} and A_{STR} to be the smallest sets satisfying the recursion equations:

$A_{NAT} \cong 1 + A_{NAT}$ with coproduct injections $z : 1 \to A_{NAT}$ and $s : A_{NAT} \to A_{NAT}$.

$A_{BOOL} \cong 1+1$ with coproduct injections $t : 1 \to A_{BOOL}$ and $f : 1 \to A_{BOOL}$.

$A_{STR} \cong 1 + (A_{STR} \times A_{NAT})$ with coproduct injections $\lambda : 1 \to A_{STR}$ and $append : A_{STR} \times A_{NAT} \to A_{STR}$, and projections $head : A_{STR} \times A_{NAT} \to A_{NAT}$ and $tail : A_{STR} \times A_{NAT} \to A_{STR}$.

The semantics of the operations is given by the following expressions where tr, p_1, p_2 and id are truly polymorphic primitives, where for any sets X and Y:

$tr : X \to 1$ is the unique function to the singleton set 1.

$p_1 : X \times Y \to X$, and $p_2 : X \times Y \to Y$ are the indicated projections.

$id : X \to X$ is the identity function on X.

For each $\sigma \in \Sigma$ with $\nu(\sigma) > 0$, we give $\xi(\sigma)$ as a mediating morphism

$$\xi(\sigma) = [\![\xi(\sigma)_{NAT}, \xi(\sigma)_{BOOL}, \xi(\sigma)_{STR}]\!] : \\ ((A_{NAT} \times (\coprod A)^{\nu(\sigma)-1}) + (A_{BOOL} \times (\coprod A)^{\nu(\sigma)-1}) + (A_{STR} \times (\coprod A)^{\nu(\sigma)-1})) \to \coprod A$$

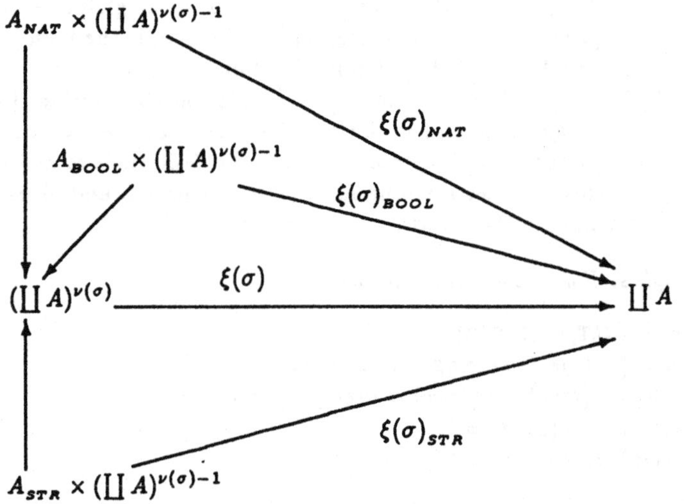

The functions $\xi(\sigma)_k : (\coprod A)^{\nu(\sigma)} \to \coprod A$, for $\sigma \in \Sigma$ and $k \in K$, are generally given as a mediating morphism for A_k (or $A_k \times \coprod A$), e.g., $\xi(pred)_{NAT} = [0, i_{NAT}] : A_{NAT} \to \coprod A$, exploiting the fact that $A_{NAT} \cong 1 + A_{NAT}$:

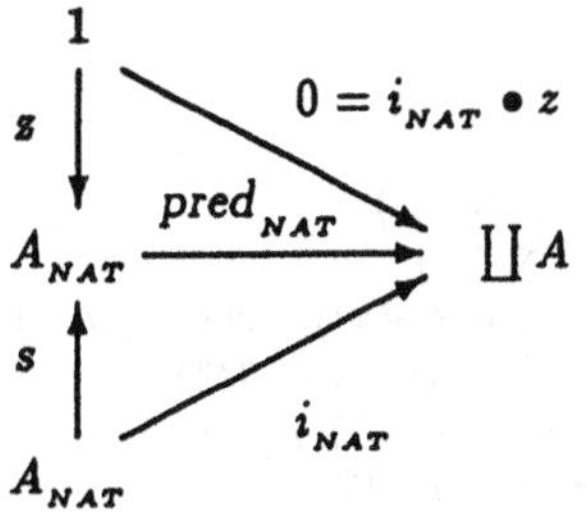

However, $\xi(add)_{STR}$ is an exception, it uses a mediating morphism for $(A_{STR} \times A_{NAT}) + (A_{STR} \times A_{BOOL}) + (A_{STR} \times A_{STR})$.
Here are the functions $\xi(\sigma)$ for this example:

$\xi(0) = i_{NAT} \bullet z : 1 \to \coprod A.$
$\xi(true) = i_{BOOL} \bullet t : 1 \to \coprod A.$
$\xi(false) = i_{BOOL} \bullet f : 1 \to \coprod A.$
$\xi(empty) = i_{STR} \bullet \lambda : 1 \to \coprod A.$
$\xi(succ)_{\mathtt{NAT}} = i_{NAT} \bullet s : A_{NAT} \to \coprod A.$
$\xi(pred)_{\mathtt{NAT}} = [0,\ i_{NAT}] : A_{NAT} \to \coprod A.$
$\xi(add)_{\mathtt{NAT}} = [p_2,\ succ \bullet add \bullet (i_{NAT} \times id)] : A_{NAT} \times \coprod A \to \coprod A.$
$\xi(mult)_{\mathtt{NAT}} = [0 \bullet p_1,\ add(mult \times p_2) \bullet (pred \times \langle p_2,\ p_2\rangle) \bullet (i_{NAT} \times p_2)]$
$: A_{NAT} \times \coprod A \to \coprod A.$
$\xi(succ)_{\mathtt{BOOL}} = [false,\ true] : A_{BOOL} \to \coprod A.$
$\xi(pred)_{\mathtt{BOOL}} = [false,\ true] : A_{BOOL} \to \coprod A.$
$\xi(add)_{\mathtt{BOOL}} = [true \bullet p_1,\ p_2] : A_{BOOL} \times \coprod A \to \coprod A.$
$\xi(mult)_{\mathtt{BOOL}} = [p_2,\ false \bullet p_1] : A_{BOOL} \times \coprod A \to \coprod A.$
$\xi(succ)_{\mathtt{STR}} = [false,\ i_{NAT} \bullet head] : A_{STR} \to \coprod A.$
$\xi(pred)_{STR} = [empty,\ i_{NAT} \bullet tail] : A_{STR} \to \coprod A.$
$\xi(add)_{STR} = [\![i_{STR} \bullet append,\ i_{STR} \bullet p_1,\ i_{STR} \bullet p_1]\!] : A_{STR} \times \coprod A \to \coprod A.$
(Note that the mediating morphism here is the one for $\coprod A$ rather than the one for A_{STR}.)
$\xi(mult)_{STR} = [p_2,\ add \bullet (mult \times id) \bullet (i_{STR} \bullet p_1,\ p_3,\ i_{NAT} \bullet p_2)] : A_{STR} \times \coprod A \to \coprod A.$

The idea now is that given a method name σ and a string $\overline{a} \in A^{\nu(\sigma)}$, the choice of which method to apply is determined by examining the class membership of the first component of $\overline{a}$.

A detailed example of a calculation is shown in Figure 1, where *add* is applied to the arguments $\langle 2, 2\rangle$.

Proposition 10. *We make the following claims concerning the functions 0, true, false, empty, succ, pred, add and mult defined above. For the present purposes we interpret* $\coprod A$ *as the set* $\mathrm{N} + \{true,\ false\} + \mathrm{N}^*$.

- *Each function* σ *is defined for all tuples in* $(\coprod A)^{\nu(\sigma)}$.
- *0 is the constant zero.*

Fig. 1. Calculation of *add*(2,2)

$$
\begin{aligned}
& add(2,2) \\
&= add(\langle s(s(z)), \mathtt{NAT}\rangle, \langle\, s(s(z)), \mathtt{NAT}\rangle\,) \\
&= add_{NAT}(\, s(s(z)),\ \langle s(s(z)), \mathtt{NAT}\rangle\,) \\
&= [p_2,\ succ \bullet add \bullet (i_{NAT} \times id)](\, s(s(z)),\ \langle s(s(z)), \mathtt{NAT}\rangle\,) \\
&= succ \bullet add \bullet (i_{NAT} \times id)(\, s(z),\ \langle s(s(z)), \mathtt{NAT}\rangle\,) \\
&= succ \bullet add(\, \langle s(z), \mathtt{NAT}\rangle,\ \langle s(s(z)), \mathtt{NAT}\rangle\,) \\
&= succ \bullet add_{NAT}(\, s(z),\ abrs(s(z)), \mathtt{NAT}\,) \\
&= succ \bullet [p_2,\ succ \bullet add \bullet (i_{NAT} \times id)](\, s(z),\ \langle s(s(z)), \mathtt{NAT}\rangle\,) \\
&= succ \bullet\ succ \bullet add \bullet (i_{NAT} \times id)(\, z,\ \langle s(s(z)), \mathtt{NAT}\rangle\,) \\
&= succ \bullet\ succ \bullet add(\, (\langle z, \mathtt{NAT}\rangle,\ \langle s(s(z)), \mathtt{NAT}\rangle\,) \\
&= succ \bullet\ succ \bullet add_{NAT}(\, (\ z,\ \langle s(s(z)), \mathtt{NAT}\rangle\,) \\
&= succ \bullet\ succ \bullet [p_2,\ succ \bullet add \bullet (i_{NAT} \times id)](\, z,\ \langle s(s(z)), \mathtt{NAT}\rangle\,) \\
&= succ \bullet\ succ \bullet p_2(\, *,\ \langle s(s(z)), \mathtt{NAT}\rangle\,) \\
&= succ \bullet succ(\, \langle s(s(z)), \mathtt{NAT}\rangle\,) \\
&= succ \bullet succ_{NAT}(\, s(s(z))\,) \\
&= succ \bullet i_{NAT} \bullet s(\, s(s(z))\,) \\
&= succ \bullet i_{NAT}(\, s(s(s(z)))\,) \\
&= succ(\, \langle s(s(s(z))), \mathtt{NAT}\rangle\,) \\
&= succ_{NAT}(\, s(s(s(z)))\,) \\
&= i_{NAT} \bullet s(\, s(s(s(z)))\,) \\
&= i_{NAT}(\, s(s(s(s(z))))\,) \\
&= \langle s(s(s(s(z)))), \mathtt{NAT}\rangle \\
&= 4
\end{aligned}
$$

- *true is the truth value "true"*
- *false is the truth value "false".*
- *empty is the empty string.*
- *the function succ is the successor function on* N, *the negation function on* {*true, false*}, *and the function hd on* N^* *which, given the empty string in* N^*, *returns the Boolean value false, but applied to a string* $w = n \cdot u \in \mathrm{N}^*$, *returns* n *(the first element of* w*).*
- *the function pred is the predecessor function on* N, *the negation function on* {*true, false*}, *and the function tl on* N^* *which, given the empty string in* N^*, *returns the empty string, but applied to a string* $w = n \cdot u \in \mathrm{N}^*$, *returns the string* u.
- *the function add is addition on the* N×N, *is conjunction on* $\{true,\ false\}^2$, *is the function from* $\mathrm{N}^* \times \mathrm{N} \rightarrow \mathrm{N}^*$ *that takes* $\langle w, n\rangle$ *to the string* $n \cdot w$, *and with the second argument fixed to be true it is the function even* : N → N *such that*

$$even(n) = \begin{cases} true \text{ if } n \text{ is an even number} \\ false \text{ if } n \text{ is an odd number} \end{cases}$$

- *the function mult is multiplication on* N×N, *is disjunction on* {*true, false*} *and is concatenation on* $\mathrm{N}^* \times \mathrm{N}^*$.

Observations:

1. In the definition of add_{STR} we made use of a mediating morphism on $\coprod A$ (in effect, a case statement based on class membership). This provided a way to make an implicit injection with several arguments, in this example the injection $append : A_{STR} \times A_{NAT} \rightarrow A_{STR}$, into a method. We took a conservative approach to this definition in which all the components of the mediating morphism, except the NAT component, had the same value $i_{STR} \bullet p_1$. This corresponds to a simplified case statement of the form `If type of second argument is NAT then e1 else e2`. Note that the meaning of such a statement is independent of the size of K.
   Restricting the program to mediators of this kind would have practical consequences if we were to implement this for a computer. It would both simplify the implementation and obviate the need to recompile each time a new class was added to K.
   However, it is also possible to get interesting results by not so restricting the use of $[\cdots]$. For example we could take

$$\xi(add)_{STR} = [i_{STR} \bullet append,\ [true \bullet p_2,\ false \bullet p_2],\ [p_2,\ add \bullet (add \times id) \bullet (i_{STR} \bullet p_1,\ p_3,\ i_{NAT} \bullet p_2)]] : A_{STR} \times \coprod A \rightarrow \coprod A.$$

   then we get

$$\langle add, \mathrm{STR} \cdot \mathrm{NAT} \rangle = append,$$

$$\langle add, \mathrm{STR} \cdot \mathrm{BOOL} \rangle = \begin{cases} true \text{ if the string is empty} \\ false \text{ if the string is not empty} \end{cases}$$

$$\langle add, \mathrm{STR} \cdot \mathrm{STR} \rangle = \text{concatenation}.$$

Remarks

1. The kind of overloading we have here is very closely related to the concept of a virtual method in C++. However in C++ it is viewed as a kind of inheritance, whereas here we just view it as overloading.
2. Note that we have produced a very highly encapsulated language by limiting where the implicit injections and projections can be used. Note, however, that this is not part of the message paradigm per se, i.e., we can view the message paradigm as just an overload system – a particular means for overloading method names and resolving that overloading.
3. The concept of element used here is both more and less powerful than the concept of object employed in Smalltalk. It is more powerful in that we make use of both $+$ and $\times$. It is less powerful in that our elements lack memory. This lack can be remedied by going to a more elaborate concept of language – see my papers on $\mathbf{LD^3}$.

6 Coercion and Inheritance

In this section we explore a notions of inheritance based on coercion and overloading. We take the viewpoint here that (one version of) inheritance is essentially the idea that if k' inherits from k then this means there is a way to coerce elements of class k' into elements of class k in such a way that we can apply a method named σ from class k, to the resulting coerced elements and get what appears to be a method in class k' with name σ.

For most of this section we continue to restrict our attention to an essentially functional language framework – mainly to further emphasize the separation between overloading, inheritance, and the object concept (data types with memory).

6.1 Orderings

Definition 11. Let K be a set and $\leq$ a partial order on K. Given $k, k' \in K$ we say they have a *least upper bound*, (*greatest lower bound*) $k'' = k \sqcup k'$, $(k \sqcap k')$ if there exists $k'' \in K$ such that $k, k' \leq k''$ ($k'' \leq k, k'$) and for any $k''' \in K$, $k, k' \leq k'''$ ($k''' \leq k, k'$) implies $k'' \leq k'''$ ($k''' \leq k''$).

We say that $\langle K, \leq \rangle$ is an *upper semi-lattice* is $k \sqcup k'$ exists for all $k, k' \in K$.

Let $\langle K, \leq \rangle$ be an upper semi-lattice, then given $u \in K^*$ we write $\sqcup u =_{def} \bigsqcup \langle u(i) \mid i = 1, \ldots, |u| \rangle$.

6.2 Basic Overloading via Simple Coercions

Definition 12. Given K with a partial ordering $\leq$ view $\langle K, \leq \rangle$ as a category. Then a *coercion system* for A with respect to $\leq$ is a functor

$$\begin{aligned} c : \langle K, \leq \rangle &\rightarrow \mathbf{Set} \\ k &\mapsto A_k \\ (k' \leq k) &\mapsto c_{k',k} : A_{k'} \rightarrow A_k. \end{aligned}$$

Note that what the functorality says is that if $k'' \leq k' \leq k$ then $c_{k',k} \bullet c_{k'',k'} = c_{k'',k}$ and that $c_{k,k} = 1_{A_k}$.

Let $A = \langle A_k \mid k \in K \rangle$ be a K-indexed set of sets. Recall that in Set, for any $n \in \mathrm{N}$,

$$(\coprod A_k)^n \cong \coprod \langle A^u \mid u \in K^n \rangle$$

Definition 13. Let $\langle K, \leq \rangle$ be an upper semi-lattice and let c be a coercion system for K with respect to $\leq$. Given $n \in \mathrm{N}$, $\tau : K \rightarrow K$, and a K-indexed family of maps $\langle \alpha_k : A_k^n \rightarrow A_{\tau(k)} \rangle$ define a new map

$$\begin{aligned} \alpha : (\coprod A_k)^n &\rightarrow (\coprod A_k) \\ (\langle a_1, \ldots, a_n \rangle \in A^u) &\mapsto \alpha_{\sqcup u}(c_{u(1), \sqcup u}(a_1), \ldots, c_{u(n), \sqcup u}(a_n)). \end{aligned}$$

We call α the *overload* of $\langle \alpha_k \mid k \in K \rangle$ *via* c.

Proposition 14. *Let $\leq$ be a partial order on K, such that $\langle K, \leq \rangle$ forms an upper semi-lattice, let c be a coercion system for K with respect to $\leq$, let $n \in \mathrm{N}$, let $\tau : K \rightarrow K$, and let $\langle \alpha_k : A_k^n \rightarrow A_{\tau(k)} \rangle$ be a K-indexed family of maps, then the overload, α, of $\langle \alpha_k \mid k \in K \rangle$ via c is well defined.*

Proof. Since $\langle K, \leq \rangle$ is an upper semi-lattice it follows that for any $u \in K^n$ that $\sqcup u = \bigsqcup \langle u(i) \mid i = 1, \ldots, n \rangle$ exists and that $c_{u(i),\sqcup u} : A_{u(i)} \rightarrow A_{\sqcup u}$ also exists. Thus if $\langle a_1, \ldots, a_n \rangle \in A^u$ then $\langle c_{u(1),\sqcup u}(a_1), \ldots, c_{u(n),\sqcup u}(a_n) \rangle \in A^n_{\sqcup u}$ and so $\alpha_{\sqcup u}(c_{u(1),\sqcup u}(a_1), \ldots, c_{u(n),\sqcup u}(a_n))$ is defined.

Example 10. Given K and the coercion system c as above, we can define an "overloaded coercion" $c^k : (\coprod A_j) \rightarrow (\coprod A_j)$ for each $k \in K$ where $n = 1$, and, for each $j \in K$,

$$c_j^k = \begin{cases} c_{j,k} & \text{if } j \leq k \\ c_{j,j} = 1_{A_j} & \text{otherwise} \end{cases}$$

Note that this makes

$$\tau(j) = \begin{cases} k \text{ if } j \leq k \\ j \text{ otherwise} \end{cases}$$

What c^k does is coerce an element in a class $k' \leq k$ into an element of class k, leaving elements of any class $k'' \not\leq k$ as they are.

Example 11. Assume we have an operation

$$\begin{gathered} type_n : (\coprod A_k)^n \rightarrow K^n \\ (\langle a_1, \ldots, a_n \rangle \in A^u) \mapsto u. \end{gathered}$$

If K is a set of r elements then for any $n \in \mathrm{N}$, K^n has r^n elements. We can use $type_n$ to define α by means of a case statement with r^n cases, one case for each $u \in K^n$:

```
α(P1,...,Pn)
    Case X=typeₙ(P1,...,Pn) of
        . . .
      X=u : α⊔u(c_{u(1),⊔u}(a1),...,c_{u(n),⊔u}(an))
        . . .
    end.
```

However, by making use of the "overloaded coercions" c^k given in example 10 we can reduce it to r cases, that is, one case for each $k \in K$:

```
α(P1,...,Pn)
    Case X=⊔(typeₙ(P1,...,Pn)) of
        . . .
      X=k : α_k(c^k(a1),...,c^k(an))
        . . .
    end.
```

Thus, in as much as this informal programming reflects what would happen in practice, considerable simplification can result from judicious use of overloading.

Example 12. For a more concrete example of what we have done above let

$$K = \{\texttt{INTeger}, \texttt{REal}, \texttt{COMplex}\}$$

with the total ordering

$$\texttt{INT} \leq \texttt{RE} \leq \texttt{COM},$$

with, for each $k \in K$, the appropriate carrier A_k and the arithmetic operations

$$+_k, *_k, -_k, /_k : A_k \times A_k \rightarrow A_k$$

and with the "usual coercion functions"

$$c_{I,R} : A_{INT} \rightarrow A_{RE}$$

and

$$c_{R,C} : A_{RE} \rightarrow A_{COM}$$

Using the technique of the preceding example we get overloaded coercions *Re* and *Co* and overloaded arithmetic operation +,*,-, and / by direct application of the above scheme. The corresponding case statements are as follows:

```
Re(P1)
   Case X=type₁(P1) of
      X=COM : P1
      X=RE  : P1
      X=INT : c_IR(P1)
   end.

Co(P1)
   Case X=type₁(P1) of
      X=COM : P1
      X=RE  : c_RC(P1)
      X=INT : c_RC(c_IR(P1))
   end.
```

and, for $f \in \{+, *, -, /\}$,

```
f(P1)
   Case X=⊔(type₂(P1,P2)) of
      X=COM : f_COM(Co(P1),Co(P2))
      X=RE  : f_RE(Re(P1), Re(P2))
      X=INT : f_INT(P1, P2)
   end.
```

6.3 Multiple Coercion Systems

Generally speaking, given a collection of classes K there will be more than one possible coercion system associated with K and subsets of K.

Example 13. Consider the example of $K = \{\texttt{INTeger}, \texttt{REal}, \texttt{COMplex}\}$ given in Example 12 with ordering $\texttt{INT} \leq \texttt{RE} \leq \texttt{COM}$. Consider the REals as being floating point numbers represented by pairs $\langle m, e\rangle \in A_{INT} \times A_{INT}$ (m for *mantissa*, and e for *exponent*), rather than as "real reals". We interpret the pair $\langle m, e\rangle$ as the number $m * 10^e$ so, for example $\langle 314, -2\rangle$ corresponds to the decimal 3.14, and 720 could be represented as $\langle 720, 0\rangle$ or as $\langle 72, 1\rangle$. Consider the COMplex numbers as being represented by pairs $\langle r, i\rangle \in A_{RE} \times A_{RE}$ (r for *real-part*, and i for *imaginary-part*) then we have coercions

$$\begin{gathered} m, e : A_{RE} \rightarrow A_{INT} \\ m : \langle n, p\rangle \mapsto n \\ e : \langle n, p\rangle \mapsto p \end{gathered}$$

and

$$\begin{gathered} r, i : A_{COM} \rightarrow A_{RE} \\ r : \langle n, p\rangle \rightarrow n \\ i : \langle n, p\rangle \rightarrow p \end{gathered}$$

given by the evident projections. These coercions do not form a partial ordering on K, much less an upper semi-lattice, since there are multiple edges between elements. However they do form a directed acyclic graph, where (as in most categorical treatments) a graph is allowed to have more than one edge between the same pair of vertices. None-the-less, we can extract a variety of upper semi-lattices which can be used, perhaps even in conjunction with the coercion system described earlier, to define functions.

In particular, given the operations of addition (+) and multiplication (*) on A_{INT}, we can use them to define the multiplication on A_{RE} as follows:

> Let $+_m : A_{RE} \times A_{RE} \rightarrow A_{INT}$ denote the overload of INT-addition via the coercion m. That is, for an reals $r_1, r_2 \in A_{RE}$, $r_1 +_m r_2 =_{def} m(r_1) +_{INT} m(r_2)$.
> Let $+_e : A_{RE} \times A_{RE} \rightarrow A_{INT}$ denote the overload of INT-addition via the coercion e. That is, for an reals $r_1, r_2 \in A_{RE}$, $r_1 +_e r_2 =_{def} e(r_1) +_{INT} e(r_2)$.
> Let $*_m : A_{RE} \times A_{RE} \rightarrow A_{INT}$ denote the overload of INT-multiplication via the coercion m. That is, for an reals $r_1, r_2 \in A_{RE}$, $r_1 *_m r_2 =_{def} m(r_1) *_{INT} m(r_2)$.
> Let $*_e : A_{RE} \times A_{RE} \rightarrow A_{INT}$ denote the overload of INT-multiplication via the coercion e. That is, for an reals $r_1, r_2 \in A_{RE}$, $r_1 *_e r_2 =_{def} e(r_1) *_{INT} e(r_2)$.

Then, forgetting about roundoff, the RE-multiplication of $r_1, r_2 \in A_{RE}$ is:

$$r_1 *_{RE} r_2 = \langle r_1 *_m r_2,\ r_1 +_e r_2\rangle.$$

which, of course, is very close to the "usual way" of writing it as:

$$r_1 *_{RE} r_2 = \langle m(r_1) *_{INT} m(r_2),\ e(r_1) +_{INT} e(r_2)\rangle$$

To do RE-addition takes more apparatus, namely conditionals, a $\leq$ predicate and subtraction, the essential idea is:

$$r_1 +_{RE} r_2 = \begin{cases} \langle r_2 +_m (r_1 *_{RE} \langle 1, (r_1 -_e r_2)\rangle), e(r_1)\rangle & \text{if } r_1 \geq_e r_2 \\ \langle r_1 +_m (r_2 *_{RE} \langle 1, (r_2 -_e r_1)\rangle), e(r_2)\rangle & \text{otherwise.} \end{cases}$$

Doing it the "usual way" we would write:

$$r_1 +_{RE} r_2 = \begin{cases} \langle m(r_2) +_{INT} (m(r_1) *_{INT} 10^{e(r_1) -_{INT} e(r_2)}),\ e(r_1)\rangle \text{ if } e(r_1) \leq_{INT} e(r_2) \\ \langle m(r_1) +_{INT} (m(r_2) *_{INT} 10^{e(r_2) -_{INT} e(r_1)}),\ e(r_2)\rangle \text{ otherwise.} \end{cases}$$

Note that doing it the "usual way" requires us to have an operation for forming exponentials. Thus the overloaded version, in addition to being more succinct, requires fewer operations on A_{INT}. However, in practice, this exponential operation would probably be implemented by shift operation (which, in the "practical world" is generally inexpensive).

Similarly, we can define COM-addition and COM-multiplication in terms of appropriate overloadings, $+_r$, $+_i$, $*_r$, $*_i$ etc., of RE-addition and RE-multiplication.

Remarks:

1. The above example shows how we can use inherited operations, as defined at the beginning of this section, to produce new operations. That is we employ $+_m$, $+_e$, $+_r$, $+_i$, etc. to produce new operations $+_{RE}$, $*_{RE}$, $+_{COM}$, $*_{COM}$ which, to use the terminology of Smalltalk, "override" the inherited operations.
2. The fact that RE can inherit $+_{INT}$ in two ways, i.e., as $+_m$ and as $+e$ is an example of what is commonly called *multiple inheritance*. However this example has the unusual feature that we are inheriting in two ways from the same class!

References

1. Luca Cardelli. Amber. Technical Memorandum 11271-840924-10TM, AT&T Bell Laboratories, September 1984.
2. Luca Cardelli and Peter Wegner. On understanding types, data abstraction, and polymorphism. *Computing Surveys*, 4:471–522, 1985.
3. Giuseppe Castagna, Giorgio Ghelli, and Giuseppe Longo. A calculus for overloaded functions with subtyping. Technical Report LIENS - 92 -4, LIENS, Laboratoire d'Informatique de l'Ecole Normale Superiure, February 1992.
4. Hans-Dieter Ehrich and Amilcar Sernadas. Fundamental object concepts and constructions. In *Proceedings of IS-CORE Workshop WS'91, London, Sept. 16-18, 1991*, 1991.
5. Joseph A. Goguen and David Wolfram. On types and foops. In *Proceedings IFIP TC-2 Conference on Object Oriented Databases*, 1991.
6. Adele Goldberg and David Robson. *Smalltalk-80: The Language and its Implementation.* Addison-Wesley, Reading, MA, 1983.
7. Borland International. *Turbo Pascal® Version 6.0 User's Guide.* Borland Int'l, Scotts Valley, CA, 1990.
8. Bertrand Meyer. *Object-Oriented Software Construction.* Prentice-Hall International Series in Computer Science. Prentice-Hall, New York, NY, 1988.
9. John C. Mitchell. Toward a typed foundation for method specialization and inheritance. In *Proceedings of the 17th POPL*, pages 109–124. ACM, 1990.
10. Bjarne Stroustrup. *The C++ Programming Language.* Addison-Wesley Series in Computer Science. Addison-Wesley, Reading, MA, 1987.
11. Bjarne Stroustrup. *The C++ Programming Language.* Addison-Wesley Series in Computer Science. Addison-Wesley, Reading, MA, 2nd edition, 1991.

12. Eric G. Wagner. Categorical semantics, or extending data types to include memory. In H.-J. Kreowski, editor, *Recent Trends in Data Type Specification: 3rd Workshop on Theory and Applications of Abstract Data Types Selected Papers*, pages 1–21. Informatik-Fachberichte 116, Springer-Verlag, 1984.
13. Eric G. Wagner. Semantics of block structured languages with pointers. In *Proceedings of the 3rd Annual Workshop on the Mathematical Foundations of Programming Language Semantics*. LNCS 298, Springer Verlag, 1987.
14. Eric G. Wagner. An algebraically specified language for data directed design. In *Proceedings of the First International Conference on Algebraic Methodology and Software Technology*, pages 145–163. University of Iowa, 1989.
15. Eric G. Wagner. On declarations. In H. Ehrig, H. Herrlich, H.-J. Kreowski, and G. Preuss, editors, *Categorical Methods in Computer Science*, pages 261–277. LNCS 393, Springer-Verlag, 1989.
16. Eric G Wagner. An algebraically specified language for data directed design. *Theoretical Computer Science*, 77:195–219, 1990.
17. Eric G. Wagner. All recursive types defined using products and sums can be implemented using pointers. In *Proceedings of Conference on Algebraic Logic and Universal Algebra in Computer Science, Jun1-June4 1988, Iowa State University, Ames, Iowa*, pages 111–132. Springer - Verlag LNCS 425, 1990.
18. Eric G. Wagner. Generic types in a language for data directed design. In H. Ehrig, K.P. Jantke, F. Orejas, and H. Reichel, editors, *Proceedings of the 7th Workshop on Specification of Abstract Data Types (Wusterhausen/Dosse, Germany, April 1990)*, pages 341–361. LNCS 534, Springer Verlag, 1991.
19. Eric G. Wagner. Generic classes in an object-based language. In *Recent Trends in Data Type Specification*, pages 330 - 344. LNCS 655, Springer Verlag, 1992.
20. Eric G. Wagner. Some mathematical thoughts on languages for data directed design. In Charles Rattray and Robert G. Clark, editors, *The Unified Computation Laboratory: Modeling, Specifications, and Tools*, pages 3–26. The Institute of Mathematics and Its Applications Conference Series, New Series Number 35, Clarendon Press, Oxford, 1992.

A SMoLCS Based Kit for Defining High-Level Algebraic Petri Nets *

Mohamed Bettaz[1] and Gianna Reggio[2]

[1] Institut D'Informatique Universite De Constantine – Algerie
[2] Dipartimento di Informatica e Scienze dell'Informazione
Università di Genova – Italy

Introduction

Petri nets are a description method for concurrent systems supported by graphic representations; their combination with abstract data types (shortly adt's) appear to be motivated by the need to explicitly specify complex data structures inherent to real systems and concrete applications.

Nowadays there is a large amount of proposals for combining Petri nets with adt's, see e.g. [5, 6, 8, 10, 12, 13, 1, 16, 17], concerning either variants of classical net or nets with new more complex concurrent features (as true concurrent Petri nets). The two formalisms may be linked in various ways. The following proposals are often found in the literature; an "algebraic net" is:

- a net schema (defined as usual) plus marking and labelling functions defined over concrete algebras;
- a net schema (defined as usual) plus marking and labelling functions defined over algebras abstractly denoted by algebraic specifications;
- a combination of a net schema and of the data aspects defined using a pure algebraic approach.

Here we use the words "high-level algebraic Petri net" (shortly HLA net) in the third case, i.e. for those nets using concepts from the field of algebraic specifications for defining labellings, markings and the net behaviour.

Our aim is to develop a "kit", i.e. a set of coordinated theoretical tools for formally defining varieties of HLA nets together with their *dynamic behaviour* (the allowed sequences of transition firings), called in the following *token game*, for a large class of varieties. Clearly also non-high-level and/or non-algebraic varieties of nets could be defined, since obviously black/coloured tokens and inscriptions consisting in natural numbers could be algebraically specified.

Precisely, using the kit, we characterize a particular variety of nets, say XYZ, by appropriate parameters (e.g. defining the form of the transitions, how to choose the transitions to fire, ...), and a particular net of such variety with an initial marking, say N, by other parameters (e.g. defining its tokens, places, transitions, ...); then we build a parametric specification that instantiated with such parameters returns the token game of N. All that is graphically represented in Fig. 1. Moreover the kit can

* This work has been supported by "Progetto Finalizzato Sistemi Informatici e Calcolo Parallelo" of C.N.R. (Italy) and by Esprit-BRA W.G. COMPASS n. 6112.

be extended to cope also with semantics over nets; unfortunately for lack of room we cannot present here this part, see [11].

Fig. 1. A schematic view of the kit

The kit is based on the SMoLCS methodology for the specification of concurrent systems ([3, 4]). SMoLCS has been proved very suitable to this aim since it is an integrate method for specifying processes and adt's and offers the possibility of giving modular and parametric process specifications. Moreover SMoLCS is not based either on a particular kind of concurrency (e.g. interleaving plus binary handshaking communications) or on a particular semantics for the process (e.g. strong bisimulation), but it allows to directly specify how the process components of a system interact among them and which processes should be considered semantically equivalent.

We expect that using this kit it is possible:

- To define a large class of varieties of HLA nets, also the one with non-standard concurrent features, as those of [10]. Since, it is easy to see classical (set based) nets as HLA ones, the kit could be used also for defining classical nets with new concurrent features.
- To relate and compare in a unique setting different varieties of HLA nets.
- To associate with existing varieties of Petri nets a corresponding HLA version; and so, perhaps, to define new varieties of interesting Petri nets.
- To use the software tools, developed for the SMoLCS specifications (see [2]), for the rapid prototyping new (under development) HLA varieties; thus helping also the task of tuning the definition of such new varieties.

This work of defining Petri nets using SMoLCS brings together two different models for concurrency: the Petri nets and the structured concurrent labelled transition systems used by SMoLCS, and so it could also be a starting point for studying the relationships between them; for example [9] presents a specification methodology based on this work which allows to refine in a canonical way a system specified by a Petri net into a distributed realization described using SMoLCS.

Also Meseguer in [15] presents an overall algebraic definition of a particular variety of (coloured) Petri nets using rewriting logic; but there the emphasis is different, he is more interested in showing the generality of his specification formalism than in defining algebraically relevant varieties of nets.

Sect. 1 is a short overview on (HLA) nets, while in Sect. 2 we briefly present the SMoLCS methodology and in Sect. 3 the kit. For lack of room here we cannot show all interesting applications of the kit, in Sect. 4 we just show how to define using the kit an existing variety of HLA nets the CATNets of [10] and a new variety of HLA nets with priorities.

1 Summary of High-Level Algebraic Petri Nets

Petri nets have been developed during the years 1960-62 by C.A. Petri for modelling notions relative to synchronized actions. In the beginning, mainly Place/Transition nets using indistinguishable tokens ("black dots") have been studied.

From a formal point of view a Place/Transition net is an oriented bipartite graph. The set of vertices of such graph is given by $P \cup T$, where P is a set of objects named *places* and T a set of objects named *transitions*. The set of arcs is contained in $(P \times T) \cup (T \times P)$. Each place is annotated by a value representing the number of tokens associated with it and called its *marking*. An arc joining a place with a transition is annotated by a value representing the (input) place minimal marking necessary for enabling the transition. This value also defines (implicitly) the number of tokens that have to be removed if the transition is actually fired. An arc joining a transition with a place is annotated by a value representing the number of tokens that have to be added to the (output) place when the transition is fired.

Given a Place/Transition net with an initial marking, the sequences of firings of of the various enabled groups of transitions is said the *token game* of the net.

Although Place/Transition nets have sufficient power for modelling the control structures of most of the practical systems they are not adequate for modelling systems handling elaborated data structures. This led to developing a number of hybrid net/data models, associating a set of variables with the net and/or attributes with the tokens, which may be modified by transitions firings. The main drawback of hybrid models is that extensions are not conform to the spirit of Petri nets, and that analysis techniques and tools developed for simple nets are no longer applicable. This is probably behind the ideas which have led to developing the so called *high-level* Petri nets in which tokens are data items and arcs and transitions are inscribed with symbolic expressions. The earliest of these are Predicate/Transition nets and Coloured nets. In a coloured net transition firing depends not only on the amount of tokens present in input places but also on their colours. This restriction concerns also removed tokens as well as added ones. A Predicate/Transition net may be seen as a schema of Coloured nets, in the sense that inscriptions are defined at a more abstract level, like for instance defining colour "filtering" by equations associated with transitions.

The main reason for the success of high-level nets is probably that they make it possible to achieve more compact specifications while keeping the possibility of using a wide variety of analysis techniques.

The advent of HLA nets may be seen as a new approach combining the strengths of Petri nets with those of abstract data types. However many of the concepts devised during several years to cope with data structuring in Petri nets, turn out to be representable by well-established concepts from the field of algebraic specifications.

This section is not devoted to recalling the various varieties of HLA nets (see e.g.: [10, 16, 5, 13, 17, 12]). The reader interested in a more detailed study of such nets may, for instance, consult [1].

Let us also remark that, like in Predicate/Transition nets, in HLA nets not only places and arcs are annotated but also transitions. In [12], for instance transitions are annotated by boolean expressions named transition conditions, while in [13] transitions are annotated by equations. Moreover places, transitions and arcs may be annotated not only by single values or expressions but also by sets of inscriptions. In [10] for instance, an input arc is annotated by two distinct inscriptions defining respectively the tokens enabling a transition and those removed by the transition firing in an explicit way. In several varieties of nets, sets of inscriptions are associated with places in order to define their markings, their capacities and even capacities w.r.t. types of markings. According to these extensions a transition becomes enabled when some condition (determined by the inscriptions) on the input places marking is satisfied, the condition associated with the transition is true, and the capacity of the output places is not exceeded by transition firing.

Another feature is the level of abstraction used in syntactic notations. In certain varieties of nets, the marking and the various labelling functions are defined over abstract data types (isomorphim classes of algebras), usually given by an algebraic specification, thus leading to specifications of classes of systems. In other nets the mentioned functions are defined over concrete algebras rather suitable for defining concrete systems.

The several variants of HLA nets may also be distinguished by the way in which their dynamic behaviour is defined. It is worth mentioning that, depending on the level of abstraction used in the syntactic notation, this behaviour is usually defined in one of the following three ways; by defining firing rules similar to those of "low-level" (usual) Petri nets, by defining proper firing rules, or via interpretation into semantically oriented models.

Thus, summarizing, in general, we assume that for defining a HLA net of a certain variety we need to give:

- a conditional algebraic specification (admiting an initial model) of the tokens;
- a net schema, a graph whose nodes are the places and the transitions, decorated by various inscriptions defined using algebraic "ingredients" (as terms and atoms). Fig. 2 presents the general form for the part of a schema connected to a transition. There $P_1, \ldots, P_j$ ($j \geq 0$) are the places appearing only in the preconditions, $P_{j+1}, \ldots, P_q$ ($q \geq j$) those appearing only in the postconditions and $P_{q+1}, \ldots, P_r$ ($r \geq q$) those appearing both in the pre and in the postconditions; for all i $cond_i$ is a term of sort $mset(token)$ representing the tokens that place P_i must contain for allowing the transition to fire, $destr_i$ is a term of sort $mset(token)$ representing the tokens eliminated by place P_i during the transition firing, $taken_i$ is a term of sort $mset(token)$ representing the tokens received by place P_i during the transition firing, and $trans\_cond$ is a conjuction of atoms representing the condition under which the transition may fire.
- the admissible place markings, since in general a place cannot contain whatever multiset of tokens (e.g. in some case there is a limit on the number of the contained tokens, while in other only tokens of a certain sort may mark a place;

- which groups of enabled transitions are allowed to fire simultaneously (the net dynamic behaviour).

Using the kit such ingredients may be defined in an overall algebraic setting.

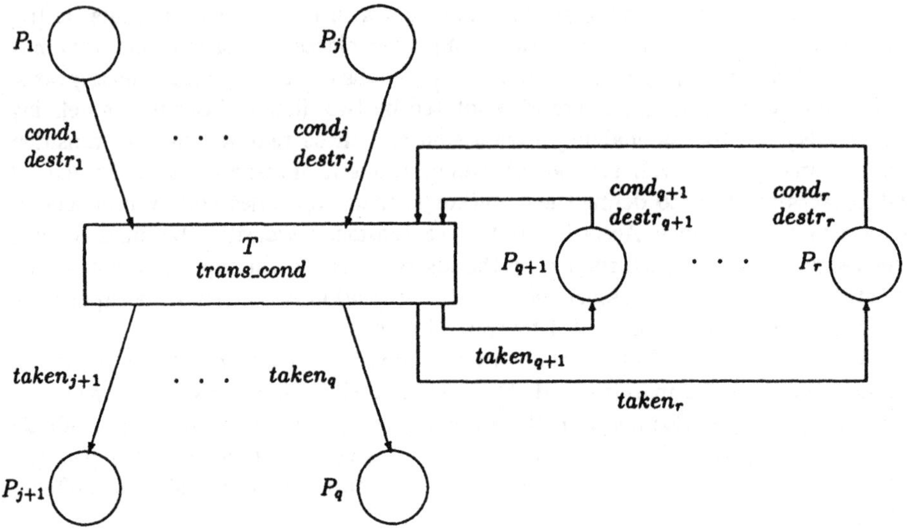

Fig. 2. A generic transition of a net

2 A Short Introduction to SMoLCS

The core of the SMoLCS approach has been developed, mainly by E. Astesiano and G. Reggio at the University of Genova, with a significant contribution by M. Wirsing of the University of Passau, since 1983. While the core of the method has been unchanged, significant improvements and additions have been made since, especially for what concerns semantics, tools and specifications at higher-level of abstraction.

SMoLCS has been applied to significant case-studies, the most important being the specification of the underlying concurrent model in the formal definition of full Ada and two case-studies proposed by ENEL (Italian National Electricity Board).

Here we briefly report the main points of SMoLCS relevant to its use for the definition of the kit, for a full view see, e.g., [3, 4].

Processes are modelled by *labelled transition systems* (shortly *lts*'s). An lts is a triple $(STATE, LAB, \rightarrow)$, where $STATE$ and LAB are two sets and $\rightarrow \subseteq STATE \times LAB \times STATE$; the elements of $STATE$ are the states (intermediate situations of interest) of the processes, $\rightarrow$ represents the possible moves of the processes and the elements of LAB are used to label the moves. Notice that $\rightarrow$ represents move capabilities, i.e. if $(s, l, s') \in \rightarrow$ (written $s \xrightarrow{l} s'$), then a process in the state (situation) s has the capability of passing to state s' performing a move whose interaction with the external (w.r.t. the process) world is represented by l; thus l represents both conditions on the external world for the move to become effective and the transformation of the external world due to such move.

Given an lts we can associate with each process the so called *transition tree*; precisely, a labelled tree whose nodes are decorated by states, whose arcs are decorated by labels, where the order of the branches is not considered, two identically decorated subtrees with the same root are considered as a unique one and there is an arc decorated by l between two nodes decorated respectively by s and s' iff $s \xrightarrow{l} s'$.

Processes are specified by algebraic specifications of lts's and are themselves data as any other; thus they can be manipulated by functions and processes.

SMoLCS supports the user-defined specification of any kind of concurrent structure, communication mechanism (from message passing to shared data) and execution modes (from interleaving to priorities). This support is provided by modularization, hierarchization and parameterization mechanisms for defining and combining specifications of parts of a system, with possibly reusable components of any kind (data, actions, communication and execution mode schemas).

Formally a process is specified by a dynamic specification (i.e. an algebraic specification of an lts), which is as follows.

- A *dynamic signature* $D\Sigma$ is a pair (Σ, DS) where:
  * $\Sigma = (S, OP, PR)$ is a predicate signature,
  * $DS \subseteq S$ (the elements in DS are the *dynamic sorts*, i.e. the sorts corresponding to states of lts's),
  * for all $st \in DS$ there exist a sort $l\text{-}st \in S - DS$ (the sort of the labels) and a predicate $\_ \xrightarrow{\_} \_ : st \times l\text{-}st \times st \in PR$ (the transition predicate).
- A *dynamic algebra* on $D\Sigma$ (shortly $D\Sigma$-algebra) is just a Σ-algebra.
- A pair $(D\Sigma, AX)$, s.t. $D\Sigma$ is a dynamic signature and AX a set of formulae of the form $\wedge_{i=1,\ldots,n}\alpha_i \supset \alpha_{n+1}$ (conditional axioms), where α_i are atoms, i.e., have the form either $t = t'$ or $Pr(t_1, \ldots, t_n)$ with Pr predicate symbol, is called a *(conditional) dynamic specification*.
  The axioms may refer both to static aspects (e.g., values, states of the system) and to the dynamic aspects, i.e. concerning the transitions predicates.
  A conditional dynamic specification has always an initial model which defines the associated lts.

Notice that by algebra we mean usually a total many-sorted algebra with predicates, see [14]; however there are no problems to use, for example, partial or order-sorted algebras.

A support to modular specification of concurrent systems is then given accordingly to the following schema, where we outline the methodological aspects, leaving apart the algebraic formalism.

A *concurrent system* (i.e. a structured process where several active components [other processes] interact among them) is algebraically specified by an lts as follows. The states are a multiset of states of the active components (process), written $p_1 \mid \ldots \mid p_n$.

The moves are specified in several steps, where at each step some partial moves are defined using those defined at the previous step; at the first step the partial moves are defined starting from the moves of process components. It is shown that any specification of a concurrent system may be reduced to a canonical form consisting of the composition of three particular steps, respectively for defining *synchronous moves*, *composing* such moves and *monitoring*, i.e. for deciding which compositions of synchronous moves become moves of the system.

Appropriate algebraic parameterized schemas are given for expressing the three steps; ultimately the specification of a system is a dynamic specification which is an instantiation of a parameterized specification, where the parameters refer to various user defined aspects of the systems concerning dynamics and data. The axioms defining the transition relations for the three steps have particular forms.

By associating with processes an lts we give an operational semantics: two processes are operationally equivalent whenever the associated transition trees are the same. However in most cases such semantics is too fine, since it takes into account all details of the process activity. It may happen that two processes which we consider semantically equivalent have associated different trees (e.g., when the internal moves are not relevant). Thus SMoLCS allows also to define various semantics on the specified systems using a general way to give an observational semantics to a conditional dynamic specification; this approach is very well-suited since it generalizes the Milner-Park's bisimulation technique.

3 A Kit for Defining High-Level Algebraic Petri Nets

Here we present the "kit", i.e. a set of coordinated theoretical tools for formally defining varieties of HLA nets together with their *dynamic behaviour* (the allowed sequences of transition firings), called in the following *token game*, for a large class of varieties. Until now, all varieties of HLA nets that we known (see the various cited papers) could be defined using this kit; also non-high-level and/or non-algebraic nets could be defined, since obviously black/coloured tokens and inscriptions consisting in natural numbers could be algebraically specified.

Precisely, using the kit, we characterize a particular variety of nets, say XYZ, by appropriate parameters (e.g. defining which groups of transitions may fire simultaneously, ...), and a particular net of such variety with an initial marking, say N, by other parameters (e.g. defining the net tokens, places, transitions, ...); then we build a parametric specification that instantiated with such parameters returns the token game of N. All of that is schematically represented in Fig. 1.

Following the SMoLCS methodology we see the token game of a net as the behaviour of a concurrent system and specify such system by a conditional dynamic specification TOKEN_GAME, whose initial model is an algebraic version of an lts (a dynamic algebra) formalizing the net behaviour for all possible initial markings.

TOKEN_GAME as a parameterized specification, whose parameters (schematically represented in Fig. 3) formalize the features of the variety of nets (those on the left) and of the particular net (those on the right) that we are considering.

For specifying a concurrent system, we need to determine its active components and to describe their interactions following the three SMoLCS steps. In this case the active components are the places of the net, their dynamic activity consists in changing their marking by taking part in the firing of the transitions and their mutual interactions are determined by the net transitions.

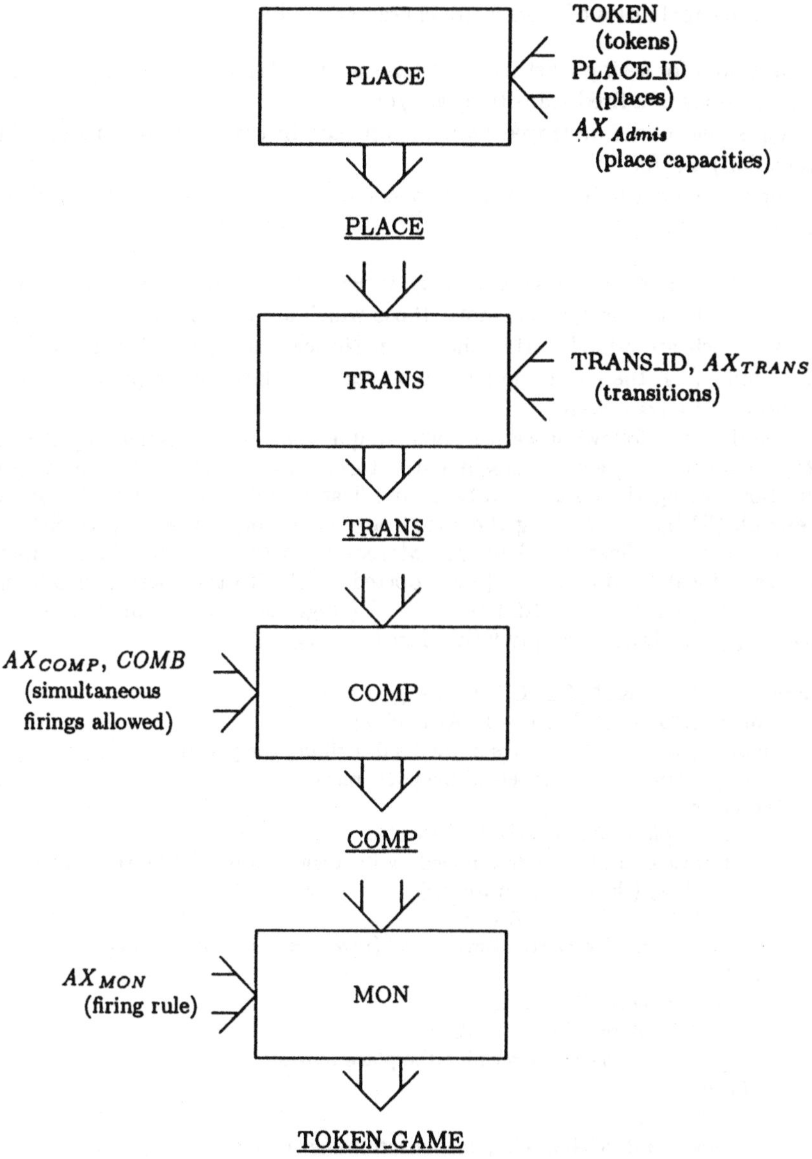

Fig. 3. A schematic view of TOKEN_GAME and of its parameters

The Active Components of TOKEN_GAME The places of the net correspond to the active components of the concurrent system defining the token games and are defined by the parametric dynamic specification PLACE, whose parameters are: an algebraic specification of the tokens of the net TOKEN (with a sort *token*); an algebraic specification PLACE_ID (with a sort *place-id*) stating which are the places of the net and a set of axioms AX_{Admis} defining a predicate "*Admis*: *place-id* × *mset*(*token*)" stating which are the admissible markings of each place.

The move capabilities of a place are characterized by:

- being tested for seeing whether it contains some tokens (when it appears in the preconditions of a fired transition) and/or
- having some tokens destroyed (when it appears in the preconditions of a fired transition) and/or
- taking some other tokens (when it appears in the postconditions of a fired transition);

thus each place move is characterized by three multisets of tokens: those which should contain for performing the move, those which are destroyed during the move and those which are added during the move. Notice that some of these multisets may be empty (e.g. the third one for the moves of a place taking part only in the preconditions of a transition).

Here and in the following we use some simple constructs, inspired by ASL see [18], to give algebraic specifications in a structured way as: $\mathrm{SP}_1 + \mathrm{SP}_2$ denoting the specification having the sorts operations, predicates and axioms of both SP_1 and SP_2; **enrich** SP **by** ... denoting the specification obtained by adding to SP some sorts, operations, predicates and axioms. Moreover, **MSET** denotes the parametric algebraic specification of multisets (not reported here) with the operations $\emptyset$ (empty multiset), $\_ \mid \_$ (union), $\_ - \_$ (difference), $\{\_\}$ (singleton) and the predicate $\_ \subseteq \_$; usually $\{x_1\} \mid \ldots \mid \{x_n\}$ is simply written $x_1 \mid \ldots \mid x_n$.

spec PLACE(TOKEN, PLACE_ID, AX_{Admis}) =
  enrich MSET(TOKEN) + PLACE_ID **by**
  dsorts *place* -- states of the lts describing the places
  sorts *l-place* -- labels of the place moves
  opns
    $\_ : \_ : \textit{place-id} \times \textit{mset(token)} \rightarrow \textit{place}$
  -- a state of a place is determined by its identification and by the actual
  -- marking (the contained tokens)
    $\_\ HAS\ \_\ GIVES\ \_\ TAKES\ \_ :$
      $\textit{place-id} \times \textit{mset(token)} \times \textit{mset(token)} \times \textit{mset(token)} \rightarrow \textit{l-place}$
  preds
    $Admis : \textit{place-id} \times \textit{mset(token)}$
    $\_ \xrightarrow{\_} \_ : \textit{place} \times \textit{l-place} \times \textit{place}$
  -- transition relation describing the place moves
  axioms
    AX_{Admis}
    $cond \subseteq mt \wedge Admis(pi, (mt - destr) | taken) \supset$
      $$pi : mt \xrightarrow{pi\ HAS\ cond\ GIVES\ destr\ TAKES\ taken} pi : (mt - destr) | taken$$

The Synchronous Actions of TOKEN_GAME The synchronous actions (minimal groups of moves of the active components) of the concurrent system describing the token game of a net correspond to the firings of single transitions. Such synchronous actions are formalized by an lts specified by the parametric dynamic specification TRANS (the name recalls that correspond to the net transitions) given below, whose parameters are: an algebraic specification TRANS_ID (with a sort *trans-id*) stating which are the net transitions and a set of axioms AX_{TRANS}, one for each transition, describing the arcs connecting it to the places with the relative inscriptions (thus the net schema).

The axiom corresponding to a transition T of the general form of Fig. 2 is:

$$\bigwedge_{1\le i\le j} \; p_i \xRightarrow{P_i\ HAS\ cond_i\ GIVES\ destr_i\ TAKES\ \emptyset} p'_i \wedge$$
$$\bigwedge_{j+1\le i\le q} \; p_i \xRightarrow{P_i\ HAS\ \emptyset\ GIVES\ \emptyset\ TAKES\ taken_i} p'_i \wedge$$
$$\bigwedge_{q+1\le i\le r} \; p_i \xRightarrow{P_i\ HAS\ cond_i\ GIVES\ destr_i\ TAKES\ taken_i} p'_i \wedge trans\_cond \supset$$
$$p_1 \mid \dots \mid p_j \mid p_{j+1} \mid \dots \mid p_q \mid p_{q+1} \mid \dots \mid p_r \xrightarrow{T} p'_1 \mid \dots \mid p'_j \mid p'_{j+1} \mid \dots \mid p'_q \mid p'_{q+1} \mid \dots \mid p'_r$$

spec TRANS(PLACE, AX_{TRANS}, TRANS_ID) =
  enrich MSET(PLACE) + TRANS_ID **by**
  dsorts *mset(place)*
  preds
    $\_ \xrightarrow{\_} \_ : mset(place) \times trans\text{-}id \times mset(place)$
  -- transition relation describing the synchronous actions
  axioms
    AX_{TRANS}

where PLACE is an instantiation of the parametric specification PLACE given in the previous subsection.

Synchronous Actions Composition of TOKEN_GAME The composition step of the concurrent system corresponding to the token game of a net describes which groups of enabled transitions may be fired together and which is the effect of their simultaneous firings. Also this step is formalized by an lts, whose moves correspond to the allowed synchronous action compositions, specified by the parametric dynamic specification COMP given below.

The various way of composing actions (i.e. synchronous actions and in turn compositions of synchronous actions) represented by means of the corresponding labels are given by some operations $Comb_1, \dots, Comb_k$ (for simplicity here we assume that they are all binary operations but we can also consider combinators with different arities). How to compose synchronous actions is given by a set of axioms AX_{COMP} of the form either

$cond(t, t') \supset Comb_j(t, t') = t''$, for some j, $1 \le j \le k$

defining the action combinators, or

$$\bigwedge_{i=1,\dots,n} mp_i \xrightarrow{t_i} mp'_i \wedge cond(t_1, \dots, t_h) \supset$$
$$mp_{r_1} \mid \dots \mid mp_{r_h} \mid mp \xrightarrow{t} mp'_{s_1} \mid \dots \mid mp'_{s_k} \mid mp$$

defining the effect of the compound actions, where $cond(t, t')$, $cond(t_1, \dots, t_h)$ are conjuctions of atoms, $\{r_1, \dots, r_h\} \subseteq \{1, \dots, n\}$, $\{s_1, \dots, s_k\} \subseteq \{1, \dots, n\}$ and t is a term obtained by combining the terms $t_1, \dots, t_h$ using only the operations $Comb_1$, $\dots$, $Comb_k$. where t_i's and t are terms, *cond* a formula, mp_i, mp'_i's variables not appearing in *cond*, $\{r_1, \dots, r_h\} \subseteq \{1, \dots, n\}$ and $\{s_1, \dots, s_k\} \subseteq \{1, \dots, n\}$.

The above form is very general, but it include various useful and interesting ways of composing synchronous actions, as:

- parallel composition: the axioms have the form

$\bigwedge_{i=1,\ldots,n} mp_i \xrightarrow{t_i} mp'_i \wedge cond \supset mp_1 \mid \ldots \mid mp_n \mid mp \xrightarrow{t} mp'_1 \mid \ldots \mid mp'_n \mid mp$;

- sequential composition: the axioms have the form

$mp \xrightarrow{t} mp' \wedge mp' \xrightarrow{t'} mp'' \wedge cond \supset mp \xrightarrow{t''} mp''$;

- sequential composition of serializable actions: the axioms have the form

$mp \xrightarrow{t_1} mp'_1 \wedge mp \xrightarrow{t_2} mp'_2 \wedge$

$mp'_1 \xrightarrow{t_2} mp' \wedge mp'_2 \xrightarrow{t_1} mp' \wedge cond \supset mp \xrightarrow{t} mp'$.

This very general form of composition is needed for example to define either the true concurrent nets of [10] or nets where groups of enabled disjoint transitions (i.e. involving disjoint sets of places) are allowed to fire simultaneously.

spec COMP(<u>TRANS</u>, $\{Comb_1, \ldots, Comb_k\}$, AX_{COMP}) =
    enrich <u>TRANS</u> **by**
    opns
        $Comb_1, \ldots, Comb_k$: *trans-id* × *trans-id* → *trans-id*
    axioms
        AX_{COMP}

where <u>TRANS</u> is an instantiation of the parameterized specification TRANS given in the previous subsection.

The Monitoring of TOKEN_GAME The final moves of the concurrent system describing the token game of a net consist of the execution of one of the compositions of synchronous actions (composition of net transitions) described in the previous step; so at this step we can decide which of such compositions are allowed to fire. Also this step is formalized by an lts, specified by the parametric dynamic specification MON given below.

spec MON(<u>COMP</u>, AX_{MON}) =
    enrich <u>COMP</u> **by**
    preds
        _ $\overset{-}{\rightsquigarrow}$> _: *mset(place)* × *trans-id* × *mset(place)*
    axioms
        AX_{MON}

where <u>COMP</u> is an instantiation of the specification COMP given in the previous subsection and AX_{MON} is a set of axiom of the form

$mp \xrightarrow{t} mp' \wedge cond(t, mp \mid mp_1) \supset mp \mid mp_1 \overset{t}{\rightsquigarrow\!>} mp' \mid mp_1$

with $cond(t, mp \mid mp_1)$ conjiuction of atoms. The places in mp_1 are those not involved in the firing of the (group of) transitions.

The Whole Definition of TOKEN_GAME Using the parametric specifications defined in the previous subsection, now we are able to give the parametric specification TOKEN_GAME:

TOKEN_GAME(TOKEN, PLACE_ID, AX_{Admis},
        TRANS_ID, AX_{TRANS},
        COMB, AX_{COMP},
        AX_{MON}) =
MON(<u>COMP</u>, AX_{MON})

where $\underline{\text{COMP}} = \text{COMP}(\underline{\text{TRANS}}, COMB, AX_{COMP})$,

$\underline{\text{TRANS}} = \text{TRANS}(\underline{\text{PLACE}}, \text{TRANS\_ID}, AX_{TRANS})$ and

$\underline{\text{PLACE}} = \text{PLACE}(\text{TOKEN}, \text{PLACE\_ID}, AX_{Admis})$.

The initial model I of an appropriate instantiation of TOKEN_GAME (that exists, since it is a conditional specifications, see [18]) is a (dynamic) algebra determining an lts, with states $I_{mset(place)}$ (corresponding to the various markings of the net), labels $I_{trans\text{-}id}$ corresponding to possible groups of transitions which may fire together and transition relation $\overset{I}{\rightsquigarrow}$ describing the net firing sequences.

Composing Nets The kit offers also a way to define a complex net putting together the specifications associated with its subparts using the well-known operations for modularly defining algebraic specifications, as sum, rename and instantiations of parametric schemas.

For example let N_1 and N_2 be two nets of the same variety and TK_1, TK_2 be the specifications of their token games given using the kit. Now the specification of token game of the net N_3, which is the composition of N_1 and of N_2 (i.e. the net having the tokens, the places and the transitions of both N_1 and of N_2, where the common ones are taken once) is simply $TK_3 = TK_1 + TK_2$.
Recall that "+" is the ASL-like sum of specifications, thus in TK_3 the sorts *token*, *place-id*, *trans-id*, ... of TK_1 and of TK_2 are identified and have both the elements specified in TK_1 and those TK_2.

4 Using the Kit

The CATNets Defined Using the Kit We use our kit to define the CATNets of [10]; they are HLA nets following the schema of Sect. 1, whose most distinctive feature is that at each step groups of enabled transitions which are "truly concurrent" (i.e. that after firing one of them, the others may still fire) are fired simultaneously.

The parameters for instantiating TOKEN_GAME in this case are as follows.

The tokens

> **spec** TOKEN =
> **enrich** TOK **by**
> **sorts** *token*
> **opns**
> $\{ S_{tok}: tok \rightarrow token \mid tok \text{ sort of TOK } \}$

The places

> **spec** PLACE_ID =
> **sorts** *place-id*
> **opns**
> $P_1, \ldots, P_k: \rightarrow place\text{-}id$ -- $P_1, \ldots, P_k$ are the the places of the net

The admissible place markings They are defined by the following axioms:

$mt \subseteq mt' \supset Admis(P, mt)$;

for each place P whose capacity is represented by the ground term mt';

$\{Admis(P, S_{tok}(t_1) \mid \ldots \mid S_{tok}(t_r)) \mid r \geq 0\}$

for each place P with infinite capacity whose associate sort is *tok*.

The transitions

> **spec** <u>TRANS_ID</u> =
> **sorts** *trans-id*
> **opns**
> $T_1, \ldots, T_h$: $\rightarrow$ *trans-id* -- $T_1, \ldots, T_h$ are the net transitions

The axioms defining the transitions are given as explained in Sect. 3.

The transition composition There are two transition compositors: _ // _ (parallel composition) and _ ; _ (serializable sequential composition) and the set of axiom defining the transition compositions is

$t;t' = t';t \quad t;(t';t'') = (t;t');t''$

$t//t' = t'//t \quad t//(t'//t'') = (t//t')//t''$

- -";" and "//" are commutative and associative

$mp \xrightarrow{t} mp' \supset mp \mid mp_1 \xrightarrow{t} mp' \mid mp_1$

$mp_1 \xrightarrow{t_1} mp_1' \wedge mp_2 \xrightarrow{t_2} mp_2' \supset mp_1 \mid mp_2 \xrightarrow{t_1//t_2} mp_1' \mid mp_2'$

- - if two disjoint transitions are both enabled, then they may fire simultaneously

$mp \xrightarrow{t_1} mp_1' \wedge mp \xrightarrow{t_2} mp_2' \wedge mp_1' \xrightarrow{t_2} mp' \wedge mp_2'' \xrightarrow{t_1} mp' \supset$

- - if t_1 and t_2 are enabled and t_2 is enabled after firing t_1 and t_1 is enabled after
- - firing t_2 then

$$mp \xrightarrow{t_1;t_2} mp'$$

- - t_1 and t_2 may be sequentially composed

The transitions which are actually fired

$mp \xrightarrow{t} mp' \supset mp \mid mp_1 \overset{t}{\rightsquigarrow} mp' \mid mp_1$

In [11] it is shown that this definition of CATNets coincides with the one of [10].

High-Level Algebraic Nets with Priorities We use our kit to define a new variety of HLA nets following the general schema of Sect. 1, where the transitions are totally ordered w.r.t. a degree of urgency $<$ (that we call priority order) to be intended as follows: whatever in a net with a certain marking two transitions are enabled, say T and T', s.t. $T < T'$ in the priority order, then it cannot happen that T is fired while T' is not. These HLA nets have been inspired by the classical nets with priorities of [7].

For what concerns the firing of transitions we assume in this case that at each step only one transition may fire (thus there is no way to compose transitions) and that in the case of several enabled transitions the maximum one w.r.t. the priority order is chosen; however using the kit we may consider also the case where several enabled transitions fire together respecting the priorities.

In Fig. 4 we present an example of these nets describing a buffer, where reading takes priority over writing; with such marking first READ will fire, then WRITE will fire twice.

The parameters for instantiating TOKEN_GAME are as follows.

The tokens and the places They are defined as in the previous subsection.

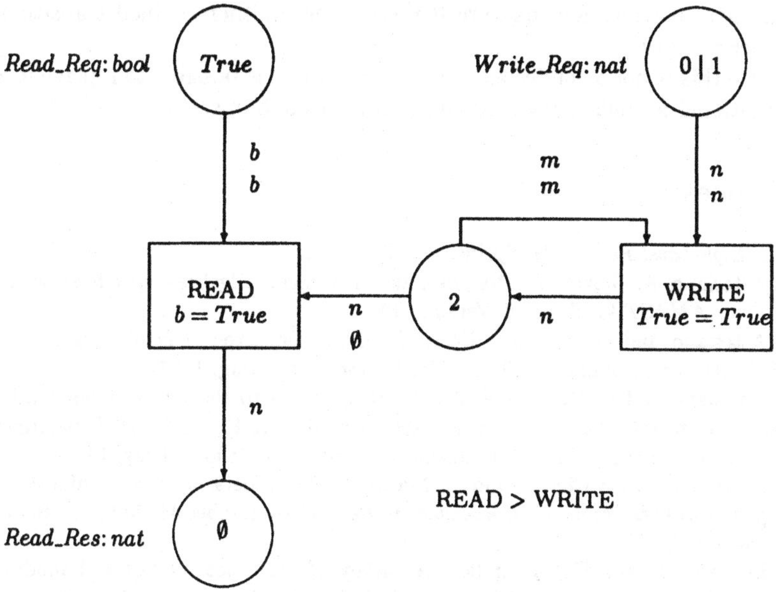

Fig. 4. A buffer specified using a HLA net with priorities

The admissible place markings They are defined by the following axioms:
$\{Admis(P, S_{tok}(t_1) \mid \ldots \mid S_{tok}(t_r)) \mid r \geq 0\}$
for each place P whose associate sort is *tok*.

The transitions Assume that the priority order of the net is $T_1 < \ldots < T_h$.

spec <u>TRANS_ID</u> =
  sorts *trans-id*
  opns
    $T_1, \ldots, T_n$: → *trans-id*
  preds
    _ < _: *trans-id* × *trans-id*
  axioms
    $T_1 < T_2 \quad \ldots \quad T_{h-1} < T_h$

The axioms defining the transitions are given as explained in Sect. 3; e.g. the axiom associated with the transition WRITE of the net in Fig. 4 is

$$pb \xRightarrow{Cont\ HAS\ m\ GIVES\ m\ TAKES\ n} pb' \wedge$$
$$pw \xRightarrow{Write\_Req\ HAS\ n\ GIVES\ n\ TAKES\ \emptyset} pw' \supset pb \mid pw \xrightarrow{\text{WRITE}} pb' \mid pw'$$

The transition composition The set of combinators and the set of axioms defining the transition composition are empty, since in this case no transitions can be fired simultaneously.

The transitions which are actually fired

$$mp \xrightarrow{t} mp' \wedge (\nexists t', \underline{mp}, \underline{mp'} \,.\, t' > t \wedge \underline{mp} \subseteq mp \mid mp_1 \wedge \underline{mp} \xrightarrow{t'} \underline{mp'}) \supset$$
$$mp \mid mp_1 \overset{t}{\leadsto} mp' \mid mp_1$$

(an enabled transition may fire if there is no another enabled transition with higher priority)
Notice this is not a conditional axiom, however it is possible to replace it with a conditional formula using auxiliary predicates and operations.

References

1. ___. *High-Level Petri Nets.* Springer Verlag, 1991.
2. E. Astesiano, A. Giovini, F. Morando, and G. Reggio. Algebraic specification at work. In *Proc. AMAST'91.* Springer Verlag, 1992.
3. E. Astesiano and G. Reggio. SMoLCS-driven concurrent calculi. In *Proc. TAPSOFT'87, Vol. 1,* number 249 in L.N.C.S. Springer Verlag, 1987.
4. E. Astesiano and G. Reggio. A structural approach to the formal modelization and specification of concurrent systems. Technical Report PDISI-92-01, Dipartimento di Informatica e Scienze dell'Informazione, Università di Genova, Italy, 1992.
5. E. Battiston, F. De Cindio, and G. Mauri. OBJSA nets: a class of high-level nets having objects as domains. In *Advances in Petri Nets,* number 340 in L.N.C.S. Springer Verlag, 1988.
6. L. Berardinello and F. De Cindio. A survey of basic net models and modular net classes. In *Advances in Petri Nets,* L.N.C.S. Springer Verlag, 1992. To appear.
7. E. Best and M. Koutny. Petri net semantics of priority systems. *T.C.S.*, 96, 1992.
8. M. Bettaz. An association of algebraic term nets and abstract data types for specifying real communication protocols. In *Recent Trends in Data Type Specification,* number 534 in L.N.C.S. Springer Verlag, 1991.
9. M. Bettaz, A. Choutri, and G. Reggio. A life-cycle for parallel and distributed systems based on two models of concurrency. In *Proc. of Second Euromicro Workshop for Parallel and Distributed Processing.* IEEE Computer Society, 1993. To appear.
10. M. Bettaz and M. Maouche. How to specify nondeterminism and true concurrency with algebraic term nets. In *Recent Trends in Data Type Specification,* number 655 in L.N.C.S. Springer-Verlag, 1992.
11. M. Bettaz and G. Reggio. A SmoLCS based kit for defining the high-level algebraic Petri nets and their semantics. In Preparation, 1993.
12. J. Billington. Many-sorted high level nets. In *Proceedings of the Third International Workshop on Petri Nets and Performance Models,* Japan, 1989.
13. C. Dimitrovici and U. Hummert. Composition of algebraic high-level nets. In *Recent Trends in Data Type Specification,* number 534 in L.N.C.S. Springer Verlag, 1991.
14. J. Goguen and J. Meseguer. Models and equality for logic programming. In *Proc. TAPSOFT'87, Vol. 2,* number 250 in L.N.C.S. Springer Verlag, 1987.
15. J. Meseguer. Rewriting as a unified model of concurrency. *TCS,* 96, 1992.
16. W. Reisig. Petri nets and algebraic specifications. *TCS,* 80, 1991.
17. J. Vautherin. Parallel system specifications with coloured Petri nets and algebraic data types. In *Advances in Petri Nets,* number 266 in L.N.C.S. Springer Verlag, 1987.
18. M. Wirsing. Algebraic specifications. In *Handbook of Theoret. Comput. Sci.*, volume B. Elsevier, 1990.

Institutions for Very Abstract Specifications*

M. Cerioli and G. Reggio

Dipartimento di Informatica e Scienze dell'Informazione, Università di Genova
Viale Benedetto XV, 3 – 16132 Genova – Italy
e-mail: {cerioli, reggio}@disi.unige.it

Introduction

This paper is a first attempt at the definition of a set of operations on specification frameworks, supporting the modular construction of formal software specification methodologies.

Since obviously a formalism providing tools to deal with all possible software specification features, if any, would be a *monster* and would become out of date in a short time, in our opinion the first step, in order to produce formal specifications, is to get a framework including all the features needed by the particular problem under examination, but as simple as possible. Following an obvious reuse principle, the best way to get such a framework is to assemble pieces of formalisms, studied once and forever, or to tune an available formalism, adding only the "local" features.

As a simple example, think of lifting an existing algebraic approach, where just sentences without variables can be used to axiomatize the data types, to a richer formalism, where also formulae with variables are at hand.

In this paper, following the well-established approach by Goguen and Burstall (see e.g. [4, 5]), specification frameworks are formalized as *institutions*; thus enrichments and assembling of formalisms become, in this setting, operations among institutions.

The need for such a modular approach to the formalism construction has already been sporadically addressed in the literature. Consider for instance the *duplex institutions* by Goguen and Burstall [5], where an institution is built whose sentences comes from two input institutions, also applied in the database field by Fiadeiro and Reichwein [11]. Another example is the *extension by universal closure* by Sannella and Tarlecki [12], of a given institution and a set of its signature morphisms, where sentences are enriched along these signature morphisms regarding the extra-symbols as variables universally quantified. Moreover the *institution of implementation specifications* by Beierle and Voss [3] enrich an institution by tools to deal with implementation.

Here we present two more operations on institutions, that are originated by abstracting from the definition of several institutions for *very abstract specifications* in the field of concurrency: very abstract entity specifications [1], very abstract entity specifications with temporal logic [2], very abstract entity specifications with event

* This work has been partially supported by Esprit-BRA W.G. n.6112 Compass, Progetto Finalizzato Sistemi Informatici e Calcolo Parallelo of C.N.R. (Italy), MURST-40% Modelli e Specifiche di Sistemi Concorrenti

logic [1, 9], each one in several variants, like with first-order, conditional, equational logic, with partial, non-strict, generalized models and so on.

Let us informally discuss the meaning of "very abstract". Every institution $\mathcal{I}$ defines some syntactic structures and offers a formal framework where to discuss, work on, and specify models on such syntaxes, giving an interpretation to the various syntactic elements (quite often algebras of some kind on signatures). Now we want to define a "very abstract institution", where to be able to express properties about not only the models on such syntaxes (i.e. about the interpretations), but also the syntaxes themselves (i.e. about the structure of the models). In this new setting we can characterize larger classes of models, having not all the same syntax, but whose syntaxes satisfy some conditions; thus we call specifications in this new institution very abstract.

An application of the very abstract operation in the field of abstract data types is the prove that the hyper-loose algebraic specifications by Pepper (see [7]), whose models on Σ are Σ'-algebras on some Σ' "extending" Σ, is an institution. **GIANNA** A specification in this institution describe classes of algebras sharing a common syntax and satisfying properties on such common part, but with possibly some more structure, analogously to software realizations of a module, that are allowed to have, besides the operations required by the interface, further internal operations. However the sentences in this institution are the same as in the parameter institution, so that properties on the syntax of the specifications cannot be imposed. Extending also the sentences, here we get the institution of very abstract data types, which supports the specification of high-level requirements on modules also about their interfaces (e.g. constraints either in the number of operations or on the number of arguments of the operations, due to limits of the admissible implementations).

Let us consider, now, the institution of entity algebras, see [8], providing a formal framework for algebraic specifications of concurrent systems, where some signature operations are used to explicitly describe the concurrent structure (i.e. to define the system components, both static and dynamic, and the system architecture). Thus very abstract specifications (built on the entity institution) describe classes of entity algebras on possibly different signatures, i.e. formal models of systems with possibly different concurrent structures, satisfying common properties.

Besides these examples, the very abstract operation has many other interesting and useful concrete applications, already used in some industrial case studies of the specification, at different levels of abstraction, of a substation for the electric power distribution (see [10]).

The definition of the very abstract operation can be modularly described as the composition of two basic operations on institutions: ABSTRACT, that abstracts the models on a signature Σ, by regarding as abstract Σ-models the actual models on each "extension" of Σ, and EXTEND, that extends the set of sentences, so that formulas about signature properties are allowed (but this operation is far more general and can be used, for example, to add in a uniform way logical operators, e.g. the equality).

The arguments of ABSTRACT are an institution and a family of signature "extensions", that are signature morphism satisfying some technical conditions. Thus, as the other parameters only depends on the signature category, the proof of the existence of such parameters can be shared by all institutions with the same syntactic part. In particular here we show the construction of signature extensions for the many-sorted signatures (with predicates), so that the same construction can be used for most "algebraic" institutions (e.g. institutions with partial or non-strict models and with every logic).

The paper is organized as follows. The operations ABSTRACT and EXTEND are introduced in Sect. 1 and 2, respectively. In Sect. 3 we apply them to get some interesting very abstract institutions, including the very abstract entity institution and the very abstract data types institution.

1 Abstracting Models w.r.t. Syntax

This section is devoted to the definition of an operation ABSTRACT that applied on a logical framework $\mathcal{I}$ yields a framework over $\mathcal{I}$, where more abstract specifications can be given, characterizing larger classes of models, that are required to provide a semantic counterpart for the specification syntax, but can have some extra-structure. A classical example of such a specification is the mathematical habit of regarding rings or fields as groups, without explicitly forgetting the product (the unity and the inverse) operations; indeed the models of the meta-specification "groups" need to have a group structure, but are as well allowed to have more operations. A more applicative example is the definition of software modules realizing a data type; indeed any such module is required to associate a function with each operation of the data type, but it is quite common in the practice to have (private) local definitions, different for every actual module, giving to the module an extra-structure.

1.1 The Parameters of ABSTRACT

Using the concept of *institution* (see e.g. [4, 5]) to represent logical frameworks, we define an operation on institutions yielding a new institution with the same syntax of its argument, i.e. with the same signatures and sentences, but whose models are, for each signature, the models of the original institution on each "extension" of the signature.

Let us recall the definition of institution (see e.g. [4]) and then introduce the basic ingredients needed to generalize the class of models on a signature.

Definition 1. An *institution* $\mathcal{I}$ consists of a category **Sign** of *signatures*, a functor Sen: **Sign** $\to$ **Set** giving the set of *sentences* over a signature, a functor Mod: **Sign** $\to$ $\mathbf{Cat}^{\mathbf{Op}}$ giving the category of *models* on a signature, and a *satisfaction relation* $\models \subseteq |Mod(\Sigma)| \times Sen(\Sigma)$ for each Σ object in **Sign**, sometimes denoted by $\models_\Sigma$, such that for each morphism $\phi: \Sigma \to \Sigma'$ in **Sign**, the *satisfaction condition*

$$M' \models_{\Sigma'} Sen(\phi)(\xi) \iff Mod(\phi)(M') \models_\Sigma \xi$$

holds for each M' in $|Mod(\Sigma')|$ and each ξ in $Sen(\Sigma)$. □

Let us fix an institution $\mathcal{I} = (\mathbf{Sign}, Sen, Mod, \models)$ and discuss the parameters for getting a institution $\mathcal{H}$ = ABSTRACT$(\mathcal{I}, \ldots)$ based on $\mathcal{I}$. These elements and their properties are summarized in tables enclosed by boxes.

Intuitively in $\mathcal{H}$ a signature Σ represents the minimal structure that its models have, but the models can have a richer structure than the one explicitly described by Σ; thus the Σ-models in $\mathcal{H}$ are the Σ'-models in $\mathcal{I}$, for some Σ' which "extends" Σ. In most examples signatures are structured (families of) sets, so that extensions are simply set-inclusions and hence correspond to a particular subclass of signature morphisms; this leads to consider the class of these morphisms, called *admissible*, as one of the ABSTRACT parameters. Note that two minimal requirements have to be imposed on this class: that the identities are admissible, corresponding to the intuition that each signature is the trivial extension of itself, and that the class of admissible morphisms is closed under composition, because extending an extension should result in an extension, too.

$\mathbf{HAMor} = \{\mathbf{HAMor}(\Sigma, \Sigma')\}_{\Sigma, \Sigma' \in |\mathbf{Sign}|}$ s.t. for all $\Sigma, \Sigma', \Sigma'' \in |\mathbf{Sign}|$

- $\mathbf{HAMor}(\Sigma, \Sigma')$ is a (possibly empty) set of morphisms from Σ into Σ';
- $Id_\Sigma \in \mathbf{HAMor}(\Sigma, \Sigma)$ (identities are admissible morphisms)
- if $m \in \mathbf{HAMor}(\Sigma, \Sigma')$ and $m' \in \mathbf{HAMor}(\Sigma', \Sigma'')$, then $m' \cdot m \in \mathbf{HAMor}(\Sigma, \Sigma'')$

Admissible morphisms

Here and in the following we write $m: \Sigma \hookrightarrow \Sigma'$ to denote that m is an admissible morphism from Σ into Σ'; moreover we simply write $A_{|m}$ for $Mod(m)(A)$. Given $\Sigma, \Sigma' \in |\mathbf{Sign}|$, we say that Σ' *extends* Σ iff there exists an admissible morphism in $\mathbf{HAMor}(\Sigma, \Sigma')$.

It is now possible to define the abstract models on any signature Σ, that are pairs $<A, m>$, for $m: \Sigma \hookrightarrow \Sigma'$ and $A \in |Mod(\Sigma')|$; note that we need to keep track of the way Σ' extends Σ, because in general Σ' may be an extension of Σ in different ways, as several morphisms with the same domain and codomain can be admissible.

Let us consider now the arrows between these new models, in order to get a category. Since abstract models are pairs, also a morphism between two such models, say from $<A, m_1: \Sigma \hookrightarrow \Sigma'>$ into $<B, m_2: \Sigma \hookrightarrow \Sigma''>$, is a pair of arrows between the corresponding components. The second element is an arrow from m_1 into m_2 (seen as objects of the comma category $\Sigma \downarrow \mathbf{Sign}_{\mathbf{HAMor}}$, where $\mathbf{Sign}_{\mathbf{HAMor}}$ is the sub-category of $\mathbf{Sign}$ with arrows in $\mathbf{HAMor}$), i.e. an admissible morphism $m: \Sigma' \hookrightarrow \Sigma''$ in $\mathbf{HAMor}$ s.t. the following diagram commutes

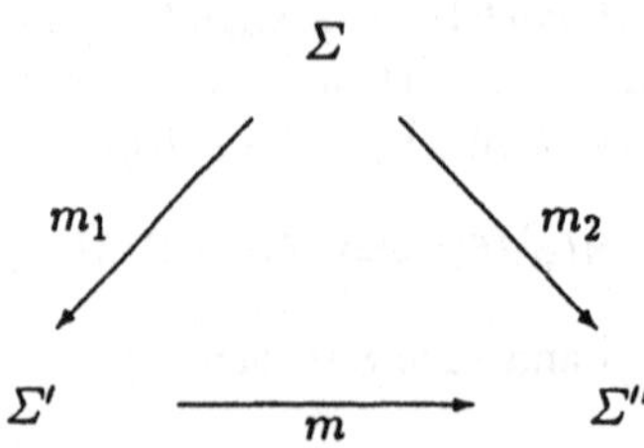

Thus, if such an m exists, B is an algebra on an extension of the actual signature of A and hence it is natural to choose as first component of the model morphism, a Σ-morphism from A into $B_{|m}$, preserving all the structure of A and not only the minimal required by Σ.

There is (at least) another natural choice of the model morphisms in $HMod(\Sigma)$, that is to have as morphisms from $<A, m_1 : \Sigma \hookrightarrow \Sigma'>$ into $<B, m_2 : \Sigma \hookrightarrow \Sigma''>$ the Σ-morphisms in $Mod(\Sigma)$ from $A_{|m_1}$ into $B_{|m_2}$. However in this way the morphisms do not depend on the extra-structure of Σ' and Σ'', and hence two abstract models, $<A, m>$ and $<B, m>$ on the same extension can be isomorphic if their restriction along m are such, while A and B are not even related by a homomorphism either way. Instead, following our choice, two abstract models (on the same extension) are isomorphic in the new institution iff they are isomorphic in the starting institution, accordingly with the intuition that the nature of the specified models is the same and in the new institution we are only able to specify "bigger" classes of original models.

Definition 2. For every $\Sigma \in |\mathbf{Sign}|$, the category $HMod(\Sigma)$ is defined by:

Objects $|HMod(\Sigma)| = \{<A, m> \mid m \in \mathbf{HAMor}(\Sigma, \Sigma'), A \in |Mod(\Sigma')|\}$;
Morphisms $HMod(\Sigma)(<A, m_1 : \Sigma \hookrightarrow \Sigma'>, <B, m_2 : \Sigma \hookrightarrow \Sigma''>) =$
$\{<p, m> \mid m \in \mathbf{HAMor}(\Sigma', \Sigma''), m \cdot m_1 = m_2 \text{ and } p \in Mod(\Sigma')(A, B_{|m})\}$;
Identities $Id_{<A, m:\Sigma \hookrightarrow \Sigma'>} = <Id_A, Id_{\Sigma'}>$;
Composition $<p, m : \Sigma' \hookrightarrow \Sigma''> \cdot <q, m' : \Sigma'' \hookrightarrow \Sigma'''> = <p \cdot q_{|m}, m' \cdot m>$. □

A graphical view of this composition is given below.

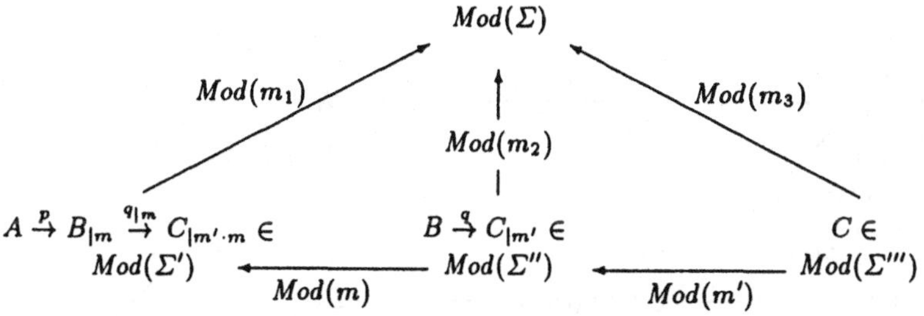

Proposition 3. *For every $\Sigma \in |\mathbf{Sign}|$, $HMod(\Sigma)$ is a category.* □

In order to generalize the above definition of $HMod(\Sigma)$ to a functor on **Sign**, a family of functors $HMod(\phi)$, for every $\phi \in \mathbf{Sign}(\Sigma_1, \Sigma_2)$, has to be defined, preserving identities and composition. To define such any $HMod(\phi)$, since the Σ_2-objects in $\mathcal{H}$ are $\mathcal{I}$-models on extensions of Σ_2, we need a uniform way of building extensions of Σ_1 starting from the Σ_2-extensions. Thus in the following definition we introduce a new ingredient for the $\mathcal{H}$-construction.

It is worth to note that the conditions 1 and 2 are needed for $HMod(\phi)$ to be a functor, while 3, 4 and 5 are needed for $HMod$ to be a functor, too, i.e. that preserves composition and identities in **Sign**.

Definition 4. A *backward extension* on a class **HAMor** of admissible morphisms in **Sign**, consists of a signature $\mathtt{sig}(\phi, m)$, a morphism $\mathtt{mor}(\phi, m) : \mathtt{sig}(\phi, m) \to \Sigma_2'$ and an admissible morphism $\mathtt{amor}(\phi, m) : \Sigma_1 \hookrightarrow \mathtt{sig}(\phi, m)$ for each signature morphism $\phi: \Sigma_1 \to \Sigma_2$ and each admissible morphism $m: \Sigma_2 \hookrightarrow \Sigma_2' \in$ **HAMor** satisfying the following conditions [2]:

1. The following diagram commutes, i.e. $m \cdot \phi = \mathtt{mor}(\phi, m) \cdot \mathtt{amor}(\phi, m)$:

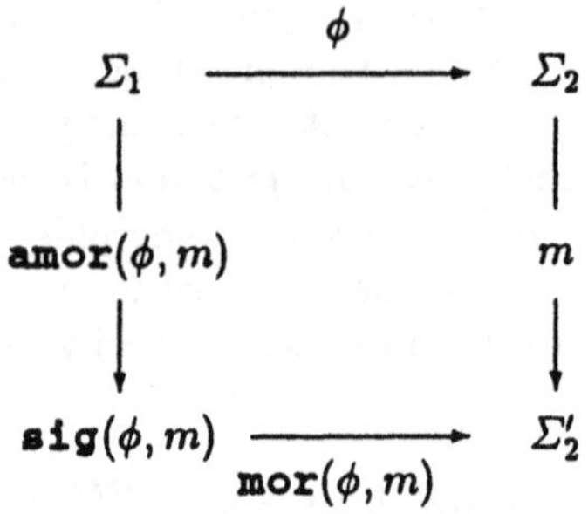

2. The choice of **sig**, **mor** and **amor** is natural w.r.t. the second argument:
   (a) $\mathtt{sig}(\phi, m' \cdot m) = \mathtt{sig}(\mathtt{mor}(\phi, m), m')$;
   (b) $\mathtt{mor}(\phi, m' \cdot m) = \mathtt{mor}(\mathtt{mor}(\phi, m), m')$;
   (c) $\mathtt{amor}(\phi, m' \cdot m) = \mathtt{amor}(\mathtt{mor}(\phi, m), m') \cdot \mathtt{amor}(\phi, m)$;

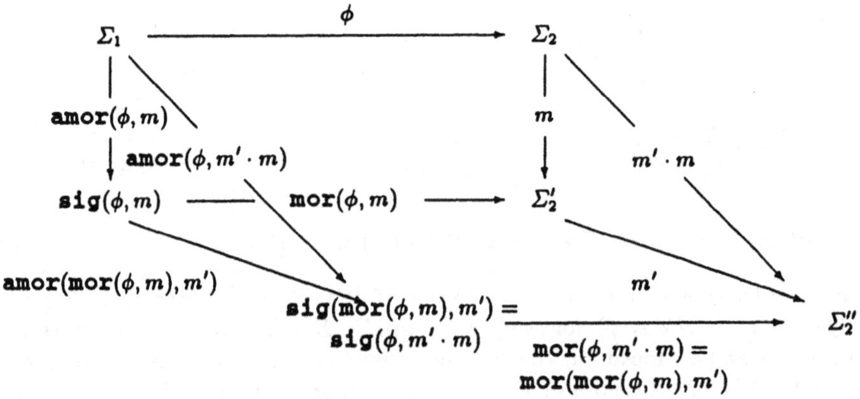

3. The choice of **sig**, **mor** and **amor** is natural w.r.t. the first argument:
   (a) $\mathtt{sig}(\phi_2 \cdot \phi_1, m) = \mathtt{sig}(\phi_1, \mathtt{amor}(\phi_2, m))$;
   (b) $\mathtt{mor}(\phi_2 \cdot \phi_1, m) = \mathtt{mor}(\phi_2, m) \cdot \mathtt{mor}(\phi_1, \mathtt{amor}(\phi_2, m))$;
   (c) $\mathtt{amor}(\phi_2 \cdot \phi_1, m) = \mathtt{amor}(\phi_1, \mathtt{amor}(\phi_2, m))$;

[2] Note that the (a)-conditions at points 2, 3, 4 and 5 folllow from the corresponding (b)-conditions (and/or from the (c)-conditions) and are mentioned for the sake of clearness.

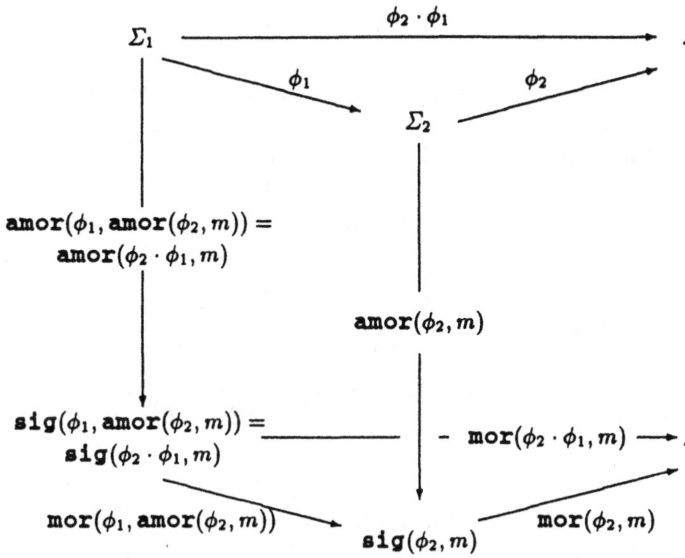

4. The identity as first argument is preserved:
   (a) $\mathbf{sig}(Id_{\delta_0(m)}, m) = \delta_1(m)$;
   (b) $\mathbf{mor}(Id_{\delta_0(m)}, m) = Id_{\delta_1(m)}$;
   (c) $\mathbf{amor}(Id_{\delta_0(m)}, m) = m$.
5. The identity as second argument is preserved:
   (a) $\mathbf{sig}(\phi, Id_{\delta_1(\phi)}) = \delta_0(\phi)$;
   (b) $\mathbf{mor}(\phi, Id_{\delta_1(\phi)}) = \phi$;
   (c) $\mathbf{amor}(\phi, Id_{\delta_1(\phi)}) = Id_{\delta_0(\phi)}$. □

Since any backward extension on **HAMor** is sufficient to define a model functor, a backward extension is the last parameter of the operation we are describing.

sig, **amor**, **mor**
Backward extensions on **HAMor**

Proposition 5. *Let $\mathcal{I}$ = (**Sign**, Sen, Mod, $\models$) be an institution and* **sig**, **amor**, **mor** *be a backward extension on a class* **HAMor** *of admissible morphisms. For every $\phi \in$ **Sign**(Σ_1, Σ_2), let $HMod(\phi): HMod(\Sigma_2) \to HMod(\Sigma_1)$ be defined by:*

- *on objects*
  $HMod(\phi)(<A, m: \Sigma_2 \hookrightarrow \Sigma_2'>) =$
  $<Mod(\mathbf{mor}(\phi, m))(A), \mathbf{amor}(\phi, m): \Sigma_1 \hookrightarrow \mathbf{sig}(\phi, m)>$
  for every $<A, m> \in |HMod(\Sigma_2)|$, i.e. the admissible morphism m is translated into the admissible morphism provided by the backward extensions and the model A is accordingly translated along the (model-interpretation of) the extension of ϕ, as the front side of the following picture shows (the back side reminds the syntactic counterpart):

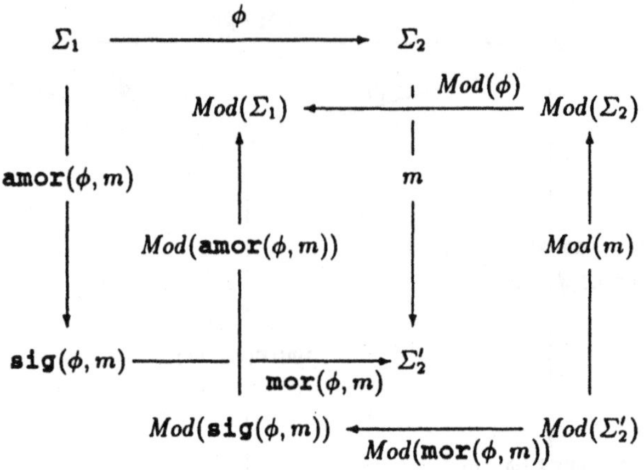

– *on morphisms*
HMod$(\phi)(<p,m>) = <Mod(\mathtt{mor}(\phi,m_2))(p), \mathtt{amor}(\mathtt{mor}(\phi,m_2),m)>$
for every $<p,m> \in HMod(\Sigma_2)(<A, m_2\colon \Sigma_2 \hookrightarrow \Sigma_2'>, <B, m_3\colon \Sigma_2 \hookrightarrow \Sigma_2''>)$, *accordingly with the translation of models; a complexive picture is given below;*

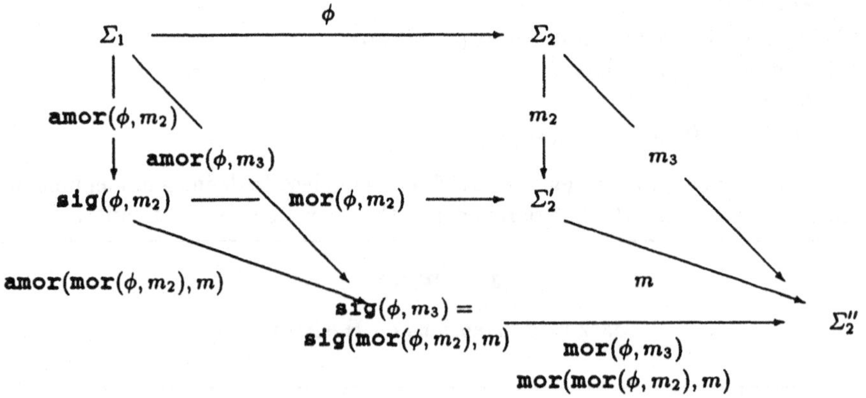

Then HMod(ϕ) *is a functor.* □

Putting together the definitions of *HMod*(Σ) and *HMod*(ϕ) we finally get a functor from **Sign** into $\mathbf{Cat}^{\mathbf{op}}$.

Proposition 6. *Under the hypothesis and using the notation of proposition 5, HMod is a functor from* **Sign** *into* $\mathbf{Cat}^{\mathbf{op}}$. □

As the sentences of the result institution are the same as the one of the parameter institution, the validity relation for "new" models can be defined in terms of the "old" validity relation and hence we do not need any other parameter in order to define the ABSTRACT operation.

1.2 The ABSTRACT Operation

$$\mathsf{ABSTRACT}(\mathcal{I}, \mathbf{HAMor}, \mathtt{sig}, \mathtt{amor}, \mathtt{mor}) = (\mathbf{Sign}, Sen, HMod, \models^H)$$

where **HAMor** is a family of admissible morphisms, **sig**, **amor** and **mor** are a backward extension on **HAMor**, *HMod* is given as in Prop. 6, $\models^H$ is defined by:
for each model $<A, m: \Sigma \hookrightarrow \Sigma'>$ in $|HMod(\Sigma)|$ and each ξ in $Sen(\Sigma)$

$$<A, m> \models^H_\Sigma \xi \iff A \models_{\Sigma'} Sen(m)(\xi) \iff A_{|m} \models_\Sigma \xi.$$

The ABSTRACT operation

Proposition 7. *Let* $\mathcal{I} = (\mathbf{Sign}, Sen, Mod, \models)$ *be an institution,* **HAMor** *be a family of admissible morphisms, and* **sig**, **amor** *and* **mor** *be a backward extension on* **HAMor**. *Then* $\mathsf{ABSTRACT}(\mathcal{I}, \mathbf{HAMor}, \mathtt{sig}, \mathtt{amor}, \mathtt{mor})$ *is an institution.* □

Remark. Note that, besides the institution $\mathcal{I}$ itself, the arguments of the ABSTRACT operation only depend on the signature category; thus the "non-canonical" part, i.e. the choice of **HAMor**, **sig**, **amor** and **mor**, can be shared by the institutions with the same signatures, disregarding the models and the sentences. In particular in section 3 a choice for **sig**, **amor** and **mor** backward extension on the embeddings as admissible morphisms is presented in the case of many-sorted signatures (with predicates), that applies, hence, in most significant institutions.

2 Enriching sentences by derived ones

Another useful operation to modularly build institutions consists of enriching the sentences by regarding as sentences on a signature Σ the sentences on a larger signature $EXT(\Sigma)$. A canonical example is adding equality to first-order logic, by coding the equality as a predicate.

As in general we may able to enrich only the sentences built over particular signatures and the "new" sentences may be incompatible with some "old" signature morphisms, a subcategory of signatures has to be selected as signature category of the result of this operation.

On the semantic side a canonical way of extending the models, in order to define the validity of the new sentences by a standard interpretation of the extra-symbols, is needed: this extension is given by a natural transformation *Ext* transforming models on Σ into models on $EXT(\Sigma)$, disregarding the model morphisms that are not involved in the definition of validity.

Let us summarize the arguments and the result of this operation.

Given an institution $\mathcal{I}$, a subcategory $\mathbf{Sign}_E$ of $\mathbf{Sign}$ with embedding $E: \mathbf{Sign}_E \to \mathbf{Sign}$, a functor $EXT: \mathbf{Sign}_E \to \mathbf{Sign}$ and a natural transformation $Ext: set \cdot Mod \cdot E \to set \cdot Mod \cdot EXT$ (set is the functor dropping from a category all morphisms different from the identities)

$$\mathsf{EXTEND}(\mathcal{I}, \mathbf{Sign}_E, EXT, Ext) = (\mathbf{Sign}_E, Sen_E, Mod_E, \models^E)$$

where $Sen_E = Sen \cdot EXT$, $Mod_E = Mod \cdot E$ and $A \models^E_\Sigma \theta$ iff $Ext(A) \models_{EXT(\Sigma)} \theta$.

The EXTEND operation

Proposition 8. *Let $\mathcal{I}$, $\mathbf{Sign}_E$, EXT and Ext be as in the above table; then* $\mathsf{EXTEND}(\mathcal{I}, \mathbf{Sign}_E, EXT, Ext)$ *is an institution.* □

3 Examples

3.1 The institution of hyper-loose specifications

Let $\mathcal{FOE} = (\mathbf{FOESign}, FOESen, FOEMod, \models^{FOE})$ denote the institution of many-sorted first-order logic with equality; in the sequel we assume that **FOESign** is the category of *abstract* signatures, i.e. the quotient of the usual category of first-order signatures w.r.t. isomorphisms, so that Σ stands for the class of signatures isomorphic to Σ.

The institution of the hyper-loose (many-sorted first-order with equality) specifications, introduced in [7], is the very abstract institution over $\mathcal{FOE}$ defined below using only the operation ABSTRACT; we do not use EXTEND in this case, since we do not need to extend the sentences.

Following Sect. 1 we give the parameters for the operation ABSTRACT.

Morphisms characterizing the signature extensions. The elements of **YAMor** are the embeddings between many-sorted signatures, i.e.:

$$\mathbf{YAMor}_{\Sigma,\Sigma'} = \{em: \Sigma \hookrightarrow \Sigma' \mid em \text{ is injective}\}.$$

Backward extension. Let $\phi: \Sigma_1 \to \Sigma_2$ be a morphism in **FOESign** and $em: \Sigma_2 \hookrightarrow \Sigma'_2$ be an admissible morphism in **YAMor**. The idea behind the definition of the backward extension of Σ_1 is to add to Σ_1 all components of $\Sigma'_2 - \Sigma_2$, as it is graphically represented below[3].

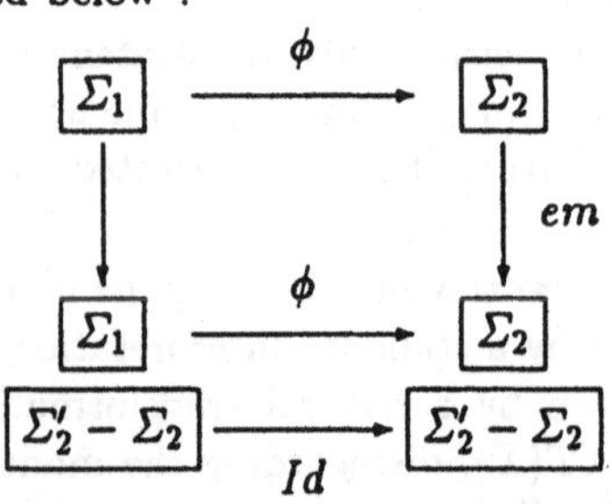

[3] Here, as in the sequel, we assume that representative of different signature classes do not share any symbol, so that the union of Σ_1 and $\Sigma'_2 - \Sigma_2$ is disjoint.

- $\mathbf{ysig}(\phi, em) = (S, OP, PR)$, where:
  * $S = Sorts(\Sigma_1) \cup (Sorts(\Sigma'_2) - Sorts(\Sigma_2))$
  * For all $s_1, \ldots, s_n, s_{n+1} \in S$
    $OP_{s_1 \ldots s_n, s_{n+1}} = Opns(\Sigma_1)_{s_1 \ldots s_n, s_{n+1}} \cup$
    $\bigcup_{s'_i = \overline{\phi}(s_i),\ i=1,\ldots,n+1} (Opns(\Sigma'_2)_{s'_1 \ldots s'_n, s'_{n+1}} - Opns(\Sigma_2)_{s'_1 \ldots s'_n, s'_{n+1}})$
    where $\overline{\phi}(s) = \phi(s)$ if $s \in Sorts(\Sigma_1)$, s otherwise.
  * For all $s_1, \ldots, s_n \in S$
    $PR_{s_1 \ldots s_n} = Preds(\Sigma_1)_{s_1 \ldots s_n} \cup$
    $\bigcup_{s'_i = \overline{\phi}(s_i),\ i=1,\ldots,n} (Preds(\Sigma'_2)_{s'_1 \ldots s'_n} - Preds(\Sigma_2)_{s'_1 \ldots s'_n})$.

  It is obvious to see that $\mathbf{ysig}(\phi, em)$ is a many-sorted signature.
- $\mathbf{yamor}(\phi, em)$ is the embedding of Σ_1 into $\mathbf{ysig}(\phi, em)$, i.e. $\mathbf{yamor}(\phi, em)(s) = s$, $\mathbf{yamor}(\phi, em)(Op) = Op$, $\mathbf{yamor}(\phi, em)(Pr) = Pr$, for all s, Op, Pr.
- $\mathbf{ymor}(\phi, em)$ is the morphism from $\mathbf{ysig}(\phi, em)$ into Σ'_2 is defined as follows:
  * on sorts:
    $\mathbf{ymor}(\phi, em)(s) = em(\phi(s))$, if $s \in Sorts(\Sigma_1)$, s otherwise;
  * on operations:
    $\mathbf{ymor}(\phi, em)(Op) = em(\phi(Op))$ if Op is in $Opns(\Sigma_1)$, Op otherwise;
  * on predicates:
    $\mathbf{ymor}(\phi, em)(Pr) = em(\phi(Pr))$ if Pr is in $Preds(\Sigma_1)$, Pr otherwise.

Proposition 9. **ysig**, **yamor** *and* **ymor** *defined above are a backward extension on* **YAMor**. □

$\mathcal{Y} = \mathsf{ABSTRACT}(\mathcal{FOE}, \mathbf{YAMor}, \mathbf{ysig}, \mathbf{ymor}, \mathbf{yamor})$
The institution of hyper-loose specifications

3.2 An institution for the very abstract specifications of data types

The idea is to extend the institution $\mathcal{Y}$ with appropriate formulae for expressing requirements on the (extra part of the) signatures of the very abstract models. It is obvious that there are different ways to choose these requirements; here we present a rather general and powerful choice, that we think appropriate for many reasonable applications. Our idea is to give the possibility to express both purely syntactic conditions on the extra part of the models (e.g. requiring the (non) existence of an operation or a predicate whose functionality satisfies some conditions) but also semantic one (e.g. requiring the (non) existence of an operation or a predicate whose interpretation satisfies some conditions, as commutativity). The practice of using very abstract specifications of abstract data types (shortly VAS) will show whether this choice is appropriate possibly suggesting improvements and modifications.

Then the institution for VAS is built by applying the operation EXTEND of Sect. 2 to the institution $\mathcal{Y}$ and the underlying idea is to take as new formulae on a signature Σ the formulae of classical first-order logic with equality on the signature enriching Σ by sorts, operations and predicates for handling the syntactic elements on Σ (e.g.: sorts, operations, predicates, variables, terms, formulae, ...) and their interpretations.

Now we list the parameters for EXTEND.

The extendible signatures. The above kind of sentence extension may be done on each many-sorted signature, so we do not restrict the objects of **FOESign**; however we have to restrict the admissible signature morphisms. For example let θ be the formula "$\exists x, y\colon sort\,.\, x \neq y$", Σ_1 be the signature having just one sort, *srt*, Σ_2 be the signature having two sorts, respectively srt_1 and srt_2, no operations and no predicates and $\phi\colon \Sigma_1 \to \Sigma_2$ be the signature morphism defined by $\phi(srt_1) = srt = \phi(srt_2)$. Now θ is false on all algebras in $YMod(\Sigma_1)$, while its translation along ϕ holds on the algebras in $YMod(\Sigma_2)$.

VSign is the category whose objects are the same of **FOESign** and whose only morphisms are the isomorphisms of **FOESign** and VE: **VSign** $\to$ **FOESign** is the embedding functor.

The extended signatures. $SYNT$: **VSign** $\to$ **VSign** is the functor defined by:

- on objects:

$$
\begin{array}{ll}
\multicolumn{2}{l}{SYNT((S, OP, PR)) =} \\
(S \cup & \{sort, atom, formula,\} \cup \{opn_{w,s}\}_{\substack{w \in S^*, s \in S \\ OP_{w,s} \neq \emptyset}} \cup \{pred_w\}_{\substack{w \in S^* \\ PR_w \neq \emptyset}} \\
\cup & \{seq_w\}_{\substack{w \in S^* \\ PR_w \neq \emptyset \text{ or } OP_{w,s} \neq \emptyset}} \cup \{var_s\}_{s \in S} \cup \{term_s\}_{s \in S} \cup \ldots \\
\multicolumn{2}{l}{OP \cup \{s\colon \to sort \mid s \in S\} \cup \{Op\colon \to opn_{w,s} \mid Op \in OP_{w,s}, w \in S^*, s \in S\}} \\
\cup & \{Pr\colon \to pred_w \mid Pr \in PR_w, w \in S^*\} \cup \\
\cup & \{\_(\_)_{w,s}\colon opn_{w,s} \times seq_w \to term_s \mid w \in S^*, s \in S\}, \cup \ldots \\
\multicolumn{2}{l}{PR \cup \{Holds\colon formula, \ldots\})}
\end{array}
$$

  For lack of room we do not give the complete definition of the extended signature, however it is easy to understand how to complete it with the remaining sorts, operations and predicates.

- on morphisms:
  the obvious extension leaving the new symbols inaffected
  $SYNT(\phi)(\sigma) = \phi(\sigma)$ if $\sigma \in \Sigma$, otherwise $SYNT(\phi)(\sigma) = \sigma$.

It is easy to see that $SYNT$ is a functor.

Interpretation of the extended signatures. For all $\Sigma \in |set(YMod(\textbf{VSign}))|$
$Synt_\Sigma\colon |YMod(\Sigma)| \to YMod(SYNT(\Sigma))$ is the functor defined by:

- on objects:
  if $A \in |\textbf{YAMor}(\Sigma)|$, i.e. A is a Σ_1-algebra where $\Sigma_1 = (S, OP, PR)$, then, fixed for every sort $s \in S$ a denumerable set of variables X_s, $Synt_\Sigma(A) = B$, where
  $B_{sort} = S$, $B_{var_s} = X_s$, $B_{opn_{w,s}} = OP_{w,s}$, $B_{pred_w} = PR_w$,
  $B_{formula}$ = the set of all first-order formulae on Σ_1 and X,
  ...
  $op^B = op^A$ if $op \in OP_{w,s}$ for some w, s,
  ...
  $Holds^B(\theta) = A \models^{FOE} \theta$,
  ...

– on morphisms:
  Obvious.

Since the morphisms in **VSign** are isomorphisms, obviously *Synt* is a natural transformation.

Example 1. We specify the fundamental requirements on a module for handling labelled transition trees without completely fixing the interface. The designer in charge of realizing such module is allowed to devise a nice choice of extra constructors for trees, but it cannot add operations modifying parts of a tree, so that it is possible to give implementations where repeated common subtrees are shared.

spec $LTT =$
  enrich $LAB, STATE$ **by**
  sorts $tree, sons$
  opns
  – fixed components of the interface
    $\Lambda: \to sons$
    $<\_,\_>\&\_: lab \times tree \times sons \to sons$
    $T: state \times sons \to tree$
  axioms
  – properties of the fixed part of the interface
    $<l,t>\&<l,t>\&sons = <l,t>\&sons$
    $<l_1,t_1>\&<l_2,t_2>\&sons = <l_2,t_2>\&<l_1,t_1>\&sons$
  – properties of the variable part of the interface
    – each constructor for *tree* is derived
    $\forall op: opn_{w,tree} \,.\, (\exists t : term_{tree} \,.\, Holds(op(x_1,\dots,x_n) = t) \wedge$
      $Operations(t) \subseteq \{<\_,\_>\&\_, T\} \cup Opns(STATE) \cup Opns(LAB))$
    – each constructor for *sons* is derived
    $\forall op: opn_{w,sons} \,.\, (\exists t : term_{sons} \,.\, Holds(op(x_1,\dots,x_n) = t) \wedge$
      $Operations(t) \subseteq \{<\_,\_>\&\_, T\} \cup Opns(STATE) \cup Opns(LAB))$

For example the operation $1_{Ary}: state \times lab \times tree \to tree$ building unary trees and defined by $1_{Ary}(s,l,t) = T(s, <l,t>\&\Lambda)$ can be added to the interface, while the following one, replacing some subtrees, cannot:

$$Replac: tree \times lab \times tree \to tree$$
$$Replac(T(s,sns),l,t) = T(s, Replac'(sns,l,t))$$
$$Replac': sns \times lab \times tree \to sns$$
$$Replac'(\Lambda,l,t) = \Lambda$$
$$Replac'(<l,t>\&sns,l,t') = <l,t'>\&Replac'(sns,l,t')$$
$$l \neq l' \supset Replac'(<l,t>\&sns,l',t') = <l,t>\&Replac'(sns,l',t')$$

3.3 Very Abstract Entity Specifications

The institution of entity algebras, where "entity" stands for processes, either simple or structured (i.e. several processes interacting together), see [8],

$$\mathcal{E} = (\mathbf{ESign}, ESen, EMod, \models^{E})$$

provides a formal framework for the process specification.

Here, for lack of room, we cannot give full details and the motivations of $\mathcal{E}$. From a formal point of view $\mathcal{E}$ is a "subinstitution" of $\mathcal{FOE}$, in the sense that:

- **ESign** is a subcategory of **FOESign**,
- *ESen* is the restriction of *FOESen* to **ESign**,
- for all $E\Sigma \in |\mathbf{ESign}|$, $EMod(E\Sigma)$ is a subcategory of $FOEMod(E\Sigma)$, whose objects are called *entity algebras* and $EMod(\phi: E\Sigma_1 \to E\Sigma_2) = FOEMod(\phi: E\Sigma_1 \to E\Sigma_2)$,
- $EA \models^E \theta \Leftrightarrow EA \models^{FOE} \theta$.

The concurrent structure of the entities modelled by an $E\Sigma$-entity algebra (i.e. which are the process components and how are assembled) is determined by some of the operations of $E\Sigma$; thus very abstract specifications (built on the entity institution) describe classes of entity algebras on possibly different signatures, i.e. processes with possibly different concurrent structures, satisfying common properties.

$\mathcal{VE}$ is given by using the two operations ABSTRACT and EXTEND as follows (see [1] for a full definition).

$$\mathcal{YE} = \text{ABSTRACT}(\mathcal{E}, \mathbf{EAmor}, \mathtt{esig}, \mathtt{eamor}, \mathtt{emor})$$

where **EAmor** includes the elements of **YAMor** which are also morphisms in **ESign**; **esig**, **eamor**, **emor** are the restrictions of **ysig**, **yamor**, **ymor** to **ESign** and **EAmor** (in [8] it is shown that such restrictions are well-defined, i.e. they return signatures and morphisms in **ESign**).

$$\mathcal{VE} = \text{EXTEND}(\mathcal{YE}, \mathbf{VESign}, COMPS, Comps)$$

where **VESign** is the subcategory of **ESign** s.t. it has the same objects and if in **VESign** there exists a morphism from $E\Sigma_1$ into $E\Sigma_2$, then the $E\Sigma_1$- and $E\Sigma_2$-entity algebras describe systems with similar concurrent structure. *COMPS* adds to an entity signature some predicates for testing which are the subcomponents of the entities (as *Is_Sub_Entity* in the following example) and *Comps* is defined accordingly.

Example 2. We specify the class of all structured processes where deadlocks never happen without making assumptions on their concurrent structure (i.e. without "over specification") by a very abstract entity specification.

spec *NO_DEADLOCKS* =
- basic signature

esorts *system* – we have at least entities of sort *system*

axioms
- if a system cannot perform any activity, then

$\nexists es', l \,.\, es \xrightarrow{l} es' \supset$
- each of its subcomponents cannot perform any activity

$\forall ec \,.\, (ec \; Is\_Sub\_Entity \; es \supset \nexists ec', l' \,.\, ec \xrightarrow{l'} ec')$

e_1 *Is_Sub_Entity* e_2 holds whenever e_1 is a subcomponent of e_2. □

Conclusions and further work

We have presented two operations on institutions, that allow to build institutions for very abstract specifications. From the practice of formal methods for software specification, it is easy to intuit that several other operations are needed in order to get meta-framework where to be able to modularly build formalisms; some more operations are presented in [6], but these are case studies rather than an organic presentation of a reasonable set of operations.

Another relevant point that we do not face here is the study of the properties of the ABSTRACT and EXTEND operations and in particular their relationships with the various notions of arrows between institutions (like horizontal/vertical composition).

References

1. E. Astesiano and G. Reggio. Entity institutions: Frameworks for dynamic systems, 1993. inpreparation.
2. E. Astesiano and G. Reggio. A metalanguage for the formal requirement specification of reactive systems. In *Proc. of FME'93*, number 670 in L.N.C.S., Berlin, 1993. Springer-Verlag.
3. C. Beierle and A. Voss. Viewing implementations as an institution. In *Proc. of Category Theory and Computer Science*, number 283 in L.N.C.S., Berlin, 1987. Springer-Verlag.
4. R. Burstall and J. Goguen. Introducing institutions. In *Logics of Programming Workshop*, number 164 in L.N.C.S. Springer Verlag, Berlin, 1984.
5. R. Burstall and J. Goguen. Institutions: Abstract model theory for specification and programming. *Journal of the Association for Computing Machinery*, 39(1), 1992.
6. M. Cerioli and G. Reggio. Algebraic-oriented institutions. In *Proc. AMAST'93*, Workshops in Computing. Springer Verlag, Berlin, 1993.
7. P. Pepper. Transforming algebraic specifications. In *Proc. AMAST'91*, Workshops in Computing. Springer Verlag, Berlin, 1992.
8. G. Reggio. Entities: an institution for dynamic systems. In *Recent Trends in Data Type Specification*, number 534 in L.N.C.S. Springer Verlag, Berlin, 1991.
9. G. Reggio. Event logic for specifying abstract dynamic data types. In *Recent Trends in Data Type Specification*, number 655 in L.N.C.S. Springer Verlag, Berlin, 1993.
10. G. Reggio, A. Morgavi, and V. Filippi. Specification of a high-voltage substation. Technical Report PDISI-92-12, Dipartimento di Informatica e Scienze dell'Informazione - Università di Genova, Italy, 1992.
11. G. Reichwein and J. Fiadeiro. A semantic framework for interoperability. Technical report, Departemento de matematica, Instituto superior técnico, Universidade técnica de Lisboa, 1992.
12. D. Sannella and A. Tarlecki. Specifications in an arbitrary institution. *Information and Computation*, 76, 1988.

About the "correctness" and "adequacy" of PLUSS specifications

Christine Choppy

LRI, C.N.R.S. U.R.A. 410 & Université Paris-Sud
91405 Orsay Cedex, France

Abstract. In the context of algebraic specifications written in Pluss, this paper investigates various issues raised by the question: "Is my specification correct?". Up to now the only ways to check the adequacy of a specification with respect to the problem to be solved are through running a prototype on appropriate examples, or through the use of the specification to prove consequent (expected) properties. Before this problem may be fully addressed, issues regarding the specification consistency and the correctness of the prototype w.r.t. the specification must be studied. In this paper, various issues concerning checking consistency and proving properties of PLUSS specifications are presented. It is investigated how general properties can be proved using an appropriate presentation of the specification that may be understood by a prototyping tool. While this study is done in the framework of the PLUSS specification language, it should be clear that most of the issues considered here arise in a similar way with other specification languages.

1 Introduction

The interest of writing formal specifications is widely acknowledged. Among other advantages, it induces a deeper understanding of the problem to be solved, and a better use of abstraction that leads to better software design -through the use of decomposition and modularization/encapsulation. However, it is clear that there is no formal way to prove that a specification actually provides an adequate description of the problem to be solved. The reason for this is that we lack a "former" formal description of the problem that would be supposed to be correct and that could be used to check the specification (the only documents established prior to a formal specification are informal ones). Therefore, a way to try to solve this problem is often to build a prototype (software) from the specification, and to run this prototype over "interesting" cases. This validation process may be considered as "specification testing", where the specification is examined through the behaviour of the derived prototype. Another way is to try to prove that a given property is a consequence of the properties already expressed in the specification.

One issue then is how to derive a prototype from a specification (for instance, when dealing with algebraic specifications, rewriting, logic programming and code generation techniques are currently used). A further issue is how to check that the obtained prototype actually reflects the specification semantics (i.e. that it is a model of the specification).

While one benefit of the use of formal specifications is that it should be possible to check their consistency (and, consequently, actually be possible to build some appropriate software implementation -for instance a prototype- of a formal specification), the way to actually check this consistency is less often described. This last point requires appropriate methods and corresponding tools that are not always available.

In this paper, various issues regarding checking consistency and proving properties of PLUSS specifications are presented. First a brief overview of the PLUSS specification language syntax and semantics is provided. The PLUSS specification building primitives that will be considered in this paper are: enrichment, parameterization, instanciation and renaming. The semantics of a PLUSS specification is defined as a class of models (Σ-algebras) that satisfy the axioms of the specification, that are finitely generated w.r.t. the generators, and that comply with constraints relative to both hierarchy and modular construction. We then examine what kind of properties of PLUSS specifications can be checked. Since it is not possible in general to provide a finite first-order axiomatization that reflects the semantics of a PLUSS specification, the only point that may be checked as regards the consistency of a PLUSS specification is the consistency of the axioms. We then examine how general properties can be proved using an adequate presentation of the specification that may be understood by the selected prototyping tool.

2 The PLUSS algebraic specification language

In this section we provide a brief overview of the PLUSS specification language syntax and semantics. However, we shall restrict ourselves to presenting those characteristics of PLUSS that will be used in the work reported here (for more details see e.g. [8, 4, 5]).

2.1 The PLUSS specification building primitives

In all specification modules, the axioms are expressed by first order logic formulas. In achieved specification modules (**spec**) the distinguished subset of generators is specified separately from the other operations of the signature and is introduced by the keyword **generated by**.

The *enrichment* primitive, denoted by the keyword **use**, provides a straightforward way to add new domains, objects, properties, to a specification. Similar enrichment primitives are present in other algebraic specification languages [9, 12, 15, 23, 3, 26]. *Parameterization* saves the writing of many instances of the same specification. In the example given in Fig. 1, ELEM is a *formal parameter* specification (**Par**), LIST (ELEM) is a *parameterised specification* (**Generic spec**), and L-IDENT is an *instance* of LIST (ELEM) where

ELEM is instanciated by IDENT through a "fitting morphism m" that maps "Elem" to "Ident"; in addition, a *renaming* of the sort "List" into "L-ident" and of the operation "Empty" into "none" is performed in order to customize names for this particular instance. It should be noted that, when dealing with PLUSS achieved specifications, the "meaning" of renaming is aliasing [6, 32] (while renaming in some other languages may mean copying). Such parameterization/instanciation primitives are available in most other algebraic specification languages [15, 3, 26]. In some languages [23], there is no explicit parameterization mechanism. However, some other constructions "make possible much of the reuse for which parameterization is advocated" [22].

Generic spec : LIST (ELEM) ;
  sort : List ;
  generated by :
    Empty : ⟶ List;
    _ : Elem ⟶ List;
    "this is a coercion : any Elem is a one element List"
    _ _ : Elem * List ⟶ List;
    "this is an anonymous operation to add an Elem to a List"
  operation :
    _ union _ : List * List ⟶ List;
    "the _'s indicate the argument locations"
  predicates[1]:
    _ is in _ : Elem * List;
    _ all in _ : List * List;
  axioms :
    "omitted here due to lack of space"
end LIST (ELEM) .

par : ELEM ;
  sort : Elem ;
end ELEM .

spec : L-IDENT ;
  use : LIST (ELEM ⇒ IDENT by m) ;
    where : m : Elem ⇒ Ident ;
  renaming : List into L-ident, Empty into none ;
end L-IDENT .

Fig. 1. An example of parameterization and instanciation.

After this short overview of the PLUSS syntax and specification-building primitives, we will now focus on its semantics.

[1] Predicates are just a synctactical convention to denote Boolean-valued functions. Any specification that introduces predicates implicitely uses a "predefined" Boolean specification.

2.2 The stratified loose semantics of PLUSS

Several choices have to be made when designing the semantics of an algebraic specification language. A first issue is the approach chosen to describe the

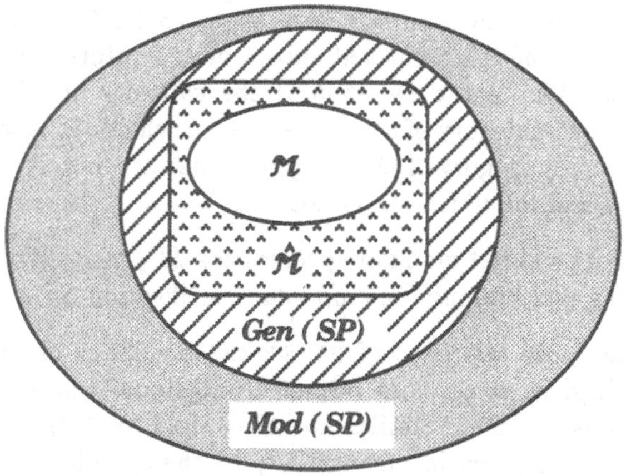

Fig. 2. Models associated to a specification

semantics [33]: the semantics of a PLUSS specification is defined as some class of *models* that are Σ-algebras (where Σ is the signature of the specification)[2]. Another point is the choice of a *loose* semantics (in this case the semantics of a specification is a class of models) as opposed to an initial [13, 12] or final [34] approach where only one model (up to isomorphism) is considered. A further characteristic of the PLUSS semantics is to provide means for expressing the semantics of a specification modularly (as opposed to expressing the semantics of a "flat" specification, where the specification structuration is flattened). Obviously the models (Σ-algebras) of a specification should satisfy the axioms (such models belong to *Mod*(*SP*) in Fig. 2). It is usual to add a further condition by only considering finitely generated models w.r.t. the signature of the specification. In the case of PLUSS achieved specifications, only models that are finitely generated w.r.t. the operations declared as generators are considered (such models belong to *Gen*(*SP*) in Fig. 2): this guarantees that for any model, all values will be denotable as some composition of these generators (an important consequence of this constraint is that *structural induction restricted to the generators* is a correct proof principle). The semantics of PLUSS introduces as well some hierarchical constraints (cf. the so called "no junk" and "no confusion" properties) - such models belong to $\widehat{\mathcal{M}}$ in Fig. 2-. Finally, constraints

[2] In some sense, PLUSS is a "meta-specification" language, i.e. various instances of PLUSS can be derived according to the chosen underlying institution (cf. e.g. [33]). However, in the sequel, it is assumed that formulas are arbitrary first-order Σ-sentences, and models are (total) Σ-algebras.

to reflect the modular structure of the specification are introduced ($\mathcal{M}$ in Fig. 2). Consequently, the class of models of a PLUSS specification is, in general, strictly included in the class of finitely generated models (w.r.t. the generators) that satisfy the axioms (cf. Fig. 2). A more precise definition of the PLUSS semantics is given below.

An algebraic (flat) specification SP is a triple $(S, \Sigma, \mathcal{A}x)$ where (S, Σ) is a signature, $\Omega \subset \Sigma$ is the distinguished subset of generators, and $\mathcal{A}x$ is a finite set of Σ-formulas. We denote by $Mod(\Sigma)$ the category of all Σ-algebras, by $Mod(SP)$ the full sub-category of all Σ-algebras for which $\mathcal{A}x$ is satisfied, and by $Gen(SP)$ the full sub-category of all Σ-algebras that are finitely generated w.r.t. the generators Ω and for which $\mathcal{A}x$ is satisfied.

Let us now consider a PLUSS modular specification SP_2 made of one specification module ΔSP that enriches only one modular specification SP_1.

According to the loose approach of PLUSS, the semantics of the specification SP_1 will be defined as some class $\mathcal{M}_1$ of Σ_1-algebras (where Σ_1 denotes the signature associated to SP_1). Similar notations hold for SP_2. Since we assume that SP_2 is defined as an enrichment of SP_1 by the specification module ΔSP, we have $\Sigma_1 \subseteq \Sigma_2$. Let $\mathcal{U}$ denote the usual forgetful functor from Σ_2-algebras to Σ_1-algebras.

With the help of this simple context, our intuition about the adequate models of the PLUSS modular specification SP_2 can be summarized as follows [5]:

1. Any model of the "large" specification SP_2 must also provide, through the forgetful functor $\mathcal{U}$, a correct model of the sub-specification SP_1, i.e. we should have: $\mathcal{U}(\mathcal{M}_2) \subseteq \mathcal{M}_1$ ("no junk").
2. Any model of the sub-specification SP_1 should be extendible to a model of the larger specification SP_2, i.e. we should have: either $\mathcal{M}_2 = \emptyset$, or $\mathcal{U}(\mathcal{M}_2) \supseteq \mathcal{M}_1$ ("no confusion").
3. It should be possible to implement the specification module ΔSP without knowing which specific realization of the sub-specification SP_1 has been (or will be) chosen. Thus, the various specification modules should be implementable **independently** of each other.

The first two requirements can be easily achieved by embedding some appropriate *hierarchical constraints* into the semantics of the **use** enrichment specification-building primitive. Roughly speaking, it is sufficient to require the following property:

> *Either* $\mathcal{M}_2 = \emptyset$ *(in which case the specification module* ΔSP *will be said to be hierarchically inconsistent) or* $\mathcal{U}(\mathcal{M}_2) = \mathcal{M}_1$.

The third requirement, however, cannot be achieved without providing a suitable (loose) semantics to **specification modules** themselves (and not only to specifications as a whole).

Definition (Stratified loose semantics)(cf. [4]): Given a modular specification SP_2 defined as the enrichment of some modular specification SP_1 by a specification module ΔSP, the semantics of the specification module ΔSP and of the modular specification SP_2 are defined as follows:

Basic case: If the sub-specification SP_1 is empty (hence the specification SP_2 is reduced to the specification module ΔSP), then:
- The semantics of the specification SP_2 is by definition the initial models of $Gen(SP_2)$, if any; if $Gen(SP_2)$ has no initial model, then SP_2 is said to be *inconsistent*.
- The semantics of the specification module ΔSP is defined as being the functors $\mathcal{F}$ from the category **1** to $Gen(SP_2)$, which maps the object of **1** to the initial models of $Gen(SP_2)$.[3]

General case: Let us denote by $\mathcal{M}_1$ the class of models associated to the modular specification SP_1, according to the current definition.
- The semantics of the specification module ΔSP is defined as being the class $\mathcal{F}_1^2$ of all the mappings $\mathcal{F}$ such that:
  1. $\mathcal{F}$ is a (**total**) functor from $\mathcal{M}_1$ to $Gen(SP_2)$.
  2. $\mathcal{F}$ is a right inverse of the forgetful functor $\mathcal{U}$, i.e.: $\forall M_1 \in \mathcal{M}_1 : \mathcal{U}(\mathcal{F}(M_1)) = M_1$.

  If the class $\mathcal{F}_1^2$ is empty, then the enrichment is said to be *hierarchically inconsistent*.
- The semantics of the whole specification SP_2 is defined as being the class of all the models in the image of the functors $\mathcal{F}$:
  $$\mathcal{M}_2 = \bigcup_{\mathcal{F} \in \mathcal{F}_1^2} \mathcal{F}(\mathcal{M}_1).$$

The class $\mathcal{M}_2$ of the models of the specification SP_2 is said to be **stratified** by the functors $\mathcal{F}$ (an example will be given at the end of this section).

It is important to note that with this PLUSS stratified loose semantics, the *hierarchical constraints* mentioned above are satisfied. More precisely, as soon as the specification module ΔSP is hierarchically consistent, we have $\mathcal{U}(\mathcal{M}_2) = \mathcal{M}_1$. Consequently, both the so-called "*no junk*" and "*no confusion*" properties are guaranteed. In other words, we know that the "old" carrier sets (i.e. the carrier sets of sorts defined in SP_1) will contain no "new" value, and that "old" values which may be distinct before (in at least one model of SP_1) should not be forced to be equal by the new specification module ΔSP.

It should be noted that other algebraic specification languages, such as e.g. ACT-ONE [12], ASL [35], Larch [23], OBJ2 [15], offer various enrichment primitives that may reflect in various degrees the "*no junk*" and "*no confusion*" constraints (e.g. the enrichment primitives "using", "extending", "protecting" in OBJ2, or

[3] As usual, the category **1** denotes the category containing only one object, which can be interpreted as a Σ_1-algebra for an empty signature Σ_1. Note that initial models are isomorphic up to unique isomorphism, and functors that map the object of **1** to an initial model are deduced from one another through a unique natural transformation.

the enrichment primitives "assumes, "imports", "includes" in the 1986 version of Larch).

Hence, the semantics of a PLUSS specification results from both *explicit* and *implicit* features. The *explicit part* of the semantics is that the models of the specification should satisfy the axioms. The *implicit part* of the semantics result from the following constraints:

1. Only finitely generated models w.r.t. the generators are considered.
2. Only models that comply with the hierarchical constraints are considered ("no junk", "no confusion").
3. Only models that are in the image of the functors are considered.

To better understand the impact of the third constraint, let us consider $\widehat{\mathcal{M}_2} = \{\Sigma_2\text{-algebras } M_2 \mid M_2$ finitely generated w.r.t. Ω_2, $M_2 \models \mathcal{A}x_2$, and $\mathcal{U}(M_2) \in \mathcal{M}_1\}$, and assume that $\mathcal{U}(\widehat{\mathcal{M}_2}) \supset \mathcal{M}_1$ (hence $\mathcal{U}(\widehat{\mathcal{M}_2}) = \mathcal{M}_1$). This class $\widehat{\mathcal{M}_2}$ reflects the first two constraints, but not the third one. Obviously $\mathcal{M}_2 \subseteq \widehat{\mathcal{M}_2}$, but in general this inclusion is strict. Let us illustrate this last point with the example in Fig. 3. As shown in Fig.4, two mappings $\mathcal{F}$ and $\mathcal{F}$' are candidates. Since $\mathcal{F}$ is not a functor (there is no morphism between the models of its image), $\mathcal{M}_2$ is simply $\mathcal{F}$'$(\mathcal{M}_1)$ (hence, $\mathcal{M}_2 \neq \widehat{\mathcal{M}_2}$). Another approach to

```
spec : S2 ;
      use : S1 ;
   sort : s2 ;
   generated by :
      c, d : ⟶ s2 ;
   axiom :
      ax : a = b | c = d ;
end S2 .
```

```
spec : S1 ;
      use : BOOL ;
   sort : s1 ;
   generated by :
      a, b : ⟶ s1 ;
end S1 .
```

Fig. 3. Illustration of the functorial aspect of the semantics.

modularity was used in [28], where any total mapping is allowed and not only functors (that should preserve morphisms between models) [4]. It is important to note that, as soon as $\widehat{\mathcal{M}_2} \neq \emptyset$, for any model M_2 in $\widehat{\mathcal{M}_2}$ there always exists a total mapping from $\mathcal{M}_1$ to $\widehat{\mathcal{M}_2}$ such that M_2 belongs to the image of this mapping (due to the Zorn axiom). Hence in the non functorial approach of [28], the class of models allowed (for "well-structured" specifications [5]) is $\widehat{\mathcal{M}_2}$.

[4] For a discussion about the interest of mappings vs functors, see [20].

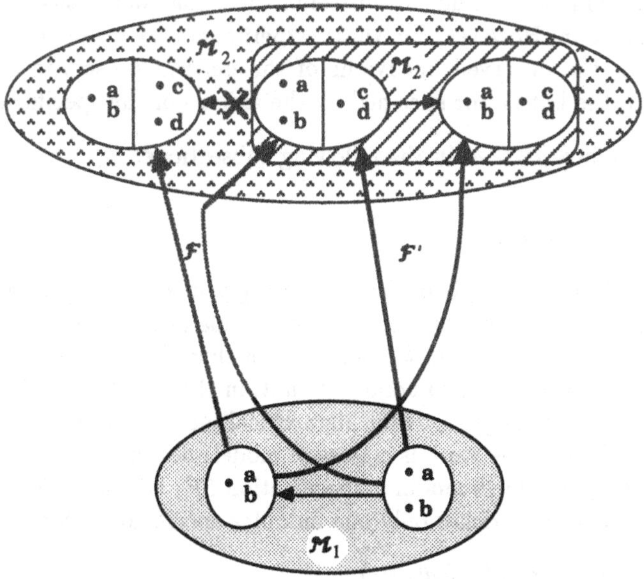

Fig. 4. Taking the functorial constraint into consideration

3 Specification validation

As stated in the introduction, once a formal specification of the problem to be solved is written, the obvious question to be raised is: "Is my specification "correct"? ". While the meaning of this question, stated in this way, is unclear (cf. Section 1), other questions (corresponding to quite different goals) may be addressed :

Question 1 : "Is this specification consistent? (Does this specification have models?)". As a matter of fact, in many approaches the correctness of a specification is defined as its consistency. Various issues related to the consistency of PLUSS specifications are studied below.

Question 2 : "Is this specification sufficiently complete ?" In other words, is the set of operators of the specification adequately defined.

Question 3 : "Does this specification correspond to the problem to be specified?" In practice, it is difficult to provide a formal expression of this question that is satisfactory [5]. Often then, this question is addressed indirectly, through experiments run on a prototype derived from the specification. These experiments allow one to observe the behaviour (of the

[5] [21] states that, when there exists a mathematical model for an abstract data type, a (correctness) proof is possible. The adequacy between the specification and the mathematical model is then proved through the isomorphism between the initial algebra of the specification and the mathematical model. However, this approach does not apply to other (more frequent) situations where there is no available mathematical model.

prototype) and may show evidence of compliance/non compliance with the expected behaviour. However, for these experiments to make sense, it is important that the observed behaviour of the derived prototype actually corresponds to the behaviour specified by the axioms of the specification.

These questions are investigated in the following subsections.

3.1 Checking consistency

Obviously a crucial issue is to know when some given PLUSS specification is consistent, hence when some PLUSS specification module is *hierarchically consistent*. From a general point of view, it is well-known that this is an undecidable problem. However, we would like to point out that, in the PLUSS stratified loose framework, there are various grounds for hierarchical inconsistency that can be distinguished according to the various classes of models described in Fig. 2. Let us assume again that the PLUSS modular specification SP_2 is made of one specification module ΔSP that enriches only one modular specification SP_1.

Consistency at the level of $Mod(SP_2)$
As usual, inconsistency may result from the axioms introduced by the specification module. While the consistency of a set of axioms is undecidable in general, it is well-known that, in the case of equations or positive conditional equations, a semi-decision procedure is obtained through completion [27, 16, 29, 18]. From a practical point of view, the completion process may prove more efficient in showing evidence of inconsistency (hence it is useful in a specification "debugging" approach), even though it may not succeed in proving consistency because the completion process either does not terminate or cannot be completed in an acceptable amount of time and space [19].

Consistency at the level of $Gen(SP_2)$
It is well-known that there exist consistent theories with no finitely generated model [6] (w.r.t. the full signature) [36]. It is very easy as well to exhibit some cases where the theory is consistent, has finitely generated models (w.r.t. the full signature) but no finitely generated models w.r.t. the declared generators (cf. examples in [10]). When the axioms are equations or positive conditional equations, the existence of an initial model (quotient of the term algebra by the least congruence generated by the axioms) is ensured, and this model is by construction finitely generated w.r.t. the full signature. Otherwise, there is, to our knowledge, no obvious way to check the existence of a finitely generated model (either w.r.t. Σ or w.r.t. Ω).

Consistency at the level of $\widehat{\mathcal{M}_2}$
Moreover, in PLUSS, hierarchical inconsistency may result from an improper structure of the specification. In some cases, there may be no total mapping from $\mathcal{M}_1$ to $Gen(SP_2)$, since some model M_1 of SP_1 might not be extendible to a model of SP_2. A typical example of such a situation is the following

[6] It suffices to consider a specification with a signature reduced to a sort s, a constant c of sort s, and the axiom $\exists$ x:s, x $\neq$ c .

one [1] : if we assume that SP_1 specifies natural numbers (with $\mathcal{M}_1 \supseteq \{\mathbf{N}, \mathbf{Z}/\mathbf{nZ}\}$), specifying a "<" operation in ΔSP (the example is given in [10]) will result in a hierarchically inconsistent specification module ($\mathbf{Z}/\mathbf{nZ}$ cannot be extended to a model of $Gen(SP_2)$ and the requirement $\mathcal{U}(\mathcal{M}_2) \supseteq \mathcal{M}_1$ is not satisfied). Thus, this "<" operation should rather have been defined in the appropriate specification module, i.e. in the module where the natural numbers are defined. It is worth noting that the "flat" version of this specification (e.g. with only one module) is consistent. Therefore, there is no way to detect the former inconsistency through mere analysis of the axioms. The only way to prevent these inconsistencies from arising is to enforce some structuration rules that can be syntactically checked.

Consistency at the level of $\mathcal{M}_2$

A further ground for inconsistency is the functorial semantics provided for specification modules. In some cases, even when the hierarchical constraints are satisfied, and even when there exist some total mappings from $\mathcal{M}_1$ to $Gen(SP_2)$, it may happen that none of these mappings is a functor (i.e. morphisms are not preserved). In such a case the specification module is inconsistent [5]. Fig. 5 provides an example where, although the hierarchical constraints are satisfied ($\widehat{\mathcal{M}_2} \neq \emptyset$: $\widehat{\mathcal{M}_2}$ contains the two leftmost algebras in Fig. 4), there is no mapping that is a functor (hence, $\mathcal{M}_2 = \emptyset$). To find sufficient conditions that will ensure the existence of functors (when $\widehat{\mathcal{M}_2} \neq \emptyset$) is a topic that obviously requires further investigation.

```
spec : S2 ;
   use : S1 ;
  sort : s2 ;
  generated by :
    c, d : ⟶ s2 ;
  axiom :
    ax : a = b | c = d ;
    ax1 : a = b ⇒ c ≠ d ;
    ax2 : c = d ⇒ a ≠ b ;
end S2 .
```

```
spec : S1 ;
   use : BOOL ;
  sort : s1 ;
  generated by :
    a, b : ⟶ s1 ;
end S1 .
```

Fig. 5. An example of modular inconsistency

It is clearly not possible in general to find a finite first order axiomatization that would present the theory associated with a Pluss specification. While the *explicit part* of the semantics (the axioms) may, in some cases, be checked (w.r.t. consistency), this is not the case for the *implicit part*. It is worth noting that these difficulties arise with other algebraic specification languages that share similar constraints (in particular, their semantics is not expressed through presentations). There is clearly some tradeoff between the expressive power of the language and the ease to check the specification consistency.

Up to now it was enough to consider, as in Section 2.2, a modular specification with a simple structure (SP_2 is obtained through ΔSP that enriches only one modular specification SP_1). In general, one deals with more complex specifications involving other specification building primitives such as (i) multiple enrichment of several specifications by one specification module, and/or (ii) instanciation of parameterized specifications. In the case of multiple enrichment (i), the specification consistency does not raise new difficulties assuming that modular compatibility and adequate structuration hold [5]. In the case of instanciation (ii), the main new issue is to check that the actual parameter specification is correct w.r.t. the formal one, in other words, to check that the class of the models of the actual parameter specification is included in the class of the models of the formal parameter specification (or that the axioms of the formal parameter specification are consequences of the axioms of the actual parameter specification). Hence proving the correctness of parameter passing mainly consists in proving properties that are consequences of the available axioms (cf. Section 3.3).

3.2 Checking "relative completeness" of operations

While the sufficient completeness property of a specification is usually worth checking, this issue when dealing with a PLUSS specification is meaningless since only models that are finitely generated w.r.t the generators are considered (hence, by definition, they have no junk values).

One motivation for the restriction to finitely generated models w.r.t. the generators is to avoid overspecification of some operations [5, 2]. The same preoccupation is shared in the Larch Shared Language to let the user have "intentionally incomplete" specifications [19]. Hence, the situation here is quite similar for PLUSS and the Larch Shared Language.

However, in some cases, "incompleteness" might result from a specification error (for instance, when the axiom x+s(y) = s(x+y) is given and the axiom x+0=0 is forgotten). Since, in most cases, the intent of the specifier is to provide a complete definition of the operation, it is of practical interest to provide means to check it. In our example, one way to check the "relative completeness" of the operation + would be to prove that *generated by 0,s,+ implies generated by 0,s*.

As a matter of fact, Larch provides another way to state that some operation is, in the intent of the specifier, completely "defined" with the **converts** (and **exempting**) clauses. In our example, one would like to check that *converts +* is true. While the practical interest of the **converts** clause is obvious, is is rather difficult to understand whether *converts +* is equivalent to or stronger than *generated by 0,s,+ implies generated by 0,s*.[7]

[7] In [19], the meaning of the **converts** clause is explained as follows: "given any fixed

3.3 Checking properties and/or behaviour

As mentioned in Section 1, an approach to check the adequacy of a specification as regards to the problem to be specified is through "testing" a prototype derived from the specification, that is through running this prototype on well-chosen cases. In order to use this approach, one needs to (i) select appropriate experiments, (ii) derive a prototype from the specification, (iii) run this prototype on the selected experiments. However, these issues cannot be considered independently of each other:

- The choice of the means used to derive the prototype depends on the prototyping technique selected (when the prototyping technique chosen is rewriting, rewrite rules have to be generated from the specification axioms, when logic programming techniques are used, a logic program needs to be produced, when using some theorem prover, acceptable formulas have to be generated from the specification, ...).
- The choice of the prototyping technique may depend on the kind of observations one wants to perform (e.g. use rewriting to obtain normal forms, use logic programming to obtain appropriate sets of values for variables, use theorem proving to prove some property).
- The choice of the prototyping technique depends on the specification and on the style of the axioms (e.g. axioms with existential quantifiers are usually not adequate for use in rewriting, while they can be acceptable for some theorem prover).

In all cases, the specification has to be analyzed to produce, in a suitable format: a signature, and adequate formulas (rewrite rules, logic program, equations and deduction rules ...). It is now clear that, to produce a prototype, one needs to find an appropriate translation of the specification. Two issues must be addressed : how to take into account the specification building primitives, and how to translate the formulas. Since we are working in the context of *modular* specifications, one issue is how to "put together" the various elements of information obtained from the various modules. The class of models $\mathcal{M}$ of a PLUSS specification *SP* is, in general, strictly included in the class *Gen*(*SP*) of Σ-algebras that are finitely generated w.r.t. the generators and that satisfy the axioms. In section 3.1, it was noted that there is usually no finite first order presentation of the theory associated to a PLUSS specification. However, if it is possible to produce a sensible presentation $\mathcal{P}res$ associated with a PLUSS specification that has a larger class of models than $\mathcal{M}$, then any property proved correct for all models of $\mathcal{P}res$ will be correct for all models in $\mathcal{M}$. This presentation $\mathcal{P}res$ may correspond to a "flattened" version of the PLUSS specification. The issues raised here are mostly similar to those raised by the computation of a suitable term rewriting system in symbolic evaluation tools. Hence, we believe that the solutions adopted for the symbolic evaluation tools in the environment

interpretations for the other operators, all interpretations of f that satisfy the specification axioms are the same."

ASSPEGIQUE+ [11] will prove useful, namely the way we are dealing with the **renaming, parameterization** and **instanciation** primitives of PLUSS.

When generating some adequate formulas, one has to be aware that some choices are made that induce a choice at the operational level. In particular, this also means that one is no longer in the context of a class of models, but in the context of some particular model.

When rewriting is used, the issue is to produce a rewriting system. With this goal, a first approach is to restrict oneself to axioms that are equations or conditional equations [24, 25, 27, 14, 16, 29]. In fact, using well-known logic laws, it is possible to admit a larger class of formulas (as done in [31, 11] where formulas with *iff*, disjunctions, etc., are, as much as possible, converted to several conditional equations). An equivalent rewriting system may be obtained when it is possible to orient the axioms into finitely terminating rewriting rules, and when it is possible to perform completion successfully. When rewriting involves a convergent system of non conditional (or positive conditional) rules, the "operational" model corresponds to the "flat" (i.e. the structuration of the specification is flattened) initial model. It is shown in [25] that specifications with positive/negative conditional equations (i.e. their premise is a conjunction of equations/disequations) admit "quasi-initial" models. Going back to the specification given in Fig. 3, the axiom $\mathrm{a} = \mathrm{b} \mid \mathrm{c} = \mathrm{d}$ is logically equivalent to either $\mathrm{a} \neq \mathrm{b} \Rightarrow \mathrm{c} = \mathrm{d}$, or to $\mathrm{c} \neq \mathrm{d} \Rightarrow \mathrm{a} = \mathrm{b}$. While the two latter forms are usable with conditional rewriting, choosing one of them implies the choice of a particular model of computation (cf. Fig. 4). This happens because operationally the translation of $\mathrm{a} \neq \mathrm{b} \Rightarrow \mathrm{c} = \mathrm{d}$ is : when normal-form(a) $\neq$ normal-form(b) then $\mathrm{c} \rightarrow \mathrm{d}$. In this case, the middle model of Fig. 4 is selected, while if the translation were : $\mathrm{c} \neq \mathrm{d} \Rightarrow \mathrm{a} = \mathrm{b}$, the left model would be selected [30]. When dealing with flat specifications, choosing one or the other of these two translation may seem rather arbitrary and without great significance. However, in the context of PLUSS modular specifications, such a choice is not "harmless" since the second translation leads to a model which is not in $\mathcal{M}_2$. Both models are quasi-initial, but only one of them belongs to $\mathcal{M}_2$.

When theorem proving is used the class of formulas allowed and the various elements of information needed depend on the theorem prover. For instance, in order to use LP [17, 18], one will provide the signature, equations, induction rules (e.g. : *assert Nat generated by 0,s*), and deduction rules (e.g. : *assert when* $i + j == i + k$ *yield* $j == k$, or: *assert S partitioned by* $\in$, or: *assert when (forall e)* $e \in x == e \in y$ *yield* $x == y$). Until recently conditional equations were not used in LP. Therefore, conditional equations had to be translated using either *if-then-else formulas* or *deduction rules (assert when ... yield ...)*. Unfortunately, such a (naive and direct) translation was not adequate: even when the semantical meaning of the axiom could be preserved, the operational content was quite different, and the proof mechanisms were not easy to use. This was a main motivation (among others) to introduce conditional equations into the latest version of LP.

4 Conclusion

The validation of the formal specification of a system is obviously a crucial step before the development process starts. In this paper, we have shown that, when considered carefully, this issue is refined into three questions: "Is this specification consistent?", "Is this specification sufficiently complete?", "Does this specification correspond to the problem to be specified?".
The first one can be formulated in a precise and mathematical way. However, depending on the semantics of the specification language, in general it is impossible to give an answer to it in practice unless careful restrictions on the specification style are enforced. The two other questions should be considered with a pragmatic understanding. Relative completeness is a tricky issue since one often wants to combine "intentionally incomplete" parts and "intentionally complete" parts in a specification. The adequacy of the specification regarding the problem/system considered can only be checked again on pragmatic grounds. The use of various tools to examine these questions is particularly important in order to formulate "concretely" (e.g. by stating explicitely the proofs to be performed) the issues to be checked. In [11] and [7] the adequacy of the specification of a transit node in a telephonic network is precisely investigated along these lines, and the usefulness of the ASSPEGIQUE+ and LP tools in this respect is shown.

Acknowledgements
This work is partially supported by a joint CNRS-NSF grant, and the E.E.C. ESPRIT Working Group COMPASS. Special thanks are due to Michel Bidoit for many fruitful discussions and careful reading of previous versions of this paper. It is a pleasure to thank Adrian Bondy for his help regarding the english language, and Anne Deo-Blanchard and Hubert Comon for their help with one of the examples.

References

1. G. Bernot. Good functors... are those preserving philosophy. In *Proc. of the Summer Conference on Category Theory and Computer Science*, pages 182–195. Springer-Verlag L.N.C.S. 283, 1987.
2. G. Bernot and M. Bidoit. Proving the correctness of algebraically specified software: Modularity and Observability issues. In *Proc. of the 2nd International Conference on Algebraic Methodology and Software Technology (AMAST)*, 1991.
3. D. Bert, P. Drabik, and R. Echahed. Manuel de référence de LPG. Technical Report 17, IMAG-LIFIA, 1987.
4. M. Bidoit. The stratified loose approach: A generalization of initial and loose semantics. In *Recent Trends in Data Type Specification, Selected Papers of the 5th Workshop on Specifications of Abstract Data Types*, pages 1–22. Springer-Verlag L.N.C.S. 332, 1987.
5. M. Bidoit. Pluss, un langage pour le développement de spécifications algébriques modulaires. Thèse d'Etat, Université Paris-Sud, 1989.

6. M. Bidoit, C. Choppy, C. Roques, and F. Voisin. About the semantics of renaming in PLUSS, 1994. In preparation.
7. M. Bidoit, C. Choppy, and F. Voisin. Validation d'une spécification algébrique du nœud de transit par prototypage et démonstration. en préparation, 1993.
8. M. Bidoit, M.-C. Gaudel, and A. Mauboussin. How to make algebraic specifications more understandable? An experiment with the Pluss specification language. *Science of Computer Programming*, 12(1), 1989.
9. R.M. Burstall and J.A. Goguen. Putting theories together to make specifications. In *Proc. of the 5th International Joint Conference on Artificial Intelligence (IJCAI)*, pages 1045–1058, 1977.
10. C. Choppy. Is my specification "correct"? A study with PLUSS specifications. L.R.I. Research Report 817, 1993.
11. C. Choppy, D. Bert, M. Bidoit, R. Echahed, C. Roques, and F. Voisin. Rapid prototyping with algebraic specifications: A case study. L.R.I. Research Report 844, 1993.
12. H. Ehrig, W. Fey, and H. Hansen. ACT ONE: an algebraic specification language with two levels of semantics. Technical Report 83–03, TU Berlin FB 20, 1983.
13. H. Ehrig and B. Mahr. *Fundamentals of algebraic specification 1. Equations and initial semantics*, volume 6 of *EATCS Monographs on Theoretical Computer Science*. Springer-Verlag, 1985.
14. R. Forgaard and J. Guttag. REVE: a term rewriting system generator with failure-resistant Knuth-Bendix, 1984. Proc. of an NSF workshop on the rewrite rule laboratory, and Report n° 84GEN008, General Electric.
15. K. Futatsugi, J.A. Goguen, J.-P. Jouannaud, and J. Meseguer. Principles of OBJ2. In *Proc. of the 12th ACM Symposium on Principles of Programming Languages (POPL)*, pages 52–66, 1985.
16. H. Ganzinger and R. Schafers. System support for modular order-sorted Horn clause specifications. In *Proc. of the 12th International Conference on Software Engineering*, pages 150–159, 1990.
17. S. Garland and J. Guttag. An overview of LP, the Larch Prover. In *Proc. of the Third International Conference on Rewriting Techniques and Applications*, pages 137–151. Springer-Verlag L.N.C.S. 355, 1989.
18. S. Garland and J. Guttag. A Guide to LP, The Larch Prover. Technical Report 82, DEC-SRC, 1991.
19. S. Garland, J. Guttag, and J. Horning. Debugging Larch Shared Language Specifications. *IEEE Transactions on Software Engineering*, 16(9):1044–1057, 1990.
20. M.-C. Gaudel. Structuring and modularizing algebraic specifications : the PLUSS specification language, evolutions and perspectives. In *Proc. of the 9th Symposium on Theoretical Aspects of Computer Science (STACS)*, pages 3–23. Springer-Verlag L.N.C.S. 577, 1992.
21. J.A. Goguen, J.W. Thatcher, and E.G. Wagner. An initial approach to the specification, correctness, and implementation of abstract data types. In R.T. Yeh, editor, *Current Trends in Programming Methodology*, volume 4, pages 80–149. Prentice Hall, 1978.
22. J. Guttag, J. Horning, and A. Modet. Report on the Larch Shared Language: Version 2.3. Technical Report 58, DEC-SRC, 1990.
23. J.V. Guttag and J.J. Horning. Report on the Larch shared language. *Science of Computer Programming*, 6(2):103–134, 1986.
24. S. Kaplan. Simplifying conditional term rewriting systems. *Journal of Symbolic Computation*, 4:295–334, 1987.

25. S. Kaplan. Positive/negative conditional rewriting. In *Proc. of the Symposium on Mathematical Foundations of Computer Science.* Springer-Verlag L.N.C.S., 1988.
26. T. Lehmann and J. Loeckx. The specification language of OBSCURE. In *Recent Trends in Data Type Specification, Selected Papers of the 5th Workshop on Specification of Abstract Data Types*, pages 131–153. Springer-Verlag L.N.C.S. 332, 1987.
27. P. Lescanne. Computer experiments with the REVE term rewriting systems generator. In *Proc. of the 10th ACM Symposium on Principles of Programming Languages (POPL)*, 1983.
28. T. Moineau. Réutilisation de logiciel : une approche algébrique, son application à Ada et les outils associés. Thèse de Doctorat, Université Paris-Sud, 1991.
29. J.-L. Rémy and H. Zhang. REVEUR 4: a system for validating conditional algebraic specifications of abstract data types. In *Proc. of the 6th European Conference on Artificial Intelligence (ECAI)*, pages 563–572, 1984.
30. C. Roques. PLUSS, validation de spécifications algébriques modulaires par prototypage par réécriture. L.R.I. DEA Report, 1990.
31. C. Roques. L'environnement ASSPEGIQUE+: Le valideur. L.R.I. Research Report 727, 1992.
32. C. Roques. Modularité dans les spécifications algébriques, Théorie et application. Thèse de Doctorat, Université Paris-Sud, 1994.
33. D.T. Sannella and A. Tarlecki. Building specifications in an arbitrary institution. In *Proc. of the International Symposium on Semantics of Data Types.* Springer-Verlag L.N.C.S. 173, 1984.
34. M. Wand. Final algebra semantics and data type extensions. *Journal of Computer and System Sciences*, 19:27–44, 1979.
35. M. Wirsing. Structured algebraic specifications: A kernel language. *Theoretical Computer Science*, 42(2):124–249, 1986.
36. M. Wirsing, M. Broy, W. Dosch, H. Partsch, and P. Pepper. On hierarchies of abstract data types. *Acta Informatica*, 20:1–33, 1983.

Semantic Constructions in the Specification Language Glider

S. Clérici, R. Jiménez, F. Orejas
Facultat d'Informàtica, Universitat Politècnica de Catalunya
Pau Gargallo 5, (08028) Barcelona, SPAIN

1. Introduction

Designing a specification is an activity consisting in building a formal and complete description of a problem from an informal, often incomplete and sometimes contradictory set of requirements. Therefore, during this process, the specifier may have to take "design" decisions to ignor certain requirements that would produce an inconsistency, or to add assumptions in order to ensure completeness. These design decisions may be incorrect with respect to the customer's wishes. In this case, some of the work will have to be re-done. As a consequence, designing a requirements specification cannot be seen as a "linear" process as it is, simplistically, often seen, i.e. a process in which, at each moment we have a full description of a subproblem that we, continuously, enlarge until the full problem is specified. Rather, when designing a specification, at any moment we have to deal with "incomplete" specifications describing only partially some aspects of a (sub)problem. Also, in subsequent steps we may refine these specifications by *completing* them, or we may have to backtrack and re-do part of the work. Therefore, a language aimed at giving support to the specification design process should offer the possibility of dealing with such a kind of incomplete specifications providing the operations for completing them. Also, it should facilitate modular structures that can faithfully reflect the design process of a given specification, so that backtracking may be limited to where the first inadequate design decision was taken.

In [CO 88, OSC 89, CO 91a], taking as a testbed the experimental language GSBL, we thoroughly studied the refinement relation associated with adding detail to an incomplete specification and concluded that it provided an inheritance relationship at the specification level playing the same rôle as "standard" inheritance in O-O design. A similar conclusion can also be found in [Gog 91]. This relationship is one of the bases of Glider, the specification language of the ICARUS project. Being specific, Glider is an algebraic specification language following the tradition of Clear [BG 77, BG 80]. Its basic construction is the *Cluster* for defining new types and operations. As usual, clusters may be parameterized. The logic underlying Glider is, essentially, first order partial logic. However, the language provides some additional constructions that increase its expressive power, such as the possibility of dealing with continuous (infinite) streams. In particular, streams allow us to describe time-varying objects in a simple manner.

New types may be defined directly or by inheritance. Direct definitions are "standard" algebraic specifications, i.e. a signature and a set of axioms extending some previous specifications. Definitions by inheritance are of two kinds: they may consist in adding detail to an "incomplete" specification (specialization inheritance) or in "restricting" a previously defined type (restriction inheritance). The former corresponds to the inheritance relationship discussed above, while the latter is especially valuable when building specifications in a model-oriented manner, a style also supported by Glider.

A specification in Glider has, in principle, loose semantics, i.e. its models may be not isomorphic. This corresponds to considering that the specification may be "incomplete". In this sense, "complete" specifications would have isomorphic semantics (for instance, initial), and completing (refining) a specification would mean restricting its associated class of models. Within an incomplete specification some parts may be considered to be completely defined (for instance, the booleans may be considered as fully defined within a larger and incomplete specification). The semantics of specifications in which some parts are completely defined is stated in terms of *constraints* [REI80, BG80]. In fact, the semantics of a specification is defined at two levels: at the model level, in terms of the set of models it denotes, and at the specification level, in terms of a *presentation* (a signature + a set of axioms) and a set of constraints defining the parts of the specification that must be interpreted monomorphically (up to isomorphism). This allows the simultaneous descripcion of the meaning of specification-building operations in terms of the resulting specifications and as constructions on models (or model classes).

The rest of the paper is organized as follows. In section 2 we provide a brief overview of Glider. In section 3, we introduce the basic semantic notions for Glider. Section 4 discusses the two forms of inheritance provided. In section 5 we show the use of continuous streams and how they are handled semantically. Finally, in section 6 we compare Glider with other specification languages drawing some conclusions.

Due to lack of space the presentation is necessarily a bit sketchy. In this sense, we cannot provide much detail about the use of the language (the interested reader may access several interesting case studies developed within ICARUS), nor can we study deeply the semantic issues introduced in the paper (this can be found in [Ore 90, JOP 91, ForSem 90, ForSem 91, CO 91b]). Instead, we have tried to present, in a rigourous manner, an introduction to Glider and its (we think) most interesting features. The reader is assumed to have some knowledge of the basic techniques used in Algebraic Specification (see, for instance [EM 85]). The notation and terminology used are the standard in that area.

ACKNOWLEDGEMENTS The design of Glider has been a collaborative effort within the ICARUS project involving many people, among whom we would like to cite E. Dubois, Ph. Du Bois, J.P. Finance, N. Levy, A. Rifaut, J. Souquieres and A. van Lamsweerde. This research has been partially supported by the Esprit Project ICARUS (ref. 2537) with complementary funding from the Spanish National Program TIC (ref. 0359-CE).

2. Overview of Glider

In this section we provide an introduction to the main constructions of Glider. The presentation will be rather informal, by means of examples together with some explanations to provide intuition. In the following sections more details on the semantics of these constructions will be given.

There are two kinds of modular constructions in Glider: *Clusters and Packages.* Clusters are the basic specification units and are used for defining new types (sorts) and operations. Conversely, packages are just used for grouping clusters and controlling visibility. Not being concerned in this paper with the static semantics aspects of Glider, packages will not be discussed further.

Type clusters are the constructions for defining new sorts. Every type cluster defines exactly a new sort (the sort of interest of the cluster) and, probably, some operations over this new sort. Below there are two simple examples of type clusters:

```
TYPE CLUSTER P_ORD
    OPERATION _≤_
      arity P_ORD × P_ORD → BOOL
      asserts  a≤a
               a≤b & b≤a ⇒ a=b
               a≤b & b≤c ⇒ a≤c
      hints  a, b, c: P_ORD
END P_ORD

TYPE CLUSTER INTEGER
    is generated by
    OPERATION 0
      arity  → INTEGER
    OPERATION succ
      arity  INTEGER → INTEGER
    OPERATION pred
      arity  INTEGER → INTEGER
      asserts  pred(succ(n)) = n
               succ(pred(n)) = n
      hints   n: INTEGER
END INTEGER
```

The former is a loose specification whose models are all partially ordered sets. Conversely, the latter is a monomorphic specification having the integers as its only model (up to isomorphism). This different interpretation is established by the clause *is generated by.* The *hints* clause says the variables and its type used in the *asserts* clause.

Operation clusters are used to define new operations over previously defined sorts. For example, below you can find an operation cluster defining new operations over the integers.

```
OPERATION CLUSTER INT_EXT
    OPERATION _+_
      arity   INTEGER × INTEGER → INTEGER
      asserts    0 + n = n
                 succ(n) + m = succ(n + m)
                 pred(n) + m = pred(n + m)
      hints    n, m: INTEGER
    OPERATION _-_
      arity   INTEGER × INTEGER → INTEGER
      asserts    n - 0 = n
                 n - succ(m) = pred(n - m)
                 n - pred(m) = succ(n - m)
      hints    n, m: INTEGER
END INT_EXT
```

As can be seen from the example above, any cluster may refer to sorts and operations defined "before" (taking into account some visibility rules not discussed here). This is the case of INT_ EXT that uses the sort INTEGER and the operations *0*, *succ* and *pred* from the cluster INTEGER defined above. This means that every cluster is seen as an extension of the previously defined clusters. This includes a number of data types considered to be "built-in" (BOOLEAN, INTEGER, CHAR, ...).

The semantics of the example above is again monomorphic. This is due to the fact that there is only one model (up to isomorphism) of INT_EXT extending the integers. However, not all operation clusters have monomorphic semantics, even if extending monomorphic types. For instance, below you can find such an example:

```
OPERATION CLUSTER CHOICE_INTEGER
    OPERATION choice
      arity SET_OF_INTEGER → INTEGER
      asserts  choice(S) ∈ S
      pre  not(empty(S))
      hints  S: SET_OF_INTEGER
END CHOICE_INTEGER
```

This cluster specifies the requirements for an operation for choosing elements out of a set of integers. Its semantics is loose since any possible choice function defines an admissible model. Note that the operation defined is partial since, according to the *pre* clause, it is only defined on non-empty sets.

Clusters may be parameterized, for instance below there is an example of a parameterized specification of sets (note that we do not require equality on the formal parameter, since it is assumed that equality is defined on every sort):

```
TYPE CLUSTER TRIV
END TRIV
```

TYPE CLUSTER SET [ELEM: TRIV]
  is generated by
  OPERATION { }
    arity → SET [ELEM]
  OPERATION add
    arity SET [ELEM] × ELEM → SET [ELEM]
    asserts add(add(s, e), e') = add(add(s, e'), e)
      add(add(s, e), e) = add(s, e)
    hints e, e': ELEM s: SET [ELEM]
  OPERATION _∈_
    arity ELEM × SET [ELEM] → BOOL
    asserts ¬(e ∈ { })
      e = e' ⇒ e ∈ add(s, e')
      e ≠ e' ⇒ (e ∈ add(s, e') = e ∈ s)
    hints e, e': ELEM s: SET [ELEM]

...

END SET

Actually, SET is also considered to be predefined, and so are the parameterized data types BAG, SEQ, CP (Cartesian Product), TBL (Tables) and UNION (Disjoint Union). This allows the specifier to use GLIDER in a "model-oriented style" of specification (e.g. à la VDM or Z). Another, especially interesting, predefined parameterized data type is STREAM, for defining (possibly) infinite sequences of values. This data type will be discussed in more detail in section 5.

The instantiation of a parameterized cluster is defined, as usual, by defining fitting morphisms between the formal and actual parameters[1]. For instance, below you can find an example of instantiation of the parameterized cluster ORD_SEQ:

TYPE CLUSTER ORD_SEQ_INT **is** ORD_SEQ[INT]
  with ≥ **for** ≤
END ORD_SEQ_INT

Where, assuming that ORD_SEQ[X:P_ORD] specifies the parameterized type of (ascending) ordered sequences of X, ORD_SEQ_INT defines the (descending) sequences of integers.

As stated in the introduction, in Glider we may use two kinds of inheritance relationships to build specifications. The first one, which we may call *specialization inheritance* allows us to define a new specification by adding detail to a previous one. A simple example could be the following:

---

[1]A parameterized specification in Glider may have more than one parameter. This is needed because clusters can only define one sort. As a consequence, the result of parameter passing is not a pushout but a colimit.

TYPE CLUSTER T_ORD **is subtype of** P_ORD
    asserts $a \leq b \vee b \leq a$ -- totality axiom
    hints a, b: T_ORD
END T_ORD

This specification has as models all totally ordered sets, i.e. all partially ordered sets satisfying, in addition, the totality axiom.

The second kind of inheritance allows us to define new types by *restricting* previously defined ones. For instance, the following could be a definition of the natural numbers:

TYPE CLUSTER NATURAL **is** INTEGER
    asserts $n \geq 0$
    hints n: NATURAL
END NATURAL

The intuition here is that the new type includes all the integers n satisfying $n \geq 0$. A more detailed discussion of both kinds of inheritance relationships can be found in section 4.

3. Basic constructions in Glider

The semantics of Glider is defined at two levels. At the specification level, a cluster denotes a *presentation* (a signature Σ and a set of axioms Ax) and a set of *constraints*, where these constraints restrict the possible interpretations of some parts of the specification. At the model level, the meaning of a cluster is a class of models, in particular the class of all (partial) Σ-algebras satisfying the given sets of axioms and constraints. For simplicity, from now on, we will assume that clusters are not parameterized.

Being specific, let us assume that we have defined a cluster T, including a sort of interest t and a set of operations Op. Furthermore, let us assume that T is an extension of clusters T1, ..., Tn. Then the semantics of T is defined as follows:

- *At the specification level* Let (Σ', Ax') be the result of "putting together" (technically, a colimit, as in [BG 80]) the presentations denoted by T1,...,Tn and let C' be the result of putting together the corresponding sets of constraints, then the meaning of T, $[T]_{Spec}$, consists of the presentation (Σ, Ax'$\cup$ Ax), where Σ is the signature obtained enriching Σ' by the new sort t and operations, i.e. $\Sigma = \Sigma' + (\{t\}, Op)$, and the set of constraints C' $\cup$ C, where C is the set of constraints introduced by T (in fact, this set contains at most one constraint).

- *At the model level* Let M' be the class of models obtained by "putting together" (technically, a general form of amalgamated sum [EBCO 91]) the model classes denoted by T1,..., Tn, then the meaning of T, $[T]_{Mod}$, is the class of all Σ-algebras A such that

a) A satisfies the axioms in Ax and the constraints in C

and b) the restriction of A to the sorts and operations in Σ' is a model in M', i.e. $A|_{\Sigma'} \in M'$.

For instance, given the cluster P_ORD defined above, its semantics at the specification level consists of a presentation (Σ, Ax), where Σ is a signature including the sorts BOOL and P_ORD and all the boolean operations plus the new operation $\leq$, and Ax includes all the boolean axioms plus the new axioms defining a partial order. P_ORD is an extension of the BOOL cluster and has as its constraints the restriction that its models can only have exactly the values of the constants True and False in the BOOL type. This is because P_ORD does not introduce any new constraint. At the model level, the models of P_ORD are all Σ-algebras whose BOOL part coincides exactly with the standard boolean values and where $\leq$ is a partial order on sort P_ORD.

The two semantics can be shown to be compatible in the following sense:

Theorem [JOP 91]

Given a cluster T, such that $[T]_{Spec} = ((\Sigma, Ax), C)$, we have:

$$[T]_{Mod} = \{A \in Alg_\Sigma \,/\, A \models Ax \text{ and } A \models C\}$$

Constraints are introduced by type clusters including the *is generated by* clause and by parameterized clusters. Also, clusters defined by inheritance may introduce constraints, however this will be discussed in more detail in section 4. Constraints introduced by clusters are the so-called *data constraints* or *free generating constraints* [BG 80, Rei 80, EWT 82] (when dealing with *streams* a slightly different kind of constraint is considered, see section 5). Given a presentation P, a free generating constraint over P is a pair of presentations (P1, P2) such that $P1 \subseteq P2 \subseteq P$ (this can be slightly generalized) and it states that the "interesting" models, i.e. the models satisfying the constraint, must fulfil the condition that their P2 restriction is freely generated from their P1 restriction. That is an algebra $A \in PAlg(P)$ satisfies a constraint (P1, P2), denoted $A \models (P1, P2)$ iff $(A|_{P1})^{|P2} \cong A|_{P2}$, where $-^{|P2}$ denotes the free construction associated with the inclusion $P1 \subseteq P2$.

When P1 is the empty specification, a constraint ($\emptyset$, P2) is often called an initial constraint. In this case, A satisfies ($\emptyset$, P2) iff its P2 restriction coincides with the initial P2 algebra, i.e. $T_{P2} \cong A|_{P2}$. For example, the constraint included in the semantics of P_ORD is the initial constraint ($\emptyset$, BOOL). As a consequence, the models of P_ORD must satisfy the condition that their BOOL part coincides with the initial BOOL-algebra.

The free generating constraint introduced by a type cluster T including an *is generated by* clause is (P', P), where P' is the result of putting together the presentations denoted by all clusters extended by T, and P is the presentation denoted by T. On the other hand, the constraint introduced by a parameterized cluster T is (PAR, P), where PAR is the presentation denoted by the formal parameter and P is the presentation denoted by T. For example, the SET cluster introduces the constraint (TRIV, SET). This constraint is satisfied by an algebra A iff its SET restriction, $A|_{SET}$, coincides with $P_F(A_{TRIV})$ (finite parts of the TRIV-values in A).

It must be noted that, given a cluster T and assuming that T must introduce the constraint (P1, P2), it may happen that (P1, P2) does not have an associated free construction. The reason is that Glider allows us to write arbitrary first order specifications and existence of free constructions is only ensured in the case of Horn clause specifications. Now, if this case happens T would be considered *erroneous*, although a tool for checking this kind of error will hardly ever be constructed.

4. Inheritance in Glider

In programming languages, types have only one meaning, i.e. they denote sets of values. However, in a specification language we may associate two different kinds of meanings to types: the set of models associated with the specification defining the type and the set of values associated with the type's sort of interest in each model. In this sense, there are two possible kinds of subclass/subtype relationships at the specification level: subclasses as set of models inclusion[2] and subclasses as subsorts. The latter, because of its similarity to subtyping in programming languages, has now a long tradition in algebraic specification (see, for instance, [GM 89, SNGM 89]). The former is related with several notions of specification refinement (see e.g. [ST 89]) and has proved to be very useful for incremental specification design, especially at the requirements level [CO 88, Gog 91].

The two forms of inheritance that we introduced in section 2 are based on these two kinds of subclass relationship: inheritance by specialization is based on the subclass relationship associated with model classes, while inheritance by restriction is associated with subsorting. Now, being specific, the two inheritance constructions work as follows:

4.1 Inheritance by specialization

If we define

TYPE CLUSTER T1 **is** T2
...
END T1

possibly including some new operations, Op, and axioms, Ax. Then, the semantics at the specification level of T1 is formed by the presentation h(P2)+(Op, Ax) and the set of constraints h(C), where (P2, C) is the specification level semantics of T2 and h is a renaming on the signature of P2 defined:

---

[2]Actually, the definition of this subclass relationship is slightly more involved. In our context, if SP1 is a subclass of SP2 it may happen that SP1 has a larger signature than SP2. Then we say that SP1 is a subclass of SP2 if for every A in Models(SP1) it holds that $A|_{\Sigma 2}$ is in Mod(SP2). This can be generalized by allowing arbitrary signature morphisms from $\Sigma 2$ to $\Sigma 1$.

$$h(x) = \text{if } x{=}t2 \text{ then } t1 \text{ else } x$$

where t1 and t2 are, respectively, the sorts of interest of T1 and T2. The model level semantics can be defined accordingly. For example, the semantics of the definition of T_ORD seen in section 2 would be similar to the following:

```
TYPE CLUSTER T_ORD
    OPERATION _≤_
      arity T_ORD × T_ORD → BOOL
      asserts  a≤a
               a≤b & b≤a ⇒ a=b
               a≤b & b≤c ⇒ a≤c
               a≤b v b≤a
      hints  a, b, c: T_ORD
END T_ORD
```

Specialization inheritance may be multiple. For instance, if we have the following definition:

```
TYPE CLUSTER  TOTREL
    OPERATION _≤_
      arity TOTREL × TOTREL → BOOL
      asserts  a≤b v b≤a
      hints  a, b: TOTREL
END TOTREL
```

Then T_ORD may also be defined as follows:

```
TYPE CLUSTER T_ORD is P_ORD, TOTREL
END T_ORD
```

The meaning of this definition is a straightforward extension of the semantics for the single inheritance case. In particular, the meaning of a type cluster T defined by multiple inheritance from T1,..., Tn (also including new operations, Op, and new axioms, Ax) would be defined in terms of the presentation h(P')+(Op, Ax) and the set of constraints h(C), where (P2, C) is now the result of putting together, after identification of their sorts of interest, the specification level semantics of T1,..., Tn and h is a renaming on the signature of P' defined:

$$h(x) = \text{if } x{=}t' \text{ then } t \text{ else } x$$

where t is the sort of interest of T and t' is the sort of interest of P'.

4.2 Inheritance by restriction

When we write a definition like the one below:

```
TYPE CLUSTER  LIMITED_INTEGER  is subtype of  INTEGER
    asserts  0 ≤ x ≤ 100
    hints  x: LIMITED_INTEGER
END LIMITED_INTEGER
```

the intuition is that we are specifying a subtype (subsort) of the integers including all the values from sort INTEGER satisfying the property $0 \leq x \leq 100$. However, when defining the semantics of Glider we have preferred not to deal with true subsorting. Instead, our choice has been to "simulate" the subsorting by means of the use of implicit coercions and retractions, in a way similar to what was done in some early versions of OBJ [GJM 85]. Being specific, given the definition:

TYPE CLUSTER T **is subtype of** T1
asserts P
...
END T

its meaning could be seen as the definition of a new sort LIMITED_INTEGER, one predicate *is_limited_integer?* (defined in terms of the invariant) and coercion and retraction operations with empty names, one from LIMITED_INTEGER into INTEGER and the other one in the opposite direction. The latter being defined only when the predicate *is_limited_integer?* is true. Both operations are assumed to be injective and each one is the inverse of the other one. That is, the above specification of LIMITED_INTEGER would be equivalent to the following "standard" cluster:

```
TYPE CLUSTER  LIMITED_INTEGER
     is generated by
     OPERATION coerc
        arity  LIMITED_INTEGER → INTEGER
        asserts   coerc(n) = coerc(m) ⇒ n = m
        hints    n, m: LIMITED_INTEGER
     OPERATION retr
        arity  INTEGER → LIMITED_INTEGER
        pre    is_limited_integer?(n)
        asserts    retr(n) = retr(m) ⇒ n = m
                   retr(coerc(p)) = p
                   coerc(retr(n)) = n
        hints    n, m: INTEGER  p: LIMITED_INTEGER
     OPERATION is_limited_integer?
        arity  INTEGER → BOOL
        asserts 0 ≤ x ≤ 100
        hints    x: INTEGER
END LIMITED_INTEGER
```

with the additional feature of assuming that the two operations *coerc* and *retr* are anonymous, i.e. they have "empty" names. As a consequence, the term X+1, with X:LIMITED_INTEGER, would denote the application of the plus operation to the conversion of X to type INTEGER and to 1. Moreover, the result is of type INTEGER but if it satisfies the invariant it may also be seen of type LIMITED_INTEGER, again by the implicit application of the anonymous retraction.

Although Glider is an algebraic specification language, it also promotes the model-oriented style of specification (à la VDM or Z). In this sense, inheritance by restriction plays an important rôle since, together with the pre-defined types, it allows the *extensional* definition of sets of values. A very simple example of this can be found in the NATURAL specification shown in section 2.

5. Streams

In order to support, in a simple manner, the definition of objects that "evolve in time", Glider provides the predefined (parameterized) type of streams, where a stream is a (possibly) infinite sequence.The modelling of "evolving" objects by means of infinite sequences has now some tradition in the area of functional programming. At the specification level, this technique was exploited within the PROSPECTRA Project to describe distributed processes (e.g. see [Bro 88]). The idea consists in representing the evolving object by a stream describing its history, i.e. the sequence of successive states of the object. For instance, the specification of a cinema may have the following form:

```
TYPE CLUSTER CINEMA
  is OBJECT [SEATS:SET[ SEAT], MOVIE*:STRING,
               SOLD-SEATS*:SET[SEAT]]
...
END CINEMA
```

where OBJECT is the name given in Glider to the streams data type, that is we are defining a stream of triples. In addition, if a field is marked with an '*' this denotes that it may vary, i.e. in this case we know that, in the model denoted by the specification, the field SEATS is always the same one for all the components of any stream.

Streams have a special status in Glider: they are the only predefined data type that cannot be defined using Glider itself. The reason is that, if we take the stream specification and we attach to it the standard Glider semantics, then the model that we obtain only includes the standard sequences. Nevertheless, streams are treated in Glider in a rather uniform way: associated with the stream specification there is a constraint that, given a set of values, states how streams over these values are built; in a similar manner as the constraint associated with SEQ states how sequences are built. The difference lies in the nature of the constraints. As we have seen, the constraints for "standard" types are defined in terms of free constructions. For the stream data type, the associated constraint is defined in terms of a *continuous free construction*, i.e. a free construction over categories of continuous algebras. To be precise, in [JOP 91] we extended results in [GTW 77, Mol 85] showing the existence of free constructions associated with the logic of continuous (in)equational specifications working as intended.

It must be remarked that mixing the two kinds of constraints in a single framework does not provide any additional complication, since all semantic constructions are independent of the kind of constraints used [EBCO 91].

6. Conclusions and related work

Glider is a specification language in the tradition of Clear [BG 77, BG 80]. In this sense, it has many things in common with other algebraic specification languages. Actually, there are no original constructions in Glider, since the aim of the ICARUS project was not to provide innovative constructions for specification languages. Rather, within ICARUS, the language was only a tool to support the research in methods for specification design. The decision to design Glider was taken after considering that none of the known languages was fully adequate for the purposes of the project. In this sense, Glider was designed taking into account the needs of ICARUS and making use of the existing specification language "technology".

Glider owes much to Clear. As with all other algebraic specification languages most of its constructions are based on those of Clear. Its semantics using constraints derives from Clear, and a notion similar to Clear's *environments* is used for expressing *sharing* in the semantics of Glider (although this issue has not been discussed in this paper). Defining the semantics at two levels has its origins in LOOK [ETLZ 82] and in Act One [EM 85]. Inheritance by specialization was taken from GSBL [CO 88, CO 91a], but similar notions can be found in OBJ [FGJM 85], LOOK and Larch [GH 86]. Finally, inheritance by restriction and streams can be found in PAnndA-S, the specification language of the PROSPECTRA project [KH 90].

To conclude, it must be said that the combination of all these features makes Glider a specification language which is very powerful and expressive, but not especially complex. Actually, as can be glimpsed in this paper, Glider has extremely simple and uniform semantics.

6. References

[BG 77] Burstall, R.M.; Goguen, J.A.: "Putting theories together to make specifications", Proc. V IJCAI, Cambridge Mass., 1977, pp. 1045-1058.

[BG 80] Burstall, R.M.; Goguen, J.A.: "The semantics of Clear, a specification language", Proc. Copenhagen Winter School on Abstract Software Specification, Springer LNCS 86, pp. 292-332, 1980.

[Bro 88] Broy, M.: "An example for the design of distributed systems in a formal setting: the lift problem". Report MIP-8802, Universität Passau, 1988.

[CO 88] Clerici, S.; Orejas, F.: "GSBL: An algebraic specification language based on inheritance" in ECOOP'88 S. Gjessing y K. Nygaard' (eds.), Springer-Verlag Lecture Notes in Computer Science 322 (1988) pp. 78-92.

[CO 91a] Clerici, S.; Orejas, F.: "The specification language GSBL" in 'Recent trends in data type specification' (H. Ehrig, K. Jantke, F. Orejas, H. Reichel (eds.)) Springer-Verlag Lecture Notes in Computer Science 534, 1991, pp. 31-51.

[CO 91b] Clerici, S.; Orejas, F.: First Definition of the Formal Semantics of the ICARUS Process Language (system's funcionalities), Icarus-Forsem Report 009-R, 1991.

[EBCO 91] Ehrig, H.; Baldamus, M.; Cornelius, F.; Orejas, F.: "Theory of algebraic module specifications including behavioural semantics, constraint and aspects of generalized morphisms", Inv. Paper, Proc. 2nd AMAST Conference Iowa City, May 1991, to appear also in Springer LNCS.

[EM 85] Ehrig, H.; Mahr, B.: "Fundamentals of algebraic specification 1", EATCS Monographs on Theor. Comp. Sc., Springer Verlag, 1985.

[ETLZ 82] Ehrig, H.; Thatcher, J.W.; Lucas, P.; Zilles, S.N.: "Denotational and initial algebra semantics of the algebraic specification language LOOK", draft report, IBM Research, 1982.

[EWT 82] Ehrig, H.; Wagner, E.G.; Thatcher, J.W.: "Algebraic constraints for specifications and canonical form results", Institut für Software und Theoretische Informatik, T.U. Berlin Bericht Nr. 82-09, 1982.

[FGJM 85] Futatsugi, K.; Goguen, J.A.; Jouannaud, J.-P.; Meseguer, J.: "Principles of OBJ2", Proc. 12th POPL, Austin 1985.

[Forsem 90] Semantic definition of Glider, Icarus-Forsem Report 004-R, 1990.

[Glider1] First description of the ICARUS language kernel for the product level, FUN-Namur, INRIA/CRIN - Nancy, PRLB - Brussels, 1989.

[Glider2] First version of the ICARUS product and process language for the specification of system functionalities, FUN-Namur, INRIA/CRIN - Nancy, PRLB - Brussels, 1990.

[Glider3] Second version of the ICARUS product , process and rationale language for the specification of system functionalities, Part I: the Glider Language, FUN-Namur, INRIA/CRIN - Nancy, PRLB - Brussels, 1990.

[Glider4] GLIDER Manual, FUN-Namur, Sema Group - Brussels, 1990.

[GH 86] Guttag, J.V.; Horning, J.J.: "Report on the Larch shared language", Science of Computer Programming 6, 2 (1986) 103-134.

[GJM 85] Goguen, J.A.; Jouannaud, J.P.; Meseguer, J.: "Operational semantics of order-sorted algebra", Proc. ICALP'85, Nafplion, Springer LNCS 194 (1985) 221-231.

[GM 89] Goguen, J.A.; Meseguer, J.: "Order-sorted algebra I: Equational deduction for multiple inheritance, overloading, exceptions and partial overloaded operations", SRI Int., Comp. Sc. Lab. Rep., SRI-CSL-89-10, 1989.

[Gog 91] Goguen, J.A.: "Types as Theories". Topology and Category Theory in Computer Science, Clarendon Press. Oxford, 1991.

[GTWW 77] Goguen, J.A.; Thatcher, J.W.; Wagner, E.W.; Wright, J.B.: "Initial Algebra Semantics and Continuous Algebras". J. ACM 24, 1 (1877), 68-95.

[JOP 91] Jiménez, R.; Orejas, F.; Peña, R.: "Some more algebraic constructs for the semantics of Glider", Icarus-Forsem Report 009-R, 1990.

[KH 90] Krieg-Brückner, B.; Hoffmann, B. (eds.) PROgram development by SPECification and TRAnsformation. Part I: Methodology, Part II: Language Family, Part III: System. PROSPECTRA Reports M.1.1.S3-R-55.2, -56.2, -57.2. Universität Bremen (to appear in Springer LNCS).

[Mol 85] Möller, B.: "On the Algebraic Specification Of Infinite Objects - Ordered and Continuous Models of Algebraic Types". Acta Informatica 22, 537-578, 1985.

[Ore 90] Orejas, F.: "Some basic algebraic constructs for the semantics of Glider", Icarus-Forsem Report 003-N, 1990.

[OSC 89] Orejas, F.; Sacristan, V.; Clerici, S.: "Development of algebraic specifications with constraints", Proc. Workshop in Categ. Methods in Comp. Sc. Springer LNCS 393 (1989).

[REI 80] Reichel, H.: "Initially restricting algebraic theories", Proc. MFCS 80, Springer LNCS 88 (1980), pp. 504-514.

[SNGM 89] Smolka, G.; Nutt, W.; Goguen, J.; Meseguer, J.: "Order sorted equational computation", Resolution of equations in algebraic structures, Vol. 2. Academic Press 1989. pp. 299-367.

[ST 89] Sannella, D.; Tarlecki, A.: "Toward formal development of ML programs: foundations and methodology", Proc. TAPSOFT 89 (Barcelona), Springer LNCS 352 (1989) 375-389.

On Certification of Specifications for TROLL *light* Objects

Stefan Conrad *

Technische Universität Braunschweig, Informatik, Abt. Datenbanken
Postfach 3329, D-38023 Braunschweig, Germany
e-mail: conrad@idb.cs.tu-bs.de

Abstract. In this paper we informally present a certification calculus for the object specification language TROLL *light*. The language supports the state- and behavior-oriented specification of information systems. It allows orthogonal construction of large systems from subsystems. The certification calculus provides a basis for verifying properties of specified objects. Besides an introduction to this calculus we show how formulae of this calculus can be derived from TROLL *light* specifications. The transformation from specification language into calculus shall later be done automatically. Furthermore, we demonstrate proving of object properties by means of an example.

1 Introduction

In the last years a lot of research has paid attention to object-oriented specification. Analogously to algebraic specification of data types [EM85, EM90, Wir90, e.g.] object-oriented specification aims at providing a theoretical foundation for the development of larger software systems. A lot of work has been done up to now to investigate theoretical foundations of object-orientation, e.g., [SE91, ES91, FM91b]. At first glance, object-orientation and algebraic specification seem to be two areas based on quite different paradigms. However, it was shown that these two areas are closely related, that there are a lot of analogies between them, and that they can profit a lot from each other, e.g. [ESS90, GR90, Reg90, EGS92].

Besides theoretical foundations also concrete specification languages are needed. In this paper we choose TROLL *light* [CGH92] for the specification of objects. TROLL *light* is a simplified dialect of TROLL [JSHS91, JSH91]. It offers a minimal number of basic concepts for the specification of objects, because it was designed with the aim to facilitate investigation of problems concerning prototyping of specifications and reasoning about specified objects. For these purposes TROLL itself seems to be too extensive.

* Work reported here has been partially supported by the German Ministry for Research and Technology (BMFT) under Grant No. 01 IS 203 D (project "KorSo", i.e., correct software) and by CEC under Grant No. BRA 6112 (COMPASS II).

In TROLL *light* the structure of objects is given by subobjects and attributes. (First-order) Constraints can be specified to restrict the possible object states. The dynamic of objects is modeled by events which could be regarded as abstractions of object state transitions. Valuation rules determine the effect of events as changes of attribute values. The specification of behavior patterns restrict the possible occurrences of events by imposing possible life cycles to objects. Interaction between objects (i.e., synchronous event calling in TROLL *light*) is the way how objects can communicate. TROLL *light* allows to compose objects (resp. systems) from subobjects (resp. subsystems) in an orthogonal way [HCG94].

For this language we informally present a certification calculus in a style similar to [Fia88, FM91a, FM91b]. This calculus enables us to formulate properties of specified objects and to prove such properties by using axioms which can be derived from their specification. Clearly, a formal transformation from specification language to certification calculus is needed, which is also sketched in this paper. Proving properties formulated in the presented certification calculus shall later be supported by a theorem prover resp. a proof assistant system.

Here, we present a simplified version of our calculus, for example, we disregard negation. Moreover, we do not formally deal with model-theoretical or proof-theoretical semantics of our calculus in this paper. This is done extensively in [Con93].

In the sequel we first want to introduce our running example, i.e., an object description by means of TROLL *light*. Then we briefly present the certification calculus. Afterwards, we deal with the transformation of basic TROLL *light* constructs into formulae of the certification calculus. This transformation is demonstrated by a simple example. To round off the presentation of the calculus and the transformation, basic inference rules for our calculus are presented. The proof of a simple object property gives an example for the use of our certification calculus. In the conclusions we briefly discuss the relation between TROLL and TROLL *light* and we give some remarks concerning future work.

2 The Runing Example: Objects Representing Authors

Instead of giving a detailed introduction to TROLL *light*, we prefer to present our running example used throughout this paper and to explain only those concepts of TROLL *light* which are necessary to understand the paper. A detailed, informal introduction to TROLL *light* is given in [CGH92]. Furthermore, [GCH93] sketches a computational model and [HCG94] deals with specifying in a modular way using TROLL *light*. In addition, [DG94] gives a brief and concise overview of TROLL *light*.

The following object description (called *template*) models authors having a name, a date of birth and some numbers of sold books distinguished by years. Such `author` objects may be created and they may change their names (but only once in the course of a life). Moreover, the number of sold books for some year can be stored resp. can be updated. Finally, an `author` object may die.

```
TEMPLATE Author
  DATA TYPES  String, Date, Nat;
  ATTRIBUTES  Name : string;
              DateOfBirth : date;
              SoldBooks(Year:nat) : nat;
  EVENTS      BIRTH create(Name:string, DateOfBirth:date);
                    changeName(NewName:string);
                    storeSoldBooks(Year:nat, Number:nat);
              DEATH destroy;
  CONSTRAINTS DEF(SoldBooks(Y))  IMPLIES  SoldBooks(Y) <= 10000;
  VALUATION   [create(N,D)] Name=N, DateOfBirth=D;
              [changeName(N)] Name=N;
              [storeSoldBooks(Y,C)] SoldBooks(Y)=C;
  BEHAVIOR    PROCESS authorlife1 =
                ( storeSoldBooks -> authorlife1 |
                  changeName -> authorlife2 |
                  destroy -> POSTMORTEM );
              PROCESS authorlife2 =
                ( storeSoldBooks -> authorlife2 |
                  destroy -> POSTMORTEM );
              ( create -> authorlife1 );
END TEMPLATE;
```

The constraint specified for author objects demands that for each year the number of sold books must not exceed 10,000 (provided that the number for that year is defined at all). In the VALUATION section of the template the effect of events on attributes is described. In the BEHAVIOR part the admissible life cycles are specified. It can easily be seen that a *changeName* event may only occur at most once in the life of an author object.

We can also consider a TROLL *light* template as a set of axioms describing the structure and behavior of objects. These axioms include the axioms of used data types, static integrity constraints, valuation constraints for events (describing the transitions from object states to other object states by event execution), and restrictions on life cycles. With respect to this view of object specifications a translation into a suitable calculus is an obvious intention.

3 The Certification Calculus

In this section we will give an informal presentation of our certification calculus. This calculus is based on the work of J. Fiadeiro and T. Maibaum [Fia88, FS90, FM91a, FM91b, FM92] who have developed a general framework for object calculi and on the work of A. Sernadas, C. Sernadas, and J.F. Costa [SSC92] who presented an *Object Specification Logic*, called OSL. In the main we have adopted parts of their approaches and suited them to our specification language TROLL *light*. Here, we abstain from a formal introduction of the calculus because the central point of this paper is the transformation from TROLL *light* into this calculus. Furthermore, the authors mentioned before gave very detailed descriptions of their calculi and logics.

For simplicity, we shall only consider simple TROLL *light* templates, i.e., templates without subobject declarations and without object-valued attributes.

We assume a fixed *data signature* containing data sorts, function symbols, and predicate symbols to be given. Especially, there is an equality predicate symbol for each data sort. The data signature covers the data types used in TROLL *light* templates. Furthermore, we assume a given algebra which interprets the data sorts, functions, and predicates of the data signature. We demand that each carrier set includes a special value $\perp$, denoting undefinedness.

Next, we extend the data signature to a *template signature* by adding the attribute symbols, event symbols, and o-machine-state symbols declared in the template. Therefore, we need additional sorts: An *object sort* for each template, a corresponding *event sort*, and a corresponding sort for *o-machine states.*

Since it is a main goal of our work to be able to reason about several objects at a time we have introduced objects sorts. In consequence, we must add a parameter to each specified subobject, attribute, and event name for referring to the corresponding objects.

In order to formulate properties of objects within the calculus we need *terms* as basic building blocks which can be composed to *propositions.* Combining propositions in an adequate way we obtain *formulae.* Formulae are the means of our calculus to express object properties. Then, proving object properties means to derive formulae from a given set of formulae. This given set is the result of the transfomation described in Sect. 4.

Terms may be built from typed variables and function symbols as usual. Furthermore, event symbols and o-maschine-state symbols may be used to construct terms in the same way as done with function symbols. Terms constructed by event symbols are terms of the corresponding event sort. Typical examples for terms are:

$$42$$
$$authorlife1$$
$$storeSoldBooks(1992, 42)$$

where 42 is a term of (data) sort *nat*, $authorlife1$ is a term of the o-maschine-state sort for `author` objects and $storeSoldBooks(1992, 42)$ is event term for `author` objects.

From terms we can now proceed to *propositions.* Propositions are mainly given by predicate expressions $p(t_1, \ldots, t_n)$ (with p a predicate symbol and t_i appropriate terms). Furthermore we allow negation (i.e., $\neg P$) and the use of positional operators (i.e., $[t_o.t_e]P$, where t_o is a term denoting an object and t_e a term describing an event for this object). A proposition $[t_o.t_e]P$ could be read as "if the next event occurring in object t_o is t_e then P holds afterwards". We distinguish between two kinds of predicate symbols: rigid and non-rigid ones (i.e., state-independent resp. state-dependent predicate symbols). For instance, rigid predicate symbols are given by the used data type specification (e.g., $\leq$ for integers), whereas attributes of objects are modeled by non-rigid predicates. Furthermore we have non-rigid predicates for dealing with enabledness and occurrence of events (*enable* and *occur*). For instance,

$$SoldBooks(A, 1992, 42)$$
$$\neg\, enable(A.changeName(\text{"}Smith\text{"}))$$
$$[A.create(N, D)]Name(A, N)$$

are obviously propositions for **author** objects.

The next step is to introduce *formulae*. As mentioned above formulae are the real means of our calculus to describe object properties. Such formulae are Gentzen-formulae (Gentzen-clauses) built from propositions, i.e., $P_1, \ldots, P_n \rightarrow Q_1, \ldots, Q_m$ is a formula if $P_1, \ldots, P_n, Q_1, \ldots, Q_m$ are propositions. A formula $P_1, \ldots, P_n \rightarrow Q_1, \ldots, Q_m$ has to be understood such that if all propositions $P_1, \ldots, P_n$ hold in an object state then one of the propositions $Q_1, \ldots, Q_m$ holds in the same state, too. In contrast to propositions formulae are not state-dependent, i.e., they are true if and only if they hold for every possible object state. The following formulae describe possible properties of **author** objects:

$$\begin{array}{ll} (1) & Name(A, \text{"}Jones\text{"}) \rightarrow SoldBooks(A, 1994, 0) \\ (2) & \rightarrow [destroy]Name(A, \bot) \\ (3) & SoldBooks(A, Y, N),\ \leq(N + M, 10000) \\ & \qquad \rightarrow enable(A.storeSoldBooks(Y, M)) \end{array}$$

Formula (1) claims that for each state in which the name of an author is "*Jones*", the value of the author's *SoldBooks* attribute is 0 for the year 1994 in the same state. Formula (2) states that, after the occurrence of the death event *destroy*, the value of the attribute *Name* is always undefined (for any author). By formula (3) we make the permission of an event $storeSoldBooks(Y, M)$ for an author A to depend on the satisfaction of the propositions $SoldBooks(A, Y, N)$ and $\leq(N + M, 10000)$ for the same instantiation of the variables Y and M.

Now, we can describe objects corresponding to a template by a set of formulae. In fact, the transformation presented in Sect. 4 yields for a TROLL *light* template a set of formulae as result. For reasoning about objects, inference rules are needed. In Sect. 6 we briefly present basic inference rules for the propositional part of our calculus.

Finally, a remark concerning the sorts of *o-machine states* is necessary. A suitable interpretation for such a sort is a carrier set which includes a value for each possible process state (or *o-machine state*) an object can take. These states can be extracted from the process specification in the BEHAVIOR part of the corresponding template.

4 Transforming Specifications into Formulae

In the sequel we assume a simple TROLL *light* template to be given. In this template there are no subobjects, no object-valued attributes, and no interaction. Hence, we have to deal with constraints, valuations and behavior. Thereby, we can concentrate on presenting the basic concepts of the transformation from specifications into formulae of our calculus. An extension for derived attributes (specified in the `DERIVATION` part) is straightforward and can easily be integrated. Subobjects, interaction, and object-valued attributes require further consideration. Their transformation into our calculus does not impose any special problem.

Besides axioms obtained from the constraints, valuations, and behavior specification in a TROLL *light* template, axioms for the used data types have to be added. For instance, the transitivity of the predicate $\leq_{<nat,nat>}$ has to be formulated as a formula of the certification calculus (for convenience, we use infix notation for $\leq_{<nat,nat>}$):

$$(X \leq_{<nat,nat>} Y),\ (Y \leq_{<nat,nat>} Z)\ \rightarrow\ (X \leq_{<nat,nat>} Z)$$

Because we assume that the used data types are specified elsewhere (for example using an algebraic specification language like ACT ONE [EM85] or SPECTRUM [BFG+92]), we do not further deal with axioms obtained from data types. The set of these axioms is denoted by DT_{axioms} and is assumed to be given.

Constraints:
As constraints we allow simple formulae without any positional operator. This is because constraints express state-independent properties. Of course, the constraints of a template must be consistent, i.e., it must be possible to fulfill all of them at the same time. These constraints lead to axioms which hold in every state of an object during its life time, i.e., an object must not reach a state in which one of the constraints is violated. Such constraints have to be transformed to formulae of the calculus. If we can convert a constraint to a set of formulae having the form

$$A_1 \wedge \ldots \wedge A_n \ \Rightarrow\ B_1 \vee \ldots \vee B_m$$

with A_i and B_j being propositions, these formulae correspond to formulae of our calculus:

$$(\,A_1, \ldots, A_n \rightarrow B_1, \ldots, B_m\,).$$

Here, we do not want to investigate which class of constraints can be transformed into an equivalent set of such formulae (this has already been done in several textbooks on classical logic). However, it seems to be evident that this class is sufficiently large for realistic specification tasks.

The set of positional formulae which can be derived by transforming the constraints given in a TROLL *light* template, is denoted by C_{axioms}.

Valuations:
In TROLL *light* specifications a valuation formula describes the change of attributes caused by the occurrence of some event. Thereby, valuation formulae describe the state transitions of objects where an object's state is determined by the values of its attributes (and its *o-machine state*). As pointed out in [KM89, e.g.] we have to distinguish between the *description* and the *prescription* of object behavior. By description we mean information about the effect of events, i.e., the changes they cause to attributes. By prescription we mean information about the permission of events, i.e., when some event may occur. TROLL *light* separates these two kinds of information into the `VALUATION` part (for the descriptive information) and the `BEHAVIOR` part (for the prescriptive information).

A TROLL *light* valuation formula consists of a precondition, an event term, and a sequence of equations:

$$\{ \; precond \; \} \; [e] \; eq_1 , \; \dots \; , \; eq_m$$

The precondition *precond* is optional and may only be a formula without any temporal or positional operator (as described above for constraints). The equations eq_i are equations of the form $a(t_1, \dots, t_k) = t$ where a is an attribute symbol and $t_1, \dots, t_k$ are suitable parameter terms for a. The terms $a(t_1, \dots, t_k)$ and t must be of the same sort. In the certification calculus each equation eq_i can be expressed as a proposition (with O a variable of the object sort corresponding to the considered template)

$$[O.e]a(O, t_1, \dots, t_k, t)$$

If a precondition *precond* is given, it must be transformed to a proposition PC (this may require to add further formulae in order to derive PC). For the valuation formula we get the following positional formula:

$$PC \; \rightarrow \; [O.e]a(O, t_1, \dots, t_k, t)$$

However, this is not the only kind of formula which can be generated for a `VALUATION` section of a template. Obviously, we can also state that the value of an attribute b which is not manipulated by any valuation rule for an event e remains unchanged:

$$b(O, P_1, \dots, P_l, V) \; \rightarrow \; [O.e]b(O, P_1, \dots, P_l, V)$$

Clearly more complicated cases can arise, but, here, we do not want to go into further details.

As shown, valuation formulae can be transformed to formulae of our calculus. The set of positional formulae obtained by transforming the valuation formulae is denoted by V_{axioms}.

Behavior:
Deriving axioms from the `BEHAVIOR` section of a TROLL *light* template is not as straightforward as for constraints and valuation formulae. The behavior specification combines the specification of process state transitions (or, as we prefer to say, o-machine state transitions) and the specification of permission for events in dependence on o-machine states and, eventually, on the object's state. Each TROLL *light* behavior specification can be written in the following form:

$$
\begin{array}{llll}
\texttt{PROCESS}\ P_1 & = & (\ \{pc_{1,1}\}\ e_{1,1}\ \texttt{->}\ P_{1,1} & | \\
 & & \quad \ldots\ | & \\
 & & \quad \{pc_{1,n_1}\}\ e_{1,n_1}\ \texttt{->}\ P_{1,n_1}\ ); & \\
\vdots & & & \\
\texttt{PROCESS}\ P_k & = & (\ \{pc_{k,1}\}\ e_{k,1}\ \texttt{->}\ P_{k,1} & | \\
 & & \quad \ldots\ | & \\
 & & \quad \{pc_{k,n_k}\}\ e_{k,n_k}\ \texttt{->}\ P_{k,n_k}\ ); &
\end{array}
$$

$$(\ \{pc_{b_1}\}\ e_{b_1}\ \texttt{->}\ P_{b_1}\ \ |\ \ \ldots\ \ |\ \ \{pc_{b_l}\}\ e_{b_l}\ \texttt{->}\ P_{b_l}\ );$$

The process names $P_1, \ldots, P_k$ denote o-machine states. All $P_{i,j}$ and P_{b_i} must be in $\{P_1, \ldots, P_k\} \cup \{\texttt{POSTMORTEM}\}$, where `POSTMORTEM` denotes the o-machine state after death. The event terms $e_{b_1}, \ldots, e_{b_l}$ must be built from event symbols marked as birth events.The other event terms must not be birth event terms. The preconditions $pc_{i,j}$ and pc_{b_i} are optional.

With respect to the abstract behavior specification given above, here, the process names P_1, ..., P_k, and `POSTMORTEM` denote different o-machine states. In order to distinguish TROLL *light* syntax from the syntax of the calculus we will do not use a symbol *postmortem* in the calculus. Instead, we introduce the symbol *vacant* denoting the state of an object in which the object is not alive.

In order to simplify the derivation of axioms from behavior specification, we introduce an implicit attribute state. This attribute has the current o-machine state of the considered object as value. Now, we derive the following axioms describing the specified behavior (PC_{b_i} resp. $PC_{i,j}$ denotes a proposition obtained by transforming the (optional) preconditions pc_{b_i} resp. $pc_{i,j}$):

- for each $e_{b_i} \in \{ e_{b_1}, \ldots, e_{b_l} \}$:

$$state(O, vacant),\ PC_{b_i}\ \rightarrow\ enable(O.e_{b_i}),$$

$$state(O, vacant),\ PC_{b_i}\ \rightarrow\ [O.e_{b_i}]state(O, P_{b_i})$$

- for each $P_i \in \{ P_1, \ldots, P_k \}$ and for each $e_{i,j} \in \{ e_{i,1}, \ldots, e_{i,n_k} \}$:

$$state(O, P_i),\ PC_{i,j}\ \rightarrow\ enable(O.e_{i,j}),$$

$$state(O, P_i),\ PC_{i,j}\ \rightarrow\ [O.e_{i,j}]state(O, P_{i,j})$$

For each precondition which is omitted in the specification we can omit the corresponding proposition PC within the formulae given above. The set of all positional formulae derived by transforming the behavior part of the considered TROLL *light* template is denoted by B_{axioms}.

The logical description of objects (corresponding to a given TROLL *light* template) is given by the set $DESC = DT_{axioms} \cup C_{axioms} \cup V_{axioms} \cup B_{axioms}$.[2]

5 An Example

In this section we will present the transformation of a TROLL *light* template into the certification calculus by example. For this purpose we will reuse the template for `author` objects given in Sect. 2. Because the transformation is rather straightforward we will essentially restrict ourselves to present the results of the transformation.

First, we have to give the prerequisites before we can construct terms, propositions, and formulae. The template signature consists of:

- the data sorts *string*, *date*, and *nat* together with the following predicate symbols (here indexed by their parameter sorts):

  $DEF_{<string>}$, $DEF_{<date>}$, $DEF_{<nat>}$, $\leq_{<nat,nat>}$, $=_{<nat,nat>}$, $=_{<date,date>}$, $=_{<string,string>}$.

  These data sorts and predicate symbols constitute the data signature. Function symbols and further predicate symbols are not required for this example.
- attribute symbols declared in the template:

  $Name_{<\mathtt{author}>,string}$, $DateOfBirth_{<\mathtt{author}>,date}$, $SoldBooks_{<\mathtt{author},nat>,nat}$.

- and the following event symbols:

  $create_{<string,date>}$, $changeName_{<string>}$, $storeSoldBooks_{<nat,nat>}$, $\mathtt{destroy}_{<>}$.

For simplicity we will omit the indices, i.e., the parameter and result sorts, because there are no ambiguities.

We will use the following variables: A, C, D, N, Y. The variables C and Y are of sort *nat*, A is of sort `author`, D is of sort *date*, and N is of sort *nat*.

Now, we can derive formulae from the template specification:

1. **Constraints:**
   The given constraint is equivalent to the following formula:

   $$SoldBooks(A, Y, N),\ DEF(N) \quad \rightarrow \quad \leq(N, 10000)$$

   Of course, the chosen constraint is quite simple so that it can be transformed without complications. As mentioned in Sect. 4 more complicated constraints can be specified in TROLL *light*. Then the transformation becomes more complex. Here, we abstain from demonstrating such a complex

[2] In the terminology of [FM91a, FM91b] the template signature Σ_T of some template T and the logical description $DESC_T$ corresponding to that template constitute a *theory presentation* $(\Sigma_T, DESC_T)$ for objects of the template T.

transformation because this kind of transformation is almost the same as it has often be done in classical logics.

2. **Valuations:**
The following formulae can be derived from the VALUATION section of the example template. Please note that the first valuation rule of the Author template manipulates two attributes, therefore, we need two formulae in our calculus:

$$\begin{array}{l} \rightarrow [A.create(N,D)]Name(A,N) \\ \rightarrow [A.create(N,D)]DateOfBirth(A,D) \\ \rightarrow [A.changeName(N)]Name(A,N) \\ \rightarrow [A.storeSoldBooks(Y,C)]SoldBooks(A,Y,C) \end{array}$$

Furthermore, there are formulae for expressing that in case of an event occurrence other attributes remain unchanged. Here, we give only one formula as an example. This formula states that a *storeSoldBooks* event does not affect the value of the attribute *Name*:

$$Name(A,N) \rightarrow [A.storeSoldBooks(Y,C)]Name(A,N)$$

3. **Behavior:**
From the behavior specification we can determine the set of o-machine state symbols: $\{authorlife_1, authorlife_2, vacant\}$. Now, we can derive the following axioms describing behavior (recall that *state* is an implicit attribute for the o-machine state):

$$\begin{array}{lcl} state(A,vacant) & \rightarrow & enable(A.create(N,D)) \\ state(A,vacant) & \rightarrow & [A.create(N,D)]state(A,authorlife_1) \\ state(A,authorlife_1) & \rightarrow & enable(A.storeSoldBooks(Y,C)) \\ state(A,authorlife_1) & \rightarrow & [A.storeSoldBooks(Y,C)]state(A,authorlife_1) \\ state(A,authorlife_1) & \rightarrow & enable(A.changeName(N)) \\ state(A,authorlife_1) & \rightarrow & [A.changeName(N)]state(A,authorlife_2) \\ state(A,authorlife_1) & \rightarrow & enable(A.destroy) \\ state(A,authorlife_1) & \rightarrow & [A.destroy]state(A,vacant) \\ state(A,authorlife_2) & \rightarrow & enable(A.storeSoldBooks(Y,C)) \\ state(A,authorlife_2) & \rightarrow & [A.storeSoldBooks(Y,C)]state(A,authorlife_2) \\ state(A,authorlife_2) & \rightarrow & enable(A.destroy) \\ state(A,authorlife_2) & \rightarrow & [A.destroy]state(A,vacant). \end{array}$$

By adding axioms for the used data types we get the set $DESC_{\texttt{Author}}$ which is the logical description of author objects. After the presentation of basic inference rules for our calculus we will continue this example by demonstrating the proof of a simple property of author objects.

6 Basic Inference Rules

In this section we present the basic inference rules for the propositional part of our calculus. These deduction rules shall help to get a better understanding of the (proof-theoretical) semantics underlying our calculus. A formal presentation of the semantics of TROLL *light* resp. of the certification calculus will happen in separate papers. The object calculi given in [Fia88, FS90, FM91a, FM91b, FM92, etc.] were starting points for the development of our calculus. In consequence, the deduction system of our calculus is an adaption and modification of the ones for these calculi. Therefore, we only present basic inference rules for our calculus in Fig. 1. Due to the fact that we do not have state-dependent terms our derivation system is much more simpler.

$$\frac{}{P \rightarrow P}\ \texttt{(axiom)} \qquad \frac{R, P_1, \ldots, P_n \rightarrow Q_1, \ldots, Q_m}{P_1, \ldots, P_n \rightarrow Q_1, \ldots, Q_m, \neg R}\ \texttt{(negR)}$$

$$\frac{P_1, \ldots, P_n \rightarrow Q_1, \ldots, Q_m}{R, P_1, \ldots, P_n \rightarrow Q_1, \ldots, Q_m, R'}\ \texttt{(ext)} \qquad \frac{P_1, \ldots, P_n \rightarrow Q_1, \ldots, Q_m, R}{\neg R, P_1, \ldots, P_n \rightarrow Q_1, \ldots, Q_m}\ \texttt{(negL)}$$

$$\frac{P_1, \ldots, P_n \rightarrow Q_1, \ldots, Q_m, R \qquad R, P'_1, \ldots, P'_k \rightarrow Q'_1, \ldots, Q'_l}{P'_1, \ldots, P'_k, P_1, \ldots, P_n \rightarrow Q_1, \ldots, Q_m, Q'_1, \ldots, Q'_l}\ \texttt{(cut)}$$

$$\frac{P_1, \ldots, P_n \rightarrow Q_1, \ldots, Q_m}{[o.e]P_1, \ldots, [o.e]P_n \rightarrow [o.e]Q_1, \ldots, [o.e]Q_m}\ \texttt{(nex)}$$

Fig. 1. Basic inference rules.

The rules `(axiom)`, `(ext)`, `(negR)`, `(negL)`, and `(cut)` are standard rules which are included in this or a similar form in each usual Gentzen-style calculus. Only the rule `(nex)` need some explanation. This rule allows us to introduce a positional operator into each proposition of a formula. Soundness of the calculus is not violated by this rule because if $P_1, \ldots, P_n \rightarrow Q_1, \ldots, Q_m$ is satisfied in each state then, of course, it is also satisfied in a state after the occurrence of an arbitrary event.

We have only presented a few basic inference rules of a deduction system for our certification calculus. Further rules must be added in order to have a deduction system which is powerful enough for reasoning about object properties.

7 Proving a Simple Property

Here, we demonstrate the proving of a property by means of our calculus. We have chosen a very simple property because otherwise we would have to introduce too much further details of our calculus.

The property to be proven is that the order of a *storeSoldBooks* event and a *changeName* event in an author object does not matter with regard to the value of the object's attribute *Name*. We will show this by proving the following two formulae:

$$(1) \quad \rightarrow [A.storeSoldBooks(Y,C)][A.changeName(N)]Name(A,N)$$

$$(2) \quad \rightarrow [A.changeName(N)][A.storeSoldBooks(Y,C)]Name(A,N)$$

We start with the proof of formula (1). The transformation of the VALUATION section of the Author template has yielded the following formula (cf. Sect. 5):

$$\rightarrow [A.changeName(N)]Name(A,N)$$

By applying the (nex)-rule using the event $A.storeSoldBooks(Y,C)$ we obtain:

$$[A.storeSoldBooks(Y,C)]true \rightarrow [A.storeSoldBooks(Y,C)][A.changeName(N)]Name(A,N)$$

Now we can eliminate the antecedent by applying the (cut)-rule to this formula and $\rightarrow [A.storeSoldBooks(Y,C)]true$ (the latter formula is an instantiation of a tautology of our calculus: $\rightarrow [O.E]true$). The result is formula (1):

$$\rightarrow [A.storeSoldBooks(Y,C)][A.changeName(N)]Name(A,N)$$

The second part is deriving formula (2). We start with another formula yielded by the transformation in Sect. 5:

$$Name(A,N) \rightarrow [A.storeSoldBooks(Y,C)]Name(A,N)$$

By applying the (nex)-rule using the event $A.changeName(N)$ we obtain:

$$[A.changeName(N)]Name(A,N) \rightarrow [A.changeName(N)][A.storeSoldBooks(Y,C)]Name(A,N)$$

Next, we we can apply the (cut)-rule to this formula and to the formula $\rightarrow [A.changeName(N)]Name(A,N)$ which is also yielded by the transformation:

$$\rightarrow [A.changeName(N)][A.storeSoldBooks(Y,C)]Name(A,N)$$

Thereby, we have also proven formula (2). In consequence, formula (1) and (2) are derivable from the formulae describing author objects, i.e., they also describe properties of author objects.

Of course, this is only a very simple example intended to demonstrate some fundamental principles of proving object properties within our certification calculus. Proofs of such an extend can still be done by hand. However, for more complex proofs this work becomes more and more tedious and faulty. Therefore, an obvious step for our certification calculus will be the combination with a theorem prover or proof assistant system. This is a central point of our current work in the KORSO project. In particular, we are "implementing" the calculus for *Isabelle* [Pau90]. This is because *Isabelle* is a generic proof system which should help us to avoid a complicated transformation of our calculus into another calculus implemented by some theorem prover, for example, first-order predicate calculus in *Tatzelwurm* [KZ90]. However, we intend to use such a theorem prover for first-order predicate calculus for consistency checks of constraints and preconditions within templates. This seems to be necessary in order to obtain a meaningful set of formulae as result of transforming specifications into our calculus.

8 Concluding Remarks

In this paper we have informally presented a certification calculus for reasoning about object properties from their specifications. Then we have described a transformation of TROLL *light* templates to formulae of that calculus. In designing our calculus we have adopted various ideas especially from [FM91a, FM91b, SSC92]. In order to make the calculus suitable for our specification language TROLL *light* some modifications were necessary.

Here, the presentation of the transformation has been restricted to simple TROLL *light* templates, i.e., templates for objects which have no subobjects and no object-valued attributes. Because of these restrictions it also was not necessary to deal with interaction. A further feature of TROLL *light*, derived attributes, can easily be treated. Such rules for deriving attributes from other attributes can be understood as constraints stating that in every object state the value of the derived attribute can be evaluated from the values of other attributes.

An interesting question is which properties our calculus has. Therefore, adequate model-theoretical and proof-theoretical semantics have been developed such that we can prove soundness for our calculus [Con93]. Up to now we have not aimed at completeness and, in fact, strong completeness seems to be unreachable (cf. [SSC92]).

As specification language we have taken TROLL *light* [CGH92, GCH93, HCG94] which is a core language for specifying objects. TROLL *light* stems from TROLL [JSH91, JSHS91]. However, TROLL (as well as other object specification languages known to us) has too much concepts for developing a first reasonable calculus. TROLL *light* offers a uniform view of objects. Classes are considered to be objects, too. Thereby, class concepts, like class attributes, metaclasses, or heterogeneous classes, are not explicitly needed in TROLL *light*.

Besides further work on the calculus a comparison of TROLL *light* with other specification approaches will be necessary. For example, the object specification languages presented in [Wie91] (CMSL), [Ara91] (based on propositional temporal logic), and [BBE+90] (Mondel) are candidates for this comparison.

Acknowledgement:

Special thanks to my KORSO colleagues Grit Denker, Hans-Dieter Ehrich, Martin Gogolla, Rudolf Herzig, and Nikolaos Vlachantonis for fruitful discussions and helpful comments on earlier versions of this paper. Moreover, A. Sernadas, C. Sernadas, and several partners of the KORSO-project have contributed to improve this paper by remarks and questions.

References

[Ara91] C. Arapis. Temporal Specifications of Object Behavior. In B. Thalheim, J. Demetrovics, and H.-D. Gerhardt, editors, *Proceedings 3rd. Symp. on Mathematical Fundamentals of Database and Knowledge Base Systems MFDBS'91*, pages 308–324. Springer, LNCS 495, 1991.

[BBE+90] G. v. Bochmann, M. Barbeau, M. Erradi, L. Lecomte, P. Mondain-Monval, and N. Williams. Mondel: An Object-Oriented Specification Language. Département d'Informatique et de Recherche Opérationnelle, Publication 748, Université de Montréal, 1990.

[BFG+92] M. Broy, C. Facchi, R. Grosu, R. Hettler, H. Hussmann, D. Nazareth, F. Regensburger, and K. Stølen. The Requirement and Design Specification Language SPECTRUM — An Informal Introduction (Version 0.3). Technical Report TUM–I9140, Technische Universität München, 1992.

[CGH92] S. Conrad, M. Gogolla, and R. Herzig. TROLL *light*: A Core Language for Specifying Objects. Informatik-Bericht 92–02, Technische Universität Braunschweig, 1992.

[Con93] S. Conrad. *Ein Basiskalkül für die Verifikation von Eigenschaften synchron interagierender Objekte* (A Basic Calculus for Verifying Properties of Synchronously Interacting Objects; in German). Submitted as PhD thesis, Technische Universität Braunschweig, 1993.

[DG94] G. Denker and M. Gogolla. Translating TROLL *light* Concepts to Maude. In F. Orejas, editor, *Proc. 9th Workshop on Abstract Data Types - 4th Compass Workshop (WADT/Compass'92)*. Springer LNCS, 1994. *(this volume)*.

[EGS92] H.-D. Ehrich, M. Gogolla, and A. Sernadas. Objects and their Specification. In M. Bidoit and C. Choppy, editors, *Proc. 8th Workshop on Abstract Data Types (ADT'91)*, pages 40–65. Springer, Berlin, LNCS 655, 1992.

[EM85] H. Ehrig and B. Mahr. *Fundamentals of Algebraic Specification 1: Equations and Initial Semantics*. Springer, Berlin, 1985.

[EM90] H. Ehrig and B. Mahr. *Fundamentals of Algebraic Specification 2: Modules and Constraints*. Springer, Berlin, 1990.

[ES91] H.-D. Ehrich and A. Sernadas. Fundamental Object Concepts and Constructions. In Saake and Sernadas [SS91], pages 1–24.

[ESS90] H.-D. Ehrich, A. Sernadas, and C. Sernadas. From Data Types to Object Types. *Journal on Information Processing and Cybernetics EIK*, 26(1-2):33–48, 1990.

[Fia88] J. Fiadeiro. *Cálculo de Objectos e Eventos*. PhD thesis, Instituto Superior Técnico, Technical University of Lisbon, 1988.

[FM91a] J. Fiadeiro and T. Maibaum. Temporal Reasoning over Deontic Specifications. *Journal of Logic and Computation*, 1(3):357–395, 1991.

[FM91b] J. Fiadeiro and T. Maibaum. Towards Object Calculi. In Saake and Sernadas [SS91], pages 129–178.

[FM92] J. Fiadeiro and T. Maibaum. Temporal Theories as Modularisation Units for Concurrent System Specification. *Journal Formal Aspects of Computing*, 4(3):239–272, 1992.

[FS90] J. Fiadeiro and A. Sernadas. Logics of Modal Terms for System Specification. *Journal of Logic and Computation*, 1(2):187–227, 1990.

[GCH93] M. Gogolla, S. Conrad, and R. Herzig. Sketching Concepts and Computational Model of TROLL *light*. In A. Miola, editor, *Proc. 3rd Int. Conf. Design and Implementation of Symbolic Computation Systems (DISCO'93)*, pages 17–32. Springer, Berlin, LNCS 722, 1993.

[GR90] M. Große-Rohde. Towards Object-Oriented Algebraic Specifications. In H. Ehrig, K.P. Jantke, F. Orejas, and H. Reichel, editors, *Recent Trends in Data Type Specification*, pages 98–116. Springer, LNCS 534, 1990.

[HCG94] R. Herzig, S. Conrad, and M. Gogolla. Compositional Description of Object Communities with TROLL light. In C. Chrisment, editor, *Proc. Basque Int. Workshop on Information Technology (BIWIT'94)*. Cepadues Society Press, France, 1994.

[JSH91] R. Jungclaus, G. Saake, and T. Hartmann. Language Features for Object-Oriented Conceptual Modeling. In T.J. Teorey, editor, *Proc. 10th Int. Conf. on Entity-Relationship Approach*, pages 309–324. E/R Institute, 1991.

[JSHS91] R. Jungclaus, G. Saake, T. Hartmann, and C. Sernadas. Object-Oriented Specification of Information Systems: The TROLL Language. Informatik-Bericht 91–04, Technische Universität Braunschweig, 1991.

[KM89] S. Khosla and T. Maibaum. The Prescription and Description of State Based Systems. In B. Banieqbal, H. Barringer, and A. Pnueli, editors, *Temporal Logic in Specification*, pages 243–294. Springer, LNCS 398, 1989.

[KZ90] T. Käufl and N. Zabel. Cooperation of Decision Procedures in a Tableau-Based Theorem Prover. *Revue d'Intelligence Artificielle*, 4(3):99–125, 1990.

[MKK91] R.A. Meersman, W. Kent, and S. Khosla, editors. *Object-Oriented Databases: Analysis, Design & Construction (DS-4), Proc. IFIP WG 2.6 Working Conference, Windermere (UK) 1990*. North-Holland, 1991.

[Pau90] L.C. Paulson. Isabelle: The Next 700 Theorem Provers. In P. Odifreddi, editor, *Logic and Computer Science*, pages 361–385. Academic Press, 1990.

[Reg90] G. Reggio. Entities: An Institution for Dynamic Systems. In H. Ehrig, K.P. Jantke, F. Orejas, and H. Reichel, editors, *Recent Trends in Data Type Specification*, pages 246–265. Springer, LNCS 534, 1990.

[SE91] A. Sernadas and H.-D. Ehrich. What is an Object, after all? In Meersman et al. [MKK91], pages 39–70.

[SS91] G. Saake and A. Sernadas, editors. *Information Systems — Correctness and Reusability, Workshop IS-CORE '91, ESPRIT BRA WG 3023, London.* Informatik-Bericht 91–03, Technische Universität Braunschweig, 1991.

[SSC92] A. Sernadas, C. Sernadas, and J.F. Costa. Object Specification Logic. Internal report, INESC, University of Lisbon, 1992.

[Wie91] R. Wieringa. Equational Specification of Dynamic Objects. In Meersman et al. [MKK91], pages 415–438.

[Wir90] M. Wirsing. Algebraic Specification. In J. Van Leeuwen, editor, *Handbook of Theoretical Computer Science, Vol. B*, pages 677–788. Elsevier, North-Holland, 1990.

Translating TROLL *light* Concepts to Maude

G. Denker, M. Gogolla*

Technische Universität Braunschweig, Informatik, Abt. Datenbanken
Postfach 3329, D–38023 Braunschweig, Germany
e-mail: {denker|gogolla}@idb.cs.tu-bs.de

Abstract. The specification language TROLL *light* is designed for the conceptual modeling of information systems. Maude is a logic programming language, which unifies the two paradigms of functional and concurrent object-oriented programming. Because of the very similar features offered by both languages, we present a translation from TROLL *light* concepts into the Maude language in order to compare the languages. Apart from presenting the translation, the languages are briefly described and illustrated by examples.

1 Introduction

Various approaches for the specification of complex software systems have appeared recently, for example: Specification of functions (VDM, Z [Jon86, BHL90]), abstract data types [EM85, EGL89, EM90, Wir90], predicate logic and extensions like temporal and modal logic [MP91], semantic data models [HK87], and process specification (CCS [Mil80], CSP [Hoa85], petri nets [Rei85]).

Our main concern is the conceptual modeling of information systems, and it seems that in isolation all these approaches are not appropriate for this task. The result of the conceptual modeling process should be a first precise characterization of the part of the world to be modeled, the so-called Universe of Discourse (UoD). If we look at an example UoD we find out that it consists of complex structured entities with time-varying behavior. Such entities usually exist concurrently and interact with each other. This is where the idea of object-oriented specification gives rise to an approach in order to represent the real-world entities as formal objects in a specification language. We work with the language TROLL *light* [CGH92, GCH93] which is a dialect of TROLL [JSHS91]. Both languages are based on recent results for semantic foundations of object-oriented specification [SE91, EGS92, ESS92, EDS93]. Structure as well as behavior of real-world entities can be characterized in TROLL *light*. Other languages for the specification of objects are for example OBLOG [SSG+91], CMSL [Wie91], and GLIDER [DBRW91, CJO92], OS [Bre91], FOOPS [GM87], MONDEL [BBE+90].

* Work reported here was partially supported by CEC under ESPRIT-II Basic Research Working Group No. 6112 COMPASS, under ESPRIT BRA WG 6071 IS-CORE, and by the German Ministry for Research and Technology (BMFT) under Grant No. ITS 9002 D/ 01 IS 203 D KORSO.

Maude [Mes92b] is a logic programming language, which unifies the two paradigms of functional and concurrent object-oriented programming. As a language feature Maude offers object-oriented modules through which classes can be formalized with their structural and behavioral characteristics.

Because of the very similar features offered by both languages, we present a translation from TROLL *light* concepts into the Maude language with examples and informally give a general translation schema. In some cases there exists only a small difference in the expressiveness of the concepts, whereas in other cases the difference results from special design decisions. Apart from presenting the translation, the languages are briefly described and illustrated by examples.

The structure of our paper is as follows. In Sect. 2 the concepts of our specification language TROLL *light* are described in more detail. In Sect. 3 we explain the basic features of the language Maude and give new representations for object configurations and in Sect. 4 for identifiers. Moreover we illustrate by examples the main ideas of translating TROLL *light* into Maude in Sect. 4 and give a general translation schema. Sect. 5 closes the paper by giving some concluding remarks.

2 Concepts of TROLL *light*

TROLL *light* is a language for the specification of objects. In general, TROLL *light* objects are associated with a possibly infinite number of attribute names, a possibly infinite number of sub-object names, and a finite number of object machine states which control object behavior. In a given state, a finite number of attribute names will take defined values, a finite number of sub-object names will be connected with defined sub-objects, and the object machine (o-machine in the sequel) will be in a certain state.

The possible attribute names, the possible sub-object names, and the o-machine states are fixed by object descriptions, which are called templates in TROLL *light*. Besides that a template also determines how state transitions between object states are to be carried out, i.e., templates comprise object behavior. State transitions are caused by event occurrences. Here the events which may occur during the life of an object have to be fixed by a finite number of event generators within a template.

In a given o-machine state an event occurrence is admissible only if a corresponding o-machine state transition rule is provided within a template. A template always contains a finite number of such o-machine state transitions. Hence an o-machine can be viewed as a finite event-driven sequential automaton. The effect of event occurrences on attributes are fixed by valuation rules, and the effect of event occurrences on other objects is fixed by interaction rules.

Further features potentially addressed within a template include means for the description of (static) integrity constraints, derived attributes, and preconditions for o-machine state transitions or for the application of valuation rules and interaction rules.

All in all a template has the following structure:

```
TEMPLATE
  DATA TYPES     decl. of data types used in current template
  TEMPLATES      decl. of other templates used in current template
  SUBOBJECTS     decl. of sub-object names
  ATTRIBUTES     decl. of attribute names
  EVENTS         decl. of event generators
  CONSTRAINTS    conditions on object states
  VALUATION      effect of event occurrences on attributes
  DERIVATION     derivation rules for derived attributes
  INTERACTION    synchronization of events in different objects
  BEHAVIOR       specification of allowed life cycles
END TEMPLATE
```

In the sequel we show by a small example how information systems may be specified by writing templates.

Let us assume that an information system is to be described, which shall contain data about author objects. For every author the name, the date of birth, and the number of books sold by year have to be stored. An author may change the name only once in the life. An appropriate TROLL *light* specification would be:

```
TEMPLATE Author
  DATA TYPES    String, Date, Nat;
  ATTRIBUTES    Name:string; DateOfBirth:date;
                SoldBooks(Year:nat):nat;
  EVENTS        BIRTH create(Name:string, DateOfBirth:date);
                      changeName(NewName:string);
                      storeSoldBooks(Year:nat, Number:nat);
                DEATH destroy;
  VALUATION     [create(S,D)] Name=S, DateOfBirth=D;
                [changeName(S)] Name=S;
                [storeSoldBooks(Y,N)] SoldBooks(Y)=N;
  BEHAVIOR      PROCESS authorlife1 =
                  ( storeSoldBooks -> authorlife1 |
                    changeName -> authorlife2 |
                    destroy -> POSTMORTEM );
                PROCESS authorlife2 =
                  ( storesSoldBooks -> authorlife2 |
                    destroy -> POSTMORTEM );
                ( create -> authorlife1 );
END TEMPLATE;
```

Attributes reflect observable properties of author objects, and events denote events which can happen during the life of an author. The effect of events on attributes is specified by valuation rules. Possible life cycles of authors are fixed by process descriptions. The corresponding o-machine is visualized in Fig. 1.

We may assume that the information system will be populated by lots of authors

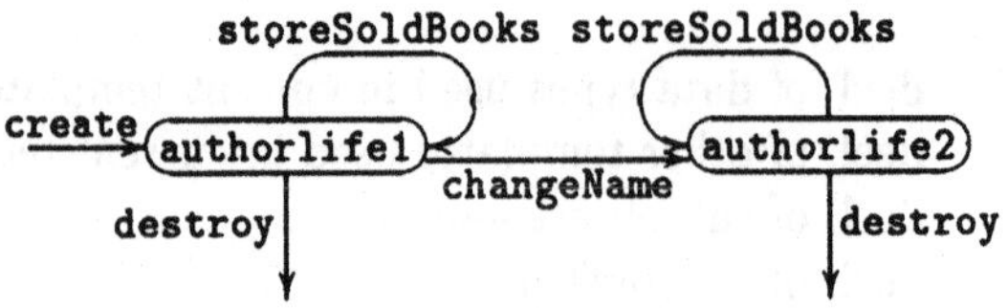

Fig. 1. Behavior of authors

so that these authors must be managed by a higher-level object. To this end usually classes are introduced in many object-oriented approaches. TROLL *light* does not support an explicit class concept. Classes are viewed as composite objects instead, and therefore classes have to be described by templates again.

```
TEMPLATE Authorclass
  DATA TYPES    String, Date, Nat;
  TEMPLATES     Author;
  SUBOBJECTS    Authors(No:nat):author;
  ATTRIBUTES    NumberOfAuthors:nat;
  EVENTS        BIRTH createClass;
                      addObject(No:nat,Name:string,
                                DateOfBirth:date);
                      removeObject(No:nat);
                DEATH destroyClass;
  VALUATION     [createClass] NumberOfAuthors=0;
                [addObject] NumberOfAuthors=NumberOfAuthors+1;
                [removeObject] NumberOfAuthors=NumberOfAuthors-1;
  INTERACTION   addObject(N,S,D) >> Authors(N).create(S,D);
                removeObject(N) >> Authors(N).destroy;
END TEMPLATE;
```

An object of type `Authorclass` will hold many author objects as private components or sub-objects. In this example a natural number serves as a key for the identification of sub-objects. Please note that in contrast to many other data models, in TROLL *light* keys need not be related to attributes of objects they identify. Adding an object to an author class means to create a new sub-object, and removing an object from an author class means to destroy the sub-object.

An object of type `Authorclass` may be sub-object of a higher object again, and so on. For example, a template `Libraryworld` may be specified which contains a class of authors, a class of books, and two libraries as sub-objects (see [CGH92]).

3 The logic programming language Maude

The programming language Maude is a direct result from the requirement to integrate concurrent programming with paradigms like functional and object-oriented programming. Maude's semantic framework is conditional rewriting logic which is a logic to reason about change in a concurrent system. Since rewriting is naturally concurrent, this logic deals adequately with one intrinsic part of object-oriented systems, namely concurrency.

Modules in Maude are theories in rewriting logic so that concurrent object-oriented computation coincides with logical deduction. Deduction is done modulo some structural axioms in order to catch in an abstract way the essential aspects of object-oriented systems. We will illustrate this by examples later on.

Maude contains three kinds of *modules*: **functional modules**, **system modules**, and **object-oriented modules**. The functional sub-language of Maude is similar to OBJ3 [GW88]. The syntax and semantics of object-oriented modules is reducible to that of system modules; they only provide a notational convenience for object-oriented applications by supporting appropriate language features. In contrast to functional modules system modules provide the specification of non-functional behavior. Maude has a parameterization mechanism and also supports multiple class inheritance.

In the sequel we illustrate the main concepts of Maude by examples which will be needed subsequently for the translation. All given modules are specified in order to translate the running example from Sect. 2. Therefore we change original Maude notions and give new representations, such as for the `CONFIGURATION` and `ID` modules below.

First we will have a look at **functional modules**. Consider the following Maude functional module specifying the abstract data type `SETOFTUPLE` (Maude keywords are underlined):

```
fmod SETOFTUPLE is
  protecting TUPLE .
  sort SetOfTuple .
  subsort Tuple < SetOfTuple .
  op _in_: Tuple SetOfTuple -> Bool .
  op _U_: SetOfTuple SetOfTuple -> SetOfTuple [assoc id:0 comm].
  op _\_: SetOfTuple Tuple -> SetOfTuple .
  vars S S': Set .
  vars T T': Tuple .
  sct S U T: SetOfTuple if not T in S .
  eq T in 0 = false .
  eq T in (T' U S)= if T == T' then true else T in S fi .
  eq S\0 = S .
  eq 0\T = 0 .
  eq (S U T')\T = if T == T' then S else T' U (S\T) fi .
endfm
```

The given functional module defines sets of tuples (e.g., of natural numbers) with the union, minus, and element of functions. The union function is declared to be commutative, associative, and has 0 as the identity element. Rewriting is done modulo these structural axioms so that besides the sort constraint sct we need no further equations. We assume that the module TUPLE is specified somewhere in the way that it protects the natural numbers and provides at least a constructor function `[ , ]: Nat Nat -> Tuple` and a selector function `first: Tuple -> Nat` returning the first component of a tuple. These operations will be needed in the next example. The line protecting TUPLE imports this module as a submodule of SETOFTUPLE, and asserts that no new data elements to old sorts (here Tuple) will be introduced (no "junk") and that the original equality relation between data elements will not be altered (no "confusion"). Moreover sort declarations, which describe the data sorts manipulated by this module, and subsort declarations, which describe how the sorts are related, are given: `sort SetOfTuple` and `subsort Tuple < SetOfTuple`. Functions with their domain and co-domain sorts provided by the module (here union function, minus function, and element of function for sets) are introduced by the keyword op . Variables used for defining equations are declared with their corresponding sorts in the vars part. The sort constraint sct accomplishes that the addition of a tuple to a set of tuples yields a set (of tuples) if and only if the tuple has not been already element of the original set. Equations eq establish the effect of the operations.

Up to now importing modules by means of protecting introduces no semantic modifications. But there exists also the possibility that importing (possibly renamed) modules is accompanied with semantic modifications, i.e., new data elements to old sorts could occur and/or new relationships between old data elements could be defined. This can be done via an using module importation. We will explain this in the following example:

```
fmod MAPNAT2NAT is
  using SETOFTUPLE *( sort SetOfTuple to MapNat2Nat) .
  op U: MapNat2Nat Tuple -> MapNat2Nat .
  ...
endfm
```

The specification *uses* the SETOFTUPLE module in such a way that the sort SetOfTuple is renamed to MapNat2Nat. In order to keep the example small we omit details. The functional dependencies forcing sets of tuples of natural numbers to become a map between natural numbers have to be specified via suitable equations. Through these new equations semantic modifications are introduced.

As another possibility we might want to specify modules which do not behave in a functional way. In fact non-functional behavior is intrinsic to object-oriented systems. For example, several reachable configurations (or say system states) are possible if we start from an initial state. This kind of behavior is supported by system and object-oriented modules.

As a first example we just want to specify such system configurations. The state of a concurrent system is represented as a multi-set of objects and messages, where objects are described as terms giving their class membership and their attribute values. A system configuration made up of concurrently existing objects and messages is formalized via a **system module**:

```
mod CONFIGURATION is
  protecting ATTRIBUTES ID.
  sorts Configuration Object Msg .
  subsorts Object Msg < Configuration .
  op __: Configuration Configuration -> Configuration
                                          [assoc id: 0 comm] .
  op <_:_|_>: OId CId Attributes -> Object .
  var IDSET : IdSet .
  var OID : OId .
  var CID : CId .
  var ATTS : Attributes .
  sct <OID:CID|ATTS> : Object if not OID in IDSET .
  rl <OID:CID|ATTS> => <OID:CID|ATTS> addId(OID,IDSET) .
endm
```

Two modules are imported by CONFIGURATION: we assume the ATTRIBUTES module to be specified somewhere else and specify the ID module in the following section. The __ operator, which is commutative, associative, and has 0 (representing a system without objects and messages) as its identity element, structures the state of a concurrent object-oriented system as a multi-set of objects and messages. Deduction, that is to say computation, is done modulo these given axioms. The "object-generating" operation <_:_|_> demands an object identifier, a class identifier, and the specific attributes (name-value pairs) of the new object. Object and class identifiers are subsorts of Id as specified later on. The sort constraint in combination with the specified rule assures that new objects are only created if their identifier is unique in the sense that before the creation it is not in the set of current object identifiers and afterwards it is added to this set. To assure that IDSET always contains all identifiers of currently existing objects this rule has to be applied each time new objects are created. The addId operation is specified in the ID module as we will see in the following. Here we changed the original notion of Meseguer (cf Sect. 4 in [Mes92a]) in order to deal with our identification mechanism more adequately. Meseguer proposes a system-wide counter as identification mechanism what is not appropriate for our approach since we use logical names as object identifiers. More details are given in the next section where the module ID is defined.

Object-oriented modules only provide a notational convenience compared with system modules. They support some common object-oriented notions, like object, message, class, etc., but their syntax and semantics can be reduced to that of system modules (for details see [Mes92a], Sect. 4.2). By means of object-oriented modules, classes can be defined, in which the structural and behavioral aspects of class members are specified via attributes and messages, respectively. The effects of messages (with or without interaction) on objects are determined by conditional term rewriting rules. Object-oriented modules look like the following:

<u>omod</u> *name* <u>**is**</u>
  <u>**extending**</u> *module names*
  <u>**protecting**</u> *(renamed) module names*
  <u>**class**</u> *class name* | *attribute decl.*
  <u>**subclass**</u> *class names*
  <u>**msgs**</u> *message decl.*
  <u>**vars**</u> *variable decl.*
  <u>**rl**</u> *rule decl.*
<u>endom</u>

where all italic items have to be specified by the user. The protecting part of object-oriented modules corresponds to that of functional modules. This means no semantic modifications are introduced. The <u>**extending**</u> mechanism in combination with rules can be used to express inheritance aspects. More exhaustive examples for object-oriented modules will follow later on.

Maude offers a lot of other language facilities. For example modules can be parameterized and class inheritance is directly supported by its order-sorted type structure in object-oriented modules. We will not go into details since we do not need these facilities for our purpose.

4 TROLL *light* to Maude – Translation by example

The translation of TROLL *light* concepts to Maude is relevant to implementation aspects. After modeling the UoD as a system of concurrently existing and interacting objects formalized with TROLL *light*, we yield a collection of TROLL *light* templates. Based on this abstract description steps towards more concrete descriptions yielding an implementation should be done. It is conceivable to take Maude [Mes92a] as such an implementation basis. Programming languages used as an implementation basis for TROLL *light* should both be able to deal with the concepts of object-orientation and be efficiently implementable. Maude among other languages seems to fulfil these requirements.

Now we explain our ideas of translating TROLL *light* concepts to Maude with the examples given in Sect. 2. This means we will work with `Authorclass`, `Author` as the given template collection where `Authorclass` is the schema template. Afterwards we will mention some general aspects of the translation.

We already mentioned the identifier problem in the previous section. The **CONFIGURATION** module deals with different kinds of identifiers, and since object-oriented modules define classes an identification mechanism for class members is required. On the other hand we set up a specification in TROLL *light* as a collection of templates, where the identification mechanism via logical names is user-definable. Since our aim is to translate TROLL *light* templates to object-oriented modules in Maude we have to deal with the identifier problem adequately. At first sight this seems to be difficult since there exists no global identifier sort in TROLL *light*. But all possible object identifier, or logical names in our notion, are defined in the **SUBOBJECTS** part. As a solution we suggest the introduction of a module **ID** which provides among other things an object identifier sort **OId** and a class identifier sort **CId**. Possible sub-object names are presented via suitable operations with co-domain sort **OId**. We illustrate this with an example.

The specified object sorts **Authorclass** and **Author** will correspond to class types in Maude as we will see in a while. The possible object identities **Authors(No:nat)** as established in the **SUBOBJECTS** part will be reflected by a module **ID** which makes object identifiers available. In the example we yield the following functional module:

```
fmod ID is
  protecting SET*( sort Set to IdSet, sort Elt to Id,
                   op _U_ to addId) .
  sorts Id OId CId AuthorclassId AuthorId IdSet .
  subsorts OId CId < Id .
  subsort AuthorId AuthorclassId < OId .
  op INIT: -> AuthorclassId .
  op Authors: AuthorclassId Nat -> AuthorId .
endfm
```

Since in TROLL *light* a given template collection represents a hirarchy of templates fixed through sub-object relationships there is always one distinguished template, the so-called schema template, of which all other templates are direct or indirect sub-templates. **INIT** is a special operation to generate an instance of the given schema template, in our example the **Authorclass** template. Class identifiers are automatically defined by object-oriented modules as we will see later on.

O-machine states (e.g., **authorlife1** etc.) are essential for the description of object behavior. Maude does not provide a special feature to express constraints on objects behavior as we are used to it in TROLL *light*. In order to give a correct translation we make o-machine states explicit (by defining a sort **OMState** plus adequate generator functions) and use them later in rules in object-oriented Maude modules to express the dependencies between o-machine states and possible object state transitions. In the given example **authorlife1**, **authorlife2**, **authorclasslife**, and **POSTMORTEM** are defined as possible object-machine states. They are also reflected via a functional module:

```
fmod OMSTATE is
  sorts OMState AuthorState AuthorclassState .
  subsorts AuthorState AuthorclassState < OMState .
  op authorlife1 : -> AuthorState .
  op authorlife2 : -> AuthorState .
  op authorclasslife : -> AuthorclassState .
  op POSTMORTEM : -> OMState .
endfm
```

The above translation, yielding the modules CONFIGURATION, ID, and OMSTATE, is necessary in general for the rest of the work. In the following each TROLL *light* template will be translated to an object-oriented Maude module and each Maude module received in this way imports at least the first two modules. OMSTATE only has to be imported if o-machine states are specified.

We proceed with translating Author and Authorclass, respectively, to object-oriented Maude modules. We will start with the Author template which is translated into the following Maude module:

```
omod AUTHOR is
  extending CONFIGURATION .
  protecting ID OMSTATE MAPNAT2NAT STRING NAT DATE .
  class Author | Name: String,
                 DateOfBirth: Date,
                 SoldBooks: MapNat2Nat,
                 omstate: AuthorState .
  msg create : AuthorId String Date -> Msg .
  msg changeName : AuthorId String -> Msg .
  msg storeSoldBooks : AuthorId Nat Nat -> Msg .
  msg destroy : AuthorId -> Msg .
  var OIDSET : OIdSet .
  var AID : AuthorId .
  var MNN : MapNat2Nat .
  vars Y N: Nat .
  var D : Date .
  vars S S': String .
  rl create(AID,S,D) =>
     <AID:Author|Name:S,DateOfBirth:D,omstate:authorlife1> .
  rl changeName(AID,S) <AID:Author|Name:S',omstate:authorlife1>
     => <AID:Author|Name:S,omstate:authorlife2> .
  rl storeSoldBooks(AID,Y,N)
     <AID:Author|SoldBooks:MNN,omstate:authorlife1>
     => <AID:Author|SoldBooks: MNNU[Y,N],omstate:authorlife1> .
  rl storeSoldBooks(AID,Y,N)
     <AID:Author|SoldBooks:MNN,omstate:authorlife2>
     => <AID:Author|SoldBooks: MNNU[Y,N],omstate:authorlife2> .
  rl destroy(AID) <AID:Author|ATTS> => 0.
endom
```

First of all we have to import the CONFIGURATION and ID modules to each object-oriented module which we receive as a translation from a TROLL *light* template. The essential notions of object, message, and identifier are necessary for each of them. As soon as o-machine states are introduced in the TROLL *light* template we also have to import OMSTATE. Furthermore, for the author template we need the sort MapNat2Nat, specified in the previous section, in order to express the parameterized attribute SoldBooks(Year:nat):nat, which could also be viewed as an attribute SoldBooks:set(tuple(nat,nat)) with additional constraints expressing the functionality implicit in the former attribute expression. The sort MapNat2Nat comprises the required functional dependency. The sorts String, Date, and Nat which are needed for several attribute and message definitions are protected by module importation.

By means of the object-oriented Maude module AUTHOR a class Author is defined, and instances are described via four attributes: Name, DateOfBirth, SoldBooks, and omstate. Obviously we have to explicitly model the o-machine state as an attribute in order to adequately express dependencies between o-machine states and possible state transitions in Maude. In contrast to that these states are inherent in TROLL *light* specifications, but not visible. Though in TROLL *light* the object's state is given through its attribute values, its sub-objects, and the current o-machine state only the attribute values and sub-objects are directly observable. However, it is possible to deduce the current o-machine state from a given fixed life cycle.

TROLL *light* events are translated more or less one to one to messages in Maude. We only have to follow the rule that each message requires an object identifier, because we describe a class of objects, where single objects are distinguished via their identifiers. This also holds for the special BIRTH and DEATH events, so that all events set one more parameter: an Maude object identifier.

In Maude all used variables have to be declared in the <u>vars</u> section. We do without variable declarations in TROLL *light* templates, because the right sorts always can be determined from the defined attributes and events, and no difficulties are to be feared.

The remaining TROLL *light* parts to translate, i.e., VALUATION, BEHAVIOR, and, for Authorclass, INTERACTION must all be modeled by rules in Maude modules. So the first rule connected with the BIRTH event not only says that after the occurrence of create(AID,S,D) a new object of type Author with identifier AID, and with attributes Name=S and DateOfBirth=D is generated (something which is expressed in the valuation part of the TROLL *light* template), but also that afterwards the o-machine state is equal to authorlife1 (what is stated in the behavior part of the corresponding TROLL *light* template).

Combining the valuation formula for the changeName event of the TROLL *light* specification with the stated behavior, i.e., changeName can only occur if the o-machine state is equal to authorlife1, gives the second rule. Similar considerations lead to the third and fourth rule about the storeSoldBooks event. The last rule states that a system consisting of an author <AID:Author|ATTS> and an event which destroys this author object proceeds to a system without any object and event. Please note that 0 is the identity element of the `__` operation in CONFIGURATION.

Now we translate the Authorclass template. New aspects are introduced through the specified sub-objects part in conjunction with the interaction formulas.

```
omod AUTHORCLASS is
  extending CONFIGURATION .
  protecting ID AUTHOR STRING NAT DATE .
  class Authorclass | NumberOfAuthors: Nat .
  msg createClass : AuthorclassId -> Msg .
  msg addObject : AuthorclassId Nat String Date -> Msg .
  msg removeObject : AuthorclassId Nat -> Msg .
  msg destroyClass : AuthorclassId -> Msg .
  var ACID : AuthorclassId .
  ...
  rl createClass(ACID) =>
     <ACID:Authorclass|NumberOfAuthors:0> .
  rl addObject(ACID,N,S,D) create(Authors(ACID,N),S,D)
     <ACID:Authorclass|NumberOfAuthors: N' =>
     <ACID:Authorclass|NumberOfAuthors: N'+1>
     <Authors(ACID,N):Author|Name:S,DateOfBirth:D,
       omstate:authorlife1> .
  rl removeObject(ACID,N) destroy(Authors(ACID,N))
     <ACID:Authorclass|NumberOfAuthors: N'>
     <Authors(ACID,N):Author|ATTS>
     => <ACID:Authorclass|NumberOfAuthors: N'-1>
  rl destroyClass(ACID) <ACID:Authorclass|NumberOfAuthors: N'> => 0.
endom
```

We will focus our interest especially on interaction formulas and how they are translated. If we have a look at the Authorclass template, we would translate the valuation formula for addObject, corresponding to the considerations already done, like this:

```
rl addObject(ACID,N,S,D) <ACID:Authorclass|NumberOfAuthors:N'> =>
   <ACID:Authorclass|NumberOfAuthors:N'+1> .
```

But because of the given interaction formula

```
addObject(N,S,D) >> Authors(N).create(S,D)
```

we have to adapt this rule to

```
rl addObject(ACID,N,S,D) create(Authors(ACID,N),S,D)
   <ACID:Authorclass | NumberOfAuthors: N'> =>
   <ACID:Authorclass | NumberOfAuthors: N'+1>
   <Authors(ACID,N):Author|Name:S,DateOfBirth:D,omstate:authorlife1>.
```

We will speak in the sequel of "rule adaption" caused by interaction formulas. The rule for the `removeObject` event is produced analogously.

At this point we loose some information of the corresponding TROLL *light* template collection. The given template collection {`Authorclass`, `Author`} with `Authorclass` as its schema template implies that authors can only be created and destroyed local to an author class. This kind of implicit functionality cannot be expressed with Maude. This seems to be a difference originated by our special design decision that systems are built as a complex object, an instance of the schema template, of which all the other objects are sub-objects in some way.

In summary we can give the following general translation schema:

object sorts →	class types
sub-object symbols →	constructor functions for identities
attributes →	attributes
events →	messages (one more parameter)
behavior →	object machine states + rules
interaction →	"rule adaption"

Object sorts become class types in Maude since each TROLL *light* template which defines an object sort is translated to an object-oriented Maude module which defines a class. Sub-object symbols provide an identification mechanism for instances via logical names. We reflected this via the `ID` module. It is always possible to determine the correct `ID` module from a given template collection in the following way. Appropriate identifier sorts have to be provided for each template; all these identity sorts will be subsorts of `OId`. Each sub-object symbol corresponds to a constructor operation for identities, where `INIT` has to be added as a constructor function for a schema template instance. TROLL *light* events can be directly translated to Maude messages, and we only have to pay attention that for each event one more parameter is needed to indicate the class instance the event refers to. The translation of TROLL *light* attributes is also easy. They are mapped one to one to Maude attributes, where an additional attribute of sort `OMState` must be included if o-machine states are specified in the behavior part.

Although most TROLL *light* concepts are expressed by Maude features some concepts like `CONSTRAINTS` or `DERIVATION` or even more complex `VALUATION` or `INTERACTION` formulas remain to be analyzed. We comment on the chances to translate full TROLL *light* to Maude in the next section.

5 Conclusions

Some concepts of TROLL *light* specifications have not been considered up to now. Let us have a look at `CONSTRAINTS` and try to give a taste what kind of formulas we have to deal with and how they will be translated. Maybe we want to specify that author classes are required to have at least one author. We can do this in TROLL *light* as follows

```
CONSTRAINTS CNT(Authors)>0
```

CNT is a predefined aggregate function which counts all elements of a set. At each point of time only a finite number of sub-objects exist and the given formula restricts all possible author class object states in the way that at least one element has to be in the set with all author identifiers. To translate this we have to provide an operation that counts the number of identifiers of sort `AuthorId` in the set `IdSet`. Surely this is manageable if we introduce such an operation in the `ID` module, but perhaps the translation becomes less direct or intuitive. Similar considerations for derivation formulas and more complex interaction or valuation formulas let us presume that Maude's language features are expressible enough to cover all TROLL *light* concepts.

Acknowledgements

Thanks to our KORSO colleagues Stefan Conrad, Hans-Dieter Ehrich, Rudolf Herzig, and Nikolaos Vlachantonis for fruitful discussions. Futhermore, the comments and questions of our SG1-IS-CORE colleagues helped a lot to improve this paper.

References

[BBE+90] G. v. Bochmann, M. Barbeau, M. Erradi, L. Lecomte, P. Mondain-Monval, and N. Williams. Mondel: An Object-Oriented Specification Language. Département d'Informatique et de Recherche Opérationnelle, Publication 748, Université de Montréal, 1990.

[BHL90] D. Bjorner, C.A.R. Hoare, and H. Langmaack, editors. *VDM'90: VDM and Z — Formal Methods in Software Development.* Springer, LNCS 428, 1990.

[Bre91] R. Breu. *Algebraic Specification Techniques in Object Oriented Programming Environments.* Springer, LNCS 562, 1991.

[CGH92] S. Conrad, M. Gogolla, and R. Herzig. TROLL *light*: A Core Language for Specifying Objects. Informatik-Bericht 92-02, TU Braunschweig, 1992.

[CJO92] S. Clerici, R. Jimenez, and F. Orejas. Semantic Constructions in the Specification Language GLIDER. Workshop on Abstract Data Types, 1992.

[DBRW91] E. Dubois, P. Du Bois, A. Rifaut, and P. Wodan. *GLIDER Manual.* Facultés Universitaires de Namur, Namur (B), 1991. ICARUS Deliverable.

[EDS93] H.-D. Ehrich, G. Denker, and A. Sernadas. Constructing Systems as Object Communities. In M.-C. Gaudel and J.-P. Jouannaud, editors, *Proc. TAPSOFT'93: Theory and Practice of Software Development*, pages 453–467. LNCS 668, Springer, Berlin, 1993.

[EGL89] H.-D. Ehrich, M. Gogolla, and U.W. Lipeck. *Algebraische Spezifikation abstrakter Datentypen - Eine Einführung in die Theorie.* Teubner, Stuttgart, 1989.

[EGS92] H.-D. Ehrich, M. Gogolla, and A. Sernadas. Objects and their Specification. In M. Bidoit and C. Choppy, editors, *Proc. 8th Workshop on Abstract Data Types (ADT'91)*, pages 40–65. Springer, Berlin, LNCS 655, 1992.

[EM85] H. Ehrig and B. Mahr. *Fundamentals of Algebraic Specification 1: Equations and Initial Semantics.* Springer, Berlin, 1985.

[EM90] H. Ehrig and B. Mahr. *Fundamentals of Algebraic Specification 2: Modules and Constraints*. Springer, Berlin, 1990.

[ESS92] H.-D. Ehrich, G. Saake, and A. Sernadas. Concepts of Object-Orientation. In *Proc. of the 2nd Workshop of "Informationssysteme und Künstliche Intelligenz: Modellierung", Ulm (Germany)*, pages 1–19. Springer IFB 303, 1992.

[GCH93] M. Gogolla, S. Conrad, and R. Herzig. Sketching Concepts and Computational Model of TROLL *light*. In A. Miola, editor, *Proc. 3rd Int. Conf. Design and Implementation of Symbolic Computation Systems (DISCO'93)*, pages 17–32. Springer, Berlin, LNCS 722, 1993.

[GM87] J. A. Goguen and J. Meseguer. Unifying Functional, Object-Oriented and Relational Programming with Logical Semantics . In B. Shriver and P. Wegner, editors, *Research Directions in Object-Oriented Programming*, pages 417–477. MIT Press, 1987.

[GW88] J.A. Goguen and T. Winkler. Introducing OBJ3. Research Report SRI-CSL-88-9, SRI International, 1988.

[HK87] R. Hull and R. King. Semantic Database Modelling: Survey, Applications, and Research Issues. *ACM Computing Surveys*, 19(3):201–260, 1987.

[Hoa85] C.A.R. Hoare. *Communicating Sequential Processes*. Prentice-Hall, Englewood Cliffs (NJ), 1985.

[Jon86] C.B. Jones. *Systematic Software Developing Using VDM*. Prentice-Hall, Englewood Cliffs (NJ), 1986.

[JSHS91] R. Jungclaus, G. Saake, T. Hartmann, and C. Sernadas. Object-Oriented Specification of Information Systems: The TROLL Language. Informatik-Bericht 91-04, TU Braunschweig, 1991.

[Mes92a] J. Meseguer. A Logical Theory of Concurrent Objects and its Realization in the Maude Language. In G. Agha, P. Wegener, and A. Yonezawa, editors, *Research Directions in Object-Based Concurrency*. MIT Press, 1992. To appear.

[Mes92b] J. Meseguer. Conditional Rewriting as a Unified Model of Concurrency. *Theoretical Computer Science*, 96(1):73–156, 1992.

[Mil80] R. Milner. *A Calculus of Communicating Systems*. Springer, Berlin, 1980.

[MP91] Z. Manna and A. Pnueli. *The Temporal Logic of Reactive and Concurrent Systems; Specification*. Springer-Verlag, New York, 1991.

[Rei85] W. Reisig. *Petri Nets: An Introduction*. Springer, Berlin, 1985.

[SE91] A. Sernadas and H.-D. Ehrich. What Is an Object, After All? In R. Meersman, W. Kent, and S. Khosla, editors, *Object-Oriented Databases: Analysis, Design and Construction (Proc. 4th IFIP WG 2.6 Working Conference DS-4, Windermere (UK))*, pages 39–70, Amsterdam, 1991. North-Holland.

[SSG+91] A. Sernadas, C. Sernadas, P. Gouveia, P. Resende, and J. Gouveia. OBLOG — Object-Oriented Logic: An Informal Introduction. Technical report, INESC, Lisbon, 1991.

[Wie91] R. Wieringa. Equational Specification of Dynamic Objects. In R.A. Meersman, W. Kent, and S. Khosla, editors, *Object-Oriented Databases: Analysis, Design & Construction (DS-4), Proc. IFIP WG 2.6 Working Conference, Windermere (UK) 1990*, pages 415–438. North-Holland, 1991.

[Wir90] M. Wirsing. Algebraic Specification. In J. Van Leeuwen, editor, *Handbook of Theoretical Computer Science, Vol. B*, pages 677–788. Elsevier, North-Holland, 1990.

Algebraic High Level Nets
Petri Nets Revisited *

Hartmut Ehrig, Julia Padberg and Leila Ribeiro

Technical University Berlin, Sekr. FR 6-1 , FB 13, Franklinstr. 28/29
10587 Berlin, Germany

Abstract. Petri nets, well established as a fundamental model of concurrency and as a specification technique for distributed systems, are revisited from an algebraic point of view. In a first step Petri nets can be considered as monoids with well-defined algebraic semantics. Secondly they can be combined with algebraic specifications leading to the concept of algebraic high-level nets with suitable compositionality results. The main idea of this paper is to present a revised version of algebraic high-level nets (AHL-nets) and to introduce AHL-net-transformation systems. This is a concept of high-level replacement systems for AHL-nets allowing to build up AHL-nets from basic components and to transform them using rules or productions in the sense of graph grammars. This is illustrated by extending the well-known example of "dining philosophers" to a "restaurant of dining philosophers". Moreover we are able to extend main results from the theory of graph grammars, including local Church-Rosser, parallelism and canonical derivation theorems, to AHL-net-transformation systems. This allows to analyze concurrency in nets not only on the token level but also on the level of transformations of the net structure.

1 Introduction

Petri nets were introduced in the early 60's by Petri [Pet62] as a method for description and analysis of non-sequential processes. Since then most of the studies concentrated only on condition/event and place/transition systems. Although Petri nets are able to express "true concurrency" using a partial order of events the main draw back was the lack of a suitable algebraic theory to calculate the behavior of processes. Today there is a large amount of theory for description and analysis of different kinds of Petri nets (see [Jen81, Rei85, Roz87, Sta90]) and also an elegant algebraic approach to Petri nets considered as monoids in [MM90]. In view of practical applications to the specification of concurrent and

* Research for the paper was partially granted by the ESPRIT Basic Research Working Group COMPASS and COMPUGRAPH, the Brazilian Research Council (CNPq) for Leila Ribeiro and the German Research Council (DFG) for Julia Padberg. We are grateful to several members of these ESPRIT working groups for fruitful cooperation on the topics of this paper.

distributed systems it turned out to be important to combine process descriptions and data type specification techniques. One of the most important examples is the specification language LOTOS [LOT87] based on the combination of CCS with ACT ONE. The combination of Petri nets and algebraic specifications was started in [Vau86] as an extension of colored Petri nets in the sense of [Jen81]. Other interesting examples for the combination of process description techniques with algebraic specification are stream processing functions [Bro85], process algebras [BK86], the SMOLCS-approach [AR87], projection specifications [EPB+87], OBJSA-nets [BCM88], and Hennessy's algebraic theory of processes [Hen88]. The combination of Petri nets and algebraic specifications was extended in [Kra89, Hum89, Rei91, DHP91, EGH92] leading to the notion of algebraic high-level nets, short AHL-nets.

In fact, the investigation of Petri nets from an algebraic point of view within the last few years was quite successful. But this development was only partially noticed by the Petri net and the algebraic specification communities. The first aim of this paper is to discuss in Sect. 1 the main common objections against Petri nets from an algebraic point of view and to revisit Petri nets showing how far these problems have been solved already.

In Sect. 3 we present a revised version of AHL-nets and their operational behavior. We show that this kind of high-level nets is a suitable abstraction of place/transition nets using the well known example of Dijkstra's "dining philosophers" [Dij71].

The main new concept introduced in this paper is the notion of AHL-net transformation systems which allow to study high-level refinements of AHL-nets. In fact, AHL-net transformation systems are a special case of high-level replacement systems recently introduced in [EHKP92] as a categorical generalization of graph grammars [EP91a]. In order to be able to apply the theory in [EHKP91] we show in Sect. 4 of this paper suitable categorical properties of the category of AHL-nets. In Sect. 5 we introduce AHL-net transformation systems, present a refinement of the "dining philosophers" to a "restaurant of dining philosophers" and – as an application of the theory of high-level replacement systems – we obtain a local Church-Rosser, parallelism and canonical derivation theorems for AHL-net-transformation systems. This allows us to analyze concurrency in AHL-nets not only on the level of transitions but also on the level of transformations of the net structure.

Finally let us point out that categorical techniques are essentially used in this paper because the investigation of AHL-net transformation systems is based on categorical properties of high-level replacement systems [EHKP91, EHKP92]. The advantage of a categorical treatment of place/transition nets was demonstrated especially in [MM90] and has motivated to extend these concepts to AHL-nets rather than to use standard set theoretical notions only.

2 Petri Nets Revisited

In this section we start with some common objections against Petri nets from an algebraic point of view. In a second step we analyze each of these objections in more detail, show how far the corresponding problems have been studied in the literature already and sketch also some new solutions which will be studied in the subsequent sections in more detail.

2.1 What are the Problems with Petri Nets?

Some main objections against Petri nets as a model for concurrency and as a specification technique for distributed systems from an algebraic point of view are given in the following three slogans:

1. *Petri Nets are not Algebraic.*
   This common objection means that usually Petri nets and their operational behavior are not defined within a suitable algebraic framework and that specially there is no suitable algebraic semantics.
2. *Petri Nets lack Abstraction*
   This means that the concept of Petri nets is a low level concept, comparable with machine level programming languages, which does not allow higher level abstraction, structuring principles and suitable compositionality which are essential for specification of distributed systems.
3. *The Net Structure of Petri Nets is not Dynamic*
   This common objection means that usually the net structure of a Petri net is considered to be fixed and that these are no suitable techniques for stepwise refinement of net items and net structure as usual in top-down or bottom-up development techniques.

In the following we will analyze how far these objections are really justified and what has been done concerning these problems in the last few years. The answer will be presented again in slogans (see the headlines of 2.2 to 2.5), but in this case together with a more detailed algebraic reasoning.

2.2 Petri Nets are Monoids

This slogan is the title of a famous paper [MM90] by Meseguer and Montanari which states that in contrast to our first objection in 2.1, Petri nets can be considered as monoids and hence as one of the most basic algebraic structure.

Recall that the usual textbook definition (see [Rei85]) of a place/transition net, short P/T-net, is a 3-tuple (P, T, F) where P is a nonempty, finite set of places, T a finite set of transitions and F is a mapping $F : (P \times T) \uplus (T \times P) \rightarrow \mathbb{N}$ that yields the casual dependency relation of the transitions and the places. F represents the pre- and postconditions for the firing of the transitions.

The algebraic way to describe a P/T-net is to view the pre- and postconditions not as a mapping from pairs to natural numbers (that represent the numbers of tokens involved in the switchings of transitions) but as functions from transitions to the free commutative monoid $P^{\oplus}$ over the places of the net [MM90]: $pre, post : T \to P^{\oplus}$. For example, $pre(t1) = 3p_1 \oplus p_2$ means that for the transition $t1$ to switch it is necessary that place p_1 has at least 3 tokens and place p_2 at least one token. This algebraic presentation of P/T-nets is the starting point in [MM90] to define also suitable algebraic semantical domains and constructions. First of all, P/T-nets together with pairs (f, g) of functions $f : T_1 \to T_2$ and monoid homomorphisms $g : P_1^{\oplus} \to P_2^{\oplus}$ compatible with *pre* and *post* define a category **Petri** (static P/T-nets). Then the nets are extended by a monoid structure on transitions (parallel transitions) and idling tokens (reflexive transitions) leading to the category **CMonRPetri** (marking graphs) and a free construction F_1 : **Petri** $\to$ **CMonRPetri** assigning to each P/T-net the corresponding marking graph. Finally sequential composition $t_1; t_2$ of transitions t_1 and t_2 with $post(t_1) = pre(t_2)$ is added leading to a category **CatPetri** (computation graphs) and a free construction F_2 : **CMonRPetri** $\to$ **CatPetri**. Thus the composition $F_{12} = F_2 \circ F_1$: **Petri** $\to$ **CatPetri** is again a free construction assigning to each place/transition net its computation graph.

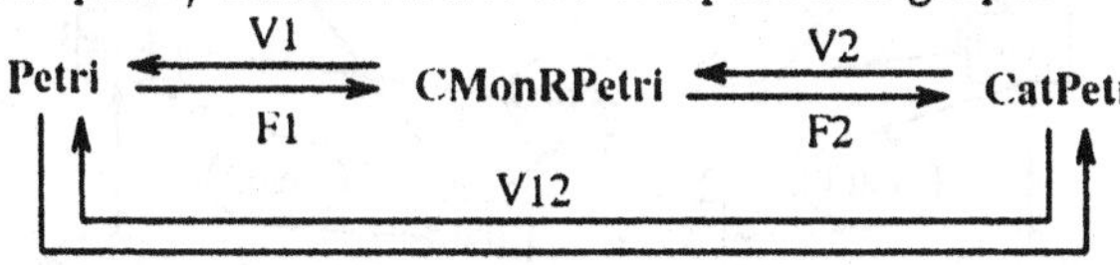

The category **Petri** is cocomplete and composition of nets can be expressed in terms of colimits. Since F_1, F_2 and F_{12} are free constructions w.r.t. the corresponding forgetful functors V_1, V_2 and V_{12} they preserve colimits. This means that both the marking graph and the computation graph semantics of P/T-nets are compositional, which is a very desirable semantical property.

As indicated in [MM90] already we can replace the free commutative monoid $P^{\oplus}$ in the definition by the free abelian group $P^{\circledcirc}$. This allows the use of subtraction and hence application of methods from linear algebra to compute invariants of P/T-nets.

2.3 Petri Nets are Abelian Groups

A place/transition net based on groups, short P/T-G-net, $N = (P, T, pre, post)$ consists of sets P and T (places and transitions, respectively) and functions $pre, post : T \to P^{\circledcirc}$, where $P^{\circledcirc}$ is the free abelian group over P with addition $\oplus$ and subtraction $\ominus$. The G in the name P/T-G-net stands for *group*.

An element of $P^{\circledcirc}$ is called *marking* of a P/T-G-net. The marking $m_1 = 2p_1 \oplus 3p_2$ means that we have 2 tokens in place p_1 and 3 tokens in place p_2. In fact, in this model we can also have negative markings like $m_2 = \ominus p_3$ corresponding to a negative number of tokens in p_3. This allows to formulate the successor marking m' of m after switch of transition t by $m' = m \ominus pre(t) \oplus post(t)$. In fact, we could replace the two functions *pre* and *post* by one function *switch* $= post \ominus pre$ leading to $m' = m \oplus switch(t)$. The idea to use abelian groups can also be applied to colored nets in the sense of [Jen81]. This is studied in [Hum89, DH90].

As an example for P/T-G-nets, the well known Dijkstra's "dining philosophers" [Dij71] will be presented. This can be modeled as a place/transition net shown in Fig. 1. In this example the weight of each transition is one, that means, all the arrows should be labeled with ones, but as it is the same for all of them, we skip these labels.

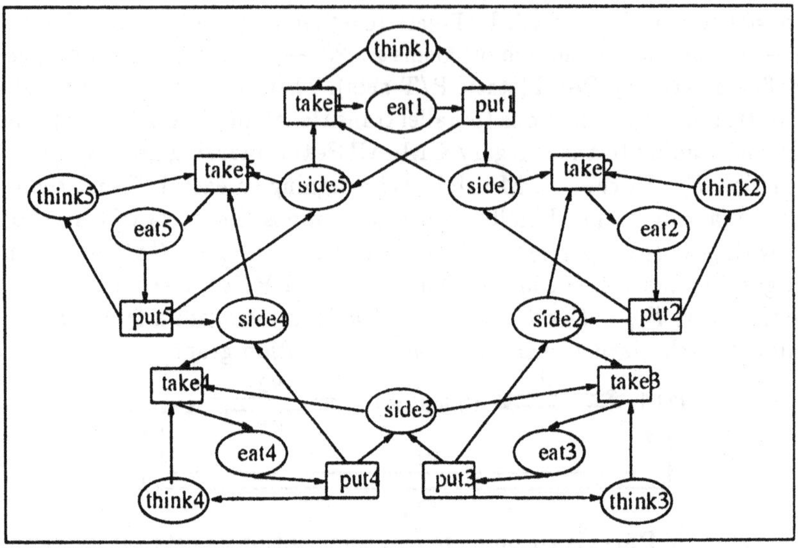

Figure 1. DIPHI: "Dining philosophers" place/transition net

The corresponding **P/T-G net** $DIPHI = (P, T, pre, post)$ is:
$P = \{think1, \ldots, think5, eat1, \ldots, eat5, side1, \ldots, side5\}$
$T = \{take1, \ldots, take5, put1, \ldots, put5\}$
$pre : T \rightarrow P^{\circledast} = \{take1 \mapsto think1 \oplus side1 \oplus side5, put1 \mapsto eat1, \ldots\}$
$post : T \rightarrow P^{\circledast} = \{take1 \mapsto eat1, put1 \mapsto think1 \oplus side1 \oplus side5, \ldots\}$

We can derive some properties of P/T-G-nets, called *invariants*. The *P-invariants* can be interpreted as sums of tokens that remain constant under switching of transitions, and the *T-invariants* as switching sequences preserving their initial marking. From an algebraic point of view the construction of P- and T-invariants can be considered a functor from the category **PT-G-Net** of P/T-G-nets into the category **Ab-Group** of abelian groups, e.g.

$$\text{P-INV} : \mathbf{PT\text{-}G\text{-}Net} \rightarrow \mathbf{Ab\text{-}Group}^{op}$$

In [Hum89, DH90, DHP91] it is shown for colored nets that the corresponding functor is cocontinuous (i.e., preserves colimits), specially pushouts of nets are transformed into pullbacks of abelian groups. This allows to compute invariants in a compositional way.

Of course, the notion of P/T-G-nets is an abstraction of the usual notion of P/T-nets which includes also initial markings and enabling of transitions, i.e. a transition can only be switched if we have $m \geq pre(t)$ for the present marking

m. In fact, these additional features and also capacities restricting the minimum and maximum number of tokens allowed in each place can be added within the algebraic framework of P/T-G-nets leading to the notion of P/T-G-nets with capacities introduced in [EGH92].

2.4 Algebraic High-Level Nets are Abstractions of Petri Nets

Now let us reconsider the second common objection mentioned in 2.1 which claims that Petri nets lack abstraction. In fact, several different notions of high-level nets have been introduced in the last years already (see [JR92]). We will focus specially on algebraic high-level nets, a combination of nets with algebraic specifications.

The first important step to achieve a higher level of abstraction for Petri nets is the concept of colored Petri nets introduced by Jensen [Jen81]. This concept allows colored tokens, i.e., different kinds of tokens in the places, and also colored transitions, i.e., different modes under which transitions can be switched. If different kinds of tokens are represented by data elements of an algebraic data type, arcs of the nets are labeled by terms with variables of the corresponding algebraic specification and a mode of a transition is given by an assignment for the variables of the terms on adjacent arcs of the transition we obtain the notion of algebraic high-level nets (see [Hum89, DH90, DHP91, Rei91, EGH92]).

The essential idea of combining Petri nets with algebraic specifications was given already by Vautherin in [Vau86]. In Sect. 3 of this paper we present a revised version of algebraic high-level nets and a flattening construction *FLAT* from algebraic high-level nets to P/T-G-nets which is compatible with markings and switching behavior on both levels.

In Sect. 3 we will present an AHL-net *AN* for the "dining philosophers" such that *FLAT*(*AN*) is equivalent to the P/T-G-net given in Sect. 2.3. This illustrates our slogan that AHL-nets are abstractions of P/T-G-nets. The flattening construction allows to extend all notions, like marking graphs and invariants from P/T-nets to AHL-nets. For a given AHL-net *AN* we can compute the marking graph and the invariants for the corresponding P/T-G-net *FLAT*(*AN*). On the other hand it is also useful to study these notions directly for high-level nets as done for invariants in [Hum89, DH90, Rei91].

In [Hum89] and [DH90] the flattening construction is defined as a functor from algebraic high-level nets to colored nets. It is shown that this functor is cocontinuous and can be combined with a cocontinuous functor computing invariants. This shows that invariants for AHL-nets can be computed in a compositional way. A slightly different technique for computing invariants for Petri nets with algebraic specifications is given in [Rei91].

2.5 Net Transformation Systems are High-Level Refinements for Petri Nets

Finally let us reconsider the last objection against Petri nets considered in 2.1 claiming that the net structure of Petri nets is not dynamic and does not allow suitable refinements. In fact, there are several attempts to define refinements of places and transitions in nets, which might be considered as low level refinements. We want to consider also high-level refinements leading to the notion of net transformation systems.

Net transformation systems have been introduced for P/T-nets and AHL-nets in [Pad92]. They are based on productions $p : L \rightarrow R$, where the left hand side L and the right hand side R are nets in the corresponding category. Similar to Chomsky grammars and graph grammars a production $p : L \rightarrow R$ is applied to a net N by finding a suitable occurrence of L in N and replacing L by R leading to a new net N'. This kind of replacement can be considered as a high-level refinement of nets. In Sect. 5 of this paper we will study transformation systems for AHL-nets. In fact, we are able to extend main results from the theory of graph grammars, including local Church-Rosser, parallelism and canonical derivation theorems, to AHL-net-transformation systems using the general theory of high-level replacement systems [EHKP91]. This allows to analyze concurrency in nets not only on the token level but also on the level of transformations of the net structure, what is very important for stepwise refinement of algebraic high-level nets as specifications for distributed systems.

3 Algebraic High-Level Nets

As discussed already in Sect. 2.4, algebraic high-level nets, short AHL-nets, are a combination of place/transition nets and algebraic specifications. In an AHL-net tokens are specified by the algebraic specification part. The pre- and postcondition functions define not only how many tokens are involved in each switching of a transition, but also which tokens are involved. AHL-nets allow a higher level of abstraction as we will see in the "dining-philosophers"' example presented as an AHL-net in this section.

Definition 1 (AHL-Net). An algebraic high-level net , short AHL-net,

$$AN = (SPEC, P, T, pre, post, A, cond)$$

consists of a specification $SPEC = (S, OP, E)$, sets P and T (places and transitions, respectively), functions $pre, post : T \rightarrow (T_{OP}(X) \times P)^{\circledast}$, assigning to each $t \in T$ an element of the free abelian group over the cartesian product of terms $T_{OP}(X)$ with variables in X and the set P of places, a $SPEC$-algebra A and a function $cond : T \rightarrow \mathcal{P}_{fin}(EQNS(SIG))$ assigning to each $t \in T$ a finite set $cond(t)$ of equations over $SIG = (S, OP)$, the signature of $SPEC$.

The *pre* (*post*) function assigns to each transition a sum of terms together with their places that are consumed(created) by switching this transition. The set of equations assigned to each transition by *cond* represents the conditions that must be satisfied for each transition to switch (see Definition 2).

Remark. For simplicity we assume that the set of variables X used in the term algebra $T_{OP}(X)$ is essentially the same for all AHL-nets. In fact, X is obtained by a fixed set X_{fix} of variables which is indexed by the set of sorts S of the signature $SIG = (S, OP)$, i.e. $X = \{x_s | x \in X_{fix}, s \in S\} \cong X_{fix} \times S$.

This notion of AHL-nets is a revised version of corresponding notions in [Vau86], [Hum89], [DHP91] and [EGH92]. Previously the notion of AHL-nets was based on AHL-net schemes, i.e. AHL-nets without algebra A, and schemes as well as nets were sorted. The latter means that for each place $p \in P$ we have a unique sort $s \in S$ such that only terms and data elements of sort s are allowed for place p. Our revised version is mixed-sorted because it allows terms and data elements of different sorts for each place. This is more flexible for applications and easier in the mathematical notation. The other slight difference – already advocated in [EGH92] – is the fact that we are able to define the switching behavior of AHL-nets directly while previously it was defined only via a semantical construction in terms of colored Petri nets in the sense of Jensen [Jen81]. An extended notion of AHL-nets including initial markings and capacities is given in [EGH92].

Example 1 (AHL-Net for Dining Philosophers). For the P/T-G-net of the "dining philosophers" given as an example in the Sect. 2.3, a corresponding AHL-net $AHLDIPHI = (\underline{\underline{dihpi}}, P, T, pre, post, A_{\underline{\underline{diphi}}}, cond)$ is given in full detail as follows:

$\underline{\underline{\text{diphi}}}$ =

sorts: philo,stick
opns: $p1, \ldots, p5 :\rightarrow philo$
$s1, \ldots, s5 :\rightarrow stick$
$ls, rs : philo \rightarrow stick$
eqns: $ls(p1) = s1, ls(p2) = s2, ls(p3) = s3, ls(p4) = s4, ls(p5) = s5,$
$rs(p1) = s5, rs(p2) = s1, rs(p3) = s2, rs(p4) = s3, rs(p5) = s4$

variables $x_{philo}, y_{stick}, z_{stick} \in X$
$P = \{THINK, EAT, SIDE\}$
$T = \{TAKE, PUT\}$
$pre = \{TAKE \mapsto (x_{philo}, THINK) \oplus (y_{stick}, SIDE) \oplus (z_{stick}, SIDE),$
$PUT \mapsto (x_{philo}, EAT)\}$
$post = \{TAKE \mapsto (x_{philo}, EAT),$
$PUT \mapsto (x_{philo}, THINK) \oplus (ls(x_{philo}), SIDE) \oplus (rs(x_{philo}), SIDE)\}$
$A_{\underline{\underline{diphi}}}$:
$A_{philo} = \{uta, anne, elli, ingo, orfeu\}$ $ls_A(x)$ = last letter of x, for $x \in A_{philo}$
$A_{stick} = \{a, e, i, o, u\}$ $rs_A(x)$ = first letter of x, for $x \in A_{philo}$
$cond = \{TAKE \mapsto \{ls(x_{philo}) = y_{stick}, rs(x_{philo}) = z_{stick}\}, PUT \mapsto \emptyset\}$

This can be graphically represented as it is shown in Fig. 2. In each transition we add to the name the set of equations that must hold for this transition to switch. The labels of the arcs represent the elements of the places which are involved in the switching of the transitions. Each label should be written as an element of $(T_{OP}(X) \times P)^{\circledcirc}$ but we avoid this in the graphical representation by writing, for example, $y_{stick} \oplus z_{stick}$ instead of $(y_{stick}, SIDE) \oplus (z_{stick}, SIDE)$.

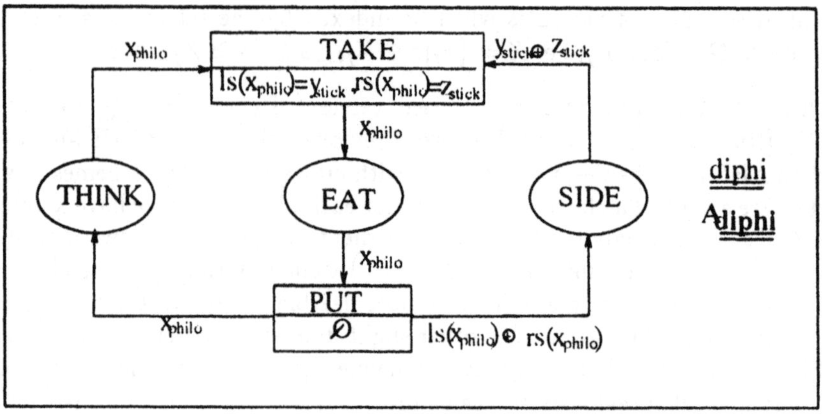

Figure 2: AHLDIPHI: Dining phisosophers' AHL-net

Definition 2 (Switching of Transitions in AHL-Nets). Given an AHL-net $N = (SPEC, P, T, pre, post, A, cond)$ as presented in Definition 1 we define:

1. The set of place vectors PV, also called marking group of AN, is the free abelian group $PV = (A \times P)^{\oplus}$. Within this context A is considered to be the disjoint union of all carrier sets of the algebra A, i. e. $A = \biguplus_{s \in S} A_s$.
   An element of PV is called a marking of the AHL-net AN.
2. The set of consistent transition assignments, is $CT = \{(t, ass_A) | t \in T, ass_A : Var(t) \to A$ s.t. A satisfies the equations $cond(t)$ with variables $Var(t)$ under the assignment $ass_A\}$. $Var(t)$ is the set of variables that occur in the condition equations $cond(t)$ and in the *pre* and *post* conditions $pre(t)$ and $post(t)$ for each transition $t \in T$.
3. The A-induced functions $pre_A, post_A : CT \to PV$ of the AHL-net AN are defined for all $(t, ass_A) \in CT$ by

$$pre_A(t, ass_A) = ASS_A(pre(t)) \text{ and } post_A(t, ass_A) = ASS_A(post(t))$$

   where $ASS_A = (T_{OP}(Var(t)) \times P)^{\oplus} \to (A \times P)^{\oplus} = PV$ is defined on generators by $ASS_A(term, p) = (ass_A(term), p)$ for each $p \in P$, and $term \in T_{OP}(Var(t))$.
4. Given a marking $m \in PV$ and a consistent transition assignment $(t, ass_A) \in CT$ the successor marking $m' \in PV$ of m is defined by

$$m' = m \ominus pre_A(t, ass_A) \oplus post_A(t, ass_A)$$

Remark. The switching of transitions in AHL-nets can easily be extended to define marking graphs with nodes colored by markings and edges by consistent transition assignments. Moreover it seems possible to extend the corresponding categorical constructions of [MM90] given in Sect. 2.2 from P/T-nets to AHL-nets. For this purpose we have to extend the flattening construction below to a cocontinuous functor from the category of AHL-nets to the category of P/T-G-nets (see remark of 3) and the constructions in [MM90] from the monoid case to P/T-G-nets.

Fact 3 (Flattening). *For each AHL-net AN there is a P/T-G-net FLAT(AN), called flattening of AN, which is behavioral equivalent to AN in the sense that both have the same marking groups and successor markings.*

Construction: For each AHL-net $AN = (SPEC, P, T, pre, post, A, cond)$ we have $FLAT(AN) = (P_F, T_F, pre_F, post_F)$ with $P_F = (A \times P)$, $T_F = CT$, $pre_F = pre_A$ and $post_F = post_A$, as it is shown in the diagram on the right.

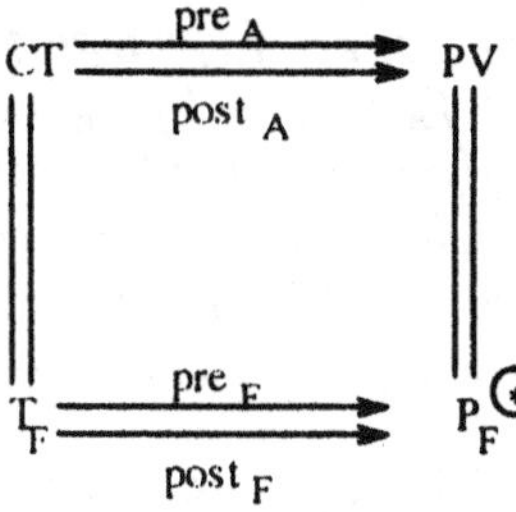

Proof. AN and $FLAT(AN)$ have the same marking group: $PV = (A \times P)^{\circledast} = P_F^{\circledast}$ by the construction of $FLAT(AN)$. As they also have the same transitions $CT = T_F$ and *pre* and *post*- functions, the successor markings defined by the formula $m' = m \ominus pre(t) \oplus post(t)$ are obviously the same. □

Remark. Although the construction of $FLAT(AN)$ may suggest that AN and $FLAT(AN)$ are almost equal, they are essentially different concerning the sets of places and transitions and the corresponding net structure which is illustrated by the example in 2. The flattening construction can be extended to a functor between suitable categories of AHL-nets and P/T-G-nets. In [Hum89, DH90] a similar functor is constructed from algebraic high-level nets to colored nets. This functor is used to define the semantics of algebraic high-level nets in terms of colored nets and shown to be cocontinuous such that the semantics becomes compositional.

Example 2 (Flattening of Dining Philosophers). The flattened net of the AHL-net $AHLDIPHI$ for the "dining philosophers" given in Example 1 is equal - up to isolated places - to the P/T-G-net $DIPHI$ presented in Sect. 2.3. Therefore we can say that AHLDIPHI is a higher level presentation or abstraction of $DIPHI$.

4 Categorical Properties of AHL-Nets

In this section we define the category of AHL-nets. Similar categories were examined concerning cocompleteness in [Hum89] and [DH90], but in this paper our interest is focused on other properties, which arise in the context of high-level replacement systems, short HLR systems. In fact AHL-net transformation systems are an instantiation of high-level replacement systems. The categorical properties, which we show in this section allow to conclude important theorems for net transformation systems in the next section.

In fact we have to deal with morphisms between algebras of different specifications. To deal sensibly with these morphisms we have to introduce *generalized homomorphisms*. These are a special case of generalized morphisms introduced in the context of specification logics [EBO91] and indexed categories [TBG87].

Definition 4 (Generalized Homomorphism). Given the category **SPEC** of specifications with $SPEC_i = (S_i, OP_i, E_i)$ and algebras $A_i \in Cat(SPEC_i)$ for $\{i = 1, 2\}$, then a generalized homomorphism $g : A_1 \rightarrow A_2$ consists of a pair $g = (f_{SPEC}, f_A)$ where $f_{SPEC} : SPEC_1 \rightarrow SPEC_2$ is a specification morphism, and $f_A : A_1 \rightarrow V_{f_{SPEC}}(A_2)$ is a homomorphism and $V_{f_{SPEC}} : Cat(SPEC_2) \rightarrow Cat(SPEC_1)$ the forgetful functor.

Composition of two generalized homomorphisms $g = (f_{SPEC}, f_A) : A_1 \rightarrow A_2$ and $g' = (f'_{SPEC}, f'_A) : A_2 \rightarrow A_3$ is given by: $g' \circ g = (f_{SPEC} \circ f'_{SPEC}, V_{f_{SPEC}}(f'_A) \circ f_A) : A_1 \rightarrow A_3$

This leads to the category **GALG** of algebras and generalized homomorphisms.

Remark. The category **GALG** is complete and cocomplete (see [TBG87], [Hum89] and [EBO91]). Colimits in **GALG** are rather tricky to construct, (see [TBG87], [EBO91]) and the full verification w.r.t. the properties required for HLR systems in order to be able to apply the results of [EHKP91, EHKP92] is still open. Thus we consider a restricted subcategory $\mathbf{GALG}_{iso}$ of **GALG** where all homomorphisms on algebras are isomorphisms. Although this restriction seems to be quite drastic, it is sufficient for interesting examples and yields interesting results. This is due to the fact that pushouts of algebras in $\mathbf{GALG}_{iso}$ are given by amalgamation of algebras(see [EBO91]). Amalgamation is defined for algebras of different specifications, if the corresponding reduct algebras are identical; here we do allow isomorphisms, thus we obtain a slightly more general kind of amalgamation.

With this notion of morphisms we subsequently can define morphisms of AHL-nets and hence the category **AHLNET** of AHL-nets.

Definition 5 (Category AHLNET). The category **AHLNET** of algebraic high-level nets consists of all AHL-nets $N = (SPEC, P, T, pre, post, A, cond)$ where $SPEC = (S, OP, E)$ (see Definition 1) as objects represented by

$$\mathcal{P}_{fin}(EQNS(SIG)) \stackrel{cond}{\longleftarrow} T \underset{post}{\overset{pre}{\rightrightarrows}} \quad (T_{OP}(X) \times P)^{\circledast}$$

A morphism $f : N1 \rightarrow N2$ is a quadruple $f = (f_{SPEC}, f_P, f_T, f_A)$ where

- $f_{SPEC} : (SIG1, E1) \rightarrow (SIG2, E2)$ is a specification morphism with $f^{\#}_{SPEC}(E1) \subseteq E2$
- $f_T : T1 \rightarrow T2$ and $f_P : P1 \rightarrow P2$ are functions
- $(f_{SPEC}, f_A) : A1 \rightarrow A2$ is a generalized homomorphism and $f_A : A1 \rightarrow V_{f_{SPEC}}(A2)$ is an isomorphism in **Cat(SPEC1)**.

such that the following diagram commutes componentwise

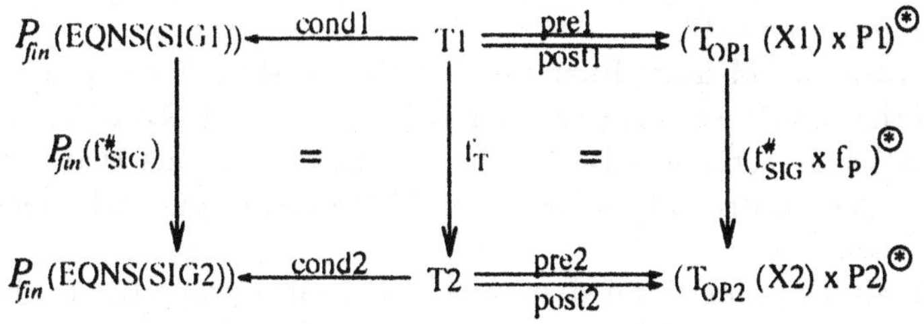

Remark. In order to extend the flattening construction in Fact 3 to a functor $FLAT$: **AHLNET** $\rightarrow$ **PT-G-Net** we also have to require that f_{SPEC} induces a bijection of variables $Var(t) \cong Var(f_T(t))$ for all $t \in T_1$.

Now we are able to formulate important categorical properties of the category **AHLNET** which on one hand allow to construct arbitrary colimits and hence horizontal structuring of AHL-nets and on the other hand correspond to HLR1-properties in [EHKP91, EHKP92] which will be used in Sect. 5 to show important properties of AHL-net transformation systems.

Theorem 6 (Categorical Properties of AHLNET).
The category **AHLNET** *together with the class* $\mathsf{M}_{\mathbf{AHLNET}}$, *short* M *of all morphisms* $f = (f_{SPEC}, f_T, f_P, f_A)$ *where* f_{SPEC} *is strict and injective and* f_T, f_P *are injective satisfies the following properties:*

1. **AHLNET** *is cocomplete*
2. *Inheritance of* M*-morphisms under pushouts*
3. *Existence of* M*-pullbacks*
4. *Inheritance of* M*-morphisms under pullbacks*
5. *"*M*-pushout-pullback-decomposition property"*

   Given the diagram on the side we have: if $(1+2)$ *is a pushout*, (2) *is a pullback and* $A \rightarrow C$, $B \rightarrow D$, $E \rightarrow F$, $B \rightarrow E$ *and* $D \rightarrow F$ *are* M*-morphisms, then also* (1) *is a pushout.*

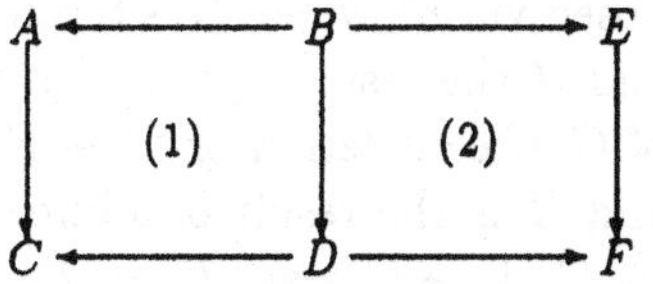

6. *Pushouts of* M*-morphisms are pullbacks*

Remark. Strictness of f_{SPEC} means $(f^{\#}_{SPEC})^{-1}(E_2) = E_1$. As pointed out in [EP91b] strictness is essential to obtain Property 6 within the category of specifications of type 2, i.e. $(f^{\#}_{SPEC})(E_1) \subseteq E_2$. Using the usual, more general version of specification morphisms where $f^{\#}_{SPEC}(E_1)$ is required to be deducible from E_2, called type 1 in [EP91b], it is still open to find a suitable class M of specification morphisms so that the Property 6 is valid for the general category of specifications.

Proof. 1. **AHLNET is cocomplete** where all colimits can be constructed separately in each component. For cocompleteness in the algebra component see [TBG87] and [EBO91].

2. **Inheritance of M-morphisms under pushouts** is due to the same property of the component categories **SPEC**, bf SET and $\mathbf{GALG}_{iso}$.
3. **Pullbacks** are constructed componentwise using the fact that the functors used in the construction $(T_{OP}(X) \times P)^{\circledS}$ preserve pullbacks for injective morphisms.

The remaining properties 4–6 are due to the same properties of the component categories **SPEC**, **SET** and $\mathbf{GALG}_{iso}$ (see [EP91b]). More details of the proof are given in [PER93]. □

5 AHL-Net Transformation Systems

Replacement in net transformation systems can be defined similar to replacement in graph grammars (see [Ehr79]). The key idea of replacement in both cases is a double pushout construction, where each pushout corresponds to a gluing construction which will be explained below.

Productions for transformation system are consisting of a left side (to be deleted), a right side (to be added) and a common gluing net (or interface). They are given as three nets together with two morphisms $p = L \leftarrow K \rightarrow R$. These morphisms belong to a distinguished class M of morphisms. $\mathsf{M} = \mathsf{M}_{\mathbf{AHLNET}}$ was defined already in the last section. In order to apply a production via a morphism $L \rightarrow G$ to a given net a gluing condition has to be satisfied. This condition makes sure that after deleting there remains a well-defined net C, called context net, such that the given net G is a pushout of L and C via K.

A direct transformation, denoted by $G \stackrel{p}{\Longrightarrow} H$, is given by two pushouts as shown in the diagram on the right. During a direct transformation the AHL-nets L and C (resp. R and C) are composed via K, where C is the context net and H the resulting net. C is the result of G after deletion of "$L - K$" from G and H is the result of adding '$R - K$" to C. $L \rightarrow G$ resp. $R \rightarrow H$ are called occurrence in G resp. H.

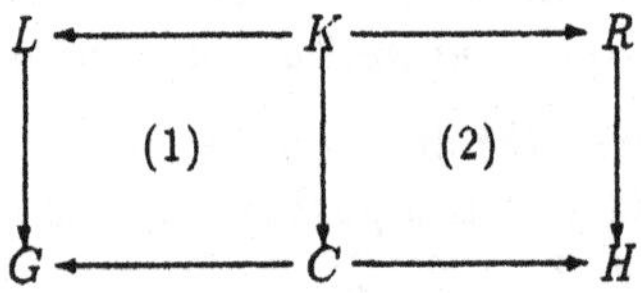

A transformation sequence is given by a sequence of direct transformations.

These concepts are formalized in the following definition which is a special case of high-level replacement systems in [EHKP91]. Note, that transformations are called derivations in [Ehr79], [EHKP91], [EKT92].

Definition 7 (AHL-netTransformation Systems). 1. A production $p = (L \leftarrow K \rightarrow R)$ in **AHLNET** consists of a pair of nets (L, R), called the left- and right-hand side, respectively, and a net K, called the gluing net or interface, and two morphisms $K \to L$ and $K \to R$ belonging to the class $M_{\mathbf{AHLNET}}$.

2. Given a production p as above and a net C, called the context net, together with a morphism $K \to C$ a direct transformation $G \overset{p}{\Longrightarrow} H$ from a net G to a net H via p is given by two pushouts $L \to G \leftarrow C$ and $C \to H \leftarrow R$ in the category **AHLNET**.
3. A transformation sequence $G \overset{*}{\Longrightarrow} H$ (short: transformation or derivation) from G to H means $G \cong H$ or a sequence of $n \geq 1$ direct transformations $G = G_0 \overset{p_1}{\Longrightarrow} G_1 \overset{p_2}{\Longrightarrow} \ldots \overset{p_n}{\Longrightarrow} G_n = H$.
4. An AHL-net transformation system $H = (P, AN_0)$ based on (**AHLNET**, $M_{\mathbf{AHLNET}}$) consists of a set of productions P and a start net AN_0 in **AHLNET**.

Example 3 (Restaurant of Dining Philosophers). The following refinements of the net AN in Example 1 illustrate an AHL-net transformation system consisting of two productions with start net AN :

1. philosophers that are thinking can start a discussion circle, if there are two of them, or they can join a discussion circle. Discussing philosophers can leave a circle, if there are at least two members left, or else they can finish the discussion circle. In both cases they resume thinking again.
2. a philosopher that has finished eating can think or read, if a book is available. If she stops reading, she puts the book back, and either thinks again or waits until she may eat again.

These two refinements differ from each other, as the first only concerns the place THINK, whereas the second also concerns the transitions.

The first refinement can be formulated by the following production in Fig. 3, where each AHL-net is represented similar to Example 1.

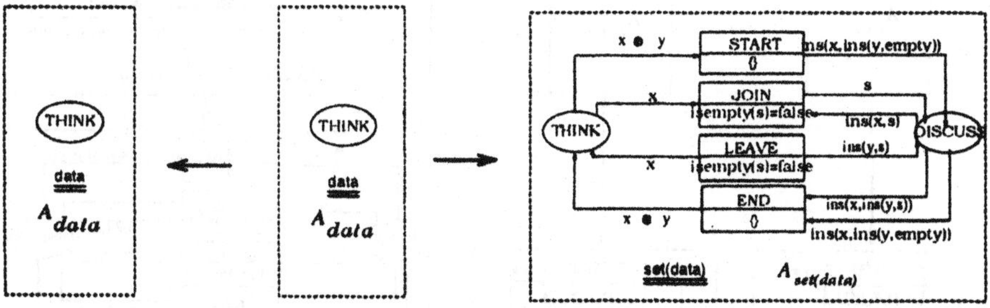

Figure 3: "Discussing" production

The specifications and algebras indicated in Fig. 3 are: a specification data consisting of one sort, 5 constants and no equations with the initial data-algebra $\mathbf{A}_{\mathbf{data}}$ and the standard specification for set(data) with the initial set(data)-algebra $\mathbf{A}_{\mathbf{set(data)}}$.

This production expresses the fact that nothing is deleted but a subnet is added, so that merely the place THINK is concerned. The equations given together with the transitions make sure that there is no philosopher talking to herself.

The second refinement is given in Fig. 4.

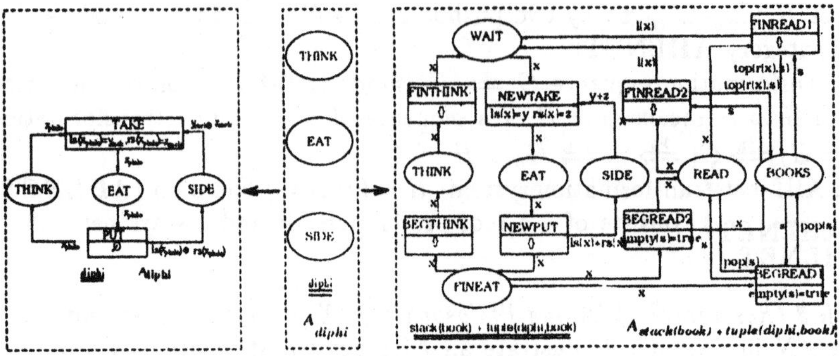

Figure 4: "Reading" production

with specifications diphi (see Example 1), book (consisting of a sort *book* and constants representing the books) and standard specifications for stack and tuple.

A direct transformation with the first production is given in in Fig. 5.

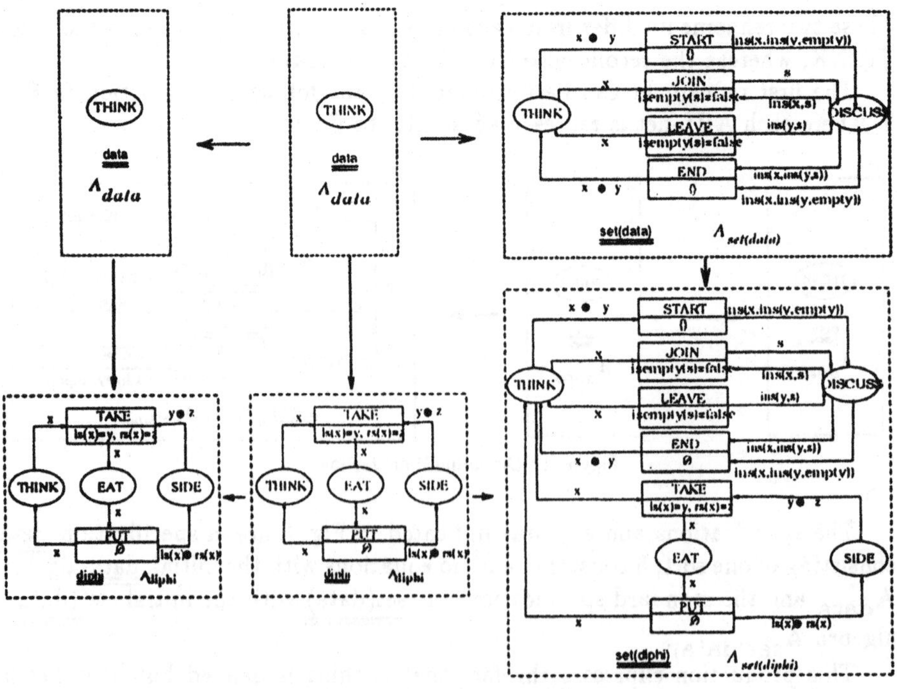

Figure 5: "Discussing" transformation

Note, that the algebra $\mathbf{A}_{\mathbf{set(diphi)}}$ is constructed by amalgamation $\mathbf{A}_{\mathbf{set(diphi)}} = \mathbf{A}_{\mathbf{set(data)}} +_{A_{data}} \mathbf{A}_{\mathbf{diphi}}$.

Finally let us consider the following important results, concerning commutativity and parallelism of productions and transformations, well-known from graph grammars and high-level replacement system.

In the context of this paper we can only give an informal statement of these important results. For a formal version in the context of graph grammars, net transformation system and high-level replacement systems we refer to [Ehr79], [EHKP91], [EKT92].

1. **Local Church-Rosser Theorem I** states the fact that two parallel independent transformations (those where the occurrence of both productions are overlapping in the gluing items only) can be sequentialized in any order. **Local Church-Rosser Theorem II** means that two sequential independent transformations can be computed in any order. Given the sequential independent transformation $G \overset{p}{\Longrightarrow} H \overset{p'}{\Longrightarrow} X$, then we have the sequential independent transformation $G \overset{p'}{\Longrightarrow} H' \overset{p}{\Longrightarrow} X$ as well.
2. **Parallel productions** are constructed by the componentwise disjoint union (coproduct) of two productions p and p' and is denoted by $p + p'$. The **Parallelism Theorem** asserts that there are two operations ANALYSIS and SYNTHESIS, that are inverse to each other:
   (a) ANALYSIS: a parallel transformation can be analyzed into two sequential independent transformation sequences that result in the same net;
   (b) SYNTHESIS: two sequential independent transformations can be synthesized into one parallel transformation yielding the same result;

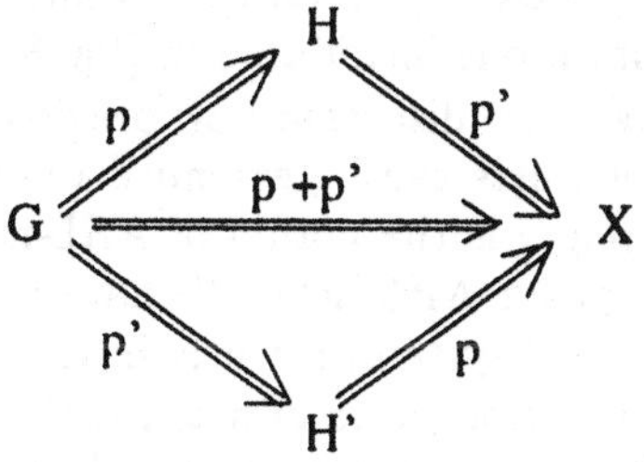

3. **Canonical Transformations**, called canonical derivations in [EKT92] can be constructed by applying SYNTHESIS and ANALYSIS of the Parallelism Theorem several times to a given transformation sequence. An operation SHIFT is defined by composition of SYNTHESIS and ANALYSIS, such that two consecutive transformation steps which are sequentially independent are exchanged. The SHIFT operation defines an equivalence relation for transformation sequences. Hence equivalent canonical parallel transformation sequences that are leftmost parallel can be constructed. If the bijective correspondence of SYNTHESIS and ANALYSIS is given, the canonical transformation sequence is unique, else there might be several different canonical sequences. The **Canonical Derivation Theorem** in [EKT92] states the fact that for each parallel transformation sequence there is a unique canonical which is equivalent to the given one.

Remark. Note, that if $\mathrm{M}_{\mathbf{AHLNET}}$ merely consists of injective specification morphisms, then the bijective correspondence of ANALYSIS and SYNTHESIS does not hold. Hence the canonical transformation may not be unique.

Theorem 8 (Properties of AHL-Net Transformation Systems). *For AHL-net transformation system based on* (**AHLNET**, $\mathsf{M}_{\mathbf{AHLNET}}$) *we have the following results:*

1. *Local Church-Rosser Theorem I*
2. *Local Church-Rosser Theorem II*
3. *Parallelism Theorem*
4. *Canonical Derivation Theorem*

Proof. Direct consequence of Theorem 6 and the general results for high-level replacement systems in [EHKP91] and [EKT92]. □

The significance of these results was pointed out already in Sect. 2.5.

6 Conclusion

In this paper we have revisited P/T-nets from an algebraic point of view in the sense of Meseguer and Montanari [MM90] and introduced a revised version of algebraic high-level nets, which is a combination of Petri nets and algebraic specifications introduced in [Vau86] and studied in more detail recently.

We have discussed how previous semantical constructions for different kinds of Petri nets can be extended to our revised version. The main new concept of this paper is the notion of AHL-net-transformations as a high-level refinement concept for AHL-nets. We have applied the categorical theory of high-level replacement systems recently introduced in [EHKP91] to obtain several non trivial results for our kind of net transformation systems.

It remains open to extend the categorical semantics of P/T-nets given in [MM90] to AHL-nets, to compare our high-level refinement concept for nets with other refinement concepts for Petri nets studied in the literature, to study AHL-net transformation systems for more general morphisms in **AHLNET** and more detail with respect to different semantical concepts for AHL-nets (e.g. relationships to stream processing functions [BS92]) , and to extend the theory to AHL-nets with initial markings and capacities as defined in [EGH92]. First results concerning markings were given already in [RP93].

References

[AR87] E. Astesiano and G. Reggio. An outline of the SMolCS approach. In M. Venturini Zilli, editor, *Mathematical models for the semantics of parallelism*, volume 280 of *Lecture Notes in Computer Science*. Springer Verlag Berlin, 1987.

[BCM88] E. Battiston, F. De Cindio, and G. Mauri. OBJSA nets: a class of high-level nets having objects as domains. In G. Rozenberg, editor, *Advances in Petri nets*, volume 340 of *Lecture Notes in Computer Science*, pages 20–43. Springer Verlag Berlin, 1988.

[BK86] J. A. Bergstra and J. W. Klop. Algebra of communicating processes. In *CWI Monographs I*, 1986. Proc. CWIU Symp. Math. and Comp. Sci.

[Bro85] M. Broy. Specification and top-down design of distributed systems. In H. Ehrig, C. Floyd, M. Nivat, and J. Thatcher, editors, *Proc. TAPSOFT'85*, volume 185 of *Lecture Notes in Computer Science*, pages 4–28. Springer Verlag Berlin, 1985.

[BS92] M. Broy and T. Streicher. Modular functional modelling of Petri nets with individual tokens. Technical Report INFO-10-90-I35-450/1. - FMI, Technical University of Munich, 1992.

[DH90] C. Dimitrovici and U. Hummert. Composition of algebraic high-level nets. In *Proc. of the 7th ADT-Workshop*, Wusterhausen/Dosse, 1990. LNCS 534(1991).

[DHP91] C. Dimitrovici, U. Hummert, and L. Petrucci. Composition and net properties of algebraic high-level nets. In *Advances of Petri Nets*, volume 483 of *Lecture Notes in Computer Science*. Springer Verlag Berlin, 1991.

[Dij71] E.W. Dijkstra. Hierarquical ordering of sequential processes. In Perrot HOARE, editor, *Operating systems techniques*. Academic Press London New York, 1971.

[EBO91] H. Ehrig, M. Baldamus, and F. Orejas. New concepts for amalgamation and extension in the framework of specification logics. In *Proc. ADT-Workshop Durdan*, pages 199 - 221, Durdan, 1991. LNCS 655.

[EGH92] H. Ehrig, M. Große-Rhode, and A. Heise. Specification techniques for concurrent and distributed systems. Technical Report 92/5, Technical University of Berlin, jan. 1992. Invited paper for 2nd Maghr. Conference on Software Engineering and Artificial Intelligence, Tunis,1992.

[EHKP91] H. Ehrig, A. Habel, H.-J. Kreowski, and F. Parisi-Presicce. From Graph Grammars to High Level Replacement Systems. In H. Ehrig, H.-J. Kreowski, and G. Rozenberg, editors, *4th Int. Workshop on Graph Grammars and Their Application to Computer Science*, volume 532 of *Lecture Notes in Computer Science*, pages 269–291. Springer Verlag Berlin, 1991.

[EHKP92] H. Ehrig, A. Habel, H.-J. Kreowski, and F. Parisi-Presicce. Parallelism and concurrency in High Level Replacement Systems. *Math. Struct. in Comp. Sci.*, 1:361–404, 1992.

[Ehr79] H. Ehrig. Introduction to the algebraic theory of graph grammars. In *1st Int. Workshop on Graph Grammars and their Application to Computer Science and Biology*, volume 73 of *Lecture Notes in Computer Science*, pages 1–69. Springer, 1979.

[EKT92] H. Ehrig, H.-J. Kreowski, and G. Taentzer. Canonical Derivations in High-Level Replacement Systems. Technical Report 6/92, University of Bremen, 1992.

[EP91a] H. Ehrig and F. Parisi-Presicce. Algebraic specification grammars: adjunction between module specifications and graph grammars. *Lecture Notes in Computer Science*, 532:292–310, 1991.

[EP91b] H. Ehrig and F. Parisi-Presicce. Nonequivalence of Categories for Equational Algebraic Specifications in View of High-Level Replacement Systems. Technical Report 91/16, Technical University of Berlin, Dep. of Comp. Sci.,

1991. Short version in Proc. 3rd Conf. on Algebraic and Logic Programming, Pisa, 1992.

[EPB+87] H. Ehrig, F. Parisi-Presicce, P. Boehm, C. Rieckhoff, C. Dimitrovici, and M. Große-Rhode. Algebraic data type and process specifications based on projection spaces. *Theoretical Computer Science*, 332:23–43, 1987.

[Hen88] M. Hennessy, editor. *Algebraic theory of processes*. The MIT Press, Combridge, Massachussets, 1988.

[Hum89] U. Hummert. *Algebraische High-Level Netze*. PhD thesis, Technical University of Berlin, Dep. of Comp. Sci., 1989.

[Jen81] K. Jensen. Coloured petri nets and the invariant method. *Theoretical Computer Science*, 14:317–336, 1981.

[JR92] K. Jensen and G. Rozenberg, editors. *High-level Petri nets: theory and application*. Springer, 1992.

[Kra89] B. Kraemer. *Concepts, syntax and semanticas of Segras, a specification language for distributed systems*. PhD thesis, Technical University of Berlin, Dep. of Comp. Sci., 1989.

[LOT87] LOTOS - A formal description technique based on temporal ordering of observational behaviour. Information Processing Systems - Open Systems Interconnection ISO DIS 8807, jul. 1987. (ISO/TC 97/SC 21 N).

[MM90] J. Meseguer and U. Montanari. Petri nets are monoids. *Information and Computation*, 88(2):105–155, oct. 1990.

[Pad92] J. Padberg. Theory of High-Level Replacement Systems with Application to Petri Nets. Diplomarbeit, Technical University of Berlin, 1992.

[PER93] J. Padberg, H. Ehrig, and L. Ribeiro. Algebraic high-level net-transformation systems. Technical Report 93-12, Technical University of Berlin, 1993.

[Pet62] C.A. Petri. *Kommunikation mit Automaten*. PhD thesis, Schriften des Institutes für Instrumentelle Mathematik, Bonn, 1962.

[Rei85] W. Reisig. *Petri nets*. Springer Verlag, 1985.

[Rei91] W. Reisig. Petri nets and algebraic specifications. *Theoretical Computer Science*, 80:1–34, 1991.

[Roz87] G. Rozenberg. Behaviour of elementary net systems. In W. Brauer, W. Reisig, and G. Rozenberg, editors, *Advances in Petri nets 1986*, volume 254 of *Lecture Notes in Computer Science*, pages 60–94. Springer Verlag Berlin, 1987.

[RP93] L. Ribeiro and J. Padberg. Compatibility results for the formal development of concurrent systems using algebraic high-level nets. Submitted to SE/AI-Conf, Marroco, 1993.

[Sta90] P. Starke. *Analyse von Petri-Netz-Modellen*. Teubner Verlag, 1990.

[TBG87] A. Tarlecki, R.M. Burstall, and J.A. Goguen. Some fundamental algebraic tools for the semantics of computation. Part III: Indexed categories. Technical report, University of Edinburgh, 1987.

[Vau86] J. Vautherin. Parallel specification with coloured Petri nets and algebraic data types. In *Proc. of the 7th European Workshop on Application and Theory of Petri nets*, pages 5–23, Oxford, England, jul. 1986.

2-Categorical Specification of Partial Algebras

Martin Große-Rhode   Uwe Wolter

Technische Universität Berlin
Fachbereich 20, Sekr. FR 6–1
Franklinstraße 28/29
D–10587 Berlin
Germany
email: mgr@cs.tu-berlin.de

Abstract

The purpose of this paper is to present a short survey of possible results of an application of general concepts from categorical algebra to the specification of partial algebras with conditional existence equations. The general concept, which models theories (= formulas and equivalence classes of terms) as categories, is extended to 2–categories, such that rewriting between terms can be made explicit. To make clear the benefits of such an approach the results are presented in the usual terminology of algebraic specifications.

1 Introduction

The aim of this paper is to use concepts from categorical algebra to obtain a clear and extendable description of partial algebras and their specification. For the more general case, categorical algebra provides such a clear and extendable methodology, which could briefly be described as follows.

- A theory is a category with a certain structure, called the syntactic category. (E.g. an equational theory of total many sorted operations is a category with finite products, a Horn theory of partial many sorted operations is a category with finite limits.)
- A specification is a presentation of such a category.
- An algebra is a structure preserving functor from the syntactic category into the category of sets, i.e. an interpretation of the theory (sorts, terms, equations etc.) in sets and functions.
- A homomorphism is a natural transformation between such functors.

This approach can be extended to specification morphisms and parameterized specifications quite easily, since specification morphisms are themselves structure preserving functors. Thus the forgetful functor is just functor composition, and the existence of a free construction (for the essentially algebraic case) can be concluded from general category theoretic results. The advantage of this approach is that an enrichment of the categorical structure leads to an enrichment of the logical frame and allows to formulate corresponding results within the same methodology (syntactic category, functor category etc.).

This approach has been worked out broadly within the theory of sketches in [BW85], resp. for categorical (intuitionistic/first order/higher order) logic in [Joh77], [MR77] and [LS86]. Pioneering papers for essentially algebraic theories are [KR72, GU71, Fre72, Fre73].
In [PW91], [See87] and others this approach has been extended to 2-categories, i.e. categories with arrows between arrows, to model rewriting of terms explicitly. Thus, beyond the syntactical and the semantical level, the logical part of a specification framework is made explicit. On the semantical side the extension to 2–categories allows to interprete directed equations by a reflexive–transitive relation which need not be equality. An example is given in section 4.

The purpose of this paper is

- to develop "2-categorical algebra" for specifications with conditional existence equations of partial algebras in a purely algebraic way, and
- to give a short survey of possible results in the language of algebraic specifications.

The paper is organized as follows: In section 2 first the definition of 2-categories and appropriate finite limits in 2-categories are recalled. Then specifications are translated into presentations of 2-categories with finite limits and a rule system for the construction of the corresponding syntactical category is presented. For sake of simplicity we have restricted ourselves to 2-categories with at most one 2-cell between morphisms. This means that we only model whether one term rewrites to another term, and not distinguish between different rewrites with the same result. The appropriate extension to the more general case is discussed in the conclusion. In section 3 this approach is used to extend the notions of specification and specification morphism. An interpretation of the categorical algebra approach concerning models and homomorphisms as functors and natural transformations is given in section 4. Section 5 compares the categorical deduction calculus from section 2 with a more intuitive calculus.

2 Syntactic 2-Categories and their Presentations

A 2-category may on one hand be considered as a category with "categories as hom-sets" such that composition becomes a functor. On the other hand it may be considered as an amalgamation of three categories (base, horizontal, and vertical) with three types of objects and morphisms respectively. Both lead, of course, to the same notion of a category with arrows between arrows (the 2-cells), which can be composed horizontally and vertically. We cite the latter definition from [PW91].

Definition 2.1 (2-Category)

A 2-category $\mathcal{A}$ consists of a set of objects $\mathcal{A}_0$, a set of morphisms $\mathcal{A}_1$ and a set of 2-cells $\mathcal{A}_2$ subject to the requirements TC–1 through TC–6 listed below.

TC–1 The horizontal category $\mathcal{A}^h$ has $\mathcal{A}_0$ as its set of objects and $\mathcal{A}_2$ as its set of morphisms. Horizontal composition is denoted $\circ$

TC–2 The vertical category $\mathcal{A}^v$ has $\mathcal{A}_1$ as its set of objects and $\mathcal{A}_2$ as its set of morphisms. Vertical composition is denoted $\bullet$

TC–3 A 2-cell α goes between morphisms whose vertical identities have the same horizontal domain and codomains; precisely,

$$\mathrm{dom}^h\mathrm{id}^v(\mathrm{dom}^v\alpha) = \mathrm{dom}^h\mathrm{id}^v(\mathrm{codom}^v\alpha) = \mathrm{dom}^h\alpha$$

and

$$\mathrm{codom}^h\mathrm{id}^v(\mathrm{dom}^v\alpha) = \mathrm{codom}^h\mathrm{id}^v(\mathrm{codom}^v\alpha) = \mathrm{codom}^h\alpha$$

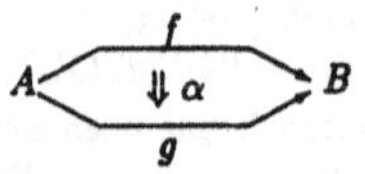

TC–4 A 2-cell that is a horizontal identity must also be a vertical identity; precisely, for an object A,

$$\mathrm{id}^h A = \mathrm{id}^v(\mathrm{dom}^v\ \mathrm{id}^h A)$$

which is necessarily also $\mathrm{id}^v(\mathrm{codom}^v\ \mathrm{id}^h A)$. This says that if α has the property that for all β that compose with α horizontally on the right,

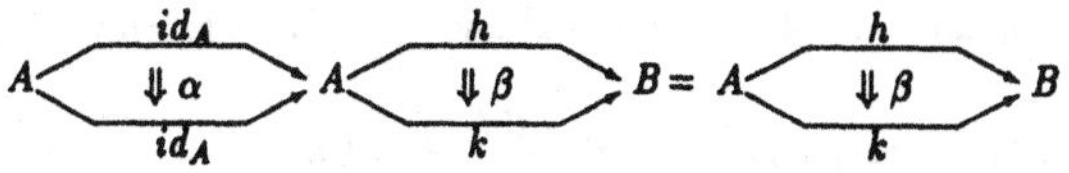

(the arrows marked id_A are forced to be that by TC–5), then for all γ that compose with α vertically on the right

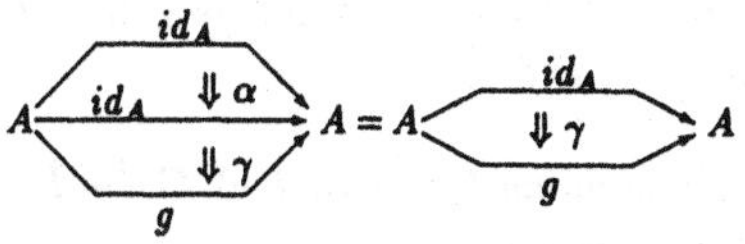

and similarly composing suitable β and γ on the left.

TC–5 For 2-cells α and β with $\mathrm{cod}^h\alpha = \mathrm{dom}^h\beta$ (so they are horizontally composable)

$$\mathrm{id}^v\mathrm{dom}^v(\beta \circ \alpha) = \mathrm{id}^v\mathrm{dom}^v\beta \circ \mathrm{id}^v\mathrm{dom}^v\alpha$$
$$\mathrm{id}^v\mathrm{codom}^v(\beta \circ \alpha) = \mathrm{id}^v\mathrm{codom}^v\beta \circ \mathrm{id}^v\mathrm{dom}^v\alpha$$

The composites on the right of each equation exist by TC–3. This axiom is illustrated like this:

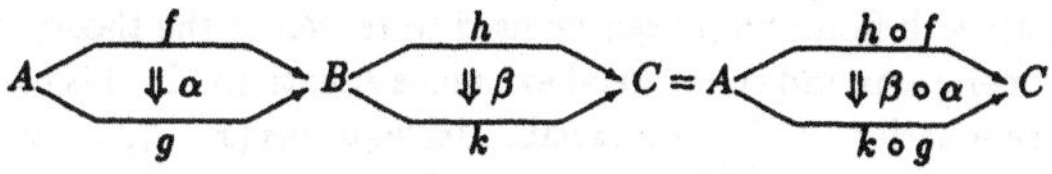

The notation "$h \circ f$" and "$k \circ g$" refer to the composition in the base category defined below.

TC–6 (The interchange law.) For 2-cells α, β, γ and δ for which the composites $\beta \circ \alpha, \delta \circ \gamma, \gamma \bullet \alpha$ and $\delta \bullet \beta$ are all defined,

$$(\delta \circ \gamma) \bullet (\beta \circ \alpha) = (\delta \bullet \beta) \circ (\gamma \bullet \alpha)$$

That these composites are defined follows from TC–5. The interchange law is applicable to a situation that looks like this:

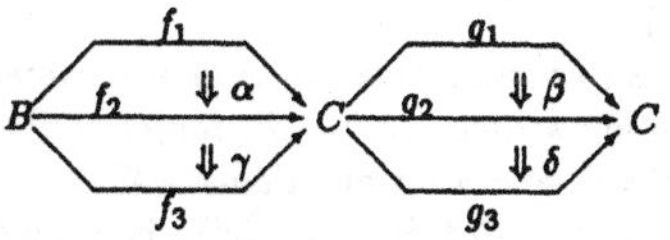

The base category $\mathcal{A}^b$ can be derived from the definition above as follows: It has $\mathcal{A}_0$ as its set of objects and $\mathcal{A}_1$ as its set of morphisms. The domain and codomain are given by $\mathrm{dom}^b = \mathrm{dom}^h(\mathrm{id}^v)$ and $\mathrm{codom}^b = \mathrm{codom}^h(\mathrm{id}^v)$. The composition is denoted $\circ$ and is defined by

$$g \circ f = \mathrm{dom}^v(\mathrm{id}^v g \circ \mathrm{id}^v f)$$

The base identity id^b for an object A turns out to be $\mathrm{dom}^v(\mathrm{id}^h A)$, which is $\mathrm{codom}^v(\mathrm{id}^h A)$.

Among the various possibilities to define limits in 2-categories (see [Kel89]) we have to select the one which corresponds to the intended construction of a syntactic 2–category consisting of formulas, terms and rewritings. Thus products are defined as usual, whereas equalizers are replaced by so called inserters (see [Kel89] resp. the definition below). These model the fact that a directed equation $t \stackrel{e}{=} t'$ does not mean that t and t' have the same semantics, but that t rewrites to t' (compare the definition of models in section 4).

Definition 2.2 (FL-2-category)

A 2-category $\mathcal{A}$ is an FL-2-category if its base category has finite products and $\mathcal{A}$ has inserters, which are specified as follows.

An inserter of two parallel morphisms $A \xrightarrow{f} B$ and $A \xrightarrow{g} B$ is given by

- an object In(f,g), a morphism $In(f,g) \xrightarrow{in(f,g)} A$ and a 2-cell $f \circ in(f,g) \xRightarrow{in^{\bullet}(f,g)} g \circ in(f,g)$ such that
- for each morphism $C \xrightarrow{h} A$ and 2-cell $f \circ h \xRightarrow{\varphi} g \circ h$ there is a unique morphism $C \xrightarrow{fac(h,\varphi)} In(f,g)$ with $in(f,g) \circ fac(h,\varphi) = h$ and $in^{\bullet}(f,g) \circ fac(h,\varphi) = \varphi$, and
- for each pair of parallel morphisms $C \xrightarrow{k} In(f,g)$, $C \xrightarrow{k'} In(f,g)$ and 2-cell $in(f,g) \circ k \xRightarrow{\beta} fac(in(f,g) \circ k')$ with $(in^{\bullet}(f,g) \circ k) \bullet (f \circ \beta) = (g \circ \beta) \bullet (in^{\bullet}(f,g) \circ k')$ a unique 2-cell $k \xRightarrow{fac^{\bullet}(k,k',\beta)} k'$ with $in(f,g) \circ fac^{\bullet}(k,k',\beta) = \beta$.

As in the one dimensional case products and inserters yield weighted pullbacks.

In the interpretation of categorical algebra, extended to 2-categories, a 2-category represents a theory, where objects are formulas, morphisms are terms and 2-cells are rewritings. As shown in [KR72, Poi85] e.g., a category with finite limits can be used to represent the theory derivable from a specification with partial operations and conditional existence equations. In this case objects are finite conjunctions of existence equations with finite variable declarations $(x_1 : s_1, \ldots, x_n : s_n, t_1 \stackrel{e}{=} t_1' \wedge \ldots \wedge t_k \stackrel{e}{=} t_k')$ $:=(w,\varphi)$, and a tuple of terms $< r_1, \ldots, r_m > := r$ represents a morphism $(w,\varphi) \xrightarrow{[r]} (v,\psi)$ (with $(v,\psi) := (x_1 : s_1', \ldots, x_m : s_m', p_1 \stackrel{e}{=} p_1' \wedge \ldots \wedge p_l \stackrel{e}{=} p_l'))$ if $(w,\varphi) \vdash (w, \psi[x_1/r_1, \ldots, x_m/r_m])$ (where substitution takes place in all terms and for all variables simultaneously). In the 2-categorical decription we have the same objects, where the existence equations, however, are interpreted as directed existence equations. Morphisms are terms instead of equivalence classes of terms as above, and 2-cells are rewritings. Thus a specification can be considered as a presentation of an FL-2-category; then the definition of an FL-2-category yields a derivation calculus for conditional existence equations.

Let's first recall the usual definition of a specification to fix notation.

Definition 2.3 (Specification)
A specification *SPEC=(S,OP,AX)* consists of a set S of sortnames, a set OP of operation symbols with *source* and *target* function $source : OP \rightarrow S^*$, $target : OP \rightarrow S$ (written $\sigma : s_1 \ldots s_n \rightarrow s$ if $source(\sigma) = s_1 \ldots s_n$ and $target(\sigma) = s$), and a set of axioms AX.
An axiom $(x_1 : s_1, \ldots, x_n : s_n; t_1 \stackrel{e}{=} t_1' \wedge \ldots \wedge t_k \stackrel{e}{=} t_k' \rightarrow r \stackrel{e}{=} r')$ is given by a list of variable declarations $x_1 : s_1, \ldots, x_n : s_n$, a conjunction of directed existence equations $t_1 \stackrel{e}{=} t_1' \wedge \ldots \wedge t_k \stackrel{e}{=} t_k'$ as premise and a single directed existence equation $r \stackrel{e}{=} r'$ as conclusion, where $t_1, t_1', \ldots t_k, t_k', r, r'$ are terms w.r.t. OP with variables from the set $\{x_1, \ldots, x_n\}$.

As an example we use a specification nat of the natural numbers with predecessor, in an ACT ONE–like syntax.

```
type nat=
    sorts   nat
    opns    0:   → nat
            s(ucc):nat → nat
            p(red):nat → nat
    axioms  0≐0;
            for all x1 in nat:
            s(x1)≐s(x1);
            for all x1,x2 in nat:
            x1≐s(x2) → p(x1)≐x2
end
```

The first two axioms state that the constant 0 is defined and that succ is a total function. The third axiom specifies the predecessor pred by a conditional existence equation (which is not really necessary, but yields an example for a conditional existence equation).

Now a specification is transformed into a presentation of an FL-2-category in two steps.

First the signature is represented:

- Each sort $s \in S$ is represented as an object $(s, \emptyset)$
- For each pair of objects $(w, \emptyset)$ and $(v, \emptyset)$ an object $(wv, \emptyset)$ is introduced (This rule is needed to supply source objects for the spans of operation symbols in the next rule.)
- Each operation symbol $\sigma : w \to s \in OP$ is represented by a span (a new object and two morphisms) $(w, \emptyset) \xleftarrow{x} (w, \sigma(x) \stackrel{e}{=} \sigma(x)) \xrightarrow{\sigma(x)} (s, \emptyset)$

To represent the axioms one first has to construct terms, then the premises and conclusions, which are (finite conjunctions of) existence equations. Therefor the 2-categorical rules (given below) for composition, inserters etc. have to be used. To construct a term $\sigma(t)$ from a given term t and an operation symbol σ the formal inverse image $(v, t \stackrel{e}{=} t \wedge \sigma(t) \stackrel{e}{=} \sigma(t)$ of their domains $(v, t \stackrel{e}{=} t)$ and $(w, \sigma(x_w) \stackrel{e}{=} \sigma(x_w)$ is constructed. Then the morphisms t and $\sigma(x_w)$ can be composed by substitution $\sigma(x) \circ t := \sigma(x)[x/t] = \sigma(t)$. Semantically this corresponds to taking the inverse image of the domain of the partial function A_σ under the partial term function A_t. The inverse image is also used to model syntactically the logical $\wedge$ resp. intersections.

The inserter rule introduces syntactical representations $(w, t \stackrel{e}{=} t')$ of solution sets

$$(w, t \stackrel{e}{=} t') \xrightarrow{x_w} (w, t \stackrel{e}{=} t \wedge t' \stackrel{e}{=} t') \underset{t'}{\overset{t}{\rightrightarrows}} (v, \emptyset)$$

With this construction

- each axiom $(w, \varphi \to \psi) \in AX$ is represented as a morphism $(w, \varphi) \xrightarrow{x} (w, \psi)$ (if (w, φ) and (w, ψ) have already been introduced).

The nat-example above as a presentation of an FL-2-category looks as follows:

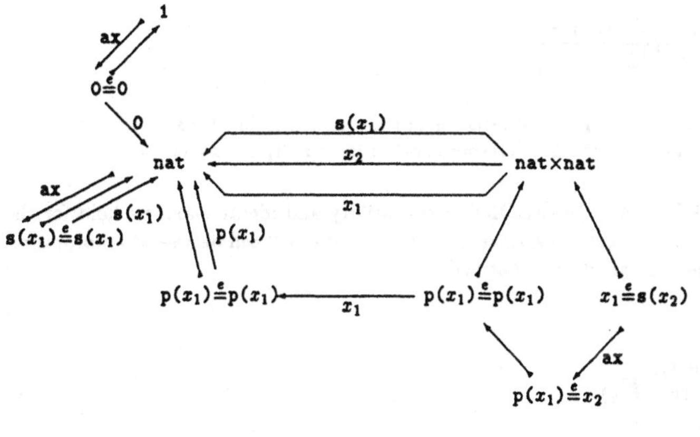

Explanation: The labels of the inclusion morphisms x_{nat} and $x_{nat \times nat}$ are omitted, the corresponding arrows are depicted as $\rightarrowtail$. The variable declarations are also omitted in the figure:
the existence equation $0 \stackrel{e}{=} 0$ has no variables;
$s(x_1) \stackrel{e}{=} s(x_1)$ and $p(x_1) \stackrel{e}{=} p(x_1)$ have one variable x_1:nat;
$x_1 \stackrel{e}{=} s(x_2)$, $p(x_1) \stackrel{e}{=} x_2$ and $p(x_1) \stackrel{e}{=} p(x_1)$ underneath nat×nat have the variables x_1, x_2:nat.

Furthermore the latter existence equation is a weighted pullback of $p(x_1)\stackrel{e}{=}p(x_1) \longrightarrow$ nat and the projection nat × nat $\xrightarrow{x_1}$ nat. The existence equation $p(x_1)\stackrel{e}{=}x_2$ is an inserter of $p(x_1)\stackrel{e}{=}p(x_1) \rightarrow$ nat× nat $\xrightarrow{x_1}$ nat and $p(x_1)\stackrel{e}{=}p(x_1) \xrightarrow{x_1} p(x_1)\stackrel{e}{=}p(x_1) \xrightarrow{p(x_1)}$ nat. The arrow nat× nat $\xrightarrow{s(x_1)}$ nat is obtained by the composition nat× nat $\xrightarrow{x_1}$ nat $\xrightarrow{ax = x_1} s(x_1)\stackrel{e}{=}s(x_1) \xrightarrow{s(x_1)}$ nat. The three axioms are labelled by ax.

To construct the whole syntactic category the same 2-categorical rules are used. Beyond the definition of the syntactic category the rules form a correct and complete derivation calculus, since the syntactic category contains all axioms derivable from the specification in their 2-categorical representation $(w, \varphi) \xrightarrow{x_w} (w, \psi)$. For the 1-dimensional analogon this is shown e.g. in [CGRW92].

A rule $\frac{P_1, \ldots, P_n}{Q_1, \ldots, Q_m}$ is given by a list of premises $P_1, \ldots, P_n$ and a list of conclusions $Q_1, \ldots, Q_m$, where each P_i and Q_j resp. states the existence of an object, morphism or 2-cell.

The first three rules introduce the specification items into the category.

{sort , *for each sort* $s \in S$}

$$\frac{}{(s, \emptyset)}$$

{operator , *for each operator symbol* $\sigma : w \rightarrow s \in OP$ }

$$\frac{(w, \emptyset), (s, \emptyset)}{(w, \emptyset) \xleftarrow{x_w} (w, \sigma(x)\stackrel{e}{=}\sigma(x)) \xrightarrow{\sigma(x)} (s, \emptyset)}$$

{axiom , *for each finite implication* $(w, t_1\stackrel{e}{=}t_2 \rightarrow r_1\stackrel{e}{=}r_2) \in AX$ }

$$\frac{(w, t_1\stackrel{e}{=}t_2), (w, r_1\stackrel{e}{=}r_2)}{(w, t_1\stackrel{e}{=}t_2) \xrightarrow{x_w} (w, r_1\stackrel{e}{=}r_2)}$$

DEFINITION OF THE BASE CATEGORY: According to the definition of composition as substitution in the rule *base composition*, composition is associative and has the corresponding variables as identities.

{base identities}

$$\frac{(w, t_1\stackrel{e}{=}t_2)}{(w, t_1\stackrel{e}{=}t_2) \xrightarrow{x_w} (w, t_1\stackrel{e}{=}t_2)}$$

{base composition}

$$\frac{(w, t_1\stackrel{e}{=}t_2) \xrightarrow{t} (v, r_1\stackrel{e}{=}r_2) \xrightarrow{r} (u, p_1\stackrel{e}{=}p_2)}{(w, t_1\stackrel{e}{=}t_2) \xrightarrow{r \circ t := r[x_v/t]} (u, p_1\stackrel{e}{=}p_2)}$$

Where $v = s_1 \ldots s_k$, $t =< t_1, \ldots, t_k >$, the variables of r are contained in $\{x_1 : s_1, \ldots, x_k : s_k\}$ and $r[x_v/t]$ is an abbreviation for the simultaneous substitution $r[x_1/t_1, \ldots, x_k/t_k]$.

DEFINITION OF THE VERTICAL CATEGORY: Associativity and identity axioms hold for the vertical as well as for the horizontal category, since there is at most one 2-cell between to morphisms, i.e. 2-cells with equal source and target are identified.

{vertical identities}

$$\frac{(w, t_1\stackrel{e}{=}t_2) \xrightarrow{t} (v, r_1\stackrel{e}{=}r_2)}{(w, t_1\stackrel{e}{=}t_2) \xrightarrow{t \Longrightarrow t} (v, r_1\stackrel{e}{=}r_2)}$$

{vertical composition}

$$\frac{(w, t_1\stackrel{e}{=}t_2) \xrightarrow{t \Longrightarrow r \Longrightarrow p} (v, r_1\stackrel{e}{=}r_2)}{(w, t_1\stackrel{e}{=}t_2) \xrightarrow{t \Longrightarrow p} (v, r_1\stackrel{e}{=}r_2)}$$

DEFINITION OF THE HORIZONTAL CATEGORY: Horizontal identities are already given as $(w, t_1\stackrel{e}{=}t_2) \xrightarrow{x_w \Longrightarrow x_w} (w, t_1\stackrel{e}{=}t_2)$ by the *vertical identity* rule.

{horizontal composition}

$$\frac{(w,t_1\stackrel{e}{=}t_2)\xrightarrow{t\Longrightarrow t'}(v,r_1\stackrel{e}{=}r_2)\xrightarrow{r\Longrightarrow r'}(u,p_1\stackrel{e}{=}p_2)}{(w,t_1\stackrel{e}{=}t_2)\xrightarrow{r\circ t\Longrightarrow r'\circ t'}(u,p_1\stackrel{e}{=}p_2)}$$

DEFINITION OF THE WEIGHTED LIMITS: Products, terminal object, inserters and inverse images. The latter are a special case of weighted pullbacks and are introduced to have inverse images and instances of existence equations explicit. Note that, according to the definition of composition as substitution, the uniqueness conditions w.r.t. the universal property of inserters and inverse images are automatically fullfilled. Products are only defined for sorts, since general products can then be derived via inverse images.

{products of sorts}

$$\frac{(s_1\ldots s_n,\emptyset),(s_{n+1}\ldots s_{n+k},\emptyset)}{\begin{array}{l}(s_1\ldots s_{n+k},\emptyset)\\ (s_1\ldots s_{n+k},\emptyset)\xrightarrow{x_{1,\ldots,n}}(s_1\ldots s_n,\emptyset)\\ (s_1\ldots s_{n+k},\emptyset)\xrightarrow{x_{n+1,\ldots,n+k}}(s_{n+1}\ldots s_{n+k},\emptyset)\end{array}}$$

{product introduction}

$$\frac{(v,t_1\stackrel{e}{=}t_2)\xrightarrow{t}(s_1\ldots s_n,\emptyset),(v,t_1\stackrel{e}{=}t_2)\xrightarrow{t'}(s_{n+1}\ldots s_{n+k},\emptyset)}{\begin{array}{l}(v,t_1\stackrel{e}{=}t_2)\xrightarrow{<t,t'>}(s_1\ldots s_{n+k},\emptyset)\\ (v,t_1\stackrel{e}{=}t_2)\xrightarrow{x_{1,\ldots,n}\circ<t,t'>=t}(s_1\ldots s_n,\emptyset)\\ (v,t_1\stackrel{e}{=}t_2)\xrightarrow{x_{n+1,\ldots,n+k}\circ<t,t'>=t'}(s_{n+1}\ldots s_{n+k},\emptyset)\end{array}}$$

{product elimination}

$$\frac{(u,r_1\stackrel{e}{=}r_2)\xrightarrow{r}(w_1w_2,\emptyset)}{(u,r_1\stackrel{e}{=}r_2)\xrightarrow{r=<x_{w_1}\circ r,x_{w_2}\circ r>}(w_1w_2,\emptyset)}$$

{terminal object}

$$\frac{}{(\lambda,\emptyset)}$$

{terminal object introduction}

$$\frac{(w,t_1\stackrel{e}{=}t_2)}{(w,t_1\stackrel{e}{=}t_2)\xrightarrow{<>}(\lambda,\emptyset)}$$

{terminal object elimination}

$$\frac{(w,t_1\stackrel{e}{=}t_2)\xrightarrow{t}(\lambda,\emptyset)}{(w,t_1\stackrel{e}{=}t_2)\xrightarrow{t=<>}(\lambda,\emptyset)}$$

{inserter}

$$\frac{(w,t_1\stackrel{e}{=}t_2)\xrightarrow{t}(v,r_1\stackrel{e}{=}r_2),(w,t_1\stackrel{e}{=}t_2)\xrightarrow{t'}(v,r_1\stackrel{e}{=}r_2)}{\begin{array}{l}(w,t_1\stackrel{e}{=}t_2\wedge t\stackrel{e}{=}t')\xrightarrow{x_w}(w,t_1\stackrel{e}{=}t_2)\\ (w,t_1\stackrel{e}{=}t_2\wedge t\stackrel{e}{=}t')\xrightarrow{t\Longrightarrow t'}(v,r_1\stackrel{e}{=}r_2)\end{array}}$$

{inserter introduction 1}

$$\frac{\begin{array}{l}(u,p_1\stackrel{e}{=}p_2)\xrightarrow{p}(w,t_1\stackrel{e}{=}t_2)\\ (u,p_1\stackrel{e}{=}p_2)\xrightarrow{t\circ p\Longrightarrow t'\circ p}(v,r_1\stackrel{e}{=}r_2)\end{array}}{(u,p_1\stackrel{e}{=}p_2)\xrightarrow{p}(w,t_1\stackrel{e}{=}t_2\wedge t\stackrel{e}{=}t')}$$

{inserter introduction 2}

$$\frac{\begin{array}{l}(u,p_1\stackrel{e}{=}p_2)\xrightarrow{p,p'}(w,t_1\stackrel{e}{=}t_2\wedge t\stackrel{e}{=}t')\\ (u,p_1\stackrel{e}{=}p_2)\xrightarrow{p\Longrightarrow p'}(w,t_1\stackrel{e}{=}t_2)\end{array}}{(u,p_1\stackrel{e}{=}p_2)\xrightarrow{p\Longrightarrow p'}(w,t_1\stackrel{e}{=}t_2\wedge t\stackrel{e}{=}t')}$$

{inverse images}

$$\frac{\begin{array}{l}(w, t_1 \stackrel{e}{=} t_2) \xrightarrow{t} (v, r_1 \stackrel{e}{=} r_2) \\ (v, p_1 \stackrel{e}{=} p_2) \xrightarrow{x_v} (v, r_1 \stackrel{e}{=} r_2)\end{array}}{\begin{array}{l}(w, t_1 \stackrel{e}{=} t_2 \wedge p_1 \circ t \stackrel{e}{=} p_2 \circ t) \xrightarrow{t} (v, p_1 \stackrel{e}{=} p_2) \\ (w, t_1 \stackrel{e}{=} t_2 \wedge p_1 \circ t \stackrel{e}{=} p_2 \circ t) \xrightarrow{x_w} (w, t_1 \stackrel{e}{=} t_2)\end{array}}$$

{inverse image introduction 1}

$$\frac{\begin{array}{l}(u, m_1 \stackrel{e}{=} m_2) \xrightarrow{m} (w, t_1 \stackrel{e}{=} t_2) \\ (u, m_1 \stackrel{e}{=} m_2) \xrightarrow{m'} (v, p_1 \stackrel{e}{=} p_2) \\ (u, m_1 \stackrel{e}{=} m_2) \xrightarrow{m' \Longrightarrow t \circ m} (v, r_1 \stackrel{e}{=} r_2)\end{array}}{\begin{array}{l}(u, m_1 \stackrel{e}{=} m_2) \xrightarrow{m} (w, t_1 \stackrel{e}{=} t_2 \wedge p_1 \circ t \stackrel{e}{=} p_2 \circ t) \\ (u, m_1 \stackrel{e}{=} m_2) \xrightarrow{t \circ m \Longrightarrow m'} (v, p_1 \stackrel{e}{=} p_2)\end{array}}$$

{inverse image introduction 2}

$$\frac{\begin{array}{l}(u, m_1 \stackrel{e}{=} m_2) \xrightarrow{m, m'} (w, t_1 \stackrel{e}{=} t_2 \wedge p_1 \circ t \stackrel{e}{=} p_2 \circ t) \\ (u, m_1 \stackrel{e}{=} m_2) \xrightarrow{m \Longrightarrow m'} (w, t_1 \stackrel{e}{=} t_2) \\ (u, m_1 \stackrel{e}{=} m_2) \xrightarrow{t \circ m \Longrightarrow t \circ m'} (v, p_1 \stackrel{e}{=} p_2)\end{array}}{(u, m_1 \stackrel{e}{=} m_2) \xrightarrow{m \Longrightarrow m'} (w, t_1 \stackrel{e}{=} t_2 \wedge p_1 \circ t \stackrel{e}{=} p_2 \circ t)}$$

3 Specifications and Specification Morphisms Revisited

A specification *SPEC=(S,OP,AX)* as defined in the preceeding section has been used to present an FL-2-category. In general a presentation of an FL-2-category consists of a set of generators for each type *object, morphism* and *2-cell*, and a set of relations for each type. A generator is nothing but a name for an element of the corresponding type, a relation is an equation between expressions of the corresponding types. E.g. $source(\sigma)$ and $s_1 \times s_2$ are expressions of type *object* if s_1, s_2 are generators of type *object* and σ is a generator of type *morphism*. From this point of view a specification can be analyzed as follows.

- S is a set of generators of type *object*.
- OP is a set of generators of type *morphism* (generating the inclusion of the domains and the partial operations themselves) and type object (generating the domains of the partial operations); *source* and *target* are relations of type *object*.
- AX is a set of generators of type *morphism* and relations of type *object* (premise and conclusion as source and target of an axiom).

Note that there are no generators of type *2-cell* and no relations of type *morphism* or *2-cell*. For the latter, however, this would not make sense anyway, since we have only considered existence of 2-cells as important.

To consider a specification as a presentation (generators and relations) now makes possible the extensions listed below of the notion of specification, without change concerning the theory (FL-2-category) generated by a specification or model (structure preserving functor, see next section):

generators of type

object are sortnames

morphism are operation symbols, axioms

2-cell are directed equations

relations of type

object are *source* and *target* function, which now may have any existence equation as value; e.g. a predicate p can be modelled as a partial function with codomain the

empty product $p : s_1 \ldots s_n \to \lambda$. Semantically this means a partial function to the one point set; i.e. the mapping is trivial, but the domain of the mapping is the extension of the predicate;
premises and conclusions of axioms as before;
general sort equations $(w, \varphi) = (v, \psi)$; an application e.g. could be an equation like
$(\mathtt{record}, \emptyset) = (\mathtt{field}_1, \mathtt{size}(f) \leq n) \times \ldots \times (\mathtt{field}_n, \emptyset)$

morphism are equations (as opposed to directed equations), e.g. if one wants to express equalities like commutativity or associativity for certain operators, which are not subject to rewriting; these equations are then strong equations, i.e. both sides are equal if both are defined, thus a strong equality does not force existence of a term;

2-cell (since parallel 2-cells are identified anyway, there is no sensible interpretation of relations between 2-cells in this context.)

This leads to the following definition.

Definition 3.1 (Generalized Specification)
A generalized specification *SPEC=(S,SE,OP,E,AX)* consists of

- a set S of sortnames,
- a set SE of sort equations $(w, \varphi) = (v, \psi)$,
- a set OP of operation symbols $\sigma : (w, \varphi) \to (v, \psi)$,
- a set E of equations $(w, t = t')$ and
- a set AX of axioms $(x_1 : s_1, \ldots, x_n : s_n; t_1 \stackrel{e}{=} t'_1 \wedge \ldots \wedge t_k \stackrel{e}{=} t'_k \to r_1 \stackrel{e}{=} r'_1 \wedge \ldots \wedge r_l \stackrel{e}{=} r'_l)$

The (extended) definition of a specifiation as presentation yields a definition of a specification morphism immediately: a *specification morphism* is a triple of functions which maps generators to generators such that the relations are preserved. In the usual interpretation this means:
A specification morphism $h = (h_S, h_{OP}) : SPEC=(S,OP,AX) \to SPEC'=(S',OP',AX')$ consists of two functions $h_X : X \to X'$ ($X \in S, OP$), such that

- $source'(h_{OP}(\sigma)) = h_S(source(\sigma))$ for all $\sigma \in OP$
- $target'(h_{OP}(\sigma)) = h_S(target(\sigma))$ for all $\sigma \in OP$
- $(h^*_S(w), h^*_{OP}(\varphi) \to h^*_{OP}(\psi)) \in AX'$ for all $(w, \varphi \to \psi) \in AX$

(The extension to generalized specifications is obvious.)

However, this definition is very strict in that axioms have to be mapped to axioms which are present in the target specification *SPEC'*, and not to derived ones. A more satisfactory definition can be obtained if one takes Kleisli morphisms instead, i.e. a specification morphism $h : SPEC \to SPEC'$ is a morphism from the specification *SPEC* to the theory generated by *SPEC'*.

Definition 3.2 (Specification Morphism)
1) A specification morphism $h = (h_S, h_{OP}) : SPEC=(S,OP,AX) \to SPEC'=(S',OP',AX')$ consists of two functions $h_X : X \to X'$ ($X \in S, OP$), such that

- $h_S : S \to$ Existence Equations$(SPEC')$, i.e. $h_S(s) = (w', \varphi')$
(the existence equations (w', φ') are the type expressions of type *object* w.r.t. *SPEC'*, which subsume e.g. products $(s'_1 \ldots s'_n, \emptyset)$)
- $h_{OP} : OP \to Terms(OP')$, i.e. $h_{OP}(\sigma) = t'$ is a term w.r.t. OP', where the sort of t' equals $h_S(target(\sigma))$ and t' may contain variables of the sorts $h^*_S(source(\sigma))$
(i.e. t' has an equivalent functionality as σ via h).

- $(h_S^*(w), h_{OP}^*(\varphi) \to h_{OP}^*(\psi))$ is derivable from *SPEC'* for all $(w, \varphi \to \psi) \in AX$.

2) A generalized specification morphism $k : SPEC \to SPEC'$ (w.r.t. general specifications *SPEC=(S,SE,OP,E,AX)*, *SPEC'=(S',SE',OP',E',AX')*) is a specification morphism $k = (k_S, k_{OP}) : SPEC \to SPEC'$ with the additional properties

- $(k_S^*(w), k_{OP}^*(\varphi)) = (k_S^*(v), k_{OP}^*(\psi))$ for all $(w, \varphi) = (v, \psi) \in SE$
- $k_S^*(w) \xrightarrow{k_{OP}^*(t)'} k_S(s) = k_S^*(w) \xrightarrow{k_{OP}^*(t')} k_S(s)$ for all $(w, t = t') \in E$

4 Models and Homomorphisms

In categorical algebra the category of models of a theory is just the category of structure preserving functors from the theory to a category with (at least) the same structure. To carry over this notion of model to 2-categorical theories and the usual semantical domain SET, we first have to construct an FL-2-category 2-SET from SET.

Definition 4.1 (2-SET)
The category 2-SET is given as follows

OBJECTS are ordered sets $(M, \geq)$, where $\geq \subseteq M \times M$ is a reflexive and transitive relation on M.

MORPHISMS are order preserving functions $f : (M, \geq) \to (N, \sqsupseteq)$, i.e. functions $f : M \to N$ with $x \geq y \Rightarrow f(x) \sqsupseteq f(y)$ for all $x, y \in M$.

2-CELLS are pointwise extensions of the relations to functions, i.e. for two functions $f, g : (M, \geq) \to (N, \sqsupseteq)$ there is a 2-cell $f \Rightarrow g$ iff for all $x \in M$ $f(x) \sqsupseteq f(y)$, otherwise there is none. Thus the set of 2-cells between two morphisms is either a singleton or empty.

The induced definitions of functors and natural transformations yield the following definition of models and homomorphisms for a specification.

Definition 4.2 (Models and Homomorphisms)
1) A *SPEC*-model $A = ((A_s)_{s \in S}, (A_\sigma)_{\sigma \in OP})$ is given by

- a family of carriers $(A_s, \geq_s)$ (for all $s \in S$) and
- a family of partial order preserving functions

$$(A_{s_1}, \geq_{s_1}) \times \cdots \times (A_{s_n}, \geq_{s_1}) \supseteq (dom\ A_\sigma, \geq_{d\sigma}) \xrightarrow{A_\sigma} (A_s, \geq_s)$$

(for all $\sigma : s_1 \ldots S_n \to s \in OP$), i.e. a subset $(dom\ A_\sigma, \geq_{d\sigma})$ of the corresponding product of carriers $(A_{s_1}, \geq_{s_1}) \times \cdots \times (A_{s_n}, \geq_{s_1})$ together with an order preserving function $A_\sigma : (dom\ A_\sigma, \geq_{d\sigma}) \to (A_s, \geq_s)$, such that each axiom is satisfied in A.

- A satisfies an existence equation $(w, t \stackrel{e}{=} t')$ if the term functions A_t and $A_{t'}$ are both defined and $A_t \geq_s A_{t'}$. A satisfies a conditional existence equation $(w, t_1 \stackrel{e}{=} t_1' \wedge \ldots \wedge t_k \stackrel{e}{=} t_k' \to r \stackrel{e}{=} r')$ if

$$\bigcap_{1 \leq i \leq k} \{\vec{a} \in A_w | A_{t_i}(\vec{a}) \geq_v A_{t_i'}(\vec{a})\} \subseteq \{\vec{a} \in A_w | A_r(\vec{a}) \geq_s A_{r'}(\vec{a})\}$$

2) A model A of a generalized specification moreover has to satisfy

- $\{\vec{a} \in A_{s_1} \times \ldots \times A_{s_n} | A_{t_i}(\vec{a}) \geq_s A_{t'_i}(\vec{a}), 1 \leq i \leq k\} =$
  $= \{\vec{a} \in A_{s'_1} \times \ldots \times A_{s'_m} | A_{r_j}(\vec{a}) \geq_s A_{r'_j}(\vec{a}), 1 \leq j \leq l\}$
  for all $(s_1 \ldots s_n, t_1 \stackrel{e}{=} t'_1 \wedge \ldots \wedge t_k \stackrel{e}{=} t'_k) = (s'_1 \ldots s'_m, r_1 \stackrel{e}{=} r'_1 \wedge \ldots \wedge r_l \stackrel{e}{=} r'_l) \in SE$
- $A_t \stackrel{s}{=} A_{t'}$ for all $(w, t = t') \in E$

3) A homomorphism $h : A \to B$ of *SPEC*-models A and B is given by

- a family of total order preserving functions $h_s : (A_s, \geq_s) \to (B_s, \geq_s)$ (for all $s \in S$) such that
- if $< a_1, \ldots, a_n > \in \text{dom } A_\sigma$, then
- $< h_{s_1}(a_1), \ldots, h_{s_n}(a_n) > \in \text{dom } B_\sigma$ and
- $h_s(A_\sigma(a_1, \ldots, a_n)) = B_\sigma(h_{s_1}(a_1), \ldots, h_{s_n}(a_n))$
  for all $\sigma : s_1 \ldots s_n \to s \in OP$

The unevitable stack–example:

```
type stack =
     sorts  elem, stack
     opns   empty:   → stack          {total}
            push:elem stack → stack   {total}
            pop:stack → stack         {total}
            top:stack → elem
     axioms for all x in elem, for all s in stack:
            top(push(x,s)) ≐e x ;
            pop(push(x,s)) ≐e s
end
```

(where the comments total are used as an abbreviation for the corresponding existence equations)

has e.g. the following two models A and B.

$A_{elem} := (M, =)$ (any nonempty set with the identity relation)
$A_{stack} := (M^*, =)$ (the free monoid with the identity relation)
$A_{empty} := \lambda$ (the empty word)
$A_{push}(m, s) := sm$

$$A_{pop}(s) := \begin{cases} s & \text{if } s = \lambda \\ s' & \text{if } s = s'm \end{cases}$$

$$A_{top}(s) := \begin{cases} \text{undefined} & \text{if } s = \lambda \\ m & \text{if } s = s'm \end{cases}$$

$B_{elem} := (M, =)$ (like A)
$B_{stack} := (M^* \times \mathbf{N}, \sqsupseteq)$ (strings with pointer)
where $(m_1 \ldots m_n \ldots m_k, n) \sqsupseteq (m'_1 \ldots m_{n'} \ldots m'_l, n')$ iff $n = n'$ (or $n \geq k$ and $n' \geq l$), $m_i = m'_i$ $(1 \leq i \leq n)$ and $k \geq l$, i.e. $stack_1 \sqsupseteq stack_2$ if $stack_1$ has the same contents as $stack_2$ (left to the pointer position n) and more garbage (the inaccessible part right to the pointer position).
$B_{empty} := (\lambda, 0)$

$$B_{push}(x, (m_1 \ldots m_k, n)) := \begin{cases} (m_1 \ldots m_n x m_{n+1} \ldots m_k, n+1) & \text{if } n < k \\ (m_1 \ldots m_k x, n+1) & \text{if } n \geq k \end{cases}$$

$$B_{pop}((m_1 \ldots m_k, n)) := \begin{cases} (m_1 \ldots m_k, n) & \text{if } n = 0 \\ (m_1 \ldots m_k, n-1) & \text{if } k > n > 0 \\ (m_1 \ldots m_k, k-1) & \text{if } n \geq k \end{cases}$$

$$B_{top}((m_1 \dots m_k, n)) := \begin{cases} \text{undefined} & \text{if } n = 0 \text{ or } k = 0 \\ m_n & \text{if } n \geq 1 \text{ and } k \geq 1 \end{cases}$$

There is a homomorphism $h : B \to A$ since A is a quotient of B w.r.t. the congruence induced by $\sqsupseteq$ on B. h deletes the garbage, i.e. $h(m_1 \dots m_n \dots m_k, n) = m_1 \dots m_n$. In the other direction there is no homomorphism because the terms `empty` and `pop(push(x,empty))` have the same value λ in A, but the different values $(\lambda, 0)$ and $(x, 0)$ in B. Especially, A is not an initial stack-model.

5 Another Derivation Calculus

From a theoretical point of view the categorical rules are satisfactory as a derivation calculus. If a theory is a category with finite limits its model category is the category of finite limit preserving functors, which is well investigated and standard categorical results can be taken over directly. For computational purposes, however, it is obviously very inefficient. In [Wol90] U.Wolter proposed another derivation calculus, which replaces the structural rules by axioms and is thereby reduced to one rule to generate new axioms: the axiom-application-rule. Presented as a rule scheme for a syntactic category it looks as follows: The rules for the introduction of the specification (*sort, operator* and *axiom*), the definition of the base category (*base identity* and *base composition*) and the structural rules for the finite limits (*products of sorts* through *inverse image introduction*) are the same as the categorical rules in section 2. The rules for the construction of the 2-cells, however, are replaced by representations of axioms for the tautologies:

{transitivity}

$$\frac{(www, x_1 \stackrel{e}{=} x_2 \wedge x_2 \stackrel{e}{=} x_3), (www, x_1 \stackrel{e}{=} x_3)}{(www, x_1 \stackrel{e}{=} x_2 \wedge x_2 \stackrel{e}{=} x_3) \xrightarrow{x_{www}} (www, x_1 \stackrel{e}{=} x_3)}$$

Here we have used the abbreviations $x_1 := x_{1 \dots n}$, $x_2 := x_{n+1 \dots 2n}$, $x_3 := x_{2n+1 \dots 3n}$ and $w := s_1 \dots s_n$.

{congruence}

$$\frac{(w, t_1 \stackrel{e}{=} t_2) \xrightarrow{t_1, t_2} (v, r_1 \stackrel{e}{=} r_2) \xrightarrow{r} (u, \emptyset), (w, r \circ t_1 \stackrel{e}{=} r \circ t_2)}{(w, t_1 \stackrel{e}{=} t_2) \xrightarrow{x_w} (w, r \circ t_1 \stackrel{e}{=} r \circ t_2)}$$

{reflexivity}

$$\frac{(w, \emptyset), (w, x_w \stackrel{e}{=} x_w)}{(w, \emptyset) \xrightarrow{x_w} (w, x_w \stackrel{e}{=} x_w)}$$

The only rule which constructs new 2-cells from given ones is now

{instances}

$$\frac{(w, t_1 \stackrel{e}{=} t_2) \xrightarrow{t} (v, r_1 \stackrel{e}{=} r_2) \xrightarrow{r \Longrightarrow r'} (u, p_1 \stackrel{e}{=} p_2)}{(w, t_1 \stackrel{e}{=} t_2) \xrightarrow{r \circ t \Longrightarrow r' \circ t} (u, p_1 \stackrel{e}{=} p_2)}$$

Since the axioms are represented as morphisms a special case of the *instances*-rule is the *axiom application*-rule:

{axiom application}

$$\frac{\begin{array}{l}(v, \emptyset) \xleftarrow{t_1 \Longrightarrow t_2} (w, t_1 \stackrel{e}{=} t_2) \xrightarrow{x_w} (w, r_1 \stackrel{e}{=} r_2) \xrightarrow{r_1 \Longrightarrow r_2} (z, \emptyset) \\ (u, p_1 \stackrel{e}{=} p_2) \xrightarrow{p} (w, t_1 \stackrel{e}{=} t_2)\end{array}}{(u, p_1 \stackrel{e}{=} p_2) \xrightarrow{r_1 \circ p \Longrightarrow r_2 \circ p} (z, \emptyset)}$$

6 Conclusion

Two main points in a 2-categorical appraoch to specification of partial algebras have only been touched very briefly in this paper: The first one is parameterization, general structuring mechanisms and compositionality of the semantics w.r.t. the syntax. In [CGRW92] these topics have been worked out in detail for the one dimensional case, probably there are no severe problems in carrying these results over to the two dimensional case. However, the work still has to be done. The second point is the restriction to at most one 2-cell between parallel morphisms in this paper. Since 2-cells are constructed according to certain 2-categorical rules their different roles could be exhibited if this restriction is removed. This would lead to a formalism which makes possible to reason about different rewrites, their composition, strategies etc., which will be subject of subsequent papers.

References

[BW85] Michael Barr and Charles Wells. *Toposes, triples, and theories.* Springer Verlag, 1985.

[CGRW92] Ingo Claßen, Martin Große-Rhode, and Uwe Wolter. Categorical concepts for parameterized partial specifications. Technical Report 92-42, TU Berlin, 1992.

[Fre72] Peter Freyd. Aspects of topoi. *Bull. Austr. Math. Soc.*, (7):1–72, 1972.

[Fre73] Peter Freyd. Aspects of topoi, corrections. *Bull. Austr. Math. Soc.*, (8):467–480, 1973.

[GU71] P. Gabriel and F. Ulmer. *Lokal präsentierbare Kategorien.* Springer Lecture Notes in Mathematics 221, 1971.

[Joh77] P. T. Johnstone. *Topos Theory.* Academic Press, 1977.

[Kel89] G. M. Kelly. Elementary observations on 2–categorical limits. *Bulletin Australian Mathematical Society*, (39):301–317, 1989.

[KR72] H. Kaphengst and H. Reichel. Operative Theorien und Kategorien von operativen Systemen. In *Studien zur Algebra und ihren Anwendungen.* Akademie Verlag, 1972.

[LS86] J. Lambek and P. J. Scott. *Introduction to higher order categorical logic.* Cambridge studies in advanced mathematics. Cambridge University Press, 1986.

[MR77] M. Makkai and G.E. Reyes. *First order categorical logic*, volume 611 of *Lecture Notes in Mathematics.* Springer Verlag, 1977.

[Poi85] Axel Poigné. Algebra categorically. *Lecture Notes in Mathematics*, (240):76–102, 1985.

[PW91] A.J. Power and Charles Wells. A formalism for the specification of essentially algebraic structures in 2–categories. Technical report, University of Edinburgh, 1991.

[See87] R. A. G. Seely. Modeling computations: A 2-categorical framework. In *Symposium on Logic in Computer Science*, pages 65–71. IEEE, 1987.

[Wol90] Uwe Wolter. An algebraic approach to deduction in equational partial horn theories. *J. Inf. Process. Cybern. EIK*, 27(2):85–128, 1990.

A Behavioural Algebraic Framework for Modular System Design with Reuse[1]

Rolf Hennicker, Friederike Nickl
Institut für Informatik, Ludwig-Maximilians-Universität München
Leopoldstr. 11B, 80802 München, GERMANY

Abstract. A formal framework for the design of modular software systems is presented which incorporates the idea of reusing software components in new applications. The approach is based on structured algebraic specifications with behavioural semantics. In order to provide a clean interconnection mechanism for specifications, behavioural specifications with import interfaces are considered and their composition with respect to the behavioural requirements of the import interface is defined. A simple implementation notion for behavioural specifications with import interface is presented which is compatible with the composition of specifications. Hence it is guaranteed that separately developed implementations of parts of an abstract system specification can be automatically composed to a globally correct system implementation. Based on these concepts, reusable components are defined as (unordered) trees of behavioural specifications with import interfaces such that two consecutive nodes are related by the implementation relation. A formal method for the systematic reuse of components in new applications is proposed. The method consists of four steps which describe how to construct for a given abstract system specification a modular implementation by reusing existing implementations available as leaves of appropriate reusable components. The method is demonstrated by a detailed example.

1 Introduction

The advantages of a modular construction of large software systems are commonly accepted: a modular design increases the understandability of a system, supports the reuse of single modules in different applications and allows the separate realization of modules by different programmers. In this paper we will introduce an algebraic framework for the construction of modular systems which is based on behavioural semantics, and, using this framework, we will develop a formal method for the systematic reuse of components in new applications (***design with reuse***).

Behavioural semantics
Intuitively, behavioural semantics is a generalization of the standard model class semantics since it describes not only the models (in the classical sense) of a specification but provides freedom for abstraction from the non observable properties of a system specification. The principle idea of behavioural semantics is to interpret the equations occurring in arbitrary first-order axioms not as identities but as behavioural equivalences of objects (cf. [Reichel 85], [Orejas, Nivela 90], [Bernot, Bidoit 91]). As an important consequence behavioural semantics allows to use a simple notion of implementation for specifications which expresses the intuitively clear idea that an implementation is correct if it produces correct observable output. In our framework implementations are treated also as formal specifications, but if they are written in a constructive style they can be translated into a functional programming language like ML (cf. [Milner et al. 90]).

Modular system design
In this paper we combine behavioural semantics with the modular construction of implementations for large system specifications. In order to allow the parallel and independent development of implementations for the single constituents of a modular specification we need a clean interconnection mechanism for specifications. Therefore we consider pairs (SP_0, SP) of structured behavioural specifications where SP_0 is called the "import interface" of SP. A specification (SP_0, SP) is called *correct* if SP is consistent, i.e. admits at least one behavioural model, and if SP preserves its import interface SP_0, i.e. the behavioural models of SP_0 can be extended to behavioural models of SP. The composition of specifications (SP_0, SP) and (SP_0', SP') with import

[1] This research has been partially sponsored by the German BMFT-project KORSO

interfaces is defined with respect to a composition morphism which connects the import interface SP_0 of SP with the (imported) specification SP' whereby the requirements of SP_0 (which are determined by the behavioural semantics of SP_0) must be satisfied by the imported specification. It is an important fact that the composition preserves the correctness of specifications.
The implementation relation between behavioural specifications with import interfaces is defined in such a way, that by every implementation of an abstract specification (SP_0, SP) the import interface SP_0 has to be preserved. More precisely this means that any behavioural model of the import interface SP_0 can be extended to a behavioural model of the concrete implementation. As a consequence correct compositions of abstract specifications induce automatically correct compositions on the implementation level, i.e. separately developed implementations of parts of an abstract system specification can be automatically composed to a consistent configuration of the whole system. This property is of crucial importance in the case where new systems are constructed by reusing existing components, since it allows to integrate single reused implementations in a consistent way.

Reusability
For the definition of a reusable component we follow the idea of [Wirsing 88] where reusable components are defined as (unordered) trees of algebraic specifications (written in the algebraic specification language ASL) such that two consecutive nodes are related by a formal implementation relation. This idea is motivated by the fact that for the correct reuse of a software module in new applications it is necessary to have an abstract description of its behaviour. Such a description is provided by the root of a reusable component while the leaves represent different concrete implementations.
In contrast to [Wirsing 88], [Wirsing et al. 89] we use here the more powerful behavioural implementation notion and the nodes of a reusable component are specifications with import interfaces. This has the important advantage that (using the interconnection mechanism for specifications with import interfaces) the composition of single reused "implementation pieces" yields a consistent system configuration. In [Wirsing et al. 89] where, based on [Wirsing 88], a first approach for the design with reuse was given the consistency of modular system implementations could not yet be guaranteed. This property, however, is of crucial importance in the formal method for the systematic reuse of components in new applications which we propose in this paper: the method consists of four steps which describe how to construct for a given abstract system specification a modular implementation by reusing existing implementations available as leaves of appropriate reusable components. The theory of reusable components with import interfaces ensures that the resulting composition of "reused implementations" yields a correct and consistent implementation of the given system specification.

2 Algebraic preliminaries

We assume the reader to be familiar with the basic notions of algebraic specifications (cf. e.g. [Ehrig, Mahr 85]) such as the notions of *signature* $\Sigma = (S, F)$, *signature morphism* $\sigma: \Sigma \to \Sigma'$, *subsignature* $\Sigma \subseteq \Sigma'$, *total* Σ*-algebra* $A = ((A_s)_{s\in S}, (f^A)_{f\in F})$ (with carrier sets A_s and total functions f^A) and *term algebra* $W_\Sigma(X)$ over an S-sorted family $X = (X_s)_{s\in S}$ of sets of variables. The *restriction* of a Σ'-algebra A w.r.t. a signature morphism $\sigma: \Sigma \to \Sigma'$ is denoted by $A|_\sigma$. In particular, the restriction of A to a subsignature $\Sigma \subseteq \Sigma'$ is denoted by $A|_\Sigma$. Analogously, if C is a class of Σ'-algebras then the restriction of C w.r.t. a signature morphism $\sigma: \Sigma \to \Sigma'$ is the class $C|_\sigma = \{A|_\sigma \mid A \in C\}$ and the restriction of C to a subsignature $\Sigma \subseteq \Sigma'$ is the class $C|_\Sigma = \{A|_\Sigma \mid A \in C\}$.
It is a well known fact that the category SIGN of signatures and signature morphisms has pushouts. In this paper we are concerned with particular pushout diagrams of the form

$$\begin{array}{ccc}
\Sigma_0 & \xrightarrow{\iota} & \Sigma \\
\sigma \downarrow & & \downarrow po_1(\iota, \sigma) \\
\Sigma' & \xrightarrow{po_2(\iota, \sigma)} & PO(\iota, \sigma)
\end{array}$$

where $\Sigma_0 \subseteq \Sigma$ is a subsignature and ι is the inclusion morphism. In the following it is assumed that for any subsignature $\Sigma_0 \subseteq \Sigma$ and signature morphism $\sigma: \Sigma_0 \rightarrow \Sigma'$ we have selected a fixed pushout $PO(\iota, \sigma)$ with signature morphisms $po_1(\iota, \sigma)$ and $po_2(\iota, \sigma)$ such that $\Sigma' \subseteq PO(\iota, \sigma)$ is a subsignature and $po_2(\iota, \sigma)$ is the inclusion morphism. (Since $\Sigma_0 \subseteq \Sigma$ is a subsignature, one can show that this choice of the pushout is possible.)

3 Structured behavioural specifications

In the following we consider structured algebraic specifications with behavioural semantics. The syntax of the specification building operators which will be used here is essentially derived from the algebraic specification language ASL (cf. [Wirsing 86]). But, in contrast to ASL, the semantics of structured specifications is not based on the standard models of a specification but on the class of all behavioural models. The essential idea behind behavioural semantics is that the equations occurring in the first-order axioms of a specification are not interpreted as identities but as behavioural equivalences of objects where two objects are called behaviourally equivalent if they cannot be distinguished by experiments with observable result. For the formal definition of our concept we use the behavioural satisfaction relation (cf. also [Reichel 85], [Orejas, Nivela 90], [Bernot, Bidoit 91]) which is based on the notion of observable Σ-context. Thereby an observable Σ-context is any term c over a given signature Σ which is of observable result sort and which contains, besides other variables, exactly one distinguished "input" variable (cf. [Hennicker, Nickl 92]).

3.1 Definition Let $\Sigma = (S, F)$ be a signature, $Obs \subseteq S$ be a set of observable sorts, $X = (X_s)_{s \in S}$ be an S-sorted family of countably infinite sets X_s of variables of sorts s, A be a Σ-algebra, $\alpha: X \rightarrow A$ be an arbitrary valuation and let $t, r \in W_\Sigma(X)$ be terms of the same sort s. Then the *behavioural satisfaction relation* (denoted by $\models_{beh}$) is defined as follows:

1. $A, \alpha \models_{beh} t = r$ if and only if
   for all observable Σ-contexts c with variables disjoint from the variables of t and r the following holds: $A, \alpha \models \forall\ Var(c): c[t] = c[r]$ where $\models$ denotes the usual satisfaction relation of first-order predicate calculus and Var(c) denotes the set of variables occurring in c.
2. The behavioural satisfaction relation for arbitrary first-order formulas which can be built over equations using the connectives $\neg$, $\wedge$, etc. and using the existential and universal quantifiers is defined (as usual) by induction over the structure of the formulas.
3. Let ϕ be an arbitrary first-order formula over Σ. Then:
   $A \models_{beh} \phi$ if and only if $A, \alpha \models_{beh} \phi$ for all valuations $\alpha: X \rightarrow A$.

Using the behavioural satisfaction relation the behavioural equivalence of objects is defined as follows:

4. Let $a, b \in A$ be objects of the same sort s. a, b are called *behaviourally equivalent* if and only if for two variables x and y of sort s and for the valuation α with $\alpha(x) = a$, $\alpha(y) = b$ the following holds: $A, \alpha \models_{beh} x = y$. ♦

Figure 1 shows the syntax and the behavioural semantics of structured specifications with specification building operators for enrichment, renaming, export, restriction and combination (sum) of specifications. Thereby the behavioural semantics of a structured specification SP is determined by its signature, denoted by *sig(SP)*, by its set of observable sorts, denoted by *obs-sorts(SP)* and by its class of *behavioural models*, denoted by *Beh(SP)*. The class of behavioural models of SP is also called *behaviour class* of SP. For the construction of the behaviour class the behavioural satisfaction relation is used (instead of the usual satisfaction relation) and reachabilty constraints are interpreted up to behavioural equivalence of objects (*behavioural reachability!*). Some proof-theoretical aspects of the approach are discussed in the conclusion (cf. section 7).

Syntax	*Signature*	*observable sorts*	*Behaviour class*
(0) Basic Specification: **sorts** S **obs-sorts** Obs **cons** C **opns** F **axioms** E <u>conditions:</u> $Obs \subseteq S$, C is a set of constructors F a set of operations such that $\Sigma = (S, C \cup F)$ is a signature, E is a set of first order formulas over Σ	Σ (see left box)	Obs	$\{ A \in Alg(\Sigma) \mid$ $A \models_{beh} e$ for all axioms $e \in E$ and A is behaviourally reachable on range(C) with C $\}$ (where range(C) = $\{s \in S \mid (f: s_1 \times \ldots \times s_n \to s) \in C\}$)
(1) Enrichment: **enrich** SP **by** **sorts** S **obs-sorts** Obs **cons** C **opns** F **axioms** E <u>conditions</u>: $Obs \subseteq sorts(SP) \cup S$, $\Sigma=(sorts(SP) \cup S, opns(SP) \cup C \cup F)$ is a signature, E is a set of first order formulas over Σ	Σ (see left box)	$obs\text{-}sorts(SP) \cup Obs$	$\{ A \in Alg(\Sigma) \mid$ $A\|_{sig(SP)} \in Beh(SP)$, $A \models_{beh} e$ for all axioms $e \in E$ and A is behaviourally reachable on range(C) with C $\}$ (where range(C) = $\{s \in S \mid (f: s_1 \times \ldots \times s_n \to s) \in C\}$)
(2) Renaming: **rename** SP **by** ρ <u>conditions:</u> $\rho: sig(SP) \to \Sigma$ is a bijective signature morphism	Σ	$\rho(obs\text{-}sorts(SP))$	$\{ A \in Alg(\Sigma) \mid A\|_{\rho} \in Beh(SP)\}$
(3) Export: **export** Σ **from** SP <u>conditions:</u> $\Sigma \subseteq sig(SP)$ is a subsignature	Σ	$sorts(\Sigma) \cap$ $obs\text{-}sorts(SP)$	$Beh(SP)\|_{\Sigma}$
(4) Restriction: **restrict** SP **on** S_0 <u>conditions:</u> $S_0 \subseteq sorts(SP)$	sig(SP)	obs-sorts(SP)	$\{ A_0 \in Alg(sig(SP)) \mid A_0$ is behaviourally reachable on S_0 with F and A_0 is a subalgebra of some behavioural model $A \in Beh(SP)$ which differs from A only on the carrier sets $(A_0)_s$ of sort $s \in S_0$.$\}$
(5) Sum: SP + SP'	$sig(SP) \cup sig(SP')$	$obs\text{-}sorts(SP) \cup$ $obs\text{-}sorts(SP')$	$\{ A \in Alg(sig(SP) \cup sig(SP')) \mid$ $A\|_{sig(SP)} \in Beh(SP)$ and $A\|_{sig(SP')} \in Beh(SP')\}$

Figure 1: Syntax and semantics of structured behavioural specifications

4 Behavioural specifications with import interfaces

A central objective of our approach is to provide a clean interconnection mechanism for structured behavioural specifications which allows a consistent composition of separately developed implementations of parts of a modular specification. For that purpose we associate to any specification a distinguished "import interface" which may be refined (i.e. described in more detail) in another specification. All sorts and operations which do not belong to the import interface are considered to be "ready for implementation" since they cannot be refined by composition with other specifications but can only be implemented on a more concrete level of abstraction. The non imported part of a specification possibly relies on the properties of the import interface of the specification.
Technically, a behavioural specification with import interface is a pair (SP_0, SP) of structured behavioural specifications where SP_0 specifies the import interface of SP. The signature of SP_0 consists of all sorts and operations of SP for which a detailed specification is left open to a further (subtask) specification and the semantical requirements which are imposed on any refinement of SP_0 are represented by the behavioural semantics of the import interface SP_0. A specification (SP_0, SP) is called *correct* if SP is consistent (i.e. admits at least one behavioural model) and if SP preserves its import interface SP_0 (i.e. any behavioural model of SP_0 can be extended to a behavioural model of SP).

4.1 Definition (1) A *behavioural specification with import interface* is a pair (SP_0, SP) of structured behavioural specifications such that $sig(SP_0) \subseteq sig(SP)$. SP_0 is called *import interface* of SP.

(2) A behavioural specification (SP_0, SP) is called *correct*, if $Beh(SP) \neq \emptyset$ and if $Beh(SP_0) \subseteq Beh(SP)|_{sig(SP_0)}$. ♦

The semantics of a behavioural specification (SP_0, SP) with import interface is determined by the behavioural semantics of the specifications SP and SP_0 (cf. section 3). In the following we assume that any import interface contains a usual specification BOOL of the truth values.

4.2 Example The following specification ($GREX_0$, GREX) is a correct specification of memory structures with direct access. Any element of sort *grex* can be seen as a memory which stores elements of the underlying set of *values* at special positions (marked by *indices*). The characteristic operations are the constant *emptygrex* denoting the empty grex, the *update* operation which inserts an element at some position in a grex, the operation *isaccessible* which tests for a grex *g* whether a value is assigned to a given index *i* and the operation *get* which selects for a grex *g* and an index *i* the entry at position *i*. If there is no entry for a given index *i* then the *get* operation yields the constant *const* as result. The import interface $GREX_0$ consists of a given specification BOOL for the truth values enriched by the sorts *index* for the indices, *value* for the values of indices and by the constant *const*. Both sorts, *index* and *value*, are declared as observable sorts whereas the sort *grex* itself is not observable.

spec $GREX_0$ = **enrich** BOOL **by** **sorts** {index, value} **obs-sorts** {index, value} **opns** const: → value **endspec**

```
spec GREX = enrich GREX0 by
  sorts
    { grex }
  cons
    { emptygrex: → grex,
      update: grex, index, value → grex }
  opns
    { isaccessible: grex, index → bool,
      get: grex, index → value }
axioms
    { update( update(g, i, w), i, v) = update(g, i, v),
      i ≠ j ⇒
      update( update(g, j, w), i, v) = update( update(g, i, v), j, w),
      isaccessible( emptygrex, i) = false,
      isaccessible(update(g, i, v), i) = true,
      i ≠ j ⇒ isaccessible(update(g, j, v), i) = isaccessible(g, i),
      get( emptygrex, i) = const,
      get(update(g, i, v), i) = v,
      i ≠ j ⇒ get(update(g, j, v), i) = get(g, i) }   endspec   ♦
```

The most important operation on specifications with import interfaces is their composition. A specification (SP_0, SP) can be composed with a specification (SP_0', SP') if the (behavioural) requirements of the import interface SP_0 of SP are satisfied by SP'. Formally, the composition of (SP_0, SP) with (SP_0', SP') is defined via a signature morphism σ: sig(SP_0) $\rightarrow$ sig(SP') which connects the import interface SP_0 with the imported specification SP' such that for all behavioural models M' $\in$ Beh(SP') the restriction of M' w.r.t. σ is a behavioural model of SP_0, i.e. $Beh(SP')|_\sigma \subseteq Beh(SP_0)$. The import interface SP_0' of the imported specification becomes the new import interface of the composed specification. In summary, we give the following definition for the composition of behavioural specifications with import interfaces:

4.3 Definition Let (SP_0, SP) and (SP_0', SP') be specifications with import interfaces SP_0, SP_0' respectively.

1. A *composition morphism* σ: (SP_0, SP) $\rightarrow$ (SP_0', SP') is a signature morphism σ: sig(SP_0) $\rightarrow$ sig(SP') such that $Beh(SP')|_\sigma \subseteq Beh(SP_0)$ holds.

2. Let σ: (SP_0, SP) $\rightarrow$ (SP_0', SP') be a composition morphism. Then

   compose (SP_0, SP) ***with*** (SP_0', SP') ***via*** $\sigma =_{def}$ (SP_0', SP_{res})

   where sig(SP_{res}) = PO(ι, σ) is the pushout of the following square in the category of signatures (cf. section 2):

$$\begin{array}{ccccc} & & sig(SP_0) & \xrightarrow{\ \iota\ } & sig(SP) \\ & & \downarrow \sigma & & \downarrow po_1(\iota,\sigma) \\ sig(SP_0') & \xrightarrow{\ \iota'\ } & sig(SP') & \xrightarrow{\ po_2(\iota,\sigma)\ } & PO(\iota,\sigma) \end{array}$$

   (ι and ι' are the inclusion morphisms w.r.t. sig(SP_0) $\subseteq$ sig(SP) and sig(SP_0')$\subseteq$sig(SP')),

obs-sorts(SP_{res}) $=_{def}$ $po_2(\iota,\sigma)$(obs-sorts(SP')) $\cup$ $po_1(\iota, \sigma)$(obs-sorts(SP) \ sorts(SP_0)),

Beh(SP_{res}) $=_{def}$ $\{A \in Alg(PO(\iota, \sigma)) \mid A|_{po_1(\iota, \sigma)} \in Beh(SP) \text{ and } A|_{po_2(\iota, \sigma)} \in Beh(SP')\}$.

(Remember that we have assumed in section 2 that the pushout is chosen in such a way that $po_2(\iota, \sigma)$ is the inclusion morphism sig(SP') $\subseteq$ PO(ι, σ). Hence the observable sorts of SP_{res} consist of the observable sorts of the imported specification SP' together with (up to renaming w.r.t. $po_1(\iota, \sigma)$) all observable sorts of SP which do not belong to the sorts of SP_0. SP_{res} is called amalgamated union (cf. [Ehrig, Mahr 85]) of SP and SP' with respect to ι and σ.) ♦

The following proposition states that compositions preserve the correctness of specifications (for the proof see proposition 4.5 in [Hennicker, Nickl 92]):

4.4 Proposition Let (SP_0, SP) and (SP_0', SP') be correct specifications and let σ: (SP_0, SP) $\rightarrow$ (SP_0', SP') be a composition morphism.
Then ***compose*** (SP_0, SP) ***with*** (SP_0', SP') ***via*** σ is a correct specification. ♦

Up to now, as a structuring operator for behavioural specifications with import interfaces we have only considered the composition since this is the most typical operator for this kind of specifications. In the following all structuring operators for specifications defined in section 3 (besides "+") are extended to behavioural specifications with import interfaces. In section 6 these operators will be used for the adaptation of reused implementations. (Note that we do not extend the "+" operator since for the combination of specifications with import interfaces we can and should use the composition operator.)

4.5 Definition Let (SP_0, SP) be a specification with import interface SP_0 and let S, Obs, C, F, E, ρ, Σ as in the definitions (0) - (4) of the structuring operators in figure 1.

(1) ***enrich*** (SP_0, SP) ***by sorts*** S ***obs-sorts*** Obs ***cons*** C ***opns*** F ***axioms*** E $=_{def}$
(SP_0, **enrich** SP **by sorts** S **obs-sorts** Obs **cons** C **opns** F **axioms** E),

(2) ***rename*** (SP_0, SP) ***by*** $\rho =_{def}$ (**rename** SP_0 **by** ρ_0, **rename** SP **by** ρ)
where ρ: sig(SP) $\rightarrow \Sigma$, ρ_0: sig(SP_0) $\rightarrow \rho$(sig(SP_0)) with $\rho_0(x) = \rho(x)$,

(3) ***export*** Σ ***from*** $(SP_0, SP) =_{def}$
(**export** $\Sigma \cap$ sig(SP_0) **from** SP_0, **export** Σ **from** SP),

(4) ***restrict*** (SP_0, SP) ***on*** S $=_{def}$ (SP_0, ***restrict*** SP ***on*** S) if $S \subseteq$ sorts(SP) \ sorts(SP_0) . ♦

4.6 Proposition Let (SP_0, SP) be a correct specification and let all specification expressions in definition 4.5 be well-formed. Then the specifications (2) - (4) of the definition are correct. A sufficient condition for the correctness of (1) is the persistency of the enrichment $\Delta =_{def}$ **sorts** S **obs-sorts** Obs **cons** C **opns** F **axioms** E (i.e. Beh(SP) = Beh(**enrich** SP **by** Δ)$|_{sig(SP)}$). ♦

Proof: The proof is straightforward using the semantics of the underlying specification building operators (cf. section 3).

5 Implementation of behavioural specifications with import interfaces

In the last section we have considered the so-called *horizontal structure* of specifications where large specifications can be designed by the application of several structuring operators such as composition, enrichment, renaming etc.. In the following we are more concerned with the *vertical structure* of specifications and program development in order to allow refinements (also called implementations) of specifications. Thereby it should be possible to construct local implementations of parts of an abstract system specification independently from each other such that the composition of local implementation pieces according to the structure of the abstract system specification yields automatically a correct implementation of the whole system. Since in our framework the composition of specifications is constructed via their import interface this can be achieved by requiring that the (semantics of the) import interface of a specification has to be preserved by any implementation. This means that a programmer who is responsible for a subtask must implement only the non imported part of a specification while the import interface of the abstract specification must not be restricted by any implementation. Then, if all "implementation pieces" are locally correct specifications it is guaranteed that no conflicts will occur when composing separately developed implementations according to the structure of an abstract system specification.

5.1 Definition Let (SP_0, SP) and (SP_0-IMPL, SP-IMPL) be correct specifications with import interfaces SP_0, SP_0-IMPL respectively. (SP_0-IMPL, SP-IMPL) is called *implementation* of (SP_0, SP) (written (SP_0, SP) ~~~> (SP_0-IMPL, SP-IMPL)) if the following conditions are satisfied:

(1) sig(SP-IMPL) = sig(SP), obs-sorts(SP) $\subseteq$ obs-sorts(SP-IMPL) and Beh(SP-IMPL) $\subseteq$ Beh(SP),

(2) sig(SP_0-IMPL) = sig(SP_0) and Beh(SP_0) $\subseteq$ Beh(SP_0-IMPL). ♦

Condition (1) requires that the signatures of the abstract and the implementing specification coincide (which can be achieved, for instance, using the export operator), that all observable sorts of the abstract specification are observable sorts of the implementation as well and that all behavioural models of the implementing specification are behavioural models of the abstract specification. Since we deal with behavioural semantics the latter condition provides a flexible implementation

notion which formalizes the intuitive idea that an implementation is correct if it satisfies the desired input/output behaviour. But unfortunately this condition does not guarantee the global consistency of a modular implementation if single consistent implementations are composed. Therefore we need condition (2) which says that an implementing specification has a less restrictive import interface than the abstract specification (in most examples both interfaces are even syntactically equal). As a consequence of this condition it is guaranteed that any behavioural model of the abstract import interface SP_0 can be extended to a behavioural model of the implementation SP-IMPL and hence SP-IMPL will be compatible with any refinement of SP_0. The extendibility of the models of SP_0 to a model of the implementation SP-IMPL is related to the correctness condition for module specifications in ACT TWO (cf. [Ehrig, Mahr 90]) where it is required that the body of a module (which gives an implementation of the export interface in terms of the import interface) is a strongly persistent extension of the import specification.
Note that the implementation relation is defined only for correct specifications. This means in particular that any implementation is consistent, i.e. admits at least one behavioural model. Obviously, the implementation relation is transitive.

5.2 Example In the following the specification ($GREX_0$, GREX) of example 4.2 is implemented by a specification ($GREX_0$, GREX-IMPL) which implements grexes by sequences of pairs consisting of an index and its associated value. The sequences of pairs are constructed using the concatenation operator *.o.* .

```
spec GREX-IMPL = export sig(GREX) from
  enrich GREX0 by sorts { grex }
    cons                                       axioms
      { emptygrex: → grex,                       { g o emptygrex = emptygrex o g = g,
        <.,.>: index, value → grex,                (g o h) o k = g o (h o k),
        .o.: grex, grex → grex }                   update(g, i, v) = <i, v> o g,
    opns                                           isaccessible(emptygrex, i) = false,
      { update: grex, index, value → grex,         isaccessible(<i, v> o g, i) = true,
        isaccessible: grex, index→ bool,           i≠j ⇒ isaccessible(<j, v> o g, i) = isaccessible(g, i),
        get: grex, index → value}                  get(emptygrex, i) = const,
                                                   get(<i, v> o g, i) = v,
                                                   i≠j ⇒ get(<j, v> o g, i) = get(g, i) } endspec
```

($GREX_0$, GREX-IMPL) is an implementation of ($GREX_0$, GREX) since memory structures can only be observed via the values of indices and hence one can show that the implementation behaviourally satisfies all axioms of the abstract specification. (All other conditions of the implementation definition are obviously satisfied.) ♦

The following central proposition ensures the compatibility of the composition of specifications with the implementation relation (for the proof see proposition 5.3 in [Hennicker, Nickl 92]):

5.3 Proposition
Let (SP_0, SP) ~~~> (SP_0-IMPL, SP-IMPL) and (SP_0', SP') ~~~> (SP_0'-IMPL, SP'-IMPL) be two implementation relations and let σ: (SP_0, SP) → (SP_0', SP') be a composition morphism. Then σ: (SP_0-IMPL, SP-IMPL) → (SP_0'-IMPL, SP'-IMPL) is a composition morphism and

compose (SP_0, SP) ***with*** (SP_0',SP') ***via*** σ ~~~>
  compose (SP_0-IMPL, SP-IMPL) ***with*** (SP_0'-IMPL,SP'-IMPL) ***via*** σ

is an implementation relation. (In particular, ***compose*** (SP_0-IMPL, SP-IMPL) ***with*** (SP_0'-IMPL, SP'-IMPL) ***via*** σ is a correct, and hence consistent, specification.) ♦

The next proposition states that all operators on behavioural specifications with import interfaces of definition 4.5 are compatible with the implementation relation (for the proof see proposition 5.5 in [Hennicker, Nickl 92]):

5.4 Proposition Let (SP_0, SP) ---> (SP_0-IMPL, SP-IMPL) be an implementation relation. Moreover, let all specification expressions below be well-formed. Then the following holds:

(1) If $\Delta =_{def}$ **sorts** S **obs-sorts** Obs **cons** C **opns** F **axioms** E is a persistent enrichment of SP (cf. proposition 4.6) and if obs-sorts(SP) = obs-sorts(SP-IMPL) then
enrich (SP_0, SP) ***by*** Δ ---> ***enrich*** (SP_0-IMPL, SP-IMPL) ***by*** Δ holds.

(2) ***rename*** (SP_0, SP) ***by*** ρ ---> ***rename*** (SP_0-IMPL, SP-IMPL) ***by*** ρ holds.

(3) ***export*** Σ ***from*** (SP_0, SP) ---> ***export*** Σ ***from*** (SP_0-IMPL, SP-IMPL) holds.

(4) ***restrict*** (SP_0, SP) ***on*** S ---> ***restrict*** (SP_0-IMPL, SP-IMPL) ***on*** S holds. ♦

6 Formal reusability concepts

In this section we introduce the concept of reusable components and we propose a method for the reuse of components which extends the approach of [Wirsing 88], [Wirsing et al. 89] to behavioural semantics and to specifications with import interfaces. In particular the use of import interfaces guarantees the consistency of compositions of reused, local implementations (cf. proposition 5.3) which was not guaranteed in [Wirsing et al. 89].

6.1 Reusable components

The central problem to be considered here is the following one: given an abstract system specification which is constructed by the composition of several specifications with import interfaces (in the following also called modules) and by the application of some structuring operators such as enrich, rename etc. What we want is to construct an implementation of the whole system specification by reusing existing implementations as local implementation pieces for the single modules and then to compose these implementation pieces to a consistent implementation of the whole system. In order to tackle this problem, we are faced with (at least) two major issues:

(1) How can we identify existing implementations which are appropriate to be reused?
(2) How can we adapt and integrate reused implementation pieces into a consistent system implementation?

Considering the first issue, we require that a reusable component is not just a single implementation (with many implementation details which are not relevant for understanding the behaviour of the component) but a reusable component consists at least of two parts: a concrete implementation and an abstract description of its behaviour which is better suited for a correct understanding and identification of a component. Hence, in our framework a reusable component could be defined as a pair (SP_0-ABSTRACT, SP-ABSTRACT) ---> (SP_0-IMPL, SP-IMPL) where (SP_0-IMPL, SP-IMPL) is an implementation of (SP_0-ABSTRACT, SP-ABSTRACT). More generally, in accordance with [Wirsing 88], we define a reusable component as an (unordered) tree of behavioural specifications with import interfaces where two consecutive nodes are related by the implementation relation. The root of the tree is the most abstract problem description and the leaves represent different concrete implementations. Hence it is possible to deal with several abstraction levels and to choose between different implementations.
Considering the second issue (2) from above a reused implementation (which has been selected as one of the leaves of a reusable component) must first be adapted to the requirements of the particular application. In our framework this can be achieved by applying specification operators (cf. definition 4.5) to the reused implementations. For the consistent integration of the (modified) reused implementations we can then use our composition operator. In summary we give the following definition of reusable component:

6.1 Definition A reusable component is an (unordered) tree of *correct* behavioural specifications with import interfaces such that any son node ($SP0_{son}$, SP_{son}) is an implementation of its father node ($SP0_{father}$, SP_{father}), i.e. ($SP0_{father}$, SP_{father}) ~~~> ($SP0_{son}$, SP_{son}). The root of a reusable component RC is denoted by *root(RC)*. ♦

6.2 Example

1. The reusable component

RC-GREX $=_{def}$ ($GREX_0$, GREX) ~~~> ($GREX_0$, GREX-IMPL)

gives an implementation of the abstract specification ($GREX_0$, GREX) of memory structures by sequences of pairs consisting of an index and its associated value (cf. example 5.2).

2. Another example which will be used in the next subsection is the following reusable component

RC-SP-n $=_{def}$ (SP_0-n, SP-n) ~~~> (SP_0-n, RECORD-n)

which consists of an abstract object-oriented specification (SP_0-n, SP-n) of objects with n attributes $a_1, \ldots, a_n$ of some observable sort s_a and methods *set_a$_i$* (for i = 1, ..., n) for changing the values of the attributes and of a constructive implementation of the abstract specification by records with n components. The import interface is the specification SP_0-n which contains the sort s_a for the attribute values and a constant c of sort s_a. The constant c serves as an initial attribute value for an initial object, called *init*, of sort s.

```
spec SP0-n = enrich BOOL by sorts {sa} obs-sorts {sa} opns { c: → sa} endspec
```

```
spec SP-n =
enrich SP0-n by
   sorts { s }
   opns
      { ai: s → sa,
        set_ai: s, sa → s | i = 1, ..., n} ∪
      { init : → s }
   axioms
      { ai(set_ai(x, y)) = y | i = 1, ..., n} ∪
      { ai(set_aj(x, y)) = ai(x) |
            i = 1, ... , n; j = 1, ... , n; i ≠ j } ∪
      { ai( init ) = c | i = 1, ..., n}
   endspec
```

```
spec RECORD-n =
export sig(SP-n) from enrich SP0-n by
   sorts { s }
   cons { <. , ... , . >: sa, ..., sa → s }
   opns { ai: s → sa,
          set_ai: s, sa → s | i = 1, ..., n } ∪
        { init : → s }
   axioms
        { ai(<y1, ..., yn>) = yi | i = 1,... , n} ∪
        { set_ai(<y1, ..., yi, ..., yn>, y) =
              <y1, ..., y, ..., yn> | i = 1,... , n } ∪
        { init = <c, ..., c> }
   endspec
```

6.2 A formal method for the systematic reuse of components

Let us assume that an abstract modular design specification is given which is constituted by the composition of several correct specifications with import interfaces (modules). It is the goal of our method to construct a modular implementation of the given abstract specification by reusing existing implementations available as leaves of appropriate reusable components. The method procedes in four steps:

First step: We search for any module (SP_0, SP) of the given design specification an existing reusable component RC whose root can be adapted to the given module. More precisely, this means that we will match any module (SP_0, SP) with the root specification root(RC) of an appropriate reusable component RC. Thereby a matching is performed by a sequence $op_1, \ldots, op_n$ of specification operators (cf. definition 4.5) which are successively applied to the specification root(RC). The matching is correct if (SP_0, SP) ~~~> $op_1(\ldots op_n(root(RC))\ldots)$ is an implementation relation.

Second step: In the second step, for any reusable component RC whose root is matched with a module (SP_0, SP) of the design specification we select a leaf, say SP_{leaf}, of RC which will be reused for the implementation of (SP_0, SP).

Third step: Now, for any selected implementation SP_{leaf} the operations op_1, ..., op_n which have been used for the matching in the first step are applied to SP_{leaf}, i.e. we construct the specification $op_1(\ldots op_n(SP_{leaf})\ldots)$. By proposition 5.4, if all enrichments occurring in op_1, ..., op_n are persistent and satisfy the condition on the observable sorts of proposition 5.4 (1), then $op_1(\ldots op_n(root(RC))\ldots)$ ~~~> $op_1(\ldots op_n(SP_{leaf})\ldots)$ is an implementation relation and hence, in particular, $op_1(\ldots op_n(SP_{leaf})\ldots)$ is a correct specification. Moreover, since the implementation relation is transitive and since the matching was correct we obtain that (SP_0, SP) ~~~> $op_1(\ldots op_n(SP_{leaf})\ldots)$ is an implementation relation. Hence we have constructed locally correct implementations for each module (SP_0, SP) of the design specification by reusing existing implementations which we have found as leaves of some appropriate reusable components.

Fourth step: In the last step all local implementations of the single modules are composed according to the structure of the abstract design specification. Proposition 5.3 and 5.4 guarantee that the result is a correct and consistent implementation of the whole system specification.

An approach for the reuse of existing programs (viewed as models of a specification) has been given in [Gaudel, Moineau 88]. The relationship "isreusable for" between a specification SP_r and a "goal" specification SP_g in [Gaudel, Moineau 88] can be compared to the existence of a matching in our first step if the matching is constructed first by a persistent enrichment, then by a renaming and finally by an export operation.

6.3 An example for the application of the method

The design specification which serves for the demonstration of our reuse method is a modular specification of a book library consisting of four modules which are (horizontally) composed.
The first module, called ($LIBRARY_0$, LIBRARY), specifies the basic transactions in a book library (such as inserting new books, lending books and returning books) without giving any details about books or users of the library. Consequently the import interface $LIBRARY_0$ of this module contains the sorts *book* for the books and *user* for the users of the library. This module is composed with modules (IMP, BOOK) and (IMP, USER) specifying books together with their attributes (such as *title* and *author*) and users resp. together with their attributes (such as *name* and *address*). All attribute values are strings. The import interface IMP of both modules contains, besides the predefined specification BOOL, the sort *string* and a constant *emptystring*. (The exact specification of strings is left open. It can be achieved, for instance, by composition with a predefined string module. However this is not important for the example.)
We start by presenting the module ($LIBRARY_0$, LIBRARY). As already mentioned above, $LIBRARY_0$ contains the sorts *book* and *user*. For convenience, we also include a constant *nobody* of sort *user* to be able to tackle the case, when a book in the library is not lent to anybody.

spec $LIBRARY_0$ = **enrich** BOOL **by sorts** {book, user} **obs-sorts** {book, user} **opns** {nobody: → user} **endspec**

In the specification LIBRARY, a library is characterized by two functions on books: A boolean valued function *belongs_to_lib*, which yields *true* on those books which belong to the library, and a function *borrower* with result sort *user* which yields for a book in the library either *nobody* (meaning that the book is not lent to anybody) or the user who has borrowed the book.
Notice that for sake of simplicity we consider only such libraries, where every book is held only once. This is reflected by the fact that for each book at most one borrower is considered. There are three operations on a library: new books may be inserted (by the *insert*-operation), books may be lent to users (by the *lend*-operation) and users may return books (by the *return*-operation).

The effect of each of these operations with respect to the library-characterizing functions *belongs_to_lib* and *borrower* is specified by the axioms of the specification: The effect of the *insert*-operation is specified in the axioms (1) -(5). If a book does already belong to a library then the *insert*-operation has no effect (due to our assumption that a book is held only once in the library). By the *lend*-operation a new borrower for a book is entered only if the book belongs to the library and is not lent to anybody (cf. axiom (7)). By the *return*-operation the borrower of a book is cancelled (i.e. is set to *nobody*) only in case the book belongs to the library and the user who returns the book is the borrower of the book (cf. axiom (11)). Neither the *lend*- nor the *return*-operation changes the set of books belonging to the library (cf. axioms (6) and (10)). It is easy to see that ($LIBRARY_0$, LIBRARY) is a correct behavioural specification.

spec LIBRARY = **enrich** $LIBRARY_0$ **by sorts** { lib }
  opns {belongs_to_lib : lib, book → bool,
    borrower : lib, book → user,
    insert : lib, book → lib,
    lend, return : lib, book, user → lib,
    emptylib : → lib }
  axioms
  { (1) belongs_to_lib(insert(l, b), b) = true,
  (2) b ≠ b' ⇒ belongs_to_lib(insert(l, b), b') = belongs_to_lib(l, b'),
  (3) belongs_to_lib(l, b) = false ⇒ borrower(insert(l, b), b) = nobody,
  (4) belongs_to_lib(l, b) = true ⇒ borrower(insert(l, b), b) = borrower(l, b),
  (5) b ≠ b' ⇒ borrower(insert(l, b), b') = borrower(l, b'),

  (6) belongs_to_lib(lend(l, b, u), b') = belongs_to_lib(l, b'),
  (7) belongs_to_lib(l, b) = true ∧ borrower(l, b) = nobody ⇒ borrower (lend(l, b, u), b) = u,
  (8) belongs_to_lib(l, b) = false ∨ borrower(l, b) ≠ nobody ⇒ borrower(lend(l, b, u), b) = borrower(l, b),
  (9) b ≠ b' ⇒ borrower(lend(l, b, u), b') = borrower (l, b'),

  (10) belongs_to_lib(return(l, b, u), b') = belongs_to_lib(l, b'),
  (11) belongs_to_lib(l, b) = true ∧ borrower(l, b) = u ⇒ borrower(return(l, b, u), b) = nobody,
  (12) belongs_to_lib(l, b) = false ∨ borrower(l, b) ≠ u ⇒ borrower(return(l, b, u), b) = borrower(l, b),
  (13) b ≠ b' ⇒ borrower(return(l, b, u), b') = borrower(l, b'),

  (14) belongs_to_lib(emptylib, b) = false,
  (15) borrower(emptylib, b) = nobody } **endspec**

In the module (IMP, BOOK) books are characterized by two attributes, one for the *author* and one for the *title* of a book. The attribute values can be assigned by the operations *set_author* and *set_title*. The module (IMP, USER) contains besides the attributes *name* and *address* and their corresponding operations *set_name* and *set_address* also a constant *emptyuser* which is needed to model *nobody* in the library module. It is obvious that (IMP, BOOK) and (IMP, USER) are correct behavioural specifications.

spec IMP = **enrich** BOOL **by sorts** {string} **obs-sorts** {string} **opns** {emptystring : → string} **endspec**

spec BOOK =
 enrich IMP **by sorts** {book}
  opns { author : book → string,
    title : book → string,
    set_author : book, string → book,
    set_title : book, string → book,
    emptybook : → book} .
  axioms
   { author(set_author(b, s)) = s,
    author(set_title (b, s)) = author (b),
    author(emptybook) = emptystring,
    title(set_author (b, s)) = title(b),
    title(set_title (b, s)) = s,
    title(emptybook) = emptystring } **endspec**

spec USER =
 enrich IMP **by sorts** {user}
  opns { name : user → string,
    address : user → string,
    set_name : user, string → user,
    set_address : user, string → user,
    emptyuser: → user}
  axioms
   { name(set_name(u, s)) = s,
    name(set_address(u, s)) = name(u),
    name(emptyuser) = emptystring,
    address(set_name(u, s)) = address(u),
    address(set_address(u, s)) = s,
    address(emptyuser) = emptystring } **endspec**

In order to obtain a specification of the entire library system, first the modules specifying books and users are composed w.r.t. the composition morphism ι which is the identity on sig(IMP). Hence the compostion defines the union of both specifications over their common import interface IMP.

spec BOOK_USER = ***compose*** (IMP, BOOK) ***with*** (IMP, USER) ***via*** ι ***endspec***

Since each single module is a correct specification, proposition 4.4 guarantees that BOOK_USER is a correct behavioural specification which has, by definition 4.3, the import interface IMP. Finally, the entire system is defined as

spec LIBRARY_BOOK_USER = ***compose*** ($LIBRARY_0$, LIBRARY) ***with*** BOOK_USER ***via*** σ ***endspec***

where σ is the identity on sig($LIBRARY_0$) \ {nobody} and maps *nobody* to *emptyuser*. Obviously, σ is a composition morphism. Hence, since each single module is a correct specification proposition 4.4 ensures that LIBRARY_BOOK_USER is a correct behavioural specification.

In the following we will apply our method for reuse described in section 6.2 in order to obtain a consistent modular implementation of the given design specification LIBRARY_BOOK_USER:

First step: We will match any module of the specification LIBRARY_BOOK_USER with the root of an appropriate reusable component:

(a) The module (IMP, USER) can easily be matched with the root of the reusable component RC-SP-2 of example 6.2.2 by renaming (SP_0-2, SP-2) by the signature morphism ρ_{USER}, where ρ_{USER} = [string/s_a, emptystring/c, user/s, name/a_1, address/a_2, set_name/set_a_1, set_address/set_a_2, emptyuser/ init]

It is easy to show that (IMP, USER) ~~~> ***rename*** (SP_0-2, SP-2) ***by*** ρ_{USER}.

(b) Analogously we have (IMP, BOOK) ~~~> ***rename*** (SP_0-2, SP-2) ***by*** ρ_{BOOK}, where ρ_{BOOK} = [string/s_a, emptystring/c, book/s, author/a_1, title/a_2, set_author/set_a_1, set_title/set_a_2, emptybook/ init]

(c) The grexes specified by GREX in example 4.2 can be seen as functions from an index set into a set of values and the libraries specified by LIBRARY are characterized by functions on books. Therefore, RC_GREX (cf. example 6.2.1) is an appropriate component on which libraries may be modelled: the sort *lib* corresponds to *grex*, *book* corresponds to *index* and *user* to *value*. The function *borrower* corresponds to the *get*-function and the *belongs_to_lib*-predicate to *isaccessible*. The *insert*-operation can be modelled by an update with the user *nobody*, provided the book to be inserted does not yet belong to the library. The *lend*- and *return*-operations are modelled by updating a library with a new user for a book (or with the user *nobody* resp.) provided the preconditions specified in LIBRARY hold. This leads to the following matching performed on ($GREX_0$, GREX) which is the root of the component RC_GREX:

export sig(LIBRARY) ***from***
    enrich (***rename*** ($GREX_0$, GREX) ***by*** ρ_{GREX}) ***by*** ***opns*** OP_{LIB} ***axioms*** AX_{LIB}

where ρ_{GREX} = [book/index, user/value, nobody/const, lib/grex,emptylib/emptygrex,
    belongs_to_lib/isaccessible, borrower/get],

OP_{LIB} = { insert: lib, book → lib, lend, return : lib, book, user → lib}

AX_{LIB} = { belongs_to_lib(l, b) = false ⇒ insert(l, b) = update(l, b, nobody),
    belongs_to_lib(l, b) = true ⇒ insert(l, b) = l,
    belongs_to_lib(l, b) = true ∧ borrower(l, b) = nobody ⇒ lend(l, b, u) = update(l, b, u),
    belongs_to_lib(l, b) = false ∨ borrower(l, b) ≠ nobody ⇒ lend(l, b, u) = l,
    belongs_to_lib(l, b) = true ∧ borrower(l, b) = u ⇒ return(l, b, u) = update(l, b, nobody),
    belongs_to_lib(l, b) = false ∨ borrower(l, b) ≠ u ⇒ return(l, b, u) = l }

Since the above enrichment is persistent, the resulting module is correct. Moreover, from the specification of the operations in GREX it follows that all laws of LIBRARY are (behaviourally) satisfied in this module. Hence we have obtained an implementation of the module ($LIBRARY_0$, LIBRARY). This means that we have matched the module ($GREX_0$, GREX) with the module ($LIBRARY_0$, LIBRARY) by performing a renaming and an enrichment on the root of the reusable component RC-GREX.

Second step: In the first step we have matched the modules (IMP, BOOK) and (IMP, USER) with the root of the component RC-SP-2 and we have matched the module ($LIBRARY_0$, LIBRARY) with the root of the component RC-GREX. Therefore, in the second step, we choose two times the leaf (SP_0-2, RECORD-2) of RC-SP-2 and once the leaf ($GREX_0$, GREX-IMPL) of RC-GREX.

Third step: All matching operations which are applied in the first step to the roots of the components RC-SP-2 and RC-GREX are now applied to the leaves of RC-SP-2 and RC-GREX which yields the following modules:

spec USER-IMPL = ***rename*** (SP_0-2, RECORD-2) ***by*** ρ_{USER} ***endspec***

spec BOOK-IMPL = ***rename*** (SP_0-2, RECORD-2) ***by*** ρ_{BOOK} ***endspec***

spec LIB-IMPL = ***export*** sig(LIBRARY) ***from***
enrich (***rename*** ($GREX_0$, GREX-IMPL) ***by*** ρ_{GREX}) ***by*** ***opns*** OP_{LIB} ***axioms*** AX_{LIB}
endspec

Then, by proposition 5.4 and by the transitivity of the implementation relation, we have:

(IMP, USER) ---> USER-IMPL, (IMP, BOOK) ---> BOOK-IMPL, ($LIBRARY_0$, LIBRARY) ---> LIB-IMPL

Fourth step: We now compose the local implementations obtained in the third step according to the structure of the given design specification LIBRARY_BOOK_USER.

spec BOOK_USER_IMPL = ***compose*** BOOK_IMPL ***with*** USER_IMPL ***via*** ι ***endspec***

spec LIBRARY_BOOK_USER_IMPL = ***compose*** LIB_IMPL ***with*** BOOK_USER_IMPL ***via*** σ ***endspec***

Now proposition 5.3 guarantees that LIBRARY_BOOK_USER_IMPL is an implementation of the whole design specification LIBRARY_BOOK_USER. In particular LIBRARY_BOOK_USER_IMPL is a correct (and therefore also consistent) specification.

7 Conclusion

The presented approach provides a formalism to modular system specification and implementation which is based on behavioural semantics. As an important objective of this work we have investigated a clean concept for the behavioural composition of specifications and a behavioural implementation notion such that locally correct implementations of parts of a system specification can be automatically composed to a globally correct system implementation. The compatibility of separately developed implementations is particularly important in the context of software reuse where already existing implementations should be reusable for new applications.

An important objective of further research is the investigation of a proof-theoretical framework for structured behavioural specifications. The problem is that usual proof rules like the preservation of the validity of formulas by enrichment and export do in general not hold in the behavioural case. For instance, if an enriched specification allows to distinguish more elements of primitive sort than the original one, then the behavioural validity of an equation in the primitive specification may not be preserved by the enrichment. If, however, all observations which are possible in the larger specification can be reduced to primitive observations (i.e. the enrichment is observationally sufficiently complete), then the behavioural validity of arbitrary first-order formulas is respected by enrichments. The situation is different, if we consider the export operator. In this case the behavioural validity of inequations is in general not preserved, because the restriction to a subsignature allows usually less observations. For instance, a list-specification (over the naturals) which is used for the implementation of sets of naturals satisfies the inequation add(succ(zero), add(zero, empty)) ≠ add(zero, add(succ(zero), empty)). However, if we forget the list selectors which give access to the first element and to the rest of a list, then the resulting specification satisfies (and should satisfy) the corresponding equation. Hence, for developing a proof theory the idea is to relativize the behavioural satisfaction relation such that behavioural equality may be considered w.r.t. a subsignature of a specification.

Our main topics *observability*, *modularity* and *reusability* were also studied in other approaches of the literature. For instance [Orejas, Nivela 90] and [Bernot, Bidoit 91] provide frameworks for modular specification with behavioural semantics, the former approach using behaviour constraints and the latter using the stratified loose semantics which reflects the modular construction of realizations. Formal reusability concepts were investigated by [Cramer et al. 91] where modules in the sense of ACT TWO are equippped with additional imperative and concurrency views and in the approach of [Gaudel, Moineau 88] where a specification SP_r is called "reusable" for a specification SP_g if there is a persistent adaptation functor which turns any implementation of SP_r into an implementation of SP_g. In [Gaudel, Moineau 88] implementations are treated as models of a specification while in our approach implementations are regarded as low-level, constructive specifications. This has the consequence that we can reason about several abstraction levels in the same formalism where programs are just the final product of a series of implementation steps.
The separate development and reuse of implementations is also pursued by [Sannella et al. 90] where the composition of implementations can be achieved by application of a (possibly higher order) parametric algebra to another parametric algebra. In contrast to specifications of parametric algebras specifications with import interfaces in our sense may be used as parameterized specifications which can be actualized by the composition operator. Our constructions guarantee that local consistency extends to global consistency which is not ensured by ASL-like parameterization (cf. [Wirsing 86]).

References

[Bernot, Bidoit 91] G. Bernot, M. Bidoit: Proving the correctness of algebraically specified software: modularity and observability issues. Proc. AMAST '91, 2nd International Conference on Algebraic Methodology of Software Technology, Technical Report of the University of Iowa, 1991.

[Cramer et al. 91] J. Cramer, W. Fey, M. Goedicke, M. Große-Rhode: Towards a formally based component description language - a foundation for reuse. Structured Programming, Vol. 2, No. 12, Springer Verlag, 1991.

[Ehrig, Mahr 85] H. Ehrig, B. Mahr: Fundamentals of algebraic specification 1. EATCS Monographs on Theor. Comp. Science, Vol. 6, Springer Verlag, 1985.

[Ehrig, Mahr 90] H. Ehrig, B. Mahr: Fundamentals of algebraic specification 2. EATCS Monographs on Theor. Comp. Science, Vol. 21, Springer Verlag, 1990.

[Gaudel, Moineau 88] M. C. Gaudel, Th. Moineau: A theory of software reusability. In: H. Ganzinger (ed.): Proc. ESOP '88. Lecture Notes in Computer Science 300, 115-130, 1988.

[Hennicker, Nickl 92] R. Hennicker, F. Nickl: A behavioural algebraic framework for modular system design with reuse. Technical report 9206, Institut für Informatik, Ludwig-Maximilians-Universität München.

[Milner et al. 90] R. Milner, M. Tofte, R. Harper. The definition of Standard ML. MIT Press, 1990.

[Orejas, Nivela 90] F. Orejas, M. P. Nivela: Constraints for behavioural specifications. In: H. Ehrig, K. P. Jantke, F. Orejas, H. Reichel (eds): Recent Trends in Data Type Specification, *Proc. 7th Workshop on Specification of Abstract Data Types*, Wusterhausen/Dosse, April 1990. Lecture Notes in Computer Science 534, 220-245, 1990.

[Reichel 85] H. Reichel: Initial restrictions of behaviour. IFIP *Working Conference*, The Role of Abstract Models in Information Processing, 1985.

[Sannella et al. 90] D.T. Sannella, S. Sokolowski, A.Tarlecki: Toward formal development of programs from algebraic specifications: parameterization revisited. Forschungsberichte des Studienganges 6/90, Univ. Bremen, 1990.

[Wirsing 86] M. Wirsing: Structured algebraic specifications: a kernel language.*Theor.Comp.Science* 42,123-249, 1986.

[Wirsing 88] M. Wirsing: Algebraic description of reusable software components. In: E. Milgrom, P. Wodon (eds.): Proc. COMPEURO '88. IEEE Computer Society, 834, Computer Society Press, 300-312, 1988.

[Wirsing et al. 89] M. Wirsing, R. Hennicker, R. Stabl: MENU - an example for the systematic reuse of specifications. In: C. Ghezzi, J. A. McDermid (eds.): *Proc.* ESEC '89, 2nd European Software Engineering Conference, Warwick, September 1989. Springer 387, 20-41, 1989.

On fibred adjunctions and completeness for fibred categories

Claudio Hermida
Computer Science Department,
Aarhus University.
e-mail: chermida@daimi.aau.dk

November 14, 1993

Abstract

We show how the completeness and cocompleteness of the total category of a fibration can be inferred from that of the fibre categories and its base. Our results are somewhat stronger than those in [BGT91] and they are obtained as direct consequences of an important property of general fibred adjunctions. Our aim is to show that fibred category theory can provide insight into constructions of relevance in algebraic specifications, *e.g.* limits and colimits of many-sorted algebras, by explaining them at a natural level of abstraction.

1. Introduction

In [BGT91], Tarlecki *et al.* present, in a tutorial fashion, indexed categories as applied in algebraic specifications, in particular in the theory of institutions [GB90]. The examples presented there include many-sorted algebraic signatures, many-sorted algebras and theories and presentations in an institution. An indexed category induces a total category (loosely speaking, the 'disjoint sum' of its fibres) and the authors go on to show sufficient conditions for this category to be (co)complete, thereby obtaining proofs of (co)completeness for some of the examples mentioned before. However the conditions for completeness and cocompleteness are rather asymmetric, *i.e.* duality is not explicit.

In this paper, we present slightly stronger versions of the abovementioned results as consequences of a factorisation property of general fibred adjunctions, *i.e.* an adjunction between fibrations over possibly different bases. Fibrations – also referred to as fibred categories – and indexed categories are essentially equivalent notions, although the former are technically more convenient to work with. The above mentioned asymmetry for completeness and cocompleteness of fibred categories is best understood by looking at cofibrations as well as fibrations, and letting duality do the work – see Corollaries 3.5 and 3.8. As pointed out in [BGT91] the (co)completeness results, in the sharper version we present here, were already contained in [Gra66]. However our proofs are different (and simpler), since the property of general fibred adjunctions we use is not present there.

Besides the applications of indexed categories in algebraic specification presented in [BGT91], it is worth mentioning a few other applications of fibrations of relevance to computer science. [Win90] contains applications of fibrations to the semantics of concurrency via (labelled) transition systems; finite completeness and cocompleteness of the (total) fibred category are put to use in this context as well as (vertical) fibred adjunctions. More significantly, fibrations are the key ingredient in the categorical semantics of (proof-theoretic) logics and type theories; see [Jac91] for a comprehensive account. Actually, we discovered Thm. 3.4 below when analysing logical relations [Mit90] categorically, motivated by [MR91]; such analysis fits within the application of fibred categories to (the semantics of) logic just mentioned. See [Her93] for details.

One further application which fits within the algebraic specification tradition is the description of strong data types, or data types with parameters, as in [Jac93b]. The description essentially relies on initial algebras for endofunctors on a distributive category, and can be used to obtain structural induction principles for the corresponding datatypes, as explained in [Her93].

Since we do not assume familiarity with either indexed categories or fibrations, we include some background material about both in §2. None of the material in that section is original. §3 deals with general fibred adjunctions and completeness. It contains the main technical result of the paper, namely Thm. 3.4, and the above mentioned characterisation of (co)completeness for the total category of a (co)fibration. This material is essentially the contents of Chapter 3 in [Her93], where full proofs can be found. Since the purpose of this paper is mainly to show how to apply Thm. 3.4 to the situation at hand, we omit the tedious technical details of its proof.

The paper is meant to be reasonably self-contained, but we do assume familiarity with basic notions of category theory, which can be found in [Mac71]. There are ocasional references to the concept of 2-category, the paradigmatic example being *Cat*, in which for any two categories, the set of functors is itself a category whose morphisms are natural transformations. However, this level of abstraction is not essential to understand the paper since we express the definitions and results on an elementary level. Anyway, the interested reader may be willing to consult [KS74] for the basics on 2-categories.

2. Basics of fibred and indexed categories

This section reviews some standard basic concepts and properties concerning indexed categories and fibrations. The presentation follows [Jac91, Jac93a, Her93], where the reader may find considerably more information and references. The examples are mostly drawn from [BGT91]. We begin by fixing some notation which will be used throughout. Categories will generally be denoted **A**, **B**, *etc.* *Set* will denote the category of sets and functions (relative to some given universe, as in [Mac71, p.21]) and *Cat* denotes the 2-category of categories, functors and natural transformations.

The notion of fibration or fibred category, introduced in [Gro71], captures the concept of a category varying over (or indexed by) another category. Before giving the actual definition, we recall the analogous situation for sets, which may help convey the intuition about the categorical concept. A family $\{X_i\}_{i\in I}$ of sets indexed by a set I corresponds to a function $X : I \to \mathit{Set}$. We may think of this as a 'set' X varying over I. It can be equivalently presented as a function $p : X \to I$, since such a function gives rise to the family $\{X_i = p^{-1}(i)\}_{i\in I}$ and conversely, given a family $\{X_i\}_{i\in I}$ we get $p : \coprod_{i\in I} X_i \to I$, where $\coprod_{i\in I} X_i$ is the disjoint union of the X_i's and p maps an element in X_i to i. It is clear that such constructions (between morphisms into I and I-indexed families) are inverse to each other. We can summarise this situation by the following isomorphism of categories:

$$\mathit{Set}/I \cong \mathit{Set}^I$$

where Set/I denotes the usual slice category of morphisms into I and commutative triangles, and Set^I is the category of functors from I (regarded as a discrete category) to Set. These two equivalent views of indexed families of sets have their categorical counterparts: a function $X : I \to Set$ is generalised to an indexed category, *cf.* Def. 2.1, while a function $p : X \to I$ is generalised to a fibration, *cf.* Def. 2.6. The isomorphism above becomes then an equivalence between fibred and indexed categories, *cf.* Prop. 2.10 below. Despite this equivalence, the notion of fibration is technically more convenient, as forcibly argued in [Bén85]. We start off with the definition of indexed category, since it seems to be the more intuitive of the two notions.

2.1. Indexed categories

We recall the definitions of indexed categories and their associated morphisms: indexed functors and indexed natural transformations. The purpose is to set up a (2-)category of indexed categories where we can deal with the structure of indexed categories in a similar way as we do with an ordinary category within Cat. The standard reference for indexed categories is [PS78].

2.1. Definition (Indexed category). Given a category $\mathbf{B}$, a $\mathbf{B}$-*indexed category* is a pseudo-functor $\mathcal{F} : \mathbf{B}^{op} \to Cat$, *i.e.* it is given by the following data

- For every object $A \in |\mathbf{B}|$, a category $\mathcal{F}A$ (usually called a *fibre*).
- For every arrow $f : A \to B$ in $\mathbf{B}$, a *reindexing* functor $\mathcal{F}(f) = f^* : \mathcal{F}B \to \mathcal{F}A$, together with natural isomorphisms $\gamma_A : 1_{\mathcal{F}A} \cong 1_A^*$ and $\delta_{f,g} : f^* \circ g^* \cong (g \circ f)^*$ satisfying the following coherence conditions: for $u : A \to B$, $v : B \to C$ and $w : D \to A$ in $\mathbf{B}$

$$\begin{aligned} \delta_{u,1_B} \circ u^*\gamma_B &= 1_{u^*} \\ \delta_{1_A,u} \circ \gamma_A u^* &= 1_{u^*} \\ \delta_{w,v\circ u} \circ w^*\delta_{u,v} &= \delta_{u\circ w,v} \circ \delta_{w,u}v^* : w^* \circ u^* \circ v^* \to (v \circ u \circ w)^* \end{aligned}$$

2.2. Remark. The coherence conditions above express associativity and identity laws. Their role will become clear with Prop. 2.10.iii. Quite often these isomorphisms are actual identities, in which case we have a *strict* indexed category, which amounts simply to a functor $\mathcal{F} : \mathbf{B}^{op} \to Cat$. This simpler version is the only one considered in [BGT91]. Even when this case is seemingly standard for the examples in *ibid.*, the more general case is important, at least for the definition of completeness conditions – see §2.3.

2.3. Examples.

(i) (*Many-sorted sets*) Consider the following functor $SS : Set^{op} \to Cat$

$$\begin{aligned} SS(I) &= Set^I \\ SS(f : I \to J) &= (X : J \to Set) \mapsto (X \circ f : I \to Set) \end{aligned}$$

Note that the objects of a fibre $SS(I)$ correspond to families of sets, as remarked before. The functor $SS(f : I \to J)$ performs reindexing along f. The coherent isomorphisms are simply identities.

(ii) (*Many-sorted algebraic signatures*) Consider the functor $(\_)^+ : Set \to Set$, which assigns to a set S the free semigroup it generates, *i.e.* the set S^+ of all finite non-empty sequences of elements of S. The functor $\mathcal{AS} = \mathcal{SS} \circ ((\_)^+)^{op} : \mathit{Set}^{op} \to \mathit{Cat}$ is then an indexed category; its fibres $\mathcal{AS}(S)$ correspond to S-sorted algebraic signatures, *i.e.* for every non-empty sequence $s_1, \ldots, s_n \in S^+$ (regarded as arity or rank $s_1, \ldots, s_{n-1} \to s_n$), a set of operation symbols (of that rank). A reindexing functor $\mathcal{AS}(f : S \to S')$ transforms S'-sorted signatures into S-sorted signatures by renaming sorts according to f.

For an ordinary category, we can deal with some of its structure, e.g. (co)limits, in terms of functors and natural transformations; these are required to define the important notion of adjunction. Similarly, in order to talk about structure in an indexed category, we need the notions of indexed functor and indexed natural transformation, so that we can define indexed adjunctions. We will denote adjunctions (standard, indexed and fibred) by $F \dashv G : \mathbf{B} \to \mathbf{A}$ (via η, ϵ), where $F : \mathbf{A} \to \mathbf{B}$ is left adjoint to $G : \mathbf{B} \to \mathbf{A}$ (with unit η and counit ϵ, which we will frequently leave implicit) [Mac71, Thm.2.(v),p.81].

2.4. **Definition.** Let $\mathcal{F} : \mathbf{B}^{op} \to \mathit{Cat}$ and $\mathcal{G} : \mathbf{B}^{op} \to \mathit{Cat}$ be indexed categories.

- An *indexed functor* $\mathcal{H} : \mathcal{F} \to \mathcal{G}$ consists of:
  (i) For every $A \in |\mathbf{B}|$, a functor $\mathcal{H}(A) : \mathcal{F}(A) \to \mathcal{G}(A)$
  (ii) For every $u : A \to B$, a natural isomorphism $\phi_u : \mathcal{G}(u) \circ \mathcal{H}(B) \dot{\to} \mathcal{H}(A) \circ \mathcal{F}(u)$,
  satisfying the following coherence conditions: for $u : A \to B$, $v : B \to C$:

$$\begin{aligned} \phi_{1_A} \circ H(A)\gamma_A &= \gamma_A H(A) \\ \phi_{v \circ u} \circ H(A)\,\delta_{u,v} &= \delta_{u,v} H(C) \circ u^* \phi_v \circ \phi_u v^* \end{aligned}$$

- An *indexed natural transformation* $\alpha : \mathcal{H} \Rightarrow \mathcal{H}'$, for indexed functors $\mathcal{H}, \mathcal{H}' : \mathcal{F} \to \mathcal{G}$, consists of a natural transformation $\alpha_A : \mathcal{H}(A) \dot{\to} \mathcal{H}'(A)$ (for every object $A \in |\mathbf{B}|$) such that for every $u : A \to B$, $\mathcal{G}(u)\alpha_B = \alpha_A \mathcal{F}(u)$ (modulo the ϕ_u's)

2.5. **Remark.** Having defined indexed functors and indexed natural transformations, the notion of indexed adjunction is then analogous to the standard notion of adjunction between categories. We can give the following description, which the reader might find more intuitive: given indexed functors $\mathcal{H} : (\mathcal{F} : \mathbf{B}^{op} \to \mathit{Cat}) \to (\mathcal{G} : \mathbf{B}^{op} \to \mathit{Cat})$ and $\mathcal{H}' : (\mathcal{G} : \mathbf{B}^{op} \to \mathit{Cat}) \to (\mathcal{F} : \mathbf{B}^{op} \to \mathit{Cat})$, $\mathcal{H}$ is an indexed left adjoint to $\mathcal{H}'$ iff:

- For every $A \in |\mathbf{B}|$, $\mathcal{H}_A \dashv \mathcal{H}'_A$.
- For every $u : A \to B$, the pair $(\mathcal{F}(u), \mathcal{G}(u))$ preserves the adjunctions, *i.e.* it is a (pseudo-)map of adjunctions from $\mathcal{H}_B \dashv \mathcal{H}'_B$ to $\mathcal{H}_A \dashv \mathcal{H}'_A$ similarly to [Mac71, p.97].

Thus, indexed categories over a given category $\mathbf{B}$, indexed functors and indexed natural transformations form a (2-)category $\mathcal{I}\mathit{Cat}(\mathbf{B})$, with the evident 'fibrewise' notions of composition and identities, inherited from Cat.

2.2. Fibrations

Since the primary focus of this paper will be on fibrations instead of indexed categories, we now introduce fibred categories and show their equivalence to indexed categories, so as to set the scene for work within the 'fibred' context.

2.6. **Definition** (Fibrations and cofibrations). Consider a functor $p : \mathbf{E} \to \mathbf{B}$. We have:

(i) A morphism $f : X \to Y$ in $\mathbf{E}$ is (p-)*cartesian* (over a morphism $u : A \to B$ in $\mathbf{B}$) if $p f = u$ and, for every $f' : X' \to Y$ with $p f' = u \circ v$ in $\mathbf{B}$, there exists a unique morphism $\phi_{f'} : X' \to X$ such that $p \phi_{f'} = v$ and $f' = f \circ \phi_f$. Diagrammatically,

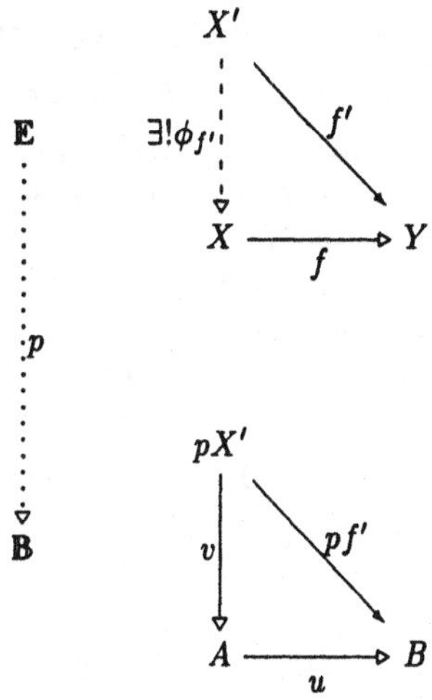

Thus, we may say a cartesian f is a 'terminal lifting' of u. We call such f a cartesian *lifting* of u.

(ii) Dually, a morphism $g : X \to Y$ is (p-)*cocartesian* (over a morphism $u : A \to B$ in $\mathbf{B}$) if $pg = u$ and, for every $g' : X \to Y'$ with $pg' = w \circ u$ in $\mathbf{B}$, there exists a unique morphism $\psi_{g'} : Y \to Y'$ such that $p \phi_{g'} = w$ and $g' = \psi_{g'} \circ g$.

(iii) The functor $p : \mathbf{E} \to \mathbf{B}$ is called a *fibration* if for every $X \in |\mathbf{E}|$ and $u : A \to pX$ in $\mathbf{B}$, there is a cartesian morphism with codomain X above u, *i.e.* such that its image along p is u. $\mathbf{B}$ is then called the *base* of the fibration and $\mathbf{E}$ its *total category*. Dually, p is a *cofibration* if $p^{op} : \mathbf{E}^{op} \to \mathbf{B}^{op}$ is a fibration, *i.e.* for every $X \in |\mathbf{E}|$ and $u : pX \to B$ in $\mathbf{B}$, there is a cocartesian morphism with domain X above u. If p is both a fibration and a cofibration, it is called a *bifibration*.

(iv) For $A \in |\mathbf{B}|$, $\mathbf{E}_A$, the *fibre* over A, denotes the subcategory of $\mathbf{E}$ whose objects are above A and its morphisms, called (p-)*vertical*, are above 1_A.

2.7. Example (Family fibration). The following standard construction of a fibration over *Set* is described in [Bén85]. It provides a simple way of understanding the origin of (the terminology for) some fibred concepts. Every category $\mathbf{C}$ gives rise to a family fibration $f(\mathbf{C}) : \mathit{Fam}(\mathbf{C}) \to \mathit{Set}$. Objects of $\mathit{Fam}(\mathbf{C})$ are families $\{X_i\}_{i \in I}$ of $\mathbf{C}$-objects, i.e. $X : I \to |\mathbf{C}|$; morphisms $(u, \{f_i\}_{i\in I}) : \{X_i\}_{i\in I} \to \{Y_j\}_{j \in J}$ are pairs consisting of a function $u : I \to J$ (in *Set*) and a family of morphisms such that $f_i : X_i \to Y_{u(i)}$ in $\mathbf{C}$. $f(C)$ takes a family of objects to its indexing set and a morphism to its first component. $(u, \{f_i\}_{i\in I})$ is cartesian when every f_i is an isomorphism. $f(C)$ is then a fibration since given $u : I \to J$ and $\{Y_j\}_{j\in J}$, $(u, \{1_{Y_{u(i)}}\}) : \{Y_{u(i)}\}_{i\in I} \to \{Y_j\}_{j\in J}$ is cartesian above u.

If a functor $p : \mathbf{E} \to \mathbf{B}$ is a fibration, we will frequently display it as $\begin{smallmatrix}\mathbf{E}\\ \downarrow p\\ \mathbf{B}\end{smallmatrix}$. A choice of cartesian lifting for every appropriate morphism in $\mathbf{B}$ is called a *cleavage* for p (which is then a *cloven* fibration) and denoted by $\overline{(\_)}$, so that for $u : A \to pX$ in $\mathbf{B}$, $\overline{u}(X) : u^*(X) \to X$ is a cartesian morphism above u. Actually any fibration can be turned into a cloven one, using the axiom of choice to obtain a cleavage. In case we have for any pair of composable morphisms u and v that $\overline{u \circ v}(X) = \overline{u}(X) \circ \overline{v}(u^*(X))$ and $\overline{1_A}(X) = 1_X$, the cleavage is a *splitting* and the fibration is *split*. Dually, if p is a cofibration, given $X \in \mathbf{E}_A$ and $u : A \to B$ in $\mathbf{B}$, we denote $\underline{(u)} : X \to u_!(X)$ a cocartesian lifting of u (at X).

A cleavage for $\begin{array}{c}\mathbf{E}\\ \downarrow p\\ \mathbf{B}\end{array}$ induces, for every $u : A \to B$ in $\mathbf{B}$, a *reindexing functor* $u^* : \mathbf{E}_B \to \mathbf{E}_A$ as follows: for $X \in |\mathbf{E}_B|$ let $u^*(X)$ be the domain of the cartesian morphism over u given by the cleavage, and for $f : X \to Y$ in $\mathbf{E}_B$ let $u^*(f) : u^*X \to u^*Y$ be the unique vertical morphism such that $f \circ \overline{u}(X) = \overline{u}(Y) \circ u^*(f)$.

Just as we did before with indexed categories, we will need notions of functors and natural transformations between fibrations.

2.8. **Definition.** Consider two fibrations $\begin{array}{c}\mathbf{E}\\ \downarrow p\\ \mathbf{B}\end{array}$ and $\begin{array}{c}\mathbf{D}\\ \downarrow q\\ \mathbf{A}\end{array}$.

- A morphism $(H, K) : p \to q$ is given by a commutative square

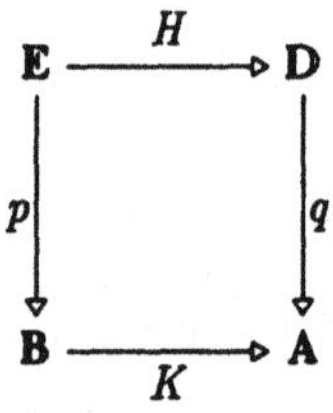

where H preserves cartesian morphisms, meaning that if f is p-cartesian, Hf is q-cartesian. (H, K) is called a *fibred 1-cell*; it determines a collection $\{H|_A : \mathbf{E}_A \to \mathbf{D}_{KA}\}_{A \in \mathbf{B}}$.

When p and q are fibrations with the same base category $\mathbf{B}$, we may consider fibred 1-cells of the form $(H, 1_\mathbf{B}) : p \to q$, which are then given by functor H such that $q \circ H = p$ and preserves cartesian morphisms. Such an H will be called a *fibred functor*, written $H : p \to q$.

- Given fibred 1-cells $(H, K), (G, L) : p \to q$, a *fibred 2-cell* from (H, K) to (G, L) is a pair of natural transformations $(\tau : H \to G, \sigma : K \to L)$ with τ above σ, meaning that $q\tau_X = \sigma_{pX}$ for every $X \in \mathbf{E}$. We will display such a fibred 2-cell as follows

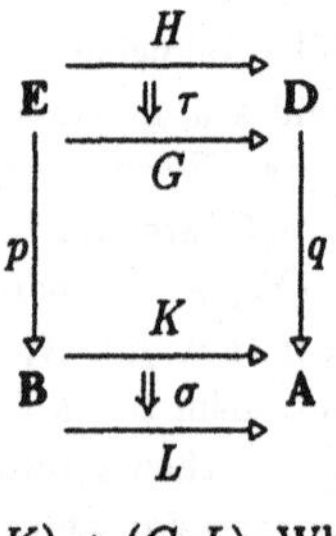

and we will write it as $(\tau, \sigma) : (H, K) \Rightarrow (G, L)$. When p and q are fibrations with the same base category $\mathbf{B}$, we may consider 'vertical' 2-cells of the form $(\tau, 1_{1_\mathbf{B}}) : (H, 1_\mathbf{B}) \Rightarrow (G, 1_\mathbf{B})$ between fibred functors H and G, which amount then to natural transformations $\tau : H \to G$ such that $q\tau = 1_p$. Such a 2-cell will be called a *fibred natural transformation*.

We thus obtain a (2-)category $\mathcal{F}ib(\mathbf{B})$ consisting of fibrations over $\mathbf{B}$, fibred functors between them (and fibred natural transformations), with compositions and identities inherited from $\mathcal{C}at$. More generally, considering fibrations over an arbitrary base category, fibred 1-cells (and fibred 2-cells) we have a (2-)category $\mathcal{F}ib$. For instance, the 'model part' of an institution morphism [GB90] is a fibred 1-cell, that is, a morphism in $\mathcal{F}ib$. Dually, we have (2-)categories $\mathcal{C}o\mathcal{F}ib$(resp. $\mathcal{C}o\mathcal{F}ib(\mathbf{B})$ of cofibrations (over $\mathbf{B}$) and (vertical) cofibred 1-cells and 2-cells.

2.9. **Remark.** Similarly to Remark 2.5, the definition of fibred 1-cells and 2-cells (resp. that of fibred functors and fibred natural transformations) determines what an adjunction between fibrations (resp. fibred adjunctions) is. We spell out fibred adjunctions: given fibrations $\begin{array}{c}\mathbf{E}\\ \downarrow p\\ \mathbf{B}\end{array}$ and $\begin{array}{c}\mathbf{D}\\ \downarrow q\\ \mathbf{B}\end{array}$, an adjunction between them is given by a pair of fibred functors $F : p \to q$ and $G : q \to p$ together with fibred natural transformations $\eta : 1_{\mathbf{E}} \dot{\to} GF$ and $\epsilon : FG \dot{\to} 1_{\mathbf{D}}$ such that $F \dashv G$ (in the standard sense, with unit η and counit ϵ).

We will now show the correspondence between (cloven) fibrations and indexed categories, due to Grothendieck, which amounts to an equivalence between the (2-)categories $\mathcal{F}ib(\mathbf{B})$ and $\mathcal{I}\mathcal{C}at(\mathbf{B})$.

2.10. **Proposition.**

(i) *Every cloven fibration* $\begin{array}{c}\mathbf{E}\\ \downarrow p\\ \mathbf{B}\end{array}$ *gives rise to an indexed category* $\mathcal{F}_p : \mathbf{B}^{op} \to \mathcal{C}at$.

(ii) *Every indexed category* $\mathcal{F} : \mathbf{B}^{op} \to \mathcal{C}at$ *gives rise to a fibration* $p_{\mathcal{F}} : \mathcal{G}\mathcal{F} \to \mathbf{B}$ (**Grothendieck construction**).

(iii) *The above correspondences yield an equivalence of (2-)categories*

$$\mathcal{I}\mathcal{C}at(\mathbf{B}) \simeq \mathcal{F}ib(\mathbf{B})$$

so that $\mathcal{F}_{p_{\mathcal{F}}} \simeq \mathcal{F}$ *and* $p_{\mathcal{F}_p} \simeq p$.

Proof. (Sketch)

(i) Given a cloven fibration $p : \mathbf{E} \to \mathbf{B}$, we obtain an indexed category $\mathcal{F}_p : \mathbf{B}^{op} \to \mathcal{C}at$ as follows:

- For every $A \in |\mathbf{B}|$, $\mathcal{F}_p A = \mathbf{E}_A$.
- For every $u : A \to B$, a cleavage $\overline{(\_)}$ induces a reindexing functor $u^* : \mathbf{E}_B \to \mathbf{E}_A$ as described before Def. 2.8. The universal property of cartesian morphisms uniquely determines natural isomorphisms $\delta_{v,u} : v^* \circ u^* \dot{\to} (u \circ v)^*$ and $\gamma_A : 1_A \dot{\to} 1^*_{pA}$, which satisfy the coherence conditions in Def. 2.1.

(ii) Given an indexed category $\mathcal{F} : \mathbf{B}^{op} \to \mathcal{C}at$ we define the total category $\mathcal{G}\mathcal{F}$, consisting of:

Objects: $\langle A, a\rangle \in |\mathcal{G}\mathcal{F}|$ iff $A \in |\mathbf{B}|$ and $a \in |\mathcal{F}A|$. That is (using a hopefully self-explanatory dependent sum notation)

$$|\mathcal{G}\mathcal{F}| = \Sigma A : \mathrm{B}.\mathcal{F}A$$

Morphisms: $\langle f, g\rangle : \langle A, a\rangle \to \langle B, b\rangle$ iff $f : A \to B$ in $\mathbf{B}$ and $g : a \to f^*(b)$ in $\mathcal{F}A$. That is

$$\mathcal{G}\mathcal{F}(\langle A, a\rangle, \langle B, b\rangle) = \Sigma f : \mathbf{B}(A, B).\mathcal{F}A(a, f^* b)$$

Identity: $\langle 1_A, \gamma_A\rangle : \langle A, a\rangle \to \langle A, a\rangle$
Composition: Given $\langle f, g\rangle : \langle A, a\rangle \to \langle B, b\rangle$ and $\langle h, j\rangle : \langle B, b\rangle \to \langle C, c\rangle$, let

$$\langle h, j\rangle \circ \langle f, g\rangle = \langle h \circ f, \delta_{f,h}(c) \circ f^* j \circ g\rangle$$

Note that the coherence conditions of Def. 2.1 are required in order to show associativity of composition and the identity laws. The projection functor $p_{\mathcal{F}} : \mathcal{GF} \to \mathbf{B}$ which takes $\langle A, a\rangle$ to A (for objects and arrows) is then a fibration: for an arrow $u : A \to B$ in $\mathbf{B}$ and an object X in $\mathcal{F}B$, we can choose as cartesian lifting $\bar{u}(X) = \langle u, 1_{u^*X}\rangle$.

(iii) Simply observe that the fibres of $p_{\mathcal{F}}$ are $\mathcal{GF}_B = \mathcal{F}B$ and the action of the reindexing functors is the same in both fibrations and indexed categories (respectively). Note also that any pair of cleavages for a given fibration give rise to naturally isomorphic indexed categories.

□

2.11. **Remarks.**

- By duality, we get an analogous result relating cofibrations $p : \mathbf{E} \to \mathbf{B}$ and (pseudo-)functors $\mathcal{G} : \mathbf{B} \to \mathcal{C}at$ ('covariant indexed categories').
- The equivalence in the above proposition clearly restricts to one between split fibrations $\begin{smallmatrix}\mathbf{E}\\ \downarrow p\\ \mathbf{B}\end{smallmatrix}$ and functors $\mathcal{F} : \mathbf{B}^{op} \to \mathcal{C}at$ (strict indexed categories). This simplified version of indexed categories is the one considered in [BGT91], with similar assumptions about indexed functors (which then amount to natural transformations).

2.12. **Remark.** The 2-categorical aspect of the equivalence in Prop. 2.10.iii implies in particular a correspondence between indexed and fibred adjunctions. Thus, a fibred adjunction $F \dashv G : p \to q$ (between $\begin{smallmatrix}\mathbf{E}\\ \downarrow p\\ \mathbf{B}\end{smallmatrix}$ and $\begin{smallmatrix}\mathbf{D}\\ \downarrow q\\ \mathbf{B}\end{smallmatrix}$) amounts to a family of adjunctions $\{F\,|_B \dashv G\,|_B : \mathbf{E}_B \to \mathbf{D}_B\}_{B \in |\mathbf{B}|}$ such that for every $u : B \to B'$, (u^{*p}, u^{*q}) is a (pseudo-)map of adjunctions from $F\,|_{B'} \dashv G\,|_{B'}$ to $F\,|_B \dashv G\,|_B$, *cf.* Remark 2.5.

2.13. **Examples.**

- The family fibration $f(\mathbf{C}) : \mathcal{F}am(\mathbf{C}) \to \mathcal{S}et$ results from applying the Grothendieck construction to the (strict) $\mathcal{S}et$-indexed category

$$\begin{array}{rcl} I & \mapsto & \mathcal{S}et^I \\ u : I \to J & \mapsto & \_ \circ u : \mathcal{S}et^J \to \mathcal{S}et^I \end{array}$$

- (Many-sorted algebraic signatures) Applying the Grothendieck construction to $\mathcal{AS} : \mathcal{S}et^{op} \to \mathcal{C}at$ from Ex. 2.3.ii we obtain the usual category of algebraic signatures **AlgSig**, whose objects are pairs $\langle S, \{\Sigma_r\}_{r \in S^+}\rangle$, where S is a set of sorts and each Σ_r is a set of operation symbols of rank r. A morphism $\langle f, g\rangle : \langle S, \{\Sigma_r\}_{r \in S^+}\rangle \to \langle S', \{\Sigma'_r\}_{r \in (S')^+}\rangle$ consists of a renaming of sorts $f : S \to S'$ and a family of operation-symbol renamings $g = \{g_r : \Sigma_r \to \Sigma'_{f^+(r)}\}_{r \in S^+}$ compatible with f.

For a functor $p : \mathbf{E} \to \mathbf{B}$, given a morphism $u : A \to B$ in $\mathbf{B}$, $X \in |\mathbf{E}_A|$ and $Y \in |\mathbf{E}_B|$, let

$$\mathbf{E}_u(X, Y) = \{f : X \to Y \text{ in } \mathbf{E} \mid pf = u\}$$

With this notation we have the following proposition:

2.14. Proposition. *Let $p : \mathbf{E} \to \mathbf{B}$ be a functor, $u : A \to B$ a morphism in $\mathbf{B}$, $X \in |\mathbf{E}_A|$ and $Y \in |\mathbf{E}_B|$.*

(i) *If p is a fibration then $\mathbf{E}_u(X, Y) \cong \mathbf{E}_A(X, u^*(Y))$ (naturally in X and Y).*

(ii) *If p is a cofibration then $\mathbf{E}_u(X, Y) \cong \mathbf{E}_B(u_!(X), Y)$ (naturally in X and Y).*

(iii) *If p is a fibration then*

$$p \text{ is a cofibration iff for every } u : A \to B \text{ in } \mathbf{B},\ u^* : \mathbf{E}_B \to \mathbf{E}_A \text{ has a left adjoint}$$

(The claims above assume a given (co)cleavage for the (co)fibration p.)

Proof. (i) and (ii) are straightforward consequences of the definition of cartesian and cocartesian morphisms respectively. For (iii),

$$\mathbf{E}_A(X, u^*(Y)) \cong \mathbf{E}_u(X, Y) \cong \mathbf{E}_B(u_!(X), Y)$$

which means that the 'coreindexings' are left adjoints to the corresponding reindexing functors, *i.e.* $u_! \dashv u^* : \mathbf{E}_B \to \mathbf{E}_A$, where $u_! : \mathbf{E}_A \to \mathbf{E}_B$ is determined dually to u^* in the proof of Prop. 2.10.i. □

Finally, we introduce the change-of-base construction which, given a functor $K : \mathbf{B} \to \mathbf{A}$ and a fibration with base $\mathbf{A}$, yields a fibration with base $\mathbf{B}$.

2.15. Proposition. *Given a fibration $q : \mathbf{D} \to \mathbf{A}$ and an arbitrary functor $K : \mathbf{B} \to \mathbf{A}$, consider a pullback diagram*

$$\begin{array}{ccc} K^*(\mathbf{D}) & \xrightarrow{q^*(K)} & \mathbf{D} \\ {\scriptstyle K^*(q)}\downarrow & & \downarrow{\scriptstyle q} \\ \mathbf{B} & \xrightarrow[K]{} & \mathbf{A} \end{array}$$

$K^*(q)$ is a fibration, with a morphism f in $K^*(\mathbf{D})$ being $K^*(q)$-cartesian iff $q^*(K)(f)$ is q-cartesian. The above diagram is therefore a morphism of fibrations (fibred 1-cell).

In the situation of the above proposition, we say that $K^*(q)$ is obtained by change of base from q along K. Note that for $B \in \mathbf{B}$, $K^*(\mathbf{D})_B \cong \mathbf{D}_{KB}$. Clearly, the same construction applies to cofibrations.

2.16. Example. Regarding the indexed categories $\mathcal{SS}$ and $\mathcal{AS}$ (Ex. 2.3) as fibrations, $p_{\mathcal{AS}}$ is obtained from $p_{\mathcal{SS}}$ by change of base along the functor $(\_)^+ : \mathcal{S}et \to \mathcal{S}et$. This example illustrates the fact that change-of-base for an indexed category $\mathcal{F} : \mathbf{B}^{op} \to \mathcal{C}at$ along a functor $K : \mathbf{A} \to \mathbf{B}$ is obtained by composition, $K^*(\mathcal{F}) \cong \mathcal{F} \circ (K)^{op}$.

This concludes the prerequisites required to deal with some notions of completeness for fibrations (resp. indexed categories) in terms of adjunctions in the (2-)categories $\mathcal{F}ib(\mathbf{B})$ (resp. $\mathcal{I}\mathcal{C}at(\mathbf{B})$), which we consider next.

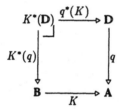

2.3. Fibrewise completeness and cocompleteness

We present fibrewise notions of completeness and cocompleteness for fibrations (and thus for indexed categories) in terms of fibred adjunctions. First, let us recall the situation with categories. Let $\mathbf{I}$ be a small category. For a category $\mathbf{C}$, a diagram of type $\mathbf{I}$ in $\mathbf{C}$ amounts to a functor $D : \mathbf{I} \to \mathbf{C}$, which is an object in the functor category $\mathbf{C}^{\mathbf{I}}$. The diagonal functor $\Delta_{\mathbf{I}} : \mathbf{C} \to \mathbf{C}^{\mathbf{I}}$ takes an object $X \in |\mathbf{C}|$ to the constant functor $\Delta_{\mathbf{I}}(X) = (I \mapsto X)$. The category $\mathbf{C}$ has $\mathbf{I}$-limits/colimits iff $\Delta_{\mathbf{I}}$ has a right/left adjoint [Mac71, p.85]. Notice that the 'only if' direction requires the axiom of choice to give an assignment of limit/colimit to every diagram of type $\mathbf{I}$.

For the analogous situation with fibrations, we need the following auxiliary result.

2.17. **Proposition.** *Given a fibration $p : \mathbf{E} \to \mathbf{B}$ and a small category $\mathbf{I}$, $p^I : \mathbf{E}^I \to \mathbf{B}^I$ is a fibration.*

Proof. A natural transformation $\alpha : F \dot{\to} G : \mathbf{I} \to \mathbf{E}$ is p^I-cartesian iff every component is p-cartesian. □

This fibration of functor categories and the change-of-base construction are used in the following definition of fibred (co)limits, due to J. Bénabou.

2.18. **Definition.** For any small category $\mathbf{I}$, a fibration $p : \mathbf{E} \to \mathbf{B}$ has fibred $\mathbf{I}$-limits (resp. colimits) iff the fibred functor $\widehat{\Delta_I} : p \to \Delta_I^*(p^I)$, uniquely determined in the diagram below, has a fibred right (resp. left) adjoint $\widehat{\Delta_I} \dashv \underleftarrow{\lim}_I$

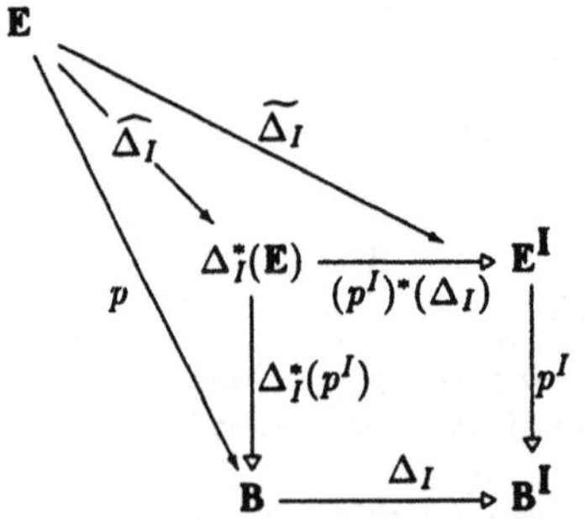

where $\Delta_I : \mathbf{B} \to \mathbf{B}^I$ and $\widetilde{\Delta_I} : \mathbf{E} \to \mathbf{E}^I$ are the diagonal functors taking objects A to constant functors $(I \mapsto A)$. A dual definition accounts for cofibred $\mathbf{I}$-limits/colimits for a cofibration.

Then, considering the fibrewise formulation of fibred adjunctions in Remark 2.12, a fibration $\begin{smallmatrix}\mathbf{E}\\ \downarrow p\\ \mathbf{B}\end{smallmatrix}$ has fibred $\mathbf{I}$-limits/colimits if every fibre has $\mathbf{I}$-limits/colimits (in their usual sense in $\mathcal{C}at$) and the reindexing functors (of any cleavage) are $\mathbf{I}$-continuous/cocontinuous (i.e. preserve $\mathbf{I}$-limits/colimits). If we were considering only split fibrations (or equivalently, strict indexed categories), the reindexing functors would have to preserve the specified limits/colimits 'on the nose', *i.e.* up to equality rather than up to isomorphism as required in the above definition.

2.19. **Example.** The fibration resulting from applying the Grothendieck construction to the indexed category $SS : \mathcal{S}et^{op} \to \mathcal{C}at$ of Ex. 2.3.i has fibred **I**-limits and colimits (for every small **I**): the fibres $SS(I) = \mathcal{S}et^{I}$ have all small limits and colimits, given pointwise, which are therefore preserved by the reindexing functors $u^* = \_ \circ u$.

We just mention that change-of-base preserves fibred limits/colimits; see [Jac91, Her93].

3. Fibred adjunctions and completeness

In this section we address the completeness of the total category of a fibration in terms of the fibrewise completeness of the fibration and the completeness of its base category. This will be done using a characterization of adjunctions in $\mathcal{F}ib$ in terms of those in $\mathcal{F}ib(\mathbf{B})$ (for suitable **B**) and those in $\mathcal{C}at$.

Let us make explicit the definition of adjunctions in $\mathcal{F}ib$ which, as already mentioned, is determined by the fact that $\mathcal{F}ib$ is a 2-category. We will call such adjunctions general fibred adjunctions.

3.1. **Definition.** Given $\begin{smallmatrix}\mathbf{E}\\ \downarrow p\\ \mathbf{B}\end{smallmatrix}$ and $\begin{smallmatrix}\mathbf{D}\\ \downarrow q\\ \mathbf{A}\end{smallmatrix}$, a *general fibred adjunction* between them is given by pair of fibred 1-cells $(\tilde{F}, F) : p \to q$ and $(\tilde{G}, G) : q \to p$ together with a pair of fibred 2-cells $(\tilde{\eta}, \eta) : (1_{\mathbf{E}}, 1_{\mathbf{B}}) \Rightarrow (\tilde{G} \circ \tilde{F}, G \circ F)$ and $(\tilde{\epsilon}, \epsilon) : (\tilde{F} \circ \tilde{G}, F \circ G) \Rightarrow (1_{\mathbf{D}}, 1_{\mathbf{A}})$ such that

(i) $\tilde{F} \dashv \tilde{G} : \mathbf{D} \to \mathbf{E}$ via $\tilde{\eta}$, $\tilde{\epsilon}$ (in $\mathcal{C}at$)

(ii) $F \dashv G : \mathbf{A} \to \mathbf{B}$ via η,ϵ (in $\mathcal{C}at$)

(iii) p and q constitute a map of adjunctions between the two above, i.e. $p\tilde{\eta} = \eta p$ (or equivalently $q\tilde{\epsilon} = \epsilon q$)

Such a fibred adjunction will be displayed in the following way

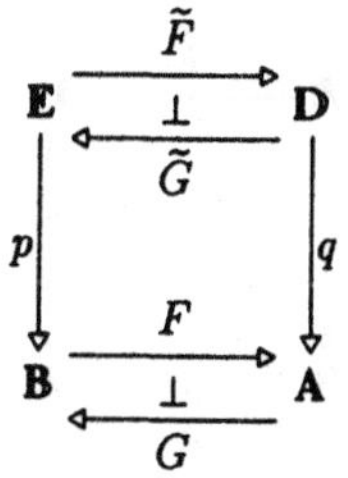

and written $(\tilde{F}, F) \dashv (\tilde{G}, G) : q \to p$. When the components of $\tilde{\eta}$ and $\tilde{\epsilon}$ are cartesian and the square $(\tilde{F}, F) : p \to q$ is a pullback, we shall call this situation a *cartesian fibred adjunction.* This terminology will be justified by Thm. 3.4.

In order to avoid going into heavy technical detail, we will simply state the main results about general fibred adjunctions we need. Full proofs may be found in [Her93], where the results are proved using mild 2-categorical reformulations of cartesian morphisms.

Firstly, change-of-base of a fibration along a left adjoint functor yields a cartesian fibred adjunction. More precisely, we have the following lemma:

3.2. **Lemma**. *Given* $\begin{array}{c}\mathbf{E}\\ \downarrow q\\ \mathbf{B}\end{array}$ *and an adjunction* $F \dashv G : \mathbf{B} \to \mathbf{A}$ *via* η, ϵ*, change-of-base along* F *yields a cartesian fibred adjunction*

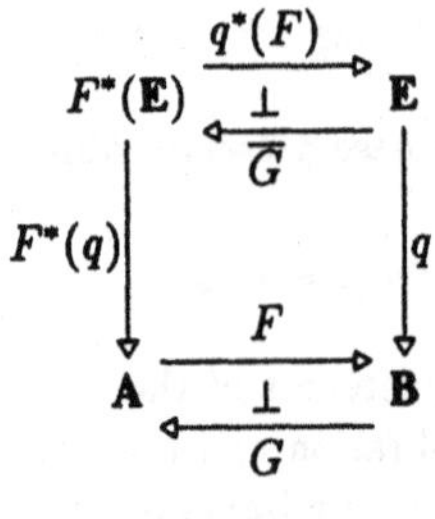

Proof. We only make explicit the cofree object. For $X \in |\mathbf{E}|$, $\overline{G}X$ is the unique object of $F^*(\mathbf{E})$ such that $q^*(F)(\overline{G}X) = \epsilon^*_{qX}(X)$ and $F^*(q)(\overline{G}X) = GqX$. Thus $\overline{G}X$ is determined by the reindexing functor ϵ^*_{qX}. □

3.3. **Remark**. Dually, change-of-base of a cofibration along a right adjoint yields cartesian cofibred adjunctions. This yields as a particular case Lemma 2 in [BGT91].

The above lemma proves one direction of the equivalence in the following theorem, which provides a factorization of general fibred adjunctions in terms of cartesian fibred adjunctions and fibred adjunctions. Cartesian fibred adjunctions are thus cartesian morphisms for a suitable fibration, with change-of-base providing a cleavage for it. Without further details, we state our main result on general fibred adjunctions, which we will apply later to obtain the purported characterisation of completeness for the total category of a fibration.

3.4. **Theorem**. *Given* $\begin{array}{c}\mathbf{E}\\ \downarrow p\\ \mathbf{B}\end{array}$, $\begin{array}{c}\mathbf{D}\\ \downarrow q\\ \mathbf{A}\end{array}$, $F \dashv G : \mathbf{A} \to \mathbf{B}$ *via* η, ϵ *and a fibred 1-cell* $(\tilde{F}, F) : p \to q$ *as shown in the following diagram*

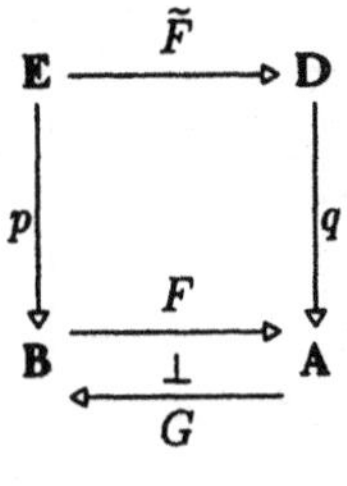

let $\widehat{F} : p \to F^*(q)$ *in* $Fib(\mathbf{B})$ *be the unique mediating functor in*

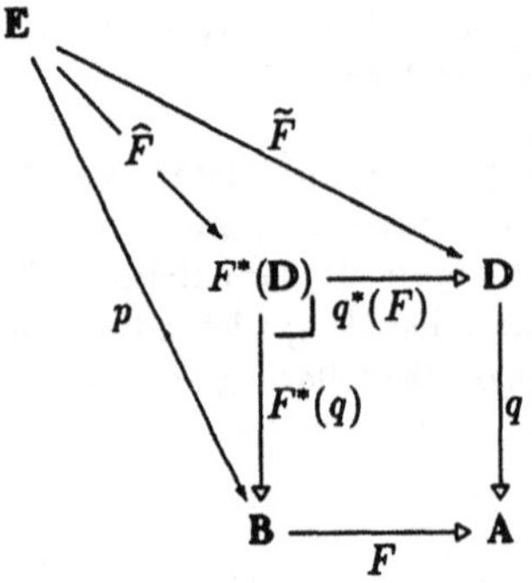

Then, the following statements are equivalent:

(i) *There exists* $\tilde{G} : \mathbf{D} \to \mathbf{E}$ *such that* $\tilde{F} \dashv \tilde{G}$ *(in Cat) and* $(\tilde{F}, F) \dashv (\tilde{G}, G) : q \to p$ *(in* $\mathcal{F}ib$*).*

(ii) *There exists* $\hat{G} : F^*(q) \to p$ *such that* $\hat{F} \dashv \hat{G}$ *(in* $\mathcal{F}ib(\mathbf{B})$*).*

Proof. We only show $(ii) \Rightarrow (i)$ since we will need the explicit description of the resulting $\tilde{G}$ later on. By Lemma 3.2, there is a $\overline{G} : \mathbf{D} \to F^*(\mathbf{D})$. We obtain the desired right adjoint by composition of adjoints: $\tilde{G} = \hat{G} \circ \overline{G}$. □

By duality, we get the following statement about adjunctions between cofibrations.

3.5. Corollary. *Given cofibrations* $p : \mathbf{E} \to \mathbf{B}$ *and* $q : \mathbf{D} \to \mathbf{A}$, $F \dashv G : \mathbf{B} \to \mathbf{A}$ *via* η, ϵ *and a fibred 1-cell* $(\tilde{G}, G) : p \to q$ *as shown in the following diagram*

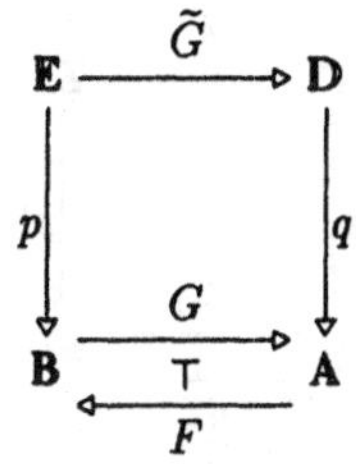

let $\hat{G} : p \to G^*(q)$ *in* $Co\mathcal{F}ib(\mathbf{B})$ *be the unique mediating functor in*

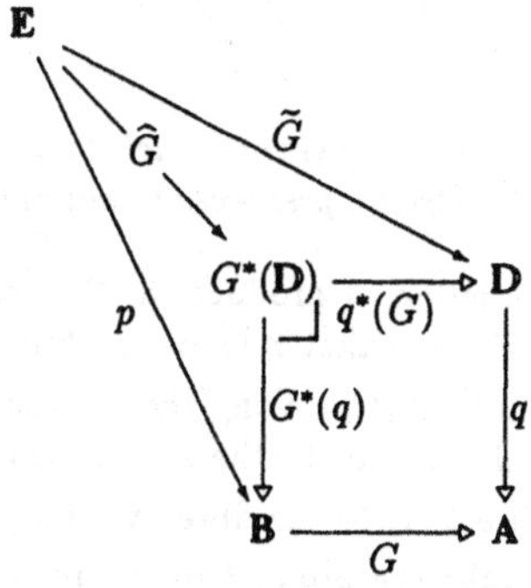

Then, the following statements are equivalent:

(i) *There exists* $\tilde{F} : \mathbf{D} \to \mathbf{E}$ *such that* $\tilde{F} \dashv \tilde{G}$ *(in Cat) and* $(\tilde{F}, F) \dashv (\tilde{G}, G) : p \to q$ *(in* $Co\mathcal{F}ib$*).*

(ii) *There exists* $\hat{F} : G^*(q) \to p$ *such that* $\hat{F} \dashv \hat{G}$ *(in* $Co\mathcal{F}ib(\mathbf{B})$*).*

Furthermore, the correspondence $\hat{F} \leftrightarrow \tilde{F}$ *is one-to-one.*

In order to apply the Thm. 3.4 to obtain completeness conditions for the total category of a fibration, we will need the following property of right adjoints in a slice category $Cat/\mathbf{B}$. The first part is essentially [Win90, Lemma 4.5] while the second part is a straightforward generalisation. $Cat^{\to}$ is the category of functors and commutative squares.

3.6. Lemma. (i) *Given* $\begin{matrix}\mathbf{E}\\ \downarrow p\\ \mathbf{B}\end{matrix}$, $\begin{matrix}\mathbf{D}\\ \downarrow q\\ \mathbf{B}\end{matrix}$, *a 1-cell* $G : q \to p$ *in* $Cat/\mathbf{B}$*, if there is* $F : p \to q$ *such that* $F \dashv G$ *in* $Cat/\mathbf{B}$ *then* G *is a fibred 1-cell, i.e.* G *preserves cartesian morphisms.*

(ii) *Given* $\begin{array}{c}\mathbf{E}\\ \downarrow p\\ \mathbf{B}\end{array}$, $\begin{array}{c}\mathbf{D}\\ \downarrow q\\ \mathbf{B}\end{array}$, *a 1-cell* $(\tilde{G}, G) : q \to p$ *in* $\mathcal{C}at^{\to}$, *if there is* $(\tilde{F}, F) : p \to q$ *such that* $(\tilde{F}, F) \dashv (\tilde{G}, G)$ *in* $\mathcal{C}at^{\to}$ *then* $(\tilde{G}, G)$ *is a fibred 2-cell, i.e.* $\tilde{G}$ *preserves cartesian morphisms.*

The above lemma means that 'right adjoints preserve cartesian morphisms'. Now we can state the following characterisation of limits in the total category of a fibration, as well as its dual for colimits and cofibrations.

3.7. Corollary. *Let* $\mathbf{I}$ *be a small category and* $\begin{array}{c}\mathbf{E}\\ \downarrow p\\ \mathbf{B}\end{array}$ *be a fibration such that* $\mathbf{B}$ *has* $\mathbf{I}$*-limits. Then* p *has fibred* $\mathbf{I}$*-limits iff* $\mathbf{E}$ *has and* p *strictly preserves* $\mathbf{I}$*-limits.*

Proof. Apply Thm. 3.4 to the following data (recall $p^I : \mathbf{E}^I \to \mathbf{B}^I$ is a fibration by Prop. 2.17)

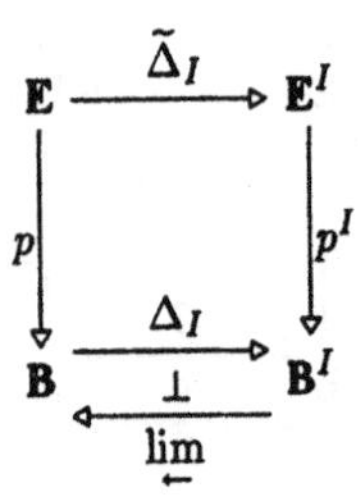

$\mathbf{E}$ has and p strictly preserves $\mathbf{I}$-limits means precisely that the above diagram can be completed to an adjunction $(\widetilde{\Delta_I}, \Delta_I) \dashv (\widetilde{\underleftarrow{\lim}}, \underleftarrow{\lim})$ in $\mathcal{C}at^{\to}$, which by Lemma 3.6.(ii) is an adjunction in $\mathcal{F}ib$. □

3.8. Corollary. *Let* $r : \mathbf{D} \to \mathbf{A}$ *be a cofibration such that* $\mathbf{A}$ *has* $\mathbf{I}$*-colimits. Then* r *has cofibred* $\mathbf{I}$*-colimits iff* $\mathbf{D}$ *has and* r *strictly preserves* $\mathbf{I}$*-colimits.*

Let us show how the construction of products in $\mathbf{E}$ (from Corollary 3.7) works. Let $\{X_i\}_{i \in I}$ be a set of objects in $\mathbf{E}$, such that $pX_i = A_i$. From Lemma 3.2, $\widetilde{\underleftarrow{\lim}}(\{X_i\}_{i \in I})$ is obtained by reindexing the family $\{X_i\}_{i \in I}$ along the corresponding instance of the counit of the adjunction $\Delta_I \dashv \underleftarrow{\lim}$, which is simply the limiting cone of the product in $\mathbf{B}$ of the A_i's. That is, we take every object X_i to the fibre over $\underleftarrow{\lim}(\{A_i\}_{i \in I})$. Then, following the construction in Thm. 3.4, we take the product of the reindexed objects within the fibre $\mathbf{E}_{\underleftarrow{\lim}(\{A_i\}_{i \in I})}$. So, for $X, Y \in |\mathbf{E}|$ (over A and B), their product is $\pi^*_{A,B}(X) \times (\pi'_{A,B})^*(Y)$ (over $A \times B$). This construction of limits and the analogous one for colimits agree with those of [BGT91], although we obtained them in a different way.

3.9. Remark.

(i) Corollary 3.7 yields a stronger version of [BGT91, Thm. 1]. More precisely, Thm. 1 asserts that if an indexed category $\mathcal{F} : \mathbf{B}^{op} \to \mathcal{C}at$ has fibred $\mathbf{I}$-limits and $\mathbf{B}$ has $\mathbf{I}$-limits, so does $\mathcal{GF}$. The corollary yields this implication plus (strict) preservation of $\mathbf{I}$-limits by p, and it also shows the converse, *i.e.* the hypotheses are necessary and not only sufficient.

(ii) Thm. 2 in *ibid.* asserts that if an indexed category $\mathcal{F} : \mathbf{B}^{op} \to \mathcal{C}at$ is such that every reindexing functor has a left adjoint has $\mathbf{I}$-colimits in every fibre and $\mathbf{B}$ has $\mathbf{I}$-colimits, so does $\mathcal{GF}$. Recall that a fibration is a bifibration (*i.e.* it is also a cofibration) iff every reindexing functor has a left adjoint (*cf.* Prop. 2.14.iii). Therefore the above mentioned theorem is a consequence of Corollary 3.8. As before, the corollary gives a converse to this theorem as well. Thus the two main results in *ibid.* can be shown as immediate consequences of our Thm. 3.4.

3.10. EXAMPLES.

(i) *Fam*(**C**) is complete whenever **C** is, by Corollary 3.7. In case **C** is cocomplete, $f(\mathbf{C})$ is also a cofibration and hence *Fam*(**C**) is cocomplete by Corollary 3.8. In any case, *Fam*(**C**) always has small sums, although they need not be preserved by $f(\mathbf{C})$. See [Jac93a] for further details on this fibration.

(ii) $\mathcal{GSS}$, the category of many-sorted sets (Ex. 2.3.i) is complete, since p_{SS} is fibred complete (Ex.2.19). Corollary 3.8 applies as well, essentially because *Set* is cocomplete – see [BGT91, Ex. 1] – and hence $\mathcal{GSS}$ is cocomplete.

(iii) The prototypical example of fibration in algebraic specifications is that of many-sorted algebras ([BGT91, Ex. 3]). Consider the functor $\mathcal{MSS} : \mathbf{AlgSig}^{op} \to \mathcal{C}at$ defined as follows:

$$\begin{aligned} \mathcal{MSS}(\Sigma) &= \mathbf{ALG}(\Sigma), \text{ the category of many-sorted } \Sigma\text{-algebras} \\ \mathcal{MSS}(\sigma : \Sigma \to \Sigma') &= -|_{\sigma}, \text{ the usual } \sigma\text{-reduct functor} \end{aligned}$$

The total category $\mathcal{GMSS}$ is then that of many-sorted algebras (with explicitly given signatures) and homomorphisms between them. As explained in *ibid.* the completeness and cocompleteness of this category can be shown by applying the above corollaries. Of course, the proof that the hypotheses of the above corollaries hold in this case is not trivial, but it belongs to the theory of algebraic structure on categories (using either sketches or monads) – see [BW85].

Conclusion

The main aim of this paper was to show how results which are relevant in the area of algebraic specifications can be understood more deeply by considering them in the context of fibred category theory and analysing the situation at a fairly general level. In particular, the results in [BGT91] about completeness and cocompleteness of total categories of fibrations are obtained as direct consequences of Thm. 3.4, which expresses an essential property of adjunctions between fibrations.

A secondary aim, which due to lack of space we might not have achieved, was to introduce the reader to fibred categories and, through the application abovementioned, show their relevance in situations which arise in the theory of algebraic specifications, particularly in the area of institutions. We apologise to the reader for the paucity of examples and informal explanations. [Her93] contains a more thorough and detailed account of some of the concepts involved (although it cannot be regarded as a tutorial introduction to the area) as well as further applications of relevance to computer science (*e.g.* logical predicates).

We think the main application of fibrations in computer science should be the categorical understanding of logical systems, including logics of programs in particular. We hope that further developments in the area will make their significance more evident. [Win90] considers fibrations (and fibred adjunctions in particular) in this light, as guidance for the design of a proof system for labelled transition systems.

Acknowledgements

Thanks to Bart Jacobs for several enlightening discussions on fibrations and for his provision of bibliographic material. Thanks to Don Sannella for his detailed comments on previous versions of the material presented here. Finally, I would like to express my gratitude to John Power for his steady encouragement and support as well as for the countless (and highly entertaining) discussions on categorical matters.

This work was supported by an Edinburgh University Postgraduate Studentship, and conducted at the Department of Computer Science of Edinburgh University.. The COMPASS project funded my attendance to the 9th WADT/4th COMPASS workshop. The diagrams were drawn with Paul Taylor's macros.

References

[Bén85] J. Bénabou. Fibred categories and the foundation of naive category theory. *Journal of Symbolic Logic*, 50, 1985.

[BGT91] R. M. Burstall, J. A. Goguen, and A. Tarlecki. Some fundamental algebraic tools for the semantics of computation. part 3: Indexed categories. *Theoretical Computer Science*, 91:239–264, 1991.

[BW85] M. Barr and C. Wells. *Toposes, Triples and Theories.* Springer Verlag, 1985.

[GB90] J.A. Goguen and R.M. Burstall. Introducing institutions. Technical Report ECS-LFCS-90-106, Laboratory for Foundations of Computer Science, Dept. of Comp. Sci., Univ. of Edinburgh, 1990. to appear in JACM.

[Gra66] J. W. Gray. Fibred and cofibred categories. In S. Eilenberg, editor, *Proceedings of the Conference on Categorical Algebra.* Springer Verlag, 1966.

[Gro71] A. Grothendieck. Catégories fibrées et descente. In A. Grothendieck, editor, *Revêtements étales et groupe fondamental, (SGA 1), Exposé VI*, volume 224 of *Lecture Notes in Mathematics.* Springer Verlag, 1971.

[Her93] C. Hermida. *Fibrations, logical predicates and related topics.* PhD thesis, University of Edinburgh, 1993. forthcoming.

[Jac91] B. Jacobs. *Categorical Type Theory.* PhD thesis, Nijmegen, 1991.

[Jac93a] B. Jacobs. Comprehension categories and the semantics of type dependency. *Theoretical Computer Science*, to appear, 1993.

[Jac93b] B. Jacobs. Parameters and parameterization in specification. *Fundamenta Informaticae*, to appear, 1993.

[KS74] G.M. Kelly and R.H. Street. Review of the elements of 2-categories. In A. Dold and B. Eckmann, editors, *Category Seminar*, volume 420 of *Lecture Notes in Mathematics.* Springer Verlag, 1974.

[Mac71] S. MacLane. *Categories for the Working Mathematician.* Springer Verlag, 1971.

[Mit90] J. Mitchell. Type systems for programming languages. In J. van Leeuwen, editor, *Handbook of Theoretical Computer Science, Volume B: Formal Models and Semantics.* North Holland, 1990.

[MR91] Q. Ma and J. C. Reynolds. Types, abstraction and parametric polymorphism 2. In S Brookes, editor, *Math. Found. of Prog. Lang. Sem.*, volume 589 of *Lecture Notes in Computer Science*, pages 1–40. Springer Verlag, 1991.

[PS78] R. Pare and D. Schumacher. Abstract families and the adjoint functor theorems. In P.T. Johnstone and R. Pare, editors, *Indexed Categories and their Applications*, volume 661 of *Lecture Notes in Mathematics.* Springer Verlag, 1978.

[Win90] G. Winskel. A compositional proof system for a category of labelled transition systems. *Information and Computation*, 87:2 – 57, 1990.

Implementing Inequality and Nondeterministic Specifications with Bi-rewriting Systems*

Jordi Levy and Jaume Agustí

Institut d'Investigació en Intel·ligència Artificial, CSIC,
Camí Sta. Bàrbara s/n, 17300 Blanes, Girona, Spain.
E-mail: levy@ceab.es and agusti@ceab.es

Abstract. Rewriting with non-symmetric relations can be considered as a computational model of many specification languages based on non-symmetric relations. For instance, Logics of Inequalities, Ordered Algebras, Rewriting Logic, Order-Sorted Algebras, Subset Logic, Unified Algebras, taxonomies, subtypes, Refinement Calculus, all them use some kind of non-symmetric relation on expressions. We have developed an operational semantics for these inequality specifications named bi-rewriting systems. In this paper we show the applicability of bi-rewriting systems to Unified Algebras and nondeterministic specifications. In the first case, we give a canonical bi-rewriting system implementing the basic theory of these algebras. In the second case, nondeterministic specifications are viewed as inclusion specifications, thus bi-rewriting is a sound, although not always complete deduction method. We show how a specification has to be completed in order to have both soundness and completeness.

1 Introduction

Term rewriting systems TRS have been usually associated with equational logic [DJ90]. Overcoming this tendency it has been shown recently [Mes90, Mes92] that the logic implicit in TRS is a generalization of equational logic, named *preorder logic* POL, or rewriting logic, which is addressed to unify a wide variety of models of concurrency. Following the new trend, we proposed in [LA93] an operative method based on rewriting techniques to automatize the deduction in the preorder logic. The inference rules defining this logic are quite similar to the ones defining the equational logic, but they do not include the symmetry rule:

$$\frac{}{t \subseteq t} \textit{ Reflexivity} \qquad \frac{s \subseteq t \quad t \subseteq v}{s \subseteq v} \textit{ Transitivity}$$

$$\frac{s_1 \subseteq t_1 \ \dots \ s_n \subseteq t_n}{f(s_1,\dots,s_n) \subseteq f(t_1,\dots,t_n)} \textit{ Monotonicity} \qquad \frac{s \subseteq t}{\sigma(s) \subseteq \sigma(t)} \textit{ Substitution}$$

An inclusion theory or specification I is defined by a finite set of inclusions $t \subseteq u$, where t and u are first order terms $\mathcal{T}(\Sigma, \mathcal{X})$ over a finite signature $\Sigma = \cup_{n \geq 0} \Sigma^n$ of function symbols and a denumerable set of variables $\mathcal{X}$.

* This work has been partially supported by the project TESEU (TIC 91-430) funded by the CICYT

The idea of applying rewriting techniques to the deduction of inclusions between terms like $t \subseteq u$ is very simple. We compute by repeatedly replacing both 1) subterms of t by *bigger* terms using the axioms and 2) subterms of u by *smaller* terms using the same axioms, until we find a path of the bi-directional search connecting t and u. To use inclusion axioms as rewrite rules we must orient them in one, the other or both directions, which produces a pair of rewriting system: one $R_{\subseteq}$ with rules oriented like $t \xrightarrow{\subseteq} u$ and the other $R_{\supseteq}$ with rules like $u \xrightarrow{\supseteq} t$. The pair $\langle R_{\subseteq}, R_{\supseteq} \rangle$ is a bi-rewriting system.

In [LA93] we started to study the theory of bi-rewriting systems, their properties and the completion process in order to ensure the termination and completeness of the bi-directional search proof procedure. These depend on two properties, the termination of both rewriting relations $\xrightarrow[R_{\subseteq}]{}$ and $\xrightarrow[R_{\supseteq}]{}$, and the commutation of them $\xleftarrow[R_{\supseteq}]{} \circ \xrightarrow[R_{\subseteq}]{} \subseteq \xrightarrow[R_{\subseteq}]{*} \circ \xleftarrow[R_{\supseteq}]{*}$. The first property is usually proved using the standard methods based on simplification orderings. The second one requires a new definition:

Definition 1. Let $\alpha_1 \xrightarrow{\subseteq} \beta_1$ in $R_{\subseteq}$ and $\alpha_2 \xrightarrow{\supseteq} \beta_2$ in $R_{\supseteq}$ be two rewriting rules (with distinct variables) and p a position in α_1, then

1. if $\alpha_1|_p$ is a non-variable subterm and ρ is the most general unifier of $\alpha_1|_p$ and α_2 then $\rho(\alpha_1[\beta_2]_p) \subseteq \rho(\beta_1)$ is a *(standard) critical pair*,
2. if $\alpha_1|_p = x$ is a repeated variable in α_1, F a term, q an occurrence in F, and $\alpha_2 \xrightarrow[R_{\subseteq}]{*} \beta_2$ is not satisfied, then $\rho(\alpha_1[F[\beta_2]_q]_p) \subseteq \rho(\beta_1)$ is an *(extended) critical pair* where ρ only substitutes x by $F[\alpha_2]_q$.

The same for critical pairs between $R_{\supseteq}$ and $R_{\subseteq}$.

In [LA93] we proved the following theorem.

Theorem 2. *Given a bi-rewriting system $\langle R_{\subseteq}, R_{\supseteq} \rangle$, if $R_{\subseteq}$ and $R_{\supseteq}$ are both terminating then the bi-rewriting system commutes iff all the critical pairs are confluent.*

The same result was extended to bi-rewriting modulo a set of nonorientable inclusions, like it is done in the equational case when we rewrite in equivalence classes. The Knuth-Bendix completion process for bi-rewriting systems has some problems (the set of extended critical pairs is in general infinite) which are the object of current work [Lev93].

In this paper we apply the bi-rewriting technique to the automatic deduction in inclusion specifications. In section 2 we complete the basic inclusion theory of Unified Algebras, that is the theory of distributive lattices, and we give a canonical bi-rewriting system for it. This example shows the problems arising from the use of extended critical pairs.

Section 3 has more theoretical interest. It has been shown that bi-rewriting is a sound and complete deduction technique for the preorder logic. The class of models of this logic are the preorder algebras. However, the models usually used in nondeterministic specifications are multialgebras. We study which conditions a specification I has to satisfy in order to be equivalent both classes of models. If this conditions are not satisfied, we propose a completion method for I. This completion introduces new rules $t \xrightarrow{\subseteq} u$, leaving the rules $t \xrightarrow{\supseteq} u$ which define the computation unchanged.

2 Implementing the Inequality Specification of Distributive Lattices

The commutativity of a bi-rewriting system requires the confluence of all the standard and extended critical pairs. The confluence of a standard critical pair, like $l \subseteq r$, can be assured adding to the system the rule $l \xrightarrow{\subseteq} r$ or $r \xrightarrow{\supseteq} l$ when it is not confluent. The same solution does not apply to the extended critical pair case because they involve inclusion schemes. The confluence of an inclusion scheme may require the addition of more than one rule and the search of the rules to add is not automatizable. Our approach to the problem is to orient the inclusion scheme in a rule scheme, and to study the new rule schemes that can be generated from it. The generation of critical pairs between rule schemes has not been solved yet. Nevertheless, in the following example we show that some particular rule instances of rule schemes may make confluent the original inclusion scheme (the extended critical pair). The rules added are sound because they are instances of rule schemes generated from extended critical pairs.

The example we present is the inequality specification of distributive lattices. This specification is the base for many other specifications or specification languages like the *Unified Algebras* [Mos89]. The presentation of the distributive lattice theory may be given by the following set of inclusions:

$$\begin{array}{ll} X \cup X \subseteq X & X \cap X \supseteq X \\ X \cup Y \supseteq X & X \cap Y \subseteq X \\ X \cup Y \supseteq Y & X \cap Y \subseteq Y \end{array}$$
$$X \cap (Y \cup Z) \subseteq (X \cap Y) \cup (X \cap Z)$$

The orientation of all these inclusions to the right results in a terminating bi-rewriting system where all *standard* critical pairs are confluent. However, the presence of the two non-left-linear rules $X \cup X \xrightarrow{\subseteq} X$ and $X \cap X \xrightarrow{\supseteq} X$ makes necessary the consideration of the *extended* critical pairs. If we only take into account, in a first step, all those extended critical pairs of the form $\langle \sigma(\alpha_1[\beta_2]_p), \sigma(\beta_1) \rangle$, which correspond to the particular case where the position q in F is the most external one $q = \lambda$, then we can generate the following sequence of new rules:

q_1 $Y \cup (X \cup Y) \xrightarrow{\subseteq} X \cup Y$
q_2 $Y \cup X \xrightarrow{\subseteq} X \cup Y$

q_3 $(X \cup Y) \cup Y \xrightarrow{\subseteq} X \cup Y$
q_4 $(X \cup Y) \cup (Y \cup Z) \xrightarrow{\subseteq} X \cup (Y \cup Z)$
q_5 $(X \cup Y) \cup Z \xrightarrow{\subseteq} X \cup (Y \cup Z)$

and the equivalent ones for $\cap$. The rules q_2 and q_5 are non-orientable and subsume the rest of rules. They make necessary the use of the bi-rewriting modulo a set of inclusions technique. These rules are symmetric –they are really equations–, therefore we can apply the standard commutative-associative closure definition [PS81]. We obtain then the following set of rules.

$$R_{\subseteq} = \begin{cases} r_1 & X \cup X \xrightarrow{\subseteq} X \\ r_1^{ext} & X \cup X \cup Y \xrightarrow{\subseteq} X \cup Y \\ r_2 & X \cap Y \xrightarrow{\subseteq} X \\ r_3 & X \cap (Y \cup Z) \xrightarrow{\subseteq} (X \cap Y) \cup (X \cap Z) \\ r_3^{ext} & X \cap (Y \cup Z) \cap T \xrightarrow{\subseteq} \big((X \cap Y) \cup (X \cap Z)\big) \cap T \end{cases}$$

$$R_{\supseteq} = \begin{cases} r_4 & X \cap X \xrightarrow{\supseteq} X \\ r_4^{ext} & X \cap X \cap Y \xrightarrow{\supseteq} X \cap Y \\ r_5 & X \cup Y \xrightarrow{\supseteq} X \end{cases}$$

$$I = \begin{cases} r_6 \; Y \cup X \xrightarrow{\subseteq} X \cup Y \\ r_7 \; (X \cup Y) \cup Z \xrightarrow{\subseteq} X \cup (Y \cup Z) \\ r_8 \; Y \cap X \xrightarrow{\subseteq} X \cap Y \\ r_9 \; (X \cap Y) \cap Z \xrightarrow{\subseteq} X \cap (Y \cap Z) \end{cases}$$

In a second step we have to consider also those rules needed to make confluent the rest of extended critical pairs.

$$F[X] \cup F[X \cup Y] \subseteq F[X \cup Y]$$
$$F[X \cap Y] \subseteq F[X] \cap F[X \cap Y]$$

First, we will study the second extended critical pair. If we orient it to the left, we obtain the rule scheme $F[X] \cap F[X \cap Y] \xrightarrow{\supseteq} F[X \cap Y]$. This rule scheme generates a standard critical pair with the rule $X \cap Y \xrightarrow{\subseteq} Y$, which is made confluent adding the rule scheme $F[X] \cap F[Y] \xrightarrow{\supseteq} F[X \cap Y]$. The overlapping of the context $F[\_]$ of this rule scheme with the left part of the rule $X \cap Y \xrightarrow{\subseteq} Y$ generates infinite many rule schemes $F[X_1, \ldots, X_n] \cap F[Y_1, \ldots, Y_n] \xrightarrow{\supseteq} F[X_1 \cap Y_1, \ldots, X_n \cap Y_n]$ for $n \geq 1$. The following (normal) rules subsume these rule schemes.

$$r_{10} \;\; X \cap (Y \cup Z) \xrightarrow{\supseteq} (X \cap Y) \cup (X \cap Z)$$
$$r_{11}^{(f)} \;\; f(X_1, \ldots, X_n) \cap f(Y_1, \ldots, Y_n) \xrightarrow{\supseteq} f(X_1 \cap Y_1, \ldots, X_n \cap Y_n) \;\; \forall f \in \Sigma^n$$

Notice that $r_{11}^{(f)}$ is really a set of rules, one for each n-ary symbol $f \in \Sigma^n$, and that r_{10} subsumes the instantiation of $r_{11}^{(f)}$ for the symbol $\cup \in \Sigma^2$.

The dual solution is not applicable to $F[X] \cup F[X \cup Y] \subseteq F[X \cup Y]$ because $X \cup (Y \cap Z) \xrightarrow{\subseteq} (X \cup Y) \cap (X \cup Z)$ and the distributive rule r_3 would lead to the non-termination of the system. This problem can be avoided using the alternative set of rules:

$$r_{12}^{(f)} \;\; f(X_1, \ldots, X_n) \cup f(Y_1, \ldots, Y_n) \xrightarrow{\subseteq} f(X_1 \cup Y_1, \ldots, X_n \cup Y_n)$$
$$r_{13}^{(f)} \;\; (X \cap f(Y_1, \ldots, Y_n)) \cup (X \cap f(Z_1, \ldots, Z_n)) \xrightarrow{\subseteq} X \cap f(Y_1 \cup Z_1, \ldots, Y_n \cup Z_n)$$

They do not subsume $F[X] \cup F[Y] \xrightarrow{\subseteq} F[X \cup Y]$, but are particular instances of this rule schema. The last rule r_{13} is non-left-linear and generates a new extended critical pair which becomes confluent if we add the following rule.

$$r_{14}^{(f)} \;\; (X \cap f(Y_1, \ldots, Y_n)) \cup (Z \cap f(V_1, \ldots, V_n)) \xrightarrow{\subseteq} (X \cup Z) \cap f(Y_1 \cup V_1, \ldots, Y_n \cup V_n)$$

Rules $r_{14}^{(f)}$ and r_1 subsume $r_{13}^{(f)}$.

Let's prove now that rules r_{12} and r_{14} makes confluent the extended critical pair $F[X] \cup F[X \cup Y] \subseteq F[X \cup Y]$. Rules $r_{12}^{(f)}$ and $r_{14}^{(f)}$ subsume $F[X] \cup F[Y] \xrightarrow{\subseteq} F[X \cup Y]$ when the schema[2] $F[\_]$ can be expressed as a composition $F[\_] = F_1[\ldots F_n[\_]\ldots]$ of schemas, where each one of this schemes satisfies $F_i[\_] = f(\ldots,\_,\ldots)$, or $F_i[\_] = E_1 \cap f(\ldots,\_,\ldots) \cap E_2$ for any symbol f different from $\cap$, and any expressions E_1, E_2. It can be proved that any scheme $F[\_]$ can be expressed as $F[\_] = G[E_1 \cap \_ \cap E_2]$ where the schema $G[\_]$ satisfies the previous condition and E_1, E_2 are two common expressions. This property allows to translate the inclusion schema (the extended critical pair) $F[X] \cup F[X \cup Y] \subseteq F[X \cup Y]$ into

$$G[X \cap H] \cup G[(X \cup Y) \cap H] \subseteq G[(X \cup Y) \cap H]$$

where $G[\_]$ can be rewritten using $F[X] \cup F[Y] \xrightarrow{\subseteq} F[X \cup Y]$. We prove then that this extended critical pair is bi-confluent using the following proof.

$$\begin{aligned} G[X \cap H] \cup G[(X \cup Y) \cap H] &\xrightarrow{\subseteq} G[(X \cap H) \cup ((X \cup Y) \cap H)] \\ &\xrightarrow{\subseteq} G[(X \cap H) \cup (X \cap H) \cup (Y \cap H)] \\ &\xrightarrow{\subseteq} G[(X \cap H) \cup (Y \cap H)] \xleftarrow{\subseteq} G[(X \cup Y) \cap H] \end{aligned}$$

A commutative and terminating bi-rewriting system for the distributive lattice theory is given by rules $r_1 \ldots r_{12}$, r_{14} and their corresponding $\cup$ and $\cap$ associative-commutative extensions.

3 Implementing Nondeterministic Specifications

It is well known that term rewriting techniques can be used to test the equivalence of terms in a equational logic specification E. The method consists in finding the normal form of both sides of the tested equality and checking if they are equal. The method is sound and complete for ground terms if the set of ground normal forms is (isomorphic to) the initial model of the specification; and for terms with variables if the set of normal forms is isomorphic to $\mathcal{T}(\Sigma, \mathcal{X})/E$ [DJ90]. It is also well known that the confluence and termination of the rewriting system resulting from orienting the equations is a sufficient condition for this completeness result.

Term rewriting techniques have also been proposed as the implementation language of nondeterministic specifications [Kap86a, Hus92]. In all these approaches the signature includes a nondeterministic choice operator —noted by $\uparrow$ in [Kap86a, Kap88], by $or(\_,\_)$ in [Hus91, Hus92], or by $\cup$ in our work— which makes nondeterministic computation lose the symmetry property. Otherwise, the rules $X \cup Y \longrightarrow X$ and $X \cup Y \longrightarrow Y$ proposed for the choice operator would allow to prove the equivalence of any two terms. Therefore, the confluence property makes no sense, and a nondeterministic specification is presented in general as a set of (non symmetric) inclusions.

[2] As usual, an schema is an expression with a *hole* in it, a selected position, denoted by an underscore "_". The schema composition $F[\_] \circ G[\_]$ is defined by the substitution of this selected position by the other schema, noted $F[G[\_]]$.

The models proposed for these specifications are based on Σ-multialgebras [Hes88, Nip86], which capture the essence of nondeterminism better than the Σ-algebras used in equational specifications.

Definition 3. A Σ-multialgebra A is a tuple $\langle S^A, \mathcal{F}^A \rangle$ where S^A is a non empty carrier set, and $\mathcal{F}^A$ is a set of set-valued functions $f^A : S^A \times \overset{n}{\dots} \times S^A \to \mathcal{P}^+(S^A)$ for each $f \in \Sigma^n$ function symbol of the signature.

Models are defined as follows.

Definition 4. Given a specification I over a signature Σ, a Σ-multialgebra A is said to be a model of I, noted $A \in MAlg(I)$, if the interpretation function $I^A_{\_}[\_] : (\mathcal{X} \to S^A) \to \mathcal{T}(\Sigma, \mathcal{X}) \to \mathcal{P}^+(S^A)$ defined inductively by

$$\begin{array}{lll} I^A_\rho[x] & = \{\rho(x)\} & \text{for any } x \in \mathcal{X} \\ I^A_\rho[f(t_1, \dots, t_n)] & = \bigcup\{f^A(v_1, \dots, v_n) \mid v_i \in I^A_\rho[t_i]\} & \text{for any } f \in \Sigma^n \end{array}$$

satisfies $I^A_\rho[t] \subseteq I^A_\rho[u]$ for any axiom $t \subseteq u$ in the specification I, and any valuation function $\rho : \mathcal{X} \to S^A$.

An inclusion $t \subseteq u$ is valid in a Σ-multialgebra model A, noted $A \models t \subseteq u$, if for any valuation ρ we have $I^A_\rho[t] \subseteq I^A_\rho[u]$.

3.1 Using Bi-rewriting Systems to Verify Specifications

Bi-rewriting systems introduced in [LA93] automatize the deduction in the *Partial Order Logic* POL (also for the rewriting logic of Meseguer [Mes92]). The models of this logic are preorder algebras, defined as follows.

Definition 5. A Σ-preorder algebra A is a triplet $\langle S^A, \subseteq_A, \mathcal{F}^A \rangle$ where S^A is a carrier set, $\subseteq_A$ is a preorder relation and $\mathcal{F}^A$ is a set of monotonic functions $f^A : S^A \times \overset{n}{\dots} \times S^A \to S^A$ for each symbol $f \in \Sigma^n$.

Definition 6. Given a specification I over Σ a Σ-preorder algebra A is said to be a model of I, noted $A \in POAlg(I)$, if the interpretation function $I^A_{\_}[\_] : (\mathcal{X} \to S^A) \to \mathcal{T}(\Sigma, \mathcal{X}) \to S^A$ defined inductively by

$$\begin{array}{lll} I^A_\rho[x] & = \rho(x) & \text{for any } x \in \mathcal{X} \\ I^A_\rho[f(t_1, \dots, t_n)] & = f^A(I^A_\rho[t_1], \dots, I^A_\rho[t_n]) & \text{for any } f \in \Sigma^n \end{array}$$

satisfies $I_\rho[t] \subseteq_A I_\rho[u]$ for any axiom $t \subseteq u$ in the specification I and any valuation $\rho : \mathcal{X} \to S^A$.

A soundness and completeness theorem, similar to the Birkhoff theorem, can be stated for this logic.

Lemma 7. *For any specification I and any pair of terms t and u we have $POAlg(I) \models t \subseteq u$ iff $I \vdash_{POL} t \subseteq u$.*

Commutative and terminating bi-rewriting systems automatize the deduction in $\vdash_{POL}$. They are a sound and complete method w.r.t. the semantics of specifications based on preorder algebras. However, $POAlg(I) \models t \subseteq u$ and $MAlg(I) \models t \subseteq u$ are not equivalent (the implication does not hold in none of both directions) as the following counter-example shows.

Example 1. A counter-example to $MAlg(I) \models t \subseteq u \Rightarrow POAlg(I) \models t \subseteq u$ is given by the following additivity axiom which is sound in multialgebra models, but not in preorder algebra models.

$$\frac{}{f(X \cup Y) \subseteq f(X) \cup f(Y)} \; Aditivity$$

The counter-example to $POAlg(I) \models t \subseteq u \Rightarrow MAlg(I) \models t \subseteq u$ is not so evident, and causes more problems. The following substitution rule is sound in preorder models, but not in multialgebra models, in the presence of repeated variables.

$$\frac{t \subseteq u}{\sigma(t) \subseteq \sigma(u)} \; Substitution$$

For instance, the deduction

$$f(X,X) \subseteq g(X) \;,\; X \subseteq X \cup Y \;,\; Y \subseteq X \cup Y \;\vdash_{POL}\; f(X,Y) \subseteq g(X \cup Y)$$

is correct in POL. However, it is not sound in a multialgebra model. The multialgebra $A = \langle S^A, \mathcal{F}^A \rangle$ defined by:

$$S^A = \{a,b\} \qquad \begin{array}{l} f^A(x,y) = if\ x = y\ then\ \{a\}\ else\ \{b\} \\ g^A(x,y) = \{a\} \\ x \cup^A y \;\; = \{x,y\} \end{array}$$

is a model of $I = \{f(X,X) \subseteq g(X), X \subseteq X \cup Y, Y \subseteq X \cup Y\}$, however $I^A_\rho[f(X,Y)] \not\subseteq I^A_\rho[g(X \cup Y)]$ for $\rho = [a \leftarrow X, b \leftarrow Y]$.

We understand variables in a specification denoting terms and being universally quantified. Therefore, we think that the substitution rule has to be sound in any specification model. Multialgebra models may satisfy this requirement if we modify the definition of interpretation and model:

Definition 8. A Σ-multialgebra A is said to be a *strong* model of a specification I, noted $A \in \overline{MAlg}(I)$, if the interpretation function $I^A_{\_}[\_] : (\mathcal{X} \to \mathcal{P}^+(S^A)) \to \mathcal{T}(\Sigma, \mathcal{X}) \to \mathcal{P}^+(S^A)$ defined inductively by

$$\begin{array}{lll} I^A_\rho[x] & = \rho(x) & \text{for any } x \in \mathcal{X} \\ I^A_\rho[f(t_1,\ldots,t_n)] & = \bigcup\{f^A(v_1,\ldots,v_n) \mid v_i \in I^A_\rho[t_i]\} & \text{for any } f \in \Sigma^n \end{array}$$

satisfies $I_\rho[t] \subseteq I_\rho[u]$ for any axiom $t \subseteq u$ in the specification I, and any valuation $\rho : \mathcal{X} \to \mathcal{P}^+(S^A)$.

Notice that the valuation function ρ ranges over sets and not only over values.

Lemma 9. *For any specification I we have $\overline{MAlg}(I) \subseteq MAlg(I)$.*

Using this smaller class of models the preorder logic entailment $\vdash_{POL}$ becomes sound.

Theorem 10. *If $POAlg(I) \models t \subseteq u$ holds, then $\overline{MAlg}(I) \models t \subseteq u$ also holds. Therefore, bi-rewriting is a sound deduction method.*

Proof. It is sufficient to prove that

$$\forall A \in \overline{MAlg} . \exists B \in POAlg . (\forall \rho . I_\rho^A[t] \subseteq I_\rho^A[u]) \Leftrightarrow (\forall \rho' . I_{\rho'}^B[t] \subseteq_B I_{\rho'}^B[u])$$

Notice that we use one implication direction to prove $A \in \overline{MAlg}(I) \Rightarrow B \in POAlg(I)$, and the opposite direction to prove $B \models t \subseteq u \Rightarrow A \models t \subseteq u$.

Any Σ-multialgebra A has a Σ-preorder algebra B naturally associated. This preorder algebra B is defined by

$$S^B \stackrel{def}{=} \mathcal{P}^+(S^A)$$
$$f^B(s_1, \dots, s_n) \stackrel{def}{=} \bigcup \{ f^A(v_1, \dots, v_n) \mid v_i \in s_i \} \text{ for any } f \in \Sigma^n$$

The carrier S_B is a power set, and the set inclusion relation $\subseteq$ used in the multialgebra model A, and the partial order relation $\subseteq_B$ used in the preorder model B are equal. We can prove by structural induction on the term t that $I_\rho^A[t] = I_\rho^B[t]$.

$$\begin{aligned} I_\rho^B[x] &= \rho(x) = I_\rho^A[x] \\ I_\rho^B[f(t_1 \dots t_n)] &= f^B(I_\rho^B[t_1] \dots I_\rho^B[t_n]) = \bigcup\{ f^A(v_1 \dots v_n) \mid v_i \in I_\rho^B[t_i]\} \\ &= \bigcup\{ f^A(v_1 \dots v_n) \mid v_i \in I_\rho^A[t_i]\} = I_\rho^A[f(t_1 \dots t_n)] \end{aligned}$$

Then the initial double implication becomes a tautology.

In the following we will study which conditions I has to satisfy in order to be $POAlg(I) \models t \subseteq u$ and $\overline{MAlg}(I) \models t \subseteq u$ equivalent.

Theorem 11. *If the specification I satisfies:*

1. *I contains the union theory as a subtheory:*
   $I \vdash_{POL} X \cup X \subseteq X,\ X \subseteq X \cup Y,\ Y \subseteq X \cup Y$.
2. *$I \vdash_{POL} t = \bigcup\{u \in Atomic(I) \mid I \vdash_{POL} u \subseteq t\}$, for any term t, where* $Atomic(I) \stackrel{def}{=} \{u \in \mathcal{T}(\Sigma, \mathcal{X}) \mid \text{ if } I \vdash_{POL} v \subseteq u \text{ then } v = u\}$.
3. *$I \vdash_{POL} f(\dots t \cup u \dots) \subseteq f(\dots t \dots) \cup f(\dots u \dots)$ for any n-ary symbol $f \in \Sigma^n$.*
4. *If $t \in Atomic(I)$ and $I \vdash_{POL} t \subseteq u \cup u'$ then either $I \vdash_{POL} t \subseteq u$ or $I \vdash_{POL} t \subseteq u'$.*

Then, whenever $\overline{MAlg}(I) \models t \subseteq u$ holds, then $POAlg(I) \models t \subseteq u$ also holds. Therefore, bi-rewriting is a complete deduction method for these specifications.

Proof. It is sufficient to prove that

$$\forall B \in POAlg . \exists A \in \overline{MAlg} . (\forall \rho . I_\rho^A[t] \subseteq I_\rho^A[u]) \Leftrightarrow (\forall \rho' . I_{\rho'}^B[t] \subseteq_B I_{\rho'}^B[u])$$

We can also associate a multialgebra A to each preorder algebra B as follows.

$$S^A \stackrel{def}{=} Atomic(S^B)$$
$$f^A(v_1,\ldots,v_n) \stackrel{def}{=} \{s \in S^A \mid s \subseteq_B f^B(v_1,\ldots,v_n)\} \text{ for any } f \in \Sigma^n$$

where for any preorder S, we define $Atomic(S) \stackrel{def}{=} \{s \in S \mid s' \subseteq s \Rightarrow s = s'\}$.[3]

Notice that in this case $\subseteq$ is the set inclusion in $\mathcal{P}^+(S^B)$, and $\subseteq_B$ is a preorder relation on S^B, and they are different relations.

Case $\forall \rho' . \exists \rho . I^A_\rho[t] \subseteq I^A_\rho[u] \Rightarrow I^B_{\rho'}[t] \subseteq_B I^B_{\rho'}[u]$.

The conditions of the theorem can be translated directly to properties of the preorder algebra B:

$$v \cup^B v \subseteq_B v \quad v_1 \subseteq_B v_1 \cup^B v_2 \quad v_2 \subseteq_B v_1 \cup^B v_2$$
$$f^B(\ldots v_1 \cup^B v_2 \ldots) \subseteq_B f^B(\ldots v_1 \ldots) \cup^B f^B(\ldots v_2 \ldots)$$
$$v = \cup^B \{v' \in Atomic(S^B) \mid v' \subseteq_B v\}$$
$$v \in Atomic(S^B) \ \wedge \ v \subseteq v_1 \cup v_2 \ \Rightarrow \ v \subseteq v_1 \ \vee \ v \subseteq v_2$$

If we define $\rho(x) \stackrel{def}{=} \{s \in S^A \mid s \subseteq_B \rho'(x)\}$ then using the properties below we can prove by structural induction on the term t that

$$I^B_{\rho'}[t] = \cup^B I^A_\rho[t]$$

where, as usual $\cup^B\{v_1,\ldots,v_n\} = v_1 \cup^B \cdots \cup^B v_n$ for any $v_1 \ldots v_n \in S^B$.

Then the monotonicity of $\cup^B$ proves that $I^A_\rho[t] \subseteq I^A_\rho[u]$ implies $I^B_{\rho'}[t] \subseteq I^B_{\rho'}[u]$.

Case $\forall \rho . \exists \rho' . I^B_{\rho'}[t] \subseteq_B I^B_{\rho'}[u] \Rightarrow I^A_\rho[t] \subseteq I^A_\rho[u]$.

The last two conditions of the theorem prove that if $t \in Atomic(I)$ and $I \vdash_{POL} t \subseteq f(u_1,\ldots,u_n)$ then there exist $v_1,\ldots,v_n \in Atomic(I)$ such that $I \vdash_{POL} t \subseteq f(v_1,\ldots,v_n)$ for any $f \in \Sigma^n$.

If we define $\rho'(x) = \cup^B \rho(x)$ then we can prove

$$I^A_\rho[t] = \{s \in S^A \mid s \subseteq_B I^B_{\rho'}[t]\}$$

for any term t by structural induction.

Then $I^B_{\rho'}[t] \subseteq_B I^B_{\rho'}[u]$ implies $I^A_\rho[t] \subseteq I^A_\rho[u]$.

The conditions of the previous theorem are usually satisfied in any nondeterministic specification I. We will find the same conditions in the next subsection where we try to prove the existence and initiality of a model based on sets of normal forms.

[3] Notice that for the free algebra of terms $T(\Sigma,\mathcal{X})/I$ this definition and the previous one becomes equivalent.

3.2 Characterizing Terms by Sets of Normal Forms

In nondeterministic computations terms can not be characterized by a unique normal form, but we will try to characterize them by its set of normal forms. In this case, a method to test inclusions of terms in a nondeterministic specification would consist in searching the set of normal forms of each side of the inclusion, and checking if one set is included in the other one. We will prove that the soundness and completeness of this *nondeterministic computation* method relies on the existence and initiality of a model of *set of normal forms* –like in the equational case with the normal form model–. The main goal of this section is to give the conditions for the existence and for the initially of this model –like it is characterized in the equational case by the confluence and termination properties–.

First we will present the formal definition of the *set of normal forms* model, SNF-model for short, and later we will study the *nondeterministic computation* method, NDC-method for short.

Nondeterministic computation is based on the computation of normal forms only using the rewriting system $R_{\supseteq}$. As we will see, the other rewriting system $R_{\subseteq}$ does not play a computational role, but its rules may be understood as semantic constraints on the class of models of the specification. The example at the end of the section shows this clearly. Adding new rules to $R_{\subseteq}$ we can prove a soundness and completeness result for the nondeterministic computation and the bi-rewriting methods w.r.t. the models of the new specification.

Given a rewriting system $R_{\supseteq}$, we will denote the set of its $R_{\supseteq}$-normal forms by $NF^{\supseteq}$ and the set of $R_{\supseteq}$-normal forms of a term t by $NF^{\supseteq}[t]$.

The *set of normal forms* multialgebra, SNF-multialgebra for short, is defined as follows.

Definition 12. Given a rewriting system $R_{\supseteq}$, the SNF-multialgebra $SNF = \langle S^{SNF}, \mathcal{F}^{SNF}\rangle$ is defined by the carrier set $S^{SNF} \stackrel{def}{=} NF^{\supseteq}$, and the set of functions $f^{SNF} : NF^{\supseteq} \times \overset{n}{\ldots} \times NF^{\supseteq} \to \mathcal{P}^{+}(NF^{\supseteq})$ defined by $f^{SNF}(t_1, \ldots, t_n) = NF^{\supseteq}[f(t_1, \ldots, t_n)]$ for each functional symbol $f \in \Sigma^n$ of the signature.

Notice that the SNF-multialgebra is defined syntactically using $R_{\supseteq}$, and independently of I. The rewriting rules of $R_{\supseteq}$ come from the orientation of some of the axioms of I. However, this fact is not enough to prove that the SNF-multialgebra is a multialgebra model of I.

Lemma 13. *Given a specification I and a rewriting system $R_{\supseteq}$, if the following conditions hold.*

1. *For any inclusion $t \subseteq u$ in I, and any substitution $\rho : \mathcal{X} \to \mathcal{NF}^{\supseteq}$, we have $NF^{\supseteq}[\rho(t)] \subseteq NF^{\supseteq}[\rho(u)]$.*
2. *If $t \in NF^{\supseteq}[f(\ldots, u, \ldots)]$, then there exists $u' \in NF^{\supseteq}[u]$ such that $t \in NF^{\supseteq}[f(\ldots, u', \ldots)]$.*

then the SNF-multialgebra is a multialgebra model of I, $SNF \in MAlg(I)$, and the interpretation function is $I_{\rho}^{SNF}[t] = NF^{\supseteq}[\rho(t)]$.

Additionally, if the following condition also holds

3. $NF^{\supseteq}[t \cup u] \subseteq NF^{\supseteq}[t] \cup NF^{\supseteq}[u]$,

then the SNF-multialgebra is a strong multialgebra model of I, $SNF \in \overline{MAlg}(I)$*, and* $I_\rho^{SNF}[t] = NF^{\supseteq}[\rho'(t)]$*, where for any* $x \in \mathcal{X}$*,* $\rho'(x) = \cup\rho(x)$*.*

Proof. First we prove that $I_\rho^{SNF}[t] = NF^{\supseteq}[\rho(t)]$ are equal. That is, $NF^{\supseteq}[\rho(t)]$ satisfies the inductive definition of multialgebra interpretation function: 1) $I_\rho^{SNF}[x] = \rho(x)$ for any variable $x \in \mathcal{X}$. As far as ρ maps variables to normal forms, $NF^{\supseteq}[\rho(x)] = \{\rho(x)\}$. 2) $I_\rho^{SNF}[f(t_1,\ldots,t_n)] = \bigcup\{f^{SNF}(v_1,\ldots,v_n) \mid v_i \in I_\rho^{SNF}[t_i]\}$, which is equivalent to $NF^{\supseteq}[f(\rho(t_1),\ldots,\rho(t_n))] = \bigcup\{NF^{\supseteq}[f(v_1,\ldots,v_n)] \mid v_i \in NF^{\supseteq}[\rho(t_i)]\}$. The inclusion $\supseteq$ is always satisfied and it can be proved using the monotonicity of f. The inclusion $\subseteq$ is proved by the second condition of the lemma.

Second the first condition of the lemma and $I_\rho^{SNF}[t] = NF^{\supseteq}[\rho(t)]$ prove that $I_\rho^{SNF}[t] \subseteq I_\rho^{SNF}[u]$ for any inclusion $t \subseteq u$ of I, and any substitution ρ.

The proof of the second part of the lemma is quite similar. In this case we need the third condition to prove $I_\rho^{SNF}[t] = \rho(x) = NF^{\supseteq}[\cup\rho(x)] = NF^{\supseteq}[\rho'(x)]$.

As we have seen in the previous subsection we can associate a preorder algebra to the SNF-multialgebra, and this preorder algebra will be a preorder model of I if the SNF-multialgebra is a strong multialgebra model of I.

Lemma 14. *If the following conditions are satisfied:*

1. *If* $I \vdash_{POL} t \subseteq u$ *then* $NF^{\supseteq}[t] \subseteq NF^{\supseteq}[u]$.
2. *If* $t \in NF^{\supseteq}[f(\ldots,u,\ldots)]$*, then there exists* $u' \in NF^{\supseteq}[u]$ *such that* $t \in NF^{\supseteq}[f(\ldots,u',\ldots)]$.
3. $NF^{\supseteq}[t \cup u] \subseteq NF^{\supseteq}[t] \cup NF^{\supseteq}[u]$,

then, the SNF-preorder algebra defined by the carrier set $S^{SNF} \stackrel{def}{=} \mathcal{P}^+(NF^{\supseteq})$ *and the set of functions* $f^{SNF}(s_1 \ldots s_n) \stackrel{def}{=} \cup\{NF^{\supseteq}[f(v_1 \ldots v_n)] \mid v_i \in s_i\}$ *is a preorder model of I.*

If in addition

4. *If* $NF^{\supseteq}[t] \subseteq NF^{\supseteq}[u]$ *then* $I \vdash_{POL} t \subseteq u$.

then the SNF-preorder model is initial in $POAlg(I)$*, and the associated SNF-multialgebra is initial in* $\overline{MAlg}(I)$*.*

Moreover, $\overline{MAlg}(I) \models t \subseteq u$ *and* $POAlg(I) \models t \subseteq u$ *are equivalent.*

Proof. The proof of the first part of the lemma is a consequence of the previous lemma. The proof for the initiality of the model relies on the completeness of $\vdash_{POL}$ w.r.t. the class of models *POAlg*. The initiality of the model SNF w.r.t. the class *POAlg*(I), and the fact that its associated multialgebra is a strong multialgebra model of I proves the last equivalence.

The conditions of this lemma reproduce the condition of theorem 11. Before reducing the four conditions of this lemma to syntactic conditions more easily provable, we will discuss its meaning.

The first condition $NF^{\supseteq}[t_1] \supseteq NF^{\supseteq}[t_2] \Rightarrow I \vdash_{POL} t_1 \supseteq t_2$ expresses the soundness of the NDC-method with respect to the specification. However, the user usually only gives the rewriting rules $R_{\supseteq}$, leaving the specification incomplete –as we will see in the examples–. This specification must be completed in order to verify this condition. Hence, we prefer to name this condition completeness of the specification with respect to the NDC-method.

The forth condition $I \vdash_{POL} t_1 \supseteq t_2 \Rightarrow NF^{\supseteq}[t_1] \supseteq NF^{\supseteq}[t_2]$ expresses the completeness of the method with respect to the specification. This condition is very easily satisfied. As it is noticed by Hussmann [Hus92] the more difficult point working with nondeterministic specifications is the soundness property of the method (or soundness of the Birkhoff theorem). Kaplan gives the theorem (theorem 2.3 in [Kap86a]) $MOD_R \models M = N$ iff $\{NF(M)\} = \{NF(N)\}$, although he does not use multialgebra models, and the theorem is stated in terms of equality, instead of inclusions.

The second property $t_2 \in NF^{\supseteq}[f(\ldots,t_1,\ldots)] \Rightarrow \exists t_3 \in NF^{\supseteq}[t_1] \,.\, t_2 \in NF^{\supseteq}[f(\ldots,t_3,\ldots)]$ is named additivity property. It is related with the use of multialgebra models. The functions in these models (from values to sets) can be extended point wise to set arguments (from sets to sets) by the additive property of the functions, obtaining a preorder model. It means that the interpretation mapping I has to be defined inductively by additivity. As we will see, to ensure this property we will require the additivity property for all the functions in the signature. This condition is also required by Hussmann [Hus92]. In fact, it becomes his DET-*additive* property by translating $t_2 \in NF^{\supseteq}[f(t_1)]$ into $f(t_1) \longrightarrow t_2 \wedge \text{DET}(t_2)$.

To reduce these four properties to syntactic ones, easier to prove, we need the following lemma.

Lemma 15. *Given a specification I containing at least the union axioms, if the orientation and completion of its axioms result in a commutative and terminating bi-rewriting system $\langle R_{\subseteq}, R_{\supseteq}\rangle$, then*

1. *If $NF^{\supseteq} \subseteq NF^{\subseteq}$, then $I \vdash_{POL} t_1 \supseteq t_2$ implies $NF^{\supseteq}(t_1) \supseteq NF^{\supseteq}(t_2)$.*
2. *If $I \vdash_{POL} t \subseteq \bigcup\{t' \mid t \xrightarrow[R_{\supseteq}]{} t'\}$ for any term $t \notin NF^{\supseteq}$, then $NF^{\supseteq}(t_1) \supseteq NF^{\supseteq}(t_2)$ implies $I \vdash_{POL} t_1 \supseteq t_2$.*
3. *If in addition the additive property $f(\ldots,X \cup Y,\ldots) = f(\ldots,X,\ldots) \cup f(\ldots,Y,\ldots)$ for any function symbol $f \in \Sigma$ holds in the specification I, and the bi-rewriting system satisfies $NF^{\supseteq}[t_1 \cup t_2] = NF^{\supseteq}[t_1] \cup NF^{\supseteq}[t_2]$ for any pair of terms t_1 and t_2, then $t_2 \in NF^{\supseteq}[f(t_1)]$ implies $\exists t_3 \in NF^{\supseteq}[t_1] \,.\, t_2 \in NF^{\supseteq}[f(t_3)]$.*

Proof. 1. Let $I \vdash_{POL} t_1 \supseteq t_2$ hold, the commutation and termination properties of $\langle R_{\subseteq}, R_{\supseteq}\rangle$ prove $t_1 \xrightarrow[\supseteq]{*} \circ \xleftarrow[\supseteq]{*} t_2$. Let $t \in NF^{\supseteq}[t_2]$ hold, we have then $t_2 \xrightarrow[\supseteq]{*} t$. The commutation and termination properties prove again $t_1 \xrightarrow[\supseteq]{*} \circ \xleftarrow[\supseteq]{*} t$. However $t \in NF^{\supseteq}$, thus, $t \in NF^{\subseteq}$ by hypothesis, and we have $t_1 \xrightarrow[\supseteq]{*} t$ and therefore $t \in NF^{\supseteq}[t_1]$.

2. The termination property and $I \vdash_{POL} t \subseteq \bigcup\{t' \mid t \xrightarrow{\supseteq} t'\}$ allow to prove by noetherian induction $I \vdash_{POL} t \subseteq \bigcup NF^{\supseteq}[t]$. The union axioms prove $I \vdash_{POL} t \supseteq \bigcup NF^{\supseteq}[t]$ and $I \vdash_{POL} \bigcup NF^{\supseteq}[t_1] \supseteq \bigcup NF^{\supseteq}[t_2]$ if $NF^{\supseteq}[t_1] \supseteq NF^{\supseteq}[t_2]$. Therefore, we have by transitivity $I \vdash_{POL} t_1 \supseteq t_2$.

3. Using the conditions of the previous point we proved $t_1 = \bigcup NF^{\supseteq}[t_1]$; and by the additional conditions of this point we have $f(\bigcup NF^{\supseteq}[t_1]) = \bigcup_{t_3 \in NF^{\supseteq}[t_1]} f(t_3)$ and $NF^{\supseteq}[\bigcup_{t_3 \in NF^{\supseteq}[t_1]} f(t_3)] = \bigcup_{t_3 \in NF^{\supseteq}[t_1]} NF^{\supseteq}[f(t_3)]$. Therefore, if t_2 belongs to this union of sets, then it belongs to one of them, that is, there exists a term $t_3 \in NF^{\supseteq}[t_1]$ such that $t_2 \in NF^{\supseteq}[f(t_3)]$.

Inspired in this SNF-model we can define a new method for checking inclusions. We name this method *nondeterministic computation* method, NDC-method for short, and we define it as follows.

Definition 16. Given a rewriting system $R_{\supseteq}$ and two terms t and u, the NDC-method is defined by $NDC(t,u) = true$ if, and only if, $NF^{\supseteq}[t] \subseteq NF^{\supseteq}[u]$.

Lemma 17. *If the conditions $I \vdash_{POL} t \subseteq u$ and $NF^{\supseteq}[t] \subseteq NF^{\supseteq}[u]$ are equivalent, the the NDC-method is sound and complete w.r.t. the class of models $POAlg(I)$.*

The following theorem is the main result of this section, and summarizes the results of all the previous lemmas.

Theorem 18. *Given a nondeterministic specification I, and a bi-rewriting system $\langle R_{\subseteq}, R_{\supseteq}\rangle$ resulting from the orientation of its axioms, if the following conditions are satisfied*

1. *the bi-rewriting system is commutative and terminating,*
2. *the axioms defining the union operator can be deduced from I,*
3. *$NF^{\supseteq} \subseteq NF^{\subseteq}$,*
4. *$I \vdash_{POL} t \subseteq \bigcup\{t' \mid t \xrightarrow{\supseteq} t'\}$ holds for any term $t \notin NF^{\supseteq}$,*
5. *$I \vdash_{POL} f(\ldots, X \cup Y, \ldots) = f(\ldots, X, \ldots) \cup f(\ldots, Y, \ldots)$ for any symbol $f \in \Sigma$*
6. *$NF^{\supseteq}[t_1 \cup t_2] = NF^{\supseteq}[t_1] \cup NF^{\supseteq}[t_2]$ for any terms t_1 and t_2,*

then the following sentences are equivalent:

$$\begin{array}{lll} POAlg(I) \models t \subseteq u & I \vdash_{POL} t \subseteq u & t \xrightarrow[R_{\subseteq}]{\bullet} \circ \xleftarrow[R_{\supseteq}]{\bullet} u \\ \overline{MAlg}(I) \models t \subseteq u & & NF^{\supseteq}[t] \subseteq NF^{\supseteq}[u] \end{array}$$

Although these conditions could seem very strange, they hold (or may hold) in most of the nondeterministic specifications. As we will see in the next example, when they do not hold is due to the incompleteness of the specification, the lack of inclusions in $R_{\subseteq}$ without computational meaning, and not to the incompleteness of the rewriting rules $R_{\supseteq}$ used to compute. In these cases it is necessary to add new axioms to the specification, which of course, reduce the number of models, and make the NDC-method and the bi-rewriting method sound and complete.

The same kind of specification completion method has been studied by Hussmann [Hus92].

3.3 An Example of Nondeterministic Specification

To show this specification completion method we will use the classical nondeterministic specification of a nondeterministic automata, in this case an automata to recognize the patterns $(0 \cup 1)^*0(0 \cup 1)^*$ and $(0 \cup 1)^*1(0 \cup 1)^*$. A first attempt to get a specification is:

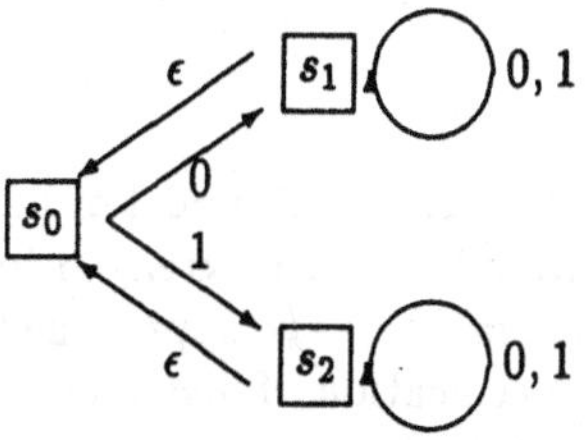

$$
\begin{array}{ll}
X \cup Y \supseteq X & X \cup Y \supseteq Y \\
trans(s_0, 0) \supseteq s_1 & trans(s_0, 1) \supseteq s_2 \\
trans(s_1, X) \supseteq s_1 & trans(s_1, X) \supseteq trans(s_0, X) \\
trans(s_2, X) \supseteq s_2 & trans(s_2, X) \supseteq trans(s_0, X) \\
prog(X, nill) \supseteq X & \\
prog(X, cons(Y, Z)) \supseteq prog(trans(X, Y), Z) &
\end{array}
$$

where all inclusions can be oriented to the right, obtaining a commutative bi-rewriting system (where $R_{\subseteq} = \emptyset$). However, it it easy to see that $trans(s_1, X)$ can be reduced by $\xrightarrow{\supseteq}$ to s_1 or to $trans(s_0, X)$, and $I \vdash_{POL} trans(s_1, X) \subseteq s_1 \cup trans(s_0, X)$ does not hold. Therefore the condition $I \vdash_{POL} t \subseteq \bigcup\{t' \mid t \xrightarrow{\supseteq} t'\}$ does not hold for all reducible terms t. This problem can be avoided adding the axiom $trans(s_1, X) \subseteq s_1 \cup trans(s_0, X)$ to the specification. The same happens with $X \cup X$ that can be reduced only to X but $X \cup X \subseteq X$ does not hold; and so on. The additivity condition makes necessary to introduce $trans(X \cup Y, Z) \subseteq trans(X, Z) \cup trans(Y, Z)$ and the same for the second argument and for *prog*. If we complete the specification in this way we obtain:

$$
\begin{array}{ll}
X \cup Y \supseteq X & X \cup Y \supseteq Y \\
X \supseteq X \cup X & \\
trans(s_0, 0) \supseteq s_1 & trans(s_0, 1) \supseteq s_2 \\
trans(s_1, X) = s_1 \cup trans(s_0, X) & trans(s_2, X) = s_2 \cup trans(s_0, X) \\
prog(X, nill) = X & \\
prog(X, cons(Y, Z)) = prog(trans(X, Y), Z) & \\
trans(X, Z) \cup trans(Y, Z) \supseteq trans(X \cup Y, Z) & \\
trans(Z, X) \cup trans(Z, Y) \supseteq trans(Z, X \cup Y) & \\
prog(X, Z) \cup prog(Y, Z) \supseteq prog(X \cup Y, Z) & \\
prog(Z, X) \cup prog(Z, Y) \supseteq prog(Z, X \cup Y) &
\end{array}
$$

which can be oriented to obtain the bi-rewriting system

$$
R_{\supseteq} = \begin{cases}
X \cup Y \xrightarrow{\supseteq} X \\
X \cup Y \xrightarrow{\supseteq} Y \\
trans(s_0, 0) \xrightarrow{\supseteq} s_1 \\
trans(s_0, 1) \xrightarrow{\supseteq} s_2 \\
trans(s_1, X) \xrightarrow{\supseteq} s_1 \\
trans(s_1, X) \xrightarrow{\supseteq} trans(s_0, X) \\
trans(s_2, X) \xrightarrow{\supseteq} s_2 \\
trans(s_2, X) \xrightarrow{\supseteq} trans(s_0, X) \\
prog(X, nill) \xrightarrow{\supseteq} X \\
prog(X, cons(Y, Z)) \xrightarrow{\supseteq} prog(trans(X, Y), Z)
\end{cases}
\qquad
R_{\subseteq} = \begin{cases}
X \cup X \xrightarrow{\subseteq} X \\
trans(X \cup Y, Z) \xrightarrow{\subseteq} trans(X, Z) \cup trans(Y, Z) \\
trans(Z, X \cup Y) \xrightarrow{\subseteq} trans(Z, X) \cup trans(Z, Y) \\
prog(X \cup Y, Z) \xrightarrow{\subseteq} prog(X, Z) \cup prog(Y, Z) \\
prog(Z, X \cup Y) \xrightarrow{\subseteq} prog(Z, X) \cup prog(Z, Y)
\end{cases}
$$

modulo the associative and commutative axioms for the union.

This new bi-rewriting system satisfies all the restrictions of the theorem 18.

The process described in this example, where a specification is completed –leaving the computational rewriting system $\xrightarrow{2}$ unchanged– corresponds to the selection of a maximally deterministic model described by Hussmann in [Hus92].

4 Conclusions

We have shown that bi-rewriting systems are a natural computational model of inequality specifications. The main results of standard rewriting have been extended to bi-rewriting. However the completion is still an open problem. We have approached the problem by solving the completion of the inequality specification of distributive lattices. The operational semantics of Unified Algebras can be based on this specification. We have also shown the usefulness of bi-rewriting systems to relate the mathematical and the operational semantics of nondeterministic specifications. Finally, we have given the conditions for the soundness and completeness of a normal form computation procedure and the bi-rewriting method, used to automatice the deduction in nondeterministic specifications. We have also given the conditions for the existence and initiality of a model based on sets of normal forms.

References

[DJ90] N. Dershowitz and J.-P. Jouannaud. Rewrite systems. In J. V. Leeuwen, editor, *Handbook of Theoretical Computer Science*. Elsevier Science Publishers, 1990.

[Hes88] W. H. Hesselink. A mathematical approach to nondeterminism in data types. *ACM Trans. Programming Languages and Systems*, 10:87–117, 1988.

[Hue80] G. Huet. Confluent reductions: Abstract properties and applications to term rewriting systems. *Journal of the ACM*, 27(4):797–821, 1980.

[Hus91] H. Hussmann. *Nondeterministic Algebraic Specifications*. PhD thesis, Institut für Informatik, Technische Universität München, München, Germany, 1991.

[Hus92] H. Hussmann. Nondeterministic algebraic specifications and nonconfluent term rewriting. *Journal of Logic Programming*, 12:237–255, 1992.

[JK86] J.-P. Jouannaud and H. Kirchner. Completion on a set of rules modulo a set of equations. *SIAM J. computing*, 15(1):1155–1194, 1986.

[Kap86a] S. Kaplan. Rewriting with a nondeterministic choice operator: from algebra to proofs. In *Proc. 1986 European Symp. on Programming*, volume 213 of *Lecture Notes in Computer Science*, pages 351–374. Springer, 1986.

[Kap86b] S. Kaplan. Simplifying conditional term rewriting systems: Unification, termination and confluence. Technical Report 316, Laboratoire de Recherche en Informatique, Universite de Paris-Sud, Orsay, France, 1986.

[Kap88] S. Kaplan. Rewriting with a nondeterministic choice operator. *J. of Theoretical Computer Science*, 56:37–57, 1988.

[LA93] J. Levy and J. Agustí. Bi-rewriting, a term rewriting technique for monotonic order relations. In *RTA'93*, volume 690 of Lecture Notes in Computer Science, pages 17–31, Montreal, Canada, 1993. Springer-Verlag.

[Lev93] J. Levy. Second-order bi-rewriting systems. Technical report, Institut d'Investigació en Intel·ligència Artificial, CSIC, 1993.

[Mes90] J. Meseguer. Rewriting as a unified model of concurrency. In *Concur'90*, Lecture Notes in Computer Science, Amsterdam, The Netherlands, 1990. Springer-Verlag.

[Mes92] J. Meseguer. Conditional rewriting logic as a unified model of concurrency. *J. of Theoretical Computer Science*, 96:73–155, 1992.

[Mos89] P. D. Mosses. Unified algebras and institutions. In *Principles of Programming Languages Conference*, pages 304–312. ACM Press, 1989.

[Nip86] T. Nipkow. Nondeterministic data types: Models and implementations. *Acta Informatica*, 22:629–661, 1986.

[PS81] G. E. Peterson and M. E. Stickel. Complete sets of reductions for some equational theories. *Journal of the ACM*, 28(2):233–264, 1981.

A Semantic Basis for Logic-Independent Transformation[1]

Junbo Liu[2]
Universität Bremen

Abstract

This paper is based on previous work by Harper, Sannella and Tarlecki who suggest a framework for giving semantic interpretations to logic representations in the LF logical framework. Besides LF, there are also other approaches that tackle the representation of logics in a meta-logic. The logic-independent aspect in the formal development of software has been investigated intensively based on abstract model theory. Less attention is paid to the proof system aspect. In this paper we treat logic-independence by considering the consequence relation that models a proof system for a logic. The existing work is generalized here to the consideration of any logic as a meta-logic, since there may be meta-logics other than LF that are more suitable and convenient for developing "object" logical systems. This generalized framework is then used for building logic-independent specifications and developments. The setting can eventually be considered as a firm semantic basis for developing logic-independent transformations.

1. Introduction

The methodology of program development by transformation integrates program (specification and) construction with verification during the development process [10][10a]. For constructing specifications in-the-large, flexible, powerful and natural structuring mechanisms are essential for making the job manageable. As indicated in [9], the structure chosen by a specifier incorporates intangible aspects of the specifier's knowledge of the problem being specified and of the relationship between parts of the problem that is vital to the understanding and use of the specification. In the early approaches [2][3], much attention has been paid to initial algebra semantics as suitable for specifying abstract data types. Also, various structuring mechanisms have been provided for building large and complex specification from smaller and simpler ones [2][3]. However, the suggested mechanisms are inadequate for specifying software systems for two reasons. Firstly, it turns out that loose specification is often preferable to the initial approach. Secondly, we may need a wide variety of logical systems for different problems(for example, equational or horn-clause logic, first-order or higher-order logics, modal or temporal logics, linear logics or operational semantics of programming languages), so that one can choose the logical system which is most suitable to the particular task (or even use several logics simultaneously). The need to use different and specialised logics may also arise in a support environment where different tools for various logics exist (proof systems, completion systems, simplifiers, etc.) or proof systems are specialised to a particular logic to achieve greater efficiency. These two additional aspects require more powerful structuring mechanisms. Results presented in [5][16][17][20] provide a solution by defining specification building operators in an arbitrary institution, where institution, as presented in [5], is used to characterize a logical system from a model theoretic view point. While this treatment is satisfactory for dealing with modular program development, even allowing for the change of logical systems at different stages of the program development, it is oriented more to program development than specification development. This fact is also highlighted in [15], where the difference between parameterized specification and specification of parametrized programs is clearly shown. The importance of this distinction is quite convincing. We believe it is a

---

1. This work is partially supported by the German Ministry of Research and Technology (BMFT) as part of the project "KORSO - Korrekte Software"

2. Universität Bremen, FB3 Informatik, Postfach 330 440, 2800 Bremen 33, Germany.
E-mail: liu@informatik.uni-bremen.de

general problem between structured specification and modular specification. Namely, specification structured toward deduction may differ from specification modularized towards implementation. Modular specification is, in general, only a special subset of structured specification, which can be implemented modularly, therefore, it is a notion related strongly to the idea of abstract model. The criterion for structured specification should be based principally on an structured reasoning, that is, the deductive aspect.

In this paper, we generalize the framework that is given in [7] for defining semantic interpretations of logic representations using the LF logical framework [6] as a meta-logic. This is because we are interested in the requirements on any logic that is used as a meta-logic, for there may be meta-logics other than LF that are more suitable as meta-logics and more convenient for developing "object" logical systems. For instance, there are also other approaches [4][13][18] that tackle the representation of logics in a meta-logic. This generalized framework is then used for building logic-independent specifications and developments. More concretely, some specification building operators in [16][17][20] are investigated again, in a logic-independent manner and relying on the extended framework. Additionally, some new specification building operators are defined that treat the inter-logic aspects of structured specifications. This setting may be eventually considered as a firm semantic basis for developing logic-independent transformations. We assume some familiarity with a few notions from category theory. See [1] [11] for all categorical definitions involved in the following sections, like the definitions of category, colimits, pushouts, products, coproducts, functors, natural transformations, etc.

2. Logical Systems and Representations

In this section, a categorical framework is taken to describe logical systems and the deductive relations one can impose on them, namely, how to represent one logical system in another one, such that proof derivation for some judgement carried out in one logic can also be obtained in the representation by another logic. For example, one may take LF [5] as a meta-logic to code equational logic or first-order logic such that valid proof trees of some judgement are simply valid terms of some type that represent judgements of object logics. The approach taken here considers logical systems mainly from a deduction point of view, which appears also in [6][7][8]. Concretely, the consequence relation is a binary relation between a subset and an element of a set of "sentences" regarded as logical formulae. This view of a logical system gives basic elements of categorical construction of semantic discourse of logical systems (from the deduction viewpoint). In the following we use ϕ and φ to denote sentences in the set of the sentences of a consequence relation, similarly Ψ and Δ to denote subsets of sentences, possibly with indices. If s: Ψ_1 --> Ψ_2 is a function, then extension to subsets is also denoted by s. The set of all subsets of a set S is denoted by $Pow(S)$ as usual. Finally, function application is expressed by juxtaposition.

Definition 2.1 (*consequence relation*) A consequence relation (*CR*) is a pair $(S, |\!-)$ where S is a set of sentences and $|\!- \subseteq Pow(S) \times S$ is a binary relation between a subset of S and an element of S.

Notice that a more categorical characterization can be given; this simple definition is taken here for brevity. In [7], the consequence relation is restricted because the main concern there is the representation of logics in LF [6]. We do not impose restrictions on the consequence relation; the meta-logic taken here can be different from LF. It is not difficult to restrict the consequence relation if a specific meta-logic is chosen later.

Definition 2.2 Let $(S, |\!-)$ be a consequence relation and let $S' \subseteq S$. The restriction of $(S, |\!-)$ to S', written $(S, |\!-) >> S'$, is the consequence relation $(S', |\!- \cap Pow(S') \times S'))$.

Definition 2.3 (*morphism of consequence relations*) A morphism of consequence relations (CR morphism) s: $(S_1, |\!-_1) \rightarrow (S_2, |\!-_2)$ is a function s: $S_1 \rightarrow S_2$ (the translation of sentences) such that if $\Delta |\!-_1 \phi$, then $s\Delta |\!-_2 s\phi$. Identity and composition are inherited from the category of sets. The CR morphism s is conservative if $\Delta |\!-_1 \phi$ whenever $s\Delta |\!-_2 s\phi$.

Proposition 2.4 Let CR be composed of the collection of consequence relations and the CR morphism between two consequence relations. ***CR*** *is a category.*

CR as a category with a consequence relation as objects and CR morphisms as morphisms describes the deductive aspect of logical systems. To be able to denote a particular logical system, we need to build an indexing domain for "constructing" that logical system. Taking the techniques presented in [5], we require for each logical system a signature category that characterizes the indexing domain of the logics. So, the logical system is formalized as a family of consequence relations indexed by a collection of signatures, which are the vocabularies for constructing sentences of the logical system. For this work, it is important that consequence be preserved in spite of the variation of signatures under the statement "truth is invariant under the change of notation". This property is guaranteed by the following functor.

Definition 2.5 (*logical system*) A logical system, or logic, is a functor $\mathcal{L}$: $\mathbf{Sig}^{\mathcal{L}} \to \mathbf{CR}$.

The category $\mathbf{Sig}^{\mathcal{L}}$ is called the *category of signatures* of $\mathcal{L}$, with its object denoted by Σ and morphism by $\sigma: \Sigma_1 \to \Sigma_2$. A signature morphism is to be thought of as specifying a "relative interpretation" of one language thhrough another. Before explaining the definition of a logical system with some examples, we refer to [8] for the justification of the relation between a institution and a logical system. This relation establishes the connection between the two different views of a logical system, namely, model theoretic and deductive. The different views of a logical system are important when discussing the purpose of structured specifications and modular specifications. The following definition of *institution* is taken from [5].

Definition 2.6 (*institution*) An institution I consists of:

- a category $\mathbf{Sig}^I$, called signatures;
- a functor $\mathbf{Sen}^I$: $\mathbf{Sig}^I \to \mathbf{Sets}$ (giving for each signature a set of sentences over it);
- a functor $\mathbf{Mod}^I$: $\mathbf{Sig}^I \to \mathbf{Cat}^{op}$ (giving for each signature a category whose objects are called signature models);
- a satisfaction relation $\models_\Sigma \subseteq |\mathbf{Mod}^I(\Sigma)| \times \mathbf{Sen}^I(\Sigma)$ for each signature Σ of $\mathbf{Sig}^I$.

  such that for each morphism $\sigma: \Sigma_1 \to \Sigma_2$ in $\mathbf{Sig}^I$, the *Satisfaction Condition*

  $$m' \models_{\Sigma_2} \mathbf{Sen}^I(\sigma)\, e \text{ iff } \mathbf{Mod}^I(\sigma)(m') \models_{\Sigma_1} e$$

  holds for each m' of $\mathbf{Mod}^I(\Sigma_2)$ and e of $\mathbf{Sen}^I(\Sigma_1)$.

Definition 2.7 An institution I determines a logical system $\mathcal{G}(I)$: $\mathbf{Sig}^I \to \mathbf{CR}$ where $\mathcal{G}(I)(\Sigma) = (\mathbf{Sen}^I(\Sigma), \models_\Sigma)$ such that for all subsets Φ and elements ϕ of $\mathbf{Sen}^I(\Sigma)$, $\Psi \models_\Sigma \phi$ iff for all models m of $\mathbf{Mod}^I(\Sigma)$, m $\models_\Sigma \phi$ whenever m $\models_\Sigma \Psi$; $\mathcal{G}(I)(\sigma) = \mathbf{Sen}^I(\sigma)$.

Proposition 2.8 For any institution I, $\mathcal{G}(I)$ defined above is indeed a logical system.

Definition 2.9 Let I be an institution and $\mathcal{L}$: $\mathbf{Sig}^I \to \mathbf{CR}$ be a logical system with, for each signature Σ of $\mathbf{Sig}^I$, $\mathbf{Sen}^I(\Sigma) = |\mathcal{L}(\Sigma)|$. We say $\mathcal{L}$ is *sound* for I if $\Psi \models^{\mathcal{L}}_\Sigma \phi$ implies $\Psi \models^I_\Sigma \phi$. If the opposite implication holds, we say $\mathcal{L}$ is *complete* for I

Example *(Many-Sorted Equational Logic)* In appendix A of [5], many-sorted logic is characterized by an institution. This institution can be used to construct the logical system of many-sorted equational logic by the method given above. However, with the new definition of logical system, we emphasize a logical system which has a corresponding proof system.

Now we are constructing the category of logics with the intention that the corresponding morphism formalizes the relation that one logic can be represented by another (from a deductive point of view). The basic idea is to precisely describe a relationship between two logical systems in the form of a translation of signatures and sentences. This means that we can consider additional properties, for example, that one deduction system can be encoded in another one such that the inference of one deduction system can be performed after "lifting" it to the other.

Definition 2.10 (*logic morphsim*) A logic morphism $\Upsilon: \mathcal{L} \to \mathcal{L}'$ is a pair $(\Upsilon^{sig}, \Upsilon^{CR})$ where Υ^{sig}: $\mathbf{Sig}^{\mathcal{L}} \to \mathbf{Sig}^{\mathcal{L}'}$ is a functor and $\Upsilon^{CR}: \mathcal{L} \to \Upsilon^{sig};\mathcal{L}'$: $\mathbf{Sig}^{\mathcal{L}} \to \mathbf{CR}$ is a natural transformation. A logic morphism is called a representation iff the functor is an embedding functor and each $\Upsilon^{CR}(\Sigma)$ is conservative for all Σ in $\mathbf{Sig}^{\mathcal{L}}$. A logic $\mathcal{L}$ is representable in a logic $\mathcal{L}'$ iff there is a representation $\Upsilon: \mathcal{L} \to \mathcal{L}'$. A representation $\Upsilon: \mathcal{L} \to \mathcal{L}'$ is surjective iff each $\Upsilon^{CR}(\Sigma)$ is surjective as a function on the underlying sets.

The condition that it is an embedding functor guarantees that the category of the signatures of the source logic is faithfully encoded in the target logic. This condition may not be necessary in general, for example, it is not required in [5] for defining an *institution morphism*. The conservativeness is explained by the following proposition.

Proposition 2.11 Let $\Upsilon: \mathcal{L} \to \mathcal{L}'$ be a representation, then for all Σ in $\mathbf{Sig}^{\mathcal{L}}$ and Ψ and ϕ in $\mathcal{L}(\Sigma)$, $\Psi \models_{\Sigma} \phi$ in $\mathcal{L}$ iff $\Upsilon^{CR}(\Sigma)(\Psi) \models_{\Upsilon^{sig}(\Sigma)} \Upsilon^{CR}(\Sigma)(\phi)$ in $\mathcal{L}'$.

This proposition gives exactly what we want from the representation, namely, to have source inference reflected in the target inference. Later, the source logic is referred to as object logic and the target logic as meta-logic.

Example (*Equational logic represented by first-order logic with equality*)
Let $\mathcal{EQ}$ and $\mathcal{FOLEQ}$ stand for equational logic and first-order logic with equality, respectively. A representation $\rho: \mathcal{EQ} \to \mathcal{FOLEQ}$ can be defined in the following way:
ρ^{sig}: $\mathbf{Sig}^{\mathcal{EQ}} \to \mathbf{Sig}^{\mathcal{FOLEQ}}$ is inclusion; ρ^{CR}: $\mathcal{EQ} \to \rho^{sig}; \mathcal{FOLEQ}$: $\mathbf{Sig}^{\mathcal{EQ}} \to \mathbf{CR}$ is inclusion, except the equal symbol in the sentence of $\mathcal{EQ}$ is translated to the equality of $\mathcal{FOLEQ}$; this can be depicted by

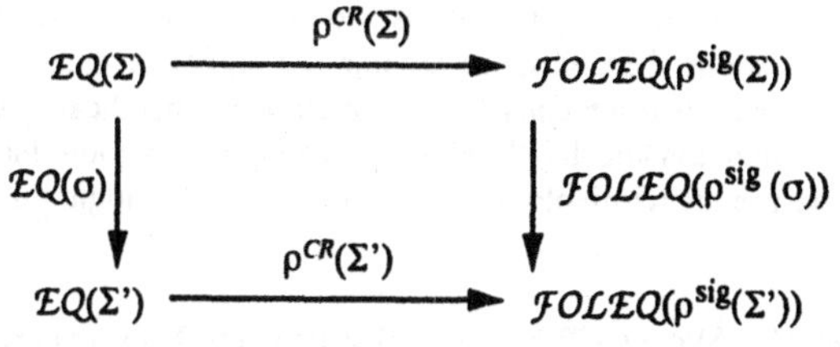

for any two signatures and signature morphism $\sigma: \Sigma \to \Sigma'$ in $\mathbf{Sig}^{\mathcal{EQ}}$. To prove that each $\rho^{CR}(\Sigma)$ is a conservative morphism is trivial in the sense that the reasoning of equality in $\mathcal{FOLEQ}$ is the same as in $\mathcal{EQ}$. Consequently we can conclude that $\mathcal{EQ}$ is representable in $\mathcal{FOLEQ}$.

Definition 2.12 Let **Log** be composed of a collection of objects and morphisms between objects. Objects are logics as functors defined above, and morphisms are logic morphisms between two logics. The identity is the pair of the identity functor on $\mathbf{Sig}^{\mathcal{L}}$ and the identity natural transformation on $\mathcal{L}$. Composition[1] is defined by

1. We use ";" for composition of functors and the composition between functors and natural transformations.

$$(\Upsilon_1^{sig}, \Upsilon_1^{CR}); (\Upsilon_2^{sig}, \Upsilon_2^{CR})) = (\Upsilon_1^{sig}; \Upsilon_2^{sig}, \Upsilon_1^{CR}; (\Upsilon_1^{sig},; \Upsilon_2^{CR}))$$

for two logic morphisms $\Upsilon_1: \mathcal{L} \rightarrow \mathcal{L}'$ and $\Upsilon_2: \mathcal{L}' \rightarrow \mathcal{L}''$.

Proposition 2.13 Log is a category.

With the category of **Log**, some analysis can be carried out, for example, what categorical constructions of logical systems can be performed, and under what conditions.

3. Specification of Logics in a Metalogical System

3.1 Specializing a Metalogic

The purpose of the representation between $\mathcal{L}$ and $\mathcal{L}'$ is to semantically characterize when we may use $\mathcal{L}'$ as an "inference engine" for $\mathcal{L}$. That is, all inferential activities in $\mathcal{L}$ are reduced to inferential activities in $\mathcal{L}'$ so that a theorem prover for $\mathcal{L}'$ can be, after modification, used for $\mathcal{L}$. Assume $\mathcal{ML}$ (standing for meta-logic) is a logic chosen as the target logic, then the representation of a logic $\mathcal{OL}$ (standing for object logic) in $\mathcal{ML}$ means that we first of all have to construct a specification $\mathcal{SPL}$ for $\mathcal{OL}$, then somehow compile this specification with $\mathcal{ML}$ to obtain a logical system $\mathcal{NL}$. $\mathcal{SPL}$ is a correct specification with respect to $\mathcal{OL}$ iff $\mathcal{OL}$ is surjectively representable in $\mathcal{NL}$. The surjection expresses the requirement that $\mathcal{ML}$ can be specialized for $\mathcal{OL}$ in the sense that the sentences of $\mathcal{NL}$ all have their origin in $\mathcal{OL}$. The question is how to compose specifications of logical systems in a meta-logic and how to compile a specification such that the result is indeed a logical system in the sense of definition 2.4. Here, for specifications of logical systems, we follow the approach in [4][6][19], namely to code all logical formulae as terms and rules as operators; moreover, a subset of terms is considered as judgements (distinguished from other syntactic terms).

We generalize the method presented in [7] for a Logical Framework to an arbitrary meta-logic. Consequently the interpretation of a specification is simply the specialization of the chosen meta-logic. That is, the category of the signatures of a specified logic is a specific subcategory of the signatures of a meta-logic, and the sentences and consequence relations of the meta-logic are restricted by the subcategory. This method is described precisely in the sequel. To allow for the specialization of a logic, we need some assumptions about the meta-logic. Firstly, we assume the signature category of a meta-logic has inclusions and that the meta-logic preserves this inclusion in the consequence relations. Secondly, we assume the signature category has pushouts along inclusions; this is needed when we construct parameterized specifications. See [7] for detailed definitions. We may further assume that the signature category has coproduct constructions (if this is required). Later, we use the terminology logic specification and logic presentation interchangeably.

Definition 3.1 Let $\mathcal{ML}$: $\mathbf{Sig}^{\mathcal{L}} \rightarrow \mathbf{CR}$ be a logical system and Σ a signature of $\mathbf{Sig}^{\mathcal{L}}$. The category that includes Σ, written $\mathbf{Sig}^{\mathcal{L}\Sigma}$, is the full subcategory of the $\mathbf{Sig}^{\mathcal{L}}$ determined by inclusion $\iota: \Sigma \rightarrow \Sigma'$, more explicitly, $\mathbf{Sig}^{\mathcal{L}\Sigma}$ has, as objects, Σ' if there is an inclusion $\iota: \Sigma \rightarrow \Sigma'$. Morphisms of $\mathbf{Sig}^{\mathcal{L}\Sigma}$ are inherited from $\mathbf{Sig}^{\mathcal{L}}$.

Definition 3.2 Let $\mathcal{ML}$: $\mathbf{Sig}^{\mathcal{ML}} \rightarrow \mathbf{CR}$ be a logical system and Σ be a signature of $\mathbf{Sig}^{\mathcal{ML}}$. The logical system $\mathcal{L}\Sigma$: $\mathbf{Sig}^{\mathcal{ML}\Sigma} \rightarrow \mathbf{CR}$ induced by Σ is

$$\mathcal{L}\Sigma(\Sigma') = \mathcal{ML}(\Sigma') \qquad \mathcal{L}\Sigma(\sigma) = \mathcal{ML}(\sigma)$$

for all Σ' and $\sigma: \Sigma_1 \rightarrow \Sigma_2$ in $\mathbf{Sig}^{\mathcal{ML}\Sigma}$.

By invoking this method of specializing a meta-logic, we obtain an object logical system which is representable in the meta-logic.

Proposition 3.3 $\mathcal{L}\Sigma$ is representable in $\mathcal{ML}$.

As already indicated in the above discussion, in practice, further restriction of $\mathcal{L}\Sigma$ is needed; since, in the sentences of $\mathcal{L}\Sigma$, there are sentences that are not judgements of the logical system to be constructed. We would like to have a method that can also exclude non-judgement sentences and restrict the consequence relation correspondingly. Firstly, let us give a definition.

Definition 3.4 $\mathcal{L}$ is soundly representable in $\mathcal{ML}$ iff there is a surjective representation from $\mathcal{L}$ to $\mathcal{ML}$.

For this work, the method in definition 3.2 is not sufficient. We need additional information for further specializing the meta-logic.

Definition 3.5 A logic presentation in a meta-logic $\mathcal{ML}$ is a pair $((\Sigma, \Im), \mathcal{ML})$ such that Σ and $\Im$ are signatures of $\mathbf{Sig}^{\mathcal{L}}$.

Definition 3.6 Let $((\Sigma, \Im), \mathcal{ML})$ be a logic presentation in the meta-logic $\mathcal{ML}$; then the logical system $\mathcal{L}\Sigma\Im$ presented by $((\Sigma, \Im), \mathcal{ML})$, is defined as

$\mathbf{Sig}^{\mathcal{L}\Sigma\Im}$ is defined by $\mathbf{Sig}^{\mathcal{L}\Sigma}$ as in the definition 3.2, and for each $\mathcal{L}\Sigma\Im$ signature Σ', $\mathcal{L}\Sigma\Im(\Sigma') = \mathcal{ML}(\Sigma') >> S$ where S is the set of sentences in $\mathcal{ML}(\Im)$, and for each $\sigma: \Sigma_1 \rightarrow \Sigma_2$ in $\mathbf{Sig}^{\mathcal{L}\Sigma\Im}$, $\mathcal{L}\Sigma\Im(\sigma) = \mathcal{ML}(\sigma) >> S$; where >> is similarly defined as in definition 2.2.

Proposition 3.7 $\mathcal{L}\Sigma\Im$ is indeed a logical system in the sense of definition 2.4.

3.2. Towards Structured Presentations

The simple way of presenting a logic in the aforementioned manner can be tedious and difficult: tedious if a logic has to be coded again and again for different purposes, difficult if a logic to be coded is very large. The method that will be investigated below considers how to provide various structuring mechanisms for overcoming the aforementioned problems. First of all, we see that all presentations in a meta-logic give a presentation category with the help of the following definition.

Definition 3.8 A presentation morphism is a morphism between two logic presentations in the meta-logical system $\mathcal{ML}$ denoted by $\sigma: ((\Sigma_1, \Im_1), \mathcal{ML}) \rightarrow ((\Sigma_2, \Im_2), \mathcal{ML})$, that is, a pair of morphisms: $\sigma_\Sigma: \Sigma_1 \dashrightarrow \Sigma_2$, and $\sigma_\Im: \Im_1 \rightarrow \Im_2$.

Definition 3.9 $\mathbf{Logpres}_{\mathcal{ML}}$ is composed of a collection of logic presentations in the meta-logic $\mathcal{ML}$, and a collection of presentation morphisms between any two logic presentations. Identity and composition are inherited from the signature of the $\mathcal{ML}$ and extended pairwise.

Proposition 3.10 $\mathbf{Logpres}_{\mathcal{ML}}$ is a category.

Definition 3.11 $I\mathcal{L}$: $\mathbf{Logpres}_{\mathcal{ML}} \rightarrow \mathbf{Log}$ is defined by

- assigning each $((\Sigma, \Im), \mathcal{ML})$ in $\mathbf{Logpres}_{\mathcal{ML}}$ to a logical system $\mathcal{L}\Sigma\Im$ (obtained by following definition 3.6) in **Log**, and

- assigning each presentation morphism $\sigma: ((\Sigma_1, \Im_1), \mathcal{ML}) \rightarrow ((\Sigma_2, \Im_2), \mathcal{ML})$ to a logic morphism $\Upsilon: \mathcal{L}\Sigma_1\Im_1 \rightarrow \mathcal{L}\Sigma_2\Im_2$ that consists of a pair $\Upsilon^{sig}: \mathbf{Sig}^{\mathcal{L}\Sigma_1\Im_1} \rightarrow \mathbf{Sig}^{\mathcal{L}\Sigma_2\Im_2}$ and $\Upsilon^{CR}: \mathcal{L}\Sigma_1\Im_1 \rightarrow \Upsilon^{sig}; \mathcal{L}\Sigma_2\Im_2: \mathbf{Sig}^{\mathcal{L}\Sigma_1\Im_1} \rightarrow \mathbf{CR}$. Υ^{sig} is constructed by the pushout of $(\sigma\Sigma: \Sigma_1 \rightarrow \Sigma_2)$ and $(\iota: \Sigma_1 \rightarrow \Sigma_1')$ for each Σ_1' in $\mathbf{Sig}^{\mathcal{L}\Sigma_1\Im_1}$. This extends also to the signature morphism. Assume $\Upsilon^{sig}(\Sigma_1') = \Sigma_2'$, then $\Upsilon^{CR}(\Sigma_1')$ is defined by taking CR morphism $\mathcal{ML}(\sigma\Sigma^{\#})$ where $\sigma\Sigma^{\#}$ is obtained by the pushout construction in $\mathcal{ML}$. We have intentionally omitted restrictions, but these can be easily added.

Proposition 3.12 $I\mathcal{L}$: $\mathbf{Logpres}_{\mathcal{ML}} \rightarrow \mathbf{Log}$ is a functor.

In the following, we will use $\mathcal{PL}$ to denote an arbitrary logic presentation. By saying a logical system $\mathcal{L}$ is presented by $\mathcal{PL}$, we mean $\mathcal{L}$ is the logical system $IL(\mathcal{PL})$ if $\mathcal{PL}$ is a presentation in the meta-logic $\mathcal{ML}$.

Definition 3.13 (*parameterized presentation*) A logic presentation pair ($\mathcal{P}1$, $\mathcal{P}2$) is called a parameterized presentation if there is an inclusion presentation morphism between $\mathcal{P}1$ and $\mathcal{P}2$. The inclusion means both components of the presentation morphism are inclusions.

Proposition 3.14 ***$Logpres_{\mathcal{ML}}$ has pushouts along inclusions.***

Definition 3.15 (*parameter passing*) Let ($\mathcal{P}1$, $\mathcal{P}2$) be a parametrized presentation and $\mathcal{P}3$ be a logic presentation such that there is a presentation morphism between $\mathcal{P}1$ and $\mathcal{P}3$. Then the presentation expressed by *instantiate* ($\mathcal{P}1$, $\mathcal{P}2$) *by* $\mathcal{P}3$ is the pushout along the inclusion.

Example We refer to the example in [7]. Here only an informal outline is given. The example is that we can construct a presentation of the logic for pure universal quantification parameterized by arbitrary formulae. By instantiating the parameter with propositional logic we get a version of first-order logic.

4. Program Specification in a Multi-Logical Environment

4.1 Theory Category

A program specification is intended to describe all the properties of all programs that may be developed from it. Taking this view, the meaning of a (program) specification is exactly a theory in the chosen logic that is used to describe these properties. Let us first give the precise definition of the theory in a logical system.

Definition 4.1 A triple $<\Sigma, \mathcal{E}, \mathcal{L}>$ is called a theory base iff Σ is a signature of the $\mathbf{Sig}^{\mathcal{L}}$ and $\mathcal{E}$ is a subset of sentences of $\mathcal{L}(\Sigma)$ whenever $\mathcal{L}$: $\mathbf{Sig}^{\mathcal{L}} \rightarrow \mathbf{CR}$ is a logical system. The closure of a theory base is a function defined as

$$\mathbf{Closure}\,(<\Sigma, \mathcal{E}, \mathcal{L}>) = <\Sigma, \{e \mid e \in L(\Sigma), \mathcal{E} \models_{\Sigma} e\}, \mathcal{L}>$$

that is also a theory base.

Definition 4.2 A theory $\mathcal{T}$ in the logical system $\mathcal{L}$ is a theory base $<\Sigma, \mathcal{E}, \mathcal{L}>$ such that $\mathbf{Closure}\,(<\Sigma, \mathcal{E}, \mathcal{L}>) = <\Sigma, \mathcal{E}, \mathcal{L}>$.

Definition 4.3 A theory morphism ι: $<\Sigma, \mathcal{E}, \mathcal{L}> \rightarrow <\Sigma', \mathcal{E}', \mathcal{L}>$ in the logical system $\mathcal{L}$ is a signature morphism ι: Σ --> Σ' such that $\mathcal{L}(\iota)(\mathcal{E})$ is included in $\mathcal{E}'$.

Definition 4.4 $\mathbf{Theo}_{\mathcal{L}}$ is composed of a collection of theories in the logical system $\mathcal{L}$ and a collection of theory morphisms between any two theories. Identity and composition are inherited from $\mathbf{Sig}^{\mathcal{L}}$.

Proposition 4.5 ***$Theo_{\mathcal{L}}$ is a category.***

In practice, there may be several logics employed for one task [5][16]. Therefore it is meaningful to construct not only the theory category for one logical system, but also a category of all categories of theories for all logical systems in **Log**.

Definition 4.6 Let Υ: $\mathcal{L} \rightarrow \mathcal{L}'$ be a logic morphism, $\mathbf{Theo}_{\mathcal{L}}$ and $\mathbf{Theo}_{\mathcal{L}'}$ categories of theories for logical systems $\mathcal{L}$ and $\mathcal{L}'$, respectively. Then $\mathcal{Th}$: $\mathbf{Theo}_{\mathcal{L}} \rightarrow \mathbf{Theo}_{\mathcal{L}'}$ is defined as follows: for each theory $\mathcal{T}$ in $\mathbf{Theo}_{\mathcal{L}}$ we assign a theory $\mathcal{T}'$ in $\mathbf{Theo}_{\mathcal{L}'}$ such that $\mathcal{T}' = \mathbf{Closure}(\Upsilon(\mathcal{T}))$ where $\Upsilon(\mathcal{T}) = <\Upsilon^{sig}(\Sigma), \Upsilon^{CR}(\Sigma)(\mathcal{E}), \mathcal{L}'>$ if $\mathcal{T} = <\Sigma, \mathcal{E}, \mathcal{L}>$. For each theory morphism η: $\mathcal{T} \rightarrow \mathcal{T}_1$ in $\mathbf{Theo}_{\mathcal{L}}$ we assign a morphism $\eta' = \Upsilon^{sig}(\eta)$: $\Upsilon(\mathcal{T}) \rightarrow \Upsilon(\mathcal{T}_1)$ in $\mathbf{Theo}_{\mathcal{L}'}$.

Proposition 4.7 ***$\mathcal{Th}$: $Theo_{\mathcal{L}} \rightarrow Theo_{\mathcal{L}'}$ is a functor.***

Definition 4.8 **Theo** is composed of a collection of all $\mathbf{Theo}_{\mathcal{L}}$ for each $\mathcal{L}$ in **Log** and collection of functors between any two $\mathbf{Theo}_{\mathcal{L}}$ and $\mathbf{Theo}_{\mathcal{L}'}$. Identity and composition are inherited from the functor category.

Proposition 4.9 Theo is a category.

The definitions of categories of theories form the semantic basis for interpreting the structured program specifications defined in the sequel.

4.2 Theory Presentation as Specification

To specify a program to be written or a problem to be solved, we have to have some syntactic sugar for readability and understandability. Here we simply take a modified theory base as a theory presentation or specification. Roughly speaking, a specification is then a triple including the signature of a theory, a set of sentences to present the theory, and a logic presentation to indicate which logical system is employed for building the intended theory. For logics with finite signatures, a finite presentation can be designed.

Definition 4.10 (*specification*) A specification is a theory presentation that is a triple $<\Sigma, \mathcal{E}, \mathcal{LP}>$ where Σ is a signature of the $\mathbf{Sig}^{\mathcal{L}}$ and $\mathcal{E}$ is a subset of sentences of $\mathcal{L}(\Sigma)$, whenever $\mathcal{LP}$ is a logic presentation and $\mathcal{L}$: $\mathbf{Sig}^{\mathcal{L}} \to \mathbf{CR}$ is the logical system presented by $\mathcal{LP}$.

For each specification, we can give its interpretation in the category $\mathbf{Theo}\mathcal{L}$, if the logic presented in the specification is $\mathcal{L}$.

Definition 4.11 (*denotation*) The denotation of a specification $<\Sigma, \mathcal{E}, \mathcal{LP}>$ is the theory $\mathcal{T}$ in $\mathbf{Theo}\mathcal{L}$ where $\mathcal{L}$ is the logic presented by $\mathcal{PL}$, and $\mathcal{T} = \mathbf{Closure}(<\Sigma, \mathcal{E}, \mathcal{L}>)$.

This interpretation of specifications gives us the deductive semantics of program specifications in the sense that by writing a theory presentation (specification) we denote all properties that are included in the corresponding theory. Finally we put specifications together along specification morphisms defined below.

Definition 4.12 (*Specification Morphism*) A specification morphism ρ: $\mathcal{SP} \to \mathcal{SP}'$ is a pair $(\rho^{sig}, \rho^{\Upsilon})$ such that ρ^{sig} is signature morphism between signatures of $\mathcal{SP}$ and $\mathcal{SP}'$ and is also a theory morphism between the their denotations; ρ^{Υ} is a logic presentation morphism between their logic presentations. A specification morphism is an inclusion iff ρ^{sig} and $\rho^{\Upsilon}$are both inclusions, moreover ρ^{sig} induces an inclusion between sentences of specifications.

It is obvious that specifications, and the morphisms between them, form a category. We denote this by $\mathbf{Spec}_{\mathcal{ML}}$. The existence of pushouts along inclusions in the category of logic presentation can then be extended to the pushouts of specifications along inclusions.

Proposition 4.13 Spec$\mathcal{ML}$ has pushouts along inclusions.

4.3 Specification Building Operators

Large specifications are unreadable and complex specifications are unmanageable, so they are not suitable for development and redevelopment in the context of software construction. Many mechanisms have been provided for structuring specifications so that large specifications are built from smaller ones and complex specifications from simpler ones. Here, we pay special attention to the specification building operators in [17][20] for their power in structuring specifications. For instance, as pointed out in [5][16], if the language of structured specifications admits translations and inverse image along logics, then we can combine specifications from several different logical systems. In the following we concentrate on the specifications built from various logics based on one meta-logic.

Definition 4.14 (*Concrete Syntax of Structured Specifications*)

$$
\begin{aligned}
\mathcal{SP} == \; & <\Sigma, \mathcal{E}, \mathcal{LP}> \\
& \mathcal{SP} \cup \mathcal{SP} \\
& \textit{enrich } \mathcal{SP} \textit{ by } <\Sigma, \mathcal{E}, \mathcal{LP}> \\
& \textit{translate } \mathcal{SP} \textit{ by } \sigma \\
& \textit{change logic } \mathcal{SP} \textit{ by } \rho \\
& \textit{parameterize } \mathcal{SP} \textit{ with } \mathcal{SP} \\
& \textit{instantiate } \mathcal{SP} \textit{ with } \mathcal{SP}
\end{aligned}
$$

First of all we explain , informally, the purpose of each specification building operator. The starting point is, of course, a basic specification (which has already been defined in the previous section). If we write two specifications for one object, we can join them together by $\cup$. *Enrich* can be used to extend an existing specification keeping all the properties of the "old" specification. *Translate* is quite useful for renaming. *Change logic* allows a specification written in one logic to be presented as a specification in another logic. *Parameterization* gives the possibility for abstraction. In the following we present well-formedness rules and denotations of specifications, which are adequate for the proof search described in the next section.

Definition 4.15 (*Well-formedness and Denotations of Structured Specifications*)

$\mathcal{SP} \cup \mathcal{SP}'$

is well formed iff two specifications have the same logic system and signatures. The denotation is **Closure**($<\Sigma, \mathcal{E}, \mathcal{L}>$) where $\mathcal{E}$ is the union of the sets of sentences in **Closure**($\mathcal{SP}$) and **Closure**($\mathcal{SP}'$) respectively.

enrich $\mathcal{SP}$ *by* $<\Sigma, \mathcal{E}, \mathcal{LP}>$

is well formed iff the logic $\mathcal{L}$ of $\mathcal{SP}$ is presented by $\mathcal{LP}$, and, for the signature Σ' of the theory denoted by $\mathcal{SP}$, if there is no morphism between Σ and Σ', and $<\Sigma'', \mathcal{E}, \mathcal{LP}>$ is a basic specification, where Σ'' is the coproduct of Σ and Σ'. The denatation is **Closure**($<\Sigma'', \mathcal{E}, \mathcal{L}>$), where $\mathcal{E}$ is the union of the sentences in the denotation of $\mathcal{SP}$ and $<\Sigma'', \mathcal{E}, \mathcal{LP}>$, respectively.

translate $\mathcal{SP}$ *by* σ

is well formed iff $\mathcal{SP}$ has the signature Σ and we have $\sigma: \Sigma \rightarrow \Sigma'$. The denotation is **Closure**($\mathcal{L}(\sigma(\mathcal{T}))$) where $\mathcal{L}$ is the logic of $\mathcal{SP}$ and $\mathcal{T}$ is the denotation of $\mathcal{SP}$.

change logic $\mathcal{SP}$ *by* σ

is well formed iff the logic presentation of $\mathcal{SP}$ is $\mathcal{PL}$ and $\sigma: \mathcal{PL} \rightarrow \mathcal{PL}'$ is a logic presentation morphism. $\Upsilon: \mathcal{L} \rightarrow \mathcal{L}'$ is the induced logic morphism by σ where $\mathcal{L}$ and $\mathcal{L}'$ are logics presented by $\mathcal{PL}$ and $\mathcal{PL}'$, respectively. The denotation is **Closure**($<\Upsilon^{sig}(\Sigma), \Upsilon^{CR}(\Sigma)(\mathcal{E}), \mathcal{L}'>$) where $<\Sigma, \mathcal{E}, \mathcal{L}>$ is the denotation of $\mathcal{SP}$.

parameterize $\mathcal{SP}$ *with* $\mathcal{SP}'$

is well formed iff there is an inclusion morphism $\iota: \mathcal{SP}' \rightarrow \mathcal{SP}$.

instantiate $\mathcal{SP}$ *with* $\mathcal{SP}''$

is well formed iff $\mathcal{SP}$ is in the form *parameterize* $\mathcal{SP}$ *with* $\mathcal{SP}'$ and there is a specification morphism $\rho: \mathcal{SP}' \rightarrow \mathcal{SP}''$. The denotation is **Closure**($\mathcal{SP}^*$) where $\mathcal{SP}^*$ is the pushout of $\iota: \mathcal{SP}' \rightarrow \mathcal{SP}$ and $\rho: \mathcal{SP}'' \rightarrow \mathcal{SP}'$.

Now we can a construct structured specification that can be interpreted within the theory category of logical systems. Multi-logical program specifications are considered in the sense that one may use several logical systems simultaneously for one task. Of course, various additional structuring mechanism are possible, for instance, to use of more than one metaloigcal system. We will consider these extensions in future work.

5. Proof Search and Specification Development

5.1 Proof Search with Structured Specifications

One of the most important purposes of structured specifications, as mentioned earlier, is to support structured reasoning. We consider now how the various structured specifications, presented above, can be used for structured reasoning.

Definition 5.1 (*proof search*) Proof search is defined as the relation $\mathcal{SP} \models \phi$, that is, to check if ϕ is in the theory of $\mathcal{SP}$. We assume the well-formedness of ϕ with respect to $\mathcal{SP}$.

Structured Reasoning requires that we split a proof search in this form into smaller ones if it is constructed from smaller specifications. We take the structured proof search in [7] and modify it for our case.

***Proposition** 5.2 Let $\mathcal{SP}$ be a structured specification and ϕ a well-formed sentence w.r.t. $\mathcal{SP}$. Then the proof search $\mathcal{SP} \models \phi$ is equivalent to the following structured proof search by analyzing the structure of $\mathcal{SP}$. Notice that each case has its applicability condition, which, if it can not be established, means we cannot proceed with the structured proof search.*

1. *enrich $\mathcal{SP}$ by $<\Sigma, \mathcal{E}, \mathcal{LP}> \models \phi$, where $\mathcal{SP} \models \phi$ if ϕ is a sentence of $\mathcal{SP}$;*
2. *translate $\mathcal{SP}$ by $\sigma \models \phi$ if there exists a Φ such that $\mathcal{SP} \models \Phi$ and $\sigma(\Phi) \models \phi$;*
3. *instantiate (parameterize $\mathcal{SP}$ with $\mathcal{SP}'$) with $\mathcal{SP}'' \models \phi$ if $\phi=\sigma(\varphi)$, where σ is a theory morphism between $\mathcal{SP}'$ and $\mathcal{SP}''$, and $\mathcal{SP} \models \varphi$;*
4. *change logic $\mathcal{SP}$ by $\sigma \models \phi$ if $\phi=\Upsilon(\varphi)$ and $\mathcal{SP} \models \varphi$, where Υ is the induced logic morphism.*

5.2 Towards Modular Specifications

We assume that if two specifications $\mathcal{SP}1$ and $\mathcal{SP}2$ are related, then there is a theory morphism between them. Let us denote this as $\mathcal{Rel}(\mathcal{SP}1, \mathcal{SP}2)$. According to the definition given earlier we can interpret them in the institution induced by the logical systems $\mathcal{L}1$ and $\mathcal{L}2$ of $\mathcal{SP}1$ and $\mathcal{SP}2$, respectively. This consideration establishes the relation between specifications based on the abstract model theory in [5] and the structured specifications developed here. It is natural to define a modular specification with respect to the model-oriented definition. Firstly we recall some definitions from [5].

Definition 5.3 Let $\mathcal{F}: \mathcal{T}1 \to \mathcal{T}2$ be a theory morphism. then a $\mathcal{T}1$-model $\mathcal{A}$ is $\mathcal{F}$-protected iff it has a free extension $\mathcal{A}^{\$}$ along $\mathcal{F}$ such that the universal morphism is an isomorphism.

Definition 5.4 (*Modular Specification*) $\mathcal{Rel}(\mathcal{SP}1, \mathcal{SP}2)$ is called modular iff $\mathcal{F}: \mathcal{T}1 \to \mathcal{T}2$ is the related theory morphism in the sense that $\mathcal{T}1$, $\mathcal{T}2$ are the denotations of $\mathcal{SP}1$ and $\mathcal{SP}2$, respectively. Moreover every $\mathcal{T}1$-model $\mathcal{A}$ is $\mathcal{F}$-protected.

Here a very theoretical criterium is taken to provide the definition of modular specification. This decision guarantees, mainly, the strict re-use of the implementation of one specification by another. In practise, the situation could be different, there maybe more powerful reuse concepts available in the implementation and therefore, looser definition at the specification level is admissible for modular specifications.

Definition 5.5 (*Refinement*) Let $\mathcal{SP}1$ and $\mathcal{SP}2$ be two specifications. We say $\mathcal{SP}2$ is a refinement of $\mathcal{SP}1$, denoted by $\mathcal{SP}1 \Longrightarrow \mathcal{SP}2$, iff there is a representation Υ between $\mathcal{L}1$ and $\mathcal{L}2$, where $\mathcal{L}1$ and $\mathcal{L}2$ are logics of $\mathcal{SP}1$ and $\mathcal{SP}2$ respectively, such that $\mathcal{SP}2 \models \Upsilon(\mathcal{SP}1)$. $\Upsilon(\mathcal{SP}1)$ denotes all the translated sentences of $\mathcal{SP}1$.

The first step of specification development should then be the restructuring of specifications such that the requirements of modularity are satisfied. We believe, therefore, that in a formal development process, program development can be delayed until after the development of modular specifications.

6. Conclusion

We have presented in this paper an approach generalising previous work [5][7] for developing logic-independent specifications in a structured way. By distinguishing structured vs. modular specification, we have re-considered specification building operators based on arbitrary logical systems, that is, logical systems that are defined from a deduction point of view.

There are various extensions and further work to be done. Firstly, as indicated in [7] and further developed in [8], the logical system given here only reflects the intention that a sentence be "closed". To take the techniques developed in [8], we can also cope with free variables. There is some other work towards categorical construction of logical presentation [4]; how to define logic-independent specification building operators in that framework is also worth investigating. We also have to further complete the various possible definitions of modular specifications. We are also interested in proof and transformation techniques for developing modular specifications. Eventually we will design a transformation system based on this framework.

Acknowledgments: Thanks go to Bernd Krieg-Brückner and Don Sannella for their suggestions and encouragement, to Burkhart Wolff for discussions. Collaboration with Owen Traynor provided many of the ideas.

7. References

[1] M. Arbib, E. Manes. Arrows, Structures, and Functors - the Categorical Imperative. New York, London: Academic Press 1975.

[2] H. Ehrig, B. Mahr. Fundamentals of Algebraic Specification I: Equations and Initial Semantics. EATCS Monographs on Theoretical Computer Science New York: Springer (1985).

[3] H. Ehrig, B. Mahr. Fundamentals of Algebraic Specification II. EATCS Monographs on Theoretical Computer Science New York: Springer (1990).

[4] P. Gardner. Representing Logics in Type Theory. Phd Thesis, LFCS Report ECS-LFCS-92-227, Dept. of Computer Science, Uni. of Edinburgh.

[5] J.A. Goguen, R.M. Burstall. Institutions: Abstract Model Theory for Specification and Programming. J. ACM, vol. 39, NO. 1, pp 95 -146 (Jan. 1992).

[6] R. Harper, F. Honsell, G. Plotkin. A Framework for Defining Logics. Proc. 2nd IEEE Symp. on Logic in Computer Science, Conell, pp 194-204 (1987).

[7] R. Harper, D. Sannella, A. Tarlecki. Structure and Representation in LF. LFCS Report ECS-LFCS-89-75, Dept. of Computer Science, Uni. of Edinburgh.

[8] R. Harper, D. Sannella, A. Tarlecki. Logic Representation in LF. Proc. 3nd Summer Conference in Category Theory and Computer Science, LNCS 389, pp 250 - 272 (1989).

[9] B. Krieg-Brückner, D. Sannella. Structuring Specifications in-the-Large and in-the-Small: Higher-Order Functions, Dependent Types and Inheritance in SPECTRAL. Proc. TAPSOFT 91, LNCS 582(1991).

[10] B. Krieg-Brückner, E. Karlsen, J. Liu, O. Traynor. The PROSPECTRA Methodology and System: Uniform Transformational (Meta-) Development. VDM '91: Formal Software Development Methods, S. Prehn W.J. Toetenel (eds.), LNCS 552, pp 362 - 397.

[10a] B. Hoffmann, B. Krieg-Brückner (eds.): PROgram development by SPECification and TRAnsformation: Methodology, Language Family, System. LNCS 680 (1993).

[11] J. Lambek, P.J. Scott. Introduction to Higher Order Categorical Logic. Cambridge studies in advanced mathematics 7, Cambridge University Press 1986.

[12] Z. Luo. An Extended Calculus of Constructions. Phd Thesis, LFCS Report ECS-LFCS-90-118, Dept. of Computer Science, Uni. of Edinburgh.

[13] J. Meseguer. General Logics, Proc. of the Logic Colloquium '87, H. D. Ebbinghaus et al. (eds.), North Holland.

[14] F. Pfenning. Logic programming in the LF logical framework. In G. Huet and G. Plotkin (eds.): Logical Frameworks. Cambridge University Press 1991.

[15] D. Sannella, S. Sokolowski, A. Tarlecki. Toward formal development of programs from algebraic specifications: parameterization revisited. Report 6/90, Informatik, Universität Bremen (1990).

[16] D. Sannella, A. Tarlecki. Towards formal development of programs from algebraic specifications: implementations revisited. In H. Ehrig et al.(eds.): TAPSOFT 87 LNCS 249 pp 96 - 110 (1987).

[17] D. Sannella, M. Wirsing. A kernel language for algebraic specifications and implementations LNCS 158, pp 413 - 427 (1983).

[19] L. Paulson. The foundations of a generic theorem prover. Technical Report 130, Computer Laboratory, University of Cambridge.

[19] L. Paulson. Logics and Computation: interactive proof with Cambridge LCF. Cambridge Tracts in Theoretical Computer Science 2, Cambridge University Press 1987.

[20] M. Wirsing. Structured Algebraic Specifications: a kernel language. TCS 42, pp 123 - 249 (1986).

Unified Algebras and Abstract Syntax

Peter D. Mosses

Computer Science Department, Aarhus University
Ny Munkegade Bldg.540, DK–8000 Aarhus C, Denmark

Abstract. We consider the algebraic specification of abstract syntax in the framework of unified algebras. We illustrate the expressiveness of unified algebraic specifications, and provide a grammar-like notation for specifying abstract syntax, particularly attractive for use in semantic descriptions of full-scale programming languages.

1 Introduction

The algebraic specification framework of *unified algebras* is somewhat unorthodox: both individuals and sorts are treated as values, so operations can be applied to sorts as well as to individuals. Moreover, no distinction is made between a singleton sort and its only element. The empty sort serves as a convenient representation of undefinedness.

Signatures of unified algebras are merely ranked alphabets. Axioms of specifications are (definite) Horn clauses involving equality, sort inclusion, and individual inclusion. The usual functionalities of operations, which are signature components in most frameworks, can easily be specified as axioms. Models of unified specifications are distributive lattices with bottoms, equipped with a distinguished (usually discrete) subset of individuals, together with inclusion-preserving functions. Specifications have initial models. Initial constraints can be specified, providing a simple form of parameterization. For formal details, see [10]; for examples, see [12, Appendix E].

Unified algebras are claimed to have significant advantages over conventional frameworks, in particular concerning the treatment of polymorphism and genericity. Here, we show how unified algebras allow the specification of abstract data types that provide an elegant and flexible treatment of *abstract syntax*.

Abstract syntax is used primarily in formal semantic descriptions of programming languages; other applications include syntax-directed editing and program transformation systems. Essentially, abstract syntax ignores details concerned with unambiguous parsing and lexical symbols, and focuses on the compositional tree structure of parsed phrases. Thereby it provides a simple interface between (context-free) concrete syntax and semantics.

There are various ways of specifying abstract syntax. With some of them, for instance McCarthy's original formulation [9], specifications resemble ordinary algebraic specifications of constructor, selector, and discriminator operations. With others, they resemble ordinary context-free grammars. It has also been shown how to transform grammars into many-sorted algebraic specifications, obtaining the corresponding abstract syntax as initial many-sorted algebras [3].

What is 'wrong' with these previous approaches to specifying abstract syntax? Well, the ones that look like ordinary algebraic specifications are not sufficiently perspicuous when used on large-scale programming languages. The ones that look like ordinary grammars are usually quite perspicuous, but their algebraic interpretation is somewhat clumsy; they are also rather *rigid*, in that nonterminal symbols cannot be replaced by the corresponding alternatives without disturbing the meaning of the specification.

We shall see that with unified algebras, a grammar is *itself* a set of axioms for an algebraic specification: there is no need for any transformation. The advantages of this approach include: it is straightforward to allow algebraic sort constructors corresponding to *regular expressions*; abstract syntax is naturally *order-sorted*; nonterminal symbols can be *substituted* by their alternatives without disturbing the specified algebra; and the *micro-syntax* of lexical symbols can be accommodated without bother.

The contribution of this paper is threefold. It illustrates the use of the expressiveness of unified algebraic specifications, thereby motivating this framework in relation to conventional frameworks. It provides an algebraic notation for specifying abstract syntax that is particularly attractive for use in semantic descriptions of realistic, large-scale programming languages. Finally, the algebraic sort constructors given here are generally useful in specifications of abstract data types: they allow a simple treatment of operations with variable numbers of arguments, e.g., an operation that constructs a list from n components for any n.

The paper is organized as follows. Section 2 summarizes the notation used in unified algebraic specifications, defines the notion of a unified algebra, and discusses constraints. Section 3 considers previous approaches to abstract syntax. Section 4 gives a unified algebraic specification of an abstract data type of trees. Section 5 proves that the given specification is consistent, by defining a nontrivial model; it also considers initial models of the specification. Section 6 provides a simple illustration of the unified algebraic specification of abstract syntax, and argues that the approach has some beneficial pragmatic qualities that previous approaches lack.

2 Unified Algebras

The following definitions are from [10] (except that 'elements' are now called 'individuals').

Definition 1. A *signature* Σ for a unified algebra is a set of operation *symbols*, each symbol having the *rank* determined by the number of place-holder signs '_' that it contains. Signatures of unified algebras always include the symbols _ | _ and _ & _ of rank 2, and the symbol nothing of rank 0.

Definition 2. A *unified algebra* A has a *universe*, which is a distributive lattice [4] with a bottom value, together with a distinguished subset $I_A \subseteq A$ of *individuals*. The partial order of the lattice is denoted by $\leq_A$. For each operation symbol f in the signature Σ of A, there is a monotone (total) function f_A on the universe of the lattice, with $\_ \mid \_A$ being the join operation of the lattice, $\_ \& \_A$ the meet, and $\mathsf{nothing}_A$ the bottom of the lattice.

Notice that the operations are not required to be strict or additive, nor to preserve the property of individuality. Moreover, we do not insist that the lattices serving as universes of unified algebras have tops.

Technically, the framework of unified algebras is 'unsorted'. However, *all* the values in the universe of a unified algebra may be thought of as sorts, with the individuals corresponding to singleton sorts. The partial order of the lattice represents sort inclusion; join is sort union and meet is sort intersection. The individuals do *not* have to be the atoms of the lattice, just above the bottom: for instance, the meet of two individuals is below both of them, but need not be identified with the bottom value. Those values that do not include any individuals at all, such as the bottom value, are vacuous sorts, often representing the lack of a proper result that arises from applying an operation to unintended arguments. A special case of a unified algebra is a *power algebra*, whose universe is a power set, ordered by set inclusion, with the singletons as individuals [10].

Definition 3. The *axioms* of a unified algebraic specification are definite Horn clauses, written $e_1; \cdots; e_n \Rightarrow e$, where the antecedents $e_1, \cdots, e_n$ and the consequent e are equations $t_1 = t_2$, inclusions $t_1 \leq t_2$, or *individual* inclusions $t_1 : t_2$ between terms. The terms are built from the operation symbols in the signature of the specification and from *variables*. Each axiom is treated as if all the variables occurring in it are universally quantified.

For perspicuity, we use *mixfix* notation when writing terms, replacing the placeholder signs '_' in symbols by the arguments and inserting grouping parentheses when necessary for disambiguation. It is convenient to assume that infixes associate to the left, so that further parentheses can be omitted.

Definition 4. An axiom $e_1; \cdots; e_n \Rightarrow e$ of a unified specification is *satisfied* by a unified algebra A (of the same signature) if whenever all the antecedents $e_1, \cdots, e_n$ hold in A, so does the consequent e. An equation $t_1 = t_2$ holds in A when the terms t_1, t_2 have identical values (whether or not these values are individuals, proper sorts, or vacuous). An inclusion $t_1 \leq t_2$ holds when the value of t_1 is below that of t_2 in the partial order of the sort lattice. An individual inclusion $t_1 : t_2$ holds when the value of t_1 is not only included in that of t_2, but also in the distinguished subset of individuals I_A. A unified algebra that satisfies all the axioms of a specification is called a *model* for the specification.

Unified algebraic specifications always have initial models, because they are essentially just unsorted Horn clause logic (with equality) specifications: the structure of unified algebras is entirely captured by a set of Horn clauses, given in the Appendix. One reason for not restricting attention to the power algebras mentioned above is that then specifications—even very simple ones—would fail to have initial models. For example, let a and b be specified to be individuals, and let c : a | b,. so that c is an *individual* included in the union a | b; since individuals are singleton sets in power algebras, this forces *either* c=a *or* c=b, and there is clearly no initial model for the specification.

Although it can be shown that unified algebras provide a *liberal* institution, with the usual notion of reduct functor, it is problematic to define useful constraints in unsorted frameworks, because the ordinary reduct functor only forgets operations—never values. However, by using a *more forgetful* reduct functor (treating all ground terms as if they were sorts) one can simulate the way that many-sorted and order-sorted forgetful functors deal with values, thereby providing *bounded data constraints* whose effect is similar to that of ordinary data constraints in conventional frameworks. See [10] for the details.

3 Abstract Syntax

Let us briefly consider some previous approaches to abstract syntax. At the end of this section, we shall discuss the relationship between concrete and abstract syntax.

McCarthy [9] was the first to formulate a notion of abstract syntax. There he proposed the use of syntax that differs from context-free grammars (BNF) by being "analytic rather than synthetic; it tells how to take a program apart, rather than how to put it together". The syntax should also be independent of the notation used to represent sums, etc., in program texts.

This idea is realized by introducing predicates to distinguish between different constructs. For simple arithmetic expressions, one might have the predicates isvar(t), isconst(t), issum(t), and isprod(t). For each predicate, one introduces selector functions, such as addend(t) and augend(t) for terms t satisfying issum(t). Finiteness of terms can be expressed by the convergence of a recursively defined predicate expressed using the introduced predicates and selector functions.

McCarthy also considers "languages which have both an analytic and a synthetic syntax satisfying certain relations". The synthetic syntax uses constructor functions, such as mksum(t,u) and the relations are specified by equations, such as addend(mksum(t,u)) $= t$.

The specification of abstract syntax in Meta-IV, the meta-notation of VDM [2], exploits a systematic naming convention for predicates and constructor functions: is-$A(o)$ tests whether an object o is of type A, mk-$A(o_1,\ldots,o_n)$ constructs objects of type A from appropriate arguments. Types are specified in a notation close to BNF. E.g., for arithmetic expressions one may specify:

Expr = Var | Const | Sum | Prod
Sum :: Expr Expr
...

Equations are interpreted as domain equations. The | stands for simple, nondiscriminated union; the :: ensures that objects created by the corresponding constructor function are distinct from those created by other constructors. Here the constructor function mk-Sum(l,r) is implicitly declared, and one can select the two subexpressions of a sum s by pattern-matching, as in let mk-Sum(l,r) $= s$ in .... Meta-IV also allows explicit selector functions to be introduced, as in:

Sum :: s-left:Expr s-right:Expr .

Meta-IV goes on to allow the use of domain operators for tuples (A^*, $A+$), optional domains ($[A]$), power sets (A-**set**), finite maps, partial functions, and total functions.

The form of abstract syntax used in connection with syntax-directed editing in [5, 15] is based on *phyla* and constructor operators. A phylum is simply a set of terms, and the operators map terms to terms. Phyla may not overlap. Specifications may be factored, so arithmetic expressions could be specified as:

expr = Var(ID) | Const(INT) | Sum, Prod(expr,expr)

where ID and INT are predefined lexical phyla, specified using regular expressions. In the ASF+SDF formalism [6], abstract syntax is derived from the context-free grammar that is used to specify concrete syntax, for example:

ID	→	EXP
NAT	→	EXP
EXP "+" EXP	→	EXP {left}
EXP "*" EXP	→	EXP {left}
"(" EXP ")"	→	EXP {bracket}

Abstract syntax trees are then generated automatically from parsed strings.

Denotational semantics (see [16] for a comprehensive text, or [11] for an introduction) has exploited various meta-notations for specifying abstract syntax. Scott and Strachey [17] originally paid scant respect to syntax: they used ambiguous, indexed grammars, written in a variant of BNF; they assumed that languages come equipped with grouping parentheses so that the compositional structure of a phrase could always be made precise when necessary. For example:

I ∈ Iden
K ∈ Const
E ∈ Expr
O ∈ Oper
E ::= I | K | E_0 O E_1 | (E)
O ::= + | *

Later Stoy [18] interpreted such grammars as defining sets of parse trees, and pointed out that they may be just as abstract as McCarthy's abstract syntax, if the grammar is chosen appropriately.

The initial algebra approach to abstract syntax (and semantics) [3] shows the existence of initial algebras for each many-sorted signature Σ using a concrete representation of trees. By identifying abstract syntax with an isomorphism class of initial algebras, independence from representational details is obtained, and algebraic homomorphisms from abstract syntax to target algebras having the same signature are uniquely defined. To specify an abstract syntax, one merely gives the signature Σ. It was shown that one can obtain signatures systematically from context-free[1] grammars, by mapping each nonterminal A of a grammar G to a sort symbol, and regarding each production $A_0 \rightarrow u_0 A_1 u_1 \ldots A_n u_n$ (where the u_i are sequences of terminal symbols) as an operation symbol from argument sorts $A_1, \ldots, A_n$ to sort A_0. The initial algebras with this signature are essentially parse trees for derivations in G (whether or not the grammar is ambiguous).

We see that most of the approaches considered above have the emphasis on *synthetic* abstract syntax, where notation is provided for constructing abstract phrases. Moreover, several approaches directly exploit context-free grammars, where terminal symbols are used to distinguish between different constructs.

This departure from McCarthy's original concept of abstract syntax, which was primarily analytic, has been found to be beneficial in various applications. No abstractness is hereby lost—providing one doesn't insist on a precise correspondence between the symbols used in grammars for concrete syntax and for abstract syntax—because in *all* approaches, even in McCarthy's, one has to choose *some* symbols for naming operations, and it is neither more nor less abstract to choose, say, mk-Sum with prefix notation in some algebraic signature, than to choose + with infix notation in the corresponding context-free grammar.

Since the grammars used for abstract syntax are not intended for parsing, they may be ambiguous (hence simpler) and yet still specify sorts of abstract syntax trees precisely. And when one does want to relate concrete syntax to abstract syntax, the relation is much easier to see when the terminal symbols used in the grammar for abstract syntax are suggestive of the corresponding concrete symbols.

However, there is still one mismatch: in practice, the concrete syntax of real programming languages is usually specified with grammars that exploit some form of *regular expressions*, as in so-called Extended BNF. It appears that only the Meta-IV approach to abstract syntax caters for the trees with unbounded branching that naturally arise from parsing according to such grammars. And although one could generalize the translation from grammars to signatures in the initial algebra approach to cope with regular expressions, the resulting signatures would be quite messy, with a new sort for each regular expression used in the grammar.

Thus there is a need for a simple algebraic treatment of context-free grammars allowing regular expressions, for use in specifying abstract syntax. We now proceed to provide such a treatment.

4 Trees

This section gives a unified algebraic specification of an abstract data type of (finite) trees, including operations for expressing regular sets of trees.

The first line of the specification below declares the signature of the specification. (The symbols _ | _ , _ & _ , and nothing are always implicitly in the

[1] The grammars are allowed to be infinite, so they may generate non-context-free languages.

signature.) The constant character stands for some unspecified alphabet, whose individuals are to be used as the leaves of our (otherwise unlabelled) trees. The intended interpretation of the binary operation symbol _ _ (juxtaposition) is concatenation of sequences, and the empty parentheses are to be interpreted as the empty sequence. The unary operation symbol _* is to be the Kleene-*, mapping any sort of tree T to a sort including precisely those individual sequences whose components are all of sort T; more generally, it may be applied to a sort of sequences of trees. Finally, $[\![\_]\!]$ constructs an individual tree from its branches. N.B. it is *not* a semantic function itself! (If $\mathcal{F}$ _ is a semantic function, it will still be correct to use the familiar $\mathcal{F}[\![\ldots]\!]$ in semantic equations.) Both _ _ and $[\![\_]\!]$ are to extend naturally from individuals to arbitrary sorts, e.g., (a b) is to be a sort that includes all individuals $(x\ y)$ where x and var y are individuals included in sorts a and b, respectively.

$$\textbf{introduces: } \mathsf{character}\ ,\ \mathsf{tree}\ ,\ \_\ \_\ ,\ (\ )\ ,\ \_^*\ ,\ [\![\_]\!]\ .$$

(1) $(a\ b)\ c = a\ (b\ c)$.

(2) $(\ )\ a = a$.

(3) $a\ (\ ) = a$.

(4) $a\ (b \mid c) = (a\ b) \mid (a\ c)$.

(5) $(a \mid b)\ c = (a\ c) \mid (b\ c)$.

(6) $\mathsf{nothing}\ a = \mathsf{nothing}$.

(7) $a\ \mathsf{nothing} = \mathsf{nothing}$.

(8) $a^* = (\ ) \mid (a\ a^*)$.

(9) $a^* = (\ ) \mid (a^*\ a)$.

(10) $(a\ x) \leq x \ \Rightarrow\ a^*\ x \leq x$.

(11) $(x\ a) \leq x \ \Rightarrow\ x\ a^* \leq x$.

(12) $\mathsf{tree} = \mathsf{character} \mid [\![\ \mathsf{tree}^*\ ]\!]$.

(13) $[\![\ a \mid b\ ]\!] = [\![\ a\ ]\!] \mid [\![\ b\ ]\!]$.

(14) $[\![\ \mathsf{nothing}\ ]\!] = \mathsf{nothing}$.

(15) $a : \mathsf{tree}^* \ \Rightarrow\ [\![\ a\ ]\!] : \mathsf{tree}$.

(16) $(\ ) : \mathsf{tree}^*$.

(17) $a : \mathsf{tree}^*\ ;\ b : \mathsf{tree}^* \ \Rightarrow\ (a\ b) : \mathsf{tree}^*$.

Axioms (1)–(11) are taken almost straight from [7], where they (together with some of the axioms and the rules of inference stated in our Appendix) are shown to provide a complete deductive system for equations between regular sets over an alphabet.[2] Concerning the use of Horn clauses, note that no finite set of pure equations can be a base for the equational theory of regular sets, in the absence of auxiliary operation symbols. In any case, a straightforward Horn clause specification seems preferable to an intricate equational specification, at least in regard to practical reasoning on the basis of specifications.

[2] This does not imply that the axioms are complete for proving equalities between regular expressions that are allowed to use the intersection operation _ & _ .

The framework of unified algebras provides some formal abbreviations for commonly occurring patterns of axioms. Exploiting these, the above specification can be written somewhat more succinctly:

introduces: character , tree , _ _ , ( ) , _* , ⟦ _ ⟧ .
_ _ :: tree*, tree* → tree* (*total*, *associative*, *unit is* ( ))
$a^* = (\,) \mid (a\ a^*) = (\,) \mid (a^*\ a)$.
$(a\ x) \leq x \ \Rightarrow\ a^*\ x \leq x$.
$(x\ a) \leq x \ \Rightarrow\ x\ a^* \leq x$.
tree = character | ⟦ tree* ⟧ .
⟦ _ ⟧ :: tree* → tree (*total*) .
( ) : tree* .

A 'functionality' of the form f _ :: $t_1 \rightarrow t_2$ is equivalent to the inclusion axiom f $(t_1) \leq t_2$; notice that the t_i need not be constants. Monotonicity then implies f $(x_1) \leq t_2$ for all arguments $x_1 \leq t_1$. The 'attribute' *total* on a functionality expresses that an operation is the natural (strict, additive) extension to sorts of some ordinary total operation on individuals. We don't bother to specify the functionality of _*, as it would be tree → tree*, making a tautology. Note that we must *not* specify _* to be total, as it is to be neither strict nor additive, nor to map individuals to individuals!

The above specifications are, in the absence of any explicit constraints, interpreted *loosely*: any unified algebra (with the declared signature) satisfying the stated axioms would be a model. Here, however, we intend the individuals of our models to be only the finite sequences of finite individual trees. Moreover, models should not equate individual trees that have different shapes or leaves. As usual with initial algebra approaches to specification, there should be no 'junk' and no 'confusion'.

All this can be specified by a *bounded data constraint* that leaves the individuals included in character open, while insisting that the values—both sorts and individuals—included in tree* be freely generated by these characters, relative to the specified axioms. Formally, the constraint consists of a *theory inclusion*. Unified algebraic specifications allow such constraints to be specified succinctly using references to modules. Here, we do not bother to introduce notation for modules. The desired constraint is simply the inclusion of the theory whose only explicit operation symbol is character, with no explicit axioms, in the theory presented by the above specification.

5 Correctness

It is easy to specify axioms that express intended properties of operations. Unfortunately, it is also easy make a mistake! For instance, one might specify an axiom that should hold only for a variable taking *individual* values, but not for vacuous or proper sorts. The possibility of instantiating the axiom with these sorts may then lead to unwelcome consequences—perhaps even to the identification of all values! (Such dangers are not special to unified algebras: the treatment of partial operations and errors in many-sorted algebraic specifications is notoriously tricky.)

In the case of trees, we have a good idea of what the intended models are—up to isomorphism—so we can check the correctness of our specification by defining a particular unified algebra and verifying that it satisfies all the axioms. We should also check that our model satisfies the specified bounded data constraint, which here ensures that models with the same individual characters form an isomorphism class.

For any set C (of characters) not containing the value λ let the unified algebra U be defined as follows. We use ordinary notation for mathematical definitions of sets, partial functions, and sequences of numbers and functions. In particular, sequence concatenation is written $p \cdot p'$, and ε is the empty sequence. Sequences of natural numbers p in N^* represent positions in trees; the functions f in T represent finite trees by mapping positions to labels in $C \cup \lambda$, the labels of interior nodes being always λ.

$$
\begin{aligned}
T &= \{f : N^* \stackrel{\sim}{\to} (C \cup \lambda) \mid \\
&\qquad |\mathsf{dom}(f)| < \infty; \\
&\qquad \forall p \in N^* \forall n \in N (p \cdot n \in \mathsf{dom}(f) \Rightarrow p \in \mathsf{dom}(f),\ f(p) = \lambda); \\
&\qquad \forall p \in N^* \forall n \in N (p \cdot (n+1) \in \mathsf{dom}(f) \Rightarrow p \cdot n \in \mathsf{dom}(f))\} \\
S &= T^* \\
U &= \mathcal{P}(S) \\
\leq_U &= \subseteq \\
I_U &= \{\{s\} \mid s \in S\}.
\end{aligned}
$$

For each operation symbol f in the specified signature the interpretation as a total function (of 0, 1, or 2 arguments) on U is defined as follows:

$$
\begin{aligned}
\_\,|\,\_{}_U(a,b) &= a \cup b \\
\_\,\&\,\_{}_U(a,b) &= a \cap b \\
\mathsf{nothing}_U &= \emptyset \\
\mathsf{character}_U &= \{[\varepsilon \mapsto c] \mid c \in C\} \\
\mathsf{tree}_U &= T \\
\_\ \_{}_U(a,b) &= \{x \cdot y \mid x \in a; y \in b\} \\
(\ )_U &= \{\varepsilon\} \\
\_^*{}_U(a) &= \{\varepsilon\} \cup \{x_1 \cdot \ldots \cdot x_n \mid x_1, \ldots, x_n \in a; n \geq 0\} \\
[\_]_U(a) &= \begin{cases} \emptyset, \text{ if } a = \emptyset; \\ \bigcup\{\mathsf{node}(f_0, \ldots, f_n) \mid \\ \qquad x \in a; x = f_0 \cdot \ldots \cdot f_n; f_0, \ldots, f_n \in T\}, \text{ otherwise} \end{cases}
\end{aligned}
$$

where we define the auxiliary functional node for each n by:

$$
\mathsf{node}(f_0, \ldots, f_n)(p) = \begin{cases} \lambda, & \text{if } p = \varepsilon; \\ f_i(p'), & \text{if } p = (i \cdot p'), 0 \leq i \leq n; \\ \text{undefined}, & \text{otherwise.} \end{cases}
$$

The partial functions in the set T mapping sequences $n_1 \cdot \ldots \cdot n_m$ of natural numbers $n_i \in N$ represent trees whose leaves are labelled with characters $c \in C$, and whose internal nodes are unlabelled. The function mapping only ε to a character c represents that character; that mapping only ε to λ represents the tree with no branches at all. The set S consists of sequences of functions, representing sequences of trees. (T^* is the well-known set of sequences of elements from the set T; it could be defined in terms of higher-order functions to avoid any trace of circularity, at some extra notational expense.) U is the power set consisting of all subsets of S, ordered by set inclusion, and the set I_U of individuals is the set of all singletons in U. Note that we do not take account of the natural partial order on the partial functions themselves.

The interpretation of the various operation symbols as (total) functions on U is rather straightforward, except perhaps for that of node construction: the partial function node($f_0, \ldots, f_n$) inspects the first branch number, say i, in its argument p, and applies the corresponding subtree f_i to the rest of of p; if the argument p is the empty number sequence, it returns λ.

Proposition 5. *The structure U defined above is a unified algebra, and it satisfies axioms (1)–(17) from Section 4.*

Proof. It is easy to see that U is a distributive lattice with a bottom, and that the operation symbols $\_ \mid \_$, $\_ \& \_$, and **nothing** are interpreted correctly. The operations corresponding to $\_\ \_$ and $[\![\_]\!]$ are defined as pointwise extensions to U of functions on S, which ensures that they are monotone, strict, additive, and map individual arguments to individuals. Thus axioms (4)–(7) and (13)–(15) are satisfied. Since the only functions in T that cannot be returned by node($f_0, \ldots, f_n$) are precisely those that map ε to a character c, axiom (12) is satisfied. The specified sequencing operation satisfies axioms (1)–(3) because the mathematical sequencing notation does. Similarly for axioms (8) and (9).

For axiom (10), let a and x have values $\bar{a}$ and $\bar{x}$ such that $\_\ \_{}_U(\bar{a}, \bar{x}) \subseteq \bar{x}$ holds. We have to show $\_\ \_{}_U(\_^*{}_U(\bar{a}), \bar{x}) \subseteq \bar{x}$ holds. Each element in $\_\ \_{}_U(\_^*{}_U(\bar{a}), \bar{x})$ consists of a finite, possibly-empty sequence s of partial functions formed by concatenating sequences $s_1, \ldots, s_n$ contained in $\bar{a}$ with a sequence s_0 contained in $\bar{x}$. If $n = 0$, the result follows immediately. Otherwise, consider the concatenation of s_n with s_0; from $\_\ \_{}_U(\bar{a}, \bar{x}) \subseteq \bar{x}$ this must be an element of $\bar{x}$. By a simple induction we get $s \in \bar{x}$ and the result follows. By symmetry, axiom (11) is satisfied as well.

So U satisfies the axioms of our specification, which demonstrates that the specification is consistent. But does it satisfy the bounded data constraint given in Section 4? No, it doesn't! For consider, say, the term $[\![(\ )]\!] \,\&\, [\![\ [\![(\ )]\!]\ ]\!]$. Clearly, the value of this term in U is the empty set. Almost as clearly, the equation $[\![(\ )]\!] \,\&\, [\![\ [\![(\ )]\!]\ ]\!]$ = **nothing** is not a consequence of the axioms of our specification (including those given in the Appendix). Hence U has 'confusion', so it cannot be freely generated by C relative to the specified axioms. Thinking of U as the model we are trying to characterize, we might say that our *specification* gives rise to 'junk', rather than U having 'confusion'. This specification junk consists of distinct expressible *sorts* that denote equal sets in U; however, there are no junk individuals at all. Less seriously, U has unreachable junk that cannot be expressed by ground terms, arising from the use of the (uncountable!) unrestricted powerset $\mathcal{P}(S)$, which includes various nonregular sets of character sequences, for example. This problem could be eliminated by reducing U to its smallest subalgebra.

We could try to mend this discrepancy between our specification and its intended model in several ways:

1. Add further axioms to our specification, such that all ground equations involving _&_ that are satisfied in U become consequences. We have recently proved a corresponding result [1] in the absence of node construction ⟦_⟧, and it is conjectured that the specification concerned—and its correctness proof—can be extended to the algebra considered here. Note that the axioms given by Kozen for his *action lattices* [8] relate meet only to join, not to sequencing or *. Moreover, action lattices involve *residuation* [14], which is nonmonotonic and so cannot be used as an operation in unified algebras.
2. Relax the notion of models of bounded data constraints in unified algebras, so that *extensionally-equal* sorts may always be equated in a model. This complicates the notion of a model of a constrained specification, but it might be a viable extension of the framework.
3. Define the problem away by removing _ & _ from unified algebras, so that models are merely semilattices. Then the problematic identities cannot be expressed, and the reduced U would presumably be a model of the specified bounded data constraint. The drawback here is that it is actually quite useful in practice to have _ & _ available! For instance, we might want to specify that truth-values and numbers are to be disjoint. Of course, meet could always be explicitly introduced and axiomatized when needed; but if we introduced it together with our specification of trees, our problem would promptly reappear.

Further investigation of these possibilities is out of the scope of this paper.

6 Unified Abstract Syntax

Let us now turn to the use of our notation for trees in the specification of abstract syntax. The idea is rather simple: we use sort equations to define abstract syntax as a collection of sorts of trees.

First, it is convenient to extend our specification of trees with the following notation:

introduces: string , $\_^{+}$, $\_^{?}$.

string = ⟦ character* ⟧ .

$a^{+} = a\ a^{*}$.

$a^{?} = (\ ) \mid a$.

Let us also assume a definite notation for individual characters and strings. For each printing (or blank) character c, there is supposed to be a symbol 'c' that denotes the corresponding individual in character. The symbols digit and letter can then easily be specified to denote the expected subsorts of character. Moreover, the symbol "$c_1 \ldots c_n$" abbreviates ⟦ 'c_1' ... 'c_n' ⟧, thus denoting an individual in string since strings are simply trees whose branches are all characters.[3]

Now consider the following unified algebraic specification. If one ignores the double brackets ⟦...⟧, it looks just like a context-free grammar exploiting regular expressions, with terminal symbols being written in quotes. (Although the need for the double brackets below might be considered a drawback by some, their use avoids relying on obscure precedence rules for disambiguating grouping in grammar specifications. Moreover, they make it possible to specify the elimination of 'chain-nodes' in abstract syntax trees.)

grammar:

Stmt = ⟦ Iden ":=" Expr ⟧ | ⟦ "begin" Stmt (";" Stmt)* "end" ⟧ |
⟦ "if" Expr "then" Stmt ("else" Stmt)$^?$ ⟧ .

Expr = Numl | Iden | ⟦ Expr Oper Expr ⟧ .

Oper = "+" | "−" | "*" | "=" .

Numl = ⟦ digit$^+$ ('.' digit$^+$)$^?$ ⟧ .

Iden = ⟦ letter (letter | digit)* ⟧ .

The specification of **grammar:** at the beginning formally abbreviates the specification of our general notation for trees, characters, and strings, together with the introduction of the left hand side symbols of the equations as constants in the signature. This makes the above equations well-formed axioms. Each equation defines the interpretation of a constant to be a particular subsort of tree. In general it can also be useful to have constants standing for subsorts of tree*, for instance Stmts = Stmt (";" Stmt)*.

Observe the following properties of the specification:

- The sort ⟦ Iden ":=" Expr ⟧ includes only individual trees with three branches, the second branch being always the string ":=". In contrast, the sort ⟦ "begin" Stmt (";" Stmt)* "end" ⟧ includes trees with unbounded branching.
- The sort ⟦ "if" Expr "then" Stmt ("else" Stmt)$^?$ ⟧ is entirely equivalent to the union ⟦ "if" Expr "then" Stmt ⟧ | ⟦ "if" Expr "then" Stmt "else" Stmt ⟧.
- Individuals (e.g., "begin") are mixed with proper sorts (e.g., Stmt) as arguments to the binary sequencing operation _ _ . It would be tedious if one had to use different symbols for an individual and the singleton sort which includes just that individual.
- The sorts Numl and Iden are *subsorts* of Expr, rather than component sorts. Of course if one really wants them as components, all one has to do is to enclose them in ⟦...⟧.

[3] To specify this notation for strings formally would require a schematic presentation of an infinite signature and a corresponding set of axioms.

- The sorts Numl and Iden are also subsorts of string. (This would not be the case for Numl is we had used the string "." instead of the character '.'.)
- The sort Iden includes the words "begin", "end", etc. It is in fact quite easy to define a subsort of Iden that is disjoint from such reserved words, since one can specify disjointness of sorts x and y using $x \,\&\, y =$ nothing. Of course the reserved words are a finite set, so the unreserved words are regular and could still be specified without the meet operation available—but the specification would then be *extremely* tedious!
- The 'organization' of the grammar does not affect the structure of the specified trees. For instance, we may replace the alternative ⟦ Expr Oper Expr ⟧ by ⟦ Expr "+" Expr ⟧ | ... | ⟦ Expr "=" Expr ⟧ without changing the semantics of the specification at all.

Assume that we restrict models of the above specification to initial models, using an empty bounded data constraint. This ensures that models only contain finite trees, and that distinct tree terms denote distinct trees—up to associativity and unit laws for the binary sequencing of branches. The class of specified models then gives us the intended abstract syntax. Note that the models contain all trees, with the sorts actually specified in the grammar denoting the expected subsorts.

Notice that the use of strings as 'terminal' components does not decrease the abstractness of our abstract syntax: using arbitrarily-chosen labels to distinguish between nodes with the same nonterminal component sorts instead would give isomorphic models. The strings used above suggest the corresponding terminal symbols that *might* be used in a corresponding concrete syntax; in practical applications, such as semantic descriptions of realistic programming languages, the mnemonic value of the strings can be extremely valuable.

The use of such abstract syntax in semantic descriptions is illustrated in [12]. (A slightly different signature is used there for sequences, requiring that sequence arguments to operations like _* be enclosed in angle brackets $\langle \ldots \rangle$ rather than ordinary parentheses. This avoids the 'invisible' operation symbol _ _, which tends to give rise to ambiguity when used together with action notation in action semantic descriptions.)

The sequencing and *-operations are also extremely convenient for reducing operations with varying numbers of arguments to unary ones. For example, list of _ :: item* → list allows list of $(x_1 \ \ldots \ x_n)$ for constructing a list with the components $x_1, \ldots, x_n$, for any $n \geq 0$.

7 Conclusion

We have specified an algebraic notation for trees and regular expressions, and shown that the axioms have a nontrivial model. This notation allows perspicuous and flexible specifications of abstract syntax for programming languages by extended context-free grammars, as has been illustrated. Terms in our tree notation can be used as sorts when specifying other operations, for instance when using semantic equations to define semantic functions, as in denotational or action semantics. This is made possible by the use of unified algebras, the expressiveness of which is fully exploited when specifying abstract syntax grammars: productions of the grammar are sort equations, and sort constructing operations are applied to mixtures of individuals and proper sorts. The notation for regular expressions can also be useful when specifying abstract data types with operations (such as list construction) that are naturally regarded as applied to ungrouped but ordered collections of arguments.

It may be desirable to generalize the notion of models of bounded data constraints, so that extensionally-equal sorts can be identified in a model even when their equality does not follow directly from the specified axioms in the logic of unified algebras. This would support the view, espoused by the author in [13], that it is really only the individuals themselves that matter, the sorts are there merely to classify the individuals. Sort inclusions are often significant, but sort equalities are usually irrelevant.

Acknowledgments Valentin Antimirov provided many useful comments during the preparation of this paper. The work reported here has been partially funded by the Danish Science Research Council project DART (5.21.08.03).

Appendix

The logic of unified algebras is given by the following definite Horn clauses. (The axioms characterizing distributive lattices could be given purely equationally, with $x \leq y$ being regarded as an abbreviation for $x \mid y = y$.) Recall from Section 2 that $x{:}y$ holds when x is not only included in the sort y but also x is an *individual*.

(1) $a = b \,;\, b = c \;\Rightarrow\; a = c \,.\quad a = b \;\Rightarrow\; b = a \,.\quad a = a \,.$

(2) $a \leq b \,;\, b \leq c \;\Rightarrow\; a \leq c \,.\quad a \leq a \,.$
$a \leq b \,;\, b \leq a \;\Rightarrow\; a = b \,.\quad \mathsf{nothing} \leq a \,.$

(3) $a : a \,;\, a \leq b \;\Rightarrow\; a : b \,.\quad a : b \;\Rightarrow\; a : a \,.$
$a : b \;\Rightarrow\; a \leq b \,.\quad a : \mathsf{nothing} \;\Rightarrow\; b = c \,.$

The last axiom above ensures that nothing is vacuous, except in the trivial one-point model. An alternative would be to permit falsity as a consequent in our Horn clauses, and expect initial models to exist only when some model exists.

(4) $a \mid (b \mid c) = (a \mid b) \mid c \,.\quad a \mid b = b \mid a \,.\quad a \mid a = a \,.$
$a \mid \mathsf{nothing} = a \,.\quad a \leq c \,;\, b \leq c \;\Rightarrow\; a \mid b \leq c \,.\quad a \leq a \mid b \,.$

(5) $a \,\&\, (b \,\&\, c) = (a \,\&\, b) \,\&\, c \,.\quad a \,\&\, b = b \,\&\, a \,.\quad a \,\&\, a = a \,.$
$a \,\&\, \mathsf{nothing} = \mathsf{nothing} \,.\quad c \leq a \,;\, c \leq b \;\Rightarrow\; c \leq a \,\&\, b \,.\quad a \,\&\, b \leq a \,.$

(6) $a \,\&\, (b \mid c) = (a \,\&\, b) \mid (a \,\&\, c) \,.\quad a \mid (b \,\&\, c) = (a \mid b) \,\&\, (a \mid c) \,.$

Furthermore, for each operation symbol f of rank n the following axioms are provided, for $i = 1$ to n:

$$x_i \leq x_i' \;\Rightarrow\; f(\!| x_1, \ldots, x_i, \ldots, x_n |\!) \leq f(\!| x_1, \ldots, x_i', \ldots, x_n |\!) \,.$$

Finally, the inference rules of Horn clause logic with equality are simply: *Modus Ponens* (from the formulae $e_1, \ldots, e_m$ and the clause $e_1; \ldots; e_m \Rightarrow e$ infer e); the substitutivity of terms proved equal; and the instantiation of clauses by substituting terms for variables.

References

1. V. M. Antimirov and P. D. Mosses. Rewriting extended regular expressions. Technical Monograph DAIMI PB-461, Computer Science Dept., Aarhus University, 1993. A short version is to appear in Proc. Conf. on Developments in Language Theory, ed. A. Salomaa, World Scientific Publ.
2. D. Bjørner and C. B. Jones, editors. *Formal Specification & Software Development.* Prentice-Hall, 1982.
3. J. A. Goguen, J. W. Thatcher, E. G. Wagner, and J. B. Wright. Initial algebra semantics and continuous algebras. *J. ACM*, 24:68–95, 1977.
4. G. Grätzer. *Lattice Theory: First Concepts and Distributive Lattices.* W. H. Freeman & Co., 1971.
5. G. Kahn et al. Metal: A formalism to specify formalisms. *Sci. Comput. Programming*, 3:151–188, 1983.
6. P. Klint. A meta-environment for generating programming environments. In *Algebraic Methods II: Theory, Tools, and Applications*, volume 490 of *Lecture Notes in Computer Science*, pages 105–124. Springer-Verlag, 1991.
7. D. Kozen. A completeness theorem for Kleene algebras and the algebra of regular events. In *LICS'91, Proc. 6th Ann. Symp. on Logic in Computer Science*, pages 214–225. IEEE, 1991.
8. D. Kozen. On action algebras. Technical Monograph DAIMI PB–381, Computer Science Dept., Aarhus University, 1992.
9. J. McCarthy. Towards a mathematical science of computation. In *Information Processing 62, Proc. IFIP Congress 62*, pages 21–28. North-Holland, 1962.
10. P. D. Mosses. Unified algebras and institutions. In *LICS'89, Proc. 4th Ann. Symp. on Logic in Computer Science*, pages 304–312. IEEE, 1989.
11. P. D. Mosses. Denotational semantics. In J. van Leeuwen, A. Meyer, M. Nivat, M. Paterson, and D. Perrin, editors, *Handbook of Theoretical Computer Science*, volume B, chapter 11. Elsevier Science Publishers, Amsterdam; and MIT Press, 1990.
12. P. D. Mosses. *Action Semantics*, volume 26 of *Cambridge Tracts in Theoretical Computer Science.* Cambridge University Press, 1992.
13. P. D. Mosses. The use of sorts in algebraic specifications. In *Proc. 8th Workshop on Abstract Data Types and 3rd COMPASS Workshop*, volume 655 of *Lecture Notes in Computer Science*, pages 66–91. Springer-Verlag, 1993.
14. V. Pratt. Action logic and pure induction. In *Logics in AI, Proc. European Workshop JELIA'90*, volume 478 of *Lecture Notes in Computer Science*, pages 97–120. Springer-Verlag, 1990.
15. T. W. Reps and T. Teitelbaum. *The Synthesizer Generator Reference Manual.* Springer-Verlag, third edition, 1989.
16. D. A. Schmidt. *Denotational Semantics: A Methodology for Language Development.* Allyn & Bacon, 1986.
17. D. S. Scott and C. Strachey. Toward a mathematical semantics for computer languages. In *Proc. Symp. on Computers and Automata*, volume 21 of *Microwave Research Institute Symposia Series.* Polytechnic Institute of Brooklyn, 1971.
18. J. E. Stoy. *Denotational Semantics: The Scott-Strachey Approach to Programming Language Theory.* MIT Press, 1977.

Structured Inheritance for Algebraic Class Specifications

F. Parisi Presicce[1]* and A. Pierantonio[2]

[1] Dip. Matematica Pura ed Applicata, Universitá de L'Aquila, I-67100 L'Aquila (Italy)
[2] Fachbereich 20 Informatik, Technische Universität Berlin, D-1000 Berlin (Germany)

Abstract. Inheritance is considered as a binary relation between two classes. Using an algebraic model of class specification, we distinguish between reusing inheritance and specialization inheritance, although the latter is sufficient to simulate the former. We propose mechanisms to *derive* inherited classes whose behavior can be described in a clean way in terms of the behavior of the superclasses. Among these mechanisms, the instantiation of parameters is seen as a special case of specialization inheritance but not of equal expressive power. A formalization of the intuitive notion of subtyping is then related to the stronger inheritance.

1 Introduction

The Object Oriented Methodology and the related languages in the 80's have proposed many techniques in order to enhance quality factors of software, such as *reusability, extensibility, compatibility.* The frequent use of notions such as inheritance, encapsulation and subtyping has not been followed by the development of a uniform terminology [16]. The term *inheritance*, for example, has been used to indicate the preservation of given characteristics with the addition of new ones, and the use without constraints of any kind of parts of a class. To compare the intended meaning of similar terms in various object oriented languages, we have proposed in [17] a formalization of the concept of class. This formalization is based on algebraic specifications, intended in the widest possible sense, although presented here in their simplest form for clarity of exposition. The model of class is intended to capture the corresponding features in existing languages, especially those belonging to the category of *class-centric* according to the classification in [11], and suggestions borrowed from other areas ([8]).
One of the features present in most languages is encapsulation, which allows the distinction between what the class implements and what the designer of the class chooses to be seen (and therefore used) from outside. Some of the features of a class visible to the outside may not be related to each instance of that class: a separate interface (usually included in the interface of the class containing visible data and methods) is useful to set aside the messages which can be interpreted by the instances [20]. To model genericity[13], we have included another part of the class, namely a parameter part, intended to model what are called unconstrained and

* current address : Dip. Scienze dell'Informazione, Universitá di Roma "La Sapienza", Via Salaria 113, 00198 Roma

constrained genericity. Finally, following the work on module specifications ([4]), we have suggested the presence of an explicit import interface. The import interface specifies only *what* is needed, but not *which* class is intended to provide the methods and class variables needed, leaving it to the interconnection mechanism to indicate the appropriate match, which in many languages is represented with features such as *use*. The presence of the import as well as of the class interface allows the development of a system bottom-up by successively extending already built data types, top-down by successively refining and implementing abstract data types as well as *middle-out*, where certain class (or instance) interfaces can at first be realized assuming the existence of certain functionalities expressed in the import interface; then the class interface is enriched or extended to obtain the desired methods and the import interface realized using other classes until all import interfaces are eliminated.

The model of the class consists of five parts: two interfaces, instance interface and class interface, for the two different roles of the class; another one, the import, requiring a producer for that class; a parameter part to model genericity, and an implementation part that includes the other four, in addition to the hidden features of the class. A key notion in object oriented methodology is inheritance, which allows the definition of new classes starting from variables and methods of old classes. But this definition of inheritance is not precise enough and it has been pointed out that there are different views of such a mechanism [20]. Although both called inheritance, there is no confusion between the idea of code sharing and the notion of functional specialization. With our model as basis, we are then able to distinguish between the notion of inheritance based on specialization and the notion of inheritance based on the reuse of code. We have shown in [17] that the two notions are related and that, in fact, the former is sufficient to express the latter.

In this paper we refine the model of class specification, its semantics and the specialization inheritance and survey some object oriented languages comparing them with respect to the features modeled by this notion of class and by our definitions of inheritance. The emphasis is on the languages in which the internal structure of the objects and the behavior of the methods is specified in a class and which use the message-passing metaphor.

In the following sections we introduce two new relations between pairs of classes, relations based on the use of the import interface and of the parameter part. One relation indicates whether one class produces an instance interface which satisfies the constraints set forth in the parameter part of another class. The effect of substituting the class for the parameter is shown to be a clean (i.e., whose semantical effect can be predicted) way to obtain a new class which inherits by specialization from the old one. The other relation matches the producer of some methods to a potential consumer of those methods by finding a correspondence between the class interface of a class and the import interface of another class. The effect of replacing the needed import with the provided class interface is again seen as a clean way to obtain a new class which inherits by implementation from the producer and by specialization from the consumer. The proofs are omitted and can be found in detail in [18].

2 Algebraic Model

To clarify our notation (details can be found in [7]).

- A *signature* Σ is a pair (S, OP)
- $Alg(\Sigma)$ is the category of Σ-algebras and Σ-homomorphisms
- a *signature morphism* $h : \Sigma_1 \longrightarrow \Sigma_2$ is a pair of functions $(h_S : S_1 \longrightarrow S_2, h_{OP} : OP_1 \longrightarrow OP_2)$
- a morphism $h : \Sigma_1 \longrightarrow \Sigma_2$ induces a *forgetful functor* $V_h : Alg(\Sigma_2) \longrightarrow Alg(\Sigma_1)$
- an *algebraic specification Spec* is a pair (Σ, E) consisting of a signature Σ and a set E of (positive conditional) equations
- $Alg(Spec)$ denotes the category of *Spec-algebras* and Σ-homomorphisms
- a *specification morphism* $f : Spec_1 \longrightarrow Spec_2$ is a pair (f_σ, f_E) consisting of a signature morphism $f_\sigma : \Sigma_1 \longrightarrow \Sigma_2$ and a compatible function $f_E : E_1 \longrightarrow E_2$
- the left adjoint of V_f is the free functor $Free_f : Alg(Spec_1) \longrightarrow Alg(Spec_2)$

Definition 1 (Class specification and Semantics). A *class specification* C_{spec} consists of five algebraic specifications PAR (parameter part), EXP_i (instance interface), EXP_c (class interface), IMP (import interface) and BOD (implementation part) and five specification morphisms as in the following commutative diagram.

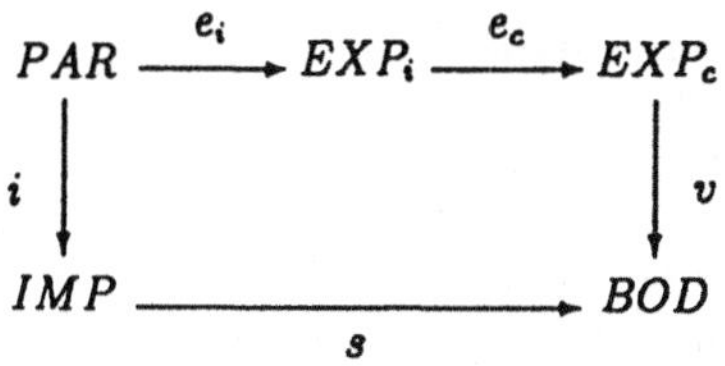

Fig. 1. Class Specification

The functor $Sem = V_v \circ Free_s$: $Alg(IMP) \longrightarrow Alg(EXP_c)$ is the *semantics* of the class specification .

Remark. The interfaces EXP_i and EXP_c describe the external access functions and their behavior: the former describes the messages which can be sent to the objects that are instances of the class, while the latter contains the methods which can be used by other classes. The specification BOD describes an implementation of the exported methods using the ones provided by the IMP specification. The import IMP contains information about *what* is needed by BOD to implement EXP_c, but not *which* class can provide it. The specification PAR models genericity, unconstrained if it consists of sorts only, constrained when the parameter is required to have operations satisfying certain properties. Other semantics (such as loose or ultraloose) for a class specification have been considered in [19].

Definition 2 (Class). A *class* $C = (C_{spec}, C_{impl})$ consists of a class specification C_{spec} and a class implementation C_{impl} such that $C_{impl} = Free_s(A_I)$ for some $A_I \in Alg(IMP)$.

Example 1. The morphisms in this example are just inclusions. In the notation we use the keywords **Parameter, Instance Interface, Class Interface, Import Interface, Body** to declare the subspecification to be added to the parts already defined. For examples, since $PAR \subseteq EXP_i$, after the keyword **Instance Interface** only $EXP_i - PAR$ is listed. When a subspecification keyword is missing, the relative specification is just the closest subspecification in the diagram.

```
STRING is Class Spec
Parameter
 sorts        data
Instance Interface
 class sort   string
 opns         EMPTY:⟶string
              MAKE:data⟶string
              RADD,LADD:string data⟶string
 eqns         RADD(EMPTY,a) = MAKE(a)
              LADD(EMPTY,a) = MAKE(a)
Import Interface
 sorts        array,nat
 opns         0:⟶nat
              SUCC:nat⟶nat
              NIL:⟶array
              (_[_]:=_):array nat data⟶array
              (_[_]):array nat⟶data
              SHIFT_l,SHIFT_r:array⟶array
 eqns         (a[i]:=e)[i] = e
              ((a[i]:=e_1)[i]:=e_2) = e_2
              ((a[i]:=e)[j]) = (a[j])
              (SHIFT_l(a)[i]) = (a[SUCC(i)])
              (SHIFT_r(a)[SUCC(i)]) = (a[i])
Body
 opns         <_,_>:array nat⟶string
 eqns         EMPTY = <NIL,0>
              MAKE(x) = <(NIL[SUCC(0)]:=x),SUCC(0)>
              RADD(<a,n>,x) = <(a[SUCC(n)]:=x),SUCC(n)>
              LADD(<a,n>,x) = <(SHIFT_l(a)[SUCC(0)]:=x),SUCC(n)>
end Class Spec
```

With this class model we intend to cover a large number of class structures as they are defined in current object oriented languages such as BETA, Smalltalk, Eiffel, POOL, Trellis/Owl. We have focused on the importance of avoiding uncontrolled code reuse without any constraint, and therefore, in the proposed model, we provide an explicit import interface. None of the languages analyzed allows to specify some requirements for the import, although BETA, Eiffel, POOL and Trellis/Owl allow the direct importing of other existing classes, incorporating (with the *use* clause) a combination mechanism. The opportunity to hide some implementational aspects gives the freedom to a class designer to modify the implementation without affecting the clients of the instances of that class. All the languages analyzed but BETA have constructs for protection of data representation. The set of all public operations of a class forms the external interface, which we call *instance interface*. Another form of protection is given to prevent another kind of client, the designer of a subclass, to access some variables, since accessing inherited variables results in a reduction of encapsulation. We have named this other interface, which contains the instance one, *class interface*. The C++, POOL, Trellis/Owl languages have an explicit class interface, distinct from the instance interface, while Smalltalk does not distinguish them and in Eiffel of [13,14] it coincides with the implementation part. In [13] a comparison between genericity and inheritance is presented. Genericity represents a good solution to achieve a good amount of flexibility with a static type system (untyped languages provide a great deal of flexibility, but all the errors can be catched only at run-time). Many languages, such as Eiffel, Trellis/Owl, POOL, BETA, and OOZE, but not C++ and Smalltalk, allow genericity, although with some differences. The only properties treated by these languages are signature properties; OOZE and OBJ allow to specify behavior with an equational language, by means of theories and views. All these languages supply an actualization mechanism in order to instantiate the generic classes.

Example 2. The left side of figure 2 represents the scheme of a C++ class where it is possible to distinguish the different external interfaces and the body part. All the listed features between the **public** and **protected** keywords represent the instance interface. All the features between the **protected** and **private** keywords represent the part of the class interface which are not listed in the instance interface but are contained in the class one. All the private features form the body of the class, i.e. all those operations which are considered local to the class. The parameter part is empty because C++ does not allow any form of genericity, while the import is empty because the imported classes are already combined by an explicit mechanism which imports each class specified after the **include** keyword. The right side of figure 2 represents the scheme of a BETA class. This language does not allow any form of protection and all its features are visible and directly accessible from the outside. As in the C++ class, BETA has no import interface; on the other hand it has the possibility to define generic classes through the notion of virtual class which can be assumed as the parameter part of a class (*SomePar* in figure 2).

Finally it is worth pointing out that the model of class specification adopted here is very similar to the notion of module specification in [9,4,8]. The essential difference is the presence of the instance interface EXP_i strictly related to the concept of object since it contains the messages which can be sent to the objects. Each module specification can be seen as a class with $EXP_i = EXP_c$ while each class can be considered a module by ignoring EXP_i. We thus have a many-one relation from classes to modules, where several classes can correspond to the same module.

3 Inheritance

Inheritance is one of the main notions of the object oriented paradigm. Its importance is widely recognized as it allows to reuse, extend and combine abstractions in order to define other abstractions by defining a new class starting from the variables and methods of other classes. The usual terminology calls the former *subclass* and

```
#include "classes.h"
class classdef {
public:
    Here are all the visible features
    ...
protected:
    Here are all the subclass visible features
    ...
private:
    Here is the implementation
    ...
};
```

```
classdef:
(# Par: virtual class SomePar; {parameter}
    All features are visible
    ...
#)
```

Fig. 2. Example of C++ and BETA class

the latter ones *superclasses*. Unfortunately in the space of languages the notion of inheritance is not homogeneous since it ranges from functional specialization to the reuse of code without any constraint. Inheritance can be considered as a technique for the implementation of an abstract data type and used as a private decision of the designer of the inheriting class, allowing omission and/or redefinition of features: we call this technique ***reusing inheritance***. On the other hand, Inheritance can be considered as a technique for defining behavioral specialization and used as a public declaration of the designer that the instances of the subclass obey the semantics of the superclass: we call this kind of inheritance ***specialization inheritance***. We give a formal distinction between these two different notions.

Definition 3 (Reusing Inheritance). Let $C1=(C1_{spec}, C1_{impl})$ and $C2=(C2_{spec}, C2_{impl})$ be classes. Then

i. $C2$ *weakly reuses* $C1$, notation $C2$ Wreuse $C1$, if there exists a morphism

$$f : EXP_{c1} \longrightarrow BOD_2,$$

ii. $C2$ *strongly reuses* $C1$, notation $C2$ Sreuse $C1$, if, in addition, $V_f(C2_{impl}) = V_{v1}(C1_{impl})$.

Example 3. According to the above definition, a new class specification, say *LIST*, is implemented by *STRING*, the class specification just introduced in example 1. What is needed is an appropriate morphism from the class interface part $EXP_{c_{string}}$ of *STRING* to the body subspecification BOD_{list} of

LIST is Class Spec
Parameter
<u>sorts</u> data
<u>opns</u> $\bot : \longrightarrow data$
Instance Interface
<u>class sort</u> list

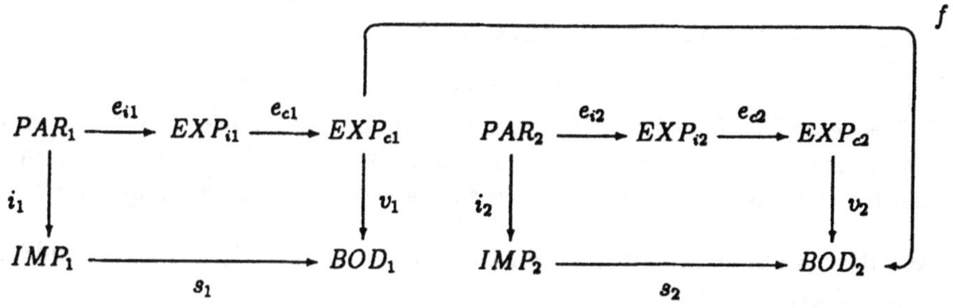

Fig. 3. Reusing Inheritance

opns EMPTY:⟶list
MAKE:data⟶list
HEAD:list⟶data
TAIL:list⟶list
APPEND:list list⟶list
eqns APPEND(l,EMPTY) = l
APPEND(EMPTY,l) = l
APPEND(l_1,APPEND(l_2,l_3) = APPEND(APPEND(l_1,l_2),l_3)
TAIL(APPEND(MAKE(a),l)) = l
HEAD(APPEND(MAKE(a),l)) = a

Import Interface

sorts array,nat
opns 0:⟶nat
SUCC:nat⟶nat
NIL:⟶array
(_[_]:=_):array nat data⟶array
(_[_]):array nat⟶data
SHIFT$_l$,SHIFT$_r$:array⟶array
eqns (NIL[i]) = ⊥
(a[i]:=e)[i] = e
((a[i]:=e_1)[i]:=e_2) = e_2
((a[i]:=e)[j]) = (a[j])
(SHIFT$_l$(a)[i]) = (a[SUCC(i)])
(SHIFT$_r$(a)[SUCC(i)]) = (a[i])

Body

opns <_,_>:array nat⟶list
eqns EMPTY = <NIL,0>
MAKE(x) = <(NIL[SUCC(0)]:=x),SUCC(0)>
CONCAT(<a_1,SUCC(n_1)>,<a_2,n_2>) =
CONCAT(<(a_1[SUCC(n_1)]:=⊥),n_1>,<(SHIFT$_l$(a_2)[SUCC(0)]),SUCC(n_2)>)
RADD(<a,n>,x) = <(a[SUCC(n)]:=x),SUCC(n)>
LADD(<a,n>,x) = <(SHIFT$_l$(a)[SUCC(0)]:=x),SUCC(n)>
TAIL(<a,SUCC(n)>) = <SHIFT$_l$(a),n>
HEAD(<a,SUCC(n)>) = (a[SUCC(0)])
RADD(s,a) = APPEND(s,MAKE(a))

LADD(s,a) = APPEND(MAKE(a),s)
end Class Spec

The second notion of inheritance, specialization inheritance, allows the enrichment of the functionalities of a class and can be modeled by morphisms from the inherited class to the inheriting class in such a way that behavior is preserved.

Definition 4 (Specialization Inheritance). Let $C1 = (C1_{spec}, C1_{impl})$ and $C2 = (C2_{spec}, C2_{impl})$ be classes. Then

i. $C2$ is a *weak specialization* of $C1$, notation $C2$ Wspec $C1$, if there exist morphisms

$$f_i : EXP_{i1} \longrightarrow EXP_{i2},$$
$$f_c : EXP_{c1} \longrightarrow EXP_{c2},$$

such that $e_{c2} \circ f_i = f_c \circ e_{c1}$ as in the commutative diagram in 4;

ii. $C2$ is a *strong specialization* of $C1$, notation $C2$ Sspec $C1$, if, in addition,

$$V_{f_c}(V_{v2}(C2_{impl})) = V_{v1}(C1_{impl})$$

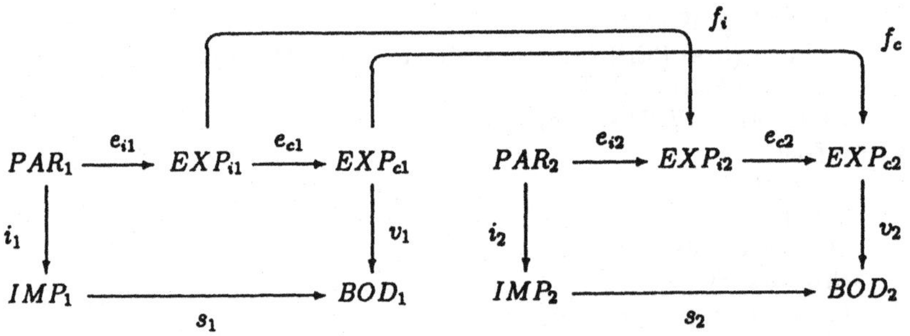

Fig. 4. Specialization Inheritance

Example 4. The class specification *STRING* turns out to be a specialization of the class specification *BASICSTRING* which we are going to introduce; in fact all the visible parts of the class specification *BASICSTRING* are enriched in *STRING*,

BASICSTRING **is Class Spec**
Parameter
<u>sorts</u> data
<u>opns</u> ⊥:⟶data
Instance Interface
<u>class sort</u> basicstring
<u>opns</u> EMPTY:⟶basicstring
MAKE:data⟶basicstring

Import Interface

<u>sorts</u> array,nat

<u>opns</u> $0{:}\longrightarrow nat$
$SUCC{:}nat \longrightarrow nat$
$NIL{:}\longrightarrow array$
$(\_[\_]{:=}\_){:}array\ nat\ data \longrightarrow array$
$(\_[\_]){:}array\ nat \longrightarrow data$
$SHIFT_l, SHIFT_r{:}array \longrightarrow array$

<u>eqns</u> $(NIL[i]) = \perp$
$(a[i]{:=}e)[i] = e$
$((a[i]{:=}e_1)[i]{:=}e_2) = e_2$
$((a[i]{:=}e)[j]) = (a[j])$
$(SHIFT_l(a)[i]) = (a[SUCC(i)])$
$(SHIFT_r(a)[SUCC(i)]) = (a[i])$

Body

<u>opns</u> $<\_,\_>{:}array\ nat \longrightarrow string$

<u>eqns</u> $EMPTY = <NIL,0>$
$MAKE(x) = <(NIL[SUCC(0)]{:=}x),SUCC(0)>$
$<a_1,SUCC(n_1)>*<a_2,n_2> =$
$<(a_1[SUCC(n_1)]{:=}\perp),n_1>*<(SHIFT_l(a_2)[SUCC(0)]),SUCC(n_2)>$

end Class Spec

There are some languages, such as C++, Smalltalk and Eiffel, where the inheritance is intended as specialization but it allows the redefinition of features. The BETA programming language does not allow the redefinition of methods but gives the possibility to extend in a subclass a method defined for the superclass. The extension consists of a portion of code specified in the subclass, but, not providing any constraints, it could violate the invariants of the superclass.

```
#include "classes.h"
class newclass : public classdef {
public:
      Here are new visible features
      and redefined methods
      ...
protected:
      Here are new subclass visible features
      and redefined methods
      ...
private:
      Here are the implementations
      of the new and the redefined methods
      ...
};
```

```
newclass: classdef
(# Par: extended class DerSomePar;
      All new visible features
      and method extensions
      ...
#)
```

Fig. 5. Example of C++ and BETA derived class

Example 5. The left side of figure 5 shows a derived class written in C++ language. The class *newClass* inherits from *classdef* and can add new methods and redefine some old methods. In the right side of figure 5 there is a BETA derived class in which we cannot redefine any methods but we can provide some method extensions. Note that the BETA language allows the enrichment of parameter part too.

4 Deriving Inheritance

In this section, we define two additional relations between class specifications and between classes (weak and strong relationships, respectively) which describe mechanisms for interconnecting class specifications and define new classes, which inherit from the old ones. The two relations correspond to instantiating the parameter part of a (generic) class and to replacing the import interface of a (*semi-virtual*) class with the class export of another class.

Definition 5 (Actualizable). Given classes $C1=(C1_{spec}, C1_{impl})$ and $C2=(C2_{spec}, C2_{impl})$ with $PAR_2 = IMP_2$

i. $C1$ is *weakly actualizable* by $C2$, denoted by $C1$ Wact $C2$, if there exists a specification morphism $f : PAR_1 \longrightarrow EXP_{i2}$
ii. $C1$ is *strongly actualizable* by $C2$, denoted by $C1$ Sact $C2$, if $C1$ Wact $C2$ with f and $V_f(V_{ec2}(V_{v2}(C2_{impl}))) = V_{ei1}(V_{ec1}(V_{v1}(C1_{impl})))$.

Remark. The binary relation Wact indicates that the parameter part of the class $C1$ can be replaced by the instance interface of the class $C2$, i.e. that the instances of class $C2$ satisfy the constraints of the parameter of $C1$. The distinction between weak and strong again separates the class specification from the class. In $C1$ Wact $C2$, a realization of the class specification $C2_{spec}$ *can* be used for the parameter part of a realization of the class specification $C1_{spec}$. On the other hand, $C1$ Sact $C2$ indicates that the realizations $C1_{impl}$ and $C2_{impl}$ of the class specification *coincide* on their PAR_1 part.

The restriction imposed on the class $C2$ that $PAR_2 = IMP_2$ is both technical and methodological. On the technical side, it makes for a cleaner construction of the class specification resulting from the replacement of the parameter part. On the methodological side, it requires that only *complete* classes, i.e. classes which do not rely on other classes for their completion of the import specification, be considered as actual parameters of generic classes. We now give a description of the result of actualizing the parameter part PAR_1 of $C1$ by $C2$. The new class specification $ACT(C1, f, C2)$ is obtained by *replacing* the parameter part PAR_1 in EXP_{i1} and EXP_{i2} with the instance and class interface, respectively, of $C2_{spec}$, and in BOD_1 with the implementation part BOD_2. The new parameter part is just the parameter PAR_2 of $C2$, which is also added to IMP_1 to obtain the new import interface.

Definition 6 (Parameter Passing). Let $Ci = (Ci_{spec}, Ci_{impl})$, $i = 1, 2$ be classes with $C1$ Wact $C2$ via $f : PAR_1 \longrightarrow EXP_{i2}$. The actualization of $C1$ by $C2$, denoted by $ACT(C1, f, C2)$, is the class specification $C3_{spec}$ as in Figure 6, (where the pushout morphisms of BOD are omitted for clarity)

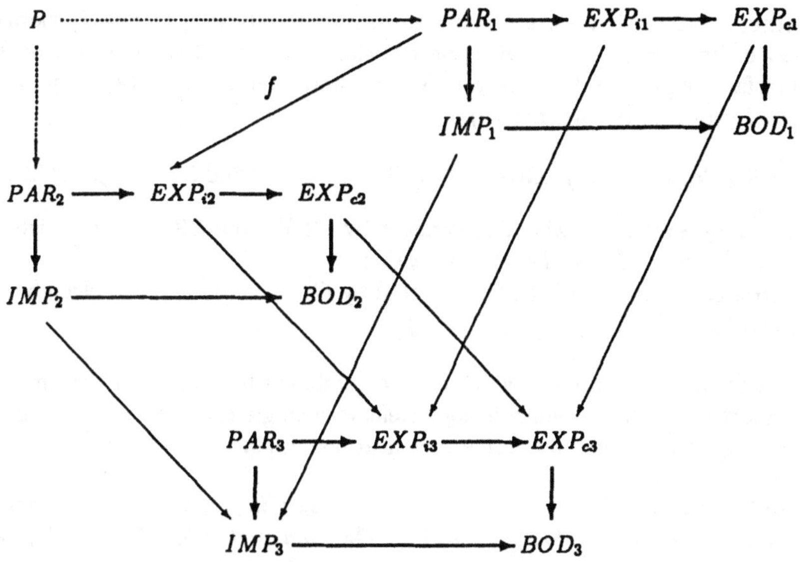

Fig. 6. Actualization

- the parameter part PAR_3 is the parameter part PAR_2 of $C2$
- the instance interface EXP_{i3} is the pushout object of f and e_{i1}
- the class interface EXP_{c3} is the pushout object of $f \circ e_{c2}$ and $e_{i1} \circ e_{c1}$
- the import interface IMP_3 is the pushout of IMP_1 and $IMP_2 (= PAR_2)$ (with respect to the intersection of PAR_1 and PAR_2)
- the implementation part BOD_3 is the pushout of BOD_1 and BOD_2 with respect to PAR_1

The specification morphisms are induced by the universal properties of the pushouts.

Theorem 7 (Induced Inheritance). *If $C1$ Wact $C2$ via f, then*

i. $ACT(C1, f, C2)$ Wspec $C1$ *and*
ii. $ACT(C1, f, C2)$ Wspec $C2$.

If the relation between $C1$ and $C2$ is strong, then it is possible to use the realization of $C1$ and $C2$ to construct a realization of $ACT(C1, f, C2)$.

Theorem 8 (Induced Strong Inheritance). *If $C1$ Sact $C2$ via f, then there exists an algebra $C3_{impl} \in Alg(BOD_{c3})$ such that*

i. $(ACT(C1, f, C2), C3_{impl})$ *is a class (still denoted by $ACT(C1, f, C2)$)*
ii. $ACT(C1, f, C2)$ Sspec $C1$
iii. $ACT(C1, f, C2)$ Sspec $C2$

The other relation that we are going to introduce relates a class $C2$, viewed as *producer* of its class interface, with another class $C1$, viewed as *consumer* of its import interface. Again we distinguish between a potential producer (weak notion) and a factual producer (strong notion).

Definition 9 (Combinable). Given $C1=(C1_{spec}, C1_{impl})$ and $C2=(C2_{spec}, C2_{impl})$

i. $C1$ is *weakly combinable* with $C2$, denoted by $C1$ Wcomb $C2$, if there exists a specification morphism $h: IMP_1 \longrightarrow EXP_{c2}$;
ii. $C1$ is *strongly combinable* with $C2$, denoted by $C1$ Scomb $C2$, if $C1$ Wcomb $C2$ via h and $V_h(V_{v2}(C2_{impl})) = V_s(C1_{impl})$.

The availability of a class $C2$ which can be combined to a class $C1$ determines an interconnection of classes which is equivalent to a single class. The construction is similar to the composition of module specifications in [8].

Definition 10 (Import Passing). Let $Ci = (Ci_{spec}, Ci_{impl})$, $i = 1, 2$, be classes with $C1$ Wcomb $C2$ via $h: IMP_1 \longrightarrow EXP_{c2}$. The *combination* of $C1$ and $C2$, denoted by $COMB(C1, h, C2)$, is the class specification $C3_{spec}$ as in the Figure 7

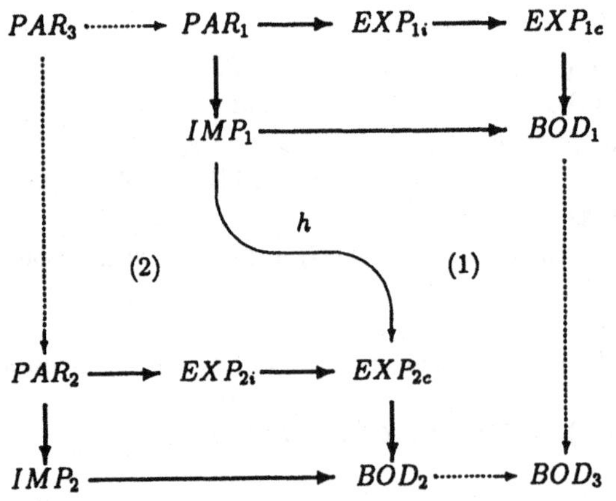

Fig. 7. Combination

where

- EXP_{i3} and EXP_{c3} are EXP_{i1} and EXP_{c1}, respectively
- IMP_3 is just IMP_2
- the new implementation part is the pushout of BOD_1 and BOD_2 with respect to IMP_1.
- the new parameter part PAR_3 is the pullback of PAR_1 and PAR_2 with respect to EXP_{c2}

The specification morphisms are deducible from the diagram.

Remark. The new class specification is obtained by ***replacing*** the import interface of $C1$ with what $C2$ ***produces.*** The new implementation part is that of $C1$ where the yet-unimplemented part IMP_1 is replaced by the implemented part of EXP_{c2}, via the ***fitting morphism*** h. The specification IMP_1 is no longer the import, having been provided by EXP_{c2}, which in turn ***needs*** IMP_2, which becomes the overall import interface.

Theorem 11 (Induced Inheritance). *If* $C1$ Wcomb $C2$ *via* h*, then*

i. $COMB(C1, h, C2)$ Wspec $C1$ *and*
ii. $COMB(C1, h, C2)$ Wreuse $C2$.

As in the case of actualization, if $C1$ Scomb $C2$, then it is possible to construct a realization of $COMB(C1, h, C2)$ using those of $C1$ and $C2$.

Theorem 12 Induced Strong Inheritance. *If* $C1$ Scomb $C2$ *via* h*, then there exists an algebra* $C3_{impl} \in Alg(BOD_{c3})$ *such that*

i. $(COMB(C1, h, C2), C3_{impl})$ *is a class (still denoted by* $COMB(C1, h, C2)$*)*
ii. $COMB(C1, h, C2)$ Sspec $C1$
iii. $COMB(C1, h, C2)$ Sreuse $C2$

There are several connections among these two relations and the interconnection mechanisms on module specifications in [4]. As was done for module specifications, it is also possible to extend the notion of Combination/Composition and Actualization to the case where one class provides only part of what another class needs. We can define in these cases notions of partial actualization and partial combination and obtain results similar to the Weak and Strong Induced Inheritance. Most of the current languages allow to import from separately written modules, but they do not provide any combination mechanism since the importing procedure requires the name of the class from which to import and produces an implicit combination of the imported code with what is being developed. The only way to require something, and then provide a supplier for it, is by means of the genericity and the actualization mechanisms.

The key notion of subtyping is often strictly related with the technique called inheritance and these concepts are sometimes confused. Apart from the terminology, it is necessary to distinguish between a technique based on the refinement of implementations, which has been presented as strong specialization inheritance, and a coercion notion, which is usually called subtyping. The first technique implies subtyping but subtyping can be considered a more general relationship. In fact, starting the definition of a class from the functionalities of another defined class and proceeding in an incremental manner new methods are added or old ones refined. This gives information about how code is shared among classes and how the programs are structured while the instances of the subclass can be viewed as more specialized superclass instances leaving room for compatible assignment rules. These rules allow to use instances of the subclass in place of the instances of the superclass.

On the other hand, it is possible to realize some abstractions with different realizations and it is therefore possible to consider the instances of a class to behave in a way similar to that of the instances of another class. The external behavior of these classes cannot show any implementation details and the representation cannot be distinguished by means of the operations of the classes. Naturally, specialized behavior can be obtained also if classes are refined by means of strong specialization. In this case, the inheritance intended as a semantics- preserving mechanism allows a restriction of the set of instances of a class by requiring that they satisfy more properties. In essence, specialization inheritance allows the definition of behavioral specialization and therefore it allows the definition of subtypes. The other deriving mechanism, the reusing inheritance, does not imply the subtyping relationship since it allows the reuse of code without any kind of constraints. Conversely, a relationship of subtyping has no implications on reusing inheritance since the former imposes no constraints on how the visible methods are implemented in the body of the class specification.

5 Concluding Remarks

The formal model of class specification presented here (a slight modification of the one proposed in [17]) is general enough to include all the features presented in the languages analyzed. Not all languages provide all the features of our model, some identifying the instance and class interface, some the class interface and the implementation, none providing an explicit import interface without an explicit reference to an existing (virtual or not) class. The class specification allows to formally distinguish between two common forms of inheritance, the reusing one and the specialization one. In fact, as shown in [17], the notion of reusing inheritance can be viewed as syntactic sugar, since it can be expressed in terms of the relation of specialization inheritance (and its inverse). We have proposed here two new relations between pairs of classes: in both cases (but with different intentions and use) it relates a class in need to be completed (either by choosing a generic part PAR or by implementing a virtual part IMP) with another class able to produce what is needed. For both relations, new hierarchies of classes can be constructed, representing the usability of certain classes in the context of other classes. These hierarchies are closely related to the inheritance hierarchies, as shown in the previous section: the producer C of an interface which satisfies the constraints of the parameter or of the import part of a class C' determines a new class which inherits from it by reusing and from C' by specialization. We believe this to be very important since it provides a restricted reuse of code where we can predict the behavior of the outcome. The notions of weak and strong specialization correspond to the inheritance and subtype notions in [5], respectively. We have presented here definitions and theorems using the simplest form of algebraic specifications, but both the formalizations and the results can immediately be extended to other frameworks based on institutions [10] other than the equational one and on different specification logics [6] such as the behavioral one.

Acknowledgment. *This research has been supported in part by the European Community under ESPRIT Basic Research Working Group COMPASS (ref.6112) and* *in part by the Consiglio Nazionale delle Ricerche under Progetto Finalizzato* Sistemi Informatici e Calcolo Parallelo, *Sottoprogetto* Linguaggi di Nuova Concezione

References

1. Alencar, A.J., Goguen, J.A.: OOZE: An Object-Oriented Z Environment. Proc. ECOOP '91, Springer Lect.Notes in Comp.Sci. 512 (1991), 180-199
2. America, P.H.M.: Inheritance and Subtyping in a Parallel Object-Oriented Language. Proc. ECOOP '87, Springer Lect.Notes in Comp.Sci. 276 (1987), 234-242
3. America,P.H.M., van der Linden, F.: A Parallel Object-Oriented Language with Inheritance and Subtyping. Proc. ECOOP/OOPSLA '90 (1990), 161-168
4. Blum, E.K., Ehrig, H., Parisi-Presicce, F.: Algebraic Specifications of Modules and their Basic Interconnections. JCSS 34, 2/3 (1987), 293-339
5. Breu, R.: Algebraic Specification Techniques in Object Oriented Programming Environments Springer Lect.Notes in Comp.Sci. 562 (1991)
6. Ehrig, H., Baldamus, M., Orejas, F.: New Concepts for Amalgamation and Extension in the Framework of the Specification Logic. TUB Technical Report (1991)
7. Ehrig, H., Mahr, B.: Fundamentals of Algebraic Specification 1. Equations and Initial Semantics. EATCS Monograph in Computer Science, Vol.6, Springer Verlag (1985)
8. Ehrig, H., Mahr, B.: Fundamentals of Algebraic Specification 2. Module Specifications and Constraints. EATCS Monograph in Computer Science, Vol.21, Springer Verlag (1990)
9. Ehrig, H., Weber, H.: Algebraic Specification of Modules. In: Neuhold E.J., Chronist G. (eds.): Formal Models in Programming. North-Holland (1985)
10. Goguen, J.A., Burstall, R.: Introducing Institutions. in Proc. Logics of Programming Workshop (1983)
11. Gabriel, R.P., White, J.L., Bobrow, D.G.: CLOS: Integrating Object Oriented and Functional Programming. Comm. ACM, 34,9 (Sept 91) 28-38
12. Kristensen, B.B., Madsen, O.L., Moller-Pedersen, B., Nygaard, K.: The BETA Programming Language. In: B.Shriver, P.Wegner (eds.): Research Directions in Object Oriented Programming. MIT Press (1987) 7-48
13. Meyer, B.: Genericity versus Inheritance. Proc. OOPSLA '86 (1986) 391-405
14. Meyer, B.: Object-Oriented Software Construction. Prentice-Hall (1988)
15. Madsen, O.L., Moller-Pedersen, B.: Virtual Classes: the Powerful Mechanism in Object-Oriented Programming. Proc. OOPSLA '89 (1989) 397-406
16. Nelson, N.L.: An Object Oriented Tower of Babel. OOPS Messenger 2,3 July 91
17. Parisi-Presicce, F., Pierantonio, A.: An Algebraic View of Inheritance and Subtyping in Object Oriented Programming. Proc. ESEC '91, Springer Lect.Notes in Comp.Sci. 550 (1991) 364-379
18. Parisi-Presicce, F., Pierantonio, A.: An Algebraic Framework to Compare and Derive the Inheritance Relation. Technical Report Dipartimento di Matematica Pura ed Aplicata, Universitá L'Aquila, May 92
19. Parisi-Presicce, F., Pierantonio, A.: An Algebraic Theory of Class Specification. (to appear)
20. Snyder, A.: Encapsulation and Inheritance in Object-Oriented Programming Languages. Proc. OOPSLA '86 (1986) 38-45
21. Schaffert, C., Cooper, T., Bullis, B., Killian, M., Wilpolt, C.: An Introduction to Trellis/Owl. Proc. OOPSLA '86 (1986) 9-16
22. Stroustrup, B.: The C++ Programming Language. Addison-Wesley (1986)
23. Wirfs-Brock, R.J., Johnson, R.E.: Surveying Current Research in Object-Oriented Design. Communication of the ACM,33,9 (Sept 90) 104-124

Towards a theory for the animation of algebraic specifications

Catharina Rieckhoff
Technische Universität Berlin,
FR 6-1, Franklinstr. 28/29
10 587 Berlin

Abstract

Conceptual ideas are developed to provide algebraic specifications with animation, i.e. graphics - possibly moving - of datas and their operations.
We are convinced that animation
helps to understand algebraic specifications easier,
supports error detection,
supports the operational view,
and improves the acceptance of specifications.
In our theory we emphasize the connection between building the terms of a specification and visualizing this term. To achive this we assign to every constant in the signature of the specification SPEC = (SIG,E) a graphic and to every operation in SIG instructions, how to manipulate the argument graphs. The assignment between terms and graphs is realized as an implementation, especially a graphical implementation by so called basic graphic algebra BaGrA, where all the graphical basic operations like linedrawing etc. and other types, are collected. The graphical implementation is compatible with the actualization of parameterized specifications. An example is given to visualize our ideas of animation.

1. Introduction

A picture says more than thousand words!
But it might be that five hundred of these words should not be said!
Therefore everyone who deals with pictures has a struggle in expressing just the right five hundred words. On the other hand we have one dimensional texts; texts like commands for the vi or equations in an algebraic specification. Sometimes awkward, rather cryptic and hard to learn or understand but precise and with a fixed meaning. Why don't we take the best of both ways? It's possible to describe with texts in an abstract, often mathematical manner and to use the natural power of pictures. The victorious career of graphical user interfaces tells something about this power.
We try to follow this idea by providing initial algebraic specifications with animation of data and their operations. We regard this as a way to significantly improve the user friendliness and acceptance of algebraic specifications. Especially by these new possibilities for rapid prototyping, so that a customer can see what you have specified!
We establish the connection between terms and graphs by implementing algebraically a given specification SPEC by a basic graph algebra. This so called BaGrA is presented first. It is necessary for the theory which follows. We'll give as an example at the end of this paper a small part of a syntax directed editor.

1.1 What we want to do and what we don't

We touch on the areas of 'programming by example' and 'program animation' (for an overview see Raeder /Ra85/ or Shu /Sh88/). But especially for the latter mentioned field of research we miss all notions of being correct for any connection between the program and their pictures, apart from any 'break points' placed somewhere in a program to make some graphs run.
For initial algebraic specifications we establish a close connection between terms and graphs by the notion of graphical implementation in a very natural way. Through this we get a sound notion of being correct. To give a foretaste of our ideas, we'll informally present a well known

example. Suppose the parameterized specification STACK(DATA) to have the usual operations like create, push, pop, and top. We will visualize a stack by a bundle of paper with empty sheets. To the pop operation of STACK belongs the corresponding graphical operation pop_G which would be animated thus: (the thick arrows don't belong to the graphs, they indicate the 'dynamics').

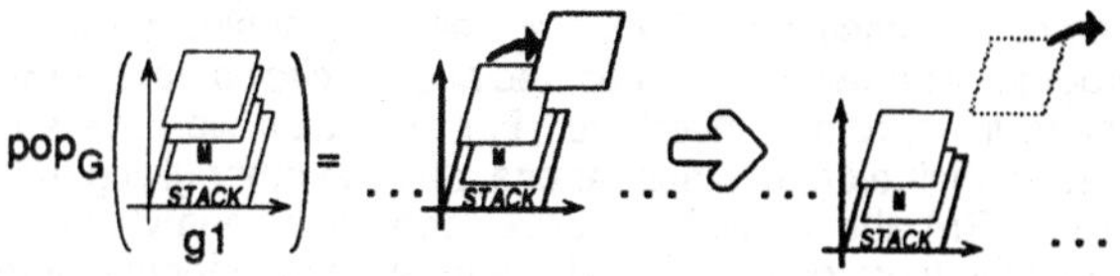

We choose as actual specification ALPHABET and as graphical implementation the letters when they appear as text. When we actualize DATA by ALPHABET, we do the same for the graphic part. Then we get automatically by actualization, as a graphical implementation for the flat STACK(ALPHABET), the 'filled' sheets (here demonstrated with the operation top).

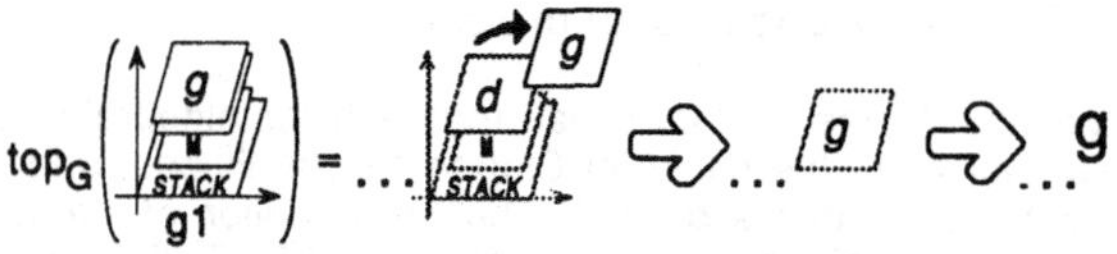

We are not aiming at the area of 'programming in the large', like general sketches for modules or flowcharts. Just as we don't create or specify graphical programming or specification languages and we don't answer to questions like which kind of graphs are the best to express this or that.

1.2 Related work

There has appeard in the last few years some systems of visualizing or animating data and algorithms (e.g. Balsa by Brown /Br88/, ANIM by Bentley and Kernighan /BK91/, Think Pad by Rubin, Golin, and Reiss /RGR85/, GARDEN by Reiss /Re86/). Especially in the field of concurrency, processes and protocols there is a need for visualizing these (Giacalone and Smolka /GS88/, Kahn and Saraswat /KS90/, the PROVIDE system by Moher /Mo88/, and the VOYEUR system by Socha, Bailey and Notkin /SBN88/). One problem is reusability; every example *looks* different and you rarely find a uniform presentation. lGenerally there is no theoretical background. Exceptions are Bolognesi and Latella in /BL89/ where they enlarge the specification language LOTOS with some very simple graphical elements to G-LOTOS, and very similiar is New and Amer in /NA89/ with the GROPE system for Estelle. In /Lö91/ M.Löwe works with graphics of algebraic specified data types, produced and handled by graph grammars, but the generated graphs have only nodes and edges. A further important work with theoretical background and the closest one to our work is given by Gogouen /Go87/. He regards the animation of data structures as very helpful for programming with 'ultra high level languages' and languages like OBJ. Also he proposes a user interface where you can perform mainly by mouse, demonstrations on how an operation works in general with the intention of defining the formal semantic of the data type. The latter goes beyond our intentions at this time.

2. The Basic Graph Algebra (BaGrA)

In the Basic Graph Algebra all functions are collected which can be used to define the graphical 'outfit' of a data type element. Its signature will be part of the definition of a graphical implementation.
We regard the BaGrA as a window or interface between the 'abstract and textual world', i.e. the terms and the 'graphical world'. The richer in operations it is, the more comfortably we arrive from terms to pictures, and the more precise our visual imagination can be for a picture or a term. Moreover the operations of BaGrA were the first thing to implement our ideas on a computer. At the TU Berlin, parts of BaGrA together with a simple user interface have been implemented in a diploma thesis /KW91/.

As domains in BaGrA we have numbers, Boolean values, texts, the plane, and combinations of these. The most important carrier set is Graph, the set of all graphs as subsets of the plane. We will meet it again in the definition of the graphical implementation.
Among the functions of BaGrA are all the graphical basic functions comparable with a drawing program: to draw points, lines, rectangles, circles, to write text, to manipulate graphs with shift, shear, fit_in, rotate, invert etc. For animation we have special functions. They yield lists of graphs, their elements appear one after the other giving the impression of a film.
This BaGrA above has been developed 'evolutionary' , i.e. we started with some functions and we added more common functions if we needed them in a few of the examples.
Our experiences with examples show, that for visualizations of parameterized specifications you really need an operation to accommodate the size of a picture, because the size of the graphs for the parameter elements, is not yet known.

3. The theoretical background

In addition to the normal initial approach for algebraic specifications we deal with partial specifications in the sense of Claßen, Große-Rhode, and Wolter /CGW92/. We admit in E existence equations and for OP the interpretation of the symbols by partial operations. The morphisms remain the total ones, so PALG(SPEC) denotes the category of all partial algebras and total homomorphism between them. The advantage of this approach is the similarity to the total one.
We model the visualization of abstract data types as an algebraic implementation, where we started from the theory for algebraic implementation of abstract data types by Ehrig, Kreowski, Mahr, and Padawitz (/EKMP82/, /EK83/). The possibility to write hidden parts especially satisfied our requirements. Only for the parameterized case did we need another notion of implementation, the idea is similar to that of Ehrich, Gogolla, and Lippeck /EGL89/.

3.1 Definition: (Implementation)

Let SPEC be included in SPEC1: $SPEC \overset{i}{\hookrightarrow} SPEC1$.
An algebra $A \in$ PAlg(SPEC1) implements $B \in$ Alg(SPEC) over $C \in$ PAlg(SIG)[1], if j, rep $\in$ PAlg(SIG) exist, such that are

rep: $C \longrightarrow B$ surjective (C represents B) and
j: $C \longrightarrow V_i(A)$ injective (C is a part of the implementing algebra).

graphical notation:

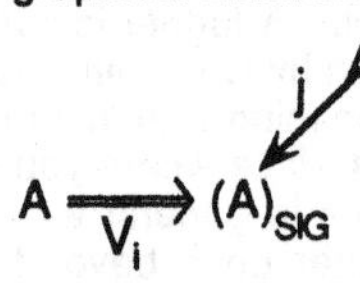

or for short[2]:

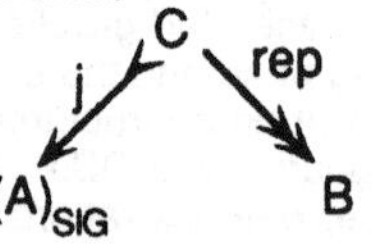

The BaGrA or a suitable quotient of it will be the implementing algebra. Its signature is part of the definition of graphical implementation. So it is clear that you can create your own BaGrA, but then it is fixed.

3.2 Definition: (Graphical Implementation)

A graphical implementation GI(SPEC) of a specification SPEC = (S,OP,E) by a SIG(BaGrA)-algebra G is a triple **GI(SPEC) = (COP, GRA, HID)** where we have:

- **COP** is a set of operation symbols ("copy-operations"), for every $s \in S$ one
  cs: Graph $\rightharpoonup$ s, Graph is a sortname in SIG(BaGrA).
- **GRA** = (GOP, GE) are the graphical operations and the equations, where the op-symbols are defined, and for compatibility with the copy operations:

---

[1] SIG is short for SIG(SPEC) and means the signature (S,OP) of a specification (S, OP, E).

[2] These diagrams work in PAlg(SIG). We omit the inclusion functor for the SPEC-algebra for readability reasons.

GOP:
for every operation symbol $N \in (OP)_{s1.....sn,s}$, $n \geq 0$, exists one
N_G : $Graph^n \twoheadrightarrow Graph$, n is the arity of N [1]
GE:
for every operation symbol $N \in (OP)_{s1.....sn,s}$, $n \geq 0$, exists one
equation of that form[2]:
$N_G(g1,.....,gn)\uparrow \Rightarrow N(cs1(g1),....., csn(gn)) = cs(N_G(g1,.....,gn))$, $n \geq 0$
and for every N_G the equations where it is defined.

- **HID** = (HS, HOP, HE) is the hidden specification, which equips the N_G's with their graphical shape.

The disjoint union of all sets of symbols we call implementation layer:
$\overline{\textbf{GI}}$ **(SPEC)** := SIG(BaGrA) + SIG(SPEC) + (Ø, COP+GOP, GE) + HID

Let SPEC = (PSPEC, BSPEC) = ((PS, POP, PE), (BS, BOP, BE)) parameterized specification with semantic F : Alg(PSPEC) ⟶ Alg(BSPEC).
From now on we suppose **F to be strongly persistent.**

3.3 Definition: (Graphical implementation, parameterized)
A graphical implementation GI(SPEC) of a parameterized specification SPEC by a SIG(BaGrA)-algebra G is a pair of graphical implementations **(GI(PSPEC), GI(BSPEC))**, where PHID = Ø and GI(PSPEC) ⊆ GI(BSPEC).

3.4 Definition: (Semantic)
The semantic of a graphical implementation is the functor

$$F_{GI} : PAlg(\overline{GI}(PSPEC)) \longrightarrow PAlg(\overline{GI}(BSPEC)).$$

Remark:
F_{GI} gives for every graphical implementation of PSPEC a graphical implementation for BSPEC. If is PSPEC = (Ø, Ø, Ø) the above definition yields for the non parameterized case the partial algebra F_{GI} (G). F_{GI} : PAlg(SIG(BaGrA)) ⟶ PAlg($\overline{GI}$ (SPEC)) is the leftadjoint (free) functor of the forgetful functor V_{BaGrA} to the inclusion SIG(BaGrA) ↪ $\overline{GI}$ (SPEC), sometimes called synthesis-functor.

3.5 Definition: (Correctness)
SPEC = (PSPEC, BSPEC) is correctly implemented graphically by G, if the following conditions hold:

PK1 $\overline{GI}$ (PSPEC) and $\overline{GI}$ (BSPEC) are specifications.

PK2 Relatively OP-complete:

Let be $X = (X_s)_{s \in PS}$, $X_s \neq \emptyset$ a set of variables for parameter sorts.
Let us suppose that PSPEC has an OP-complete graphical implementation then the following must be valid:
for all $t \in T_{SIG,s}(X)$ exist a t' and
t' = x if t = x for s ∈ PS or
$t \equiv_{\overline{GI}(SPEC)} t'$, t' is defined and t' = cs(b), b ∈ G.

---

[1] If name conflicts exist in OP by overloading with the same arity , than N_G has to be additionally indicated; e.g. with a different sort (there must be at least one).
[2] ↑ is the abbreviation for $t \stackrel{e}{=} t$, i. e. the term t exist and is defined.

PK3 Semantically correct:

For every $\overline{GI}$(PSPEC)-algebra A, which implements a PSPEC-algebra B over CP $\in$ Alg(PSIG) exists an implementation for the body containing the one for the parameter i.e.: it exists an algebra

$R \in$ PAlg(BSIG),

$j^B: R \longrightarrow V^B_{GI}(F_{GI}(A))$ injective,

$rep^B: R \longrightarrow F(B)$ surjective,

$V_i(j^B) = j^P$ and

$V_i(rep^B) = rep^P$.

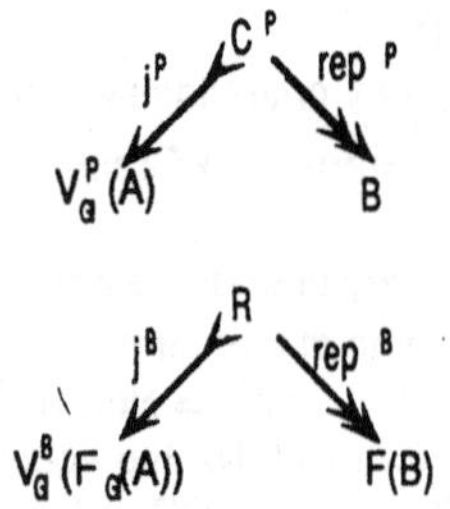

(F is the semantic of SPEC, F_{GI} the semantic on the implementation layer and V^B_{GI} the forgetful functor to the inclusion i^B_{GI}: $\overline{GI}$ (BSPEC) $\longrightarrow$ BSPEC).

PK4 F_{GI} is persistent.

In PK3 we claim that any BSIG-algebra R has to exist and a suited pair of morphisms. In the following we will construct, based on R, a standardimplementation over a C^B. C^B is the smallest algebra in the sense that for everyone of it's quotients, the correctness of the bodyimplementation doesn't hold any more, or the parameter implementation doesn't remain unchanged.

3.6 Fact: (Standardimplementation)
Let GI(SPEC) correct graphical implementation of

SPEC = (PSPEC, BSPEC), A $\in$ PAlg($\overline{GI}$ (PSPEC)), B $\in$ Alg(BSPEC).

Then exists a standardalgebra C^B which implements F(B) over $F_{GI}(A)$.

Remarks:

- Now we can speak about **the** body implementation for a given parameter-implementation.
- The algebra C^B is uniquely determined up to isomorphism by restriction in the sense of /EG91/, i.e. as an intersection over all A $\in$ PAlg(BSIG) these PSIG-restrictions yield the same.

Now we are able to define what we call animation, respectively visualization. Because of the OP-completeness we find for every term a graph in the form c(g) where c is the suited copy operation and g an element of G $\in$ ALG(SIG(BaGrA)). If g is builded by operations like move or animate we interpret g as a series of pictures, therefore we use the notion 'animation'. If it's not 'moved' then we say visualization.

3.7 Definition: (Animation)
Let SPEC = (S, OP, E) a specification,

N $\in$ OP a n-ary operation symbol (n $\geq$ 0), $t \in T_{SIG,s}$

GI(SPEC) implements SPEC correctly by G $\in$ Alg(SIG(BaGrA)).

i) g $\in$ G is called **animation of t** (by G) if

$t \equiv_{\overline{GI}\,(SPEC)} c(g)$.

ii) The set of animations of all terms with the topmost OP-symbol N is the **animation of the operation N.**

iii) The set of all animations of all OP-symbols N $\in$ OP is the **animation of SPEC.**

4. Standard parameter passing

The next step is standard parameter passing. From the graphical point of view we want the following behaviour: The actualization of a parameterized graphical implementation by an actual graphical implementation yields without any additional graphical information a new flat one, which fits to the result specification of the corresponding parameter passing on specification layer. Our theorem in the next section will ensure this behaviour. The empty HID-part in the implementation of the parameter allows actualization without conflicts.

It is given a parameterized specification SPEC = (PSPEC, BSPEC) with persistent F as semantic, an 'actual' specification ASPEC and a parameter passing morphism h: PSPEC ⟶ ASPEC. We have for every specification the graphical implementation belonging to it as a fixed SIG(BaGrA)-Algebra G.

F_{GI} : PAlg($\overline{GI}$ (PSPEC)) ⟶ PAlg($\overline{GI}$ (BSPEC)) is persistent (PK4). First we need a suited parameter passing morphism h_{GI} depending on h for the implementation layer.

4.1 Fact: (Extension of a parameter passing morphism)
We can extend a parameter passing morphism h: PSPEC ⟶ ASPEC to a signature morphism h_{GI}: $\overline{GI}$ (PSPEC) ⟶ $\overline{GI}$ (ASPEC) on the implementation layer in a unique[1] way. If we now actualize on both layers we obtain on one hand a value specification WSPEC, on the other hand GI(WSPEC). The following theorem ensures the compatibility of actualization and graphical implementation.

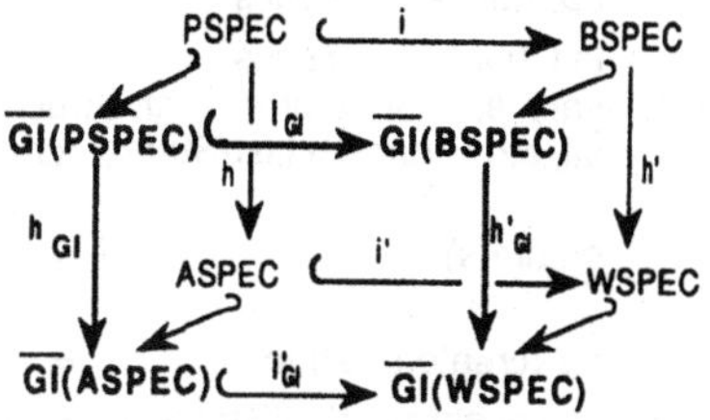

4.2 Theorem: (Standardactualization and graphical implementation)
GI(WSPEC) is a correct graphical implementation for WSPEC over G ∈ Alg(SIG(BaGrA)):

a) GI(WSPEC) is a graphical implementation for WSPEC,
 . $\overline{GI}$ (WSPEC) is a specification,
b) GI(WSPEC) is OP-complete,
c) GI(WSPEC) is semanticly correct,
d) F_{GI} is persistent with regard to G.

Remark: It is no problem to lift all the theory up to the case of parameterized parameter passing.

5. Example

We can show the skeptical reader a convincing example. For this we choose the specification of a syntax directed editor by Claßen and Löwe /CL90/. It's too large for this paper but we can take the more interesting part and try to bridge over the lacking parts with verbal explanations and of course pictures. The part we present is the specification of FOCUS, i.e. trees representing the structure of the program together with a cursor. In /CL90/ the cursor position is specified as the subtree hanging on the marked node, while the immediate contexts are stored on three stacks: the ALTERNATIVE STACK for the direct ancestor, two STRUCTURE LIST STACKS for the list of left respectively right brothers. The specification FOCUS defines the user operations for the movements of the cursor: up, down, left, and right. We'll give the graphical implementation GI(FOCUS) not in the form of pure BaGrA operations, but a sketch of how the interpretation of the graphical operations would look like on the screen (as far as it is possible to give an idea of a film on a sheet of paper).
We start with the parameterized specification STACK(DATA) with the usual operations create, push, pop, top and visualize it as a bundle of paper, the elements would be placed later on the sheets of paper. Furthermore we have PROGRAM STRUCTURES with the main constructor a[l] for the sort Structures where 'a' stands for the element in the root and 'l' for a list of structures. The constructors of the lists are empty and ∘. We will visualize the sort Structure as trees, the copy operation is $<\_>_S$.

[1] On SIG(BaGrA) h_{GI} has to be the identity.

For the following specification we need two kinds of stacks. We obtain them by actualizing DATA in STACK(DATA) by PROGRAM TOKENS (it's mainly an enumeration of constants like statement, iteration, atom, operator etc.) which yields ALTERNATIVE STACK, respectively actualizing DATA by PROGRAM STRUCTURES where we get STRUCTURE LIST STACK.

We do the same with the appropriate graphical implementations. The copy operations belonging to them are $<\_>_{AS}$ and $<\_>_{SLS}$.

FOCUS = PROGRAM STRUCTURES + ALTERNATIVE STACK +
STRUCTURE LIST STACK +

sorts: Focus

opns:

<_,_,_,_>	: Alternative-Stack Structure List-Stack Structure List-Stack Structure	⟶ Focus
create	: Structure	⟶ Focus
up, down	: Focus	⟶ Focus
left, right	: Focus	⟶ Focus

eqns: vars: s,s': Structure; sl: Structure List; a: Alternative;
stl, str: Structure List-Stack; ast: Alternative-Stack;

create(s) = <create,create,create,s>

up<create,stl,str,s> = <create,stl,str,s>
up<push(a,ast),stl,str,s> = <ast,pop(stl),pop(str),a[top(stl) ∘ s ∘ top(str)]>

down<ast,stl,str,a[λ]> = <ast,stl,str,a[λ]>
down<ast,stl,str,a[s∘ sl]> = <push(a,ast),push(λ,stl),push(sl,str),s>

left<ast,create,str,s> = <ast,create,str,s>
left<ast,push(λ,stl),str,s> = <ast,push(λ,stl),str,s>
left<ast,push(sl∘s,stl),str,s'> = <ast,push(sl,stl),push(s'∘top(str),pop(str)),s>

right<ast,stl,create,s> = <ast,stl,create,s>
right<ast,stl,push(λ,str),s> = <ast,stl,push(λ,str),s>
right<ast,stl,push(s∘sl,str),s'> = <ast,push(top(stl)∘s',pop(stl)),push(sl,str),s>

Anybody who is reading this for the first time is asked to see only by these equations how the operation up works (without looking at the next pages of course) and after that to compare their way and the method (did you sketch a picture?) instead of comprehending the graphical operation up_G in (H3). We hope you get the same result as we do, and see that it is valuable and useful to have this kind of support.

GI(FOCUS) = GI(PROGRAM STRUCTURES) + GI(ALTERNATIVE STACK) +
GI(STRUCTURE LIST STACK) +

COP: $<\_>_F$: Graph ⟶ Focus

GRA:

GOP:

$<\_,\_,\_,\_>_G$	: Graph Graph Graph Graph	⟶ Graph
$create_G$	: Graph	⟶ Graph
up_G, $down_G$	: Graph	⟶ Graph
$left_G$, $right_G$	: Graph	⟶ Graph

GE: (G1) $<g1,g2,g3,g4>_G\uparrow \;\Rightarrow$

$<<g1>_{AS},<g2>_{SLS},<g3>_{SLS},<g4>_S> \quad \stackrel{e}{=} <<g1,g2,g3,g4>_G>_F$

(G2) $create_G(g)\uparrow \quad \Rightarrow create(<g>_S) \quad \stackrel{e}{=} <create_G(g)>_F$

(G3) $up_G(g)\uparrow \quad \Rightarrow up(<g>_F) \quad \stackrel{e}{=} <up_G(g)>_F$

(G4) $down_G(g)\uparrow \quad \Rightarrow down(<g>_F) \quad \stackrel{e}{=} <down_G(g)>_F$

(G5) $left_G(g)\uparrow \quad \Rightarrow left(<g>_F) \quad \stackrel{e}{=} <left_G(g)>_F$

(G6) $right_G(g)\uparrow \quad \Rightarrow right(<g>_F) \quad \stackrel{e}{=} <right_G(g)>_F$

(G7) $<<g1>_{AS},<g2>_{SLS},<g3>_{SLS},<g4>_S>\uparrow \Rightarrow <g1,g2,g3,g4>_G\uparrow$

(G8) $create(<g>_S)\uparrow \;\Rightarrow create_G(g)\uparrow$

(G9) $up(<g>_F)\uparrow \;\Rightarrow up_G(g)\uparrow$

(G10) $down(<g>_F)\uparrow \;\Rightarrow down_G(g)\uparrow$

(G11) $left(<g>_F)\uparrow \;\Rightarrow left_G(g)\uparrow$

(G12) $right(<g>_F)\uparrow \;\Rightarrow right_G(g)\uparrow$

HID:

HE: (H1) $<g1,g2,g3,g4>_G\uparrow \;\Rightarrow$
$<g1,g2,g3,g4>_G =$
place g1, g2, g3,
and g4 side by side not
overlapping so that
Max_y(g1) = ...=
= Max_y(g4).

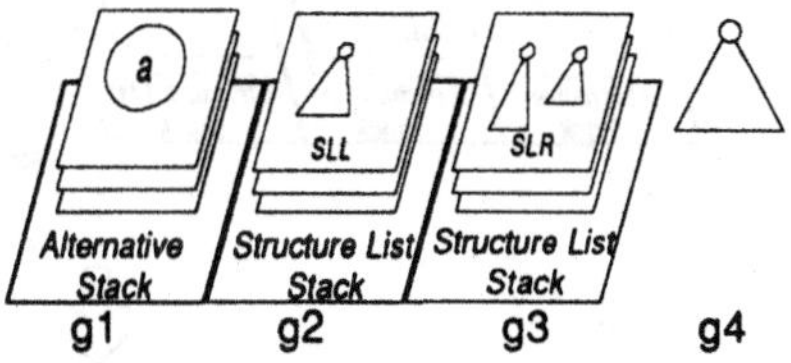

(H2) $create_G(g)\uparrow \Rightarrow create_G(g) =$

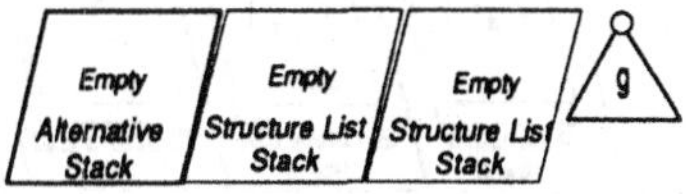

(H3) $<g1,g2,g3,g4>_G\uparrow \Rightarrow$

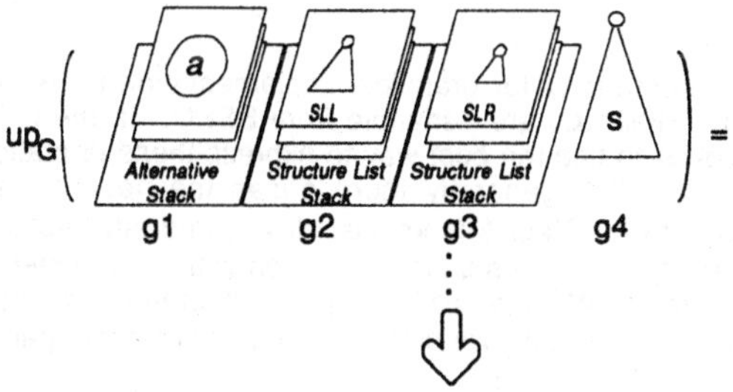

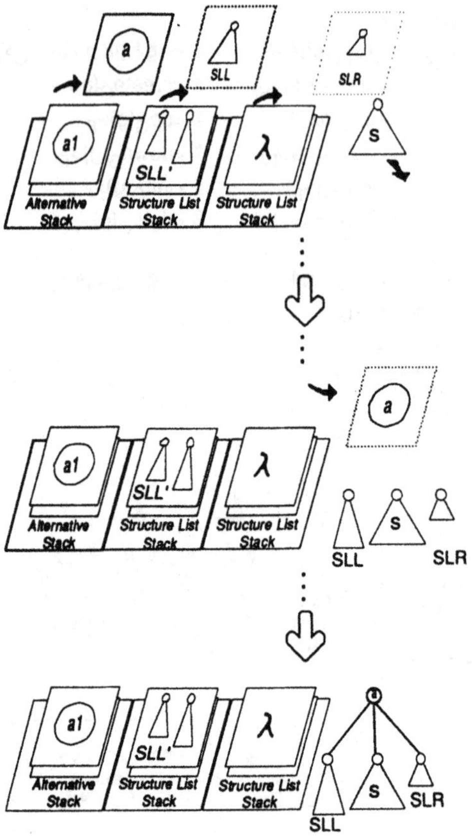

(H4) ... analogous for $down_G$, $left_G$, and $right_G$.

• End GI(FOCUS) •

In the examples, the following strategy for graphical implementation turns out to be useful. The COP and GRA parts of GI(SPEC) are derivable from SPEC. In the HID part we need creativity and imaginative power to find the best way to express these operations. During the description how an op_G looks like, generally there arises the need for some graphical auxiliary operations additional to the BaGrA-functions. If you see after some examples that you need a few of these auxiliary operations quite often, then you can transfer them to BaGrA, sometimes in a more general form. We see this like a pyramid: at the base the more common and therefore reusable functions, the more we climb the nearer and more particular we are to the specification.

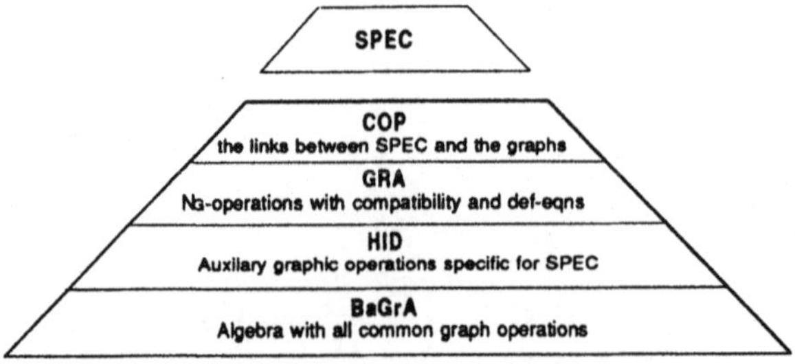

So the BaGrA will pass through evolutionary stages till it has adapted to your problems.

6. Conclusion

We provided initial algebraic specifications with animation with the notion graphical implementation. A central role plays the BaGrA, where all the graphical ground functions are collected, which can be used to define the graphical behavior of an operation in SPEC. We also have a notion when a specification is correctly implemented graphically over a SIG(BaGrA)-algebra G. Furthermore we ensured the compatibility of actualization and graphical implementation. Finally we gave as an example, an animation of a part of a syntax directed editor.

In our opinion it is very neccessary to have a suitable user interface to define the graphical operations, because the pure mathematical way we use up until now, is very awkward and tedious to write and read (and this is of course the last thing we want to achieve). We regard this as an interim state, a first step to develop the theoretical framework. The user interface can be a small but powerful description language for pictures as it was realized in a diploma thesis by R.Bardohl at TU Berlin this year /Ba93/. Or it can be a graphical user interface with a functionality of a drawing program perhaps together with a kind of recorder for the 'film scenes' and interactive components to associate terms and graphs in the right way. If we are at this point, may be the step to interchange the roles, i.e. to specify using graphs with textual support, is not as far away as it seems to be now.
In implementing a tool for animations we also have to solve problems like finding an intelligent default representation for the terms, or if it's compatible with our theoretical framework, to turn over to an icon representation, when graphs would be too small.

Acknowledgment

I'm very grateful to Prof. Hartmut Ehrig and all my colleagues in his group. Special thanks to Dr. Michael Löwe for his constant help and encouragement and to Martin Große-Rhode for his patience with all my questions.

References

/Ba93/ Roswitha Bardohl
Konzept und Implementierung der Sprache GVT zur graphischen Visualisierung von Termen algebraischer Spezifikationen; Diplomarbeit an der TU Berlin, Mai1993

/BK91/ Jon L. Bentley, Brian W. Kernighan
A System for Algorithm Animation; Computing Systems, Vol. 4, No. 1, 1991, pp. 5-30

/BL89/ Tommaso Bolognesi, Diego Latella
Techniques for the formal definition of the G-LOTOS syntax; in: Participant's Proceedings of the Ninth IFIPW WG 6.1, 6 - 9 June 1989, pp. 1-14. University of Twente - Enschede,

/Br88/ Marc H. Brown
Exploring Algorithms Using Balsa-II; IEEE Computer, May 1988, pp. 14-36.

/CGW92/ Ingo Claßen, Martin Große-Rohde, Uwe Wolter
Categorical Concepts for Parameterized Partial Specifications; TU Berlin report no. 92-42

/CL90/ Ingo Claßen, Michael Löwe
Algebraic Development of a syntax directed Editor; TU Berlin report no. 9o/37

/EG91/ H. Ehrig, M. Große-Rhode
Structural Theory of Algebraic Specifications in a Specification logic, part 1: Functorial parameterized specifications; TU Berlin, report no. 91/23, oct.91

/EGL89/ H.-D. Ehrich, M. Gogolla, U.W. Lipeck
Algebraische Spezifikationen abstrakter Datentypen
Leitfäden und Monographien der Informatik; Teubner, Stuttgart,1989

/EK83/ H. Ehrig, H.-J. Kreowski
Compatibility of parameter passing and implementation of parameterized data types
Theoretical Computer Science 27 (1983), pp. 255-286

/EKMP82/ H. Ehrig, H.-J. Kreowski, B. Mahr, P. Padawitz
Algebraic implementation of abstract data types; TCS 20 (1982), pp. 209-263

/EM85/ H.Ehrig; B.Mahr
Fundamentals of Algebraic Specifications 1, Equations and Initial Semantics
EATCS Monograph on Theoretical Computer Sciences, Vol. 6, Springer Verlag 1985

/Go87/ J.A.Gougen
Programming by Generic Example; in: Steven Kartashev and Svetlana Kartashev, (eds.), Proc. 2nd Int. Supercomputing Conf.1987, Vol.I, pp. 209-216

/GS88/ Alessandro Giacalone, Scott A. Smolka
Integrated Environments for Formally Well-founded Design and Simulation of Concurrent Systems; IEEE Transactions on Software Engineering, Vol.14, No.6, (1988), pp.787 - 801

/KS90/ Kenneth M. Kahn, Vijay A. Saraswat
Complete visualizations of concurrent programs and their executions; IEEE Workshop on Visual Languages, June 1990, Skokie,Illinois, USA, pp. 227-232

/KW91/ Gudrun König, Lutz Wrage
Grundkonzepte und Implementierung einer graphischen Darstellung von algebraisch spezifizierten Datentypen; Diplomarbeit an der TU Berlin, 1991

/Lö91/ Michael Löwe
Extended Algebraic Graph Transformation; PhD-thesis at the TU Berlin 1991

/Mo88/ Thomas G. Moher
PROVIDE: A Process Visualization and Debugging Environment; IEEE Transactions on Software Engineering, Vol.14, No.6, June 1988, pp. 849 - 857

/My90/ Brad A. Myers
Invisible Programming; IEEE Workshop on Visual Languages, June 1990, pp. 203-208

/NA89/ Darren New, Paul D. Amer
Adding Graphics and Animation to Estelle; in: Participant's Proceedings of the Ninth IFIPW WG 6.1, 6 - 9 June 1989, pp. 1-14. University of Twente - Enschede

/Ra85/ Georg Raeder
A Survey of Current Graphical Programming Techniques
IEEE Computer, Vol. 18, No.8, pp. 11-25

/Re86/ Steven P. Reiss
Visual Languages and the GARDEN System; in LNCS 282, Visualization in Programming, Workshop in Schärding/Austria, 20 - 23 May 1986, Gorny/Tauber (Eds.), pp. 178-193

/RGR85/ Robert V. Rubin, Eric J. Golin, Steven P. Reiss
Think Pad: A Graphical System for Programming by Demonstration
IEEE Software, March 1985, pp. 73-79

/SBN88/ David Socha, Mary L. Bailey, David Notkin
VOYEUR: Graphical Views of Parallel Programs; ACM SIGPLAN and SIGOPS, Workshop on Parallel and Distributed Debugging, 1988, pp. 206 - 215

/Sh88/ Nan C. Shu
Visual Programming;
Van Nostrand Reinhold Company, New York, 1988

/St91/ John T. Stasko
Using direct Manipulation to Build Algorithm Animation by Demonstration; ACM Conference Proceedings CHI'91, Reaching through Technology, Addison Wesley May 91

Second-Order Proof Systems for Algebraic Specification Languages

Pierre-Yves Schobbens *

Fac. Univ. Notre-Dame de la Paix
Institut d'Informatique
Rue Grandgagnage 21
B-5000 Namur

Abstract. Besides explicit axioms, an algebraic specification language contains model-theoretic constraints such as term-generation or initiality. For proving properties of specifications and refining them to programs, an axiomatisation of these constraints is needed; unfortunately, no effective, sound and complete proof system can be constructed for most algebraic specification languages.
In this paper, we construct non-effective second-order axiomatisations for constraints commonly found in specification languages, and simplified forms useful for the universal fragment. They are shown to be sound and complete, but not effective, since the underlying second-order logic is not effective. A good level of machine support is still possible using higher-order proof assistants.

1 Introduction

1.1 Are our specification languages too expressive?

Algebraic specification languages extend universal algebra as needed for their application to program specification:

- various typing disciplines have been proposed, the most known being many-sorted and order-sorted algebras;
- model-theoretic constraints (such as initiality) have been added in order to increase the expressive power of the language, and to eliminate trivial models.
- the specification logic, first restricted to equations, has been extended to equational Horn logic, equational clauses and first-order logic. Our results are thus designed to hold for these richer languages.

Most of these model-theoretic constraints increase the expressive power of the language beyond what is effectively axiomatizable, as shown for instance by [18] for the simple case of initial constraints on equational specifications; more cases are proved in [16].

Current research is trying to circumvent that impossibility:

* This research was mostly carried out at Centre National de la Recherche Scientifique, Centre de Recherche en Informatique de Nancy.

- Wirsing [25] uses rules with an infinite number of antecedents. His language, ASL, contains e.g. a reachability constraint (see section 3.3, A.1) which he axiomatizes by the rule:

$$\frac{\Phi[t/x] \quad \text{for all } T_F(X)}{\forall x : s.\Phi}$$

where $T_F(X)$ is the (often infinite) set of generating terms. In practice, this infinite set of terms is often treated by an informal induction.
- Another solution uses non-logical antecedents in inference rules. For instance, to axiomatize initiality on equational Horn clauses, we might use the following rule in complement to some rule expressing term generation:

$$\frac{\text{for all } \sigma.\sigma t_1, \sigma t_2 \text{ ground} \qquad \nvdash \sigma t_1 = \sigma t_2}{\vdash t_1 \neq t_2}$$

This rule uses non-provability of equations as an antecedent for provability of inequations. Thanks to the fact that the specification is Horn, this is not a circular definition. Yet, we need a decision procedure for equations to keep the system for disequations effective. In practice, we have only semi-decision procedures (such as narrowing) for some forms of specifications. When one of these complete procedures terminates without finding equal ground instances, the disequation follows. This method is thus suited to automation, but not general and very handy for manual proofs, since an exhaustive search is necessary to establish non-provability.
- These constraints, considered as logical formulae, form an institution [10]; but this does not provide proof systems. The present paper shows that this institution is a subset of the second-order logic institution.
- In this article, in contrast, we are interested in second-order axiomatizations of such theories. This approach is adequate for a larger class of logics – including first-order logic – and constraints, and is suited to computer-assisted proofs [11] (but not to automated proofs).

1.2 Second-order logic

Second-order logic interprets predicate variables as ranging over all sets. It is not effectively axiomatizable, but the inference rules known for second-order logic are often sufficient in practice, and can sometimes be used to reduce a specification with constraints to a first-order specification (e.g. in 3.1)

To take a well-known example, the term-generation constraint can be axiomatized by a second-order induction rule. When no functions (except constants) are used, this rule is easily reduced to a first-order disjunction. The paper develops similar rules for constraints found in various specification languages [8, 25, 12].

The rules are directly based on semantic characterizations of the models; they can be divided into two types, the first one encoding the definition of homomorphisms, and the other one, the notion of congruence on a term algebra. The second type is often easier to use, but is only valid for universal specifications.

These rules are obtained easily, as they just encode the set-theoretic definition of the constraints in second order logic. (The differences between set theory and second-order logic require just a few precautions, see 4.1.)

The paper informally presents the main ideas of our approach, and their application to several constraints: section 3 presents the term-generation constraints and its variants, section 4 presents initiality and its generalisations, among which an original one, section 5 presents selected variants of observationality (which is not really a constraint, since it enlarges the class of models). Mathematical definitions are found in appendixes; proofs could not be included.

2 Relativization

As second-order logic is unsorted, while the logics used in most specification languages are sorted, we use through the paper the relativization technique [9]: we introduce a unary predicate for each sort, and replace quantification $\forall x : s.\phi$ by $\forall x.s(x) \Rightarrow R(\phi)$, where $R(\phi)$ is (recursively) the relativization of ϕ. The well-sortedness of operators has to be expressed by an axiom $OPS(O)^2$ We define thus the translation $R(S)$ of a presentation $S = (\Sigma, \phi)$, where $\Sigma = (S, O, P)$, as $OPS(O) \wedge R(\phi)$. Relativization also allows a simple treatment of subsorts.

3 Term-generated models

3.1 Term-generation (CIP)

When specifying data structures, it is natural to consider only the data that can be created by the declared operators. This is the approach followed in CIP [5]. As is well known, this condition can be expressed by the second-order induction axiom $TG(\Sigma)^6$.

How could we have obtained this rule in a more methodic way? We will see below that the axiom *TERM* characterize term algebras. *TERM* itself contains an induction rule *FG* on terms. By using $I_s(V(t))$ as the inductive predicate in *FG* – where V the surjective evaluation mentioned in the definition of term generation – we obtain the rule *TG*.

3.2 Generated models (Larch)

The constraint above is too strong for hierarchical specifications, since they may forbid some models of imported or parameterized specifications. In the example of parameterized bags below, the parameter has to be interpreted loosely, although the bags have to be "term-generated" in a weak sense. To that end Larch[12, 13] contains the constraint s generated by F, where F is a set of operators with results in s. The idea is that s and F will be chosen in the new

[1] These bold numbers refer to the theorems of appendix B. Definitions are found in appendix A.

part of the specification; in the example above, s will be the sort of bags, and F will be its usual constructors *empty*, *add*.

This constraint is defined by a very similar induction rule, $GENL(s, F)$[7].

Unfortunately, this proposal does not allow mutually generated sorts.

Example 1. Even and odd natural numbers are distinguished by putting them into separate sorts:
spec *EvenOdd* =
sorts *even*, *odd*
opers $0 :\rightarrow even$
$s_e : even \rightarrow odd$
$s_o : odd \rightarrow even$
end
In this case, it becomes impossible to write down the usual induction on naturals in Larch, because we need both *odd* and *even* in a single rule.

3.3 Reachable models (ASL)

This problem is solved in ASL: it contains the more general construct **reachable** S **on** T **with** F. Mutually generated sorts are thus allowed by using a set of sorts T rather than a single sort in the syntax.

Instead of the infinite rule of [25], the following slightly generalised induction rule, $RCH(T, F)$, can axiomatize this constraint[5]. By setting $(T, F) = (S, O)$, the term-generation constraint is obtained as a special case; by restricting F to have results in T, we obtain Larch's **generated by**.

This construct does not yet allow a sort to be generated by a subset of another.

Example 2. Let us specify square numbers as a separate sort:
spec *Squares* = **with** *Int*
sorts *squares*
opers $.^2 : int \rightarrow squares$
$. : squares \rightarrow int$
axioms $\forall i : int$,
$i^2 = i * i$
...
end
We can assert **reachable** *Squares* **on** *squares* **with** $.^2$, but it is not possible to specify that the natural numbers are sufficient to obtain all squares.

3.4 Generalisation

The previous example could not be treated because ASL uses the set of sorts T both to designate the constrained sorts and to determine the sorts where variables are allowed ($S \setminus T$).

In an algebra A, a sort s is said to be *reachable* by F and S', (where S' is a set of subsorts indexed by S; s' is the element of index s) if any element a of the carrier A_s, is the value of a term of $T_F(s'_A)_{s \in S}$. A is *reachable* on $T \subseteq S$ by F and S' if all sorts $s \in T$ are reachable. This constraint is axiomatized by $FG((T,F),S')^4$. In particular, the ASL reachability constraint is obtained by taking $s' = s$ for $s \in T$, and constraining s' to be empty (by an axiom $\forall x : s'.x \neq x$) for $s \in S \setminus T$.

4 Initiality and extensions

4.1 Initial model

To avoid trivial models, the semantics of a specification is often taken to be its initial model. A model A of $\mathcal{S}$ is initial iff for every B of $\mathcal{S}$ there is a unique homomorphism $h : A \to B$. The initial model is often intuitively explained as minimizing equality ("no confusion", or more precisely "minimum confusion"). When predicates are present, a similar default is used to preserve uniqueness of the initial model [10]. Initial and free models are generalised in the last part in this section; we present them first for historical and paedagogical reasons.

First-order logic The power of second-order logic allows a direct encoding of the definition of initial model, for axioms written in many-sorted first-order logic, a subset of which is used in Clear[4] and ACT-ONE[7]. A many-sorted signature will be encoded in second-order logic by a triple of second-order variables: (sort) predicates for S, functions for O, and predicates for P. The part of the interpretation corresponding to this triple will represent an arbitrary algebra. Given two such triples, Σ and Σ', an homomorphism is a S-tuple of function h satisfying $HOM(\text{h}, \Sigma, \Sigma')$.

Initiality seems thus directly translated as $*INI(\mathcal{S})$.

Example 3. Let us look more closely at the models of $*INI$ for:
spec Nat =
sort nat
opers $0 :\to nat$
$succ : nat \to nat$
end
The initial model of this presentation is known to be isomorphic to the natural numbers. When the domain contains a single element, $*INI$ is unexpectedly satisfied: there is a single function from the singleton nat to the singleton nat'.

The problem is that Σ' ranges over subsets of the domain, while we would like it to range over sets of arbitrary cardinality. Knowing that a model of a first-order sentence is initial iff it is initial among models whose carriers are subsets of a domain that is at least denumerable[9], we just have to add an axiom DEN that ensures that the domain is at least denumerable. We conjoin it with our previous attempt to obtain an exact characterization.

When the specification is not Horn, there is often no initial model at all. This motivates the search for more sensible constraints, reviewed in section 4.3.

Furthermore, using the rule $INI(\mathcal{S})$ to make practical proofs is tedious: fortunately, a simpler rule can be used for universal sentences.

Universal sentences When the language is restricted to universal sentences, we know that the initial model is isomorphic to the quotient of T_Σ by the least congruence satisfying the axioms. This fact can be used to construct a more practical rule, where quantification over functions is eliminated. Assume that we can characterize algebras isomorphic to T_Σ by some axiom $TERM(\Sigma)$ (this will be done in section 4.2). Then we introduce a family of new binary predicates $\equiv_s$ to express the congruence on T_Σ, and we state the usual congruence axioms $EQ(\Sigma)$.

Of course, the presentation should use this congruence instead of equality, which is achieved by a simple substitution of the equality symbol by a congruence symbol of the adequate sort: $\phi[\equiv / =]$, where $\equiv$ is an abbreviation for a family $(\equiv_s)_{s\in S}$ of binary relations. We will detail and generalise this axiom in the next section; what is important is to understand its construction and structure to follow easily the sequel.

4.2 Free models

First-order logic Once again, the definition of initial model is not suitable for parameterized specifications, since it may put constraints on the parameter.

Example 4. We specify bags of some loosely specified sort of elements, plus a loose specification of containers (e.g. lists):

spec *Elem* = **sort** *elem* **end**

spec *Bag* = free with *Elem*
sort *bag*
opns $add : elem \times bag \to bag$
$empty : \to bag$
pred $. \in . : elem \times bag$
axioms $\forall e, f : elem, s : bag.$
$e \in add(e, s)$
$add(e, add(f, s)) = add(f, add(e, s))$
end

spec *Container* = **with** *Bag*
sort *cont*
opns $cons : elem \times cont \to cont$
$bagof : cont \to bag$
pred $.in. : elem \times cont$
axioms $\forall e : elem, c : cont.$
$e\ in\ cons(e, s)$
$bagof(cons(e, s)) = add(e, bagof(s))$
end

The intended models of *Containers* are the free models wrt *Bag* on *Elem*; no freeness constraint should be put on *Elem*, because it would then be void. Similarly, no constraint should be put on *Cont*, hence the importance of limiting the constraint to *Bag*.

An algebra A is said to be *free* with respect to $\mathcal{S}_2$ on $\mathcal{S}_1$ ($\mathcal{S}_1 \subseteq \mathcal{S}_2$) iff for all models A_2 of $\mathcal{S}_2$, and homomorphisms $h_1 : A|_{\Sigma_1} \to A_2|_{\Sigma_1}$ there is a unique homomorphism $h_2 : A|_{\Sigma_2} \to A_2$ satisfying $h_2|_{\Sigma_1} = h_1$.

This condition translates directly into a second-order axiom. We have the same cardinality problem as for initiality, and here we have a slightly weaker result[9], since we have at least the cardinality of the "old" sorts (S_1). As each s_i is already included in the domain, it suffices to ensure a domain at least denumerable, for which our axiom *DEN* suffices. So our final axiom is $FREE(S_2, S_1)$[11].

Universal sentences When the language is restricted to universal sentences, or any sublanguage that has the submodel property, we can show that the Σ_2-reduct of a free model is isomorphic to the quotient of $T_{\Sigma_2}(I|_{\Sigma_1})$ by the least congruence satisfying the axioms of S_2. The free construction is again a term algebra, this time using the elements of S_1 as variables. We use a copy Σ_1' of Σ_1 disjoint from Σ_2, to represent the algebra we started from. This distinction is only temporary, for if we prove persistency (see below), the two algebras can be identified.

The following facts, $TERM(\Sigma, S_1')$ characterize term algebras[8]:

- the algebra is well-typed, $OPS(O)$.
- variables are terms, $INC(S, S_1')$:
- functions have disjoint images, $DIS(O)$.
- each function is injective, $INJ(O)$.
- functions do not yield variables, $NOV(O, S_1')$.
- the algebra is reachable, $FG(\Sigma, S')$.

The congruence should respect the structure of Σ_1, as expressed by $RS(\Sigma_1')$. The free model is characterized by the least congruence and by the least extension of predicates, $LC(S_2)$.

Conjoining these conditions, we obtain *LCS*. This axiom allows us to derive exactly the same consequences than the original specification, provided we treat the goal similarly, i.e. we relativize it, and use $\equiv$ instead of $=$.[13]

To avoid this replacement, we can use use a quotient morphism; we use this technique to state persistency below.

Persistency This free model is usually considered *correct* [7] if persistency is insured, i.e. the Σ_1-reduct of the free extension wrt S_2 of any model of S_1 is isomorphic to that model.

To show persistency, we have to prove the existence of a quotient morphism from free model to the original model i.e. to prove $PER(\Sigma_2, \Sigma_1)$ from *LCS*.

Knowing persistency, we may now use a simpler rule, where S_1 and S_1' are identified. *FG* can be simplified to $RCH(S_2 \setminus S_1, O_2)$,

The axioms *INC* and *NOV* can be simply suppressed; *DIS* and *INJ* are only applied for f with result outside S_1, and similarly for the *EQ* axioms.

Example 5. Our notations have now grown to a point where most readers have difficulties to unfold them mentally, so let's do the exercise for our *Bag* example.

Here, the persistency proof obligation is trivial, since no new operator has an old result sort, and there are no equations on an old sort.

To simplify notation, we move the quantification
$\forall e, f, s, t, x. elem(e) \wedge elem(f) \wedge bag(s) \wedge bag(t) \wedge bag(x) \Rightarrow ..$
outside (which is allowed since the signature is sensible).

$$
\begin{array}{ll}
OPS & elem(default) \\
 & bag(empty) \\
 & bag(add(e,s)) \\
R(\phi) & e \in add(e,s) \\
 & add(e, add(f,s)) \equiv add(f, add(e,s)) \\
TERM & empty \neq add(e,s) \\
 & add(e,s) = add(f,t) \Rightarrow e = f \wedge s = t \\
EQ & s \equiv s \\
 & t \equiv s \Rightarrow s \equiv t \\
 & x \equiv s \wedge s \equiv t \Rightarrow x \equiv t \\
 & t \equiv s \Rightarrow add(e,s) \equiv add(e,t) \\
 & t \equiv s \Rightarrow [e \in s \Leftrightarrow e \in t] \\
LC & \forall \equiv', \in' . R(\phi') \wedge EQ' \Rightarrow (s \equiv t \Rightarrow s \equiv' t) \wedge (e \in s \Rightarrow e \in' s)
\end{array}
$$

As an exercise, let use prove $\psi = \forall e : elem, s : bag. add(e,s) \neq empty$, which is not stated in the axioms but is non-monotonically derivable since the contrary is not stated. This goal translates to $R(\psi)[\equiv / =] = \forall e, s. elem(e) \wedge bag(s) \Rightarrow add(e,s) \not\equiv empty$. Let $x \equiv' y$ be $(x \equiv y) \wedge (x = empty \Leftrightarrow y = empty)$. It is easy to check that $R(\phi')$ and EQ' are satisfied for this new equality, so that we deduce by LC that $\forall x, y. bag(x) \wedge bag(y) \wedge x \equiv y \Rightarrow [x = empty \Leftrightarrow y = empty]$. By DIS, $empty \neq add(e,s)$, hence the goal.

Now let's prove $\psi = \forall e : elem.\ e \notin empty$, which is also not stated in the axioms. The goal translates to $R(\psi)[\equiv / =] = \forall e. elem(e) \Rightarrow \neg(e \in empty)$. We instantiate $\equiv'$ by $\equiv$, and $\in'$ by $s \neq empty \wedge e \in s$ in LC. The antecedents can be eliminated:

- EQ' is derivable from EQ, except $t \equiv s \Rightarrow [(s \neq empty \wedge e \in s) \Leftrightarrow (t \neq empty \wedge e \in t)]$, which simplifies to $t \equiv s \Rightarrow (s = empty \Leftrightarrow t = empty)$, proved above.
- $R(\phi')$ is derivable using $TERM$ and $R(\phi)$.

We obtain thus $\forall e, s. elem(s) \wedge bag(s) \wedge e \in s \Rightarrow (s \neq empty \wedge e \in s)$, which simplifies to the goal.

We leave $add(e, add(e,s)) \neq add(e,s)$ and $f \in add(e,s) \Leftrightarrow (f = e \vee f \in s)$ as exercises to the reader.

4.3 Extensions of free models

The main problem of free models is that they are only guaranteed to exist for Horn specifications. In many cases there is no free model at all. Four approaches (minimal [1], quasi-free [15], circumscriptive [19] and surjective [22, 23] models) have been designed to avoid this problem; all of them are expressible in second-order logic. They are compared in [23].

5 Observability

The constraints we have seen so far are designed to strengthen the specification. In contrast, observable specifications intend to have more models. The classical example is the stack: none of the classical implementations of the stack satisfy its specification ***stricto sensu***, since $pop(push(e, s))$ differs from s through implementation details.

5.1 Partitions in Larch

Although Larch contains no concept of observability in the usual sense, it contains the construct s **partitioned by** F which has a similar motivation. It is defined by the (first-order!) axiom $PART(s, F)$. The problem is then to define how an implementation has to treat equality, but this is not in the scope of Larch, but rather of its interface languages.

5.2 Observability in ASL

ASL contains a very general observation operator, called **observe** $\mathcal{S}$ **wrt** Φ in [25, 21], where Φ is a set of first-order formulae. Intuitively, it means that the specification $\mathcal{S}$ has been too strong: for instance, $pop(push(e, s)) = s$ only means that these two stacks should not be distinguishable by equalities between elements.

For our purposes, we need a finite description of the infinite Φ. We propose a recursive definition of the following form, called an ***observation signature*** Σ_o:

- a supplementary set S_o of ***subsorts***. These subsorts are just syntactical categories for classifying terms, that will allow us to define the shape of observed formulae. The function $\sigma : S_o \rightarrow S$ gives the ***parent*** sort.
- a set of operator declarations $O_o \subset O \times (S_o \cup S)^* \times S_o$. These operator declarations defines which functions may appear in term of sort s_o: those who have a declaration that their result is in s_o. These declarations must be consistent with the original declarations, i.e. if $f : \mathbf{s} \rightarrow r \in O_o$, then $f : \sigma(\mathbf{s}) \rightarrow \sigma(r) \in O$.
- a set of observed predicate declarations $P_o \subset P \times (S_o \cup S)^*$, that define the observed formulae. Again, it must be compatible with the original declarations: if $p : \mathbf{s} \in P_o$, then $p : \sigma(\mathbf{s}) \in P$.

The set of observable formulae is defined as $\{p(\mathbf{t}) | p : \mathbf{s} \in P_o, \mathbf{t} : \mathbf{s}\}$, where $t : s$ is defined as follows:

- $t : s \Leftrightarrow t \in T^s_\Sigma(X)$, when $s \in S$;
- $t : r \Leftrightarrow t = f(\mathbf{t}), f : \mathbf{s} \rightarrow r \in O_o, \mathbf{t} : \mathbf{s}$, when $r \in S_o$.

Sorts may contain variables, while subsorts may not: they are just used to define categories of terms. In particular, it is easy to construct an observation signature with subsorts for ground terms. Another special case is the IN/OUT scheme of [21] by setting $P_o = \{=: \tau(s) \times \tau(s) | s \in OUT\}$, $O_o = \{f : \tau(s) \to \tau(s) | f : s \to r \in P\}$, where τ returns for each IN sort, the sort itself, and for other sorts, the subsort of its terms, say T_s. As noted in [24, 1], schemes based on sorts like this one are not detailed enough in practice: our scheme also allows to treat specify which operators and predicates are observed.

Given a set of formulae Φ, [25] defines an equivalence relation $A \equiv_\Phi A'$ as: there are a set of variable X and two surjective valuations $V : X \to A$, $V' : X \to A'$ such that $A \models_V \phi \Leftrightarrow A' \models_{V'} \phi$, for all $\phi \in \Phi$. (These valuations are only useful if open formulae are observable.) A is a model of **observe** S **wrt** Φ iff it is equivalent to some model A' of S.

We already have all the definitions necessary for encoding this semantic definition in second-order logic, since we can describe the terms $T_\Sigma(X)$, the set of observable terms inductively, and the valuations V, V' as surjective functions. Finally, we would have to solve the usual cardinality problems.

However, this approach can be simplified in a way similar to term-generation. The terms and valuations are indeed immaterial in this definition; the relation between the elements of the algebra is sufficient. So let's define $(C_s)_{s \in S_o \cup S}$ by $C_s(a, a') \Leftrightarrow \exists t : s. V_A(t) = a, V_{A'}(t) = a'$. Intuitively, $C_s(a, a')$ means that a and a' have the same observed behaviour. The observed subsorts $s_o(a) (s_o \in S_o)$ are defined as $\exists t : s_o. V_A(t) = a$, or equivalently as $\exists a'. C_{s_o}(a, a')$. These subsorts are an important (implicit) feature of observability: it means that some elements need not satisfy the axioms of S. For instance, in the classical implementation of stacks as pair (integer, array), pairs with a negative integer need not (and indeed do not) satisfy $pop(push(e, s)) = s$.

This family of relations must be: total, surjective, compatible with operators, minimum on subsorts. This last condition has a form similar to an induction rule; it can be used to give an explicit second-order definition of $(C_s)_{s \in S_o}$ on basis of $(C_s)_{s \in S}$. Observational equivalence can then simply be stated as $OBS(S, \Sigma_o)$. Note that when $=: s \times s$ is observable, C_s is thus a bijection. When all predicates (including equalities) are observable ($P = P_o$), C is an isomorphism.

5.3 Behavioural equality

Observability works on models, without considering the syntax of S. Another solution is to redefine equality [20, 14, 17], as indistinguishability in some contexts. Applying our method here just yields the context induction principle [14].

5.4 Ultra-looseness

Ultra-looseness [3] considers that axioms have to hold for reachable elements only. Our method also encodes this easily; it calls for a generalisation of observability and ultra-looseness based on reachable subsorts, that we leave for future work.

6 Conclusion

For most languages and constraints studied here, no effective proof system can exist [16]. We have argued that a second-order proof system is its best approximation, since it allows an exact and finite translation of specifications written in most known specification languages. Specially, it allows one to prove the equivalence of two specifications, even written in different specification languages, a feature which is out of reach of infinite proof systems. The translations proposed here have been obtained in a systematic way from the model-theoretic definition, and then simplified when possible. This work opens some questions in logic, like the description of the fragment of second-order logic used, and of its properties (a downward Löwenheim-Skolem property is expected, for instance.)

A Definitions

A.1 ASL

Syntax We consider here only the finite fragment of the ASL language. [25].

$\mathcal{S} ::= \mathcal{P}$
$\quad | \; \mathcal{S}_1 + \mathcal{S}_2$
$\quad | \; \textbf{reachable } \mathcal{S}_1 \textbf{ on } T \textbf{ with } F$
$\quad | \; \textbf{observe } \mathcal{S}_1 \textbf{ wrt } \Sigma_o$
$\quad | \; \textbf{derive from } \mathcal{S}_1 \textbf{ by } \sigma$

- all signatures are assumed to be finite,
- $\mathcal{S}, \mathcal{S}_2, \mathcal{S}_2$ are specifications,
- $\mathcal{P}$ is a finite presentation,
- T is a subset of S_1, the sorts of $\mathcal{S}_1$,
- F is a subset of O_1 the operators of $\mathcal{S}_1$,
- Σ_o is a triple (S_o, O_o, P_o) such that $\Sigma_1 \cup \Sigma_o$ is a signature.
- $\sigma : \Sigma \rightarrow \Sigma_1$ is a signature morphism.

Semantics A Σ-algebra A satisfies a sum iff $\Sigma = \Sigma_1 \cup \Sigma_2$, $A|_{\Sigma_1} \models \mathcal{S}_1$, and $A|_{\Sigma_2} \models \mathcal{S}_2$.

An algebra A is said to be *reachable on T with F*, where T is a subset of the declared sorts and F a subset of the declared operators, iff, for every sort $s \in T$, any element a of the carrier A_s is a possible value of a term of $T_F(X)$, where X_s is empty if $s \in T$, and infinite otherwise. (Such terms are called *generating terms*). A *possible value* of a term is a a such that there is a valuation V to A such that $V_A(t) = a$.

Given a set of formulae $\Phi = \{p(\mathrm{t}) | p : \mathrm{s} \in P_o, \mathrm{t} : \mathrm{s}\}$, $A \equiv_\Phi A'$ is defined as: there are a set of variable X and two surjective valuations $V : X \rightarrow A$, $V' : X \rightarrow A'$ such that $A \models_{V_A} \phi \Leftrightarrow A' \models_{V'_{A'}} \phi$, for all $\phi \in \Phi$. A is a model of **observe** $\mathcal{S}$ **wrt** Φ if it is equivalent to some model A' of $\mathcal{S}$.

Given a signature morphism σ, A is a model of **derive from** $\mathcal{S}$ **by** σ iff $\sigma(A)$ is isomorphic to A' and $A' \models_{ASL} \mathcal{S}$.

(We have suppressed many useless isorphisms[15] from [25])

The results of this paper gives an equivalent semantics by a translation in second-order logic:

$$\begin{aligned}
R(\mathcal{P}) &= OPS(O) \wedge R(\phi)\\
R(\mathcal{S}+\mathcal{T}) &= R(\mathcal{S}) \wedge R(\mathcal{T})\\
R(\textbf{reachable } \mathcal{S} \textbf{ on } T \textbf{ with } F) &= R(\mathcal{S}) \wedge RCH(T, F)\\
R(\textbf{observe } \mathcal{S} \textbf{ wrt } \Sigma_o) &= OBS(\mathcal{S}, \Sigma_o)\\
R(\textbf{derive from } \mathcal{S} \textbf{ by } \sigma) &= \exists \Sigma . R(\mathcal{S}) \wedge ISO(\sigma(\Sigma'), \Sigma)
\end{aligned}$$

A.2 Larch

The syntax of SCL, the kernel sublanguage of Larch is given by:

$\mathcal{S}$ ::= **introduces** Σ **asserts** $\{gen|part|eq\}^*$

gen ::= s **generated by** F

$part$ ::= s **partitioned by** F

eq ::= $t_1 == t_2$

According to [12], the semantics of a Larch specification is an infinite first-order theory. Specially, the semantics of s **generated by** F is to add all instances of:

$$\forall z : \mathrm{r}. \forall y : s.P \;\Leftrightarrow\; \bigwedge_{f:\mathrm{s} \to r \in F} \forall \mathrm{x} : \mathrm{s}.(\bigwedge_i P[x_i/y]) \Rightarrow P[f(\mathrm{x})/y]$$

where P is replaced by a first-order formula built over a "universal" signature, and P contains at most y, z as free variables. Consequently, the language has no natural model-theoretic interpretation: the rule above does not characterize exactly generated models, it also admits non-standard models. Furthermore, P has to range also over not yet defined formulae, hence the trick of using a "universal" alphabet.

Therefore we use in this paper the second-order version of the rules given in [12], which has a model-theoretic interpretation and is finite. The semantics R of a Larch specification is then:

$$\begin{aligned}
R(\textbf{introduces } \Sigma \textbf{ asserts } A) &= OPS(\Sigma) \wedge \textstyle\bigwedge_{g \in A} R(g)\\
R(s \textbf{ generated by } F) &= GENL(s, F)\\
R(s \textbf{ partitioned by } F) &= PART(s, F)\\
R(t_1 == t_2) &= \forall \mathrm{x}, t_1 = t_2
\end{aligned}$$

where $\mathrm{x} = vars(t_1) \cup vars(t_2)$.

A.3 Second-order axioms

In all axioms, we assume $\Sigma = (S, O, P)$.

$OPS(O)$ $\quad \bigwedge_{f:\mathrm{s} \to s \in O} \forall \mathrm{x}.\mathrm{s}(\mathrm{x}) \Rightarrow s(f(\mathrm{x}))$

$TG(\Sigma)$ $\quad RCH(S, O)$

$GENL(s, F)$	$RCH(\{s\}, F)$
$RCH(T, F)$	$\forall (I_s)_{s \in T}.[\bigwedge_{f:s \to r \in F} \forall x, s(x) \wedge I_s(x) \Rightarrow I_r(f(x))] \Rightarrow [\bigwedge_{s \in T} \forall x.s(x) \Rightarrow I_s(x)]$
$FG((T, F), S')$	$\forall (I_s)_{s \in S}.[\bigwedge_{f:s \to r \in F} \forall x, s(x) \wedge I_s(x) \Rightarrow I_r(f(x)) \wedge \bigwedge_{s \in S} \forall x.s'(x) \Rightarrow I_s(x)] \Rightarrow [\bigwedge_{s \in T} \forall x.s(x) \Rightarrow I_s(x)]$
$HOM(h, \Sigma, \Sigma')$	$HS((h, S, S') \wedge HF(h, \Sigma, \Sigma') \wedge HP(h, \Sigma, \Sigma')$
$HS((h, S, S')$	$\bigwedge_{s \in S} \forall x.s(x) \Rightarrow s'(h_s(x))$
$HF(h, \Sigma, \Sigma')$	$\bigwedge_{f:r \to s \in F} \forall x.(\bigwedge_i s_i(x_i)) \Rightarrow h_r(f(x)) = f'(h_s(x))$
$HP(h, \Sigma, \Sigma')$	$\bigwedge_{p:s \in P} \forall x.(\bigwedge_i s_i(x_i)) \wedge p(x) \Rightarrow p'(h_s(x))$
$ISO(\Sigma, \Sigma')$	$\exists h, g.HOM(h, \Sigma, \Sigma') \wedge HOM(g, \Sigma', \Sigma) \wedge \bigwedge_{s \in S} \forall x.s(x) \Rightarrow g_s(h_s(x)) = x \wedge \forall x.s'(x) \Rightarrow h_s(g_s(x)) = x$
DEN	$\exists 0, <, s.\forall x, y, z : 0 < s(x) \wedge x < s(x) \wedge \neg(x < y \wedge y < x) \wedge (x < y \wedge y < z \Rightarrow x < z)$
$FREE(\mathcal{S}_2, \mathcal{S}_1)$	$DEN \wedge \forall \Sigma'_2.R(\mathcal{S}_2)[\Sigma'_2/\Sigma_2] \Rightarrow \forall (h_s)_{s \in S_1}.HOM((h_s)_{s \in S_1}, \Sigma_1, \Sigma'_1) \Rightarrow \exists! (h_s)_{s \in S_2 \setminus S_1}.HOM((h_s)_{s \in S_2}, \Sigma_2, \Sigma'_2)$
$EQ(\Sigma)$	$RE(S) \wedge SY(S) \wedge TR(S) \wedge CF(\Sigma) \wedge CP(\Sigma)$
$RE(S)$	$\bigwedge_{s \in S} \forall x.s(x) \Rightarrow x \equiv_s x$
$SY(S)$	$\bigwedge_{s \in S} \forall x, y.s(x) \wedge s(y) \Rightarrow (x \equiv_s y \Rightarrow y \equiv_s x)$
$TR(S)$	$bwe_{s \in S} \forall x, y, z.s(x) \wedge s(y) \wedge s(z) \Rightarrow (x \equiv_s y \wedge y \equiv_s z \Rightarrow x \equiv_s z)$
$CF(\Sigma)$	$\bigwedge_{f:s \to r \in O} \forall x, x'.s(x) \wedge s(x') \wedge x \equiv x' \Rightarrow f(x) \equiv_r f(x')$
$CP(\Sigma)$	$\bigwedge_{p:s \in P} \forall x, x'_i.s(x) \wedge s_i(x'_i) \wedge x_i \equiv_{s_i} x'_i \Rightarrow [p(x) \Leftrightarrow p(x')]$
$RF(\Sigma'_1, \Sigma)$	$\bigwedge_{f':s' \to r' \in O'_1} \forall a, b.s'(a) \wedge f'(a) = b \Rightarrow f(a) \equiv_s b$
$RP(\Sigma'_1, \Sigma)$	$\bigwedge_{p':s' \in P'_1} \forall a, b.s'(a) \wedge p'(a) \Rightarrow p(a)$
$LC(\Sigma_2)$	$\forall \Delta'.EQ(\Sigma_2)[\equiv' / \equiv] \wedge R(\mathcal{S}_2)[\equiv / =][\Delta'/\Delta] \Rightarrow \Delta' \leq \Delta$
Δ	$(\equiv_s)_{s \in S_2}, (p)_{p:s \in P_2}$
$\Delta \leq \Delta'$	$[\bigwedge_{s \in S_2} \forall x, y.s(x) \wedge s(y) \wedge x \equiv_s y \Rightarrow x \equiv'_s y] \wedge [\bigwedge_{p:s \in P_2} \forall x, s(x) \wedge p(x) \Rightarrow p'(x)]$
$TERM(\Sigma, S'_1)$	$OPS(O) \wedge INC(S, S'_1) \wedge INJ(O) \wedge NOV(O, S'_1) \wedge FG(\Sigma, S')$
$INC(S, S'_1)$	$\bigwedge_{s \in S} \forall x.s'(x) \Rightarrow s(x)$
$DIS(O)$	$\bigwedge_{f \neq g:s \to r \in O} \forall x, y.s(x) \wedge s'(y) \Rightarrow \neg(f(x) = g(y))$
$INJ(O)$	$\bigwedge_{f \in O} \forall x, y.s(x) \wedge s(y) \wedge f(x) = f(y) \Rightarrow \bigwedge_{i \leq n} x_i = y_i$
$NOV(O, S'_1)$	$\bigwedge_{f:s \to r \in O} \forall x, s(x) \Rightarrow \neg r'(f(x))$
$LCS(\mathcal{S}_1, \mathcal{S}_2)$	$TERM(\Sigma_2, S'_1) \wedge RF(\Sigma'_1, \Sigma) \wedge RP(\Sigma'_1, \Sigma) \wedge EQ(\Sigma_2) \wedge R(\mathcal{S}_2)[\equiv / =] \wedge LC(\Sigma_2)$
$PER(\Sigma_2, \Sigma_1)$	$\exists (i_s)_{s \in S_1}.HOM(i, \Sigma_1, \Sigma'_1) \wedge \bigwedge_{s \in S_1} [\forall x, y.s(x) \wedge s(y) \Rightarrow [i_s(x) = i_s(y) \Leftrightarrow x \equiv_s y] \wedge \forall y.s(y) \Rightarrow \exists x.s(x) \wedge i_s(x) = y]$
$PART(s, F)$	$\forall x, y.s(x) \wedge s(y) \Rightarrow [x = y \Leftrightarrow \bigwedge_{f:s \to r \in O} \forall x.s(x) \Rightarrow \bigwedge_{s_i = s} f(x_1, \ldots, x, \ldots, x_n) = f(x_1, \ldots, y, \ldots, x_n)]$
$COR(C, \Sigma_o, \Sigma'_o)$	$CTR(C, S, S') \wedge CSR(C, S, S') \wedge CPR(C, O_o \cup O') \wedge CMS(C, \Sigma_o, \Sigma'_o)$
$CTR(C, S, S')$	$\bigwedge_{s \in S} \forall a.s(a) \Rightarrow \exists a'.s'(a') \wedge C_s(a, a')$

$CSR(C,S,S')$ $\bigwedge_{s\in S} \forall a'.s'(a') \Rightarrow \exists a.s(a) \wedge C_s(a,a')$
$CPR(C,O_o \cup O') \bigwedge_{f:s\to r\in O_o\cup O} \forall \mathbf{a},\mathbf{a}'.\bigwedge_i C_{s_i}(a_i,a_i') \wedge s_i(a_i) \wedge s_i'(a_i) \Rightarrow C_r(f(\mathbf{a}),f'(\mathbf{a}'))$
$CMS(C,\Sigma_o,\Sigma_o')\forall(R_s')_{s\in S_o}.CPR(R',O_o \cup O) \wedge \bigwedge_{s\in S} R_s' = C_s \Rightarrow \bigwedge_{s\in S_o} \forall a,a',C_s(a,a') \Rightarrow R_s'(a,a')$

B Theorems

Definition 1. Given $\mathcal{I}$, a second-order model of $OPS(\Sigma)$, its a *inverse relativization* $A = Ms(\mathcal{I})$, is defined by:

- $s_A = s_{\mathcal{I}}$;
- the multi-sorted functions and predicates are a restriction of their counterparts: $f_A = f_{\mathcal{I}}|s_{1\mathcal{I}} \times \ldots \times s_{n\mathcal{I}}$;
- predicates also: $p_A(x) = p_{\mathcal{I}}(x) \wedge s_{1\mathcal{I}}(x) \wedge \ldots \wedge s_{n\mathcal{I}}(x)$.

$\mathcal{I}$ is then a *relativization* of A.

Lemma 2. *[9] For any multi-sorted sentences* ψ,ϕ: $\phi \models_{MS} \psi$ *iff* $OPS(\Sigma) \cup R(\phi) \models_2 R(\psi)$.

Definition 3. Let $\mathcal{S}$ be a specification (denoting a class of algebras), $R(\mathcal{S})$, a second-order sentence, is a *relativization* of $\mathcal{S}$ iff whenever $A = Ms(\mathcal{I})$, $A \models \mathcal{S}$ iff $\mathcal{I} \models_2 R(\mathcal{S})$, and $R(\mathcal{S}) \models_2 OPS(\Sigma)$. (Annexes A.1-A.2 provides a definition of R that will be shown to have this property)

Theorem 4. *Whenever* $A = Ms(\mathcal{I})$, *A is reachable on T with F and S′ iff* $\mathcal{I} \models_2 R(\mathcal{S}) \wedge FG((T,F),S')$.

Corollary 5. reachable $\mathcal{S}$ on T with $F \models_{ASL} \phi$ *iff* $R(\mathcal{S}) \wedge RCH(T,F) \models_2 R(\phi)$.

Corollary 6. $\mathcal{S} \models_{CIP} \psi$ *iff* $R(\mathcal{S}) \wedge TG(\Sigma) \models_2 R(\psi)$.

Corollary 7. $A \models_{Larch} \mathcal{S}$, s generated by F *iff A is reachable on s by F*.

Lemma 8. *When* $A = Ms(\mathcal{I})$, $\mathcal{I} \models_2 TERM(\Sigma,X)$ *iff A is isomorphic to the algebra* $T_\Sigma(\biguplus_{x\in X} x_{\mathcal{I}})$.

Lemma 9. *A model I is free with respect to* S_2 *on* Σ_1 *iff it is free among the models of cardinality* $max(\omega, card(I|_{\Sigma_1}))$, *where* $card(A) = max_{s\in S}(card(s_A))$.

Lemma 10. *If* $\mathcal{I}$ *is a denumerable relativization of A, then* $A \models \mathcal{S}$ free wrt $\mathcal{S}_2$ on S_1 *iff* $\mathcal{I} \models_2 FREE(\mathcal{S}_2,\Sigma_1)$.

Corollary 11. $\mathcal{S}$ free wrt $\mathcal{S}_2$ on $S_1 \models \psi$ *iff* $FREE(\mathcal{S}_2,\Sigma_1) \models R(\psi)$.

Lemma 12. *If* $S_2 = (\Sigma_2, \phi_2)$, *where* ϕ_2 *is a universal sentence, and* $\mathcal{I}$ *is a relativization of* A, *then* $A \models S$ **free wrt** S_2 **on** S_1 *iff* $\mathcal{I} \models_2 R(S) \wedge LCS(S_2, S_1)$

Corollary 13. *If* ϕ_2 *is a universal sentence,* S *free wrt* S_2 *on* $S_1 \models \psi$ *iff* $R(S) \wedge LCS(S_2, S_1) \models_2 R(\psi)[\equiv / =]$.

Lemma 14. $A \models$ **observe** S **wrt** Σ_o *iff there is a family of binary relations (called a correspondence) between the carriers of A and the carriers of some model of* S, *that is total, surjective, compatible with operators, minimum on subsorts.*

Lemma 15. *the models of an ASL specification are closed under isomorphism.*

Lemma 16. *(Downward Löwenheim-Skolem) If* $A \models_{ASL} S$, *then there is a submodel Sk of A of cardinality at most* ω.

Lemma 17. *If* $A \models_{ASL}$ **observe** S_1 **wrt** Σ_o, *then it is equivalent to a model* A' *of* S_1 *of cardinality less than* $max(\omega, card(A))$.

Theorem 18. *When* $R(A, \mathcal{I}), \mathcal{I} \models_2 DEN$, $A \models_{ASL}$ **observe** S **wrt** Σ_o *iff* $\mathcal{I} \models_2 OBS(S, \Sigma_o)$.

References

1. M. Bidoit and G. Bernot. Proving correctness of algebraically specified software: Modularity and observability issues. In M. Nivat, C. Rattray, T. Rus, and G. Scollo, editors, *AMAST'91*, pages 139–161. Springer-Verlag, 1992.
2. M. Broy and al. The requirement and design specification language spectrum: an introduction. Technical Report TUM-I9140, Technische Universität München, 1991.
3. M. Broy and M. Wirsing. Ultra-Loose Algebraic Specification. Report MIP-8814, Universitat Passau, Fakultat Fur Mathematik Und Informatik, Aug 1988.
4. R. Burstall and J. Goguen. Semantics of CLEAR, a Specification Language. In D. Bjorner, editor, *Abstract software specifications, Proc. 1979 Copenhagen Winter School*, volume 86, pages 292–332. Springer, 1980.
5. CIP Language Group. *The Munich Project CIP – Vol. I: The Language*, volume 183 of *Lecture Notes in Computer Science*. Springer, 1985.
6. N. Denyer. Pure second-order logic. *Notre-Dame Journal of Formal Logic*, 33(2):220, 1992.
7. H. Ehrig and B. Mahr. *Fundamentals of algebraic specification : Volume 1. Equations and initial semantics*. Springer Verlag, 1985.
8. H. Ehrig and B. Mahr. *Fundamentals of Algebraic Specification 2: Module Specifications and Constraints*, volume 21 of *EATCS Monographs on Theoretical Computer Science*. Springer-Verlag, 1990.
9. H. B. Enderton. *A Mathematical Introduction To Logic*. 1972.
10. J. Goguen and R. Burstall. Institutions: Abstract model theory for specification and programming. *J. ACM*, 39(1):95–146, Jan. 1992.
11. P. de Groote. How I spent my nights in Cambridge with Isabelle. Report RR-87-1, Univ. Cath. de Louvain, Jan. 1989.

12. J. Guttag, J. Horning. Report on the Larch shared language. Technical Report 58, Digital SRC, 1990.
13. J. Guttag, J. Horning. *Larch: Languages and Tools for Formal Specification.* Springer-Verlag, 1993.
14. R. Hennicker. Context induction: a proof principle for behavioural abstractions and algebraic implementations. *Formal Aspects of Computing*, 3:326–345, 1991.
15. S. Kaplan. Positive/negative conditional rewriting. In *Conditional Term Rewriting*, volume 308 of *Lecture Notes in Computer Science.* Springer, 1988.
16. D. MacQueen and D. Sannella. Completeness of proof systems for equational specifications. *IEEE TSE*, SE-11(5), May 1985.
17. P. Nivela and F. Orejas. Initial behaviour semantics for algebraic specifications. In *Recent Trends in Data Type Specification*, number 332 in Lecture Notes in Computer Science, pages 184–207. Springer-Verlag, 1987.
18. F. Nourani. On induction for programming logics: syntax, semantics, and inductive closure. *EATCS Bulletin*, 13:51–64, 1981.
19. P. Rathmann and M. Winslett. Circumscribing equality. In *Proc. of the 8th Nat. Conf. on Art. Int. (AAAI-89)*, pages 468–473, 1989.
20. H. Reichel. Behavioural validity of conditional equations in abstract data types. In *Contrib. to General Algebra 3*, 1984.
21. D. Sannella and A. Tarlecki. On observational equivalence and algebraic specification. *JCSS*, 34(2/3), 1987.
22. P.-Y. Schobbens. Exceptions for software specification: on the meaning of "but". Report RR-89-8, Univ. Cath. de Louvain, Feb. 1989.
23. P.-Y. Schobbens. Surjective circumscription. Technical report, CRIN, Nancy, 1992; also Proc. Workshop on Non-Monotonic Reasoning, Aachen, Dec. 1993.
24. N. W. P. van Diepen. Implementation of modular algebraic specifications. In *ESOP'88*, number 300 in Lecture Notes in Computer Science. Springer-Verlag, 1987.
25. M. Wirsing. Structured algebraic specifications: A kernel language. *Theoretical Computer Science*, 42:123–249, 1986.

An Institution of Object Behaviour

Amílcar Sernadas[1,3], José Félix Costa[2,3] and Cristina Sernadas[1,3]

[1] Departamento de Matemática, IST
[2] Departamento de Informática, FCUL
[3] INESC, Apartado 10105, 1017 Lisboa Codex, PORTUGAL
E-mail: acs@inesc.pt

Abstract. An institution for a simple logic of behaviour is built using a cofibration from a category of transition systems into the envisaged category of signatures. The chosen propositional, linear temporal logic distinguishes between event occurrence and event enabling. The satisfaction condition is proved using a fibered adjunction between transition systems and their computations. The operational semantics of behaviour specifications is briefly discussed.

1 Introduction

Consolidating the conjectures in [SernadasA *et al* 92a], we study the problem of setting-up a suitable institution (see [Goguen and Burstall 84]) of linear temporal logic from a given reasonable semantic domain of object behaviour. For the sake of simplicity we work towards a propositional fragment. No major problem is expected when extending the results towards a first-order logic (for instance, like the logic outlined in [SernadasA *et al* 92b]).

The basic problem is to identify the appropriate cofibration from the given category of behaviours into the category of signatures. It should constitute an indexing mechanism (see [Tarlecki *et al* 91]) from which the semantic components of the envisaged institution should follow without much further ado (like a Grothendieck "deconstruction"). Namely, the semantic functor of the institution is defined using the functor induced by the cofibration at hand.

Many behaviour models have been proposed in the past and several of them have been adopted when studying the semantics of objects. Herein, we consider a notion of behaviour built around the notion of transition system, adapting from [Manna and Pnueli 92], instead of the naive notion of process as a set of life-cycles considered for instance in [SernadasA *et al* 92a]. Some care is needed when establishing the category of transition systems in order to ensure an adequate treatment of aggregation and hiding. Our categorial treatment of transition systems is an extension of the work in [Winskel 84].

Once the semantic domain is fixed with a suitable indexing mechanism, the development of the envisaged institution goes like this: (i) the syntax functor is defined towards the chosen language (in this case, propositional, linear temporal logic distinguishing between enabling and occurrence of events); (ii) the semantic functor is canonically established using the properties of the indexing mechanism as a cofibration; (iii) the satisfaction relation is defined using the standard Kripke technique on the set of computations of each transition system; (iv) the satisfaction condition is verified exploiting a fibered adjunction between transition systems and their computations. The use of fibered adjunctions was already advocated in [Winskel 85, 87] for relating different semantic domains.

This direct approach should be compared with the proposal in [Fiadeiro *et al* 93] where the bridge between behaviours (processes as sets of life-cycles) and theories goes through the standard interpretation structures for the chosen logic (a similar one but without distinguishing between occurrence and enabling of events).

Herein, beside working with a more general semantic domain (transition systems) and a more powerful logic, we identify a general approach to the problem: set-up a cofibration from the semantic domain into the category of signatures and establish a fibered adjunction between the elements of the semantic domain and their computations.

We assume that the reader is conversant with the field of temporal logic specification (for instance at the level of [Goldblatt 87]). We also use a little bit of category theory (the reader may find all relevant concepts in the introductory chapters of any textbook on the matter, eg [Adámek *et al* 90]). We borrow from [Winskel 87] the result on the preservation of cocartesian morphisms by left adjoints.

The underlying approach to system specification (following [SernadasA *et al* 92b]) is briefly described in Section 2. Section 3 is dedicated to the underlying semantic domain: transition systems and their computations. The envisaged institution is presented in Section 4. The concluding remarks in Section 5 include a brief discussion of the "operational" semantics of temporal specifications.

2 System specification

At first sight (see [SernadasA et al 89a,89b, SernadasA and Ehrich 91]), a system (or object) is an entity with an internal state (reflected in the values of its slots or attributes) that may interact with other systems. While so interacting a system displays some behaviour. That is, depending on its internal state, it is not always ready to provide the same services to the others and/or to ask the same services of others. The most basic unit of interaction is the event: for instance, the action event open-door may be shared by a person and a car. Therefore, the behaviour of a system may be seen as corresponding to a state-dependent menu of enabled events (at each state the set of events in which the object is "willing" to involve itself).

At this naive level of analysis, the specification of a system should include the list of its attributes (with the indication of their codomain sorts), the list of its events (with the indication of their parameter sorts if any) and the constraints on its behaviour (including the observation events that allow the examination of values of the attributes). Furthermore, the "life" of a system should correspond to a trajectory of transitions that happened since its birth to its death. Therefore, if we ignore the birth and the death issues, a computation of the system can be presented as a map from $\mathbb{Z}$ (the set of integers) into the set of its transitions.

As an illustration consider a simple *flip-flop* as a system. The *flip-flop* has a unique attribute status with two possible values: on and off. It allows only two actions: *flip* and *flop*. Therefore, it allows four events: two observation events (*status=on* and *status=off*) plus two action events (*flip* and *flop*). Observation events do not change the state of the *flip-flop*. Actions do change it. Both kinds of events may be constrained by enabling conditions. The intended behaviour of the flip-flop is easily described using a simple propositional temporal logic, as follows:

(1) $(\diamond \text{flip} \Leftrightarrow \diamond \text{status=on})$
(2) $(\diamond \text{flop} \Leftrightarrow \diamond \text{status=off})$
(3) $(\nabla \text{flip} \Rightarrow (\mathbf{X} \diamond \text{status=off}))$
(4) $(\nabla \text{flop} \Rightarrow (\mathbf{X} \diamond \text{status=on}))$
(5) $(\diamond \text{status=off} \mid \diamond \text{status=on})$
(6) $((\nabla \text{status=on} \wedge (\neg \nabla \text{flip})) \Rightarrow (\mathbf{X} \diamond \text{status=on}))$
(7) $((\nabla \text{status=off} \wedge (\neg \nabla \text{flop})) \Rightarrow (\mathbf{X} \diamond \text{status=off}))$

The propositional symbols are of the form $\diamond g$ or ∇g where g is an event (action or observation). A propositional symbol of the form $\diamond g$ (read: g is possible) indicates that the event g is enabled. A propositional symbol of the form ∇g (read: g happens) indicates the occurrence of event g.

For the the purpose of this paper, there is no need to distinguish between the two kinds of events (actions and observations). Therefore, in the sequel, we consider a single alphabet of events G generating the following alphabet of propositional symbols $\{\diamond g : g \in G\} \cup \{\nabla g : g \in G\}$. But first-order versions of this behaviour language will require that distinction, namely for imposing the functionality of attributes (see [SernadasA *et al* 92b]).

Returning to the behaviour specification above, axiom (1) states that *flip* may happen only in states where the observation ***status=on*** may also happen: that is, *flip* may happen only in states where the attribute status has value on. Axiom (2) is similar for *flop*. Axiom (3) states that if *flip* happens then in the next state the observation ***status=off*** is possible: that is, if *flip* happens then in the next state status has value off. Axiom (4) is similar for *flop*. Axiom (5) states that status is either off or on (exclusive or): deterministic functionality of the attribute status. Axioms (6) and (7) reflect the fact that the observations of status do not affect the state of the *flip-flop*.

Such a logic of behaviour with happening (∇) and enabled ($\diamond$) symbols is rich enough for describing in practice useful interacting systems. For further examples see [SernadasA *et al* 92b] where a proof system is provided for dealing with object specialization and aggregation.

Note that fairness assumptions are easily specified in this logic. For instance, if so specified, $((\mathbf{F}(\mathbf{G}\diamond g))\Rightarrow(\mathbf{G}(\mathbf{F}\nabla g)))$ states that if g is continually enabled from a certain position on then it happens infinitely many times (F stands for "sometime" and G for "always"). Clearly, we expect the formula $(\nabla g\Rightarrow\diamond g)$ to be universally true, since an event g may happen only when enabled. As we shall see, the proposed semantics does ensure the universal validity of this assertion.

3 A semantic domain

3.1 Transition systems

Definition 3.1.1. A *transition system* trs=$\langle G,S,\delta\rangle$ is a triple consisting of a set G, a set S, and a family $\delta=\{\delta_e\}_{e\in E}$, where $E=2^G$, of total maps $\delta_e:S\rightarrow 2^S$ such that $s\in\delta_\varnothing(s)$ for each $s\in S$. □

The elements of G are called *prime events*, those of E *events* and those of S *states*. Also, sets E and S are said to be the *event space* and the *state space*, respectively, of the transition system. Each function $\delta_e:S\rightarrow 2^S$ is called the *transition map for e*: it returns the set of states reachable from a given state by the occurrence of event *e*.

Comparing with [Manna and Pnueli 92], this definition of transition system is different in two accounts: (i) it allows for the occurrence of "simultaneous" prime events; and (ii) it does not impose that $\delta_\varnothing(s)=\{s\}$. The former is essential to modelling "aggregation" (parallel composition) where several prime events may occur simultaneously. And the latter is needed for coping with "abstraction" (hiding of prime events).

Definition 3.1.2. A *transition system morphism* $h:\langle G,S,\delta\rangle\rightarrow\langle G',S',\delta'\rangle$ is a pair $\langle h_G,h_S\rangle$ where $h_G:G'\to G$ and $h_S:S\to S'$ are total maps such that, for each $e\in E$, $h_S(\delta_e(s))\subseteq \delta'_{h_G^{-1}(e)}(h_S(s))$. □

The contravariance of the first component is to be expected if we anticipate that the prime events constitute the signature of a transition system: signature morphisms and semantic morphisms go in opposite directions. Furthermore, the morphism condition just states that to each "transition" $s \text{—}e\to r$ of $\langle G,S,\delta\rangle$ corresponds a transition of $\langle G',S',\delta'\rangle$.

Fact/Definition 3.1.3. Transition systems and their morphisms constitute a concrete category TrS over $Set^{op}\times Set$ with respect to the functor $GS:TrS\to Set^{op}\times Set$ mapping each $trs=\langle G,S,\delta\rangle$ onto the pair (G,S), and each $h:\langle G,S,\delta\rangle\to\langle G',S',\delta'\rangle$ onto the pair $(h_G{}^{op}:G\to G',h_S:S\to S')$. □

Fact 3.1.4. The category TrS is small complete and cocomplete. □

Since this result is not essential to the development of this paper we omit its proof herein. The product of transition systems $trs'=\langle G',S',\delta'\rangle$ and $trs''=\langle G'',S'',\delta''\rangle$ reflects their parallel composition and it is, up to isomorphism, given by a 2-source with vertex $trs'||trs''=\langle G'+G'',S'\times S'',\delta\rangle$ where, for $e\in 2^{G'+G''}$, $\delta_e(s)=\delta'_{i'^{-1}(e)}(\pi'(s))\times\delta''_{i''^{-1}(e)}(\pi''(s))$. The terminal transition system is the triple $\langle\varnothing,\{\bullet\},\delta\rangle$ where $\delta_\varnothing(\bullet)=\{\bullet\}$. Coproducts are only interesting for a given G and a given S: they reflect (external and internal) choice and are given by $trs'+trs''=\langle G,S,\delta'\cup\delta''\rangle$. And the initial transition system is the triple $\langle\varnothing,\varnothing,\delta_\varnothing\rangle$ where $\delta_\varnothing$ is the empty map.

Definition 3.1.5. The *indexing functor* $Gen:TrS\to Set^{op}$ is $\pi_1\circ GS$. □

Therefore, the functor Gen maps each $trs=\langle G,S,\delta\rangle$ onto G, and each $h:\langle G,S,\delta\rangle\to\langle G',S',\delta'\rangle$ onto $h_G{}^{op}:G\to G'$.

Fact 3.1.6. The indexing functor $Gen:TrS\to Set^{op}$ is a cofibration. Namely, given $h:G\to G'$ of Set^{op} and a transition system $trs=\langle G,S,\delta\rangle$, the cocartesian morphism for h and trs is $\underline{h}_{trs}:trs\to trs'$ defined as follows: (i) $trs'=\langle G',S,\delta'\rangle$ with $\delta'_{e'}=\bigcup_{x:(h^{op})^{-1}(x)=e'}\delta_x$ for each event $e'\in E'$; and (ii) $\underline{h}_{trs}=\langle(\underline{h}_{trs})_G,(\underline{h}_{trs})_S\rangle$ with $(\underline{h}_{trs})_G:G'\to G$ given by $(\underline{h}_{trs})_G=h^{op}$ and $(\underline{h}_{trs})_S:S\to S$ given by $(\underline{h}_{trs})_S=id_S$.

Proof: We verify first that $\underline{h}_{trs}$ is a morphism in TrS: indeed, $\delta_e(s)\subseteq \delta'_{(h^{op})^{-1}(e)}(s)$ because the latter is $\bigcup_{x:(h^{op})^{-1}(x)=(h^{op})^{-1}(e)}\delta_x(s)$ that contains $\delta_e(s)$. Moreover, $\underline{h}_{trs}$ is cocartesian: given a transition system $trs''=\langle G'',S'',\delta''\rangle$, $f:\langle G,S,\delta\rangle\to\langle G'',S'',\delta''\rangle$ of TrS and $k:G'\to G''$ of Set^{op} such that $f_G=h^{op}\circ k^{op}$, there is a unique $\underline{k}:\langle G',S',\delta'\rangle\to\langle G'',S',\delta''\rangle$ such that $f=\underline{k}\circ\underline{h}_{trs}$ with $\underline{k}_G=k^{op}$. Indeed, for the composition to hold $\underline{k}_S$ must be f_S. Finally, we have to verify that $\underline{k}=\langle k^{op},f_S\rangle$ is a morphism of TrS: $f_S(\delta'_{e'}(s'))=f_S(\bigcup_{x:(h^{op})^{-1}(x)=e'}\delta_x(s'))=\bigcup_{x:(h^{op})^{-1}(x)=e'}f_S(\delta_x(s'))$; so, $f_S(\delta'_{e'}(s'))\subseteq\bigcup_{x:(h^{op})^{-1}(x)=e'}\delta''_{f_G^{-1}(x)}(f_S(s'))$; finally, since $f_G{}^{-1}(x)=(k^{op})^{-1}((h^{op})^{-1}(x))$, the latter colapses onto $\delta''_{(k^{op})^{-1}(e')}(f_S(s'))$. □

Definition 3.1.7. Let trs=<G,S,δ> be a transition system. The *menu map* $M_{trs}:S\to 2^E$ induced by trs is defined by $M_{trs}(s)=\{e\in E:\delta_e(s)\neq\emptyset\}$. □

Fact 3.1.8. Let h:trs→trs' be a transition system morphism. Then, the following condition holds: $h_G^{-1}(M_{trs}(s))\subseteq M_{trs'}(h_S(s))$.

Proof: Let $e'\in h_G^{-1}(M_{trs}(s))$. Then: $e'=h_G^{-1}(e)$ for some $e\in M_{trs}(s)$, $\delta_e(s)\neq \emptyset$, $h_S(\delta_e(s))\neq\emptyset$, $\delta'_{h_G^{-1}(e)}(h_S(s))\neq\emptyset$, $h_G^{-1}(e)\in M_{trs'}(h_S(s))$, and, finally, $e'\in M_{trs'}(h_S(s))$. □

3.2 Computations

In order to prepare the ground for establishing the envisaged temporal institution in the next section, it is convenient to study the properties of computations of transition systems.

Definition 3.2.1. A *computation system* cos=<G,S,Ξ> is a triple consisting of a set G, a set S, and a subset Ξ of $\{\xi\in[\mathbf{Z}\to S\otimes E\otimes S]: \forall n\in\mathbf{Z}\ (\xi_{n+1})_1=(\xi_n)_3\}$, where $E=2^G$. □

As in transition systems, the elements of G are called *prime events*, those of E *events* and those of S *states*. Each element ξ of Ξ is called a *computation*: a sequence of triples, each of them a *transition* of the form <s,e,r> with s,r∈S and e∈E.

Definition 3.2.2. A *computation system morphism* h:<G,S,Ξ>→<G',S',Ξ'> is a pair $<h_G,h_S>$ where $h_G:G'\to G$ and $h_S:S\to S'$ are total maps such that $\{h(\xi):\xi\in\Xi\}\subseteq\Xi'$, where $h(\xi)_n=<h_S((\xi_n)_1),h_G^{-1}((\xi_n)_2),h_S((\xi_n)_3)>$ for each $n\in\mathbf{Z}$. □

We denote in the sequel {h(ξ):ξ∈Ξ} by h(Ξ). Thus, the computation system morphism condition is written h(Ξ)⊆Ξ'.

Fact/Definition 3.2.3. Computation systems and their morphisms constitute a concrete category CoS over $Set^{op}\times Set$ with respect to the functor $GS':CoS\to Set^{op}\times Set$ mapping each cos=<G,S,Ξ> onto the pair (G,S), and each h:<G,S,Ξ>→<G',S',Ξ'> onto the pair $(h_G{}^{op}:G\to G', h_S:S\to S')$. □

Definition 3.2.4. The *indexing functor* $Gen':CoS\to Set^{op}$ is $\pi_1\circ GS'$. □

Therefore, the functor Gen' maps each cos=<G,S,Ξ> onto G, and each h:<G,S,Ξ>→<G',S',Ξ'> onto $h_G{}^{op}:G\to G'$.

Fact 3.2.5. The indexing functor $Gen':CoS\to Set^{op}$ is a cofibration. Given h:G→G' of Set^{op} and a computation system cos=<G,S,Ξ>, the cocartesian morphism for h and cos is $\underline{h}_{cos}$:cos→cos' defined as follows:

(i) $cos'=<G',S,\Xi'>$ with $\Xi'=\{\underline{h}_{cos}(\xi): \xi\in\Xi\}$; and (ii) $\underline{h}_{cos}=<(\underline{h}_{cos})_G,(\underline{h}_{cos})_S>$ with $(\underline{h}_{cos})_G:G'\to G$ given by $(\underline{h}_{cos})_G=h^{op}$ and $(\underline{h}_{cos})_S:S\to S'$ given by $(\underline{h}_{cos})_S=id_S$.

Proof: Clearly, $\underline{h}_{cos}$ is a morphism in CoS. Moreover, $\underline{h}_{cos}$ is cocartesian: given a computation system $cos''=<G'',S'',\Xi''>$, $f:<G,S,\Xi>\to<G'',S'',\Xi''>$ of CoS and $k:G'\to G''$ of Set^{op} such that $f_G=h^{op}\circ k^{op}$, there is a unique $\underline{k}:<G',S',\Xi'>\to<G'',S',\Xi''>$ such that $f=\underline{k}\circ\underline{h}_{cos}$ with $\underline{k}_G=k^{op}$. Indeed, for the composition to hold $\underline{k}_S$ must be f_S. Finally, we have to verify that $\underline{k}=<k^{op},f_S>$ is a morphism of CoS: trivial once we recognize that by the definition of $\underline{k}$ we have $f(\xi)=\underline{k}(\underline{h}_{cos}(\xi))$ for every $\xi\in\Xi$. □

The set of computations Ξ_{trs} induced by $trs=<G,S,\delta>$ is $\{\xi\in[\mathbf{Z}\to S\otimes E\otimes S]: \forall n\in\mathbf{Z}\ (\xi_n)_3\in\delta_{(\xi_n)_2}((\xi_n)_1) \text{ and } (\xi_{n+1})_1=(\xi_n)_3\}$. In this way we can establish a functor from TrS into CoS:

Fact/Definition 3.2.6. The functor C:TrS→CoS maps each transition system $trs=<G,S,\delta>$ onto the computation system $<G,S,\Xi_{trs}>$ and each transition system morphism h from $trs=<G,S,\delta>$ into $trs'=<G',S',\delta'>$ onto the computation system morphism $h:<G,S,\Xi_{trs}>\to<G',S',\Xi_{trs'}>$ induced by the same pair $<h_G,h_S>$.

Proof: It is necessary to verify that the transition system morphism condition implies the computation system morphism condition. Indeed, let $\xi\in\Xi_{trs}$. We prove that $h(\xi)\in\Xi_{trs'}$: $\forall n\ (\xi_n)_3\in\delta_{(\xi_n)_2}((\xi_n)_1)$, $\forall n\ h_S((\xi_n)_3)\in h_S(\delta_{(\xi_n)_2}((\xi_n)_1))$, $\forall n\ h_S((\xi_n)_3)\in\delta'_{h_G^{-1}((\xi_n)_2)}(h_S((\xi_n)_1))$, and, so, $h(\xi)\in\Xi_{trs'}$. □

Definition 3.2.7. The category TCoS of *computation systems generated by transition systems* is the full subcategory of CoS whose elements are images of elements of TrS by C. The *unfolding functor* U:TrS→TCoS is defined as C. □

Fact 3.2.8. The functor U has a right adjoint T:TCoS→TrS.

Proof: For each $<G,S,\Xi>$ choose a $<G,S,\delta>$ such that $U(<G,S,\delta>)=<G,S,\Xi>$ and consider the identity $<id_G,id_S>:U(<G,S,\delta>)\to<G,S,\Xi>$. We prove that the pair $<<G,S,\delta>,<id_G,id_S>>$ is co-free over $<G,S,\Xi>$ with respect to U. Given a transition system $trs'=<G',S',\delta'>$ and a computation morphism $f:U(<G',S',\delta'>)\to<G,S,\Xi>$ there is a unique transition system morphism $g:<G',S',\delta'>\to<G,S,\delta>$ such that $<id_G,id_S>\circ U(g)=f$, namely $g=<f_G,f_S>$. Indeed, $f_S(\delta'_{e'}(s'))\subseteq\delta_{f_G^{-1}(e')}(f_S(s'))$ because: if $t'\in\delta_{e'}(s')$ there is $\xi\in\Xi_{trs'}$ such that $\xi_n=<s',\varnothing,s'>$ for $n<0$, $\xi_0=<s',e',t'>$, and $\xi_n=<t',\varnothing,t'>$ for $n>0$; so, $f(\xi)_n=<f_S(s'),\varnothing,f_S(s')>$ for $n<0$, $f(\xi)_0=<f_S(s'),f_G^{-1}(e'),f_S(t')>$, and $f(\xi)_n=<f_S(t'),\varnothing,f_S(t')>$ for $n>0$; thus, finally, since $f(\xi)$ must be a computation of $<G,S,\Xi>=U(<G,S,\delta>)$, $f_S(t')\in\delta_{f_G^{-1}(e')}(f_S(s'))$. □

The functor T:TCoS→TrS maps each computation system $cos=<G,S,\Xi>$ in

TCoS onto the transition system $<G,S,\delta>$ such that $\delta_e(s)=\{(\xi_n)_3: \xi\in\Xi, n\in\mathbf{Z}, (\xi_n)_1=s, (\xi_n)_2=e\}$ and each computation system morphism $h:<G,S,\Xi>\rightarrow<G',S',\Xi'>$ onto the transition system morphism $h:<G,S,\delta>\rightarrow<G',S',\delta'>$ induced by the same pair $<h_G,h_S>$. Let TGen': $TCoS\rightarrow Set^{op}$ be the restriction of Gen' to TCoS. Then, we have:

Fact 3.2.9. $U\vdash T:TCoS\rightarrow TrS$ is a fibered adjunction with respect to <TGen',Gen> over Set^{op}.

Proof: Clearly, $Gen\circ T=TGen'$; $TGen'\circ U=Gen$; $TGen'(<id_G,id_S>: U\circ T(cos)\rightarrow cos)$ is the identity morphism at TGen'(cos); and $Gen(<id_G,id_S>:trs\rightarrow T\circ U(trs))$ is the identity morphism at Gen(trs). □

Fact 3.2.10. U preserves cocartesian morphisms.

Proof: This is just an application of the general result on preservation of (co)cartesian morphisms by fibered adjoints — see [Winskel 87]. □

As we shall see in the next section, this result is useful when proving the satisfaction condition.

4 The institution

4.1 The category of signatures

Definition 4.1.1. The category Sig of *signatures* is the category Set. □

Each element g of a signature G is intended to correspond to a prime event. Although there are no elements in a signature for referring to events in general (composed of several prime events), no limitation arises since appropriate formulae can be used to this end: see below.

Fact 4.1.2. The category Sig is small complete and cocomplete. □

4.2 The syntax functor

Definition 4.2.1. The *propositional, linear temporal language* L_G induced by a signature G is the least set satisfying the following requirements:

- $\nabla g, \Diamond g\in L_G$, provided that $g\in G$;
- $(\neg\gamma),(X\gamma),(G\gamma)\in L_G$, provided that $\gamma\in L_G$;
- $(\gamma_1\Rightarrow\gamma_2),(\gamma_1 U\gamma_2)\in L_G$, provided that both $\gamma_1,\gamma_2\in L_G$. □

Therefore, the language only provides the means for referring directly to the enabling or occurrence of prime events. Events in general may be referred to by use of logical connectives. As usual, we extend L_G with the following abbreviations:

- $(\gamma_1\vee\gamma_2) = ((\neg\gamma_1)\Rightarrow\gamma_2)$
- $(\gamma_1\wedge\gamma_2) = (\neg((\neg\gamma_1)\vee(\neg\gamma_2)))$

- $(\gamma_1 \mid \gamma_2) = (((\neg\gamma_1)\wedge\gamma_2)\vee(\gamma_1\wedge(\neg\gamma_2)))$
- $(\gamma_1 \Leftrightarrow \gamma_2) = ((\gamma_1\wedge\gamma_2)\vee((\neg\gamma_1)\wedge(\neg\gamma_2)))$
- $(\mathbf{F}\gamma) = (\neg(\mathbf{G}(\neg\gamma)))$

For instance $(\nabla g_1 \wedge \nabla g_2)$ refers to the occurrence of an event e such that both $g_1, g_2 \in e$.

Definition 4.2.2. The *translation map* $h^\wedge: L_G \rightarrow L_{G'}$ induced by a signature morphism $h: G \rightarrow G'$ is inductively defined as follows:

- $h^\wedge(\nabla g) = \nabla h(g)$;
- $h^\wedge(\diamond g) = \diamond h(g)$;
- $h^\wedge(\neg\gamma) = (\neg h^\wedge(\gamma))$;
- $h^\wedge(\gamma_1 \Rightarrow \gamma_2) = (h^\wedge(\gamma_1) \Rightarrow h^\wedge(\gamma_2))$;
- $h^\wedge(\mathbf{X}\gamma) = (\mathbf{X}h^\wedge(\gamma))$;
- $h^\wedge(\mathbf{G}\gamma) = (\mathbf{G}h^\wedge(\gamma))$;
- $h^\wedge(\gamma_1 \mathbf{U} \gamma_2) = (h^\wedge(\gamma_1)\mathbf{U}h^\wedge(\gamma_2))$. □

Fact/Definition 4.2.3. The *syntax functor* Sen:Sig→Set maps each signature G onto the propositional, linear temporal language L_G, and each signature morphism $h: G \rightarrow G'$ onto the translation map $h^\wedge: L_G \rightarrow L_{G'}$. □

4.3 The semantic functor

Definition 4.3.1. Let G be a signature. The category TrS_G of *G-transition systems* and *G-transition morphisms* is the fiber $Gen^{-1}(G)$. The category CoS_G of *G-computation systems* and *G-computation system morphisms* is the fiber $(Gen')^{-1}(G)$. □

Fact/Definition 4.3.2. The *translation functor* $h^\sim: TrS_{G'} \rightarrow TrS_G$ induced by a signature morphism $h: G \rightarrow G'$ maps each G'-transition system trs'=<G',S',δ'> onto the codomain of the cocartesian morphism $\underline{h^{op}}_{trs'}$ for h^{op} and trs', and maps each G'-transition morphism $g': trs'_1 \rightarrow trs'_2$ onto the unique G-transition system morphism $h^\sim(g'): h^\sim(trs'_1) \rightarrow h^\sim(trs'_2)$ such that $h^\sim(g') \circ \underline{h^{op}}_{trs'_1} = \underline{h^{op}}_{trs'_2} \circ g'$. □

That is, $h^\sim$ is the functor induced by h^{op} with respect to the cofibration Gen.

Fact/Definition 4.3.3. The *semantic functor* Mod:Sig→Cat^{op} maps each signature G onto the subcategory TrS_G of TrS, and each signature morphism $h: G \rightarrow G'$ onto the translation functor $h^\sim: TrS_{G'} \rightarrow TrS_G$. □

Given a signature morphism $h: G \rightarrow G'$ and a G'-transition system trs'=<G',S',δ'>, the G-transition system $h^\sim$(trs') is called the *h-reduct* of trs'. Recalling the characterization of the cofibration Gen, it is easy to conclude: (i) the state space of the h-reduct is identical to the given state space; (ii) the reduct transition map for each $e \in G$ is defined by

$\delta_e(s)=\bigcup_{x:h^{-1}(x)=e} \delta_x(s)$: that is, when e happens on s in the h-reduct, the resulting state may be r iff there is an event x=h(e) such that the resulting state in trs' when x happens on s may be r. Furthermore, the cocartesian morphism $\underline{h^{op}}_{trs'}$ for h^{op} and trs' is the pair $<h,id_S>$.

For proving the satisfaction condition we shall also need:

Fact/Definition 4.3.4. The *translation functor* $h^{\sim}$:$CoS_{G'}$→CoS_G induced by a signature morphism h:G→G' maps each G'-computation system cos'=<G',S',Ξ'> onto the codomain of the cocartesian morphism $\underline{h^{op}}_{cos'}$ for h^{op} and cos', and maps each G'-computation system morphism $g':cos'_1 \to cos'_2$ onto the unique G-computation morphism $h^{\sim}(g):h^{\sim}(cos'_1)\to h^{\sim}(cos'_2)$ such that $h^{\sim}(g') \circ \underline{h^{op}}_{cos'_1} = \underline{h^{op}}_{cos'_2} \circ g'$. □

That is, $h^{\sim}$ is the functor induced by h^{op} with respect to the cofibration Gen'.

4.4 Satisfaction

Definition 4.4.1. Let G be a signature, φ a formula of L_G, and trs a G-transition system. The *satisfaction* of φ by $\xi\in\Xi_{trs}$ at $n\in\mathbf{Z}$ (written $\xi\vDash_n\varphi$) is inductively defined as follows:

- $\xi\vDash_n\nabla g$ iff $g\in(\xi_n)_2$;
- $\xi\vDash_n\Diamond g$ iff there is $e\in M_{trs}((\xi_n)_1)$ such that $g\in e$;
- $\xi\vDash_n(\neg\gamma)$ iff not $\xi\vDash_n\gamma$;
- $\xi\vDash_n(\gamma_1\Rightarrow\gamma_2)$ iff $\xi\vDash_n\gamma_2$ or not $\xi\vDash_n\gamma_1$;
- $\xi\vDash_n(\mathbf{X}\gamma)$ iff $\xi\vDash_{n+1}\gamma$;
- $\xi\vDash_n(\mathbf{G}\gamma)$ iff $\xi\vDash_m\gamma$ for every $m\geq n$;
- $\xi\vDash_n(\gamma_1\mathbf{U}\gamma_2)$ iff $\xi\vDash_m\gamma_2$ for some $m\geq n$ and $\xi\vDash_i\gamma_1$ for every i such that $n\leq i<m$.

Definition 4.4.2. Let G be a signature, φ a formula of L_G, and trs a G-transition system. We say that trs *satisfies* φ (written $trs\vDash_G\varphi$) iff $\xi\vDash_n\varphi$ for every $\xi\in\Xi_{trs}$ and every $n\in\mathbf{Z}$.

4.5 Structurality

Having chosen the relevant category of signatures and established the suitable syntax and semantic functors, it remains to check if the satisfaction condition is fulfilled. To this end we need the following lemmas:

Fact 4.5.1. Let G,G' be signatures, h:G→G' a signature morphism, and trs' a G'-transition system. Then, $\Xi_{h^{\sim}(trs')}=\{\underline{h^{op}}_{\Xi_{trs'}}(\xi'): \xi'\in\Xi_{trs'}\}$.

Proof: Since the left adjoint of a fibered adjunction preserves cocartesian morphisms, $U(h^{-}(trs'))=h^{-}(U(trs'))$. Therefore, since the set of computations of $h^{-}(U(trs'))$ is given by $\{\underline{h}^{op}{}_{\Xi_{trs'}}(\xi'): \xi' \in \Xi_{trs'}\}$ and the set of computations of $U(h^{-}(trs'))$ is $\Xi_{h^{-}(trs')}$ the thesis holds. □

Fact 4.5.2. Let G,G' be signatures, $h:G \rightarrow G'$ a signature morphism, and trs' a G'-transition system. Then, $M_{h^{-}(trs')}(s)=h^{-1}(M_{trs'}(s))$.

Proof: $e \in M_{h^{-}(trs')}(s)$ iff $(\bigcup_{x:h^{-1}(x)=e'} \delta'_x(s)) \neq \emptyset$ iff $\exists x\ e=h^{-1}(x)$ and $\delta'_x(s) \neq \emptyset$ iff $e \in \{h^{-1}(x): \delta'_x(s) \neq \emptyset\}$ iff $e \in h^{-1}(M_{trs'}(s))$. □

We are now ready to establish the *satisfaction condition*:

Fact 4.5.3. Let G,G' be signatures, $h:G \rightarrow G'$ a signature morphism, φ a formula of L_G, and trs' a G'-transition system. Then, $trs' \models_{G'} Sen(h)(\varphi)$ iff $Mod(h)(trs') \models_G \varphi$.

Proof:

We prove by induction on the structure of the formula φ that $\xi' \models_n h^{\wedge}(\varphi)$ iff $\underline{h}^{op}{}_{trs'}(\xi') \models_n \varphi$:

- $\xi' \models_n h^{\wedge}(\nabla g)$ iff $\xi' \models_n \nabla h(g)$ iff $h(g) \in (\xi'_n)_2$ iff $g \in h^{-1}((\xi'_n)_2)$ iff $g \in ((\underline{h}^{op}{}_{trs'}(\xi'))_n)_2$ iff $\underline{h}^{op}{}_{trs'}(\xi') \models_n \nabla g$.

- $\xi' \models_n h^{\wedge}(\Diamond g)$ iff $\xi' \models_n \Diamond h(g)$ iff $\exists\ e' \in M_{trs'}((\xi'_n)_1)\ h(g) \in e'$ iff $\exists\ e \in h^{-1}(M_{trs'}((\xi'_n)_1))\ g \in e$ iff $\exists\ e \in M_{h^{-}(trs')}([(\xi'_n)_1])\ g \in e$ iff $\exists\ e \in M_{h^{-}(trs')}(((\underline{h}^{op}{}_{trs'}(\xi'))_n)_1)\ g \in e$ iff $\underline{h}^{op}{}_{trs'}(\xi') \models_n \Diamond g$.

- $\xi' \models_n h^{\wedge}(\neg\gamma)$ iff $\xi' \models_n (\neg\ h^{\wedge}(\gamma))$ iff not $\xi' \models_n h^{\wedge}(\gamma)$ iff not $\underline{h}^{op}{}_{trs'}(\xi') \models_n \gamma$ iff $\underline{h}^{op}{}_{trs'}(\xi') \models_n (\neg\gamma)$.

- $\xi' \models_n h^{\wedge}(\gamma_1 \Rightarrow \gamma_2)$ iff $\xi' \models_n (h^{\wedge}(\gamma_1) \Rightarrow h^{\wedge}(\gamma_2))$ iff $\xi' \models_n h^{\wedge}(\gamma_2)$ or not $\xi' \models_n h^{\wedge}(\gamma_1)$ iff $\underline{h}^{op}{}_{trs'}(\xi') \models_n \gamma_2$ or not $\underline{h}^{op}{}_{trs'}(\xi') \models_n \gamma_1$ iff $\underline{h}^{op}{}_{trs'}(\xi') \models_n (\gamma_1 \Rightarrow \gamma_2)$.

- $\xi' \models_n h^{\wedge}(X\gamma)$ iff $\xi' \models_n (X h^{\wedge}(\gamma))$ iff $\xi' \models_{n+1} h^{\wedge}(\gamma)$ iff $\underline{h}^{op}{}_{trs'}(\xi') \models_{n+1} \gamma$ iff $\underline{h}^{op}{}_{trs'}(\xi') \models_n (X\gamma)$.

- $\xi' \models_n h^{\wedge}(G\gamma)$ iff $\xi' \models_n (G h^{\wedge}(\gamma))$ iff $\forall m \geq n\ \xi' \models_m h^{\wedge}(\gamma)$ iff $\forall m \geq n\ \underline{h}^{op}{}_{trs'}(\xi') \models_m \gamma$ iff $\underline{h}^{op}{}_{trs'}(\xi') \models_n (G\gamma)$.

- $\xi' \models_n h^{\wedge}(\gamma_1 U \gamma_2)$ iff $\xi' \models_n (h^{\wedge}(\gamma_1) U h^{\wedge}(\gamma_2))$ iff $\xi' \models_m h^{\wedge}(\gamma_2)$ for some $m \geq n$ and $\xi' \models_i h^{\wedge}(\gamma_1)$ for every i such that $n \leq i < m$ iff $\underline{h}^{op}{}_{trs'}(\xi') \models_m \gamma_2$ for some $m \geq n$ and $\underline{h}^{op}{}_{trs'}(\xi') \models_i \gamma_1$ for every i such that $n \leq i < m$ iff $\underline{h}^{op}{}_{trs'} \models_n (\gamma_1 U \gamma_2)$. □

5 Concluding remarks

We have shown how to build an institution for a simple logic of behaviour using a cofibration from a given (flat) category of transition systems into the envisaged category of signatures. The adopted propositional, linear temporal logic was chosen for its simplicity while still distinguishing between event occurrence and enabling. The satisfaction condition was proved using a fibered adjunction between transition systems and their computations.

It is important to note that some desirable universal requirements (eg like those related to the frame principle as used in [Sernadas *et al* 92b]) may destroy the satisfaction condition if incorporated into the logic. In that case, a weaker form of structurality may still be required, along the lines of [Maibaum *et al* 90]. Note also the "open nature" of transition systems. For instance, $(\neg\nabla g)$ is semantically entailed by $(\nabla g \Rightarrow (\mathbf{X}\nabla g'))$, since the empty event should always be enabled. A related problem concerns "fairness assumptions". The functor U we adopted for extracting the computations from each transition system is rather unfair. It is conceivable to adopt slightly different unfolding functors introducing some degree of fairness (for instance, precluding computations where the empty event is repeated for ever while other events are enabled). One wonders what will be the impact in the satisfaction condition.

Given a specification (theory presentation) <G,Γ> within the proposed institution, one may ask what should be its semantics. The traditional "loose" approach of associating to <G,Γ> the set Γ^* of all G-transition systems that satisfy each axiom in Γ is not appropriate if we want to find a "canonical" model representing in some "extreme" way all models of Γ (along the lines of [Fiadeiro *et al* 93]). Such a model is useful when providing a semantic map for a specification language built within the proposed institution.

For the semantics of life-cycles (sequences of events) it is very simple to obtain such a "canonical" model: just collect all life-cycles that satisfy the specification. But for the semantics of transition systems (or their computations) we have to face the additional problem of choosing the state space. In [Caleiro 93] it is shown how to obtain such a canonical transition system from a given temporal specification, by adapting the synthesis algorithm in [Manna and Wolper 84]. The categorial characterization of this "operational" semantics of temporal logic is under investigation.

Acknowledgments

This work was partially supported by the JNICT Projects OBCALC and FAC3, the ESPRIT BRA's IS-CORE and COMPASS, and the ESDI Project OBLOG. The authors are grateful to their many colleagues in these projects for many rewarding interactions, and, specially, to José Luiz Fiadeiro, Hans-Dieter Ehrich and Carlos Caleiro.

References

[Adámek *et al* 90]
J.Adámek, H.Herrlich and G.Strecker, *Abstract and Concrete Categories*, Wiley, 1990.

[Caleiro 93]
C.Caleiro, "Operational Semantics of Temporal Object Specifications", INESC/DMIST Research Report, June 1993, presented at the COMPASS GM'93, Dresden.

[Fiadeiro *et al* 93]
J.Fiadeiro, J.F.Costa, A.Sernadas and T.Maibaum, "Process Semantics of Temporal Logic Specification", in M.Bidoit and C.Choppy (eds), *Recent Trends in Data Type Specification: 8th Workshop on Specification of Abstract Data Types - Selected Papers*, Springer-Verlag, 1993, 40-65.

[Goguen and Burstall 84]
J.A.Goguen and R.M.Burstall, "Introducing Institutions", in E.Clarke (ed), *Logics of Programming Workshop*, Springer-Verlag, 1984, 221-256.

[Goldblatt 87]
R.Goldblatt, *Logics of Time and Computation*, CSLI, 1987.

[Maibaum *et al* 90]
T.Maibaum, J.Fiadeiro and M.Sadler, "Stepwise Program Development in π-Institutions", Imperial College, Department of Computing Research Report, 1990.

[Manna and Pnueli 92]
Z.Manna and A.Pnueli, *The Temporal Logic of Reactive and Concurrent Systems*, Springer-Verlag, 1992.

[Manna and Wolper 84]
Z.Manna and P.Wolper, "Synthesis of Communicating Processes from Temporal Logic Specifications", *ACM Transactions on Programming Languages and Systems*, 1984, 68-93.

[SernadasA and Ehrich 91]
A.Sernadas and H.-D.Ehrich, "What is an Object, After All?", in R.Meersman, W.Kent and S.Khosla (eds), *Object Oriented Databases: Analysis, Design and Construction*, North-Holland, 1991, 39-69.

[SernadasA *et al* 89a]
A.Sernadas, J.Fiadeiro, C.Sernadas and H.-D.-Ehrich, "Basic Building Blocks of Information Systems", in E.Falkenberg and P.Lindgreen (eds), *Information System Concepts: An In-depth Analysis*, North-Holland, 1989, 225-246.

[SernadasA *et al* 89b]
A.Sernadas, J.Fiadeiro, C.Sernadas and H.-D.-Ehrich, "Abstract

Object Types: A Temporal Perspective", in B.Banieqbal, H.Barringer and A.Pnueli (eds), *Temporal Logic in Specification*, Springer-Verlag, 1989, 324-350.

[SernadasA *et al* 92a]
A.Sernadas, J.F.Costa, J.L.Fiadeiro and H.-D.Ehrich, "Object Template Institution", Dagstuhl Workshop on Foundations of Information Systems Specification and Design, March 16-19, 1992.

[SernadasA *et al* 92b]
A.Sernadas, C.Sernadas and J.F.Costa, "Object Specification Logic", INESC/DMIST Research Report, June 1992, *submitted*.

[Tarlecki *et al* 91]
A.Tarlecki, R.M.Burstall and J.A.Goguen, "Some Fundamental Algebraic Tools for the Semantics of Computation. Part III: Indexed Categories", *Theoretical Computer Science*, 1991, 239-264.

[Winskel 84]
G.Winskel, "Synchronization Trees", *Theoretical Computer Science*, 34, 1984.

[Winskel 85]
G.Winskel, "Categories of Models for Concurrency", in S.D.Brookes et al (eds), *Proceedings of the Seminar on Concurrency*, Springer-Verlag, 1985, 246-267.

[Winskel 87]
G.Winskel, "Petri Nets, Algebras, Morphisms and Compositionality", *Information and Computation*, March, 1987.

Lecture Notes in Computer Science

For information about Vols. 1–709
please contact your bookseller or Springer-Verlag

Vol. 710: Z. Ésik (Ed.), Fundamentals of Computation Theory. Proceedings, 1993. IX, 471 pages. 1993.

Vol. 711: A. M. Borzyszkowski, S. Sokołowski (Eds.), Mathematical Foundations of Computer Science 1993. Proceedings, 1993. XIII, 782 pages. 1993.

Vol. 712: P. V. Rangan (Ed.), Network and Operating System Support for Digital Audio and Video. Proceedings, 1992. X, 416 pages. 1993.

Vol. 713: G. Gottlob, A. Leitsch, D. Mundici (Eds.), Computational Logic and Proof Theory. Proceedings, 1993. XI, 348 pages. 1993.

Vol. 714: M. Bruynooghe, J. Penjam (Eds.), Programming Language Implementation and Logic Programming. Proceedings, 1993. XI, 421 pages. 1993.

Vol. 715: E. Best (Ed.), CONCUR'93. Proceedings, 1993. IX, 541 pages. 1993.

Vol. 716: A. U. Frank, I. Campari (Eds.), Spatial Information Theory. Proceedings, 1993. XI, 478 pages. 1993.

Vol. 717: I. Sommerville, M. Paul (Eds.), Software Engineering – ESEC '93. Proceedings, 1993. XII, 516 pages. 1993.

Vol. 718: J. Seberry, Y. Zheng (Eds.), Advances in Cryptology – AUSCRYPT '92. Proceedings, 1992. XIII, 543 pages. 1993.

Vol. 719: D. Chetverikov, W.G. Kropatsch (Eds.), Computer Analysis of Images and Patterns. Proceedings, 1993. XVI, 857 pages. 1993.

Vol. 720: V.Mařík, J. Lažanský, R.R. Wagner (Eds.), Database and Expert Systems Applications. Proceedings, 1993. XV, 768 pages. 1993.

Vol. 721: J. Fitch (Ed.), Design and Implementation of Symbolic Computation Systems. Proceedings, 1992. VIII, 215 pages. 1993.

Vol. 722: A. Miola (Ed.), Design and Implementation of Symbolic Computation Systems. Proceedings, 1993. XII, 384 pages. 1993.

Vol. 723: N. Aussenac, G. Boy, B. Gaines, M. Linster, J.-G. Ganascia, Y. Kodratoff (Eds.), Knowledge Acquisition for Knowledge-Based Systems. Proceedings, 1993. XIII, 446 pages. 1993. (Subseries LNAI).

Vol. 724: P. Cousot, M. Falaschi, G. Filè, A. Rauzy (Eds.), Static Analysis. Proceedings, 1993. IX, 283 pages. 1993.

Vol. 725: A. Schiper (Ed.), Distributed Algorithms. Proceedings, 1993. VIII, 325 pages. 1993.

Vol. 726: T. Lengauer (Ed.), Algorithms – ESA '93. Proceedings, 1993. IX, 419 pages. 1993

Vol. 727: M. Filgueiras, L. Damas (Eds.), Progress in Artificial Intelligence. Proceedings, 1993. X, 362 pages. 1993. (Subseries LNAI).

Vol. 728: P. Torasso (Ed.), Advances in Artificial Intelligence. Proceedings, 1993. XI, 336 pages. 1993. (Subseries LNAI).

Vol. 729: L. Donatiello, R. Nelson (Eds.), Performance Evaluation of Computer and Communication Systems. Proceedings, 1993. VIII, 675 pages. 1993.

Vol. 730: D. B. Lomet (Ed.), Foundations of Data Organization and Algorithms. Proceedings, 1993. XII, 412 pages. 1993.

Vol. 731: A. Schill (Ed.), DCE – The OSF Distributed Computing Environment. Proceedings, 1993. VIII, 285 pages. 1993.

Vol. 732: A. Bode, M. Dal Cin (Eds.), Parallel Computer Architectures. IX, 311 pages. 1993.

Vol. 733: Th. Grechenig, M. Tscheligi (Eds.), Human Computer Interaction. Proceedings, 1993. XIV, 450 pages. 1993.

Vol. 734: J. Volkert (Ed.), Parallel Computation. Proceedings, 1993. VIII, 248 pages. 1993.

Vol. 735: D. Bjørner, M. Broy, I. V. Pottosin (Eds.), Formal Methods in Programming and Their Applications. Proceedings, 1993. IX, 434 pages. 1993.

Vol. 736: R. L. Grossman, A. Nerode, A. P. Ravn, H. Rischel (Eds.), Hybrid Systems. VIII, 474 pages. 1993.

Vol. 737: J. Calmet, J. A. Campbell (Eds.), Artificial Intelligence and Symbolic Mathematical Computing. Proceedings, 1992. VIII, 305 pages. 1993.

Vol. 738: M. Weber, M. Simons, Ch. Lafontaine, The Generic Development Language Deva. XI, 246 pages. 1993.

Vol. 739: H. Imai, R. L. Rivest, T. Matsumoto (Eds.), Advances in Cryptology – ASIACRYPT '91. X, 499 pages. 1993.

Vol. 740: E. F. Brickell (Ed.), Advances in Cryptology – CRYPTO '92. Proceedings, 1992. X, 593 pages. 1993.

Vol. 741: B. Preneel, R. Govaerts, J. Vandewalle (Eds.), Computer Security and Industrial Cryptography. Proceedings, 1991. VIII, 275 pages. 1993.

Vol. 742: S. Nishio, A. Yonezawa (Eds.), Object Technologies for Advanced Software. Proceedings, 1993. X, 543 pages. 1993.

Vol. 743: S. Doshita, K. Furukawa, K. P. Jantke, T. Nishida (Eds.), Algorithmic Learning Theory. Proceedings, 1992. X, 260 pages. 1993. (Subseries LNAI)

Vol. 744: K. P. Jantke, T. Yokomori, S. Kobayashi, E. Tomita (Eds.), Algorithmic Learning Theory. Proceedings, 1993. XI, 423 pages. 1993. (Subseries LNAI)

Vol. 745: V. Roberto (Ed.), Intelligent Perceptual Systems. VIII, 378 pages. 1993. (Subseries LNAI)

Vol. 746: A. S. Tanguiane, Artificial Perception and Music Recognition. XV, 210 pages. 1993. (Subseries LNAI).

Vol. 747: M. Clarke, R. Kruse, S. Moral (Eds.), Symbolic and Quantitative Approaches to Reasoning and Uncertainty. Proceedings, 1993. X, 390 pages. 1993.

Vol. 748: R. H. Halstead Jr., T. Ito (Eds.), Parallel Symbolic Computing: Languages, Systems, and Applications. Proceedings, 1992. X, 419 pages. 1993.

Vol. 749: P. A. Fritzson (Ed.), Automated and Algorithmic Debugging. Proceedings, 1993. VIII, 369 pages. 1993.

Vol. 750: J. L. Díaz-Herrera (Ed.), Software Engineering Education. Proceedings, 1994. XII, 601 pages. 1994.

Vol. 751: B. Jähne, Spatio-Temporal Image Processing. XII, 208 pages. 1993.

Vol. 752: T. W. Finin, C. K. Nicholas, Y. Yesha (Eds.), Information and Knowledge Management. Proceedings, 1992. VII, 142 pages. 1993.

Vol. 753: L. J. Bass, J. Gornostaev, C. Unger (Eds.), Human-Computer Interaction. Proceedings, 1993. X, 388 pages. 1993.

Vol. 754: H. D. Pfeiffer, T. E. Nagle (Eds.), Conceptual Structures: Theory and Implementation. Proceedings, 1992. IX, 327 pages. 1993. (Subseries LNAI).

Vol. 755: B. Möller, H. Partsch, S. Schuman (Eds.), Formal Program Development. Proceedings. VII, 371 pages. 1993.

Vol. 756: J. Pieprzyk, B. Sadeghiyan, Design of Hashing Algorithms. XV, 194 pages. 1993.

Vol. 757: U. Banerjee, D. Gelernter, A. Nicolau, D. Padua (Eds.), Languages and Compilers for Parallel Computing. Proceedings, 1992. X, 576 pages. 1993.

Vol. 758: M. Teillaud, Towards Dynamic Randomized Algorithms in Computational Geometry. IX, 157 pages. 1993.

Vol. 759: N. R. Adam, B. K. Bhargava (Eds.), Advanced Database Systems. XV, 451 pages. 1993.

Vol. 760: S. Ceri, K. Tanaka, S. Tsur (Eds.), Deductive and Object-Oriented Databases. Proceedings, 1993. XII, 488 pages. 1993.

Vol. 761: R. K. Shyamasundar (Ed.), Foundations of Software Technology and Theoretical Computer Science. Proceedings, 1993. XIV, 456 pages. 1993.

Vol. 762: K. W. Ng, P. Raghavan, N. V. Balasubramanian, F. Y. L. Chin (Eds.), Algorithms and Computation. Proceedings, 1993. XIII, 542 pages. 1993.

Vol. 763: F. Pichler, R. Moreno Díaz (Eds.), Computer Aided Systems Theory – EUROCAST '93. Proceedings, 1993. IX, 451 pages. 1994.

Vol. 764: G. Wagner, Vivid Logic. XII, 148 pages. 1994. (Subseries LNAI).

Vol. 765: T. Helleseth (Ed.), Advances in Cryptology – EUROCRYPT '93. Proceedings, 1993. X, 467 pages. 1994.

Vol. 766: P. R. Van Loocke, The Dynamics of Concepts. XI, 340 pages. 1994. (Subseries LNAI).

Vol. 767: M. Gogolla, An Extended Entity-Relationship Model. X, 136 pages. 1994.

Vol. 768: U. Banerjee, D. Gelernter, A. Nicolau, D. Padua (Eds.), Languages and Compilers for Parallel Computing. Proceedings, 1993. XI, 655 pages. 1994.

Vol. 769: J. L. Nazareth, The Newton-Cauchy Framework. XII, 101 pages. 1994.

Vol. 770: P. Haddawy (Representing Plans Under Uncertainty. X, 129 pages. 1994. (Subseries LNAI).

Vol. 771: G. Tomas, C. W. Ueberhuber, Visualization of Scientific Parallel Programs. XI, 310 pages. 1994.

Vol. 772: B. C. Warboys (Ed.),Software Process Technology. Proceedings, 1994. IX, 275 pages. 1994.

Vol. 773: D. R. Stinson (Ed.), Advances in Cryptology – CRYPTO '93. Proceedings, 1993. X, 492 pages. 1994.

Vol. 774: M. Banâtre, P. A. Lee (Eds.), Hardware and Software Architectures for Fault Tolerance. XIII, 311 pages. 1994.

Vol. 775: P. Enjalbert, E. W. Mayr, K. W. Wagner (Eds.), STACS 94. Proceedings, 1994. XIV, 782 pages. 1994.

Vol. 776: H. J. Schneider, H. Ehrig (Eds.), Graph Transformations in Computer Science. Proceedings, 1993. VIII, 395 pages. 1994.

Vol. 777: K. von Luck, H. Marburger (Eds.), Management and Processing of Complex Data Structures. Proceedings, 1994. VII, 220 pages. 1994.

Vol. 778: M. Bonuccelli, P. Crescenzi, R. Petreschi (Eds.), Algorithms and Complexity. Proceedings, 1994. VIII, 222 pages. 1994.

Vol. 779: M. Jarke, J. Bubenko, K. Jeffery (Eds.), Advances in Database Technology — EDBT '94. Proceedings, 1994. XII, 406 pages. 1994.

Vol. 780: J. J. Joyce, C.-J. H. Seger (Eds.), Higher Order Logic Theorem Proving and Its Applications. Proceedings, 1993. X, 518 pages. 1994.

Vol. 781: G. Cohen, S. Litsyn, A. Lobstein, G. Zémor (Eds.), Algebraic Coding. Proceedings, 1993. XII, 326 pages. 1994.

Vol. 782: J. Gutknecht (Ed.), Programming Languages and System Architectures. Proceedings, 1994. X, 344 pages. 1994.

Vol. 783: C. G. Günther (Ed.), Mobile Communications. Proceedings, 1994. XVI, 564 pages. 1994.

Vol. 784: F. Bergadano, L. De Raedt (Eds.), Machine Learning: ECML-94. Proceedings, 1994. XI, 439 pages. 1994. (Subseries LNAI).

Vol. 785: H. Ehrig, F. Orejas (Eds.), Recent Trends in Data Type Specification. Proceedings, 1992. VIII, 350 pages. 1994.

Vol. 786: P. A. Fritzson (Ed.), Compiler Construction. Proceedings, 1994. XI, 451 pages. 1994.

Vol. 787: S. Tison (Ed.), Trees in Algebra and Programming – CAAP '94. Proceedings, 1994. X, 351 pages. 1994.

Vol. 788: D. Sannella (Ed.), Programming Languages and Systems – ESOP '94. Proceedings, 1994. VIII, 516 pages. 1994.

Vol. 789: M. Hagiya, J. C. Mitchell (Eds.), Theoretical Aspects of Computer Software. Proceedings, 1994. XI, 887 pages. 1994.